# Revelation

# Revelation

SIGVE K. TONSTAD

**Baker Academic**
*a division of Baker Publishing Group*
Grand Rapids, Michigan

Published by Baker Academic
a division of Baker Publishing Group
PO Box 6287, Grand Rapids, MI 49516-6287
www.bakeracademic.com

Printed in the United States of America

Library of Congress Cataloging-in-Publication Data
Names: Tonstad, Sigve, author.
Title: Revelation / Sigve K. Tonstad.
Description: Grand Rapids : Baker Academic, a division of Baker Publishing Group, 2019. | Series: Paideia : commentaries on the New Testament | Includes bibliographical references and index.
Identifiers: LCCN 2019017285 | ISBN 9780801049002 (pbk.)
Subjects: LCSH: Bible. Revelation—Commentaries.
Classification: LCC BS2825.53 .T66 2019 | DDC 228/.077—dc23
LC record available at https://lccn.loc.gov/2019017285

ISBN 978-1-5409-6242-3 (casebound)

To Bruce Longenecker
*mentor and friend*

# Contents

# Figures

# Foreword

*Paideia: Commentaries on the New Testament* is a series that sets out to comment on the final form of the New Testament text in a way that pays due attention both to the cultural, literary, and theological settings in which the text took form and to the interests of the contemporary readers to whom the commentaries are addressed. This series is aimed squarely at students—including MA students in religious and theological studies programs, seminarians, and upper-division undergraduates—who have theological interests in the biblical text. Thus, the didactic aim of the series is to enable students to understand each book of the New Testament as a literary whole rooted in a particular ancient setting and related to its context within the New Testament.

The name "Paideia" (Greek for "education") reflects (1) the instructional aim of the series—giving contemporary students a basic grounding in academic New Testament studies by guiding their engagement with New Testament texts; (2) the fact that the New Testament texts as literary unities are shaped by the educational categories and ideas (rhetorical, narratological, etc.) of their ancient writers and readers; and (3) the pedagogical aims of the texts themselves—their central aim being not simply to impart information but to form the theological convictions and moral habits of their readers.

Each commentary deals with the text in terms of larger rhetorical units; these are not verse-by-verse commentaries. This series thus stands within the stream of recent commentaries that attend to the final form of the text. Such reader-centered literary approaches are inherently more accessible to liberal arts students without extensive linguistic and historical-critical preparation than older exegetical approaches, but within the reader-centered world the sanest practitioners have paid careful attention to the extratext of the original readers, including not only these readers' knowledge of the geography, history, and other contextual elements reflected in the text but also their ability to respond correctly to the literary and rhetorical conventions used in the text. Paideia commentaries pay deliberate attention to this extratextual repertoire in order to highlight the ways in which the text is designed to persuade and move its readers. Each rhetorical unit is explored from three angles: (1) introductory matters; (2) tracing the train of thought or narrative or rhetorical flow of the argument; and (3) theological issues raised by the text that are of interest to the contemporary Christian. Thus, the primary focus remains on the text and not its historical context or its interpretation in the secondary literature.

Our authors represent a variety of confessional points of view: Protestant, Catholic, and Orthodox. What they share, beyond being New Testament scholars of national and international repute, is a commitment to reading the biblical text as theological documents within their ancient contexts. Working within the broad parameters described here, each author brings his or her own considerable exegetical talents and deep theological commitments to the task of laying bare the interpretation of Scripture for the faith and practice of God's people everywhere.

Mikeal C. Parsons
Charles H. Talbert
Bruce W. Longenecker

# Preface

*Paideia* means instruction intended for a person who is in the process of growing up. Whether in secular or biblical usage the term has a practical bent: genuine *paideia* enables a person to exercise discernment and make good choices amid life's array of competing options. Given that "growing up" is a lifelong project, grasping the *paideia* of Revelation might well be, too.

Revelation is a learned book, probably the most challenging book in the library we call the Bible. Its intellectual aspirations are matched to existential needs: it is learning set forth for conditions where misrepresentation, mudslinging, and falsehood are the order of the day. The book is so sure of meeting a critical need that it declares those blessed "who read aloud . . . and those who keep what is written" (1:3). Reading this book is connected to practice. Learning is meant for living.

But Revelation is also a Pandora's box in biblical interpretation. Martin Luther called it "every mob-leader's bag of tricks," suggesting that Revelation caters to mob leaders more than to levelheaded people. Can this reputation be overcome? Luther was not alone in believing that Revelation's bizarre images lend themselves to theological trickery. Is it possible to retain primacy for this learned text and its earnest author over the restive imaginations of its readers? Are not the diverse interpretations of Revelation conclusive proof that we can erect meanings on the foundations of an ancient text, but we cannot know what the author meant? For a commentary on this book, there is the additional challenge that no other NT book engages interpreters as much in historical study, whether the history is ancient, somewhere in the middle, or deals in present-day events. If historical knowledge is an entrance requirement for reading the book intelligently, the deterrent to potential readers is formidable. One result of this is that various communities of faith cultivate resident experts who understand the book on their behalf. The communities take comfort in the belief that their designated expert understands the book even if they don't.

Mindful of these concerns, I begin with three issues in need of clarification, all of them so important that they must be set forth at the outset. First, I address Revelation's reputation as a book portraying (and relishing) violence. That there is violence in the book cannot be denied. But that is not the whole story. Most expositors attribute the violence to God, with no need to pursue other options even though other possibilities are shouting and waving at the reader from all corners of this text. And yet nothing characterizes Revelation as much as its depiction of the conflict between God and Satan. We shall therefore be guilty of a grave sin of omission if we do not question the standard view. Who is behind the violence? Who is doing the violence if it is not God? The answer to these questions leads to widely different views of the theology of the book. Where the cosmic scope is missing—*where God is doing it*—the result consolidates a theology of *retribution*. Where the cosmic perspective is respected—*where God is not doing it*—the accent falls on *revelation*. It is hard to think of any question more important.

A second issue centers on the role of the Roman Empire. While it is now common to examine the books of the NT for clues to political concerns, some "political" readings of NT books fall well short of being persuasive. Revelation has been an exception. Belief in the political errand of this book came early among interpreters. It is now a near axiom that Revelation takes aim at the Roman Empire, in general, and the emperor Nero, in particular. This view is so widely assumed that there is little need to present evidence—or to consider evidence to the contrary. In this commentary, the evidence for the "Roman Empire" reading is neither assumed nor is it left out. On the contrary, textual and historical evidence is included, scrutinized, and assessed. Here, too, much is at stake because empire-centered interpretations put at risk the theological aspiration of the book.

Is Revelation what it claims to be—a *revelation*? This is the third stage-setting question. It is related to the previous two, but the question also has separate and independent standing. A *retribution*-oriented reading or a *Roman*-centered interpretation accommodates the possibility of genuine revelation, but such readings conform better to common ideas as to the kind of literature we have in the last book of the Bible. By conventional criteria, we can see Revelation as a creative parody of the emperor Nero or as an example of *crisis literature* along the lines of other so-called apocalypses. We need a more robust notion of revelation if the circumstances are less important than they are thought to be and if Revelation [*apokalypsis*] is not a code word for a certain literary genre. The alternative posits a drama playing out on a larger screen than human history, larger too than Roman imperial reality. I struggle to find the right words with which to express it, but let it come down to this: *In this apocalypse, revelation is foremost a depiction not of a historical problem but is rather a shocking and utterly counterintuitive representation of God.* This vouches for a notion of revelation that surpasses historical contingencies, literary genre, predictive prophecy, and interpretation of visions and dreams. In the latter category, the latest incarnation could be Sigmund Freud, who like Daniel and John, was a Jew in exile and a thinker drawing up the epistemological boundaries that many take for granted today.

The plot in Revelation centers on the scroll that is sealed with seven seals (5:1). The scroll holds the attention of the heavenly council, of John, and now of us, the readers. No interpretation of Revelation can claim success if it fails to take the correct measure of the scroll. The scroll has been described as the *book of life,* a *book of deeds,* or a *book of action,* in the latter sense mostly punitive actions that God brings to bear on the world. I contend that the sealed scroll is a *book of revelation.* Given the fact that so much of its content is excruciatingly familiar (6:1–11), it can also be described as the *book of reality.* Jesus, who "has what it takes" to take the book and to break its seals (5:2–6), is the *Revealer.* The reality that only he can unravel is the problem of suffering and injustice. "How long, holy and true Lord, will it be before you act justly and vindicate our blood [shed] by those who dwell on the earth?" victims cry out when the fifth seal is opened (6:10). This question proves Revelation to be a book that addresses the most vexing existential problem, then and now, and now even more than then. But the answer, lest we miss the point, is found in the identity and character of the Revealer (5:6). It is Revelation's representation of the Revealer that certifies it as a *revelation* more emphatically than anything else that comes to light in the book.

The Paideia series generally represents commentary on *text units* rather than breaking the comments down to specific verses. Revelation is a challenge to any commentary format for the need to know the whole to understand the parts, and equally for the need to pay exquisite attention to detail. Attention to detail, in turn, means to capture nuances in translation as well as the allusive character of the composition. I have observed the *text unit* format, but I include translations of entire verses where that has seemed necessary to make the point. The symphonic composition of our book, performed in text, demands an approach that preserves the symphony.

I count it an enormous privilege to be entrusted with the task of writing a commentary on Revelation and to ponder its momentous existential questions. My gratitude goes to Jim Kinney and Bryan Dyer at Baker for allowing me to do it and to Mikeal Parsons and Bruce Longenecker, the series editors, for nurturing, much-needed correctives, and persistence. I am grateful to Wells Turner and his editorial team for carefully preparing my manuscript for publication.

I am indebted to Richard Bauckham for his written work and mentoring at the University of St. Andrews. Jon Paulien, dean of Loma Linda University and a leading Revelation scholar, has given me time and encouragement ever since I joined the religion faculty as a fledgling professor. So have the colleagues who went out of their way to welcome and mentor me at the beginning, especially Julius Nam, Johnny Ramirez, Siroj Sirajjakool, and Carla Gober. My senior colleagues Dave Larson, Richard Rice, Ivan Blazen, Jim Walters, Andy Lampkin, and Jerry Winslow have been supportive of my writing endeavors in every way. My friend Terje Bjerka has generously shared illustrations from his extensive travels; his recent illness puts a damper on the joy we would otherwise have.

The late Roy Branson had a lifelong interest in *the healing of the nations*, and his ideas and encouragement have been a great help. Bernard Taylor has provided peerless quality control on details of language, and I thank Dennis Meier in Germany for careful and constructive feedback. Nanette Wuchenich talked me into doing a Revelation class in the university community some years ago. We kept it going verse by verse for two years till we were done. This is a sweet memory. The work done at that time and the level of our discussions have made my writing much easier. I cannot leave out the gratitude felt for the moral and material assistance Ken Peterson offered at a critical stage.

Further back, now as a subliminal influence, I acknowledge my parents, especially my father, Hans, who treated me to the symphonic ending of Revelation before I knew how to read. He sowed the seeds that made me an early captive of the hope that is projected and proclaimed in this book. Most of all, I thank my friend and doctoral mentor, Bruce Longenecker, then at the University of St. Andrews and now at Baylor University. His gentleness, commitment to quality, and encouragement to persevere could well have come from the source represented as the speaker in Revelation. "I scrutinize [*elenchō*] and mentor [*paideuō*] those whom I love" (3:19). Bruce did that for me at the University of St. Andrews. In gratitude, I dedicate this book to him.

# Abbreviations

## General

| | | | |
|---|---|---|---|
| aor. | aorist | LXX | Septuagint |
| Aram. | Aramaic | no(s). | number(s) |
| BCE | before the Common (Christian) era | NT | New Testament |
| | | OT | Old Testament |
| CE | Common (Christian) era | perf. | perfect |
| cf. | *confer*, compare | repr. | reprinted |
| chap(s). | chapter(s) | rev. ed. | revised edition |
| ed(s). | editor(s), edited by, edition | sg. | singular |
| e.g. | *exempli gratia*, for example | s.v. | *sub verbo*, under the word |
| et al. | *et alii*, and others | Theod. | Theodotion's recension of the LXX |
| Gk. | Greek | | |
| Hb. | Hebrew | trans. | translated by, translation, translators |
| i.e. | *id est*, that is | | |
| lit. | literally | v(v). | verse(s) |
| loc(s). | location(s) | vol(s). | volume(s) |

## Biblical Texts and Versions

| | | | |
|---|---|---|---|
| KJV | King James Version | NJB | New Jerusalem Bible |
| NAB | New American Bible | NKJV | New King James Version |
| NASB | New American Standard Bible | NRSV | New Revised Standard Version |
| NIV | New International Version | | |

## Ancient Corpora

OLD TESTAMENT

| | | | |
|---|---|---|---|
| | | Exod. | Exodus |
| | | Lev. | Leviticus |
| Gen. | Genesis | Num. | Numbers |

| Deut. | Deuteronomy | | Mal. | Malachi |
|-------|-------------|---|------|---------|
| Josh. | Joshua | | | |
| Judg. | Judges | | **NEW TESTAMENT** | |
| Ruth | Ruth | | Matt. | Matthew |
| 1–2 Sam. | 1–2 Samuel | | Mark | Mark |
| 1–2 Kings | 1–2 Kings | | Luke | Luke |
| 1–2 Chron. | 1–2 Chronicles | | John | John |
| Ezra | Ezra | | Acts | Acts |
| Neh. | Nehemiah | | Rom. | Romans |
| Esther | Esther | | 1–2 Cor. | 1–2 Corinthians |
| Job | Job | | Gal. | Galatians |
| Ps(s). | Psalm(s) | | Eph. | Ephesians |
| Prov. | Proverbs | | Phil. | Philippians |
| Eccles. | Ecclesiastes | | Col. | Colossians |
| Song | Song of Songs | | 1–2 Thess. | 1–2 Thessalonians |
| Isa. | Isaiah | | 1–2 Tim. | 1–2 Timothy |
| Jer. | Jeremiah | | Titus | Titus |
| Lam. | Lamentations | | Philem. | Philemon |
| Ezek. | Ezekiel | | Heb. | Hebrews |
| Dan. | Daniel | | James | James |
| Hosea | Hosea | | 1–2 Pet. | 1–2 Peter |
| Joel | Joel | | 1–3 John | 1–3 John |
| Amos | Amos | | Jude | Jude |
| Obad. | Obadiah | | Rev. | Revelation |
| Jon. | Jonah | | | |
| Mic. | Micah | | **OLD TESTAMENT PSEUDEPIGRAPHA** | |
| Nah. | Nahum | | 1–2 En. | 1–2 Enoch |
| Hab. | Habakkuk | | | |
| Zeph. | Zephaniah | | **APOSTOLIC FATHERS** | |
| Hag. | Haggai | | Did. | Didache |
| Zech. | Zechariah | | Ign. Magn. | Ignatius, To the Magnesians |

# Ancient Authors

**AUGUSTINE**

Civ.   De civitate Dei (The City of God)

**CAESAR**

Bel. civ.   Bellum civile (Civil War)

**DIO CASSIUS**

Hist. rom.   Historiae romanae (Roman History)

**EUSEBIUS**

Hist. eccl.   Historia ecclesiastica (Ecclesiastical History)

Vit. Const.   Vita Constantini (Life of Constantine)

**GREGORY OF NYSSA**

Hom. Cant.   Homiliae in Canticum Canticorum (Homilies on Song of Songs)

IRENAEUS

*Haer.* *Adversus haereses (Against Heresies)*

HERODOTUS

*Hist.* *Historiae*

JOHN CHRYSOSTOM

*Adv. Jud.* *Adversus Judaeos (Discourses against Judaizing Christians)*

ORIGEN

*Cels.* *Contra Celsum (Against Celsus)*
*Hom.* *Homiliae (Homilies)*
*Princ.* *De principiis (First Principles)*

PLINY THE YOUNGER

*Pan.* *Panegyricus*

QUINTILIAN

*Inst.* *Institutio oratoria (Institutes of Oratory)*

SUETONIUS

*Aug.* *Divus Augustus (Divine Augustus)*
*Dom.* *Domitianus (Domitian)*
*Jul.* *Divus Julius (Divine Julius)*

TACITUS

*Agr.* *Agricola*
*Ann.* *Annales (Annals)*

VERGIL

*Aen.* *Aeneid*

## Series, Collections, and Reference Works

BDAG    W. Bauer, F. W. Danker, W. F. Arndt, and F. W. Gingrich. *A Greek-English Lexicon of the New Testament and Other Early Christian Literature.* 3rd ed. Chicago: University of Chicago Press, 2000.

BDF     F. Blass, A. Debrunner, and R. W. Funk. *A Greek Grammar of the New Testament and Other Early Christian Literature.* Chicago: University of Chicago Press, 1961.

CR      Corpus reformatorum. 101 vols. 1834–1907.

GNO     Gregory of Nyssa Opera. Vol. 6. Edited by H. Langerbeck. Leiden: Brill, 1960.

HALOT   *The Hebrew and Aramaic Lexicon of the Old Testament.* By L. Koehler, W. Baumgartner, J. J. Stamm, and M. E. J. Richardson. Study ed. 2 vols. Leiden: Brill, 2001.

L&N     Johannes P. Louw and Eugene A. Nida, eds. *Greek-English Lexicon of the New Testament: Based on Semantic Domains.* 2nd ed. 2 vols. New York: United Bible Societies, 1988–89.

LW      Luther's Works. Edited by H. T. Lehmann, J. Pelikan, et al. Philadelphia: Fortress; St. Louis: Concordia, 1955–.

OTP     *The Old Testament Pseudepigrapha.* Edited by J. H. Charlesworth. 2 vols. Garden City, NY: Doubleday, 1983–85.

TDNT    *Theological Dictionary of the New Testament.* Edited by Gerhard Kittel and Gerhard Friedrich. Translated and edited by Geoffrey W. Bromiley. 10 vols. Grand Rapids: Eerdmans, 1964–76.

TDOT    *Theological Dictionary of the Old Testament.* Edited by G. J. Botterweck, H. Ringgren, and H.-J. Fabry. Translated by J. T. Willis, G. W. Bromiley, D. E. Green, and D. W. Stott. 15 vols. Grand Rapids: Eerdmans, 1974–2006.

# Revelation

# Introduction

## *Finding the Door*

Revelation is a book of open doors (Rev. 3:7; 4:1; 11:19; 19:11). Why, then, is it so hard to get inside? It is unsettling to discover that some of history's most fearless door-openers made an exception for Revelation. In 1522 Martin Luther wrote, "I miss more than one thing in this book, and it makes me consider it to be neither apostolic nor prophetic. . . . For me this is reason enough not to think highly of it: Christ is neither taught nor known in it" (LW 35:398; Hofmann 1982). Not apostolic, not prophetic, Christ not known in it—these are serious blows. Luther's put-down goes further. "Again, they are supposed to be blessed who keep what is written in this book; and yet no one knows what that is, to say nothing of keeping it. This is just the same as if we did not have the book at all" (LW 35:398). If obscure content and lack of comprehension are what awaits the reader, Luther's conclusion is fair enough. Huldrych Zwingli was even more brusque, writing that "with the *Apocalypse* we have no concern, for it is not a biblical book" (CR 93:395). John Calvin rounds off the Protestant verdict by simply ignoring the book (T. Parker 1971, 77).

Imagine these Reformers standing at the head of a picket line next to Revelation's open door. The deterrent to entering would be formidable. Now, nearer to us, less visceral but no less devastating comments reinforce the negative impression. C. H. Dodd (1963, 40) said that Revelation "falls below the level, not only of the teaching of Jesus, but of the best parts of the Old Testament." Adela Yarbro Collins (1984, 156) represents Revelation as "a thin veil over the hearers' desire for vengeance on Rome," cushioning her verdict by adding that the revenge plays out mostly in the mind, as a form of mental catharsis. To John J. Collins (1998, 278), Revelation differs from the other books in the

NT for its preoccupation with unpalatable business: Jesus "did not destroy the wicked in his earthly life, but he would return with supernatural power to complete the task."

These sentiments originate in the realm of theology, and they seriously impact the reputation of the last book in the Bible. And yet they are mild-mannered compared to views held by readers coming from other quarters. Friedrich Nietzsche (1844–1900) built his philosophy on the wise conviction that an attitude of *resentment* is a toxic element in society. He considered Revelation the worst kind in this regard, calling it "that most obscene of all the written outbursts, which has revenge on its conscience" (Nietzsche 1918, 36).

Carl Gustav Jung (1875–1961), the Swiss psychiatrist, deemed the author of Revelation important enough to subject him to psychoanalysis nearly two thousand years after his death. He found John unable to separate the conscious from the unconscious as healthy people are expected to do. The collapse of this boundary led to pandemonium in the mind. "A veritable orgy of hatred, wrath, vindictiveness, and blind destructive fury that revels in fantastic images of terror breaks out and with blood and fire overwhelms a world which Christ had just endeavored to restore to the original state of innocence and loving communion with God," said Jung of his "patient" John (2002, 97). Who dares pass through a door where such monsters are on the loose? Who wants to undo what good has been accomplished by the other books in the NT, as Jung intimates? D. H. Lawrence (1885–1930) compared Revelation to the twelve disciples, calling it an oddball. Just as Jesus "had to have a Judas Iscariot among his disciples, so did there have to be a Revelation in the New Testament," he wrote (1967, 22). By this measure, Revelation ensures for Jesus permanent betrayal in print—within the canon! Among the pejorative adjectives liberally scattered throughout Lawrence's review are "repulsive," "disgusting," "beastly," and "hideous" along with labels such as "self-conceit," "self-importance," and "secret envy."

Speaking as a literary critic, Harold Bloom (1988, 4) takes Revelation to task for violence *and* lack of literary finesse: "Resentment and not love is the teaching of the Revelation of St. John the Divine. It is a book without wisdom, goodness, kindness, or affection of any kind. Perhaps it is appropriate that a celebration of the end of the world should be not only barbaric, but scarcely literate."

We now have a philosopher, a psychiatrist, a novelist, and a literary critic coming to the same conclusion. Lest these opinion-makers be found to lack the best credentials, the last word shall belong to an expert on the NT. John Dominic Crossan (2009, 209) calls Revelation "that most consistently violent text in all the canonical literature of all the world's religions."

Where, now, the door? Why take the trouble to find it? With such sentiments freshly in our minds, there should not be many people seeking entrance to Revelation. Or, as an alternative, the person willing to enter might be expected to have a certain personality type, or even a personality disorder (Carl Jung), perhaps someone who is resistant to good advice, hostile to authority, or unfazed by the violence in the book.

In some parts of the world, the stampede of people rushing to get through the door shows a determination *not to* take Luther's advice to heart. It is unwarranted to believe that Revelation caters to a certain personality type, but we certainly have *interpretations* that make the alleged violence of the book their selling point. The sixteen-volume Left Behind series by Tim LaHaye and Jerry B. Jenkins has been translated into over one hundred languages and had by 2016 sold more than 65 million copies, making it the greatest success in the history of "Christian" fiction (LaHaye and Jenkins 1995–2007). The series claims to be based on Revelation, and it is not squeamish about violence. In *Glorious Appearing*, volume 12 in the series, Jesus takes the stage as a heavenly Rambo (LaHaye and Jenkins 2004; Johns 2005, 194–214).

> Tens of thousands fell dead, simply dropping where they stood, their bodies ripped open, blood pooling in great masses. (LaHaye and Jenkins 2004, 204)

> Tens of thousands grabbed their heads or their chests, fell to their knees, and writhed as they were invisibly sliced asunder. Their innards and entrails gushed to the desert floor, their blood pooling and rising in the unforgiving brightness of the glory of Christ. (LaHaye and Jenkins 2004, 226)

> Their flesh dissolved, their eyes melted, and their tongues disintegrated. (LaHaye and Jenkins 2004, 273)

This is "Jesus" in action. "Tens of thousands"—the number does not bother the narrator. "Innards and entrails" gushing to the desert floor—the narrator takes it in stride. Dissolving flesh, melting eyes, disintegrating tongues—this is Jesus bringing history to an end with an exclamation mark. The smashing box office success of *Left Behind* has been achieved without the need to worry about dreadful violence or bad theology.

Revelation has survived despite the put-downs, on the one hand, or the tremendous interest, on the other. The door is still there. Whether to enter, what to expect, and what we shall find are pressing questions right from the beginning. We shall need a quiet corner for reflection to sort out the options and decide how to proceed. Christopher Frilingos (2004, 6) puts the dilemma of Revelation sharply into perspective. He shows that Revelation presents Jesus as a victim of violence in the book's most pivotal scene (Rev. 5:6). This feature ensures that Jesus is represented just as he is in the other books in the NT. Cruelty is rampant, but the cruelty targets *him*.

But then, later in the story, scenes come on the screen that seem to cancel out the earlier impression (14:9–11). As the drama nears the end, those who line up on the wrong side of the conflict "will drink the wine of God's wrath, poured unmixed into the cup of God's anger, and . . . be tormented with fire and sulfur in the presence of the holy angels and in the presence of the Lamb" (14:10). The severity in this depiction is undeniable, and it is aggravated by duration. The text says that "the smoke of their torture goes up forever and ever" (14:11). Frilingos chills at the violence, as do others, and he chills even more when he looks beyond the carnage itself. The spectacle, he notes, plays out *under the gaze of the Lamb*. As he reads the text, *the Lamb is a spectator, and the Lamb seems bereft of compassion*. The alleged dispassionate gaze of the Lamb makes the horrific scene more horrifying. What we see, ultimately, is not only torment by fire and sulfur but also a lack of compassion, and the absence of compassion takes control of the message. "As if to confirm the truth of the Lamb's manly bearing, the creature's posture goes unmentioned in this episode; and the gash in the Lamb's body, so apparent earlier, disappears from view" (Frilingos 2004, 81).

Hatred of opponents, hatred of Rome, and an ending that obliterates the wounds in the Lamb's body are terrifying in theological terms. Frilingos finds Revelation teeming with spectacles and spectators familiar to Roman culture, staged for dramatic effect, and likely to appeal to the masses. The analogy is imperfect, but if he is correct, there will be an element of truth to the idea that Revelation to the first audience had a *Left Behind* feel to it. The violence celebrated in the Colosseum and elsewhere in the empire had by this criterion a corollary in Revelation's depictions, with Revelation giving the savagery theological warrant. By this criterion, Revelation becomes "a cultural product of the Roman Empire, a book that shared with contemporaneous texts and institutions specific techniques for defining the world and self" (Frilingos 2004, 5). It was, says Frilingos (2004, 120), "a story that subjects of the Roman Empire loved, for they knew it well."

## Through the Open Door

The foregoing perception of Revelation has two key components: God-ordained violence and a lack of compassion. These impressions have been noticed by people who are skeptical not only of Revelation but also of the entire Christian story line. When the French writer and Nobel laureate Albert Camus (1913–60) wrote that there "is no possible salvation for the man who feels real compassion" (1991, 57), he took for granted a Christian tradition that envisions eternal torment for those who make the wrong choice and—in the face of this scenario—the need to curb instinctual compassion. Interpretations of Revelation have contributed to this outlook, possibly more than any other book in the canon. Contrary to this entrenched view, we shall find—*beyond the door*—a message quite different from the impressions noted above. *We shall encounter a surprise that will leave us speechless*, as it does to onlookers at the most critical moment in the book (8:1). Readers will be wise to do the following: be sure to find the door; don't worry about the picket line advising against entry; keep a cool head amid the *Left Behind* stampede; then prepare for insights not found in the realm of thought, only in the realm of *revelation*.

The reorientation can begin by noting that Revelation is staging a recovery in circles that used to take little interest in the book. The outpouring of massive commentaries at the turn of the millennium is proof that scholars, publishers, and readers are finding the book worth their while to a degree not seen in the past (Aune 1996–98; Beale 1999; Brighton 1999; Osborne 2002; Koester 2014). This turnaround is evident not only with respect to market success. It also extends to perceptions of the book's theology. Richard J. Bauckham (1993a, ix) says that Revelation is "a work of immense learning, astonishingly meticulous literary artistry, remarkable creative imagination, radical political critique, and profound theology." Notice how this assessment does not have the slightest trace of Luther's contempt for Revelation's theology or for Bloom's claim that the book is "scarcely literate." Bauckham frames alternative options that include how to read Revelation and what to take away from it. "Profound theology" and "astonishingly meticulous literary artistry," as Bauckham puts it, suggest a radically different perception of what lies beyond the door.

Jacques Ellul (1977, 15) confronts head-on the notion that God in Revelation orchestrates violence. He cautions, first, that "the Apocalypse specifically is not a text capable of being understood directly." The first impression is not the best and should not be the last, and the negative reviews are unreliable because they deal in first impressions. Indeed, says Ellul, "Every supposed immediate comprehension is false," and this because Revelation "is a discourse extraordinarily sophisticated." His reading does not deny that Revelation depicts violence, but he insists that the violence is not God willed or God implemented. The characters and the plot are complex, and the hurry to blame God owes to an ill-advised rush to conclusion. In the scenes of devastation in Revelation's trumpet sequence (8:2–11:19), Ellul (1977, 65) takes the view—emphatically—that it is the action of satanic powers "that in every circumstance provokes death in the Apocalypse, *and not at all, never directly, the action of God upon men.*" Violence is not denied, whether in human reality or in Revelation, but the meaning of the violence, especially the *theological* meaning, does not lie on the surface.

And yet the surface also speaks, crackling and snapping with bursts that contradict the negative views. If Revelation is received as a message for the *ear* instead of the *eye*, it will greatly affect interpretation. Unsurprisingly, Frilingos (2004, 39) takes the theatricality in Revelation to mean that the book "privileges sight." John's visions may indeed seem like a movie—the visual imagery is compelling—but it comes to us by way of the *word*, as *hearing*. In the auditory scenario, the living person "*who reads aloud the words*" (1:3) retains control of the message by use of body language, emphases, pauses, and

7

tone of voice. The message is still *seen*—we "see" when we listen or read—but the *hearing* shapes the pictures. Kayle B. de Waal (2015) argues persuasively that Revelation privileges *sound* above *sight*. Similarly, Mitchell G. Reddish (2004) describes how *hearing* the book promotes impressions that may otherwise be missed. The difference with this kind of "seeing" is incalculable. This alone—reading the book aloud—might put an end to the idea that the God of Revelation has retribution on his mind. While this view delegates tremendous responsibility to readers and hearers, this, too, is within Revelation's purview. Its disclosures are reserved for "anyone who has an ear" (2:7, 11, 17, 29; 3:6, 13, 22; 13:9), and it calls for "a mind that has wisdom" (13:18; 17:9). The book is in the business of "aural circumcision" (Kermode 1979, 3), *reading* and *hearing* cooperating to make the message come out right.

As an auditory exercise, imagine hearing three calls to attention immediately upon passing through Revelation's open doors. "*Write!*" says a booming voice shortly after entry (1:11), repeating it at critical junctures a full twelve times (1:11, 19; 2:1, 8, 12, 18; 3:1, 7, 14; 14:13; 19:9; 21:5). "*Look!*" we hear even earlier (1:7), the same exclamation repeated a full twenty-six times (1:7, 18; 2:10, 22; 3:8, 9 [2x], 20; 4:1, 2; 5:5; 6:2, 5, 8; 7:9; 9:12; 11:14; 12:3; 14:1, 14; 16:15; 19:11; 21:3, 5; 22:7, 12). "*Come!*" we hear at the very end, the key word at the conclusion spoken in a tone of voice that is urgent and welcoming (22:17). "*Come!*" is repeated twice, but the voices saying it the second time are unexpected. "And let the one who hears *say*, '*Come!*'" (22:17). The surprise at the ending is not so much the exclamation itself *but that we hear ourselves exclaiming it*. The recipient of the message is now also a proclaimer; the invitee has become an inviter. This could hardly happen except for the proclaimer's conviction that the message does not have revenge on its mind. Revelation's auditory thrust is inimical to the view that Revelation is the Judas of the NT, a tribute to violence, or a play where Jesus turns in his worst performance. Correct *reading* accompanied by keen *hearing* will be the first step to setting things right at the door and immediately beyond the door. "If anyone is endowed with an ear, hear" (13:9; cf. 2:7, 11, 17, 29; 3:6, 13, 22).

## Revelation and the Roman Empire

What was the situation in which Revelation came into being? Will the "situation"—once we figure it out—have explanatory power for the book? These used to be easy questions, and they were answered in roughly the following order.

1. Revelation is an apocalyptic book (Aune 1986).
2. Apocalyptic literature originates in situations of crisis (P. Hanson 1979, 1; Rowland 1982, 9; Cook 1995; Porter-Young 2011, 3–45).

3. There was a crisis, and we know what it was: "It is obvious that Revelation was written at a time when the Christians of Asia Minor, and probably other places as well, were being persecuted by the Roman officials for their refusal to worship the emperors, both living and dead, as gods and to worship Roma, the personification of Rome, as a goddess" (Rist 1957, 354). In fact, "the situation was desperate" (Rist 1961, 22).

This used to be the answer, and it is still the answer in the eyes of many scholars. Overall, however, the consensus that used to exist has vanished. A far more complicated picture has emerged, listed by way of Paul Duff's (2001, 5–16) overview of the options and concentrating chiefly on the "crisis" question: Was there or wasn't there a crisis?

1. There was persecution, even though there is little or no evidence for it (Fiorenza 1991, 7).
2. There was a perception of hostility, whether the perception was warranted or not (A. Collins 1984, 84–110).
3. There was no crisis, perceived or otherwise (L. Thompson 1990, 171–201).
4. There was a crisis, but not in the sense that the Roman Empire threatened the church. Instead, "the 'crisis' facing the communities of the Apocalypse can be more accurately defined as a social conflict within the churches" (Duff 2001, 14).

What changed? How did questions that used to have simple answers morph into such complexity, whether from *crisis* to *no crisis* or from threats from *without* to threats from *within*? The answer lies largely in readings of the historical record and partly in Revelation itself. External evidence dates Revelation to the latter end of the reign of the emperor Domitian (81–96 CE; Irenaeus, *Haer.* 5.30.3). This date is not certain, but it is accepted by most scholars. According to Eusebius (*Hist. eccl.* 3.14–20), the first church historian (ca. 260–340 CE), Domitian was a wicked emperor and a notorious persecutor of Christians. Thanks to the testimony of writers like Pliny the Younger (*Pan.* 48–49), Tacitus (*Agr.* 39–44), Suetonius (*Dom.* 10.2; 11.1; 13.2; 15.1), and Dio Cassius (*Hist. rom.* 67.4.7; 67.11.3), on whom Eusebius relied, Domitian acquired a reputation as an erratic, megalomaniacal, and mean ruler. But was he? Ancient writers—and modern writers too—sometimes have other motives than the truth for their version of events. *Fake news* has a long history. A society structured by relations of patronage and propaganda can easily allow truth to slip low on its scale of priorities (Nauta 2002; Wallace-Hadrill 1989). Notions of an independent press or unbiased historians in Roman times can safely be laid aside. Paul Zanker's (1990, 237) caution to readers of Roman history is well advised:

We must never lose sight of the fact that, in a world without competing news agencies and the like, the general perception of historical events was largely dependent on the official version propagated by the state. Most of what makes up our news nowadays—disasters, crises—was never mentioned. Major catastrophes, like that of Varus's legions in Germany, of course became known, but no one dwelled on them. The constantly renewed imagery of new triumphs quickly swept away such dark shadows. The language of political imagery never even made use of the reversals as warning or admonition.

Instead, we must think in terms of flattery, on the one hand, and of misrepresentation, on the other. This is not hard to imagine, given the use of political propaganda in modern totalitarian states and political advertising in countries presumed to be free and open. In Leonard Thompson's (1990, 95–115) reading of the evidence, the written record is replete with propagandistic elements. The writers who shaped Domitian's reputation invented evils during his reign as a foil for their praise of Nerva (96–98) and Trajan (98–117), the emperors who succeeded Domitian after he had been murdered in a palace coup in 96 CE. The alleged villainy of Domitian magnified the virtues of Trajan, and the latter's virtues are exaggerated (Wallace-Hadrill 1995, 145). Brian Jones (1992, 196) disputes the assertion that Domitian demanded divine appellations, and he dismisses the notion of a Domitianic persecution. Being the last emperor in the Flavian dynasty meant that the new dynasty needed army support, a clean slate, and conspicuous claims of merit to establish its legitimacy (Grainger 2003). In important respects, Domitian's track record of governance, efficiency, and judicial integrity seems above average. His legacy includes the reputation of being one of the greatest builders in Rome, his managerial imprint also preserved in such far-flung places as Asia Minor and the Near East (Thomas 2004, 23).

Domitian risked defamation "through his utter determination to govern according to his own standards, to ignore tradition whenever it did not suit him and to proclaim the senate's impotence rather than disguise it through polite platitudes" (Jones 1992, 196; F. Parker 2001, 207–31). This brings to view a man who did not playact participatory rule in the knowledge that actual power sharing was a sham. While failure to stroke the egos of the upper class can be judged a risky political strategy on a personal level, such a policy suggests that ordinary people had little to fear (Ulrich 1996; Slater 1998). Evidence for persecution *within* Revelation, as in the cry of the slain martyrs under the fifth seal (6:9–11), although taken as proof of *Roman* persecution (Biguzzi 1998b), can have other explanations. After his assassination in 96 CE, Domitian's successors set afoot a process of "damnation and mutilation," an almost unparalleled attempt to eradicate all traces of his life and handiwork. Scholars today are hard pressed even to find the base for the colossal equestrian statue of Domitian that for five years was one of the most conspicuous monuments in Rome (Varner 2004; Thomas 2004).

Figure 1. Domitian's colossal equestrian statue in Rome is lost, but the body of this bronze statue at the Museo Archeologico dei Campi Flegrei (Baia) projects power. The head is a noteworthy case of "damnation and mutilation": the head was recarved to represent Nerva, Domitian's successor. Photo from Steven L. Tuck, "The Origins of Imperial Hunting Imagery: Domitian and the Redefinition of Virtus under the Principate," *Greece and Rome* 52, no. 2 (2005): 221–45.

Courtesy of Steven L. Tuck

The revision of the dominant view and its account of persecution demand a reconsideration of the situation that led to the writing of Revelation. Persecution of Christians orchestrated from the imperial center can no longer be taken as the social setting of believers at the time. L. Thompson (1990, 166) concludes that there was no significant political unrest or evidence of class conflict. Instead, the empire "was beneficial to rich and poor provincials; and there were checks against extensive abuse of the poorer provincials by the richer ones."

## Revelation and the Roman "Situation"

Domitian is largely off the hook in the new consensus regarding Roman imperial reality at the time of the writing of Revelation: he was not the persecutor of Christians that generations of interpreters made him out to be. But the empire has not ceased to be relevant. Attention has shifted to the Roman Empire as such and to the role of the imperial cult in Asia Minor. Steven Friesen (2001, 3) notes that "nearly all commentators on the Revelation of John have acknowledged that imperial cults—that is, institutions for the worship of the Roman emperors—played a crucial role in the production of John's text." His own contribution, in a study billed as the first book-length treatment of the topic, consolidates this view. In this scenario, imperial power projection is the most important reason for "the production of John's text," even if Domitian moves out of the limelight. Specific emperors are still in view, but they are now Augustus (31 BCE–14 CE) or Nero (54–67), not Domitian. Before we assess the merits of the now-dominant view of the role of the Roman Empire, we must know more about the evidence on which this view is based.

This part of the story begins with Julius Caesar (100–44 BCE) and his adopted son Augustus (63 BCE–14 CE). Augustus was the founding father of the imperial system and the main reason for its remarkable staying power. The key elements in the Augustan state, drawn from a variety of sources (Vergil, *Aen.*; Tacitus, *Ann.*; Syme 1960; Price 1984; Zanker 1990; Galinsky 1996; Beacham 1999), include the following points.

The Roman Empire had expanded into a colossal territorial entity by the time Julius Caesar crossed the Rubicon in 49 BCE, ostensibly to break the stranglehold of dysfunctional government in addition to defending his own honor and possibly his life (Syme 1960, 1–60). This marked the de facto end of the Republic and the ascent of larger-than-life ruler figures. Caesar was charismatic and Kennedy-esque as a person; Suetonius (*Jul.* 45) writes that he was "tall, his complexion light and clear, with eyes black, lively, and quick, set in a face somewhat full; his limbs were round and strong." He was valiant as a general (*Jul.* 55), beloved by his troops (*Jul.* 68; Gardner 1967, 25); successful as a writer (Caesar, *Bel. civ.*; Suetonius, *Jul.* 56), capable as a statesman (Gelzer 1968), unabashed in his amorous exploits (Suetonius, *Jul.* 50–52), and unapologetic in his grasp for power (*Jul.* 76–79). The latter did not sit well with some members of the Roman Senate. Defense of the Republic was hardly the only motive of the conspirators who plotted his murder, but it was a cause that could be argued in the name of patriotism and tradition.

The plot misfired. In reality, the murder of Julius Caesar on the floor of the Roman Senate in 44 BCE turned out to be a boon to the imperial office and a key element in the ensuing myth construction. In life, Caesar was a dictator. Dead, "he became a god and a myth, passing from the realm of history into literature and legend, declamation and propaganda," says Ronald Syme (1960, 53). Augustus astutely saw an opening and was quick to take advantage. As the grandson of Julius Caesar's sister and the designated heir in Caesar's will, he arranged to be formally accepted by the Senate as the deceased ruler's legally adopted son. He took care to erase *Octavianus*, stressing instead that he was the son of Caesar. He deftly prevailed on the Senate to vote divine honors for the murdered Caesar, the vote said to be accompanied by astral signs that were promptly incorporated into the public iconography (Galinsky 1996, 17; Suetonius, *Aug.* 94). Augustus could now designate himself as *divi filius*, son of the divinized emperor, endowed with greater-than-human luster (Galinsky 1996, 17).

Courtesy of Österreichisches Archäologische Institut

Figure 2. Frieze from a temple in Ephesus depicting the apotheosis (deification) of Lucius Verus (161–66 CE), coregent with his adoptive brother Marcus Aurelius. Caesar was the first emperor to be accorded "divine honors." Ephesos-Museum, Vienna.

When Augustus in 31 BCE prevailed in the civil war against Mark Antony to become the sole head of the empire, he toned down the imperial character of his rule to make it appear that he was a mere *first citizen*, the subtlety bearing fruit in the form of ever increasing de facto stature (Zanker 1990, 92; Galinsky 1996, 11). Shrewdly, Augustus proclaimed the restoration of the Republic, not its eclipse, although the sham did not escape Tacitus's irony and ire (*Ann.* 1.9). The republican government continued in form even though it was undermined in practice. Augustus made it his priority to tend to the public weal, launching an ambitious program of religious and moral reform with the aim of restoring Roman greatness, piety, and virtue (Zanker 1990, 1–2). In reality, the emperor was increasingly a priestly, superhuman figure, a savior, the head of all the major cults, the Pontifex Maximus, and the link between earth and heaven (Suetonius, *Aug.* 58; Galinsky 1996, 29–39). Power and authority were reinforced through a program of storytelling in marble and ritual, the marble in the form of imposing temples that linked the emperor to the gods (Price 1984, 54–55; Friesen 2001, 33).

The ritual enactments were at one and the same time religious, entertaining, and popular. The goal was "to project onto future generations the impression that they lived in the best of all possible worlds and in the best of all times" (Zanker 1990, 4). Or, as Jupiter says to his daughter Venus in Vergil's epic poem *The Aeneid*,

13

Figures 3 and 4. Statues illustrating Augustan iconography, presenting him as a soldier and emperor in the early propaganda (left) and as priest (*pontifex maximus*) and father of the homeland (*pater patriae*) in the later representation (right).

> I set no limits to their fortunes and
> no time; I give them empire without end.
> . . . The gruesome gates of war,
> with tightly welded iron plates,
> shall be shut fast.

Jupiter's prophecy makes Rome an "empire without end." The poem mentions "Julius," referring either to Julius Caesar or using it as a code for Augustus. Either way, the Caesar will be installed "as a god in heaven as a sign of Roman supremacy in the world" (Galinsky 1996, 251). On earth, there will be peace.

In the *Res gestae divi Augustus*, written at Augustus's direction shortly before his death, Augustus piously claims that he transferred the commonwealth from his power to "the judgment of the senate and the people of Rome," retaining for himself only the distinction that he "excelled all in *auctoritas*" (Galinsky 1996, 11). *Auctoritas* has a strong moral connotation, a status reflecting the esteem in which the person is held more than distinctions sought or demanded. Augustus, too, was adept at myth making, particularly by his skill in leaving the pride of the senators intact while eroding their power. He would be remembered just as he had represented himself—as a *savior* and *healer*. The image was powerful—and more powerful than reality would support (Zanker 1990, 101, 238).

In Asia Minor, the setting of the book of Revelation, the cult of the emperor began during the reign of Augustus and took hold with less reserve than in Rome. The cult, says S. R. F. Price (1984, 24–35, 117–21), was not simply a matter of honors, hero worship, or public formality, and it was not coerced. Most of the seven cities in Revelation had imperial temples, beginning with the cult of Roma and Augustus at Pergamum in 29 BCE and a second temple for Roma and Julius Caesar in Ephesus in 27 BCE (Price 1984, 24–35, 54–62). These projects were initiated by prominent individuals in the provinces, representing a system of exchange, patronage, and narrative creation (Price 1984, 24–25, 102–14, 234–48). While ruler veneration had an antecedent in the Hellenistic world, the imperial cult came into existence because of the need for a "language" for the awesome power of Rome. As Price notes, citizens "represented the emperor to themselves in the familiar terms of divine power," and the ritual of the cult structured the world in terms of "the relationship between the emperor and the gods" (Price 1984, 248; Zanker 1990, 299). The religious character of the imperial office is not in question, nor can it be doubted that the empire was eager to inscribe its myth into the minds of citizens and slaves across the Roman world.

This background is crucial to understanding how many scholars see the Roman Empire in Revelation. According to "the Roman Imperial View," Revelation's story centers on the Roman Empire and the imperial cult. John is addressing the historical situation contemporary to him. The story is projected to climax in the death of the emperor Nero and the myth of Nero's return. Revelation 13 is the cornerstone for this conviction. Leading interpreters argue this view as an established fact. To Wilhelm Bousset (1906, 120), "The observation that the core of the prophecy in the Apocalypse refers to the then widely held expectation of Nero redivivus is in my opinion an immovable point that will not again be surrendered, the *bronze rock* of the contemporary historical interpretation against which all contrary points of view so far have been dashed to pieces." Richard Bauckham (1993a, 389) is no less certain. "The gematria [referring to the number 666] does not merely assert that Nero is the beast: it demonstrates that he is." Jan Dochhorn (2010, 115) concludes that "in the time of the seventh trumpet, at the close of the rule of a-yet-to-come Roman emperor, . . . a world ruler will arise that will threaten Christendom to its foundation. This figure is none other than the emperor Nero raised to life" (see also Klauck 2001, 683–90; Champlin 2003, 1–35).

This is the "upside" for the emperor veneration that many scholars see as the main concern in Revelation. Its ingredients are the mammoth reach of the imperial office, the lines converging in the figure of the emperor at the point where earth and heaven meet (Price 1984, 248), and the promotion and celebration of the prestige of the imperial office by the various imperial cults, culminating in the myth of Nero's death and resurrection.

### The Other Side of the "Roman Situation"

Is there a downside—and even a contrary point of view? There is definitely a downside and evidence that accommodates a different view. The downside relates to the representation and interpretation of the historical realities in the secular sources, but it is chiefly concerned with the alleged connection between the historical realities and the message of Revelation.

Was it irrelevant to emperor veneration that Julius Caesar was a notorious womanizer; had a very public affair with Servilia, Brutus's mother; and that Brutus might well have had personal motives for assassinating him (Syme 1960, 58)? Brutus was not only defending the Republic but also settling accounts with a man he had no reason to love and admire.

Did it escape public knowledge that Augustus, Caesar's adopted son, represented as a paragon of virtue in the public iconography, was less than that in private? Livia, his second wife, was taken from another man while pregnant. Tiberius, the next emperor, was another man's biological son (Suetonius, *Aug.* 62; Syme 1960, 229). Claudius (41–54) had his wife Messalina assassinated, then married Agrippina, his niece. In 49 CE, the purpose-driven couple arranged the betrothal of Octavia, Claudius's ten-year-old daughter, to Nero, then Agrippina's eleven-year-old son and soon to be Claudius's adopted son. Britannicus, Nero's "brother" by adoption, was the brother of Octavia, Nero's first wife. He was unceremoniously poisoned in his sister's presence (Beacham 1999, 193–95). Augustus succeeded in investing the imperial office with prestige, and he carefully cultivated an image of humility and piety, but his successors were less worried about such niceties. Seneca's parody of the divinization of the emperor Claudius belongs to this reckoning. His savage lampoon is in English known as *The Pumpkinification of the Deified Claudius*: Claudius was upon his death made into a pumpkin rather than a god! The emperor is said to have farted just as he lay dying, then uttered the undignified words, "Oh Lord, I think I've [soiled] myself." The narrator chimes in that Claudius "certainly [soiled] . . . everything else." Heaven shudders at the monster presenting himself for divinization. Deliberations end with the decision to send Claudius to the underworld to shuffle papers for one of Caligula's freedmen (Romm 2014, 65).

The résumé of Nero (54–67) includes *regicide, fratricide, matricide, mariticide, holocaust,* and *suicide:* the murder of his adoptive father, brother, mother, and wife, and then the Great Fire before his reign ended in suicide (Romm 2014, 33–198). Syme (1960, 439) writes that "from first to last the dynasty of the Julii and the Claudii ran true to form, despotic and murderous." The notion of a "Golden Age" during the first five years of Nero, ostensibly owing to Seneca's responsible tutelage, is not sustained in James Romm's (2014) careful account. Seneca, willingly or not, comes across as Nero's enabler. If *virtus* and *pietas* ("virtue" and "piety") were the most important constituents in emperor worship and the case for divinization, Caligula, Claudius, and Nero brought diminishing returns. For Nero, posthumous divinization was not on offer when the Senate declared him a public enemy (Romm 2014, 201). In 96 CE the Senate also denied divine honors to Domitian upon his murder by members of the palace guard (Suetonius, *Dom.* 23).

How much of this reached the public? Nero was not particularly subtle about his exploits. The evident dissembling and hypocrisy cannot be overlooked, as with the brave face of Octavia upon the murder of her brother in her presence, duly described by Tacitus. The parting kiss of Seneca by Nero before Seneca headed home to commit suicide is in the same category. Did appearances really triumph over reality, "common knowledge notwithstanding"? Why the need for surveillance by secret police that there would not be sloth in the "acclamations and pre-arranged applause" at the public

Public Domain

Carole Raddato, CC BY-SA 2.0 / Wikimedia Commons

Figures 5 and 6. Happier days? Reliefs from Aphrodisias showing Nero and Britannicus, his brother by adoption (left), and his mother Agrippina crowning her son emperor (right). Nero had Britannicus poisoned and later assassinated his mother.

games when Nero was one of the performers (Tacitus, *Ann.* 13.16; 14.56; 15.18; 16.4–5)? The stagecraft of the theater and the cult was impressive. Was it persuasive?

Proponents of "the Roman Imperial View" seem unfazed by these counterpoints, perhaps on the logic that the conduct and character of the emperors were sanitized in Asia Minor to the point that the connection between the emperor and the gods was secure. In the main, however, the possibility of self-evident unworthiness is left out. The "situated void" in Roman society represents the most egregious sin of omission (Welborn 2009, 309). "Void" means "emptiness," and the emptiness was located at the center, in full view of all citizens. L. L. Welborn applies the term to the ubiquity of slavery and the fact that death on the cross was an ever-present possibility for the slave. This "situated void" was so unflattering to the Roman self-image that decent writers avoided the subject altogether. Nonmention, however, is not the same as not seen or known. Slavery was ubiquitous throughout the empire, and the slaves were without legal protection. On the Esquiline Hill in Rome, slaves were brought in routinely by their owners to be crucified for utterly trivial offences. *Slavery* and *death on the cross*, these together, were part of the Roman power structure. Indeed, says Welborn (2009, 309), "The cross may be identified as the dark, gravitational center which, whether recognized or repressed, allotted places to all those who lived within the socio-symbolic edifice of the Roman Empire, and compelled thought to consent to those places."

Silence concerning this black hole cannot be construed as lack of awareness. Instead, it is awareness conspiring with silence concerning the black hole that would be fatal to notions of imperial worthiness, a Golden Age, and a blissful *Pax Romana*. Welborn (2009, 303) glimpses "a subject cringing around a void, simultaneously registering and repressing knowledge of the death-driven situation with which his existence was constrained" (see also Wallace-Hadrill 1982, 19–36; Bowersock 1972, 179–212; Bradley 1987). Will the emperor, the figure at the top of the pyramid, emerge worship-worthy? Was special revelation required to point out that he wasn't? Or did the facts speak for themselves, in horrified silence (Parenti 2003)?

These questions suggest what the answer ought to be. Despite the silence— and despite the evidence that this was a *willed and orchestrated* silence—voices break through to show an emperor without clothes (and sometimes the emperor as a pumpkin). Tacitus, the greatest of the Roman historians, was not fooled by appearances. *True, there was peace thereafter—bloody peace,* he wrote sarcastically of the myth of Augustan peace (Tacitus, *Ann.* 1.10.4; Zanker 1990, 187). "On the day that he died," Suetonius says of Augustus, "he called for a mirror, and had his hair combed and his lower jaw, which had fallen from weakness, propped up. Presently he summoned a group of friends and asked: 'Have I played my part in the farce of life creditably enough?'" (*Aug.*

99). The self-irony of the emperor's final act is impressive. He knew it was a farce. Did everyone else also know?

What imperial myth making aspired to achieve is not in doubt—monuments, rituals, and stagecraft all bent toward the same task—but there are a host of reasons to question whether it succeeded. Doubts in this regard call for other options with respect to Revelation's errand. What can a *Book of Revelation* add to evidence already lying in broad daylight with respect to the Roman Empire? On the logic that an argument in favor of the obvious makes the obvious *less* clear, other hypotheses have greater credence than the Nero myth. Owing no debt to the scholars who make the myth of Nero's return the centerpiece to understanding Revelation, Gerhard Maier (1981, 622) concludes that "the [myth of] Nero redivivus is anything but a *bronze rock* for interpretation; it is only a hypothesis, and a fairly clumsy one at that."

## Alternative Options

Roman imperial persecution lacks explanatory power for the "situation" in Revelation, and many scholars no longer subscribe to this view. The "replacement model," centered on the imperial cult and the myth of Nero's return, risks the same fate even though it enjoys wide scholarly esteem. Substantive objections to the Nero hypothesis are many, culminating in the damning question, "In what way is Nero the consummate opponent of Christ?" (Resseguie 1998, 56). The empire and the notion of Nero's return put forward a foot that is too small for the shoe of John's imagery (Tonstad 2006, 7–15, 41–54). Revelation's terms call for a larger character, in *quality* as much as in *quantity*, and they outline a plot that reaches beyond Roman political concerns. Other specific objections include (1) the absence of Nero in the earliest known interpretations of Revelation (Irenaeus, *Haer.* 5.30.1; 5.30.3; Tonstad 2008a); (2) textual criticism that is prejudicial to Revelation's cosmic perspective (as in Aune 1996–98, 725–26); (3) the connection between the first half of Revelation and the second half (Tonstad 2006, 108–23); (4) the tenor of Revelation's terms, particularly the *imitation* theme (Minear 1953; Tonstad 2008a); and (5) the relationship of Rev. 13 to the Synoptic apocalypse (Vos 1965, 54–111; Tonstad 2008a).

What options are left—and better? The alternative can be described succinctly.

1. Revelation's perspective is *cosmic* more than it is *Roman* (Tonstad 2006). The cosmic, nonhuman aspect in the story is more than a means by which to amplify *Roman* reality.
2. The story is shaped by the *biblical narrative* more than by imperial life in the first century (Rissi 1966, 65–70; Tonstad 2006, 208; Töniste

2016). It is essential to pay attention to the character designated as *the Ancient Serpent* (12:9; 20:2).

3. The plot of Revelation projects the theme of *imitation* more than the notion of *parody* (Minear 1953; 1968, 119). "At the end Satan's attack must be launched from a beachhead within the Church, where the earth-beast not only carries on priestly activities but displays the credentials of a prophet" (Minear 1968, 119; cf. Beale 1999, 708).

4. Revelation is truly prophetic and not only descriptive of first-century concerns. In this regard its horizon is like the Synoptic apocalypse (Vos 1965, 54–111; Beale 1999, 708; cf. Wenham 1981, 2:345–75; Tonstad 2007). This story line is already evident in the messages to the seven churches, beginning with the surprising finding that "most of the issues enumerated (and certainly the most pressing ones) are internal, intra-Christian issues" (Duff 2001, 46).

The alternative sketched above may be called "the Cosmic Conflict View" or "the Imitation View." This view is not indifferent to Roman imperial reality, but it deals with bigger concerns, and it projects on a wider screen. What lies on the surface in the form of imposing buildings and beguiling spectacles matters less than what is not seen. Nonhuman powers are at work. They are more important than the Roman emperors—more important also in the sense that the plot begins with *them*, not with Rome. Primordial aspirations of the nonhuman powers come to fruition in the eschaton. They, not the myth of Nero's return, control the story line. Biblical antecedents and images carry over into Revelation; they explain shocking twists and turns in the story better than anything *Roman* or *human* (20:1–7; Tonstad 2006, 41–54). The temporal horizon reaches beyond the present, but the most important disclosure of the book—what certifies it as *revelation*—is the revelation *in the middle* of John's spatial and temporal boundaries (5:6). With the role of the Roman Empire circumscribed, a more robust concept of *revelation* may get the space it has been denied for "the production of John's text" (Friesen 2001, 3).

## Revelation as *Revelation*

*Apokalypsis* (Rev. 1:1) is not a term for catastrophe. Looking at the word itself, it is best approached through its verbal counterpart, *apo-kalyptō*. *Apo-kalyptō* describes an *un*-covering, a removal of the lid to bring the hidden item into full view (BDAG 505, καλύπτω; A. Oepke, *TDNT* 3:563–92, ἀποκαλύπτω). The word pictures the opposite of concealment and is the reversal of concealment. In the context of Revelation, the notion of revealing what another party might wish to hide goes to the heart of the matter. When the concealed item is exposed in broad daylight, it has, in a makeshift Greek-English transliteration, been *"apo-kalypted."* Full disclosure of the kind we find in Revelation is a threat to other powers but not to God. A work that sails under the name *revelation* cannot escape scrutiny of the concept itself.

## Revelation as Exposé

Revelation as exposé begins with the realization that the book is rife with conflict. "War" *(polemos)* is one of the most important words in the book, as a noun (9:7, 9; 11:7; 12:7, 17; 13:7; 16:14; 19:19; 20:8) or as a verb *(polemeō)* with the meaning "to *wage war*" (12:7; 13:4; 17:14; 19:11). No sentence is more representative than the statement *"There was war"* (12:7). *Polemos* is the word from which the English "polemics" is derived. In Greek the word means "war," but the connotation of "polemics" in English is useful. "War" has a military connotation; "polemics" is a form of disagreement playing out in the realm of opinion and argument. This notion fits the conflict in Revelation better than an outright matchup of conflicting parties in the realm of power.

War, yes, but *who*, and *how*, and *why*? Revelation goes out of its way to characterize the felonious party. The adversary has a name—he is *"the Devil [ho Diabolos], the Satan [ho Satanas], the Ancient Serpent [ho ophis ho archaios],* and *the Deceiver of the whole world"* (12:9; 20:2; see also 2:10; 12:12; 20:10). The terms and the many aliases seem deliberate and descriptively precise. Are they also theologically significant? Should the character thus described be taken seriously? If our answer is "yes," we are in largely uncharted territory because this character is *not* given much attention in critical interpretations of Revelation (Tonstad 2006, 7–16, 41–54). Should the implied *plot* or *story* be taken seriously, too? If our answer again is "yes," we shall have more work on our hands because critical interpretations *do not* make a substantive investment in the character or the plot.

With the name comes a story. *The Devil* is "the ancient serpent" and "the deceiver of the whole world" (12:9; 20:2). The terms link the opponent in Revelation to the serpent in Genesis (Rev. 12:9; 20:2; Gen. 3:1–13). Revelation has not invented this character from scratch. Moreover, what the character is in the context of Genesis, he is also in Revelation. Both texts represent him as a *deceiver*, and both make *deception* a key element (Rev. 12:9, 10; 13:14; 18:23; 19:20; 20:3, 8, 10; Gen. 3:1, 13). The import of the story of Adam, Eve, and the serpent in Genesis is subject to debate, but Christian theology has generally made the story ground zero in its conception of "sin"—and catastrophic (Tonstad 2016a, 87–103).

Crucial parts of the story are bleached or missing in the theological tradition. A quick review is telling for what is remembered and what is left out.

## I. Remembered

She took of its fruit and ate. (Gen. 3:6)

She also gave some to her husband, who was with her, and he ate. (Gen. 3:6)

GOD: Have you eaten from the tree of which I commanded you not to eat? (Gen. 3:11)

Therefore the LORD God sent him forth from the garden of Eden. (Gen. 3:23)

## II. Left Out (Less Well Remembered)

THE SERPENT: Did God say, "You shall not eat from any tree in the garden?" (Gen. 3:1)

THE SERPENT: You will not die. (Gen. 3:4)

THE WOMAN: The serpent deceived me, and I ate. (Gen. 3:13)

GOD TO THE SERPENT: Because you have done this, cursed are you. . . . I will put enmity between you and the woman, and between your offspring and hers. (Gen. 3:14–15)

The representations above are not meant to suggest that we do not "remember" some parts in an absolute sense or that parts have been "left out" on purpose. It is enough to delineate these accounts as different emphases, but the differences are not trivial. On the side of "Remembered," the human agent is in focus. The line of action runs from the divine command to violation, and from violation to punishment for having violated the command. The character of the divine command is not subject to debate. The main problem in the story can be described as disobedience to the divine command. This version has been the dominant emphasis in the Christian "sin" memory of the story.

On the side of "Left Out," the accent falls on the role of the serpent, first, and on deception, second (Gen. 3:1, 13). In this version, the serpent is a significant character and at least equal to the human agent in the plot construct. *Misrepresentation* of the divine command, not *violation*, is the first move (Gen. 3:1). In the second version, the human agent is a *victim* and not only a *violator* of the divine command even if we maintain that the violator should not have believed the serpent. The "sin" problem is not limited to violation of the divine command (Tonstad 2016b, 207–20).

Which of these versions fits Revelation best? To opt for the second version is the easy part. It is a more demanding task to carve out room for the prospect that Revelation takes an interest in *the ancient serpent* and—far more demanding—incorporates the deception in the garden of Eden in its conception of what makes *the ancient serpent* be *the deceiver of the whole world* (Rev. 12:9; 20:2; Gen. 3:1, 13). Putting this into perspective, we are expected to work with a notion of deception that is anchored in the biblical narrative, not in Roman imperial reality. Second, the remedy must equal the problem, now a problem that makes misrepresentation a key ingredient. Why is the remedy the way it is in Revelation? Why, indeed, is *revelation* the remedy?

He "is *the Devil [ho Diabolos]*," Revelation says of the adversary (12:9; 20:2). *Diabolos* has the same root as ballistics, *throwing* something *through* another person, here with the connotation of *complaining about a person to a third party*, *bringing charges*, or simply *throwing mud* (BDAG 226–27, διάβολος). In modern English, he is *the Slanderer* or *the Mudslinger* (12:9; 20:2; cf. 13:6). For a war fought primarily in the realm of opinion, this points to a character who specializes in misrepresenting others. He conforms to what has been called "the world's most convincing portrait of Satan," as in Goethe's *Faust*: "cynicism, scoffing, negation, is the key-note of his intellectuality" (Wayne 1949, 22).

Slander is damaging to the reputation of the person who is slandered. If God were to be the target of slander, it would be damaging to God too (Tonstad 2006, 89–107). The purpose of slander is to portray a person as something they're not. This is one facet of slander—misrepresenting another person—but it is not the only element. The slanderer also projects virtues he does not have: he may even pretend to possess the virtues of the one slandered. *Misrepresentation* of the other person goes hand in hand with deceitful *self-representation*.

Slander is successful if it wins acceptance for the idea that the slanderer is *virtuous* while the other side—the good side—is the *villain*. This calls for stealth, subtlety, and tremendous audacity. Quintilian (35–ca. 96 CE), the great teacher of rhetoric in the Roman world, explains how a lawyer may yet win his case by slandering the opponent if neither the character of his client nor the merits of the case are likely to get traction before the judges.

> Let it, however, be laid down as a general rule that we should turn from that which is prejudicial to us to that which is favorable. If we are perplexed about our cause, the character of our client may aid us; if about our client, the nature of our cause. If nothing that can be a support to us presents itself [i.e., neither character nor cause], *we may seek for something to damage our adversary*, for as it is our greatest wish to gain more favor than our adversary, so it will be our next object to incur less dislike. (*Inst.* 4.1.44)

This counsel will not help the reputation of the legal profession, but it is instructive. "Going negative" is the only option for the lawyer who has a poor case and an unpleasant client to defend. Success hinges on making the other person look bad. It is not easy to fix a problem of this kind, but the solution, if found, must cut two ways: it must show that the *slanderer* is guilty of misrepresenting the other side, and it must deprive him of the veneer of virtue.

Analogies between theology and human affairs have serious limitations, but the worst that can happen is that the attempted analogy is unhelpful. How, as a thought experiment, does society handle slander? What are the constraints against speech, particularly false speech?

I. F. Stone (1989, 197–214) makes Athens in the days of Socrates a case in point, saying that Athens believed in free speech and a free "press." According to Stone, Plato (427–347 BCE) and possibly Socrates (470–399 BCE) were against the emerging democratic values in Athens that included, among other things, the right to the free expression of opinion. He makes the Athenian ideal compare favorably to the standard set in our time. "Wherever Athenians gathered, they were free to hear him [Socrates]. No KGB—or, for that matter, FBI or CIA—had to tap his telephone to learn his views. Though such institutions were already known in other parts of ancient Greece, they did not exist in Athens" (Stone 1989, 113). Modern news outlets did not exist, but Athens had public arenas where they could express themselves. "The Athenian equivalent of a free press was the theater" (Stone 1989, 114). The irony of Socrates's case, then, was that Socrates, although benefiting from the right to free expression, a right in which he may not have believed, was prosecuted for taking advantage of a right that the Athenians claimed to support.

> When Athens prosecuted Socrates, it was *untrue* to itself. The paradox and the shame in the trial of Socrates is that a city famous for free speech prosecuted a philosopher guilty of no other crime than exercising it. To invoke the memory of our own American lapses, Athens had no Alien and Sedition Laws. Athens had no little Iron Curtain like the McCarran-Walter immigration act to bar visitors with suspect ideas. . . . Athens never had an un-Athenian Activities Investigating Committee. (Stone 1989, 197)

Free speech, especially when it is put to wrongful use, is a demanding ideal. "The trial of Socrates was a prosecution of *ideas*," says Stone. "He was the first *martyr* of free speech and free thought" (Stone 1989, 197). If we make the Roman Empire another case in point, the surveillance by secret police at the public games during the reign of Nero suggests a society enamored by amusement but less smitten by the right to free speech (Tacitus, *Ann.* 13.16; 14.56; 15.18; 16.4–5). At the time when I am writing this, one of the principal countries in the Middle East has seized the offices of the largest newspaper, replacing the editorial staff with hand-picked editors who are friendly to the government. "Free speech," as the concept goes, is a rarity in the affairs of nations. Athens in the days of Socrates could be an exception, although less an exception for failing to let Socrates benefit. The United States might be another exception. In the words of Supreme Court Justice Louis D. Brandeis, the constitutional remedy for false speech is "more speech, not enforced silence" (W. Turner 2011, 126–27). For the United States, too, as for Athens, there might be times when the country blinks with respect to its own ideal.

We can now ask about speech in God's economy and for God's remedy for false speech. The Bible begins with a case of "false speech" (Gen. 3:1). It ends with a sustained showdown with *the ancient serpent*, also described as *the deceiver of the whole world* (Rev. 12:9). Does this mean that God's remedy for "false speech" is "more speech"? Does it mean that God's remedy is—*revelation*?

*Apokalypsis*, as noted, is not a word for catastrophe and not primarily a technical term. "John was writing . . . the climax of prophetic revelation, which gathered up the prophetic meaning of the Old Testament scriptures and disclosed the way in which it was being and was to be fulfilled in the last days," says Bauckham (1993a, xi). Continuity and a steadying hand make the many-faceted books of the Bible into a forward-driven story. Beyond this "gathering up" in the last book of the Bible, *apokalypsis* is "more speech" going head to head with false speech. "More speech" would then, in the realm of theology as much as in civil society, be the better way even though it is also the road less traveled. Brandeis credited the framers of the constitution of the United States for recognizing that "it is hazardous to discourage thought, hope, and imagination; that fear breeds repression; that repression breeds hate; that hate menaces stable government; that the path of safety lies in the opportunity to discuss freely supposed grievances and proposed remedies; and that the fitting remedy for evil counsels is good ones" (W. Turner 2011, 127).

Concepts like these might be included among the working hypotheses before we immerse ourselves in the seals (4:1–8:1), the trumpets (8:2–11:19), and the bowls (15:1–16:21) that make up the bulk of Revelation. If this has merit, it means that an ideal in human society is not less an ideal in matters between God and humans. It could be the other way around: when humans cringe in the face of their "more speech" ideal, God does not. Such will be the case if we see in Revelation "more speech" deployed against the terrible menace of "false speech."

## Revelation as *Unveiling*

Revelation is not only an exposé. Near the climax of the trumpet sequence, an angel appears that might easily be mistaken for a divine figure (10:1). "He held a little scroll that *had been opened* in his hand," John reports (10:2). An opened scroll suggests a disclosure at the point of completion. He "raised his right hand to heaven and swore by him who lives forever and ever, who created heaven and what is in it, the earth and what is in it, and the sea and what is in it: 'There will be no more time [*chronos*], but in the days of the sound of the seventh angel, when he is to blow his trumpet, the mystery of God will have come to completion, as he proclaimed [*euēngelisen*] to his servants the prophets'" (10:6–7).

A mystery is nearing completion—but not out of the blue! What comes to completion was "proclaimed to his servants the prophets" (10:7). The proclamation happened in advance of the time of its fulfillment and was in its earliest configuration set forth as announcement of good news (*euēngelisen*). Looking at the OT background in the prophet Amos, he says that "the Lord God does nothing without revealing [*apokalypsē*] his teaching [*paideian autou*] to his servants the prophets" (Amos 3:7 LXX, my trans.).

> **Paideia in the LXX of Amos**
>
> The Greek word *paideia* is used in the Septuagint translation of Amos 3:7 (cf. Rev. 10:7) to refer to God's providing training, education, and understanding. This is in line with its use in Revelation and expresses the aspiration of this series as well.

*Apokalypsis* is at work in the background text, and it is best understood as a disclosure policy to which God is deeply committed. A God who "does nothing without revealing his secret" ensures that revelation is anchored in God's disposition (Paul 1991, 113; cf. Tonstad 2016a, 125–41).

If we make this our reference point for asking why we have a certain communication, the focus shifts from situational factors to God. "Making known" on the part of God and "knowing" on the part of humans bring to light deep and persistent elements in the divine economy. This note is struck with emphasis at the very beginning: "*the revelation [apokalypsis] of Jesus Christ . . . to make known [deixai] . . . he made it known [esēmanen]*" (1:1). John deploys two different verbs to describe the commission, but both verbs come down to "making known." *Apokalypsis* and the notion that *God gave* are supporting terms toward the same goal (1:1).

## Temporal Horizon

Revelation's relationship to historical time has so dominated readings that the main schools of interpretation break along axes of time (Court 1979, 2–15; Pate 1998). *Preterist* interpretations argue that Revelation's *time* is chiefly the time of the author. Careful study of Roman imperial reality in the late first century is the key to the meaning of the book. This "school" sees the emperor Nero as a dominant figure (Bousset 1906, 358; Dochhorn 2010, 102–39).

### Revelation and Time

| School of thought | Temporal horizon |
| --- | --- |
| Preterism | Time of John—first-century Roman reality |
| Historicism | Time of John and beyond—continuous history |
| Futurism | Time of the end—in practice |

For preterists, the return of Nero now a remote concern, Revelation's value is not thereby exhausted. Preterists argue that the book still communicates meaningfully to situations in which Revelation's concerns are *actualized*. Systems of oppression, predation, and illicit alliances between religious interests and the interests of the state fall under its judgment even if the political power is less circumscribed than the imperial office or the religion subtler than the imperial cult. If the preterist view of *time* is a limitation, it is softened by envisioning imperial reality as a *type* with many possible incarnations. Many preterist interpretations bring important value judgments into the discussion in the form of postcolonial perspectives and criticism of empire (Keller 1996, 140–80, 275–310; Moore 2006, 97–121; Friesen 2001, 210–17; Kraybill 2010). To the extent that the preterist temporal commitment defines and specifies the *type*, however, the possibility of missing the mark is not eliminated. A preterist reading can overcome the limitation only if it succeeds in defining the *type* correctly. *Time* and *type* may prove to be so closely linked that it is impossible to get one of them right without the other.

*Futurists* hold that Revelation is mostly about the end of time, not the time of the author. In practice, this tends to be interpreted as the time of the current reader. Futurist interpreters show little concern for textual and historical controls. Despite coming to grief again and again with respect to relating Revelation's symbols to contemporary events, the appetite for such applications shows little sign of abating. Predictions have shown a knack for "turning failure into fortune," one such attempt reaching sales of twenty-eight million (Lindsey 1970). In the marketplace of prophecy in the United States, futurist interpretations have the largest market share by a wide margin. The Left Behind novels, discussed earlier, are examples of prophetic scenarios written within the futurist framework. Academic disdain for futurist approaches to Revelation is so deep-seated that respectable commentaries hardly dignify them with a bibliographic entry.

The *historicist* "school," also known as the continuous historical interpretation, claims that Revelation depicts all of history, especially history from the first century until the end of time. This view, too, claims referential specificity with respect to Revelation's symbols: each symbol should ideally have one specific fulfillment. Historicism received a boost during the Protestant Reformation for finding in Revelation resources for an anti-Catholic message. Martin Luther, too, made peace with the book in his later years, and his interpretation fits a historicist conception (LW 35:400–410). The historicist influence has since fallen on hard times (Kovacs and Rowland 2004, 19–23), in part because academic interpretations favor preterism while the popular market has embraced futurist schemes. Historicist interpretations have also paid a penalty for changing their map of events. As in futurism, history tends to climax close to the time of the interpreter (U. Smith 1884, 476–93; Stefanovic 2009a, 285–322). C. Marvin Pate (1998, 18) writes that "failed attempts to locate the fulfillment of Revelation in the course of circumstances of history has doomed it to continual revision as time passed and, ultimately, to obscurity." It is noteworthy that futurist schemes have not significantly diminished their market appeal despite ever-changing applications.

These schools are all "time bound" or "time specific," and they have in common bold lines running from the symbol to the historical reality to which a symbol is said to refer. Claims of referential specificity are less risky for preterist interpreters, given the advantage of working with historical data that are almost all in the past. But a stable historical database does not solve all its problems. Challenges to preterist readings have chiefly to do with *adequacy* and *relevance*. I have critiqued tenets of the preterist view with respect to *adequacy*: *the foot is too small for the shoe* (Tonstad 2008a). *Adequacy* and *relevance* are criteria by which all interpretations should expect to be judged. Is Nero truly the referent for the number 666 (13:18), as leading preterists claim (Bauckham 1993a, 389; Dochhorn 2010, 115)? Did John foresee the Dark Ages under the third trumpet or "the rise of rationalism, skepticism, humanism, and liberalism, with its final product of secularism," under the fifth trumpet, as envisioned in a historicist proposal? Or, in another iteration of the fifth trumpet, should we see the emergence of "deism, relativism, nihilism, rationalism, and communism" in the eighteenth century (Stefanovic 2009a, 303, 312)? If John meant to describe the eighteenth century, do these *-isms* do justice to his priorities? Will the yearning for predictive specificity reflected in these proposals pass the adequacy test? Does the number 666 (13:18) refer to a tattoo to be placed on the forehead or the hand of the unfaithful some time during the last three decades of the twentieth century, as a futurist interpreter argued with enormous market success (Lindsey 1970, 112–13)? Or, in another example of the high-wire dance of futurists, does "Armageddon" in Revelation predict a conflict over oil and the location of the decisive battle in World War III, as suggested by an interpreter billed as "the Father of Modern Biblical prophecy" (Walvoord 2007)? Still on the futurist high-wire act, should the "Armageddon" sentiments in American Christianity dictate the political priorities of the United States in the Middle East while also nourishing attitudes that are "resistant to federal authority, hostile to the traditional American politics of compromise, rejecting government controls over the banking and business systems, and profoundly suspicious of international law and peacekeeping" (Jewett 2009, 67; cf. Weber 2004; Sizer 2004)? If finding the door was the problem in approaching the book, what lies beyond the door is equally a challenge.

Revelation claims a temporal horizon that covers all of history, past, present, and future: "Now write what you have seen [past], what is [present], and what is to take place after this [future]" (1:19; van Unnik 1962–63, 86–94; Michaels 1991, 604–20). In temporal terms, the scope of Revelation runs from primordial time to the eschaton. This might be used as more than token support for the historicist aspiration, but it does not certify a specific road map of events. All the "schools" are in danger of reading Revelation's symbols as coded language for specific events rather than respecting the integrity of the symbol as symbol. Revelation has a story that needs to be told and will not let up until the task is done. The story climaxes in the implosion of evil (20:1–10) and the earth made new (21:1–6; 22:1–4). The mandate to reveal history must be taken seriously, but the claims to historical specificity must be modest. Qualitative representations of reality count, too, as is evident in the trumpet sequence (8:7–9:21). Revelation trains its sight on *values* more than *events*, and it is *God*-centered more than *time*-centered. A value-centered understanding of Revelation avoids the cynicism that results from failed predictions. Most importantly, it escapes Karl Popper's (1989–90) criticism of predictive approaches to history that fail the test of morality: they evade moral action in the present, fortified by certitude about the predicted outcome. The dogmatist counts on support in prophecy for his militant attitude, and the complacent nihilist justifies his inaction by counting on prophecy's inexorable momentum to make up the difference. "So we can be sure," Popper (1989–90, 2:274) writes, "that whatever we do will lead to the same result," putting historical prophecy in the place of conscience. It is a grave misreading to consider Revelation a partner in inculcating such attitudes.

### Retrospect and Prospect

Revelation presents *revelation* as *exposé*, but *the Revealer is more important than his exposé* in suspenseful sequences of seals, trumpets, and bowls. In the sequence of the seven seals, the figure *in the middle*, the "*Lamb standing as though it had been killed with violence*," is the ultimate revelation (5:6). He is beyond the imagination of creatures "in heaven, . . . on the earth, . . . or under the earth" (5:3); he represents the divine reality (5:5–6); and he is the pattern for moral action in the present (13:10; 14:4). He, and he alone, has "*what it takes to open the scroll and its seven seals*" (5:5), whatever we shall find them to be.

### Where, When, by Whom, Why, and How to Read Revelation

*Where, when, by whom, why, and how*: these are obligatory subjects in a commentary. Here they lay the groundwork for the three most important commitments for readers of Revelation.

#### Genre

Revelation is an *apocalyptic* book but not in the sense that it is *crisis literature* and thus typical of the apocalyptic *genre*. A straightforward generic classification fails to do justice to the complexity of the book and to answer the *why* question. However, it is not a mistake to consider Revelation an *apocalyptic* book if the purpose is to identify it as revelatory literature. Other features thought to define the apocalyptic genre are a disclosure presented in a narrative framework that opens to view a transcendent reality that is both temporal (a new age) and spatial (another world). Usually, too, the disclosure is mediated by an otherworldly being (J. Collins 1979, 9). This description has won widespread support, and much of it fits Revelation. Nevertheless, it is far from clear how these comparisons help interpretation. Pseudonymity is normally a characteristic feature of apocalypses, but Revelation is written in the actual author's *name*, "I, John" (1:1, 4, 9; 22:8). The story is anchored in a specific *place*—"I was on the island called Patmos" (1:9)—and it is addressed to "the seven churches" in Asia Minor (1:11). These specifics show the book to be neither *pseudonymous* nor *pseudo-topical* (Becker 2007). "John stands at the end of his Apocalypse looking back" (H. Maier 2002, 18). At the time of writing, he is no longer on Patmos.

Genre is supposed to bring clarity to a subject, but what is the reader to do with a book that has the characteristics of prophecy (Mazzaferri 1989, 382) and a letter (Fiorenza 1991, 23), as well as traits alleged to make it an apocalyptic work? The term *apokalypsis* was not a signifier of genre at the time of the writing of Revelation (M. Smith 1983). The potential of genre to help readers is in doubt unless one limits it to the claim announced in the opening word: a *disclosure* is in the making. Revelation resists a simple classification, the task complicated by lack of unanimity with respect to how the genre should be defined (Linton 2006, 37). Gregory Linton's conclusion is commendably nuanced. Revelation is a text that "refuses to stay in bounds," he says, and is from "John's own standpoint in the first century . . . something new and different from previous similar writings" (Linton 2006, 35, 40).

### Authorship

The author of Revelation is "John" (1:1, 4, 9; 22:8). The designation itself has not been seriously contested. "John" is not a fictitious person or a pseudonym. But which "John" was he? How many "Johns" do we have among whom to choose? How many "Johns" could write this kind of book and send it to the seven churches of Asia Minor with an air of self-authentication that all but excludes anyone mistaking his identity? What, too, is the relationship between the John of Revelation and the Gospel that carries the name "John"?

Among the "Johns" from which to choose, only two "Johns" otherwise known are considered serious contenders. The first is John the apostle; the second is John the Elder, a much less well-defined "John" than the Galilean John who was one of the two sons of Zebedee (Matt. 4:21; 10:2; 20:20; 26:37; 27:56; Luke 5:10; John 21:2; Aune 1996–98, l–li).

Figure 7. "I was on the island called Patmos" (Rev. 1:9). Patmos as seen from the present-day Monastery of St. John.

Irenaeus (ca. 130–202 CE), born in Smyrna, one of the cities of the seven churches in Revelation, refers to this John—the apostle—as the author of both the Gospel of John and Revelation. "Lastly John, the disciple of the Lord, who had leant back on His breast, once more set forth the gospel, while residing at Ephesus in Asia" (*Haer.* 3.1.2). Later in his book, Irenaeus says that this John was the one "who beheld the apocalyptic vision," and this "almost in our day, towards the end of Domitian's reign" (*Haer.* 5.30.3).

Does this help identify the author of Revelation? That we have a "John" in Revelation is not in doubt (1:1, 4, 9; 22:8). Is he the "John" who has been identified above as the Beloved Disciple and the author of the Gospel of John? Many scholars are convinced that this cannot be the case, mostly because of differences in language and genre. Dionysius of Alexandria (d. 260) used differences in language idiom as evidence *against* common authorship (Eusebius, *Hist. eccl.* 7.24.6–26). David E. Aune (1996–98, xlvii–lvi) argues that Revelation was meant to be a pseudonymous work despite the mention of "John." G. K. Beale (1999, 34–36) says that the son of Zebedee cannot be ruled out, but his identity is not important for the message of the book. Craig R. Koester (2014, 65–69, 80–83) thinks that John was an early Christian prophet but not John the son of Zebedee.

Objections to common authorship of the Gospel of John and Revelation are significant but not insurmountable. Austin Farrer (1964, 41) notes that

31

Revelation's John "writes as if there were no other John." Both books are remarkable and so in need of an extraordinary author that the list of conceivable candidates will be short. On the strength of this feature alone, it is more plausible to propose a single author for both books than to cast about for other possibilities, with John as an unknown Christian prophet in my view one of the less plausible options (Koester 2014, 65–69). The differences between the Gospel of John and Revelation can be accounted for by circumstances, resources, type of writing, and—not to be left out—actual *revelation*. When we take such matters into account, the similarities are more striking than the differences. As Luke Timothy Johnson (1999, 580) notes, "Once it is granted that the apocalyptic genre drastically reshapes the view of the world, the deep harmony in outlook and symbolization between Revelation and the other Johannine writings is all the more impressive."

The similarities are extensive, and they deal in some of the most characteristic themes of the respective books. In John, as in Revelation, the theme of cosmic conflict drives the story line. Jesus is at war with a cosmic opponent and will not let up until the opponent has been exposed and expelled (Tonstad 2008b).

> Now is the critical moment of this world, now the ruler of this world will be expelled [*ekblēthēsetai*]. (John 12:31; Brant 2011, 193)

> The great dragon was expelled [*ekblēthē*], that ancient serpent, who is called the Devil and Satan, the deceiver of the whole world—he was expelled [*ekblēthē*] to the earth. (Rev. 12:9)

As in Revelation, the adversary in the Fourth Gospel has deception and misrepresentation as his modus operandi: he "has not stood in the truth, because there is not truth in him. Whenever he speaks as he is wont, he speaks the lie [*to pseudos*], for he is a liar and the father of the lie" (John 8:44). Again, as in Revelation, the remedy against someone who does not tell the truth is *revelation*. In both books Jesus is the Revealer (John 1:18; Rev. 1:1; 5:5–6). *Witness*, a key word in John as much as in Revelation, is a virtual synonym for the revealing errand (John 5:31–36; 8:13–18; 10:25; 18:37; 19:35; Rev. 1:9; 6:9; 11:7; 12:17; 19:10; 20:4; 22:16, 18). Witness will make right what has gone wrong.

> Pilate then said to him, "Then you are not a king, are you?" Jesus answered, "You say that I am a king. For this task I was born, and for this reason I came into the world—to witness [*martyrēsō*] to the truth." (John 18:37, my trans.)

> And filled with rage against the woman, the Dragon went away to make war against the rest of her seed, those who keep the commandments of God and have the witness [*martyrian*] of Jesus. (Rev. 12:17)

Both books conceive of judgment as revelation, a "critical moment" when things obscure and bewildering will declare themselves and be shown up to be what they are.

> The hour [*hē hōra*] has come. . . . Now is the critical moment [*krisis*] of this world. (John 12:23, 31)

> For the hour [*hē hōra*] has come, the critical moment [*krisis*]. (Rev. 14:7)

"Community" vies with "cosmic conflict" as a central theme in both books. Love made manifest in community will give proof to the world "that you have sent me" (John 17:23). In Revelation, Jesus is represented as one "who walks among the seven golden lampstands" (2:1; 1:12, 13, 20), and the well-being of the community is his foremost concern. The believing community in Revelation "are those who *follow* [*hoi akolouthountes*] him wherever he goes" (Rev. 14:4), reminiscent of his call in John, "Follow [*akolouthei*] me!" (John 21:19, 22). The most affecting examples of Johannine diction are messages to the community.

> If someone loves me, he will keep my word, and my Father will love him, and we will come to him and we will make ourselves a dwelling place in his presence. (John 14:23; Brant 2011, 215)

> I have given them the glory that you gave me, that they may be one as we are one—I in them and you in me. (John 17:22–23 NIV)

> If anyone hears my voice and opens the door, I will come in and eat with him, and he with me. (Rev. 3:20)

Knocking, coming in, staying late and long, talking, getting close, eating together, becoming one—there is closeness between God and the individual believer in these passages, but God's dwelling and indwelling is actualized in *community*. This is a broad Johannine theme, and the Johannine diction in these verses is pointed and specific. "I will come in and eat with him, and he with me," we read in the message to the church at Laodicea (Rev. 3:20). This is Johannine to the core, a verbal signature as real as a person's fingerprint. "I . . . with him, and he with me" (Rev. 3:20)—and in John, "I in them and you in me" (John 17:23; cf. 14:20).

The identity of "John" in Revelation deserves a longer discussion than this, but key pieces of the evidence add up this way. "I, John" (1:9; 22:8) is a well-known figure; his identity is no mystery to the original recipients. He writes as a prophet, but his Hebraic diction does not mean that Greek is a second language, nor are his grammatical "mistakes" due to linguistic infelicity (Ozanne 1965). Instead, his style of writing is deliberately Hebraic, meant to help us "understand that we are listening to the last of the Hebrew prophets" (Hort 1908, xxxviii). His grasp of the OT is exceptional, truly an "intense and systematic meditation on the whole prophetic tradition" (Farrer 1964, 4). But his book is so closely linked to the Fourth Gospel as to make the John of that Gospel—John now the best candidate for the Beloved Disciple—merge with the writer of Revelation (Westcott 1978, ix–lxvii; R. Brown 1966, xcviii; Keener 2003, 84–104). In his farewell speech in John, Jesus tells the disciples not to be anxious because he is going away to prepare a place for them, then will return to "take you to myself, so that where I am, there you may be also" (John 14:1–3). Revelation offers an encore on this promise. The voice from the throne says that "the dwelling place of God is with human beings, and he will dwell with them, and they will be his people, and God himself shall be with them" (Rev. 21:3). They with him where he is, in heaven, is good, but "he . . . with them" here, on earth, could be more impressive. In my view, the story is complemented and completed by the same hand (John 14:1; Rev. 21:3; Ozanne 1965, 9; L. Johnson 1999, 589). The close-knit human web within which "John" is a pivotal figure and the story brought to completion in Revelation will by these criteria be inseparable. And the quest for the author, often captive to the counsel of despair, has returned an answer. Writers of such insight and perspicuity do not come in bulk. Finding one would be remarkable; finding two is a lot less plausible than finding one. But we find one.

### Date

Dating Revelation by the internal evidence is elusive because it is difficult to avoid circular reasoning (Witetschek 2012). The command to "measure the temple of God" (11:1) might be a clue if the temple in view is the earthly temple in Jerusalem at the time of the book's composition. In that case, a date before the destruction of Jerusalem in 69–70 CE falls within the range of possibility (R. B. Moberly 1992; Wilson 2005; van Kooten 2007).

However, if the language is symbolic and John has another city or temple in mind, the state of the earthly Jerusalem becomes irrelevant. If Revelation was written in response to persecution, and if Domitian instigated persecution in Asia Minor during his reign, the text and the historical evidence match up well for a date during the time of Domitian (Mounce 1977, 140; Beale 1999, 4–20). But these clues stand or fall on the assumptions on which they are based. If actual persecution is *not* the setting of Revelation, and if Domitian was *not* a large-scale persecutor, the value of these assumptions disappears. A creative remedial hypothesis posits that there was persecution of Christians during the time of *Nero* (albeit in Rome, not Asia Minor) and that Nero's influence was imprinted on the memory of Domitian (Mucha 2014). This view salvages three of the elements thought to be important to dating: persecution, the myth of Nero's return, and Domitian.

To give priority to the theological and communal mission does not advance the task of dating the book, but neither is it a disadvantage. Revelation did not end up as the climax of the canon by accident (Tõniste 2016). A late date for Revelation is compatible with a theological priority. With recourse to external evidence for specifics, this view is not in conflict with Irenaeus's contention that John's vision happened "almost in our day, towards the end of Domitian's reign" (*Haer.* 5.30.3; A. Collins 1981). Domitian was assassinated in 96 CE.

### Language

Readers versed in Greek do not have to go far into Revelation before realizing that this book does not play by the usual rules of grammar and syntax. Dionysius of Alexandria (ca. 200–265), a student of the learned Origen, said that the language and style "are not really Greek; he uses barbarous idioms, and is sometimes guilty of solecisms" (Eusebius, *Hist. eccl.* 7.25.11). Dionysius grants that the author of Revelation had the gift of knowledge but not the gift of speech. But this view underestimates John. The formal question revolves around the extent of Semitic influence, whether the author was a person of Semitic background who wrote "translation Greek." Then, beyond the formal question, is the possibility that Revelation is an exceptional artistic achievement.

A strong Semitic influence makes the best sense of Revelation's idiom (Mussies 1971; 1980; S. Thompson 1985, 108). R. H. Charles (1920, 1:cxliii) envisioned a writer who thinks in Hebrew but writes in Greek and who also "deliberately set at defiance the grammar and the ordinary rules of syntax." The result is an idiosyncratic but effective composition. The stigma of linguistic ineptitude is softened if intention, not incompetence, explains the peculiarities. C. G. Ozanne (1965, 4) claims that "the author was evidently familiar with the rules which he violated." Why, then, did he do it? Was it worth the risk to his literary and intellectual reputation, to the point of braving outright scorn? Ozanne (1965, 4) answers that "the author deliberately modelled his grammar on the pattern of the classical Hebrew of the Old Testament." If this accounts for the idiosyncrasies, incompetence is not the issue. Intention and command of the material explain him best. The story told in the Bible is coming to completion. He will be the one to do it; he will have the last word—in apparent awareness of the context in which his book belongs.

### Structure

With respect to structure, Adela Yarbro Collins (1976, 8) finds "almost as many outlines as there are interpreters." This is enough of a warning to set modest goals. Most interpreters acknowledge that Revelation has a prologue (1:1–8) and an epilogue (22:6–21). Another division falls between the messages to the seven churches and the visionary ascent to the heavenly throne room that begins in chapter 4 (Lambrecht 1979). This could be called the "Open Heaven" part (4:1–22:5).

Within the "open heaven" section, the most significant features are the recurring cycles of seven and the role played by chapter 12, both widely acknowledged to be important.

| Prologue | Letters to the Seven Churches | Open Heaven | Epilogue |
|---|---|---|---|
| 1:1–8 | 1:9–3:22 | 4:1–22:5 | 22:6–21 |

A third perspective responds to clues that break through the ebb-and-flow pattern of the cycles of seven (Dochhorn 2010, 54–59, 79–138). This perspective envisions a composition that builds progression and suspense in a more conventional way.

### The Cycles of Seven

Four cycles of seven are explicit in the book. These are the letters to the seven churches (2:1–3:22), the seven seals (6:1–8:1), the seven trumpets (8:2–11:19), and the seven bowls (15:1–16:21). The reach of the last cycle extends to the end of the book via "one of the seven angels who had the seven bowls" (17:1). This angel explains the demise of the harlot Babylon (17:1–18) and the meaning of the New Jerusalem (21:9–22:5; Giblin 1974).

The four explicit cycles account for much of the book, but they leave a gaping hole in the middle (12:1–14:20). Some interpreters plug the hole by making the middle part into a cycle of seven even though it is not labeled as such (A. Collins 1976, 19; Dochhorn 2010, 82–86). This fits everything into cycles of seven, but it is not convincing. Here, the hole will stand, awaiting some other proposal (below) for why John laid things out this way.

The striking similarity between the trumpet (8:2–11:19) and the bowl (15:1–16:21) cycles indicates repetition and some form of recapitulation, meaning that the author tells the same story over and over from various angles (Bornkamm 1937). But the recapitulation is not static. "The trumpets are worse than the seals, the bowls are worse than the trumpets" (Lambrecht 1979, 103; Fiorenza 1991, 33, 36). In all, there is a forward movement, with each cycle having an intensifying tenor over the previous one.

To what end is all this, not in the sense of "end" as "ending" but "end" as "purpose"? "End" as "ending" prioritizes the bowl cycle (15:1–16:21) and, beyond the bowls, the vision of a new heaven and a new earth (21:1–22:5). By contrast, "end" as "purpose" favors the cycle of the seven seals (4:1–8:1). "When the Lamb opened the seventh seal," says Revelation, "there was silence in heaven for about half an hour" (8:1). The silence is enigmatic by any criterion, but the scene is intrinsic to the seven seals and represents the climax of this cycle. No further event is laid out before the heavenly council. "The event," to the extent that there is one, is the stunned silence of the councillors upon the breaking of the final seal (8:1). The breaking of the seals, in turn, is itself an act of revelation and best seen as an enactment of what the whole book represents. Disclosure on God's part leads to discernment in the created realm. If we see Revelation's structure as a way to grasp this "end," the outermost cycle will be the cycle of the seven seals, not the trumpets or the bowls. By this criterion, "end" as "purpose" includes scenes showing that the revelation was a success in relation to those who witness it.

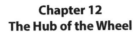

**Chapter 12**
**The Hub of the Wheel**

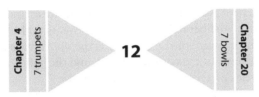

Figure 8. This diagram illustrates the centrality of chapter 12 in Revelation's structure, showing retroactive influence on chapters 4–11 and proactive influence on chapters 13–20.

### Revelation 12

The central role of chapter 12 for the structure of Revelation is widely accepted (Gunkel 1895; Prigent 1959; Gollinger 1967; A. Collins 1976, 101–42), but its explanatory potential remains largely untapped. Reading Revelation linearly from chapter 12 to chapter 20 is demanding for the profusion of detail in the story, but the coherence with respect to theme and thread is never in doubt.

What, however, is the relationship of chapter 12 to the chapters *preceding* it? At the beginning of the "Open Heaven" part (5:1–4), "the heavenly council is faced with a serious problem," says Adela Yarbro Collins (1979, 39). The crisis facing the council "is the rebellion of Satan" (A. Collins 1979, 39). This is well said. But "the rebellion of Satan" is not made explicit until Rev. 12. It follows that *a part of the story that is not told until chapter 12 wields a decisive influence on scenes much earlier in the book.* The *conflict in heaven* in Rev. 12 (12:7–12) is the implied premise for the *crisis in the heavenly council* in the earlier scene (5:1–4)! To convey the importance of chapter 12 for the whole story, it is necessary to grasp the influence of chapter 12 on the preceding chapters as much as on the chapters following.

Two pieces of evidence corroborate this representation. First, the "abrupt fresh start" (Bauckham 1993a, 15) in chapter 12 is muted by the close parallels between the trumpet and bowl cycles (8:6–11:19; 16:1–21). These parallels demonstrate thematic continuity in the story preceding chapter 12 with the scenes following it (Beale 1999, 622, 808–10; Tonstad 2006, 108–9). Second, in Rev. 12 John says that the tail of the dragon "swept down *a third* of the stars of heaven" (12:4). In the earlier trumpet sequence, there is mention of "*a third*" a full fourteen times, always referring to items in the cosmos that are darkened or destroyed (8:7–9:18). The insistent monotony of the term suggests that there is more to it than a description of fraction. When insights of Rev. 12 are applied to prior passages in Revelation, the thrust of the recurring *third* will not be a reference to *quantity*, or a probing for *what* or *where* or *when* or *how much*. Instead, it is a marker of *agency*, an answer to the question *Who?* The mantra of "thirds" in the trumpet sequence is a telltale sign of demonic activity.

What now of the "black hole" in the foregoing structural representation? The alleged "hole," deliberately mislabeled above, is no hole at all! Instead, it is the key to the message of the book. It is the *apocalypse* in miniature, an overview and synopsis of the cosmic conflict, and the lighthouse illuminating the preceding cycles of seven and those that follow.

### Structure of Revelation

Figure 9. This diagram shows the overall structure of Revelation, with four cycles of seven and the crucial "black hole" now filled by the story of the cosmic conflict.

### How to Read Revelation

Three commitments now emerge before moving in earnest beyond the door to this book. These are (1) to become a re-reader, (2) to pay attention to its allusions to the OT, and (3) to keep in mind that God is not the only one who is active in the world.

#### Becoming a Re-reader

"Curiously enough, one cannot read a book: one can only reread it. A good reader, a major reader, an active and creative reader is a re-reader," says Vladimir Nabokov (1980, 3). This is good advice with respect to reading in general, but it is a must with respect to Revelation. Its structure is a case in point, featuring a crisis in the heavenly council at the beginning of the book

(5:1–4), the reason for which is not explained until much later (12:7–9; A. Collins 1979, 39). The imaginary picket line blocking access to the door at the beginning of this chapter is unmerited, but a sign should be posted at the entrance, saying, "For Re-readers Only." Only a re-reader will have an awareness of the whole that is necessary for understanding the parts. As one reader notes, "Many of the difficulties that scholars have seen in this particular vision would have vanished, if they had once tried to draw the picture which the seer saw" (Flowers 1930, 526). The re-reader will be able to do that.

### Allusions to the Old Testament

Revelation appears to be "conceived in the very words in which it is written down; as though, in fact, the author was thinking with his pen" (Farrer 1964, 24). *Thinking* is the key word because the author was a *thinking* person, and thought was just as important as vision. His thinking was nourished by an amazing command of the OT. John obligates readers to engage with the OT background as a key to understanding (Kraft 1974, 16). Revelation's allusions are not haphazard. In line with the notion that John was a thoughtful person, his allusions are "meant to recall the Old Testament context, which thereby becomes part of the meaning that the Apocalypse conveys, and to build up, sometimes by a network of allusion to the same Old Testament passage in various parts of the Apocalypse, an interpretation of whole passages of Old Testament prophecy" (Bauckham 1993a, xi).

### God Is Not the Only One

God "is not the only one who is at work in this world—as the Apocalypse makes so abundantly clear" (Vögtle 1976, 383). Indeed! This is the third commitment in the "how to" column. *God is not the only one*—and yet interpreters reflexively and uncritically assign the calamities in the book to divine agency. *God is not the only one*—we must consider other options for who is doing what in this book. If interpreters are in the habit of making the wrong call with respect to important questions like this, there is work to do.

### Outline of Revelation

**Incentive to read (1:1–20)**

Letter opening: From whom to whom (1:1–6)

"Hope," signed Alpha and Omega (1:7–8)

From where to where (1:9–11)

Vision of the glorified Jesus, and a commission (1:12–20)

**To the one who has an ear (2:1–3:22)**

Ephesus (2:1–7)

Smyrna (2:8–11)

Pergamum (2:12–17)

Thyatira (2:18–29)

Sardis (3:1–6)

# Revelation 1:1–20

## Incentive to Read

**Introductory Matters**

Revelation meets the criteria of a letter, but it is distinctive for claiming to be sent from God (1:1). Although the subject matter is called "the revelation of Jesus Christ" (1:1), Jesus acts as the Revealer of God (1:1–2). The relationship between God as sender and Jesus as the Revealer is by this criterion like the Gospel of John (Rev. 1:1–2; John 1:1–2, 14, 18). Lesser characters in the letter chain are God's mediating angel, John, and "the seven believing communities in Asia" (1:1, 4). Everyone in the chain counts. Faithful transmission along the letter chain enables faithful representation at the point of reception. John contributes by seeing and writing (1:2, 4, 9–11), and the seven believing communities participate by reading the message out loud, hearing it, and protecting it (1:3). To our surprise, Jesus appears not only at the point of origin (1:1) but also at the point of reception, standing "in the middle of the lampstands" (1:12–13). He represents God *to* the believing communities, but the communities represent God *in* the world, as conspicuous yet vulnerable points of light (1:12–13, 20). From the very first verse, the language idiom blends

> **Revelation 1:1–20 in the Rhetorical Flow**
>
> ▶ Incentive to read (1:1–20)
>
> > Letter opening: From whom to whom (1:1–6)
> >
> > "Hope," signed Alpha and Omega (1:7–8)
> >
> > From where to where (1:9–11)
> >
> > Vision of the glorified Jesus, and a commission (1:12–20)

43

OT passages with familiar elements in the story of Jesus. We are explicitly enticed to *read*, not only the text of Revelation but also the text within the text—the OT background—and thus take possession of the message and the blessing promised (1:3).

### Tracing the Train of Thought

For a book like Revelation, "train of thought" is a hazardous concept. Readers are in for a dense bombardment of thought, but the thought is symphonic, not single instrument, and the ebb and flow of symphonic communication is how this book works. "Leaps of thought" describe the flow better than "train of thought." Like a symphony, too, the theme may be soft at first, a background whisper played softly on a clarinet, before all the instruments join in. Add to this that there is an undulating emotional tenor, that "the scenes and events . . . are repetitive and jump back and forth in time" (Sweet 1979, 58). Moreover, John's thinking "was generally done in the form of images," as Max Brod (1995, 52) says of Franz Kafka. A disorderly time line and a profusion of images are challenging. How does a reader prepare for such an encounter except by buckling up?

#### Letter Opening: From Whom to Whom (1:1–6)

**1:1–3.** *Revelation* is in character with the kind of person God is: a God who *reveals*. This note is struck with emphasis from the very beginning. **The disclosure [apokalypsis] of Jesus Christ, which God gave him to make known [deixai] to his servants what must soon take place; he made it known [esēmanen] by sending his angel to his servant John** (1:1). John deploys two different verbs to describe the commission, but either verb comes down to "making known." God is the first to speak in direct address (1:3). Then John steps up to the microphone (1:4). God is also the last one to talk (22:20), with an opportunity for all readers of the book to respond (22:21). The symmetry of direct divine speech at the beginning and ending is striking.

God's first word is a blessing. **Blessed is the one who reads aloud and those who hear the words of the prophecy, and (blessed) are those who keep what is written in it; for the time is near** (1:3). To be **blessed** in the biblical sense is more than being the recipient of a good wish, like "safe travels" or "good luck," and it means more than the promise of subjective happiness. "Bliss" is not measured on an emotional scale. The person thus described is in an enviable state and objectively in a position of privilege.

"The one who reads *aloud*" would in the first century be indistinguishable from "the one who reads" because silent reading had yet to be invented. Reading out loud would also be a matter of necessity because of the low literacy rate. Readers and hearers are included in the blessing, but appropriation comes to fruition only for "those who keep" the revelation. Two specific aspects of this text should be kept in mind in the twenty-first century. First, reading *aloud* is an act of interpretation. The human voice—in varying cadences, pitch, feeling, and emphasis—has an enormous influence on the message conveyed. Monologue, monotone, and monochrome are alien to reading out loud. Facial expression and body language are also part of the communicative arsenal of "the one who reads aloud." The opening beatitude envisions the reader and the hearers working together in a communal and collaborative venture that gives life and clarity to the message. The concept "liturgical dialogue" is helpful. Formal features to this effect are striking in the prologue and epilogue (Kavanagh 1984; Vanni 1991). Even on the printed page, Revelation is rhetorically masterful.

The blessing is for those who read and receive "the words of the prophecy." It is tempting to pause after the word *read* to make the beatitude say, "Blessed are those who read." Period. Mastery of Revelation requires reading proficiency that is at risk in an era of half sentences, sound bites, and tweets. A competent reading of "the words of the prophecy" may therefore begin with the rehabilitation of basic reading skills and with raising the prestige of reading real books. The blessing promised to the reader could have the side effect of placing reading—and books—at the center of education and culture that befits the notion of *paideia*. We cannot master this book if we do not read competently.

**1:4–6.** John is now speaking for God in a recognizable epistolary greeting to the seven churches. Yet the idiosyncrasies are conspicuous. The phrase **the one who is** [*ho ōn*] **and who was** [*ho ēn*] **and who is to come** [*ho erchomenos*] defies the rules of grammar and syntax (1:4). Why the odd wording, using the nominative instead of the genitive after the preposition *apo*, and mixing participles (*ho ōn*, "the one who is") and an indicative verb (*ho ēn*, "the he-was") in the sentence (Walther 1995; Ozanne 1965, 6–7; Koester 2014, 215)? The answer should not be that John lacks mastery of Greek. He is reproducing God's self-designation in the encounter with Moses at the burning bush, "I AM WHO I AM [*ho ōn*]" (Exod. 3:14 LXX), and he implies that God's name is indeclinable. Although God's name is identified with reference to the past (was), the present (is), and the future (is to come), the emphasis should not be God's *existence*, that God is *eternal*, or that God is *inscrutable*. The question is not whether God exists but *whether God will show up* (B. Jacob 1992, 71–74). In the original setting, "I AM WHO I AM" means that God is first and foremost the One who *is with you*. As Edmond Jacob (1971, 52) notes, "It is not the idea of eternity which is primary when the Israelites pronounce the name Yahweh, but that of presence. . . . God is he who is *with* someone" (see also Albertini 1999; den Hertog 2002). An affirmation of God's existence or self-existence fits a philosophical construct, but Revelation is more interested in God's *conduct*. This matches the situation in Exodus. Whether past, present, or future, God is *with* people: God is the One "who approaches you and helps you" (Albertini 1999, 22). The affirmation cannot find a stronger guarantee than to "define" God by what is most emphatically true of God: "I Myself am there, count on Me!" (Vriezen 1970, 180).

Equally important but less appreciated is the implied contrast—and conflict—reflected in this phrase.

| God | God's adversary |
|---|---|
| the one who was [*ho ēn*], the one who is [*ho ōn*], and the one who is to come. (1:4) | was [*ēn*] and is not [*ouk estin*] and is to come [*parestai*]. (17:8) |

Wherein the contrast? God's self-designation is anchored in fact. The adversary, by contrast, is *defined by what he pretends to be but isn't*. Whether the criterion is ontology or character, the adversary is not God. And yet the comparison is not pointless in the context of Revelation's story. A re-reader will know what is coming so as not to miss the contrast (17:8; 1:4).

The texture of conflict is not softened when Jesus is described as **the witness, the *trustworthy one* [*ho martys, ho pistos*], the firstborn of the dead, and the ruler of the kings of the earth** (Rev. 1:5a; cf. Ps. 89:27, 37 [88:28, 38 LXX]). Jesus is "faithful" (*pistos*) in the sense of carrying out his heaven-sent mission, and he is "faithful" by keeping faith with God. But the context of conflict sharpens the tenor of the description. *He* is "the *trustworthy one*" (*ho pistos*); he, not the adversary, is the one who is worthy of trust; *he* goes head-to-head with "the Mudslinger and the Antagonist, the deceiver of the whole world" (12:9). Trustworthiness is not a trivial quality compared to an adversary that has misrepresentation of God as his trademark. As "the firstborn of the dead," Jesus's resurrection is the hardware of hope, but the resurrection has death as its point of reference. *Dying* and *self-giving* gleam at the zenith of his witness.

The exclamation that follows is of a piece with the story of Jesus's self-giving (1:5b–6). It is expressed in a "hymnic-proclamatory style," implying that it is familiar to the recipients and quite possibly related to baptism (Fiorenza 1974, 222). The exclamation expands the statement that "the one who is and who was and who is to come" (1:4) is on the side of human beings in life's struggle. Liberation is accomplished by God's intervention, not by human efforts (cf. Rom. 3:24–25). The notion of being *released* or **set free from our sins** (*lysanti ek tōn hamartiōn hēmōn*) is open to a wide range of conceptions as to the plight from which liberation is needed. John, speaking in the plural for himself and the churches, accepts ownership of sin. But in this book deliverance is projected on a wide canvas. "Sin" is not only transgression with a need for forgiveness or empowerment in the face of moral weakness (Fiorenza 1974, 225). It is also misperception of what is good. The poisoned seed of misperception was the original achievement of "the ancient Serpent" (Gen.

3:1; Rev. 12:9). For sin in all its expressions, the violent death of Jesus is the means of deliverance. God's love comes first, however, and the self-giving of Jesus is the expression of God's love. The converse is false. God's love is the cause, not the result, of Jesus's self-giving.

The exclamation has a further application that is both political and priestly (Fiorenza 1974). In political terms, the reversal of fortune for the believers is spectacular, but the priestly connotation is more defining. The companies of believers in Asia Minor are participants in a new exodus. God calls them to be "for me a priestly kingdom [*basileion hierateuma*, LXX] and a holy nation" (Exod. 19:6; cf. Isa. 61:6). This means vocation and witness for the believers, not political hegemony, and the call of ancient Israel is now actualized in the churches. The astounding "transfer" of status is best understood as realization rather than supersession. Revelation's high view of the church in the first three chapters cannot be surpassed.

### *"Hope," Signed Alpha and Omega (1:7–8)*

**1:7–8.** No sooner has John paid an exclamatory tribute to **Jesus Christ** for his accomplishment than he turns to contemplate the result. **Look! He is coming with the clouds, and every eye will see him—even those who pierced him—and all the tribes of the earth will mourn deeply and sincerely because of him. That's how it will be! Amen!** (1:7). My translation requires an explanation, but the translation comes first: this text envisions the success of Jesus's mission.

Two OT texts are brought together in a verse that consists almost entirely of ancient voices. Daniel supplies the first part, "He is coming with the clouds" (Rev. 1:7a; Dan. 7:13). Relative to its size, the book of Daniel in general and Dan. 7 in particular wield a disproportionate influence on the NT: Dan. 7 is "embedded in the foundation of New Testament thought" (Dodd 1952, 69). The status and significance of the figure that "is coming with the clouds" has been the subject of much debate in the context of Daniel, but his identity is no mystery in Revelation. The one coming is Jesus Christ, carrying on his body stigmata that rule out mistaking his identity. Yet his identity in Daniel is not a foregone conclusion. The range of options spans a figure that could be *human, angelic,* or *divine* (Shepherd 2006). Given that Revelation applies the text to Jesus, two of these options must be ruled in as certain: he is *human* and *divine*, ontologically speaking (*ontology* refers to categories of being). Is he also *angelic*? Adela Yarbro Collins (1996, 159) demonstrates that Revelation "expresses an angelic Christology which is best understood in the context of the Jewish motif of the principal angel." The representation demands precision, nuance, and imagination. If Jesus's preexistence is a matter of course from the point of view of Revelation, how would the ancient writings represent him? Which conceptual and descriptive resources were available? It will be necessary to distinguish between identity and *representation*, or between identity and *manifestation*. This means that a divine figure can be represented in angelic terms without being an angel (Garrett 2008; J. Collins 1974; Gieschen 1998; Rowland 1980; 1985), in part because the options are limited. On a deeper level, the angelic representation of the preexistent Jesus might be less the result of limited resources of representation than is commonly thought. Perhaps Jesus does not mind being represented as an angel or even thought of as one (Tonstad 2016a, 67–83)? Why would it offend him to be represented as an angel when he is not bothered by being a human? To appear lower in rank than he is and not consider it shameful is consonant with the disposition of Jesus (Heb. 2:11–12; Phil. 2:5–12), and the commitment is irreversible. "The Incarnation is . . . not a temporary stage in the history of the Christ" (J. Barr 1956, 22).

The announcement that "he is coming with the clouds" refers to more than how and where he will appear in spatial terms. It also signifies *revelation* and *reversal*. Jesus made use of the text in the latter sense in the Synoptic account of his trial. "From now on you will see the Son of Man seated at the right hand of Power and coming on the clouds of heaven" (Matt. 26:64; cf. Dan. 7:13). "Son of Man," at first sight an innocuous term, gets added meaning because of the allusion to Daniel. In fact, the "Son of Man" who comes "with the clouds" encroaches on God's turf to the point that the "Son of Man" becomes a euphemism for "Son of God" (Matt. 26:64; 27:43; Ford 1968). Jesus will now be seen by "every eye," even by "those who pierced him" (1:7).

This leads to another OT allusion, this one from Zech. 12:10:

They will look on the one whom they have pierced [Hb. *dāqārû*]. (Zech. 12:10)

They will look on the one whom they have pierced [*exekentēsan*]. (John 19:37)

Every eye will see him—even those who pierced [*exekentēsan*] him. (Rev. 1:7)

Zechariah's contribution is greater than the part reproduced above, but this marks the beginning of the thought expressed. The Gospel of John and Revelation are the only NT books to include this part of the text (Tonstad 2016a, 299). The focus is sharp—the "piercing" of the figure—and the wording in John and Revelation is nearly identical. Both NT references are better representations of the Hebrew text than of the LXX, but Theodotion, Symmachus, and Aquila use exactly the same word for *pierced* as the NT, *exekentēsan* (Menken 1993; 2007; Prigent 2001, 121). This is evidence that the NT usage is concentrated in books associated with "John"—and in the John that this commentary sees as the author. It also suggests that John had mastery of the OT in Hebrew. Most of all, the identity and impact of Jesus center on the fact that he was *pierced*. From this fact, allowing the text in Zechariah to resonate, John shows how this revelation changes everything.

The impact is cosmic and profound: "all the tribes of the earth will mourn deeply and sincerely because of him" (1:7). This rendition of John's exclamation draws on more background in Zechariah, text and context.

> And I will pour out a spirit of favor and supplication on the house of David and the inhabitants of Jerusalem, and they shall look on the one whom they have pierced, and they shall mourn for him, as one mourns for an only child, and weep intensely over him, as one weeps over a firstborn. On that day the mourning in Jerusalem will be as great as the mourning for Hadad-rimmon in the plain of Megiddo. The land shall mourn, each family by itself [*kai kopsetai hē gē kata phylas*, LXX]. (Zech. 12:10–12, my trans.)

Something is afoot in this text—and something even bigger is afoot in Revelation. Attention to the OT background counters the impression that John describes a scene of retribution; that the entire world "will be forced to recognize him" (Prigent 2001, 122); or, as some commentators see it, that the scene is meant to capture that it is now "too late" (Roloff 1993, 27–28).

First, the text and its preceding context in Zechariah are eschatological. "It speaks of the 'end-time' as far as the prophet was concerned" (R. Smith 1984, 278).

Second, Zechariah describes a hostile and adversarial relationship that turns friendly by looking "on the one whom they have pierced" (Zech. 12:10). The previous hostility has focused precisely on this person, and the dramatic turnaround has to do with a reappraisal of who he is and what he represents. A new "spirit" is manifest, "a spirit of favor [*ḥēn*] and supplication [*taḥănûnîm*]." Carol L. Meyers and Eric M. Meyers (1993, 335) say of the first of these words that the recipients receive "the ability to be themselves positively disposed toward another party."

> In other words, the horror of a deed perpetrated through negative feelings of anger, jealousy, fear—whatever would cause some people to stab another—will now be mitigated by the emergence of a different, positive disposition: "favor." There seems, however, to be no accountability in terms of justice for a crime of assault (or murder); rather, an internal change comes over those responsible for the terrible act. They now become able to show favor—the "supplication" of the accompanying term. (C. Meyers and E. Meyers 1993, 335)

Attention shifts from the one who was pierced to the change in those who did the piercing. Is their mourning mere regret? Does the reversal of previous feelings come too late to make a difference? The critical point is the "reversal of previous feelings" (C. Meyers and E. Meyers 1993, 336). The people "shall look" in the sense of paying heartfelt attention to one who was earlier the object of hostility and scorn. God, who brings about the new sentiment, is also its object. "They will look" means that the people in view are now "favorably inclined toward and asking forgiveness from the one(s) whom they had previously treated with violence" (C. Meyers and E. Meyers 1993, 335). "They will mourn," says Zechariah, and the mourning is more than skin deep.

> The verbal root *spd* ("to mourn, wail") appears four times in verses 10 and 11, and a fifth occurrence in verse 12 carries the idea of mourning throughout the Catalog of Mourners in verses 12–14. This repetition of the word for "mourning," accompanied by three powerful images portraying the intensity of grief (mourning for an only child, a firstborn, and perhaps a dying god), emphasizes the dramatic change in disposition. . . . All those who have done violence to God's word (by assaulting prophets) will now feel positive (with "favor") toward prophetic figures, will ask forgiveness ("supplication") and will greatly mourn all the evil they have done in failing to heed God's spokespersons and in attempting to suppress them. (C. Meyers and E. Meyers 1993, 340–41)

Mourning of this kind is deep and healing. The "only child" (*yāḥîd*) and the "firstborn" in the text bring into view the story of the binding of Isaac in Gen. 22. The loss of any child is difficult, but "the death of an only child stands to cause exceptional depth of mourning" (C. Meyers and E. Meyers 1993, 342). The orientation and arithmetic of the most important words in Zechariah set the stage for clear and compelling theology. "With the root for 'mourn' appearing five times and the one for 'grieve' occurring twice, a total of seven terms for these emotions occur: the remorse is total" (C. Meyers and E. Meyers 1993, 342). This does not mean that the remorse is precipitated by the coming of Jesus in the clouds but that the coming of Jesus is the occasion for expressing it. On the strength of this reading of Zechariah, the translation in Revelation must be that "all the tribes [*pasai hai phylai*] of the earth will mourn deeply and sincerely because of him" (1:7; cf. Bauckham 1993a, 322). This is not futility and regret but revelation and reversal, not a "too late" scene. And John's exclamation is not the kind that makes the reader sigh, dolefully, "too bad."

Confirmation of this view comes from many quarters in Revelation (Bauckham 1993a, 238–337). "All the *tribes* [*pasai hai phylai*] of the earth" are engaged in mourning (1:7), the "tribes" here a snippet of a longer phrase that recurs with minor variations in the book (1:7; 5:9; 7:9; 10:11; 11:9; 13:7; 14:6; 17:15). Revelation's message goes forth as "eternal good news to every nation and *tribe* [*phylēn*] and language and people" (14:6). The prologue is not the only place where Revelation predicts and depicts success. In the end, praise to God will resound "from every tribe" (*ek pasēs phylēs*, 5:9), and the numbers will be there. "I looked," John says later, "and there was a great multitude that no one could count, from every nation, from all tribes [*ek pantos . . . phylōn*] and peoples and languages" (7:9).

Many readers may wonder how a successful outcome can be described in terms of mourning (L. Thompson 2000). Would not celebration and rejoicing better convey victory, if that is what we have? The answer must be no. Deep mourning, including loud wailing and body language to match it, captures the success of the revelation and the depth of the reversal better than happiness. Mourning of this kind has long been warranted but out of reach; it signifies understanding and self-understanding; it speaks of enmity acknowledged and overcome (Huesman 1961). Deep mourning as depicted in Zechariah is commensurate with the depth of conviction over sin and prior misperceptions of God. Mourning over the one who was pierced works best whether we see in it an expression of contrition, recognition, love, or gratitude. "This is how it will be!"—as revelation and promise—wrings from history an outcome that has appeared unlikely and unattainable. But it will be. "Amen!"

Again, God appears in direct speech. **"I am the Alpha [*to alpha*] and the Omega [*to ō*]," says the Lord God, who is and who was and who is to come, the Almighty** (1:8; cf. 1:4; Isa. 44:6; 48:12). This concludes the prologue.

### *From Where to Where (1:9–11)*

**1:9–11.** John, as noted, "writes as if there were no other John" (Farrer 1964, 41), and he identifies with the recipients of the letter. "He refuses a hierarchical clerical order and states his communion with them" (Bovon 2000, 698). **Tribulation** (*thlipsis*) can refer to outright persecution (1:9), but it can also describe anything that causes distraction or distress with respect to reaching the goal that is in view. Prosperity and complacency are well-known anesthetics with respect to spiritual growth, and some churches in Asia Minor were afflicted by both (3:1–6, 14–22). Lack of evidence for persecution during the reign of Domitian has necessitated a drastic reassessment of the "situation" when Revelation most likely was written (L. Thompson 1990, 171–201). It is no longer self-evident that Revelation was written in response to a crisis— *persecution*—that was obvious to all. But this does not remove the notion of *crisis* from the picture. Instead, John "wrote his book to point out a crisis that many of them did not perceive" (A. Collins 1984, 77). Lack of awareness of a problem—if the crisis is real—may be fully as serious as persecution. Persecution in the conventional sense must nevertheless remain on the believer's horizon, not because persecution was a staple of Roman imperial policy but because it is a constant in the satanic program of deception and violence (12:7–19).

John's letter-book shows a concerned pastor at work. He shares common ground with Paul, the greatest letter writer in the NT. The number *seven* implies concern for the church universal. The disclosure that John **was on the island called Patmos because of the word of God and the testimony of Jesus** (1:9) is usually taken to mean that he was there involuntarily, in forced exile, and this possibility cannot be ruled out (Eusebius, *Hist. eccl.* 3.23.1.6; Koester 2014, 242). But it is not inconceivable that he was on Patmos voluntarily, for reasons of mission. Or, in a twist on the idea of forced exile, he was "on the island called Patmos" not because of past trouble but "because" (*dia*) of work still to be done. "Because" is by this logic oriented toward the future. Patmos is a small island in the Aegean Sea, seven miles long at the longest. Ephesus, the first of the churches addressed in Revelation, is about fifty miles to the northeast of the island. The disclosure that John *was* on the island is in the aorist tense, suggesting that he had his visions while on the island but was no longer there when he wrote them down (Koester 2014, 239).

Whether voluntary or involuntary, mission or exile, John says that he was on Patmos because of "the word of God [*ton logon tou theou*] and the testimony of Jesus [*tēn martyrian Iēsou*]" (1:9). This phrase and its variants epitomize the message of the book.

the word of God and the testimony of Jesus Christ (1:2)

the word of God and the testimony they had in their possession (6:9)

the commandments of God [*tas entolas tou theou*] and . . . the testimony of Jesus [*tēn martyrian Iēsou*] (12:17)

the commandments of God [*tas entolas tou theou*] and the faithfulness of Jesus [*tēn pistin Iēsou*] (14:12)

the testimony of Jesus and the word of God (20:4)

How should these phrases be understood? First, "the word of God" (1:2, 9; 6:9; 20:4) is complemented by "the commandments of God" (12:17; 14:12). Both terms invite a broad, *theological* interpretation. In addition to "word" and "commandments," ideas like "message" or "ways" are serviceable (Aune 1996–98, 19). Revelation depicts a crisis in the heavenly council (5:1–4); it addresses the discrepancy between expectations and reality (6:9–11); and it speaks of the revelation of "the mystery of God" (10:7). If we let "the word of God" mean "the ways of God," the *word* is the reality in need of an explanation (Dehandschutter 1980, 285). Second, therefore, the two components of the phrase stand in an explanatory relationship to each other: "the testimony of Jesus" *explains* "the ways of God." The grammatical term for this is *epexegetical*, meaning that we have terms that clarify each other (Aune 1996–98, 6; Beale 1999, 184). "The testimony of Jesus" (1:2, 9; 12:17; 20:4) is complemented by "the faithfulness of Jesus" (14:12; Tonstad 2006, 16–94). Either expression has Jesus as the subject of the noun, whether "testimony" (*martyria*) or "faithfulness" (*pistis*; Trites 1977, 156; Blount 2000, 402). When we factor these insights into the translation, the explanatory power will be significant.

the word of God *as revealed by* the testimony of Jesus Christ (1:2) the word of God *as revealed by* the testimony of Jesus (1:9)

the word of God and the [*explanatory*] testimony they had in their possession (6:9)

the commandments of God and . . . the [*explanatory*] testimony of Jesus (12:17)

the commandments of God *as revealed by* the faithfulness of Jesus (14:12)

the [*explanatory*] testimony of Jesus and the word of God (20:4)

"Explanatory" is a trite term for the illumination brought by Jesus, and readers should search for better words. But the emerging picture connects "the word of God" to "the testimony of Jesus Christ" with the same one-of-a-kind, no-one-else-could-do-it relationship that exists between the Word and the Revealer in the Fourth Gospel (John 1:1, 9, 14, 18; Keener 2003, 1:360). In both books, Jesus is the embodied Torah. The riveting focal image in "the testimony of Jesus" is that he was *pierced* (1:7). This alone provides two specific insights into the ways of God: it is *self-giving*, and it is *nonviolent*.

**I was in the Spirit on the Lord's day**, says John (1:10). Being "in the Spirit" points to a visionary experience. Most interpreters take the reference to "the Lord's day" (*en tē kyriakē hēmera*) to refer to a specific day of the week. While the word "day" (*hēmera*) is missing in *Didache* (*The Teaching of the Twelve Apostles*) and in Ignatius's *Letter to the Magnesians* (ca. 110 CE), these early sources use the same adjectival form of "the Lord" (*kyriakē*) as Revelation (1:10; *Did.* 14.1; Ign. *Magn.* 9.1). Ignatius alludes to the resurrection in connection with Sunday (Ign. *Magn.* 9.1). The specific day in view is by this logic thought to be Sunday (Bauckham 1982). It is objected that *kyriakē* in the extrabiblical sources is used with nouns other than "day" (such as "way" or "manner") and that Revelation's use of *kyriakē* should not be understood in the light of later usage (Stefanovic 2011). More serious objections, especially with basis in Ignatius's letters, are incongruities in the story of his martyrdom, his obsession with conformity of belief, and his hierarchical ideal for the church, which make it hard to determine what is original and what may be later emendations.

Given that John constantly makes use of OT allusions, the possibility of an OT antecedent deserves serious consideration. Two options are evident, beginning with "my holy day" (Hb. *bəyôm qodshi*) in Isaiah, meaning the Sabbath (Isa. 58:13). Isaiah invests the Sabbath with enormous communal, social, and eschatological prestige (Isa. 56:1–8; 58:1–14; Tonstad 2009, 145–60). The other option is "the Day of the LORD" (Hb. *yôm yhwh*; Gk. *hē hēmera tou kyriou*), understood in a turning-of-the-ages eschatological sense (Joel 2:11, 31; Amos 5:18–20; Zeph. 1:4; Mal. 4:5). This "day" can also be written in shorthand, *that day* (Hb. *hayyôm hahû'*; Gk. *tē hēmera ekeinē*), as Isaiah is prone to do and as Zechariah does in the passage about mourning at the sight of the one who was pierced (Rev. 1:7; Isa. 19:18–24; Zech. 12:3–11; 13:1, 2). By this criterion, John is announcing that *that day* has arrived, coming to fulfillment in the "*apokalypsis of Jesus Christ*" (1:1). Charles Welch lands unequivocally on this view of "the Lord's day."

> The book of Revelation is taken up with something infinitely vaster than days of the week. It is solely concerned with the day of the Lord. To read that John became in spirit on the Lord's day (meaning Sunday) tells practically nothing. To read in the solemn introduction that John became in spirit in the Day of the Lord, that day of prophetic import, is to tell us practically everything. (Welch 1950, 49)

This view has merit, but John is grounded in earthly reality, and reference to a specific day of the week cannot be excluded. On the other hand, the "day" in question, whether figurative or literal, is no ordinary day. The apocalyptic event shatters all notions of business as usual, fully corresponding to *that day*: **I heard behind me a loud voice like a trumpet, saying, "Write in a book what you see and send it to the seven churches, to Ephesus, to Smyrna, to Pergamum, to Thyatira, to Sardis, to Philadelphia, and to Laodicea"** (1:10–11). A loud voice "from behind" has an antecedent in Ezekiel (3:12), but the sound of a trumpet at full blast recalls Mount Sinai (Exod. 19:16, 19; 20:18). On that occasion the blast preceded a theophany—God making an appearance. God is now making another appearance, focusing the attention of John and the churches with sights and sounds that exceed those of Sinai. Writing "to the seven churches" would be a necessity because of the distance. The OT style of writing and the parallels between the first chapters in Genesis and the last chapters of Revelation indicate that the message was meant to reach beyond the churches in Asia Minor. Richard J. Bauckham's (1993a, xi) perception that John understood himself to be writing "the climax of prophetic revelation" does not seem exaggerated. That the letter is addressed to "*the* seven churches" (*tais hepta ekklēsiais*) must be given weight, but it should also be taken with a grain of salt. Asia Minor had more than seven churches. The use of the definite article, circumscribing the seven churches as a group and almost as an existing concept, accommodates a larger view. Colossae and Hierapolis are examples of named churches known to be in the same geographical area in the first century (Col. 1:2; 4:13). This does not mean that the churches addressed in Revelation are only symbolic, but a strict literal application is too narrow. The named churches may also be *types* and *representatives* of the condition, needs, and aspirations of the church universal. This view will not negate historical and archaeological investigation into the seven churches and their respective cities, but it gives priority to the *text* and to features implying a wide audience: *To Whom It May Concern.* "Whoever has an ear, let him/ her hear what the Spirit says to the churches" (2:7, 11, 17, 29; 3:6, 13, 22).

### Vision of the Glorified Jesus, and a Commission (1:12–20)

**1:12–16. And I turned to see the voice that spoke with me** (1:12) is a sentence odd enough to give rise to a book title (Humphrey 2007, 151–94). The phrasing may have been inadvertent. John meant to say that he "turned to see the person whose voice he heard speaking," but he writes that he "turned to see the voice." We can take this to mean that the *voice* matters. For John there is seeing in a physical sense, too, but *vision* is secondary, and it operates chiefly at the point when words turn into understanding. "He saw the light," in everyday English, does not refer to literal seeing but to understanding. For John there is seeing, but for the reader today there is only the voice (= word). At Mount Sinai, to which John has already alluded, "all the people saw the voice" (Exod. 20:18 LXX), and this—seeing the voice but nothing else—is made to be a matter of great importance. "You heard the sound of words but saw no form; there was only a voice. . . . Since you saw no form when the LORD spoke to you at Horeb out of the fire, take care and watch yourselves closely" (Deut. 4:12, 15 NIV). Turning "to see the *voice*" may in this sense be prescriptive for a time witnessing "the decline of the Age of Typography and the ascendancy of the Age of Television" (Postman 2006, 8). Intrigued by the prioritizing of the voice at Mount Sinai, Neil Postman notes the peculiarity of making this an integral part of the ethical system of Israel, "*a connection between forms of human communication and the quality of a culture*" (Postman 2006, 9). By this criterion, Revelation offers itself as a resource in a reading rehabilitation program.

**And on turning, I saw seven lampstands of gold, and in the middle of the lampstands [I saw] one like the Son of Man, clothed with a robe reaching to the feet and girded about with a golden sash across his chest** (1:12–13). This is the beginning of a lengthy and detailed description of the figure's appearance and clothing, but the visual paraphernalia take on meaning because of the prior *word.* "The seven lampstands are the seven churches," John explains moments later (1:20). Two OT passages seem especially pertinent, the "lampstand" or seven-armed "candlestick" in Exodus (25:31–35; 26:35) and the vision of the lampstand in Zechariah (4:1–6). With respect to the former, Revelation's application of the "lampstands" to the church is a telling interpretation of sanctuary imagery. In Zechariah, the lampstands signify dependence, on the one hand, and empowerment, on the other. "Do you not know what these are?" an angel asks Zechariah. "No," he answers. "Not by might, nor by power, but by my spirit," comes the response (Zech. 4:5–6 NIV). Finding Jesus "in the middle of the lampstands" (*en mesō tōn lychniōn*) speaks of his importance to the church and of the church's importance to him. Jesus will be "in the middle" more than once in Revelation, and location matters (1:13; 2:1; 5:6).

Jesus "in the middle of the lampstands" means that he is close to the church (1:13; 2:1); he loves the church (3:19); and he is concerned about the integrity of the witness of the believing community (2:5). When we factor in that the one who is seen "in the middle of the lampstands" will also appear "in the middle of the throne" (5:6), the connection between heaven and earth is firm and decisive.

"One like the Son of Man" brings back the person seen earlier, the one who "is coming with the clouds" (1:7, 13). Daniel is the source of this image (Dan. 7:13), confirmation of which is supplied by the way the figure is described (Rev. 1:12–15; Dan. 10:5–6). The notion of "angel Christology" or "angelomorphic" Christology is anchored in the images used to describe Jesus in Revelation (Gieschen 1998, 51–69; Rowland 1980).

However, "*angel* Christology" is not the whole story. **His head and the hair were white as white wool, as snow; his eyes were like a flame of fire, and his feet were like gleaming bronze, refined as in a furnace, and his voice was like the sound of many waters** (1:14–15). This is "no ordinary angel." The giveaway for this is "his head and his hair" (1:14). For this part of the physiognomy, "angelic" will not suffice. In Daniel's vision of the Ancient One, "the hair of his head (was) like pure wool" (Dan. 7:9). John is not guilty of cutting and pasting OT imagery and getting it wrong. Jesus shares in the divine identity, and more evidence to this effect will be forthcoming. His feet are described by a term that is difficult to translate (*chalkolibanō*), often rendered *bronze*. The likeliest OT antecedents are in Ezekiel and Daniel (Ezek. 1:7; Dan. 10:6). The overall impression of the description is a majestic figure where divine, angelic, and—yes—human characteristics are deliberately brought together. When we compute the meaning—hair, eyes, feet, voice, and all—there can be little doubt that John has put Jesus on God's side of the line that divides created from uncreated reality.

This impression is reinforced by features that go beyond externals. **And he had in his right hand seven stars, and from his mouth came forth a sharp, two-edged sword, and his face was like the sun when it shines at its brightest** (1:16). The radiance of the face is another allusion to Daniel (10:6), but Isaiah's description of the Suffering Servant is the most compelling background for the sword (Isa. 42:1–9; 49:1–9; 50:4–9; 52:13–53:12; cf. Bellinger and Farmer 1998). "He made my mouth like a sharp sword," says the Servant (Isa. 49:2; cf. 11:4). When the Servant finds himself tormented by thoughts of futility and failure (Isa. 49:4), he is assured that he is the one by whom God's deliverance will reach "to the ends of the earth" (Isa. 49:6; cf. P. Hanson 1995, 130). Why the sense of futility? All the passages that describe the Suffering Servant show a figure that seems unimpressive and ineffectual to the naked eye (Isa. 53:1–3), and the sharp sword does nothing to mitigate this impression. Indeed, the witness of the Servant "stands so starkly in contrast to the ways of the nations and their leaders that it must be regarded either as foolishness or as an intriguing alternative to a failed strategy" (P. Hanson 1995, 45–46). Which is it, a failed strategy or the remedy for a failed strategy? The answer must be that these texts—with Revelation as the last—are united in saying that what seems like a failed strategy will work despite evidence to the contrary (Tonstad 2016b, 274–75). The weapon of the Revealer in Revelation is *witness*: he has already been defined as "the *witness*, the trustworthy one" (1:5). *Witness* in his realm means *revelation* and *persuasion*, not violence.

**1:17–20.** **And when I saw him, I fell at his feet as though I were dead** (1:17a). Daniel did, too, in almost the same manner (Dan. 10:8–9), and Ezekiel had a similar reaction (Ezek. 1:28). John's posture resembles the OT pattern, but there is no antecedent for what follows. **But he placed his right hand on me, saying, "Do not be afraid. I am the first and the last and the living one. And I was dead, and look: I am alive forever and ever, and I have the keys to death and to Hades"** (1:17b–18). Assurance and reassurance do not let up: in the right hand placed on John; in the claim regarding the speaker's identity; in the speaker's death and resurrection, henceforth "alive forever and ever"; in the confident declaration that the speaker has "the keys" that ensure the reversal of death and the exposé of "Hades." It is now clearer than before that the one who speaks for God is himself God. What God says of God, Jesus can say of himself: "I am the first and the last" (1:8, 17; 2:8; 21:6; 22:13; Bauckham 1998a, 53–54). The Revealer and the revelation cannot be separated: the medium is also the message. The terminology that puts Jesus within the divine identity resists corrosion because it echoes the most emphatic monotheistic affirmations in the OT (Isa. 41:4; 44:6; 48:12; cf. 43:10).

The task of writing will be daunting, but the subject matter is worth a book. **Write, then, what you have seen, what is, and what is to happen after this** (1:19). There is merit to the view that John is commissioned to cover "the totality of existence in its three aspects of past, present and future" (van Unnik 1962–63, 88). Likewise, his writing deals with *reality*. "It is not merely a record of what someone saw, but an account of what *is* or what is *true*, whether in the present or the future" (Michaels 1991, 619).

Before addressing the seven churches directly, **the seven stars** and **the seven golden lampstands** need to be explained: **the seven stars are** [the] **angels of the seven churches, and the seven lampstands are** [the] **seven churches** (1:20). If angels (*angeloi*) refer to heavenly beings and not to earthly "messengers," the churches have a heavenly liaison. Mediation and the role of an intermediary are features of interest, but both are assurances that heaven and earth are connected. This detail is not more important than the idea that "the lampstands are the seven churches" (1:20)—heaven's visible outposts on earth. Mediation by angels is not to be construed as a feature of *distance* when we remember that "the Son of Man" is found "in the middle of the seven lampstands of gold" (1:12–13; 2:1).

## Theological Issues

For meanings of the opening word "revelation" (*apokalypsis*, 1:1), the option that fits Revelation best has been relegated to the margins. Neither genre nor "situation" does justice to the *theological* meaning of the opening word. The claim to *revelation* is not anchored in circumstances or style but in the kind of person God is (1:1; 10:7). This view finds strong support in the OT texts echoing in the first verses.

God's intent to "make known" links Revelation to Daniel (Rev. 1:1; Dan. 2:28–30, 45). G. K. Beale (1999, 50) emphasizes the common theme of "making known" in these books. Revelation's contention that God "*made it known*" (*esēmanen*) depends on a Greek word that means "make known," "report," "communicate," "foretell," or "signify." "The clauses 'revelation . . . God showed . . . what must come to pass . . . and he *made known (sēmainō)*' occur together only in Daniel 2 and Revelation 1:1," says Beale (1999, 50). When we consider the context in Daniel, we have not only a fascinating word study but also a case report for how a message claiming to be a revelation compares to other sources of knowledge. When crunch time comes, Daniel says to King Nebuchadnezzar that "there is a God in heaven who reveals [*anakalyptōn*] mysteries, . . . and he has disclosed . . . to you what is to be [*ha dei genesthai*] . . . in order that the interpretation may be known [*esēmanthē*]" (Dan. 2:28–30 LXX).

> **Revelation 1:1**
>
> • "revelation" (*apokalypsis*)
> • "to make known" (*deixai*)
> • "he made it known" (*esēmanen*)

The thematic link between Daniel and Revelation is indisputable. While Revelation and the Greek text of Daniel both use *sēmainō* for "making known," the Semitic word in Daniel is the same word used in the conversation between God and Abraham in Genesis (Gen. 18:17–19; Beale 1999, 50; Tonstad 2016a, 128–33). In Genesis, too, the subject is God's disposition in relation to knowledge passing from the divine realm to the human sphere. Daniel expands on prior notions of things God alone knows by variants of the word *rāz* (mystery), a Persian loan word found only in Daniel (2:18, 19, 27, 28, 29, 30, 47; 4:6), with all but one occurrence in Dan. 2 (Lenzi 2009, 331, 341; Hartman and Di Lella 2005, 139–40). The mystery denoted as *rāz*, then, is "secret information that only the deity knows" (Lenzi 2009, 332).

In Dan. 2, the subject is not only what God *knows* but that God *shares*. King Nebuchadnezzar has a dream that troubles him to the point of making him sleepless (Dan. 2:1). Daniel is called upon to help when everyone else comes up short. The Hebrew exile explains to the king that "there is a God in heaven who is a revealer [*anakalyptōn*] of mysteries," providing a noun to match the verb: God is "the Revealer" (*ho anakalyptōn*; Dan. 2:28, 29 LXX, my trans.). What God *knows* and what God *shares* are by this logic two sides of the same coin. "Daniel's deity does not just happen to reveal this secret in this one particular instance," says Alan Lenzi (2009, 343). "Rather, Daniel *characterizes* the Hebrew deity as a 'revealer of secrets'; revelation of secret or hidden things is one of this deity's *defining* attributes." "Making known" is so characteristic of God as to make it a proper name: God is "the Known-Maker" (*ho anakalyptōn*).

Daniel, especially Dan. 2, has a concentration of "know" terms that is unparalleled in the Hebrew Bible (Yoder 2009). The word *yəda'*, whether in the form "knowing" or in the form "making known," occurs forty-one times in Daniel, eighteen of which are in Dan. 2. *Yəda'* is on numerous occasions mixed or linked with the word *gəlā'*. Both terms compete for the honor of being the strongest term for "making known." The Greek terms for *yəda'* vary, but *gəlā'* is usually translated by some form of *apokalyptō*, making the two words mutually reinforcing and almost synonymous. This word, so profuse in Daniel, sets the stage for the message of Revelation.

> he makes known [Aram. *gəlā'*; Gk. *apokalyptō*] . . . he knows [Aram. *yəda'*; Gk. *ginōskō*] (Dan. 2:22, my trans.)

> you . . . have made known [Aram. *yəda'*; Gk. *sēmaino, gnōrizō* (Theod.)] . . . you have made known [Aram. *yəda'*; Gk. *gnōrizō* (Theod.)] (Dan. 2:23, my trans.)

> there is a God in heaven who makes known [Aram. *gəlā'*; Gk. *apokalyptō*] (Dan. 2:28, my trans.)

In English, the recurring theme is to "make known." Without violation to the original text, Dan. 2:22–23 can be translated "You have *made known*, . . . you have *made known*," no matter which of the two terms are in view. These texts focus the thought that God "makes known," and they occur in the context of a fierce conflict over what is humanly knowable (Yoder 2009).

The most challenging and clarifying aspect of these terms in Daniel is illustrated by Nebuchadnezzar's strange dream at the beginning of the book (2:1–45). The king knows that he has dreamed. He is accustomed to think that dreams communicate messages from the gods. But he cannot find the key to his troubling dream (2:1–9)!

Has he forgotten the dream, in my view the strongest option (cf. Baldwin 1978, 98)? This fits the usual scenario, where telling the dream is part of the resolution process. Babylonian custom held that "if a man cannot remember the dream . . . his (personal) god is angry with him" (Baldwin 1978, 98). The LXX accommodates the translation, "The word is withdrawn (gone) from me" (Dan. 2:5 LXX, my trans.). If this is the king's way of saying that he cannot remember the dream, his stance during the remainder of the dispute seems more understandable.

Does Nebuchadnezzar remember what he has dreamed, using the occasion to run a quality check on the integrity of his courtiers (J. Collins and A. Collins

1993, 156–57)? This view, in my opinion less persuasive, does not weaken the critical point: God is the source of his dream and the reason for its content.

The king demands of his advisers not only that they tell him how the dream should be interpreted; he also insists that they retrieve his dream (2:9)! His insistence distills the epistemological issue to its essence: the range and source of knowledge in the human realm; the limits of human knowledge; and the idea that certain types of knowledge are in God's possession only. If the dream is communication from an outside intelligence, then it is not a product of the king's mental activity. It cannot be reduced to psychology, learning, or talent. If, too, the dream represents a message from a God who is in the business of "making known" rather than unprovoked human intellectual activity, God is free to share the message with people other than the king. Nebuchadnezzar is on to something when he insists to his state-salaried dream interpreters, "Tell me the dream, and I shall know that you can give me its interpretation" (2:9). This is a hint that his advisers have been playing games in the past (2:9).

The experts get the point. Now it is their turn to try to bring the king to his senses.

> There is no one on earth who can reveal what the king demands! In fact no king, however great and powerful, has ever asked such a thing of any magician or enchanter or Chaldean. The thing that the king is asking is too difficult, and no one can reveal it to the king except the gods, whose dwelling is not with mortals. (Dan. 2:10–11)

Their consternation is intense. Earth has no resource that can meet the king's demand! No one has ever been this unreasonable! The task is too difficult! Perhaps the gods can do it, if gods exist! Even if gods exist, there is no reason to believe that they communicate with mortals!

The king ought to fold in the face of the closely reasoned answer, but he doesn't (Dan. 2:12–13). His rage could be a form of poetic justice, payback for all the years when they pretended to explain communications from the gods while doubting that the higher powers communicate with humans. Nebuchadnezzar seems 100 percent certain that he has received a genuine message from a higher power—the dream isn't just "in his head."

To Daniel and his friends, the predicament is dire, too, but it is also an opportunity. They ask for time. They turn to prayer (Dan. 2:14–18). The result confirms Nebuchadnezzar's conviction that he has received a message from above. We find ourselves in theological territory: the message "made known" to Nebuchadnezzar in a dream is now "made known [Aram. *gălî*; Gk. *apekalyphthē* (Theod.)] to Daniel" (2:19).

The story hammers home the reality of a "Known-Maker" in the universe (Dan. 2:20–30). Daniel agrees with the court-appointed experts that no earthly or human intelligence "can show the king the mystery that the king is asking" (2:27). But he does not agree that human limitations exhaust the options. Daniel's role is modest (2:30), but the new epistemic horizon is vast. "Knowing" is within reach because, beyond the human realm, there is One who causes things to be known.

Daniel proceeds to recount to the king his dream (Dan. 2:31–36) and then its interpretation (2:37–45). The dream presents the flow of history in broad strokes. It stresses human finitude; it exposes the fleeting nature of greatness; it pictures a relentless decline; and it predicts failure with respect to establishing enduring structures (2:31–33, 37–44). Dissolution seems inherent to the human project itself: a statue standing on feet of iron and clay. The constituent elements are unable to overcome intrinsic incompatibility, partly weak, partly strong, but never able to "hold together" (2:33, 41–43). In contrast to this, the dream brings into focus the heavenly alternative.

A stone was cut out, *not by hands* [*lā' bîdayin*] (Dan. 2:34, my trans.)

A stone was cut out from the mountain *not by hands* [*lā' bîdayin*] (Dan. 2:45, my trans.)

These verses stress how the stone was *not* cut out (Hartman and Di Lella 2005, 136). And, yes—the wording justifies the translation that is usually preferred: "a stone was cut out, not by *human* hands," even though the "hands" in question are not specified as human or divine (Dan. 2:34, 45). Nevertheless, the dream envisions a kingdom that "will be brought about by God himself" (Albertz 2002, 1:186). But this is not all. *Method* as well as *agency* are contrasted with human convention, and it is especially the difference with respect to *means* that carries over into Revelation. Let the distinctive feature of God's action now read: "a stone was cut out—but not by *power*" (Dan. 2:34, 45, my trans.; 12:7; cf. J. Collins and A. Collins 1993, 399).

A series of closely linked claims appears in the OT background material that marks the entryway to Revelation. A claim to knowledge that does not have a human origin is proclaimed at the highest level of society: the king dreams, but he cannot remember his dream (Dan. 2:1–7). The claim is corroborated not by the king's belated recollection but by God revealing the dream to someone other than the king (2:14–19)! The dream depicts human history (2:31–43), revealing feet of iron and clay on which the figure stands (2:41–43). Feet of clay indicate that the structure is doomed to collapse quite apart from anything done to it from without (Goldingay 1998, 39). The stone that "was cut from the mountain" (Dan. 2:34, 45) is not an instrument of violence: the divine agency blends with the divine method. A principle other than power is at work in history, an elusive principle that is not of this world—*and not only because the one who operates it isn't human.* The stone "was cut from the mountain *without power*," showing that the "hand" at work represents a different mode of action (2:34, 45). Daniel's stagecraft is compelling and, on some points, entertaining, but the purpose is not to entertain. By Daniel's criterion, *revelation* is special knowledge given to human beings by God, and God is a "Known-Maker." The vision is certified as a revelation not only because the transmission is uniquely circumscribed but also by the content. God brings a solution to bear on the human predicament that is different in character and mode of operation.

This background perspective, although distinctive in Daniel, is much more developed, sure-footed, and conclusive in Revelation. With Daniel's terminology as building blocks, a new *revelation* (*apokalypsis*) is breaking in on the world (1:1). It is specified as "the revelation of Jesus Christ," with Jesus Christ as the subject matter. In scenes yet to come, the riddle of cosmic and human reality is as inscrutable as Nebuchadnezzar's dream (5:3). The epistemological impasse is dense and utterly disheartening (5:4). Then, when the impasse is at its most acute, God brings a *revelation* as the solution to the crisis (5:5–6). Where Daniel hints at a solution "without hands," that is, without the use of force (Dan. 2:34, 45), Revelation puts at the center of its story "a Lamb standing as if it had been killed with violence" (Rev. 5:6). Nonuse of force in Daniel and a victim of violence in Revelation show ideological common ground and affinity that goes beyond shared terminology. Of the two, the images and scenes in Revelation have no peer.

Revelation is certified as *revelation* in a currency that is resistant to forgery or imitation. Let one hundred billion human neurons go to work; let one trillion synapses sizzle at peak activity. Let the minds of all created beings allow their imagination to run wild. No one will take us to the scene in Revelation's "middle" (5:5–6). *This is truly the dream that no one can remember, and this, more than any other scene, certifies it as a revelation* (1:1; 5:5–6).

Daniel and Revelation contend for an epistemological frame of reference that challenges assumptions about human experience now as much as in the ancient world. Sigmund Freud (1856–1939) grappled with the subject in material terms—profoundly influencing our ideas of what is *knowable* and the limits to knowledge. As in Daniel, the subject matter is dreams, and, like Daniel, Freud is the Jewish resident expert on how to interpret them (Frieden 1990). A few excerpts from *The Interpretation of Dreams* will have to suffice.

> Our scientific consideration of dreams starts off from the assumption that they are products of our own mental activity. (Freud 2010, 77)

> *When the work of interpretation has been completed, we perceive that a dream is the fulfilment of a wish.* (Freud 2010, 145)

> We are not in general in a position to interpret another person's dream unless he is prepared to communicate to us the unconscious thought that lies behind its content. (Freud 2010, 260)

It will no doubt have surprised all of us to be told that dreams are nothing other than fulfilments of wishes, and not only on account of the contradiction offered by anxiety-dreams. (Freud 2010, 550–51)

Freud explores dreams that humans experience in everyday life, of course, but his circumscription of the character of dreams extends to the claims made in Daniel. Dreams—*all* dreams—"are products of our own mental activity." Dreams—*all* dreams—must be recounted by the person who had the dream to know its content, and this person must be "prepared to communicate to us the unconscious thought that lies behind its content" for the dream to be understood. Dreams—*all* dreams—"are nothing other than fulfilments of wishes." In Freud's version of psychoanalysis, dreams represent a resource for therapy, mostly in the sense of managing and defusing illicit wishes and conflicts that come to light in the dream.

Revelation, fortified by Daniel, will not abide by these constraints. In these books, God is a "Known-Maker," knocking on the door of human reality more persistently than human beings knock on heaven's door. A person wondering how such a book could come into existence is nudged to consider *God* as the best answer. To give a *theological* reason for Revelation does not negate specific needs at the time of John, exceptional opportunities, or dangers unknown. But the content exceeds what is humanly imaginable, awake or asleep, and the source is a God who makes things known.

Revelation is from the beginning a *Book of Transparency*. In the opening chapter, Revelation proclaims not only that God exists but also that God *shows up* (1:4, 8). God's self-designation anticipates the claims as well as the fallacy of God's adversary in the story (1:4, 8; 17:8). Likewise, "the faithful witness" of Jesus anticipates and epitomizes his role in contrast to the unfaithful and slanderous witness of the enemy (1:5; 12:7–9). Already at the opening exclamation, Revelation predicts the capacity of the witness of Jesus to turn a hostile relation into a relationship of trust, admiration, and love (1:7–8). God's regard for the well-being and witness of "the seven believing communities" emerges as the take-home message of the opening chapter, the chief concern of God's message to them and—through them—to the world.

# Revelation 2:1–3:22

## *To the One Who Has an Ear*

### Introductory Matters

Beware of hyperbole. This is the first piece of advice before "reading the mail," the messages to the seven believing communities in Revelation (2:1–3:22).

How, for instance, should one read the following in the letter to the community in Thyatira? "But I have this against you: you allow playing room for the woman Jezebel, who calls herself a prophet and is teaching and deceiving my servants to practice sexual immorality and to eat food sacrificed to idols" (2:20). Was there a woman named "Jezebel" in Thyatira? Was a figure equivalent to "Jezebel," "one of the Bible's most booed antiheroes" (H. Maier 2002, 173), creating havoc in a church? The OT chronicler describes a Sidonian woman who became the queen of King Ahab (1 Kings 16:31), the architect of the murder of Naboth (1 Kings 21:1–10), the persecutor of Elijah (1 Kings 18:4, 13; 19:2), and a seductress, her eyes painted and her hair adorned sensuously on the day of her reckoning (2 Kings 9:30). And then to "Jezebel" in Revelation. In a comment that is not atypical, Jürgen Roloff (1993, 54) says that "at the pinnacle of the gnostic movement, which the church apparently tolerated uncritically, stands a woman who claims to be a prophetess." This statement stops short of finding a woman by the name "Jezebel," but it finds a *woman*, an *individual*, a person claiming to be a *prophetess*, and a matching *ideology*: Gnosticism.

Let it be said again: Beware of hyperbole. Merriam-Webster defines hyperbole as "language that describes something as better or worse than it really is." Hyperbole does not indicate malice; it is part of normal speech; it can have a pedagogic function that needs reflection to be appreciated. Dictionary.com describes hyperbole as an "obvious and intentional exaggeration" or "an extravagant statement or figure of speech not intended to be taken literally." If the exaggeration is obvious and intentional, the speaker is not trying to mislead. Use of hyperbole casts doubt on the idea that "Jezebel" was a woman, an individual, and a prophetess with dubious credentials. John is *not* guilty of exaggeration if his intention is to say that the church—and possibly the church beyond Thyatira—is threatened by a phenomenon fully as serious as the biblical Jezebel. He is *not* guilty of overstating things if he has in mind the "false messiahs and false prophets," who will "deceive, if possible, even the elect," as Jesus warned in the Synoptic apocalypse (Matt. 24:24, my trans.). The hyperbole stands, and so does the legitimacy of using it.

> **Revelation 2:1–3:22 in the Rhetorical Flow**
>
> Incentive to read (1:1–20)
>
> ►To the one who has an ear (2:1–3:22)
>
>     Ephesus (2:1–7)
>
>     Smyrna (2:8–11)
>
>     Pergamum (2:12–17)
>
>     Thyatira (2:18–29)
>
>     Sardis (3:1–6)
>
>     Philadelphia (3:7–13)
>
>     Laodicea (3:14–22)

This leads to a closely related, second characteristic of the seven messages. They have a formalistic, repetitive, and almost rigid form that blends with pointed, "over-individual," "supra-individual," or even "hyper-individual" descriptions and notes to each of the churches (Popkes 1983). The form and pattern threaten to relativize the specifics, and this could be intentional. A multiplicity of problems or "heresies" collapse into a single reality, suggesting *one* problem rather than *five* or *ten*, and *one* truth rather than three, or five, or ten. This feature strengthens the need to be aware of hyperbole, as intimated in relation to the figure Jezebel.

### Form and Pattern in the Letters

| Community | Designation of the Problem Group | Specific Characterization |
| --- | --- | --- |
| Ephesus | evildoers<br>Nicolaitans | claim to be "apostles"—falsely |
| Smyrna | synagogue of Satan | claim to be "Jews"—falsely |
| Pergamum | Satan's throne<br>teaching of Balaam<br>Nicolaitans | "sexual immorality"<br>"food sacrificed to idols" |
| Thyatira | woman Jezebel<br>deep things of Satan | claim to be "prophetess"—falsely<br>"sexual immorality"<br>"food sacrificed to idols" |
| Philadelphia | synagogue of Satan | claim to be "Jews"—falsely |

We are now ready to read the letters from the beginning.

### Tracing the Train of Thought

All the messages to the seven believing communities follow the same pattern. There is first "to whom" and "from whom," the "from whom" part made up of images of Jesus in the first chapter. Then follows an "inventory" or "audit" that is either commendatory or critical. In medical terms, this would be the "diagnostic" part. Next, in harmony with impeccable medical logic, follows the "prescription" or counsel. Closing off each message, a formulaic exhortation seeks to make sure that the message has been heard correctly (2:7, 11, 17, 29; 3:6, 13, 22). This is accompanied by a promise to the person who takes the message to heart. These promises make use of images from the final two chapters in Revelation while also alluding copiously to the OT (2:7, 11, 17, 26–28; 3:5, 12, 21).

#### Ephesus

**2:1–7.** Each of the churches has an **angel** (1:20; 2:1). There are more references to angels in Revelation than in any other book in the NT (Wolff 2007). Is the angel in question an "angel" in the sense of a heavenly character, or is it a figure of speech for a human being, a "messenger"? In the category of "messenger," could the "angel" be the "congregational reader" who brings the message to the local fellowship (Ferguson 2011)? This option cannot be ruled out, but the angels of the respective fellowships are best seen as heavenly messengers (1:20). Such a figure means *linkage* between heaven and earth, akin to the connection described in the Gospel of John. If "the angels of God are ascending and descending upon the Son of Man," as in John (1:51), earth is connected to heaven: *earth has not been abandoned.* There is *access, communication,* and *presence.* A heavenly messenger in the churches in Asia Minor suggests that heaven has established an outpost on earth. Human reality is a subject of unceasing interest in heaven, and heaven is present on earth to assist human beings. In this endeavor, angels are not on their own because the essential link is the "Son of Man" (John 1:51), who is also represented as the "Son of Man" in Revelation (1:13).

**Thus says he** (*tade legei*) is a basic element in the form and pattern of the messages (2:1, 8, 12, 18; 3:1, 7, 14). It signifies "prophetic speech and royal decrees" (Koester 2014, 261), and it echoes an OT mantra for *divine* speech (Exod. 4:22; 5:1; 2 Sam. 12:7; 1 Kings 21:19). The utterance is regal, declarative, prophetic, and definitive: it does not invite a contrary point of view. But it is not speech coming from far away. The speaker is Jesus, God and human (1:13–16), dead and resurrected (1:17–19), now walking **in the middle of the seven lampstands of gold** (2:1).

The message is addressed to the believing community in **Ephesus** (2:1). Ephesus was the city closest to Patmos on the mainland and by then the leading city in Asia Minor. Augustus made Ephesus the administrative capital in that region in 29 BCE after his victory at Actium, eclipsing Pergamum (Friesen 1993, 26). While Pergamum claimed the distinction of having the first temple built in honor of the emperor in the imperial era (29 BCE) and Smyrna the second (26 CE), the Flavian temple built in Ephesus stands out conspicuously because it was built during the reign of Domitian (84–96 CE; Price 1984, 197–98; Biguzzi 1998a). The temple of Artemis, predating imperial times, was regarded as one of the seven wonders of the ancient world, "the largest edifice in the entire Hellenistic world and the first of such magnitude to be constructed entirely of marble" (Biguzzi 1998a, 279). Add to this the Great Theater, the most imposing structure in what is left of ancient Ephesus today, at peak capacity seating 25,000 spectators. Government, religion, and culture align in Ephesus with imposing results. If size, splendor, and importance were spiritual criteria for preeminence, Ephesus had it all.

But what does knowledge of the political, economic, and religious situation in ancient Ephesus contribute to our understanding of the letter? As we shall see, the explanatory power is less than one might expect. **I know your works and your effort and your perseverance—and this because you cannot tolerate evildoers. And you have tested those who say about themselves that they are apostles but are not, and you have found them to be deceitful (2:2).** This is a generous commendation, and the tribute has special force because

Courtesy of Terje Bjerka

Figure 10. The importance of ancient Ephesus can still be easily ascertained from the large amphitheater.

it shows the cost of discipleship. But how is cost computed? From where does the evident hardship come, as trials from without or as distress from within? The "evildoers" and the ones "who say about themselves that they are apostles but are not" seem to be subversive *insiders*. If emperors and imperial schemes are in view, they are at this stage far from the center of the picture. Promotion of false ideals seems to afflict the community in more than casual ways. Or, with an eye to hyperbole, false ideals are a constant danger. The misdirection is not specified, but God's ideal is. **And you have perseverance, and you are bearing up on account of my name, and that you have not grown weary** (2:3). "Name" (*onoma*) has a representative meaning (2:3, 13; 19:12, 13, 16), joining words that include "witness" (*martyria*) and "faithfulness" (*pistis*; 12:17; 14:12). The revelation of God in Jesus is the go-to reality that takes the measure of all other claims.

The believing community in Ephesus has so far heard much to gladden the heart, but a "but" is coming. **But I have against you that you have let go of your first love** (2:4). The notion of a *"first* love" gives "love" an emotional tenor, and it suggests that the good feelings that existed at the beginning of the relationship are no longer there. Contemporary neuroscience distinguishes between cognitive and emotive parts of the brain. It has been shown that damage to the emotive part leads to inaction even if cognition is intact. "Love," even "love" as an emotional state, is by this criterion indispensable to action: nothing good can happen where a community lets go of "love." If human relationships have a time line that begins on a high note—only to be overtaken by drudgery, ho-hum routines, and lack of verve—a similar loss of emotional fervor appears to be at work in the relationship between Jesus and the believers at Ephesus. Memory puts the loss into perspective. **Remember then from what you have fallen and turn around, and do the first works** (2:5). "The first love" (*tēn agapēn tēn prōtēn*) and "the first works" (*ta prōta erga*) seem interchangeable: loss of "love" registers as loss of "works" in the retrospective and, in the opposite direction, "love" recaptured will bring back "the first works." Failure to reclaim what has been lost is not optional from the point of view of Jesus (2:5). Filling the relational void is crucial to the appointed mission. God cannot be represented by a believing community bereft of love or, as some see the situation, when there is a mismatch between correct belief and emotion (Stefanovic 2009a, 118). If the community does not turn, **I will come to you and remove your lampstand from its place** (2:5).

The Ephesians are commended for not tolerating "evildoers" (2:2). The "evildoers" are identified as "those who say about themselves that they are apostles but are not" (2:2). A single reality is described from various angles by different terms. **But this you do have: that you hate the works of the Nicolaitans, which I also hate** (2:6). This, too, is a commendation, and it envisions a single reality. "Evildoers," self-designated "apostles," and "the Nicolaitans" refer to one reality rather than to three different groups. Several things favor a "lumping" over a "splitting" strategy, but we cannot ignore scholarly attempts to see "the Nicolaitans" as a definite group.

"Nicolaus, a proselyte of Antioch," is mentioned as one of the seven deacons chosen to oversee the distribution of aid according to Acts (6:5). These individuals were to be "men of good standing, full of the Spirit and of wisdom" (6:3). Is this Nicolaus the point man for the Nicolaitans in Revelation? Some of the church fathers thought so (Irenaeus, *Haer.* 1.26.3; 3.11.1; 7.24). Contemporary interpreters think the connection is warranted even though there must have been more than one "Nicolaus" among whom to choose (Brox 1965). If the Nicolaus in Acts is singled out for heavy-handed criticism in the person of his followers, things must have gone seriously wrong for him or his influence between Antioch and Ephesus. Alternatively—as a bolder theory—nothing "went wrong." Readers are expected to perceive a conflict between different visions of true faith. Ephesus is thought to be a case in point, showing a divided and polarized community. The most developed version of this hypothesis sees one branch of "Christianity" defending the open-minded and tolerant legacy of the apostle Paul against the "conservative" and uncompromising conviction in Revelation. By this logic "Nicolaus" is in Paul's camp. He may even have been the founder of the church in Ephesus, counting among his allies Priscilla and Aquila in addition to Paul (Acts 18:18–26; Heiligenthal 1991; Walter 2002). On this reading of the evidence, there were at least two groups of believers in Ephesus, each claiming the high ground in the NT, one side standing with Paul and the other with the author of Revelation. These groups were not living amicably alongside each other. As indicated by the harsh language in Revelation, they were in fierce conflict, with the message to Ephesus denying legitimacy to "the Nicolaitans" and projecting the wish to drive them to extinction by a word coming directly from Jesus (Walter 2002, 226).

This theory hangs by a precarious thread for making a connection between Nicolaus in Antioch and the Nicolaitans in Ephesus. Were the Nicolaitans Gnostics—and for that reason fairly criticized (Roloff 1993, 45)? Were they defenders of the legacy of Paul—and therefore unfairly criticized (Walter 2002, 226)? Was their message identical to "the teaching of Balaam" (Aune 1996–98, 178)? The answer can be left for later because "the Nicolaitans" make a second appearance in the message to the believers in Pergamum (2:15). The grid shown at the beginning favors other possibilities. We are unwise if we overlook the repetitive form that goes hand in hand with the "hyper-individual" message to each community (Popkes 1983). By this criterion, the identity and meaning of "the Nicolaitans" may be found in the text.

What do we have so far? First, the Ephesian community is faced with problems, but there is very little actual evidence in the letter portion that these problems are caused by Roman imperial reality (Friesen 1993, 24–37; 1995a). Although familiar with the leading Roman city in Asia Minor, John says little or nothing in the letter portion to indicate that the physical and calendrical imprint of the Roman Empire weighs heavily on him. The messages to the seven churches spring out of a communal and theological context, not in the streets of ancient Ephesus. We are encouraged to *read*. Actual *travel* on the tourist trek, an unlikely prospect from John's point of view, will not be as important as carefully touring the text.

Second, there is no straight line from city and culture—the setting of the seven communities in Revelation—to the spiritual and theological concerns in the letters. The allure of this line of inquiry has proved irresistible to many (Ramsay 1905; Hemer 1986), but the evidence falls short of the claims, as Steven J. Friesen (1995b) has shown. Third, the problem in Ephesus is *internal*, whether we describe it in social or theological terms (Duff 2001, 10–16), and it remains a problem *within* the communities even if we allow for the possibility of hyperbole. Fourth, most interpreters see "the Nicolaitans" (2:6, 15), the "teaching of Balaam" (2:14), the "woman Jezebel" (2:20), "sexual immorality" (2:14, 20), and "food sacrificed to idols" (2:14, 20) in local and human terms, triggering a quest for some group or specific aberration in the respective churches. But, again, the messages are conspicuously repetitive. This points to a general concern rather than a unique set of problems in a given community. Moreover, the *cosmic* and *theological* element has received less attention even though it is conspicuous: the "synagogue of Satan" in Smyrna (2:9), "the throne of Satan" in Pergamum (2:13), "the deep things of Satan" in Thyatira (2:24), and "the synagogue of Satan" in Philadelphia (3:9). These terms need to be explored for their contribution to, and coherence with, the cosmic scope and theological concerns of Revelation as a whole. They suggest that something terrifying is at work in history and that no community of faith is likely to be spared.

This view is enhanced by the exhortation that concludes the message to Ephesus. **Let everyone who has an ear hear what the Spirit is saying to the believing communities. To everyone who overcomes in the war [*tō nikōnti*], I will give that person to eat from the tree of life that is in the paradise of God** (2:7). This translation boosts the cosmic perspective that is often lost. While the NRSV has "to everyone who conquers [*tō nikōnti*]," the battle metaphor comes closer to the tenor of Revelation when we say "everyone who overcomes *in the war*" (2:7). Leaving the verb without an object is permissible on formal grounds, but an object is implied. Revelation will address believers as those who "overcome" and "conquer" (*tō nikōnti*), urging them to persevere, but it is implied throughout that they are engaged in a war with a nonhuman enemy (cf. 2:7, 11, 17). This is beyond doubt when Revelation specifies that "they have overcome *him*" (*enikēsan auton*; 12:11; cf. 15:2; 17:14). "Overcoming" or "prevailing" happens in relation to the adversary in the story, and it is couched in the language of conflict.

What awaits the person who prevails? The echoes of Genesis are loud and resonant. In Genesis, God is concerned that the human being (*hā'ādām*) "might reach out his hand and take also from the tree of life, and eat, and live forever" (Gen. 3:22). To forestall this, "God sent him forth from the garden of Eden. . . . [God] drove out the man; and [God] . . . placed the cherubim, and a sword flaming and turning to guard the way to the tree of life" (3:23–24).

Now, in Revelation, God announces that access to the tree of life has been restored. "I will give to her and to him to eat from the tree of life that is in the paradise of God" (2:7; cf. 22:2). It is surely to the point that "the first promise refers to the very start of the biblical narrative: the creation" (Dulk 2006, 516). Expulsion and exile at the beginning are reversed: there is now access and return. This observation is good enough in most interpretations, suggesting that for a problem defined as *expulsion*, access and return will be the solution.

But this is no more than half the story; it is incorrect to define the problem in Genesis mostly as *expulsion* (Gen. 3:23–24). Before the expulsion, there was *misrepresentation* of the divine command (3:1–2). Misrepresentation was followed by distrust, and distrust led to violation of the command (3:7–11). Only when this is factored in—the misrepresentation that preceded the distrust (3:1–2)—can the full extent of the reversal in Revelation be appreciated. Access to "the tree of life" is by this logic best understood not only as reversal of expulsion but also as defeat of the misrepresentation that brought about the expulsion (Rev. 2:7; Gen. 3:1–14, 23–24).

The message to the believing community in Ephesus establishes the pattern for all seven communities.

### Pattern of the Messages

| To whom | "To the ministering angel . . . write" | |
|---|---|---|
| From whom | Description of Jesus using images from Rev. 1, full of OT echoes | |
| Audit | Description, commendation, and rebuke | "Diagnosis" |
| Counsel | Prescription: *What to do about it* | "Treatment" |
| Call | "To the one who has an ear" | |
| Promise | Promise using images from Rev. 20–22, saturated with OT echoes | |

#### Smyrna

**2:8–11.** The outline established for the message to the community in Ephesus stands, beginning with *to whom* and *from whom* (2:8). On the "to whom" side, the mail is sent forty miles north and slightly westward to Smyrna, like Ephesus a coastal city (the coastline has since moved away from ancient Ephesus). Smyrna boasted historical roots going all the way back to Alexander the Great. It is the reputed birthplace of Homer, and it is the only one of the seven cities of Revelation to be continuously inhabited. In the wake of World War I, when maps were redrawn and empires ceased to exist, Smyrna burst into the consciousness of the world like a sonic boom. During the nineteenth century the city had become the richest, most beautiful, and most cosmopolitan city of the eastern Mediterranean, a trading center of half a million people, with an amalgam of Turks, Greeks, Armenians, Jews, and immigrant European traders. In September 1922, this came to an end in a terrifying conflagration and bloodshed as the army of the new Turkish state bore down on the city. The fire laid waste to much of the city, and the conquest led to the slaughter or expulsion of most of the non-Muslim residents. Smyrna has been called the first genocide of the twentieth century for the scale of the killing (Ureneck 2015, 23–25). Little of this is evident in modern Izmir, a thriving city and popular tourist destination, at 3.7 million inhabitants Turkey's third-largest city.

The imperial credentials of Smyrna are only slightly less impressive than those of Ephesus. The city played host to the provincial assembly and won the honor of building the Temple of Tiberius, the second imperial temple to be built in Asia Minor, after overcoming fierce competition from ten other contestants and prevailing in the final round over Sardis (26 CE; Tacitus, *Ann.* 5.55–56; Price 1984, 197–98; Friesen 2001, 46). In the Christian community, Irenaeus (*Haer.* 3.3.4) says of Polycarp that he "conversed with many who had seen Christ," saw the apostle John in person, and was later appointed bishop of Smyrna, a position he held until suffering martyrdom during the reign of Marcus Aurelius (161–180 CE) at the age of eighty-six (Eusebius, *Hist. eccl.* 4.14.2–15.36). Polycarp is thus an example of actual imperial persecution within a century of the writing of Revelation.

> ### Polycarp
>
> The story of Polycarp's martyrdom has elements that might be the stuff of legend, the fire taking "the shape of a vaulted room" that protected the martyr's body, an executioner stepping forth to kill him with a sword only to see the blood streaming forth to quench the fire (Eusebius, *Hist. eccl.* 4.14.2–15.36).

On the "from whom" side, two claims to uniqueness are made, both taken from the introductory vision (1:17–18). Jesus is **the First and the Last**. Only a person who shares the divine identity can talk like that (Bauckham 1998a). Triumph over death needs the attributes of "the First and the Last," but these attributes alone are not the reason why death has been fought into submission. The impossible possibility has come to be because Jesus **was dead** and **lived again**: *life is the prize won by self-giving* (cf. John 12:24–25). When the figure's claims to uniqueness are put into perspective, Jesus is what his antagonist is not. The adversary is not "the first and the last," and he is not a self-giving person. Jesus, by contrast, is not only "the First and the Last" but also self-giving, certified by the fact that he **was dead**. Defeat of death walks hand in hand with the defeat of the adversary's misrepresentation of God (Rev. 12:9; 20:2; Gen. 3:1).

*I know* (2:9) means awareness of the believer's circumstances and of his/her state of mind. The subjective distress is real, but appearances are not the measure of actual success or failure. The Smyrnean believers may outwardly be an unimpressive and unenviable community, but in actual fact—by heaven's objective measure—they are **rich** (2:9). This view corresponds to the blessing pronounced at the beginning of the letter: blessings and riches are not measured in material terms (1:3; 2:9). **I also know the slander** [*tēn blasphēmian*] **of those who say that they are Jews and are not, but are a synagogue of Satan** (2:9). **Distress** and **poverty** have specific content (2:9). The Smyrneans are exposed to "slander." The wording of the NRSV reflects a wise choice. *Slander* will often flash across the screen in Revelation (2:9; 13:1, 5, 6; 16:9, 11, 21; 17:3). In other instances—and less wisely—the NRSV opts for the word "blasphemy" (13:1, 5, 6; 16:9, 11, 21; 17:3). Feeling the need to make a distinction between "the blasphemy" experienced by the Smyrneans and "blasphemy" directed at God, translators make the Smyrneans face *slander* (2:9) while God is at the receiving end of "*blasphemy*" (Duff 2001, 44).

Much is lost by making this unnecessary distinction. *Slander* works perfectly well in all cases, as noun (2:9; 13:1, 5, 6; 17:3) or verb (13:6; 16:9, 11, 21). Indeed, it is the better word precisely where translators opt for "blasphemy." *Slander* is the original and essential gambit in the cosmic conflict. When Jesus says to the Smyrneans, "I know the slander" (2:9), we underread it if we take it to mean only that Jesus knows *their* experience and is aware of what *they* are going through. The one who knows "the slander" knows it firsthand: he is the one who really knows because he is the original and essential target (12:7–12; 20:2; Gen. 3:1). Peering out from the shadows of what Jesus knows is "the Slanderer" (Rev. 12:9; 20:2). "Slander" is the enemy's business in Smyrna, too.

When we allow the thought to go in this direction, the identity of "those who say that they are Jews but are not" (2:9) becomes less fraught than the option usually preferred. People said to be "Jews" may well be Jews, of course, but we should not be certain that this is the opinion in Revelation. The "Jews" in this text are an especially malignant kind. Not only are they not what they claim to be; they "are a synagogue of Satan" (2:9). This is savage rhetoric, to put it mildly. If John has real people in mind, and if the people are real Jews, this application has had devastating consequences for Jewish communities through the ages (Lohse 1993).

Are "the Jews" mentioned in the message to believers in Smyrna real Jews, however? Do we have a conflict between a group of noble Christ-followers and some or all the members of the local Jewish synagogue? This is how many interpreters see it. We are offered the option of seeing the entire Jewish community in Smyrna, stronger and better connected than the Christians, giving the small group of Christ-followers a hard time (Lambrecht 1999). Or, in a scaled-down version of this scenario, we have some "bad-apple" Jews, a militant minority in the synagogue, ganging up on the Christ-followers either directly or by colluding with the Roman authorities (Mayo 2006; Koester 2014, 275, 278). The scenario can be laid out as follows: (1) "The Jews" in question are ethnic Jews (Lambrecht 1999, 425; Mayo 2006, 51). (2) The criticism leveled at them is vicious: they "are a synagogue of Satan" (2:9). It is therefore right to ask, "Why are Christians speaking about Jews this way?" (Lohse 1993, 106). (3) The denigration does not apply to all Jews in Smyrna. Except for a few "bad apples," most of the Jews in Smyrna are the good kind (Mayo 2006, 72). (4) The history of John's characterization of real Jews started a tradition that has been calamitous for the Jews (Mayo 2006, 75). With respect to the last of these points, it is argued that the text was not meant to become the biblical repository for Christian anti-Semitism. Wholesale application to Jews has taken the text in a direction that the author did not intend. The "nonapplication" pertains to John Chrysostom's outbursts in Antioch in the fourth century that Christians should not join the Jews in their "unclean doors" or participate with them at "the table of demons" (*Adv. Jud.* 1.7.5). In this tradition, at fault too is Martin Luther, who in 1543 advised fellow Germans "to set fire to their [Jewish] synagogues or schools and to bury and cover with dirt whatever will not burn, so that no man will ever again see a stone or cinder of them" (LW 47:268). To Luther, forgiveness was needed for past lenience against the Jews and not for present severity. "This is to be done in honor of our Lord and of Christendom, so that God might see that we are Christians, and do not condone or knowingly tolerate such public lying, cursing, and blaspheming of his Son and of his Christians" (LW 47:268). If there is a line connecting John's "synagogue of Satan" in Revelation and Luther's vitriol against the Jews—even if the line is exaggerated, misguided, or invalid—the Holocaust demands unsentimental accounting from the Christian church and its reading of Scripture.

Elaine Pagels's view of the "Satan" language in the NT seeks indirectly to allay the concern that the message of Jesus to the believing community in Smyrna bears responsibility for Christian vilification of Jews. In Pagels's scenario, Satan is a *rhetorical* entity, not a real person. In the heat of conflict surrounding the followers of Jesus, the quest for a rhetorical sledgehammer gave rise to Satan. Pagels (1995, 47) argues that followers of Jesus "began increasingly to invoke the *satan* to characterize their Jewish opponents; in the process they turned this rather unpleasant angel into a far grander—and far more malevolent—figure." The key to this "Satan" is not found in the realm of ontology or the story of Lucifer's "fall." Satan's rise is explained by sociology and the need for tools with which to defeat competing beliefs. No weapon strips an opponent of dignity more effectively than to label him/her "Satan" or an agent of "Satan." Pagels points to the paradox that the people most likely to be hit with the Satan epithet are those with whom one has most in common. Satan is the "intimate enemy."

Even if this construct of "Satan" were to be accepted, it does not lessen the risk to ethnic Jews if the "synagogue of Satan" in Smyrna refers to actual Jews of one kind or another. Quite a different scenario must be considered. On the one hand, "those who say that they are Jews" are not *Jews* at all. "Jews" is a metaphor for people who claim to represent God. On the other hand, Satan is more than a figure of speech. Believers in Smyrna are served notice that Satan maintains a synagogue in their city, but the synagogue must be understood as hyperbole and metaphor. "Those who say that they are Jews" in Smyrna are like "those who say about themselves that they are apostles" in Ephesus (2:2, 9). For both "groups," Revelation gives the verdict that "they are not" what they claim to be (2:2, 9). That is, they have the appearance of being "apostles" and "Jews" and genuine representatives of God in the world, but they "are not" (2:2, 9). The problem of falsehood masquerading as truth is real in both cities, but it does not apply to these communities more than elsewhere in the world. Ephesus has "apostles" who "are not" while Smyrna has "Jews" who "are not," and the phenomenon is a staple of how Satan operates. The same story will be told in less subtle terms later in the book (13:1–18). Revelation lays it out in the letter portion, too. Interpreters who construe the "synagogue of Satan" as ethnic Jews commit an injustice to actual Jews. They also make Satan less real than he is, and they rob Revelation of its subtlety.

But Satan gets his due, with no go-between. **Do not fear what you are about to suffer,** Jesus continues (2:10). **Look, the Mudslinger** [*ho diabolos*] **is about to throw some of you into prison to tempt you to give up, and for ten days you will have affliction** (2:10). Direct mention of "the Mudslinger" does not mean that intermediaries are excluded, but the demonic agent is the primary concern. The "ten days" of affliction are meant to show that the ability of the opposing side to inflict harm is limited. Satan tempts the believers "to give up," but believers keep in mind that time is running out for him (12:12).

When we read the text as an exposé of how Satan works, there will be less temptation to search for real people to pin the "synagogue of Satan" label on them. The Jewish synagogue a few blocks down the street from one of the house churches in Smyrna is not "the Great Satan" or "the synagogue of Satan." We are dealing with figures of speech and hyperbole. The call to **be faithful until death** (2:10) is a reminder of actual danger. Urging the believers to "be faithful until death" is of one piece with "the faithfulness of Jesus" (14:12; cf. 1:5). For him, victory was achieved through victimhood. **I will give you the crown** [*ton stephanon*] **of life,** says Jesus (2:10). The "crown" that will be awarded is in this setting neither the wreath of the victor in an athletic competition nor the reward for public service, although these are occasions for the awarding of "crowns" (Koester 2014, 277). Here, the crowning happens in the context of battle. It will be awarded when the war is won.

Smyrna is wise to listen to the message addressed to it, but so is everyone else (2:11). The choice of the pronouns "anyone" and "whoever" generalizes what otherwise seems specific to a certain congregation in Asia Minor in the distant past. **Whoever prevails in the war will not be harmed by the second death** (2:11). This promise oscillates between the first pages of Genesis and the last pages of Revelation, and it calls for re-reader competence. "Death" has been the lot of humans ever since Adam and Eve took the serpent's denial of death to be true (Gen. 3:2–5). But "the *second* death" is a concept found only in Revelation (20:6, 14), and only in the portion that narrates in painstaking detail the demise of "the ancient serpent" (20:1–10). The promise to the conquerors in Smyrna "is notoriously hard to expound" (Dulk 2006, 517), particularly the idea that believers "will not be *harmed*" (2:11). Re-readers will know more on the second tour through the book. "The second death" marks the end of the cosmic war, culminating in scenes of battle that give the notion of "standing in harm's way" new meaning (20:7–10; 14:13–20). When "the second death" bears down on the world in all its demonic fury (2:11; 20:6, 14), believers "will not be harmed." There can be no better advice than to stay tuned.

It cannot be stressed too strongly that the promises to the first two communities (2:7, 11) refer to the first pages of the biblical narrative. The thrust is not Roman but *human*; it is not political but *existential*; it is not limited to *circumstances* at a certain point in time but applicable to *human reality* across the ages. In Ephesus and Smyrna, at least, the reference to the biblical narrative signals exposé and reversal of the calamity at the core of human existence. The threats to the communities of faith, which in Smyrna are said to come from "the synagogue of Satan" and "the Mudslinger" (2:9, 10), are also threats to humanity at large. In that sense, at least, the believing communities and the world are in the same boat.

### Pergamum

**2:12–17.** "To whom" is now Pergamum (2:12), situated sixty-five miles to the north of Smyrna and the most important city in Asia Minor until it was eclipsed by Ephesus. The eastward expansion of the Roman Empire was determined and relentless, but Pergamum marked a rare exception in the catalogue of conquest. Attalus III (138–133 BCE), the last of the Attalid rulers in Pergamum, was more interested in medicine, botany, and gardening than in politics, and he had no male heirs. Before his death in 133 BCE, he voluntarily bequeathed his domain to Rome. Pergamum was no small prize, and it remained the judicial center of the region even after the administrative apparatus had relocated to Ephesus. One of the most spectacular treasures of antiquity, the Pergamum Altar, was taken in its entirety to Berlin early in the twentieth century. It is the chief attraction of one of the greatest museum complexes in the world and is known as "the Pergamum Island." Pergamum had the honor of pioneering the imperial cult in Asia Minor by getting permission to build a temple dedicated to Augustus and Rome as early as 29 BCE, just two years after Augustus's defeat of Mark Antony in the Battle of Actium. On the acropolis stood a temple dedicated to Athena, the patron goddess of Pergamum. Just outside the city was a temple dedicated to Asclepius, the god of healing. This site later became an important medical center, in part due to the work of Galen (129–216), Pergamum's famous native son and the most towering medical authority in antiquity after Hippocrates. Pergamum's claim to fame is merited, its fusion of religious and political life characteristic of the time and very impressive.

Jesus introduces himself as the one wielding **the sharp two-edged sword** (2:12). This metaphor seems at first sight strange, but the book's introductory vision provides us with an explanatory reference: the sword goes out "from his mouth" (1:16). The weapon of violence turns out to be the exact opposite. "The sharp two-edged sword" and the mouth from which it goes forth refer to speech. Divine speech is a synonym for revelation. Why, then, the warlike symbol for a reality that is nonviolent and irenic? The answer must be that a sword is an implement of warfare, and there is war (12:7). It is an understatement to say that this is a "war of words," but *words* are extremely important in the campaign of "the Mudslinger" (12:9; 20:2; Gen. 3:1). Conflicting versions of truth are clashing. Behind the text is the OT figure that counts on "the rod of his mouth" and "the breath of his lips" to defeat his adversaries (Isa. 11:4). This passage (Isa. 11:1–10) might be the best example of how John weaves "a network of allusion to the same Old Testament passage in various parts of the Apocalypse" (Bauckham 1993a, xi). Jesus states that he "will make war . . . by the sword of my mouth" (2:16). Winning the war is never disconnected from *how* he wins: "*in righteousness* he governs and makes war" (19:11; cf. Isa. 11:3–5).

When Jesus begins the audit, the cosmic perspective is immediately apparent. **I know where you are residing, where Satan's throne is located** (Rev. 2:13). This opening differs slightly from the messages to Ephesus and Smyrna: to them Jesus emphasizes their "works" (2:2) and their "affliction" (2:9), respectively. Here, the concern begins with the neighborhood—"where you are residing" (2:13). Jesus claims to have reliable intelligence about their locality, and the neighborhood is bad. Interpreters have lost no time searching for the specific features in Pergamum that justify the characterization. As usual, the suspicion falls on Roman imperial realities and the imperial cult (Klauck 1992; Reddish 2004). The notion that Satan is headquartered in Pergamum is a problem if it is predicated on features of the city's religious or political life (Klauck 1992, 161; Aune 1996–98, 183), but it is not a problem if we reckon with hyperbole. We have already seen "the Mudslinger" at work in Smyrna, where believers can expect to be thrown into prison (2:10). In Pergamum, the believing community has seen Satan go a notch higher. **And you are keeping my name, and you did not deny my faithfulness even in the days of Antipas, my witness, my faithful one, who was killed among you, where Satan is residing** (2:13). This is a strong commendation for Antipas, who has embodied the faithfulness of Jesus (1:5; 14:12), and it is also a generous tribute to the community. But who committed the cruel deed that cost Antipas his life? Did the Roman authorities do it (Klauck 1992, 162–63)? Was it instigated by the Jews (Klauck 1992, 163)? Revelation does not hint at a causal link to either of these groups. The notion that "Satan's throne" is in Pergamum and that Pergamum is the city "where Satan is residing" hardly identifies a specific communal or political entity. Satan is not coming to perform at a theater near them at some point in the future. He is already there, where they live (2:13). But the geographical circumscription is not a license for readers to utter a sigh of relief that they don't live in Pergamum: "such a horrible place; thank God I don't live there." The hyper-individuality and hyper-particularity of the language break the confines of the local situation. Satan is at work in Pergamum, to be sure, with the martyrdom of Antipas to prove the length to which Satan will go, but Satan does not reside in Pergamum more than anywhere else in the world. What has happened in Pergamum is *revelatory* and *representative* of Satan's economy and government. When "Satan's throne" appears later in Revelation (13:2; 16:10), the concern is its reality and mode of operation, not its location.

The audit is favorable overall. **But I have a few things against you: you have some there who adhere strongly to the teaching of Balaam, who instructed Balak to lay a trap before the children of Israel to make them eat food sacrificed to idols and commit sexual immorality** (2:14). This indictment facilitates interpretation of all the messages on three counts. First, there is a pattern of repetition *within* each message, the same phenomenon described in different ways. In Pergamum, this means that "the teaching of Balaam" and "the Nicolaitans" are similar, perhaps the same (Klauck 1992, 165). *Likewise*, **you also have some who have bought into the teachings of the Nicolaitans** (2:15). The parallel opens a path to secrets that time has rendered inaccessible. While the footprint of the Nicolaitans has been covered by the sands of time, Balaam's legacy is fixed in print and accessible (Num. 22:5–34; 31:16). Second, there is now a pattern of repetition *across* the messages because we have Nicolaitans in Ephesus *and* in Pergamum. This can be read as though the Nicolaitans (Rev. 2:15) were a specific first-century movement with a presence in different locations, but such specificity requires a hefty dose of speculation, and it comes at the cost of muting the hyperbole. When it comes to the Nicolaitans, there is no certainty to be had (Koester 2014, 263–64), but the biblical story of Balaam fills in the picture. The short version of "the teaching of Balaam" is *unfaithfulness*. In the context of Israel's journey toward the promised land, the unfaithfulness took the form of actual sexual immorality: the Israelites "began to have sexual relations with the women of Moab," who, we are told, "invited the people to the sacrifices of their gods, and the people ate and bowed down to their gods" (Num. 25:1–2). This began immediately after Balaam departed the scene following his failed mission to curse the people of Israel (Num. 24:25). What a curse from above could not do, however, might be accomplished by cunning from below. Israelite men succumbed to sexual entrapment by Moabite women in a scheme concocted by Balaam (Num.

31:16). The scheme was only a partial success. In the end, it brought about Balaam's demise (Num. 31:8, 16).

Is the believing community in Pergamum in danger of succumbing to actual "sexual immorality" of the kind witnessed at the border of the promised land at the instigation of a latter-day Balaam? This would make no sense—certainly not if "the Nicolaitans" in Pergamum in some way espouse the theology of Paul, as some commentators believe. If actual sexual immorality is not the problem, a similar judgment applies to "food sacrificed to idols." These terms are best seen as synonyms for the same reality, neither term meant to be taken literally. The Israelite apostasy was sexual in a way that the problem in Pergamum is not, but the terminology in Revelation depicts seduction and apostasy that does not need to be sexual in nature. In the OT sexual infidelity is the favored metaphor for apostasy or idolatry, no matter which expression it takes (Duff 2001, 55; Klauck 1992, 167). The common element, even in nonsexual infidelity, is *seduction*. If Jesus wishes to say that seduction poses a risk to the believer, he could hardly have picked a better case than Balaam's strike from behind. By this criterion, "the teaching of Balaam" highlights the risk of being seduced.

There is a third way in which Pergamum's diagnosis facilitates our understanding of the other letters. A series of parallels with respect to "groups" *within* each community extends to parallels *across* the communities. The parallels *within* are described as "sexual immorality" and "food sacrificed to idols," the parallels *across* are linked by the fact that both deviations are seen in Pergamum and Thyatira—with "the Nicolaitans" also appearing in Ephesus.

**Naming Problems, or a Problem with Many Names**

| Community | Designation of the Problem Group | Specific Characterization |
|---|---|---|
| Ephesus | evildoers<br>Nicolaitans | claim to be "apostles"—falsely |
| Pergamum | Satan's throne<br>teaching of Balaam<br>Nicolaitans | "sexual immorality"<br>"food sacrificed to idols" |
| Thyatira | woman Jezebel<br>deep things of Satan | claim to be "prophetess"—falsely<br>"sexual immorality"<br>"food sacrificed to idols" |

The proposed local and specific options ignore the generalizing tendency of the messages. This casts doubts on the notion that John in Pergamum goes to battle against a tolerant, inclusive vision of Christian community in the tradition of Paul. Hans-Josef Klauck argues in great depth that the exhortation to Pergamum is a world-rejecting and world-denying vision that is too rigid and unworkable. If heeded, it will paint the believing community into a corner and consolidate a state of immaturity. They should instead accept that they live in the real world, and they must be given the means to do it in a realistic way (Klauck 1992, 181; Duff 2001, 60). A less dramatic version envisions John taking to task believers who for socioeconomic reasons are not as strict as they ought to be in their dealings with the imperial cult (Duff 2001, 69; Klauck 1992, 178). If, on the other hand, we view these messages through the lens of metaphor, John searches the OT for the most powerful and viscerally arousing images to sound a warning against the risk of spiritual seduction. Scholars have been rightly perplexed at how the messages to the seven churches relate to the body of the book (Klauck 1992, 174). Here, believers are served notice that Satan is at work in Pergamum, and the warning against seduction has a cosmic frame of reference. When we get to the main body of Revelation, the drumbeat of John's hyperbole in the letters to the seven churches will seem less mysterious.

**Turn, then** (*metanoēson oun*; 2:16). The corrective is usually translated "repent," but repentance is a form of "turning." **If not, I will come to you in a hurry, and I will make war with you by means of the sword of my mouth** (2:16). Urgency is in the air: Jesus will come "in a hurry." A "war" is being fought in the cosmos and in the streets of Pergamum: for the first time John is using the word for "making war" (*polemeō*) that re-readers will recognize as the virtual theme word of the book (2:16; 12:7; 13:4; 19:11). This war spares no one, and Jesus will engage the opposing power with his weapon of choice and the means characteristic of him—"by means of the sword of my mouth" (2:16).

*Hearing*—and hearing correctly—goes to the heart of the matter in Pergamum as in the previous two communities (2:17). Two enticing images are used for the reward that awaits those who prevail in Pergamum: **hidden manna** and **a white stone** (2:17). The "manna" recalls the story of how the Israelites were miraculously fed in the wilderness on their journey to the promised land (Exod. 16:4, 32–34). In John, Jesus spiritualizes the image, saying, "I am the living bread that came down from heaven" (John 6:51; cf. 6:31–51). "*Hidden* manna" (*tou manna tou kekrymmenou*) must likewise represent a spiritual concept: the one who gets access to "*hidden* manna" is the recipient of revelation. "Manna" is food in time of need, for the Israelites the only food in sight.

The "white stone" is not as easily identified with an OT image. One possibility is in Zechariah: on a stone with seven facets, God engraves an inscription that signifies removal of guilt (Zech. 3:9). In the Greco-Roman world, white stones were associated with voting and vindication in court (Koester 2014, 263). The fact that the "white stone" is here awarded in the context of *war* suggests vindication and victory (Iwamura 2002, 165). "Manna" that is "hidden" is joined with "a new name that no one knows," the new name to be inscribed on the "white stone." These are images of things that are "hidden" (*manna, name*), but they convey the opposite: *revelation*. However, the revelation is personalized and known only to "the one who receives it" (2:17). The "new name" suggests illumination and transformation so deep that it goes to the bedrock of character and personality (Iwamura 2002, 171). It must not be left out that the word translated "received" (*lambanō*) allows for meanings like "apprehend," "comprehend," and "make one's own" (BDAG 583–85, λαμβάνω), just as *grasp* in English is used metaphorically in the sense of *understand*. By the usual sense of "receiving," the "hidden manna" and the "white stone" are rewards that lie in the future and belong to the world to come. "Apprehension" or "comprehension," by contrast, is available in the present. If Revelation's errand is to effect transformation in the present, the latter meaning should be preferred. The "white stone" is by this token not an amulet to coddle in the future but illumination for the present, and "hidden manna" is food that can be eaten now.

### Thyatira

**2:18–29.** The mailman now turns eastward and slightly south, toward the interior and hinterland of Asia Minor. The distance from Pergamum to Thyatira is about thirty-five miles (2:18). The notion that the seven churches in Revelation track according to the Roman postal route of the first century is no longer tenable. In commercial and travel terms, Ephesus was the hub, and the other cities relate to Ephesus in a pattern corresponding to a road system radiating from the center (Guttenberger 2005, 164). In contrast to the three previous cities, Thyatira along with Philadelphia had no claim to fame. Gudrun Guttenberger (2005, 162–63) calls both towns "insignificant," saying of Thyatira that "we have a town of inferior status, economically weak, culturally impoverished . . . as well as politically powerless." "The longest and most difficult of the seven letters is addressed to the least known, least important, and least remarkable of the cities," says Colin Hemer (1986, 106). Given its insignificance, the case for including Thyatira calls for an explanation. Some argue that it was included because John had a special connection to the community; others that it afforded a pedagogical opportunity for all the churches (2:23; Guttenberger 2005, 175, 179). Acts mentions a woman by the name of Lydia, who "was from the city of Thyatira and a dealer in purple cloth" (Acts 16:14). This makes Lydia a shareholder in Thyatira's chief commercial product in the first century, textiles and the art of dyeing various types of cloth (Hemer 1986, 109).

A message from on high to a small community in an inconsequential town points to another possible reason why this community is included: The town is unimportant, but the church is not. The believing fellowship is an object of high regard to God, and *God* is very much in view on the "from whom" side of the equation. The speaker identifies himself as **the Son of God** (2:18), the only time this expression is used in Revelation. "Son" is not a term for derivation, descent, or inferiority because the speaker has already identified himself as "the First and the Last" (1:17). His appearance adds to the impression that the speaker shares the divine identity—**the eyes . . . like a flame of fire and the** feet . . . like burnished bronze (2:18). These terms appeared in the introductory vision (1:14, 15), and they come with strong OT overtones (Ezek. 1:7, 27; Dan. 10:6). The letter does not focus on inferiority to God on the part of the "Son of God." On the contrary, the focus is on likeness to God in the sense that the divine identity of Jesus makes it possible for him to reveal God in a way no one else can. In the present context, his divine credentials show that it is not below God's dignity to take interest in a small group of believers in an insignificant town. If Thyatira as a city counts for little on an imperial scale, great things are ahead for the believers. To these believers, says Jesus, "I will give to him/her authority over the nations" (2:26).

Here, too, the audit is largely positive. **I know your works [*erga*] and your love [*agapē*] and your faithfulness [*pistis*] and your service [*diakonia*] and your perseverance [*hypomonē*], and your last works are greater than the first** (2:19). This is a resounding commendation, five weighty nouns in all, the last four probably meant to give content to the works, the first word in the sequence. Thyatira's believers have seemingly reversed the inevitable spiritual decline seen in the previous churches. Unlike Ephesus, where believers have "let go of the first love" (2:4), "the last works" of believers in Thyatira "are greater than the first" (2:19). The best things in life are not necessarily headed for decay and decline. Love, faithfulness, service, and perseverance are qualities that are constantly refined in Thyatira.

The "but" soon to come is for this reason unexpected, and the severity of the "but" is shocking. **But I have this against you: you tolerate that woman Jezebel, who says of herself that she is a prophetess and is teaching and deceiving my very own servants to practice sexual immorality and to eat food sacrificed to idols** (2:20). How can the commendation stand when believers in Thyatira turn out to be guilty of such serious dereliction of duty? Let it be that a small fish manages to slip through the net of vigilance, but this is no small fish. This is *"that woman Jezebel!"* Revelation conjures up the most notorious sponsor of evil in the OT, alleging that she is on the loose in Thyatira as a resident prophetess. The Bible portrays the reign of Jezebel and Ahab as a period of religious erosion to the point that "Yahwism was in danger of becoming a pagan religion" (Bright 1976, 259). Are believers in Thyatira similarly at risk?

As noted, scholars tend to take the rhetoric at face value. "Jezebel" is a woman, a single individual operating within the believing community (Trocmé 1999; Guttenberger 2005, 171; Friedrich 2002, 203), possibly "a patroness or hostess of one of the house churches that made up the Christian community at Thyatira" (Aune 1996–98, 203; Koester 2014, 303). Her deceit is evident in her activity: she is teaching "my very own servants to practice sexual immorality and to eat food sacrificed to idols" (2:20), the same problem identified in Pergamum (2:14, 20). The libertine, disgust-arousing "prophetess" is alleged to be in a personal feud with John. He engages in a ruthless effort to take her down (Friedrich 2002, 201; Thimmes 2003, 134; Carter 2009, 33; Moore

2014, 513). To some interpreters, John exceeds the rules of fair play in this battle. "Who is the monster responsible for the mass murder of Jezebel's children?" Tina Pippin (1995, 196) asks, "And even more broadly, how did such a misogynist text make it into the Christian canon?" Can't John (and Jesus) accept that there will be differences of opinion without resorting to such harsh rhetoric? Violence seems to threaten even before John spells out what Jesus intends to do about "Jezebel's" recalcitrance (2:21–23). "The ferocity of his language against the Thyatiran prophet, as well as those who follow her, is surpassed only by his vehemence against the Whore of Babylon," writes Pamela Thimmes (2003, 140). She adds that this is "language inscribed with violence from beginning to end. It is language that consumes; it is language that permits no response or rebuttal" (Thimmes 2003, 140). In another variant of the "overreacting" theme, "Jezebel's" offense is nothing else and nothing worse than Paul's adjudication between "the weak" and "the strong" in Rom. 14 (Trocmé 1999). To yet others, John is reacting to "Jezebel's" accommodating stance toward Roman imperial realities, and his concern is well taken. "While 'Jezebel' advocated engagement with the larger society (probably with an eye to reforming from within), John recommended withdrawal into the ghetto" (Duff 2001, 60). Why the need to call the phenomenon "Jezebel," of all things?

Are these options—any of them—convincing? In my view, they fail on at least two counts. First, they are tone deaf to the hyperbole that abounds in all the messages and is particularly unsubtle in the message to Thyatira. Second, they do not do justice to the generalizing elements in the messages. On the generalizing side, Thyatira is not a unique case. At least four generalizing elements stand out:

1. Self-representation of the problem group.

   Ephesus: *say about themselves that they are apostles but are not* (2:2)

   Pergamum: *say about themselves that they are Jews but are not* (2:9)

   Thyatira: *says about herself that she is a prophetess* (but is not) (2:20)

   Philadelphia: *say about themselves that they are Jews but are not* (3:9)

Do these representations reflect three different realities, or do they point to one reality represented in three different ways?

2. John's label for the problem group.

   Ephesus: *Nicolaitans*

   Smyrna: *synagogue of Satan*

   Pergamum: *teaching of Balaam, Nicolaitans*

   Thyatira: *woman Jezebel*

   Philadelphia: *synagogue of Satan*

Do these designations correspond to four or five different realities or to one single reality?

3. "Description" of what the problem groups are doing.
    Pergamum: *food sacrificed to idols, sexual immorality*
    Thyatira: *sexual immorality, food sacrificed to idols*

This is as specific as it gets, "food sacrificed to idols" and "sexual immorality" in Pergamum, the same items in the reverse order in Thyatira. The representations preceding these descriptions make it likely that we are dealing with similar problems in all the faith communities. If "food sacrificed to idols" and "sexual immorality" are metaphors, their descriptive force needs redirection. As noted earlier, it is difficult to believe that promotion of actual "sexual immorality" would have much traction in the fledgling churches (Duff 2001, 59).

4. Theology and ideology.
    Smyrna: *the synagogue of Satan*
    Pergamum: *the throne of Satan, where Satan resides*
    Thyatira: *the deep things of Satan*
    Philadelphia: *the synagogue of Satan*

Jesus is handing out names, and it is not pretty. "Satan" is the threat common to all the communities. Affiliated with "Satan" are expressions descriptive of "people" (*synagogue*), "location" (*throne*), and "ideology" (*deep things*). *This element is the most representative for what Revelation brings to light in the letters to the churches.* While the hyperbole rings out loud and clear, its aim is not Roman imperial reality or a distinct group or movement within each of the believing communities. "Satan" is the ultimate adversary in all the messages. The entire book is written in acute awareness of Satan's activity and objectives, beginning with the seven churches.

**I gave her** [Jezebel] **time to turn, but she is not willing to turn from her sexual immorality** (2:21). Thyatira's "Jezebel" would be an extreme way of referring to an actual person, but it is appropriate for the demonic reality John is addressing and exposing. Jezebel was characterized by her determination to impose the cult of Baal on Israel's body politic, and her determination intensified in the face of evidence that she served a lost cause (1 Kings 18:39; 19:1–2; cf. Rev. 12:12). *Turning* was not in her character even though God was disposed to give even such an unpromising person an opportunity to do just that. If there is no *turning*, however, if the battle lines merely harden, terrible consequences are sure to follow.

**Look, I am throwing her on a bed, and those who commit adultery with her into great distress, unless they turn from her works, and I will kill her**

**children with death** (2:22–23a). Three things require comment and clarification in this text. First, the verbs are in the active voice. Revelation often prefers the passive voice, but this text is an exception. The passive voice highlights the action implied in the verb, but it veils the acting subject.

*Active voice*: The boy threw the stone.
*Passive voice*: The stone was thrown.

In this example, the stone and the throwing are preserved, but the thrower goes missing in the passive voice. There is no such problem here. The sentence is in the active voice, and Jesus is the acting subject.

Second, the verbs depicting Jesus's action are forceful: "throw" (*ballō*) and "kill" (*apokteinō*). "Throwing" is linked to "bed," leading interpreters to wonder whether the action depicted implies a "bed of adultery" or a "bed of illness" (Pippin 1995, 193). The former need not be excluded by preference for the latter. Indeed, the text connects adultery with illness, and it envisions progression from "sickness" to "death." "Jezebel" is "thrown" on the defensive, against her will. Her death and that of her accomplices are on the horizon. The combination of forceful verbs and ominous nouns makes for a serious message.

Third, "Jezebel" is now circumscribed as an alien character, a rhetorical embodiment of evil, an object generating feelings of disgust, to be "vomited, expelled, abjected" (Moore 2014, 522). "Those who commit adultery with her" will not come away unscathed (2:22), and worse is to follow. "I will kill her children with death" (2:23). The odd redundancy of this sentence will get a separate comment, but the action is indelicate and unsubtle. Is actual, physical killing of children in view? Or, if the "children" are "disciples" of Jezebel, are they to be physically killed? Will the believing community proceed to execute fellow members on the strength of Jesus's hostility to some of them? Or will Jesus do it himself? These options offer implausible and impossible scenarios. Language that includes "throw" and "kill" implies war, but how Jesus fights the war will not be different in Thyatira than it was in Pergamum. "I will come to you soon and make war against them by means of *the sword of my mouth*" (2:16). If there is "killing," the *word* will have to do it. Actual violence at the hands of Jesus is not in view here more than in the Gospel of John (John 12:44–49). "Throw" and "kill" means neither "throw" nor "kill" in a literal sense. Jesus is a Revealer, not an Executioner. He fights the menace called "Jezebel" by the means of *revelation*.

Fourth, with respect to the redundancy noted earlier (2:23), "I will kill" would seem to be quite enough; I will bring "death" would likewise suffice. Here we have the oddity, "I will kill with death" (*apoktenō en thanatō*). The closest OT antecedent for this turn of phrase is found in Genesis when God spells out the consequence of eating of the Tree of Knowledge. "For in the day that you eat of it you shall die" (Gen. 2:17). In this verse, too, there is apparent redundancy, "You shall certainly die" (Hb. *môt tāmût*) or "You shall die with death" (Gk. *thanatō apothaneisthe*; Gen. 2:17). This is Semitic diction for saying something with emphasis (Speiser 2008, 17). Revelation 2:23 does the same in awkward Greek.

**And all the believing communities will know that I am the one who examines "kidneys and hearts"**—the inner recesses of the person—**and I will give to each of you according to your works** (2:23b; cf. Pss. 7:9; 139:1–2, 23; Jer. 17:10). However stern Jesus's message to the believers might be, its purpose is to encourage believers to lead examined lives. Revelation is famous for noise and fiery displays, but it is capable of subdued interiority more than is appreciated. John personalizes and individualizes the words of Jesus by probing the inner recesses of a person, but he also generalizes: "all the believing communities will know" (2:23). And what will they know? Will they know that there was a "Jezebel" in Thyatira that has been dealt with in no uncertain terms, her bloody demise serving as a deterrent to others not to go there? Or, seeing "Jezebel" as the rhetorical construct that she is, will they look within more than without? Will they refrain from embarking on a witch hunt in the community and take to heart the hyperbole better than interpreters have done centuries later? Above all, will they grasp the profound ideological underpinning of John's message? **But I say to you, to the rest in Thyatira, to those who do not hold this teaching, those who have not known the deep things of Satan, I do not lay on you any other burden** (2:24).

"Satan" is a fixture and not a fiction in these messages, mentioned by name in four of the messages (2:9, 13, 24; 3:9) and otherwise appearing in the guise of some of the most unsettling characters in the OT. And "the deep things of Satan"—what are they? Are they "food sacrificed to idols" and "sexual immortality," the former in the sense that "eating food sacrificed to idols *is* practicing sexual immorality" (Thimmes 2003, 137)? Is this the best Satan can do, his "deep things" no deeper than that? Or, looking for bigger things, are "the deep things of Satan" located in the biblical narrative that is so much the concern of Revelation? That Revelation points the reader in that direction is suggested when "Jezebel" in Thyatira is characterized by the verb that is the hallmark of Satan (Friedrich 2002, 203). In the guise of being a prophetess, she is "teaching [*didaskei*] and deceiving [*plana*] my very own servants," says Jesus (2:20). One has to be good to make this happen. Satan is the ultimate theological con artist, capable of "deep things" (2:20; 12:9; 13:14; 18:23; 19:20; 20:8, 10).

Who is who in this scenario? Do the "good" ones know who they are? Do they also know who the "bad" ones are? Is "good" and "bad" manifest to those who belong to the "bad" side? Are the lines clearly demarcated on the surface? Alternatively, is "good" and "bad" a mixture known only by soul-searching on the part of the individual? After delivering his warning, Jesus acknowledges that there is virtue to be found in Thyatira: some "have not known the deep things of Satan" (2:24). **Only hold on to what you have until I come,** Jesus says to them (2:25).

The promise section of the message to Thyatira is as long and complex as the spiritual "audit" that precedes it (2:26–28). "Prevailing" in the war is less a matter of defeating the other side than to be "successful in resisting" (Friedrich 2002, 208). **Keeping** (2:26) amounts to the same, but it comes with a specific referent. If **my works** points to the work done by Jesus—the entire revelation of God in Jesus—the struggle boils down to making sure that this "work" is not eroded or lost. A shocking measure of power is promised to the believer who internalizes the revelation (2:26). Anyone who is tempted to see this promise in terms of power and unbridled exercise of force, as some do (Pippin 1995, 198; Thimmes 2003, 140), should think again. A reset is due in the affairs of the nations along the lines spelled out in Ps. 2:8–9, but the pattern is set by what God has revealed in Jesus (Rev. 5:6; 13:8). His **rod of iron** is meant for the protection of the sheep (2:26–27; 12:5), but the metaphor is demanding. This is a shepherd who is so committed to the well-being of the sheep that he lays down his life for them (John 10:11), a shepherd, too, who is not oblivious to the thief who "comes only to steal and kill and destroy" (10:10). The Johannine texture of this verse is not contrived: nothing is more characteristic in John's Gospel than the Father giving and the Son receiving (John 10:18; 13:20; 16:15; 17:7–8). We have the same thought and cadence here: **just as I received (authority) from my Father** (Rev. 2:28).

Still another promise remains for the one who prevails. **And I will give him/her the Morning Star** (2:28). "The Morning Star" is not your average star; it is a star so bright that it can be seen in daylight. The re-reader will know what this means because Jesus says at the end of the book, "I am the root and the descendant of David, the bright Morning Star" (22:16). The longer version is more complicated, and it is the longer story that is the message of Revelation. For now, a short version of the longer story will meet our need. Satan, who is referenced in the messages to the seven believing communities in Asia Minor (2:9, 13, 24; 3:9), once bore a name that did not strike fear and horror. He was once "the shining one, the son of the morning" (*ho heōsphoros ho prōi anatellōn,* Isa. 14:12 LXX; Rev. 9:1; 12:7–9). To be "the bright morning star" was part and parcel of his identity and vocational portfolio. Now, in a retrospective of the entire cosmic conflict, his light has gone out. Jesus is "the bright Morning Star" (Rev. 22:16; Isa. 14:12–20; Ezek. 28:12–19).

The message to the believing community in Thyatira demands close attention. **Let the one who has an ear hear what the Spirit is saying to the believing communities** (2:29).

### Sardis

**3:1–6. And to the angel ministering to the believing community in Sardis, write: Thus says the One who has the seven spirits of God and the seven stars** (3:1). Sardis is situated in the region of ancient Lydia, the capital of the famously rich Croesus (560–546 BCE). This was the king who asked the Oracle of Delphi for advice whether to go to war against the Persian Empire. "If Croesus goes to war, he will destroy a great empire," the oracle answered. Croesus did not stop to consider the ambiguity of the answer and went to war. And a great empire was destroyed—his own.

If Thyatira was insignificant, Sardis belonged to the greats among the seven cities in Revelation. It had history, location, beauty, and wealth comparable to cities like Ephesus and Pergamum. David E. Aune (1996–98, 218) calls it "one of the more illustrious cities of ancient Anatolia," its wealth in ancient times "based on the gold found in the river Pactolus" (see also Koester 2014, 309). To get there, the mail carrier in Revelation had to travel forty plus miles to the southeast of Thyatira. Sardis had a population estimated at 100,000 and diversity reflective of Persian, Greek, and Roman influences. The diversity was also expressed in a large Jewish community that had roots as far back as the sixth century BCE and had the largest known ancient synagogue, with a capacity of one thousand people (Aune 1996–98, 218).

Courtesy of Terje Bjerka

Figure 11. Careful work has been done to restore the Jewish synagogue in Sardis, large even by modern standards.

Revelation does not mention any of this. The body of the message to the community in Sardis is terse and clinical. It is as though the mailman has barely had time to ring the doorbell before blurting out, **I know your works—that you have a name as though you are living, but you are dead** (3:1). There is no commendation except for a short caveat later in the message (3:4). In several of the other messages and in the message to Laodicea that is yet to come, the external audit exposes a discrepancy between self-representation and reality: what a group (2:2, 9; 3:9) or a "person" (2:20), or even a church (3:17) says about themselves cannot be objectively confirmed. *This community makes no claim about itself, but it is not what it seems to be: reputation* and *reality* do not match (Fuller 1983, 303). Its "name," here best understood as reputation, is vastly better than warranted. This may be pleasing to the community, of course. Who does not want to be perceived as good and virtuous? On the other hand, who feels the need to rise higher if the report card in society is excellent? Who can help a person or a group that is only accustomed to praise and positive feedback to acknowledge that something is seriously wrong? To facilitate the required introspection, Jesus sends a message that is something between a diagnosis and an autopsy report: "You have a name as though you are living, but you are dead" (3:1).

Is there evidence to back this up? What are the details, the proof of incriminating behavior, the loss of passion, the false teaching, the recalcitrant group, the "apostles" and the "Jews" and the false prophetess mentioned in the messages to the previous communities of faith? Where are "the Nicolaitans," and "Balaam," and *"that woman Jezebel"*? Where the other messages deal in specifics and hyper-specifics, the message to Sardis does not specify. Whatever evidence there is for the indictment, it must be found at the level of self-evidence. This, in turn, will be evidence that can be accessed only by introspection. God and the believers together will have to sort this out, and they will have to do it against a societal verdict that gives the believers every reason to feel good about themselves. It is permissible to see this message as an exception to "the Rule of Specifics" that characterizes the other six, but it is also possible that the lack of specifics breaks the messages open. In this sense, the shortest and least specific message is the most effective in conveying the character of the messages: "the solemn and general admonition that each contains implies that they hold a teaching given for all time and for every church: for the Church" (Ellul 1977, 126).

The lack of specifics requires a great deal of self-analysis and imagination on the part of the recipients. We can imagine the mailman still standing in the doorway when he reads the proposed remedy, not wishing to tone down the urgency by coming inside and sitting down. **Wake up, and strengthen what remains and is about to die, for I have not found your works complete in the sight of my God** (3:2). Believers in Sardis are in a state of denial, far removed from reality, in part because society applauds them. But *"in the sight of my*

*God*," Jesus says, they are broken and incomplete (3:2). He then reminds the faithful of Sardis of their spiritual history, a history not shared with us as readers: **Remember then what you have received and heard and keep and turn. If you do not wake up, I will come like a thief, and you will not know at what hour I will come to you** (3:3). Memory is called upon to speak; memory must supply the specifics: what was said and heard and received and experienced at some point in the past. Can a knock on memory's door bring it back? Can the past become the present, *present* understood not only in relation to time but also in relation to space? What is past and now at a distance must become present in the *here* and *now*. The verbs calling for action are dynamic: *wake up, remember, received, heard, keep, turn*. The tenses of the verbs are mixed and jumbled, but the meaning is not in doubt. The verbs are all connected to the hidden landscape of memory. On the surface, the message seems terse, but in reality, it is personal and tender. There would be no call to believers in Sardis to "remember" except for the fact that Jesus *remembers*. All the crucial items in the message are predicated on awareness of a shared experience in the past. "If you do not wake up, I will come like a thief" may sound like a threat, but it is only stating the obvious. To the one who is asleep—or in a state of stupor—the arrival of the one who is to come will seem like the intrusion of a thief.

Commendation is scarce, but it is not wholly absent. **Yet you have a few names in Sardis who have not dirtied their clothes; they will walk with me in white, for they have what it takes** [*axioi eisin*] (3:4). This brings back the question raised concerning the message to Thyatira: Who is who? Do the "good" ones know who they are and the "bad" ones likewise? Do the "good" ones know who the "bad" are? Do the "good" think that this is a message for "them" and not for "us"? A message so short on specifics and so dependent on introspection is unlikely to resolve the "Who is who?" question. *Names* (*onomata*) must here mean "people," but the word is well chosen and on topic, given that the message begins by addressing those who "have a name" without content to match it. "A few" have both.

Few things are more desirable in Revelation than the prospect of walking "in white" (3:4, 5, 18; 4:4; 6:11; 7:9, 13; 19:8). The commendation is risky if understood within a conventional view of salvation. Do the "few names . . . have what it takes" in the sense that "they are worthy" (3:4)—this again in the sense that they are deserving? This risk is muted by discovering that the advantage of those who "have what it takes" (3:4) is not their virtue but their sense of need.

Walking "in white" retains a sense of healing, cleansing, and character, but it is above all a token of victory (6:11; 7:13–14). The promise to the believers in Sardis—**the one who prevails in the war**—strikes this note no less than the other messages (3:5). On first impression, **the Book of Life** appears to turn a personal relationship into a formal and legal matter, and the notion of bookkeeping may seem unnerving. The book might come in handy, however, if we come to terms with its intended use. The "book" in question is an official document that can be made available to the public if the need should arise (13:8; 17:8; 20:12, 15; 21:27). Revelation implies that there is a controversy of who should or should not be in the book. The notion that God literally proceeds "by the book" (20:12, 15) does not imply cold formality. To the contrary, it means that the economy of heaven is transparent; it is not secretive or arbitrary. "The Book of Life" is not an anxiety-arousing feature of existence but the opposite. God gives account of what God is doing and has means by which to defend with transparency decisions that are made.

The linkage of "the Book of Life" with Jesus's promise that he **will confess [*homologēsō*] his/her name before my Father and before his angels** gives additional support to this view (Rev. 3:5; cf. Matt. 10:32; Luke 12:8). The Greek word translated "confess" means "to commit oneself to do something for someone" (BDAG 708–9, ὁμολογέω). Jesus puts himself in the believer's corner, and he does it in the public square. Although it is often missed, Jesus's *affirmation* of the believer takes place against a barrage of *accusation* on the part of "the Accuser of the brothers and sisters, the one who accuses them before God day and night" (Rev. 12:10). Only when the adversarial texture and the unceasing efforts of "the Accuser" are understood will it be possible to appreciate the meaning of what Jesus is doing "before my Father and before his angels." If it is possible for a name to be removed from the Book of Life, as Revelation suggests (Royalty 2005), the criterion is not that Jesus lost interest in that name but that the person for some grievous reason dissociated from him.

When we re-read the message to believers in Sardis, God and the believer are the only ones on stage. We do not see any troublemakers. There is no mention of anything Roman, and there is "nothing in the Sardis letter to suggest that Christians in that city were harassed or persecuted by outside forces" (Duff 2001, 41).

But the need for exquisite listening is the same as before. **Let the one who has an ear hear what the Spirit is saying to the believing communities** (3:6).

### Philadelphia

**3:7–13.** Philadelphia shares with Thyatira the dubious honor of being so insignificant that scholars wonder why these cities were chosen to be among the seven (Guttenberger 2005, 162). Here, too, the answer could be that the significance of the believing community is not measured according to the importance of its city. Like Thyatira, Philadelphia was a relatively young city, its founding and name most likely going back to Attalus Philadelphus (220–138 BCE), the ruler of Pergamum. It is located about thirty miles to the southeast of Sardis, on a route that runs from Pergamum through Thyatira and Sardis to Laodicea (Hemer 1986, 153). This is in an earthquake-prone area of Turkey, and Philadelphia suffered a devastating earthquake in 17 CE. It was rebuilt as a rather modest city during the reign of Tiberius (14–37 CE), with a Christian community that "was small in number and weak economically" (Aune 1996–98, 235). As with Thyatira, little remains of ancient Philadelphia. The ruins of its basilica are, of course, more recent than the time of John.

On the "from whom" side, Jesus introduces himself as **the Whole One** (*ho hagios*), usually and legitimately translated "the Holy One" (3:7). If ontological identity is made the priority, "Holy One" works well, highlighting "the quality possessed by things and persons that could approach a divinity" (BDAG 10–11, ἅγιος). Revelation does not claim less than that on Jesus's behalf, but "whole" is a dimension of "holy," and it puts up a contrast between Jesus (whole) and human reality (broken) that is valuable for everyday use. When Revelation adds that Jesus is **the Trustworthy One** (3:7), the connotation of conflict is once more evident. This characterization is made under circumstances of slander and lies, mendacity that succeeds because it poses as something other than what it is. Under such conditions, Jesus is the only one who is "Whole" and "Trustworthy." Explicit references to **David** are found at key junctures in Revelation (3:7; 5:5; 22:16). Here, the one **who opens and no one will close, who closes and no one opens** suggests a figure who succeeds in carrying out what he sets out to do against efforts to thwart him (3:7; cf. Isa. 22:22), and he succeeds in ways that the OT precursor did not (Isa. 22:25).

Jesus's evaluation of the spiritual qualities of the Christian community in Philadelphia is entirely positive (3:8). In fact, the assessment is so positive that "Philadelphia was perhaps the strongest of the seven churches" (Blevins 1990, 620). The "open door" is a *theological* statement. God has an open-door policy that is not affected by shifting circumstances, the "open door" suggesting transparency, access, and assistance. Believers in Philadelphia do not have an advantage that is denied to others. The notion of **little strength** should be seen the same way. It, too, depicts a condition that is common to human beings. If the believers do not give up, God will make sure they are not overcome, no matter the odds against them. What they have **kept** and **not denied** is described in terms of the revelation of God in Jesus: **my** *word* [*mou ton logon*] and **my** *name* [*to onoma mou*] (3:8). These terms join a large family of words that all focus on the accomplishment of Jesus.

*revelation* of Jesus Christ: 1:1
*testimony* of Jesus Christ: 1:2; cf. 1:9; 6:9; 12:17; 19:10; 20:4
*faithfulness* of Jesus: 14:12
*works* (of Jesus): 2:26; 3:8; 15:3
*word* (of Jesus): 3:8, 10; 19:13; 22:7
*perseverance* (of Jesus): 3:10
*name* (of Jesus): 2:13; 3:8; 14:1; 19:13; 22:4

These terms all read as variants of the first term on the list: the subject is *"the revelation of Jesus Christ"* (1:1), and the call to resist attempts to destroy it. Believers in Philadelphia have done exceptionally well, but they have not been spared. The echoes of—or rather, the link to—the message to Smyrna is conspicuous. In Smyrna, Jesus tells the believers that he knows "the slander [*tēn blasphēmian*] of those who say that they are Jews and are not, but are a synagogue of Satan" (2:9). This is not malicious name-calling, in whole or in part. The "synagogue of Satan" is real, but it does not break along ethnic lines or boundaries easily visible on the surface. Messengers saying that "they are Jews" go to the heart of the matter, as we see again and again in the seven messages (2:2, 9, 20; 3:9). The so-called synagogue of Satan operates under a false flag, claiming to be what it is not. Above all, this is not a local phenomenon. The warning might as well have been addressed to Smyrna. **Look, I will make those of the synagogue of Satan who say about themselves that they are Jews and are not, but are lying—look, I will make them come and bow down before your feet, and they will know that I have loved you** (3:9). Here, as in Smyrna, the distinguishing feature of "the synagogue of Satan" is that its members "say about themselves that they are Jews and are not" (3:9). Scholars almost uniformly read this as though John is depicting a conflict between believers in Jesus and the local Jewish synagogue, the former group now equipped with rhetorical tools that will put the "Jews" irreversibly on the defensive locally (Roloff 1993, 61)—and, albeit unintentionally, saddle real Jews with a terrible burden for all time (Lohse 1993, 105–23). Within the narrow, local, and literal reading, Jesus promises the believing community a reversal of fortune: one day the "lying Jews" will show up at the door of the believers to acknowledge that the latter were right all along. Unless the concession of the "lying Jews" is construed as a conversion, this merely adds insult to injury from the point of view of Jews.

When the speech is recognized as hyperbole, **Satan** will be the villain, not the "Jews," and the "Jews" will not be identified along ethnic lines. The surface perception of a narrow, communal conflict yields the ground to a cosmic struggle. *Slander*, the theological brand of "the synagogue of Satan," will in the end be recognized for what it is (2:2; 3:9). Satan's brand of "slander" targets and finds fault with God. While vindication is in store for the believers, the larger vindication relates to God. Which of the two comes out as the most important will depend on where we let the emphasis fall. "They will know that I have loved *you*" (3:9), meaning the little group of believers in Philadelphia, is one option. The other option is theological, countering the malice and the slander at its most basic proposition: "They will know that I have *loved* you" (3:9). The latter option addresses distortions brought to bear on how God is seen and perceived. When we read this as commentary on what God is and does, doubts and misperceptions of God dissolve. "The synagogue of Satan" is headed for defeat, its existence based on malice and falsehood.

93

The big-picture, cosmic tendency does not let up (3:10). "Steadfastness" is evident in the stance of the believers, but it is **the word of *my* steadfastness**— the steadfastness of Jesus—that counts the most. The notion of being kept **from [*ek*] the hour of trial** hints that believers will not be tried, but it can also mean that they will be "kept," whatever the trial (Koester 2014, 331). This matter involves **the whole world**, not only Philadelphia. An "*hour* of trial . . . is coming," a moment that is time-ending and world-ending, and not limited to Asia Minor. History is moving toward a grand climax. Revelation's message of hope unfolds along the lines sketched on numerous occasions in the OT, particularly in Daniel (Dan. 12:1; cf. Isa. 11:10; 52:6; Jer. 30:7; Amos 5:18–20; Joel 2:1–32; S. Brown 1966, 308–14). The sentence is awkward (3:10), and it is important not to lose sight of its purpose-oriented logic, in Greek introduced by the word *hina* (in order to). No translation makes sense if "the hour of trial" (*hōra tou peirasmou*) is understood to be no more than sixty minutes **to test** [*peirasai*] **the inhabitants of the earth** (3:10), with the purpose of the test left out. John is not guilty of such a grave sin of omission; the "test" (*peirasmos*) happens to "learn the nature or character of something" or someone (BDAG 793, πειρασμός).

How imminent is "the hour of trial" (3:10)? The spatial and temporal perspective suggests that it will not happen tomorrow or the next day. "Imminence" is a tenuous concept, as is **soon** (3:11). The message drives home the urgency and the certainty, but it does not offer a date. **To everyone who prevails in the war [*ho nikōn*], I will make him/her a pillar in the temple of my God: you will not go out to the outside any more. And I will write on him/her the name of my God and the name of the city of my God, the New Jerusalem that is coming down from heaven from my God, and my name, the new one** (3:12). What honors! What a sweeping vision! And what a spectacular blend of architecture and theology, of physical components and inner meaning! To be "a pillar in the temple of my God" implies steadfastness, permanence, and honor (Wilkinson 1988, 500). "Name" is a profoundly theological term, to some extent a bullet-point version of the entire conflict. Here, the name of God revealed in Jesus appears in a series of combinations, but it is "my name, the new one" that commands special interest (3:12). As elsewhere (2:17; 5:9; 14:3; 21:1, 2, 5), "new" (*kainos*) does not need to mean "new" in an absolute sense (L. Thompson 1990, 85; Russell 1996, 208; Rossing 2005, 170). It has the connotation of restoring or repairing what has been damaged or lost. Jesus's name, "the new one" (3:12), is in this sense the most riveting conception.

The promise to "the one who prevails in the war" in Philadelphia is so dense with allusions that it threatens to choke even competent re-readers. We have "the New Jerusalem that is coming down from heaven from my God" even though we have not yet been told of the city (3:12; cf. 21:2, 10–27); we have "a pillar in the temple of my God" even though the New Jerusalem does not have a temple (3:12; cf. 21:22); we have the promise that "you will not go out to the outside any more" (3:12). Of these, the most telling is the assurance that the believer "will not go out to the outside." There, "outside the city" (14:20; cf. 21:2; 20:9), a terrifying, conflict-ending battle will take place that is not described until the last pages of the book (20:7–10). When the forces of evil assemble for the final push, the believer "will not go out to the outside." To be "a pillar in the temple of my God" and "not to go out to the outside any more" (3:12) means safety and security in the hour of battle, a fitting complement to Jesus's promise that "I will keep you from the hour of trial" (3:10). As we will see later in much greater detail, it also means that the battle will be fought *among* those who are on the outside. The big-picture conception in the last part of the message to this community comes as no surprise to interpretations already sensitized to the cosmic frame.

### Laodicea

**3:14–22.** When the messenger reaches Laodicea (3:14), the seventh and last city on the odd delivery route, he has journeyed another sixty miles to the southeast from Philadelphia. Laodicea will be the easternmost point on the way. In all, he has traveled some 320 miles if we include the 50 miles from Patmos to Ephesus. This is a roundabout way to Laodicea because the direct route from Ephesus to Laodicea is only 100 miles. Laodicea was situated on a plateau in the Lycus Valley, on a major road going east from Ephesus (Hemer 1986, 179–80; Koester 2014, 333–34). As noted earlier, the notion that the long route conforms to an actual mail delivery course is not supported by the evidence (Friesen 1995b, 300–306; Koester 2003). The city dates to the time of Antiochus II (261–246 BCE), who expanded an older settlement during his reign, naming it Laodicea after his wife or possibly his sister (Hemer 1986, 180; Aune 1996–98, 249). The city belonged to the domain of Pergamum in the second century BCE until it was bequeathed to the Romans along with the entire Attalid Kingdom in 133 BCE. Earthquakes are common in the area, two earthquakes striking Laodicea hard in the first century, in 20 CE and in 60 CE. Tacitus (*Ann.* 14.27) wrote of the last of these that "one of Asia's notable cities, Laodicea, after collapsing in an earthquake, revived without our assistance, using its own resources." To scholars of Revelation, this information has given rise to two enduring conceptions. The first is that Laodicea was a prosperous, self-sufficient, and self-satisfied city. The second is that the believing fellowship in Laodicea resembled the city in being prosperous, self-sufficient, and self-satisfied. With respect to the first of these impressions, scholars have pointed to Laodicea's textile industry, its medical school, and the manufacture of remedial ointments, among which was an eye salve consisting of "Phrygian powder" mixed with oil (Mounce 1977, 123; Rudwick 1957; Hemer 1986, 186–91; Porter 1987; Cashmore 2004). These ideas have had wide circulation, but they cast little light upon the message itself. Craig R. Koester has shown that wool and textile production were common to many of the cities named in Revelation. Pergamum's reputation as a center of healing was greater than Laodicea's, as was its reported expertise at curing eye disease. Moreover, the main banking center of the region was Ephesus, not Laodicea (Koester 2003, 417–18). Given that the items said to characterize Laodicea are not unique to this town, it is unlikely that the believing community was compromised or influenced by these purported characteristics (Koester 2003, 420). The same applies to the alleged poor quality of Laodicea's water supply, supposedly so lukewarm as to be hardly fit to drink (Koester 2003, 410). It clearly wasn't. "If Laodicea's water was lukewarm, the same would have been true at Ephesus, Smyrna, Pergamum, and Sardis" (Koester 2003, 411).

In the NT, Laodicea shares with Ephesus the distinction of being mentioned in the letters of Paul (1 Cor. 15:32; 16:8; Col. 2:1; 4:12–16). It is singled out as corecipient of the Letter to the Colossians, suggesting a close relationship between the nearby communities in Colossae, Hierapolis, and Laodicea (Col. 4:13–16). Paul sends greetings to "the brothers and sisters in Laodicea, and to Nympha and the church in her house" (Col. 4:16). These tidbits might be as true (or truer) to actual life in the Laodicean neighborhood as what we find in Revelation.

Some of the questions discussed earlier again seem relevant. We have *seven* churches—why no more? Why these communities? We have language suggestive of hyperbole, determined by theological intent more than precise description. We have a certain order—beginning, middle, and ending—indicating the pursuit of an aim that ends with Laodicea for a reason.

The message begins with a sense of finality. **Thus says the Amen, the faithful and true witness, the keeper of God's creation** (3:14). Three features describe Jesus. First, he is "the Amen." By criteria of English usage, this makes him the last word. But the OT background brings to light a word that means more than that. "Amen" is an OT designation for God and God's defining attribute (Roloff 1993, 64). "Then whoever invokes a blessing in the land shall bless by the God of faithfulness [*bēʾlōhê ʾāmēn*], and whoever takes an oath in the land shall swear by the God of faithfulness [*bēʾlōhê ʾāmēn*]; because the former troubles are forgotten and are hidden from my sight" (Isa. 65:16). This text affirms God's disposition, not only God's existence. Equally important, God is defined not by what God claims to be but by what God is seen to be. "Truthfulness," "dependability," "trustworthiness," and "faithfulness" are all pertinent to the word used in Hebrew. Aquila's Greek translation, generally thought to approximate the Hebrew closely, has the word *pepistōmenōs*, the perfect participle of the verb *pisteuein*, not in the sense "to believe" but in the sense of being "believable" and "worthy of trust" (A. Jepsen, *TDOT* 1:322, *ʾāman*; Reider 1966, 264).

The OT allusion highlights that Jesus shares in the divine identity, but the reverse is just as important. God revealed in Jesus is proof that God is what the text claims God to be. Toward this end, Jesus is "the Witness, the faithful and true one." This repeats what has already been said. When Revelation calls Jesus "the Amen," the formula is "nothing but a translation and explanation of the Hebrew word 'Amen'" (Rissi 1972, 21). The affirmation unfolds in the context of slander (2:9; 12:9; 13:6; 20:2). Jesus is not "the faithful and true witness" in sunny weather and light breeze. He is "the faithful and true witness" amid the murk and mud of slander (12:13–19). The third element, Jesus as "the keeper [*hē archē*] of God's creation," can also be translated "the beginning of God's creation" (3:14).

What will Jesus find on the last stop of the journey? Are the messages ending on a high note? The answers will depend on *how* we read. If "high note" requires a community that lives according to his hopes and expectations, the first impression will be depressing. **I know your works; you are neither cold nor hot. I wish you were either cold or hot** (3:15). "Water" is not mentioned, but the adjectives are almost universally thought to apply to water temperature, particularly water for drinking. "Hot" and "cold" are good, "lukewarm" is not. Moreover, and strengthened by years of usage, the terms are applied to the spiritual condition of the Laodicean community. On this assumption, "hot" is the desirable condition, "lukewarm" the worst. "Cold" is better than "lukewarm" because Jesus finds unbelief and opposition preferable to the in-between state that characterizes the community in Laodicea. Craig R. Koester (2003, 409) objects to this view on the logic that "an appeal for faithfulness would make sense, but a call for unbelief would not." This objection carries weight, but a counterintuitive interpretation should not be ruled out. What if Jesus, contrary to what one might expect, perceives "cold" to be a stance that offers clarity in ways "lukewarm" does not? What if Jesus, as the traditional interpretation has it, prefers opposition to halfheartedness?

"Lukewarm" is the state that won't work. **Thus, because you are lukewarm, and neither hot nor cold, I am about to vomit you out of my mouth** (3:16). Here, "vomit" is not too strong; "spit out" works, too. But the stronger word captures the visceral meaning better than **spit out**. In physiological terms, vomiting is preceded by nausea, and both are responses mediated by the autonomic nervous system. The reaction is spontaneous and involuntary: a person may try to will away nausea without being able to curb it in the slightest. Again, the reaction is visceral, not legal; spontaneous, not scripted. Koester (2003, 409), seeking to avoid the negative connotation of **cold**, argues that the metaphor "requires that both hot and cold be understood positively in contrast to being lukewarm, the negative trait that characterizes the complacency of the Laodicean Christians." By this logic, two of the options are positive, "hot" (good) or "cold" (good), both referring to states that are acceptable and desirable (Koester 2003, 415). This works as a comment on temperature of water, wine, or ingredients in a meal, but it is less persuasive if the referent is a person. "I wish *you* were either cold or hot" (3:15).

**For you say, "I am rich, I have prospered, and I have need of nothing"** (3:17). This is what Jesus finds in the last of the believing communities. While the self-representation comes in three versions, they amount to one and the same thing. In the Laodicean self-report, what "I am" and what "I have" add up to a stunning conclusion: "I have need of nothing" (3:17). Where "need of *nothing*" is the bottom line, it is not necessary to specify whether the absence of need is computed in material, personal, theological, spiritual, or ethical terms. This community revels in a sense of wholeness, securely ensconced within an all-around edifice of accomplishment. It is also worth noting that there is no mention of persecution, hardship, or external threats. The fundamental problem is lack of the sense of need, with the possibility that the condition is made worse by material prosperity.

We could leave it at this, but one question should nevertheless be asked. "For you *say*," we read. Was the Laodicean community really *saying* the words attributed to it? Would anyone in his/her right mind *say* things like that? This seems unlikely. But if the Laodiceans were not *saying* these things, why does the letter represent them as though they were? To solve this, we need to make a distinction between implicit and explicit communication. The Laodicean community is too sophisticated to say openly the things attributed to it, but it is capable of behaving in ways that convey the attitude thus described. A community that masters theological discourse might even be able to enhance their own perceived status by appropriating the Laodicean label. *Insight*, nevertheless, is what Laodicea does not have, and the message to the community may be the keenest statement of how difficult it is to see the discrepancy between self-representation and reality. In this regard the problem in Laodicea is so extreme that it makes Jesus sick to his stomach.

*Self-perception*: rich . . . have prospered . . . need of nothing

*Jesus's assessment*: wretched . . . pitiful . . . poor . . . blind . . . naked

There is a hint of judgment in the warning that **I am about to vomit you out of my mouth** (3:16), as noted, but the metaphor is physical rather than legal. Severance of relations is dictated by the condition itself. When the analysis moves to specifics, it describes the problem in existential and medical terms. We are treated to scenes of destitution and need, not sin and punishment. Jesus approaches the community in the posture of a physician and not as a judge. All the proposed remedies have a medical flavor (3:18).

When Jesus says, **I counsel** [*symbouleuō*] **you** (3:18), participation on the part of the recipient is implied (BDAG 957, συμβουλεύω). Jesus assumes that he has the attention of the Laodicean believers and that there is a willingness on their part to be counseled and to act on the counsel given. Moreover, "counsel" seems curiously mild for the severity of his rebuke. Would not "command" or "demand" serve the need better than "counsel"? On the other hand, the choice of this word makes sense if confidence-building and consent are required, and it is a good word in the context of medicine. Physicians cannot "command" or "demand." If this is what we have, Jesus's choice of word shows a master physician at work.

The counsel that follows revisits the problem of Laodicea's inflated self-image. The claim "I am rich" has been falsified, but there is a way for them to **become rich** (3:15, 18). Jesus offers to sell them **gold made red hot by fire** (3:18). "Gold" stands in opposition to "poor," while "red hot" and "fire" are contrasts to "lukewarm" or "cold," spiritual states that Jesus proposes to change. The imagery also envisions a radical refining process (Mal. 3:2–3; Isa. 48:10–11). "Clothing" alone would suffice to take care of nakedness, but Jesus offers *white* **clothing.** The connection between nakedness and shame goes back all the way to the garden of Eden (Gen. 2:25; 3:7, 10, 11). We should add that the man and the woman in Genesis show an awareness of nakedness that the Laodiceans lack (Gen. 3:10, 11; Rev. 3:18). Jesus speaks in terms that apply to the human condition. The **eye salve** (*koll[o]yrion*) offered is a supernatural remedy designed to turn someone spiritually blind into a seeing person (3:18; Berger 1985). In the OT, "the commandment of the LORD is clear, enlightening the eyes" (Ps. 19:8; cf. 119:105; John 9:6–11). *Seeing* and "enlightenment" are categories of *revelation*, and it is offered as a remedy both in Revelation and in the OT. In Revelation, the doctor makes house calls in awareness that mere knowledge of the written word will not by itself open eyes. Nothing short of divine intervention is necessary to enable the Word of God to make a human being a *seeing* person (Berger 1985, 191–92).

The tone of the letter remains personal throughout. **I scrutinize** [*elenchō*] **and counsel** [*paideuō*] **those whom I love. Be serious, therefore, and turn** (3:19). Translators are justified in using terms like "reprove" and "discipline" (NRSV), but lexical meanings of the word translated "counsel" (*paideuō*) include to provide "instruction for informed and responsible living" and "assist in the development of a person's ability to make appropriate choices" (BDAG 749, παιδεύω). By these criteria, Jesus makes rounds not only as a physician but also as a most unusual educator and mentor. The beneficiaries are "those whom I love." To whom, now, do the messages *not* apply?

**Look! I have taken up my position** [*hestēka*] **at the door, and I stand there knocking** [*krouō*]**. If anyone hears my voice and opens the door, I will come in to eat with him/her, and he/she with me** (3:20). The word for standing "at the door" is in the perfect tense. Greek grammarians say that the perfect tense is "the most important, exegetically, of all the Greek Tenses" (Moulton 1908, 140). Its use is said to reflect a deliberate choice on the part of the writer (Wallace 1996, 572). The perfect looks at an entire action from the point of view of its completion, also described as "the *continuance* of *completed action*" (BDF §340, p. 175). The statement above is a challenge because the first verb is in the perfect tense while the second verb is in the present. A sentence that says, "I stand at the door and knock" makes sense in English, with both verbs in the present tense. If we settle for this, however, we lose the nuance of the Greek where the word for "standing" is in the perfect tense. "Standing" as a completed action that continues in the present requires visualization of the person arriving at the door and then—*standing* there.

What is the point? There is the sound of knocking at the door. Is anyone home? Does anyone hear? Will the person inside, if he/she hears it, open the door? If so, Jesus will come in, and they will share a meal together. "I will . . . eat with him/her," he says, "eating" doing double duty as a reference to eating and intimacy (3:20). The Johannine diction of the phrases is unmistakable: "I will . . . eat with him and he with me, or, eat with her and she with me" (3:20; cf. John 14:23; 17:22).

Communion with Jesus in this world comes with the promise **to sit with me on my throne** in the world to come (3:21). The throne image brings into sharp focus the crux of the cosmic conflict. The rebel in the story said in his heart, "I will ascend to heaven; *I will raise my throne above the stars of God. . . . I will make myself like the Most High*" (Isa. 14:13–14, emphasis added). The rebel's scheme of rapacity and self-exaltation comes to grief—but not because God is opposed to sharing the throne with anyone (3:21; 20:4; cf. Tonstad 2016a, 67–83). This throne is a crowded place, and it has now been settled who will sit there.

And then, for the seventh time, we read the call to hear the messages aright and the reminder that the messages are intended for a wide audience. **Let the one who has an ear hear what the Spirit is saying to the believing communities** (3:22).

### Theological Issues

Three things stand out in a closing retrospective on the messages to the seven communities in Asia Minor (2:1–3:22). First, almost all the messages focus on the discrepancy between self-representation and reality, in whole or in part. In Ephesus, we have "those who say about themselves that they are apostles but are not" (2:2); in Smyrna, "those who say that they are Jews and are not" (2:9); in Thyatira, one "who says of herself that she is a prophetess" but is not (2:20); in Sardis, those who "have a name that you are living, but you are dead" (3:1); in Philadelphia, "those . . . who say about themselves that they are Jews and are not" (3:9); in Laodicea, a strongly worded rebuke of a community saying about itself, "I am rich, I have prospered, and I have need of nothing" (3:17). The gulf between self-representation and reality in the messages softens the boundary between the unfamiliar "them" and the familiar "us," making the past recognizable in the present. A flattering self-representation and a less flattering reality could well be the most important take-home message in the seven letters. If this becomes our focus, the number of addressees expands, and we will appreciate the messages more for keen psychological and spiritual perception than as a source of historical information. Two of the last three communities, Sardis and Laodicea, are in the worst bind. Along the axis of time, notions of progress and ever-increasing sophistication and self-awareness become especially challenging when the most deluded condition is saved for last. A reader in the twenty-first century might then recognize a familiar face in the mirror, in the community that says, "I am rich, I have prospered, and I have need of nothing" (3:17).

Second, we have confirmation that "most of the issues enumerated (and certainly the most pressing ones) are internal, intra-Christian issues" (Duff 2001, 46). Hyperbole in the form of particularity and hyper-particularity in some messages complicates the efforts to tie the symbols to specific individuals or groups of people in the respective communities. Crucially, the religious and institutional imprint of the Roman Empire is hard to find in this part of Revelation. If it is found at all, it is made up from assumptions and not from the text itself. The cosmic perspective, on the other hand, is textually explicit. We find it in the "synagogue of Satan" in Smyrna (2:9), in "the throne of Satan" in Pergamum (2:13), in "the deep things of Satan" in Thyatira (2:24), and in "the synagogue of Satan" in Philadelphia (3:9). Aware as we are of the discrepancy between self-representation and reality in the human realm, this is also the hallmark of things associated with Satan. A wide-screen reading will not miss the cosmic context and temporal progression. "I will keep you safe through the hour of trial that is coming on the world to put to the test the inhabitants of the earth," says the message to the community in Philadelphia (3:10). A revelation is unfolding on the stage of history, and the "trial" that is coming will bring to light "the nature or character" of those subjected to it (BDAG 793, πειρασμός). In the message to Philadelphia, the reader's wish to master the community's past confronts an exhortation to come to terms with the world's future.

Third, the concepts and the rhetoric in the messages are medical rather than legal. The medical conceptions are especially conspicuous in the message to the community in Laodicea (3:14–22). A book often thought to be preoccupied with violence and punishment is by this criterion better seen as a vision of vulnerability, disease, and healing. Jesus addresses the community as a diagnostician (3:17), and he has a medical remedy tailored to every need (3:18). In the conflict with Satan, his weapon is "the sword of (his) mouth" (2:16; cf. 1:16; 2:12). This weapon is a synonym for *revelation*. In the realm of human experience, not only in the affairs of nations, *revelation* has the capacity to bridge the gap between representation and reality that appears again and again in the book. Human *need* looms large in the messages, and the need is most acute in the last of the seven communities (3:15–17). When there is knocking on the door in Laodicea (3:20), the aim is clearly to connect with a person in need.

And yet, pausing for one last look at the person "standing at the door" (3:20), everything depends on him. Where recognition of need is lacking in the human realm, the persistence and yearning of the one knocking must be stronger than human awareness of need.

# Revelation 4:1–8:1

## The Seven Seals

**Introductory Matters**

The portion dedicated to the seven seals (4:1–8:1) begins with one of the most dramatic transitions in Revelation (4:1). From *earth* to *heaven*? No one misses that. From earthly *commotion* to heavenly *calm*? That is how many interpreters see it (Charles 1920, 1:102–3; Rowland 1982, 425; Resseguie 1998, 175). But this commonsense perception is almost certainly wrong. It should be that way, of course; there should be a contrast between earthly *strife* and heavenly *serenity*, between human *panic* and angelic *poise*, between *turmoil* and *tranquility*. Heaven should be a *haven*, the shelter against earthly distress and the solution to earth's predicament. And yet we find the exact opposite. Instead of calm and composure, there is a crisis in the heavenly council (A. Collins 1979, 39). The crisis is centered on the book sealed with seven seals (5:1). No one has what it takes to open it (5:3), even though it is hugely consequential that it be opened (5:4).

Do the heavenly councillors know the content of the sealed scroll? They seem to know it very well (6:1–11). Perhaps we know it, too. If we don't know it because of the scroll, we have other means of ascertaining that there is deception, war, famine, death, and injustice in the world (6:1–11). In that case the most vexing realities in human experience are also the subject matter of the scroll. To know that there is a throne in heaven may seem reassuring (4:2). To know that there is One sitting on the throne is also heartening (4:2). But what does it help to have a throne and One sitting on it if the world is disordered and disappointing?

Knowledge of content is not the same as understanding. The councillors don't *understand*—and thus the crisis! They, too, need a *revelation*. On this logic, the predicament of the sealed scroll enacts spectacular scenes of disclosure *within* Revelation. By way of hypothesis, we are on the threshold of three discoveries. First, earthly chaos must be understood in the light of a conflict originating in heaven—*and not as a contrast to heaven*. Second, the search for someone who can "open" the scroll entails a person who can *explain* it. Third, the call to "come up here" (4:1) is a signifier of *openness* and *access*. Access to the halls of power is not a matter of course whether in society or theology (Tonstad 2016a, 3–21). Here the "open door" suggests a God who is committed to transparency, and it gives the reader of the book a vantage point from which to understand what is revealed. "Where you stand depends on where you sit" is more than a cliché (Miles 1978). Heaven is not in denial regarding the state of the world. When we add up these things, we find ourselves submerged in the biggest existential questions of the twenty-first century, as though this book was composed with an eye to our time and need.

### Tracing the Train of Thought

#### Open Heaven: The Heavenly Council in Session (4:1–11)

**4:1–6.** After this I saw—and look!—a door stood open in heaven! And the first voice which I had heard speaking to me like a trumpet, spoke to me again, saying, "Come up here, and I will show you what must take place after this!" (4:1).

Three times in this verse I have supplied an exclamation mark that is not found in the Greek text without wishing to embellish the original. The sentence is exclamatory, but the content would be worthy of exclamation marks even if the text used less vigorous verbs and tenses. A voice that speaks "like a trumpet" must have something urgent to say, and this voice surely does. The sentence describes how God exercises power. And what is the modus operandi of the heavenly government? We have the answer right here. "A door stood open in heaven!" What is the open door but a signifier of access? What is the open door but proof of an authority that is committed to transparency? What is the open door but a signal that the heavenly authority grants what earthly authorities often deny (Moynihan 1998), even authorities that profess commitment to openness? What is this, too, but a rebuke to a theological tradition that claims God's ways to be off-limits to scrutiny? The text does not depict humans encroaching on forbidden territory. Rather, we are brought face-to-face with heaven's policy of candor.

The subject matter about to be disclosed has reference to time (4:1): "after *this.*" *This* is not specified, but a movement from present to future is implied. To be told that information about the future is on offer is a controversial prospect. This claim is not new, however (1:1, 19; 4:1), and it is reinforced by a telling verb. If awareness of future realities is the goal, there is a reason for it. The voice speaking to John promises to show him "what *must* [*dei*] take place" (4:1). This suggests a problem, a principle, or a question that is to be illuminated for reasons that fall under the headline *necessity*. The future, whatever it holds, cannot be dissociated from the past: *the necessity shrouded in future's unknowns is located in some bygone event.* Given that Revelation imparts *understanding* and not only *information*, the reference point for the necessity must be part of the disclosure. A God who invokes the logic of necessity for the horizon that is to open before John, as Revelation says again and again (1:1, 19; 4:1; 22:6), must let John in on what dictates the necessity.

For John, there is no delay in responding to the summons. **Right away I was in the spirit, and look!—there in heaven stood a throne, with one seated on the throne!** (4:2). Three more exclamation marks are in order, one for "look," another one for "throne," and a third one for the "one seated on the throne," although the one in the middle is left out in this translation. A "throne" is a symbol of government, order, and authority (Gallusz 2014). A general understanding of "throne" could highlight the contrast between order and anarchy. Did the notion of anarchy occur to readers in the first century? It surely occurs to readers in our time. Were believers (or people in general) troubled by a discrepancy between expectations and reality to the point of wondering what God is up to? The cry of the victims of violence proves as much (6:9–11). If John's vision speaks to the question of order versus anarchy, Revelation claims a seat at the table where the most vexing existential and philosophical problem of our time is discussed. Should "the throne" as such fall short of reassuring that there is order, Revelation answers that there is "one seated on the throne" (4:2). This, too, may fall short, however, and it may even aggravate the problem. How can a claim to order be sustained if order is not discernible (6:9–11)? To what notion of order is the "one seated on the throne" committed, conceding that symbols of order are not matched by order at the level of experience? Already by this criterion, the discovery of a "throne" and of "one seated on the throne" leads to more questions than it answers.

A discussion of order versus anarchy has huge implications, but this is only one half of the message. In this book, the critical question is not whether there is a "throne" or whether someone is sitting on it (4:2). Revelation says that "war broke out in heaven" (12:7). The "war" was *a contest about the throne.* The most important background text brings the contest for the throne into focus. "I will ascend to heaven," says the pretender who started the war, "*I will raise my throne above the stars of God*" (Isa. 14:13, emphasis added). While "a throne" and one "sitting on the throne" may seem reassuring, this route does not work in Revelation. Here, "the throne" *is not the solution to the problem; it is the seat of the problem.*

There can be no doubt that this is a vision of God (Rev. 4:3), composed of images of God in the OT (Exod. 24:10; Ezek. 1:26–28; 28:13). The **rainbow** in the picture suggests promise, commitment, and hope (Isa. 54:9–10). While the imagery also conveys grandeur and beauty, the rainbow, the precious stones, and the sea of glass are also indicators of transparency and not at all, as some interpreters suggest, "a reminder of the separation between God and his creation" (Brighton 1999, 121) or of "vast distance" (Swete 1908, 70). God is not enthroned at a majestic distance from other beings. The throne in the middle is flanked by **twenty-four thrones,** a multiple of twelve (Rev. 4:4). But the number is a lesser concern than the arrangement. If the throne in the middle is a seat of authority, the other thrones suggest participation and power sharing.

Choreography impressive to the eye is matched by an overwhelming output of sound (4:5). Similar blasts of light and sound are repeated three more times in the book. The first one, above, belongs to the seven seals (4:5). The next two happen at the beginning and the end of the trumpet sequence (8:5; 11:19). The last blast occurs at the end of the seven bowls (16:17–18). Together, these three cycles make up the body of Revelation. All three are accompanied by blasts of sound and light that recall the encounter with God at Mount Sinai (Exod. 19:16–20; cf. 1 Kings 19:11–12). Outwardly, the choreography might afflict Broadway with an acute case of envy, and the sound and light might suggest it best to keep distance. But the meaning is low key and to the point, and it is exactly the opposite: the call to "come up" has been heard before, in the call to Moses to "*come up* to me on the mountain" (Exod. 24:12). Despite the outward display, the message is to come close and not to keep distance. As in the OT, these are the signs accompanying revelation. A theophany—a showing forth of God—is in the making.

Access and participation are in view and more insistent than ever (4:6). The **four living creatures** are not located "around the throne, and on each side of the throne," as the NRSV says (4:6). Translating the text literally, these beings are located *in the middle of the throne* and **around the throne** (4:6b; Tonstad 2006, 119–21). The arrangement is awkward and well-nigh impossible to visualize, but it obliterates the distance between God and created beings (Blount 2009, 92). These beings, like God, seem to be "in the middle of the throne" and not only around it (4:6b). We are in a council where high-level participation is in view. Interpreters who refer to this scene mostly for proof that real authority resides in heaven and not in the Roman emperor miss that the exercise of authority in heaven is conceived along lines that are strikingly at odds with earthly imperial practice (Aune 1983; Reddish 2001, 92–93).

Do created beings possess ability equal to the trust invested in them? Must not the divine government be a take-it-or-leave-it proposition that cannot be subject to second-guessing, consent, or approval? In John's vision of the heavenly council, eyes are the most conspicuous anatomic feature of the four living creatures: they are **full of eyes in front and behind,** and their wings, too, are **full of eyes all around and inside** (4:6, 8). Eyes are a symbol of intelligence, wisdom, and discernment (Mounce 1977, 138; Blount 2009, 93; Koester 2014, 364). The text goes out of its way to emphasize that the four living creatures are *seeing* beings. Created reality is not depicted in a state of incapacity. God is committed to transparency, and intelligent beings are endowed with the ability to understand.

**4:7–11.** The imagery describing the "four living creatures" comes from Ezekiel (1:10; 10:14), from passages that contribute much to John's vision of the proceedings in the heavenly council (Ezek. 1:4–2:10). Specifically, Ezekiel describes a connection between the throne and the four living creatures that is so close and unusual that it turns the entire throne arrangement into a living, sentient entity (Ezek. 1:4–28; Zimmerli 1979, 1:127; R. Hall 1990). These beings do not have it in them to remain silent. **And day and night without ceasing they sing, "Holy, holy, holy, the Lord God the Almighty, who was and is and is to come"** (4:8). Isaiah supplies the words to the first part of the song (Isa. 6:3). We have seen the second part before (Rev. 1:8), stressing the idea that "God is he who is *with* someone" (E. Jacob 1971, 52). This means that the four living creatures are praising God for what God *does*. They are not only asserting that God *exists*.

Do these scenes confirm what many interpreters take to be the main point? Must we now conclude—perhaps with a sense of relief—that there is a welcome contrast between earth and heaven? No one has articulated this view more eloquently than R. H. Charles (1920, 1:102–3):

> But the moment we leave the restlessness, the troubles, the imperfectness, and apprehension pervading ii–iii., we pass at once in iv. into an atmosphere of perfect assurance and peace. Not even the faintest echo is heard here of the alarms and fears of the faithful, nor do the unmeasured claims and wrongdoings of the supreme and imperial power on earth wake even a moment's misgiving in the trust and adoration of the heavenly hosts. An infinite harmony of righteousness and power prevails, while the greatest angelic orders proclaim before the throne the holiness of Him who sits thereon.

Heaven is here perceived as a contrast to earth: *on earth, there is bedlam; in heaven, calm.* "The contrast between the hymns of praise to the all-powerful God in heaven and the lack of evidence of the divine will on earth must have been most evident to the readers of the apocalypse," says Christopher Rowland (1982, 425; cf. Ford 1975, 87). Heaven performs according to expectations: "order and coherence rules the universe" (Resseguie 1998, 175).

These are views of expert readers, and other scenes in Revelation appear to support them. We read of "the four living creatures" that day and night without ceasing "sing, 'Holy, holy, holy, the Lord God the Almighty, who was and is and is to come'" (4:8). Through the hymns "the work gradually moves into a crescendo and reaches a climax which becomes the proclamation of the establishment of the Kingdom of God and the enthronement of the Lamb" (Ford 1998, 208). The hymns are not musical interludes without content. Klaus-Peter Jörns (1971, 166) shows the hymns to be intrinsic to the story line, arising from the surrounding narrative and projecting back into the narrative a heightened sense of drama.

But what is the story line? Ford champions a christological emphasis. Jesus is the solution, the end point, and the aim of the hymns. He epitomizes heaven's solution to the problems of earth (Ford 1998, 207–29). Klaus-Peter Jörns (1983) stresses the antiphonal character of the hymns. *Two* voices sound the same theme, a voice of *proclamation* seeking resonance, affirmation, and amplification in voices of *acclamation* (cf. Carnegie 1982; Ruiz 1995).

These observations confirm expectations, but they fall short on one crucial point. It is true that "music plays a larger role in the Apocalypse than in any other New Testament writing" (Gloer 2001, 36). In Revelation, however, the full range of voices is *triphonal*, featuring *three* voices and not only *two*. The third voice is more than implicit; it is more than a whisper from offstage; it is not a voice that we need to hypothesize or infer. To the re-reader, the third voice provides the background and premise of the other two voices. Until we notice the voice of *accusation*, we will not make the right call with respect to the voices of *proclamation* and *acclamation*.

> *Voices of proclamation*: "And day and night without ceasing they sing, 'Holy, holy, holy, the Lord God the Almighty, who was and is and is to come'" (4:8).

> *Voice of accusation*: "And I heard a loud voice in heaven, proclaiming, 'Now have come the salvation and the power and the kingdom of our God and the authority of his Messiah, for the accuser of our brothers and sisters has been cast out [*eblēthē*], who accuses them before our God day and night'" (12:10).

Is there evidence for a third voice? *There certainly is* (12:10). Is the third voice appropriately called the voice of *accusation*? *There is no better term.*

Does the discovery and recognition of the *third* voice shatter the illusion of heavenly calm? *It does.* The transition from earth to heaven, passing through heaven's "open door," does not conform to expectations. From the ashes of earthly chaos, we are led into the fire of heavenly conflict! Heaven is not a *contrast* but an *expansion* and corollary to conditions on earth.

"And *day and night* without ceasing they sing" (4:8).
"The accuser . . . who accuses them before our God *day and night*" (12:10).

*Day and night* (4:8; 12:10)—this is the heavenly reality—an aggressive, opposing voice is heard. When we restore the voice of accusation to its rightful place, the illusion of heavenly harmony crashes to the ground. Revelation offers a front-row seat to voices that do not play the same tune, echo the same sentiments, or affirm the same reality. Even if we conclude that the voice of accusation has fallen silent (12:10), the accusations remain the reference point for the heavenly affirmations and the reason for their fervor. "The accuser" is a person who brings charges, reproach, and blame (BDAG 533, κατηγορέω). Accusations "day and night" on one side (12:10), proclamations and acclamations "day and night" on the other side (4:8–11), show a charged situation.

> **Competing Voices**
>
> Voices of proclamation—day and night (4:8)
> Voices of acclamation (4:9–11)
> Voice of accusation—day and night (12:10)

It follows from this that the proclaiming and acclaiming voices "day and night" have a reason. This is not an ordinary, humdrum day at the office, the four living creatures mindlessly repeating their mantra morning, noon, and night, like the music machines dotting Disneyland, or like the cowed members of the Communist party in the days of Joseph Stalin, as described by Aleksandr Solzhenitsyn (1918–2008) in *The Gulag Archipelago* (see sidebar). Heaven is not a contrast to earthly chaos but the point where the trouble began. A text that filled me with dread since childhood opens to other possibilities. When my imagination toyed with the idea that in the world to come everyone, "day and night," sings "holy, holy, holy" without letting up, it suggested to me a place of monotony and unrelieved boredom.

The notion of a contest of voices changes this impression completely, the balances reset by intra-textual echoes. When Revelation later says that "the accuser . . . has been *cast out* [*eblēthē*]," repeating it twice in the passage that bears on the subject (12:9, 10), the word has the connotation of something that is *exposed* and *unmasked*, on the one hand (Marcus 2000, 168), and *exorcised*, on the other (Brant 2011, 194). Both aspects are relevant to the problem at hand. *Unmasking* addresses a problem that is wrapped in deceit, *exorcism* a problem that has invaded reality to such an extent that only heaven's nimble hand knows how to dissect the normal from the abnormal.

## Praise without Ceasing, Communist Style

*"At the conclusion of the conference, a tribute to Comrade Stalin was called for. Of course, everyone stood up (just as everyone had leaped to his feet during the conference at every mention of his name). The small hall echoed with 'stormy applause, rising to an ovation.' For three minutes, four minutes, five minutes, the "stormy applause, rising to an ovation," continued. . . . However, who would dare be the first to stop? . . . And in that obscure, small hall, unknown to the Leader, the applause went on—six, seven, eight minutes! They couldn't stop now till they collapsed with heart attacks! At the rear of the hall, which was crowded, they could of course cheat a bit, clap less frequently, less vigorously, not so eagerly—but up there with the presidium where everyone could see them? The director of the local paper factory, an independent and strong-minded man, stood with the presidium.*

*"Aware of all the falsity and all the impossibility of the situation, he still kept on applauding! Nine minutes! Ten! In anguish he watched the secretary of the District Party Committee, but the latter dared not stop. Insanity! To the last man! With make-believe enthusiasm on their faces, looking at each other with faint hope, the district leaders were just going to go on and on applauding till they fell where they stood, till they were carried out of the hall on stretchers! And even then those who were left would not falter. . . . Then, after eleven minutes, the director of the paper factory assumed a businesslike expression and sat down in his seat. And, oh, a miracle took place! Where had the universal, uninhibited, indescribable enthusiasm gone? To a man, everyone else stopped dead and sat down. They had been saved!*

*"The squirrel had been smart enough to jump off his revolving wheel. That, however, was how they discovered who the independent people were. And that was how they went about eliminating them. That same night the factory director was arrested. They easily pasted ten years on him on the pretext of something quite different. But after he had signed Form 206, the final document of the interrogation, his interrogator reminded him: 'Don't ever be the first to stop applauding!'"* (Solzhenitsyn 1973, 69–70)

When the voices of *proclamation* (4:8) are heard as a counterpoint to the voice of *accusation* (12:10), the voices of *acclamation* can sound at full volume, as they do (4:9–11). The key concept in the acclamation is usually translated **worthy** (*axios*, 4:8, 11). This translation does not project what is affirmed broadly enough. *Axios* implies a comparison, originally a measuring term for "bringing up the other beam of the scales" (Gingrich and Danker 1965, s.v. ἄξιος). We need to imagine a contrast between someone who is "worthy" and one who isn't. David E. Aune (1996–98, 347) notes that *axios* means being qualified "in the sense of having the proper qualifications to perform this special task." This is a valid inference, but the most important part of the affirmation contrasts the worthiness of **the one who is seated on the throne** (4:9) with the *un*worthiness of the being who aspired to sit there (Isa. 14:12–15; Rev. 12:7–9). By this criterion, we hear the twenty-four elders acclaiming with emphasis, **You have what it takes, our Lord and God**—the opponent does not; **you created all things**—the opponent did not; **by your will they came into being and were created**—the opponent contributed nothing (4:11).

This view of what is on the mind of the members of the heavenly council needs a note on what is *not* on their minds. What *is not* on their minds is the emperor Nero and the Roman imperial cult. To let the scene apply to other claimants to "worthiness" is in order, but the heavenly council has its own frame of reference. Klaus-Peter Jörns (1971, 56–73) says the "worthy" language does not have a counterpart in cultic or imperial rituals contemporary to John. Other options also fall short, jarringly, for invoking soaring platitudes. The heavenly scene, says one, represents "the mysterious formula of the timeless divine totality" (Lohmeyer 1926, 49). To another, John attempts to "create a bridge between the timelessness of the divine existence and the subservience of creation to time" (Kraft 1974, 101). A third adds that Revelation has "continuous adoration" as a prominent feature (Mounce 1977, 138; cf. *1 En.* 39.12–14; *2 En.* 21.1). These trite comments miss the point. In reality, the heavenly council is in crisis mode. Revelation will explain why.

### Crisis in the Heavenly Council (5:1–14)

**5:1–7.** The thought that heaven brings a respite from earthly turmoil runs into strong headwinds when the scene shifts to the scroll and the concern that dominates Revelation's story.

> Then I saw in the right hand of the one seated on the throne a scroll written on the inside and on the back, sealed with seven seals; and I saw a mighty angel proclaiming with a loud voice,
>
>> "Who has what it takes
>> to open the scroll
>> and break its seals?"
>
> And no one in heaven or on earth or under the earth was able to open the scroll or to look into it. And I wept and wept profusely because no one was found to have what it takes to open the scroll or to look into it. (5:1–4)

Adela Yarbro Collins (1979, 39) says that "the first four verses of chapter 5 imply that the heavenly council is faced with a serious problem." How can this be—a problem *in heaven*? Heaven is supposed to be the solution; in heaven all problems vanish. And yet the scene in the heavenly council comes across as though there is indeed "a serious problem" (5:4). Paul J. Achtemeier (1986, 284) is on target when he observes that the summons for one who can open the scroll "is greeted with silence—unaccustomed silence."

Figure 12. William Blake's depiction of the Ancient of Days and the sealed scroll centers on the joy after it has been opened.

A. Collins (1979, 39) explains that "the problem facing the heavenly council is the rebellion of Satan which is paralleled by rebellion on earth." This insight requires re-reader awareness. The heavenly war is not described until later in the book (12:7–9; cf. 9:1–11), but there would be no crisis except for it. A linear reading of Revelation can now be seen to fail dismally. John's entry into the heavenly council happens at the point where the council is casting about for a solution to the rebellion of Satan. This is assumed by the participants in the heavenly council and must also be assumed by readers.

Heaven offers no reprieve from the problems of earth. Rather than placing John in the embrace of "an atmosphere of perfect assurance and peace" (Charles 1920, 1:102), heaven, too, is awash in problems! Heaven, and heaven in particular, is at a loss about what to do! John's response to the presentation of the scroll confirms the predicament (5:4). His tears are not the reaction of a person who has found the solution to the problems facing earth (van Unnik 1970). Rather, it describes the response of a man who has been brought face-to-face with the cause and the source of the problem—and a quandary that makes mockery of solutions!

**Heavenly Books**

• Book of *Life*
• Book of *Deeds*
• Book of *Fates*
• Book of *Action*

"The scroll" is the enigma to be solved. In a study of heavenly books in Jewish and Christian apocalyptic literature, Leslie Baynes (2012) identifies four categories of such books (see sidebar).

The first three categories are the *book of life*, containing the names of those who are found worthy; next, the *book of deeds*, containing the record of human deeds; and third, the *book of fates*, the latter rarely found in the Hebrew Scriptures (Baynes 2012, 7–8, 18; Aune 1996–98, 224). The scroll that is sealed with seven seals does not fit any of these categories. For this book, Baynes (2012, 8, 18, 150–55) suggests a separate, fourth category, a *book of action*. While asserting that "Revelation says absolutely nothing about the alleged written content of the book" (Baynes 2012, 151), she contends that

> the one thing we do know about its content is that when the Lamb opens each seal, bad things begin to happen: first the arrival of four horsemen who bring slaughter, famine, pestilence, and death (6:1–8), then a vision of martyrdom (6:9–11), and then an earthquake and the dissolution of the heavens "like a scroll rolling itself up" (6:12–16), all eschatological events of momentous portent. (Baynes 2012, 152)

In her view, there is a link to the flying scroll in Zechariah because the scrolls are written on both sides, and both function to destroy (Zech. 5:1–4). Thus the scroll in Revelation and the flying scroll in Zechariah "effect destruction on the unrighteous" (Baynes 2012, 153). This leads to the conclusion that the sealed scroll "emerges as a slayer itself, amassing catastrophic destruction as the Lamb opens its seals one by one, emitting slaughter, famine, pestilence, wild animal attack, and the very dissolution of the heavens and the earth" (Baynes 2012, 154–55). God, through the agency of the Lamb, is by this logic the acting subject of the calamities that come to light in this sequence.

This view is not sensitized to the crisis in the heavenly council (A. Collins 1979, 39), and it does not let show that God "is not the only one who is at work in this world" (Vögtle 1976, 383). For this alternative (a crisis in heaven) there are other clues. The setting is reminiscent of Ezekiel's vision of the throne

113

room (Ezek. 1:4–28), and so is the scroll (Ezek. 2:9–10; Aune 1996–98, 339; Beale 1999, 337). In Revelation, the scroll is written "on the inside and on the back" (5:1). Ezekiel's scroll is described in almost identical terms: "I looked, and a hand was stretched out to me, and a written scroll was in it. He spread it before me; it had writing on the front and on the back, and written on it were words of lamentation and mourning and woe" (Ezek. 2:9–10). Ezekiel's scroll, "its front and back . . . covered with writing" (Greenberg 1983, 60), resembles the scroll in Revelation, but its content is no secret. Densely written on both sides, the message is a litany of "lamentation and mourning and woe" (Ezek. 2:10). It has been charmingly said that "the book is so crowded with writing that not only is the inside of it full but the writing had to be continued upon the back" (Peake 1919, 259). The writing is spilling over; it is filling the page; there is hardly room enough for it all. And the meaning? Allowing the allusion to Ezekiel's scroll to hint at the answer, the content of the scroll is not good.

The scroll, we have noticed, is "sealed with seven seals" (5:1). Scrolls are sealed in other instances in the Bible, too, not in the sense of secret content but in the sense of deficient understanding (Isa. 29:10, 11, 18; Dan. 12:9–10). This view of sealed scrolls was held by the Qumran sectarians (Stefanovic 2009b, 367–68). When such a scroll is "unsealed," the benefit does not come primarily at the level of information but at the level of understanding. The person who unseals the scroll makes it intelligible (Kraft 1974, 105), and the main thing relates not to *what* is seen but to *how* it is seen.

For John, consolation is on the way.

> And one of the elders said to me,
> "Do not weep!
> Look!
> The lion of the tribe of Judah,
>     the root of David,
>     has won the war,
> so that he can open the scroll
> and its seven seals!" (5:5)

Here we could say that "the root of David has *won* [*enikēsen*]," leaving out what he has won, but this compromises the meaning (11:17; 12:7–12; 17:14; 20:7–10). The setting of war is unavoidable, and the word should be supplied. John's profusion of tears is not a mystery (5:4): *Is God about to lose the war? Does God play a weak hand in the cosmic conflict? Are the "facts on the ground," all recorded in the scroll, so damaging that nothing can bridge the gap?*

Such possibilities are the stuff of mental terror, but John is told not to weep. The one who "has what it takes to open the scroll" (5:2)—and there is only one—is "the root of David" (5:5; Isa. 11:1, 10). Isaiah depicts him as a right-maker and an agent of revelation (Isa. 11:1–10; cf. Tonstad 2016b, 370–79). He is unique for the way he makes right (Isa. 11:1–5). When his right-making is complete, "the wolf shall live with the lamb, the leopard shall lie down with the kid, the calf and the lion and the fatling together, and a little child shall lead them" (Isa. 11:6).

The beginning and the ending of this "pearl of Hebrew poetry" is striking, here in Hans Wildberger's (1991, 460–61, 465) translation.

> A shoot shall come out
> from the stump of Jesse,
> and a sprig will "sprout forth"
> from his roots. (Isa. 11:1)

> And it will happen on that day:
> Toward the root of Jesse,
> which stands there
> like a signal for the nations,
> the nations will all turn inquisitively,
> and its resting place
> shall be glory. (Isa. 11:10)

### All Eyes on the Middle

The *scroll*—it *must* be opened. But no one has what it takes to do it—*no one!* *Except* for the Lamb standing *in the middle* who has what it takes because of who he is and because *he was killed with violence.* He was prefigured in the prophet Isaiah (11:1–10), the Revealer, coming to fill the earth "with the knowledge of the Lord, as the waters cover the sea" (Isa. 11:9).

Isaiah depicts a figure rising from unimpressive and out-of-date material, "an unexpected new beginning" (Wildberger 1991, 470). Origin, character, means, and impact are all vastly surpassing what anyone could imagine.

And there he is, "the stump of Jesse" and the promised Revealer!

**And I saw in the middle of the throne, [in the middle of] the four living creatures, and in the middle of the twenty-four elders a lamb standing as though it had been killed with violence, having seven horns and seven eyes!** (5:6).

It is commonplace to perceive a contrast between the person who is announced (5:5) and his actual looks (5:6), but the link to Isaiah mutes this impression. He, too, envisioned an agent of revelation rather than a figure of power (Isa. 11:1–10; 52:13–53:12). This is Revelation's pivotal scene, the foremost revelation in the entire book. *What a shocker!*

Revelation's preoccupation with "the middle" is a stumbling block for translations (4:6; 5:6). For background, Ezekiel is the best clue. His introductory vision features "a great cloud with brightness around it and fire flashing forth continually, and *in the middle* of the fire, something like gleaming amber" (Ezek. 1:4). The figure *in the middle* must be God, but there are repeated references to "the middle" that get muted in translations. Ezekiel repeats himself,

> "*from the middle* of it [the fire],
> like from the eye or the source,
> so to speak,
> appeared something that looked like *ḥashmal*
> from *the middle* of the fire." (Ezek. 1:4, my trans.)

Equally tantalizing is the figure in the middle, *hashmal*, translated "gleaming amber" in the NRSV but left untranslated in one of the most learned commentaries (Greenberg 1983, 37).

*The middle*, as a spatial term, is also full of significance in Ezekiel's poem about "the covering cherub" (Ezek. 28:12–19, my trans.). The cherub was "on the holy mountain of God," walking back and forth "*in the middle* of stones of fire" (Ezek. 28:14, my trans.). From a state of exaltation and innocence, he was expelled from "the mountain of God" (Ezek. 28:16). The expulsion left a void "in the middle." In Moshe Greenberg's (1997, 579) translation, slightly modified, "So I barred you from the mountain of God, and I banished you, shielding cherub, *from the middle* of fire-stones." Revelation's story of cosmic conflict is conditioned by the spatial parameters of Ezekiel's vision, the account of the "covering cherub" who was "in the middle" but is no longer there.

The Lamb "in the middle" comes from "the root of David" (5:5). This certifies his human credentials. But his appearance suggests more. He has "seven horns and seven eyes" (5:6). These features attest his divine identity in the Semitic thought world of Revelation; they are symbols of power and wisdom. By these symbols, Revelation does not admit to a power deficit or a lack of caring on God's part. Most remarkable is the story inscribed on his body. He is represented "as though killed with violence" (5:6). Most translations say "slaughtered," but the connotation of violence is necessary for two reasons. First, it has already been announced that he "has won the war" (5:5). The ensuing paradox is demanding. How can the one who has been "killed with violence" emerge as the winner of the war? Being killed is the fate of the loser. Here, the apparent loser is the winner. Second, as Loren Johns (1998, 2:780) notes, being killed is part and parcel of the Lamb's identity, and "*the language is that of butchery and murder*, not ritual sacrifice." The context of the Lamb's death is the battlefield, not the temple. Richard J. Bauckham (1993b, 64) says that the slaughtered Lamb in the middle "*belongs to the way God rules the world*." This statement must be qualified by the context in Revelation. If this is "the way God rules the world," we must add that this is how God defeats the opposing side in the cosmic conflict. Looking beyond the symbols, the Lamb that has been "killed with violence" must be a self-giving person.

He went [*ēlthen*]—and he has taken [*eilēphen*](!)—the scroll from the right hand of the one who is seated on the throne (5:7). The shift in verbal tenses from the aorist to the perfect is hard to reproduce in English, but there is a rising sense of excitement from "went" to "has taken." The first verb depicts the generic act of walking as a past event, the second describes Jesus taking the scroll as a completed act with enduring results in the present. The impact on the members of the heavenly council is stunning, from dejected silence to ecstatic wonder.

**5:8–14.** John's sentence zigzags (5:8), introducing elements that are meant to complete the picture without distracting from the main subject of the action. While **the four living creatures and the twenty-four elders** are focused on the Lamb and the scroll, it is now evident that they are musically inclined. Moreover, they have **golden bowls full of incense, which are the prayers of the saints** (5:8). Earthly reality is by these tokens firmly a concern in heaven: the heavenly council is preoccupied with earthly need.

> **And they sing a new song, saying,**
> **"You have what it takes**
>   **to take the scroll**
>   **and to open its seals,**
> **for you were killed with violence**
>   **and by your blood**
>   **you liberated for God**
> **[people] from every tribe**
>   **and language**
>   **and people**
>   **and nation;**
> **and you have made them for our God**
>   **a kingdom and priests,**
> **and they will reign**
>   **on the earth."** (5:9–10)

Beginning with the last sentence, just as earthly need is known in heaven, heaven will be represented on earth by "[people] from every tribe and language and people and nation" (5:10). The priestly function is not to plead the cause of humanity before God. Instead, the priest's role is to represent heaven on earth. This view of priestly function is universal, involving all believers, with no exception for age or gender. Moreover, the believers on earth are entrusted with the vocation to which Israel was called at Mount Sinai (Exod. 19:5–6). What was not actualized in the past will now be done.

A "new song" (5:9; 14:3) is a well-known concept in the OT (Pss. 33:3; 40:3; 96:1; 98:1; 144:9; 149:1; Isa. 42:10). *New* reflects the perception of the singer: the song is *new* to the one singing it even though the subject matter of the song is not. *New* in this sense also means *renewed*, a *renaissance* for a song sung earlier. The subject matter of *new songs* in the OT is almost invariably God's faithfulness (Pss. 33:4; 40:9–10; 98:2; Isa. 42:3). This is also the case in Revelation, only now exceeding what "new" songs in the past aspired to convey. In this "new song," we hear echoes of the deliverance from Egypt. Like the Israelites, believers have been "liberated" from captivity. This captivity, however, is not physical or political as much as it is spiritual and existential. Here, the power holding people captive is "the Mudslinger," also known as "Satan" and "the deceiver of the whole world" (12:9; 20:2).

Language needs new concepts for what follows. In English, the saying "All hell broke loose" is well established. We are expected to see unprecedented scenes of chaos and pandemonium. Here, *all heaven breaks loose.*

This is the new reality: there is limitless relief, understanding, and jubilation. Two movements must be imagined, one of beings paying attention to the center; the other of jubilation spreading from the center to the periphery. A stadium, if you will, where the spectators "take the wave."

And I looked, and I heard the voice of many angels around the throne and the living creatures and the elders, and their number was myriads of myriads and thousands of thousands, singing as loud as they could,

"The Lamb
 that was killed with violence
 has what it takes
 to deserve the power and riches
 and wisdom and might
 and honor and glory
 and praise!" (5:11–12)

Working from the premise that the songs bring the story line to a crescendo, more is accomplished than the ear is accustomed to hearing. As God's revealer steps forward, the sentiment in heaven shifts from embarrassment, crisis, and silence (5:1–4) to confidence, resolution, and jubilation (5:8–14). The problem that brought about the crisis has been solved. The worthiness of the Lamb is proclaimed and acclaimed first against the background of misrepresentation and accusation, and second against death and hopelessness. The wave of euphoria that now sweeps heaven is jubilation over the defeat of the adversary. All the things that "the Lamb" is deemed worthy of receiving—"glory" being one of them—reflect the reality of someone who is vindicated and has reclaimed his good name.

The jubilation does not let up, making it clear that "the Lamb" all along has been the Revealer of "the one who is sitting on the throne" (5:13). Silence is out; exclamation and acclamation are in.

And I heard every creature in heaven and on earth and under the earth
 and in the sea, and all that is in them, singing,
"To the one who is sitting on the throne
 and to the Lamb
be the praise and the honor
 and the glory and the power
 forever and ever!" (5:13)

First, "a scroll . . . sealed with seven seals" and heaven at a loss—and now a scroll opened and heaven in a state of jubilation (5:1–4, 7–14)! First, "no one in heaven or on earth or under the earth . . . able to open the scroll or to look into it" (5:3)—and now "every creature in heaven and on earth and under the earth and in the sea . . . singing" (5:13)! First, a profusion of tears (5:4)—and now faces beaming in wonder (5:5, 8–14)! Proclamation leads to acclamation, and the acclamation comes in wave upon wave. **And the four living creatures said, "Amen!" And the elders fell down and worshiped** (5:14).

The crisis in heaven has been solved. What set off the crisis? The crisis has been solved, but how? To get to know this, the seals must be opened.

### Breaking the Seals: The First Six (6:1–17)

**6:1–17.** There are too many opinions about the sealed scroll to permit a detailed review. The most widely held view sees the scroll as a Book of Destiny of some kind (Swete 1908, 75; Charles 1920, 1:138; Mounce 1977, 142; Metzger 1993, 52). Expressing a variant of this view, Craig R. Koester (2014, 393) says that "the sealed scroll conveys God's purposes." These are broad conceptions, easy to defend and difficult to refute. On the other hand, they are agreeably reverent. God is thought to be in control, and there is no need to panic. Leslie Baynes (2012, 8, 18, 150–55) offers a variant on the Book of Destiny theme, calling the scroll a *book of action*. Others have suggested that the scroll is akin to the Book of the Covenant in Deuteronomy (Stefanovic 2009a, 167; Ford 1975, 87–88). This view envisions a scene of enthronement at which the first duty of the king is to make a copy of the Book of the Covenant and commit to upholding it (Deut. 17:18–20). Some interpreters argue that the breaking of the seals is a preliminary exercise unrelated to the actual content of the scroll (Bauckham 1993a, 248; Koester 2014, 373). Yet others say that a scroll written "on the inside and on the back" proves it to be a document that is identical on the inside and the outside—the content thus known—but matters go into effect only when the document is unsealed (Holtz 1962, 32–35; Roloff 1993, 76–77; Aune 1996–98, 341).

Three responses to these views are in order. First, a *Book of Destiny* is too general to be of much help, and it becomes increasingly problematic as the subject matter of the scroll comes into the open (6:9–11). Second, the notion of a *Doppelurkunde* with an "inside" and an "outside" version of the same message has merit, but it contributes little to the meaning of the scroll. Third, just as a Book of Destiny is too general, the idea that the scroll's content can be known only when the scroll is opened is too literalistic. The allusion to Ezekiel points to content that is known (Ezek. 2:9–10). Further evidence to this effect emerges when the Lamb breaks the seals. G. B. Caird (1999, 71) argues wisely that the process of breaking the seals is meaningless unless the accompanying events are related to the contents of the book. He is rightly unimpressed at the lack of novelty in the parade of war, famine, and death that accompanies the breaking of the seals (6:1–8). "Then on to the stage of history come only four horsemen representing disasters as old as the human race," he says disappointedly, then asks, "Is this all that we are to receive from the regnant Christ?" (Caird 1999, 82).

Whether the Book of Destiny, a book of action, or the Book of the Covenant, God is held to be the acting subject. With God as the moving force, most of the envisioned action is punitive. Leslie Baynes (2012, 154–55) sees the scroll effecting "catastrophic destruction as the Lamb opens its seals one by one." In the covenant view, the action is regarded as "covenant curses" (Paulien 1992; Stefanovic 2009a, 219–20). These curses are the consequence of disobedience, the underlying moral calculus positing a direct and proportional relationship between disobedience and punishment (Lev. 26:21–26). This scenario runs into difficulties when the voices under the fifth seal complain that *God has failed to act* (6:9–10). If God has been busy raining "destruction on the unrighteous" (Baynes 2012, 153), what are the victims complaining about?

Names better suited for the sealed scroll are a *Book of Revelation* in view of the *revelation* that is enacted when the seals are broken. The content that comes to view also qualifies it as *the Book of Reality*. How things *are*, is one thing, and that part is *known*. How things should be *understood* is another matter, and that part is *unknown*. This fits the OT background. In Ezekiel, the content of the scroll is in large measure known (Ezek. 2:9–10); in Isaiah, there is sealed content in the sense that it is not understood (Isa. 29:10–11, 18; cf. Dan. 12:9–10). A scroll appropriately seen as *the Book of Reality* will be unsealed (5:6). There is no need for breathless suspense at what the scroll will bring to light because the content is familiar (Caird 1999, 82). The Revealer cannot deny reality; he cannot explain away the content of the scroll. But he can bring a perspective to bear on a known reality that breaks the seals of incomprehension. To this end, the breaking of the seals is not a solo performance on the part of "the Lamb." While he alone "has what it takes to open the scroll and break its seals" (5:2), the members of the heavenly council are aware of the reality that needs to be unsealed.

This is evident already at the breaking of the first seal. **And I saw the Lamb open the first of the seven seals, and I heard one of the four living creatures calling out, as in a voice of thunder, "Come!"** (6:1). The scene is remarkably interactive, especially if we suppose that no one knows what's coming except the person breaking the seals. "The Lamb" opens the first seal, but "one of the four living creatures" contributes immensely to the proceedings. To whom is the "living creature" talking in such a commanding voice? The voice says, "Come!" He/she appears to be in the know, befitting beings that are "full of eyes in front and behind" (4:6). It is not persuasive to see him/her bringing an unknown, God-ordained destiny to bear on the world. Instead, heaven has mobilized to the last person for the task of revelation. In this scenario, the voice "in the middle" is not talking to his own or to some inanimate, nonsentient reality. The voice is instead calling out for a revelation—an exposé—to become manifest.

**And I looked, and wow! there was a white horse! And the one sitting on it had a bow, and a crown was given to him, and he set out conquering, dead**

**set on winning the war** (6:2). "Wow," indeed! My translation takes away the comfort that the white horse is innocent of evil. "Conquering" has an object: it is "winning *the war*" that counts. Even though "the Lamb" has already been declared the winner (5:5), the adversary has not given up hope that he can snatch victory from the jaws of defeat (cf. 12:13–18; 13:1–18).

Can this view, so different from a Book of Destiny perspective, be sustained? Despite the color white, the first horse does not dispel the impression that none of the horses is up to anything good (6:1–8). The horses and their riders come onstage as a group, configured as representations of the same reality. The image of the four horses is taken from Zechariah, and one of Zechariah's horses is white (Zech. 1:7–11; cf. 6:1–8). Color alone does not set this horse apart. Leslie Baynes (2010a) has shown that white equine imagery was prolific in the world of John for its imperial, heroic, and "savior god" connotation. To a first-century audience, white would be the color of virtue and victory. Domitian, the likely emperor of John's time, was pictured riding on a white horse. Neither the Bible nor Roman imagery contemporary to the author makes the white horse a self-evident symbol of Christ.

What else could be in view if the first horse and its rider do not represent Christ? Comparing Revelation and the Synoptic apocalypse, Louis A. Vos (1965, 181–92) answers that the white horse is best seen as a symbol of false messiahs and false prophecy. To Mathias Rissi (1964, 414–16), likewise, "the rider on the white horse appears as a part of a group that acts as demonic agents of destruction." This rider is akin to the figure of Gog, the apocalyptic last enemy whose characteristic weapon is the bow (Ezek. 39:3, 9). Deceptive activity on the part of its rider is so much the point that "the failure of modern interpreters to see the nature of counterfeit in the rider of the white horse displays the success [of] the author's literary device" (Kerkeslager 1993, 121). Pieter G. R. de Villiers (2004, 148) concludes that the rider on the white horse "is one of the most important enemies in the book. It tells of a time in which false prophets will be so powerful that they will mislead the world and even the church." A similar focus has already been evident in the messages to the seven believing communities (Rev. 2–3).

This understanding fits well with the emphasis on false messiahs and false prophets that dominates Jesus's discourse on the last things in the Synoptic Gospels.

> *The disciples' question to Jesus*: "Tell us, when will this be, and what will be the sign of your coming and of the end of the age?" (Matt. 24:3)
>
> *Jesus's reply to the disciples*: "Beware that no one leads you astray. For many will come in my name, saying, 'I am the Messiah!' and they will lead many astray. . . . For false messiahs and false prophets will appear and produce great signs and omens, to lead astray, if possible, even the elect. Take note, I have told you beforehand. So, if they say to you, 'Look! He

Figure 13. Albrecht Dürer's *Four Horsemen of the Apocalypse* is a form of exegesis: the horses appear as a group, and they all have the same ominous appearance, including the white horse.

is in the wilderness,' do not go out. If they say, 'Look! He is in the inner rooms,' do not believe it." (Matt. 24:4–5, 24–26)

War, famine, persecution, and cosmic dissolution appear in the Synoptic apocalypse, too (Matt. 24:6–10), but the most striking feature is the warning against deception. Deceit, more than destruction, takes priority in the Synoptic exposé. Jesus is, as it were, warning his followers that the adversary prefers to ride on a white horse and that he poses as someone other than who he is. Is this perspective missing from Rev. 6, otherwise thought to replicate the Synoptic apocalypse with respect to content and sequence? The "rider on the white horse" in the Synoptic apocalypse, in my deliberate tongue-in-cheek twist of the image, is precisely *not* Jesus. This leads to the strong possibility that in both places someone has stolen his horse!

Victorinus of Pettau, writing in the middle of the third century (258–260 CE), held that the white horse is "the word of preaching sent into the world by the Holy Spirit" (Victorin 1997, 79–81). This view has proved resilient and is still defended (Sweet 1979, 139; Stefanovic 2009a, 233), but it faces significant hurdles. First, the assertion that "white always, and without any exception, refers to Christ or his followers and is never used with reference to the forces of evil" (Stefanovic 2009a, 233) elevates a premise into a proof. If *this* white horse is not Christ or on the side of good, the color white is not always a signifier of good. Second, the white horse and its rider sets out "conquering and to conquer" (*nikōn kai hina nikēsē*; 6:2 NRSV). The purpose clause, signified by *hina* in Greek, indicates determination to reach a goal not yet in hand. This might work for the view that takes the white horse to symbolize the preaching of the gospel, but serious reservations remain. "The Lamb" that takes the scroll is already declared the winner (5:5). He does not need to go forth "conquering and to conquer" (6:2), given that he has already won (5:5). Indetermination on this point is resolved by making sure that "conquering" or "prevailing" retains the connection to the cosmic conflict. In my translation, the rider on the white horse sets out "conquering, dead set on winning the war" (6:2). In fact, it is a conundrum that the adversary "goes to war" again (12:17), and again (13:7), and again (16:14), and again (19:19), and again (20:8)—impervious to the certain fact of defeat (12:7–12). It is equally a puzzle that he will have victories to show for himself (11:7; 13:7). This is best understood as the counterpunch of the loser in the war: he has not yet thrown in the towel (12:13–18).

Third, for consistent representations of Jesus in Revelation, his weapon is the "sword," not the "bow" (1:16; 2:12, 16; 19:15, 21). The stance of Jesus and his followers is the stance of witness (*martyria*) rather than conquest (1:2, 9; 6:9; 11:7; 12:11, 17; 19:10; 20:4). Winning is, for the good side, always anchored in witness. Fourth, as David E. Aune (1996–98, 393–94) notes, despite the similarity between the hard-charging rider in 6:2 and the triumphant rider in 19:12, "the two cavaliers have actually very little in common." Both riders have white horses, but the rider in 6:2 has a "bow" and "crown" or wreath (*stephanos*), while the rider in 19:11–16 has a "sharp two-edged sword" in his mouth and "many diadems" (*diadēmata*) on his head. Fifth, even though the color white seems to be an enticing symbol for "the gospel," this view gets tangled when horses "red" (6:4), "black" (6:5), and "sickly green" (6:8) appear on the stage. The "gospel" view sees these horses, broadly, as "the consequences of the rejection of the gospel" (Stefanovic 2009a, 237). The world is now in the throes of "covenant curses." The underlying logic is retribution. For the sin of turning down the "white horse" and its rider, there will be punishment (Stefanovic 2009a, 241). This interpretation has the added weakness of offering an allegorical rather than a symbolic interpretation of the horses and their riders.

Sixth, the logic of retribution hits a brick wall when "the Lamb" opens "the fifth seal" (6:9). There, according to the most common translations, *victims of violence decry the absence of consequences for the perpetrators of evil* (6:10). *It is precisely absence of action that is their complaint against the way God is conducting the war* (6:9–10). To hear this concern raised when divine action is supposed to operate at full blast indicates that the four horses represent something other than *divine* action and, too, that human expectations of retribution have not been met. A *revelatory* view of the seven seals, by contrast, is consistent with the OT background texts, the Synoptic apocalypse, the notion that the four horses are a group, and representations of Jesus.

One more option should be mentioned for the white horse. This view, too, treats the four horses as one group, all of them representing disasters that go from bad to worse. In this view, "the first rider must be identified as a victorious warrior who in his form embodies aggression and conquest" (Roloff 1993, 86). This view ensures consistency of representation for the four horses, but the mandate given the rider of the white horse conflicts with the mission of the "red horse" that follows (6:3–4). Or rather, it is redundant (6:4). Like its forerunner, the two have war and conquest on their mind. This stands in contrast to the view that the white horse is stolen; it symbolizes deception; it is not redundant; the rider has "a bow" as a token of conquest; "a crown" for the pretense of being a winner; and he sets out "conquering, dead set on winning the war" (6:2). The "white horse" is not there to sow confusion at the level of representation. On the contrary, a reality meant to confuse requires precisely *this* representation. The demonic will be shorn of its most prized guise if denied the option of dressing in white.

**And when he opened the second seal, I heard the second living creature calling out, "Come!"** (6:3). Again, looking to the criteria used for assessing the first seal, is the reality coming to light good or bad? If it is bad, has the vector shifted from good to bad between the first and the second seal? If a disaster is about to happen, who or what is causing it? **And another horse came forth, flaming red, and the one sitting on it was permitted** [*edothē*] **to take peace from the earth so that people would kill one another, and a massive sword was given** [*edothē*] **to him** (6:4). Much of the action taking place is described in the passive voice. As noted earlier, the passive voice anonymizes the acting subject: we are informed of the action but not of the one doing it. The key verb is *didōmi*, a verb that has "give," "grant," "allow," or "permit" within its range of meanings (BDAG 242–43, δίδωμι). We can say that the rider on the red horse "*was given* to take peace from the earth." Likewise—preserving the exact word order in Greek—"there *was given* to him a massive sword" (6:4). The action is uncomplicated. This rider is a war-maker and warmonger, bent on killing on a large scale. But who is doing the "giving"? Scholars tend to give

God exclusive proprietary rights to this verb, calling its use in the passive voice a "divine passive," sometimes with the qualification that the expression by itself does not point to positive or negative activity (Aune 1996–98, 394–95). By this logic, God is the acting subject. The writer is thought to have such reverence for God's name that he will not say it outright. Most of the action collapses into God-ordained activity.

But this view is far too simplistic. John has not copyrighted this verb to refer to God any more than God insists on exclusive rights to the color white. A reading sensitized to conflict sees God acting by *permission* while Satan acts by *commission*. By the logic of divine *permission*, the second rider "was *permitted* to take peace from the earth" (6:4). By the logic of demonic *commission*, this rider "was *commissioned* to take peace from the earth" (6:4). These are not mutually exclusive options but actions viewed from complementary perspectives. We have "divine permission granted to evil powers to carry out their nefarious work" (Caird 1999, 81). A consistent representation and use lead to the conclusion that "all four riders represent evils which are not caused by the will of God" (Caird 1999, 81). God does not will the action to happen, but God wills the other side to show its colors. Disclosure is a matter of necessity (1:1; 4:1; 11:5; 17:10; 20:3; 22:6).

**And when he opened the third seal, I heard the third living creature calling out, "Come!" I looked, and wow! there was a black horse! And the one sitting on it had a pair of scales in his hand, and I heard a voice that seemed to originate in the middle of the four living creatures, calling out, "A quart of wheat for a denarius, and three quarts of barley for a denarius, but do not harm the olive oil and the wine!"** (6:5–6). Each "living creature" is in on the action taking place (6:1, 3, 5), taking turns keeping tabs on the four horses and their riders. The third rider deals in household economics. Following the debasement of the coinage after Nero, a "denarius" corresponded to a worker's daily wage (BDAG 223, δηνάριον). "A quart of wheat" represents the daily ration for one person (BDAG 1086, χοῖνιξ). Looking at the family budget, the provider and head of the household had bad news for the family because of the mismatch between income and expenses. Another word for this is *famine*. Barley is cheaper—"three quarts of barley for a denarius"—but a switch to cheaper grain will not make up the difference. David E. Aune (1996–98, 397) estimates price increases to "eight times the normal price for wheat and five-and-one-third times the normal price for barley." The voice "from the middle" sets a limit to the hardship that will be permitted. "Wheat" and "barley" are annual crops, damage to which may quickly be reversed. Damage to olive trees and vines takes years to undo. The overall import is an economy of destitution, in contrast to God's economy of plenty.

**And when he opened the fourth seal, I heard the voice of the fourth living creature calling out, "Come!"** (6:7). As noted, all the "living creatures" seem to know their part, executing it with perfect pitch and timing. **And I looked, and**

wow! there was a sickly green horse! And the one sitting on it bears the name Death, and Hades followed in his train. And these were permitted [*edothē*] to have power to kill a fourth of the earth—with sword, with famine, and with death, and by the wild animals of the earth (6:8). Things are not easing up; they are getting worse. The writer's "wow!" is to the point. The fourth horse may be "pale green" (NRSV), but it is better to describe the green as "sickly green." In medical terms, it would be *jaundiced* (6:8). What it brings cannot by any stretch of the imagination be described as "good." By now there is a striking correspondence between "the name" and the reality. His name is "Death," and the death-maker has "demonic" written all over him: "Hades followed in his train." "Permission," on one side, and "commission," on the other, are relevant here, too, the demonic side committed to inflict horror. As with the previous seal, a limit is set to the carnage: "a fourth of the earth" (6:8). The fourth horse and its rider are a composite of the two previous horses, given that "death" and "famine" belong to their mandate. Where he rides forth, civilization and life itself are in retreat. Predatory "wild animals" roam the earth (6:8).

It will be worthwhile to pause for a moment to assess the heavenly choreography once more. Each of the scenes is preceded by "the Lamb" breaking one of the seals (6:1, 3, 5, 7). The voice calling out operates in lockstep with the actions of "the Lamb."

> I heard one of the four living creatures calling out, as in a voice of thunder, "Come!" (6:1)

> I heard the second living creature calling out, "Come!" (6:3)

> I heard the third living creature calling out, "Come!" (6:5)

> I heard the voice of the fourth living creature calling out, "Come!" (6:7)

The choreography is precise and coordinated. Action by the one who breaks the seals is timed to coincide with exclamations on the part of the four living creatures. The thunderous "Come!" calls out to reality to reveal itself: the time has come for Satan to show his colors.

*This*—rather than attempting to pin each horse and its rider to a specific event in history, whether it be the first century in the preterist mode, the profusion of suggestions in futurist schemes, or historicist attempts to match the horses to well-defined historical periods. Revelation prioritizes representations of reality over historical specificity without denying history a fair-minded depiction. *Reality* will not be missing for the person whose short list must include the Crusades (a "white horse" event), the Black Death of the fourteenth century, the Holocaust, or Hiroshima. With this drift in the seven seals, the fifth seal will not be a non sequitur—an abrupt change of topic—to the preceding four. On the contrary, the first four seals have laid an exquisite groundwork for the question about to travel through space from earth to heaven.

The fifth seal reiterates the mismatch between expectations and reality that weighs on the heavenly council, but the problem is now expressed from a human perspective.

**And when he opened the fifth seal, I saw under the altar the victims who had been killed with violence for the word of God and the testimony [of Jesus] that they had in their possession. They cried out as loud as they could,**

> "How long, Great Majesty,
>     upright and trustworthy,
>     will it be
> before you decide to act justly [*krineis*]
>     and vindicate [*ekdikeis*] our blood
>     [shed] by those
>     who dwell on the earth?" (6:9–10)

My translation hears those "who had been killed" crying out for vindication (Mounce 1977, 159). Other translations perceive the victims crying out to God to "judge and avenge our blood on the inhabitants of the earth," suggesting a prayer for punitive action (6:10 NRSV). God has let the sufferer down either by not punishing those who made them suffer or by failing to make it up to the victim. They cried out "as loud as they could" (*phōnē megalē*) to show that they question the policy of permission. The victims' cry matters. Giancarlo Biguzzi (1998b, 212) calls their complaint "the genetic nucleus of the whole narrative cycle of the scroll." Jacques Ellul (1977, 158) takes it a notch higher, calling the prayer of the martyrs "one of the motor forces of history." To other interpreters, the outcry encompasses the problem of the entire book (Heil 1993; Lambrecht 1998). The crisis that is evident but not explicitly verbalized in heaven is now voiced loudly on earth (5:1–4; 6:10). This might be described as a "crisis of theodicy," centered on "the silence of God in the face of the intolerably triumphant 'persecutor' already diffused among the churches" (Biguzzi 1998b, 216).

What is heaven's answer? There is an answer, sort of, immediately following the question. **And to each was given a long white robe and it was said to them to rest a short time longer until [the number] would be complete, that is, [the number of] the fellow servants and their brothers and sisters who were to be killed just as they had been** (6:11). It is better English to say that "they were given" and "they were told," but I have retained the metrics of the Greek. This time, there can be no doubt that the hand that provides the "white robe" and the voice telling them "to rest a short time longer" represent heaven. But what kind of answer is this? There is no hint that heaven's permissive policy is about

127

to change. More victims are to come the way of those already killed (6:11). The notion that a numeric goal must be reached before the sordid chapter can be closed must not be taken literally. The process running to completion does not unfold according to an arithmetic measure, but there is an underlying reason. In the meantime, the victims have the "white robe." They belong to the winning side, and God will make it up to them.

The "white robe" signifies vindication. What about vengeance? Must not the perpetrators be punished for what they have done? Interpreters who hold that the victims under the altar are crying out for vengeance, and this is the vast majority, argue that the trumpet sequence is the answer to the victims' complaint. "How long?" they ask (6:10). The answer, in the words of one interpreter, is found in the seven trumpets. "Not too long [before justice is done]. I am already judging those who viciously assault and persecute my saints" (Stefanovic 2009a, 255; cf. Paulien 1988, 320; A. Collins 1976, 17, 34; May 2009). As in Exodus, God must hit the world ever harder, with devastating trumpet blasts (8:2–11:19) and with the bowls of wrath (15:1–16:21). The problem of God's apparent permissiveness is solved by showing that the permissiveness is only temporary and apparent. Justice will be done when the perpetrators of injustice face the calamities of the seven trumpets and the seven last plagues—and then, the eternal consuming fire. "In the narrow sense, justice means bringing the perpetrators of injustice to account, and in due time Revelation will show this taking place" (Koester 2014, 435).

In contrast to this view, God's permissiveness is the main problem and the reason for the crisis in the heavenly council. A series of negations are necessary to bring this out. Thus, the problem is *not* solved by retribution. The answer to the cry of the victims of violence is *not* found in the trumpets or the bowls or in some other future horizon. It is *not* what comes to light with the opening of the seals that sets the mind at ease. The seals—all of them—are themselves proof of heaven's permissive policy and *not* its remedy. The cry of the victims of violence is the boldest reminder of the policy and the existential problem that goes with it (6:9–10). The solution, again, is *not* found by breaking another seal, blowing another trumpet, or pouring out another bowl. *The solution— and there is one—is the Lamb that was killed with violence* (5:5–8). The road less traveled by him does not erase the meaning of victimhood, making it up to the victims in the form of retribution. To do this would put the meaning of God's conduct of the war at risk. The Lamb "in the middle" of the story, not the event at the end, is heaven's answer. "The Lamb is, finally, the one who does not at all create the Scourges, nor even evoke them, but who *discloses* them" (Ellul 1977, 154).

**And I looked when he opened the sixth seal, and there came a great earthquake; the sun became black as sackcloth, the entire moon became like blood, and the stars of the heaven fell to the earth as the fig tree drops its winter fruit**

when shaken by a gale. And the heaven disappeared like a scroll rolling itself up, and every mountain and island was removed from its place (6:12–14). Old Testament allusions abound in this scene. Isaiah describes a time when "the stars of the heavens and their constellations will not give their light; the sun will be dark at its rising" (13:10); "the moon will be abashed, and the sun ashamed" (24:23); and "the skies roll up like a scroll" (34:4). Chaos threatens the cosmic order as though God has abdicated and left the world to itself. Jeremiah describes scenes of *de*-creation, throwing the sequence of creation in Genesis into reverse (4:23–26). The portrayal of cosmic dissolution makes cosmology overshadow the theology of the scene. As cosmology, it is impressive to report that "the sky vanished" (Rev. 6:14). Letting the phrase say that "the heaven disappeared" (6:14) retains the sense of cosmic turmoil, but the wording lies a step closer to the theological message. *There is no heaven any longer!* It is as though God has taken his hands off the controls. The power supply of the universe has temporarily been turned off. "The middle" is abandoned or left to the adversary, and the mad galloping of the four horses is felt in the entire cosmos (Ellul 1977, 160). As with the previous seals, this scene, too, has a permissive tenor. What happens to the cosmos if God steps away (Tonstad 2007)? Earthlings take notice of the dissolution.

And the kings of the earth and the mighty and the generals and the well-to-do and the powerful, and everyone, whether slave or free, hid themselves in the caves and among the rocks of the mountains, calling to the mountains and the rocks,

"Fall on us and hide us
   from the face of the one
      who is sitting on the throne
   and from the wrath
   of the Lamb,
for the great day of their wrath
   has come,
and who is able to stand?" (6:15–17)

Everyone is represented in this scene, "slave and free," but "the mighty" predominate. With the cosmos in disarray (6:12–14), all are running for cover. "Enter into the rock and hide in the dust from the terror of the LORD, and from the glory of his majesty," Isaiah says in the text that echoes here (Isa. 2:10, 19). Does Revelation describe a scene of God's presence or of God's absence? Can it be both at the same time, the cosmic dissolution as a token of God's absence, the fear of seeing "the face" a reminder that God's face will be seen? G. B. Caird (1999, 92) finds scant reason to grant theological merit to the exclamation of those who cry out. "There is no need to find a place in John's theology for any concept of 'the wrath of the Lamb,' since it is not a phrase he uses *propria persona*, but one which he puts on the lips of the terrified inhabitants of earth. It has its source not in the true character of Christ, but in the tragic and paranoiac delusion to which they have surrendered themselves."

"You cannot see my face; for no one shall see me and live," God said to Moses (Exod. 33:20). If "God's face" refers to God as God is, the attitude toward seeing God's face depends on views held prior to seeing it. In Hosea, those who "say to the mountains, 'Cover us,' and to the hills, 'Fall on us,'" are panicking in the face of hostile forces bearing down on the land (Hosea 10:8, quote marks added). In Luke, the same text appears when Jesus talks of a day when people will call "to the mountains, 'Cover us,' and to the hills, 'Fall on us'" (23:30). In his perspective, too, restraint and inhibitions are absent. "For if they do this when the wood is green, what will happen when it is dry?" Jesus asks (Luke 23:31). What matters is what "*they* do," and the problem is absence of restraint. Revelation hints at a similar state. This is "what would be reality if God were not continually their protector, if the men who are the bearers of the Kingdom were not continually among them imperfectly, mysteriously, incognito—the Witnesses and those who pray" (Ellul 1977, 167).

"Who is able to stand?" (Rev. 6:17). As so often, OT texts illuminate the subject. For the need at hand, one text stands out. "If you, O LORD, should mark iniquities, Lord, who could stand?" (Ps. 130:3). In this text "Who is able to stand" depends on a quality in God rather than an attribute in human beings. But the question cannot be cut loose from its context, from the passages preceding it and from the text to follow. In the texts preceding it, God's permissiveness is under scrutiny. In the texts to follow, more will come to light as to God's determination to make people "able to stand" (6:17; cf. 16:14).

### Digression (7:1–17)

#### Protection (7:1–8)

**7:1–8.** Much lies between the opening of the sixth (6:12) and the seventh (8:1) seal, but it is not a time-out. Whether we call it an "intermission," "interruption," "interlude," "intercalation," or "digression," the "digression" is packed with activity (Perry 2009).

In one sense, the content of the rest of the book is compressed into the next seventeen verses (7:1–17). The cosmic conflict is brought to the surface more clearly than at any time so far (7:1–4); the redeemed are brought to safety (7:5–10); that anyone made it is one reason for wonder, another that so many did (7:5–10); who they are and how it happened are questions of intense interest (7:13–17); all this is interspersed with scenes of jubilation (7:10–12, 15). "Who is able to stand?" (6:17)—the question at the entryway to these scenes—is answered.

**After this I saw four angels standing at the four corners of the earth, holding the four winds of the earth so that no wind could blow on the earth or the sea or against any tree** (7:1). A restraining influence keeps the forces of chaos at bay. The expression "the four winds of the earth" is similar to one in the book of Daniel (Dan. 7:2). Here, the winds are subject to restraint, and the restraint is total: "no wind" on the side of causation and "every tree" on the side of effect. By this symbolism, restraint and protection work both ends of the field for the purpose in view (Rev. 7:2–3). We shall be forgiven if the commanding voice of the "angel ascending from the rising of the sun" leaves us bewildered whether heaven is *causing* "the four winds of the earth" to blow or only *permitting* it (7:2). But heaven's priority is not in doubt. Whatever it takes to put "the seal of the living God" on the foreheads of "the servants of our God" will be done. Their needs come first. Nothing will be allowed to interfere with the sealing process. Only when the seal is firmly affixed "on the servants of our God on their foreheads" (7:3) will "the four winds" have their turn.

> **Outline of
> Revelation 6:1–8:1**
>
> **Breaking the seals:
> The first six (6:1–17)**
>
> **Digression (7:1–17)**
>
> Protection (7:1–8)
>
> Homecoming (7:9–17)
>
> **The seventh seal (8:1)**

R. H. Charles (1920, 1:205) evokes the sealing drama perceptively, capturing the *timing* as well as the *meaning*:

> The sealing is to secure the servants of God against the attacks of demonic powers coming into the open manifestation. The Satanic host is about to make its final struggle for the mastery of the world. . . . The hidden mystery of wickedness, the secret source of all the haunting horrors, and crimes, and failures, and sins of the past was about to reveal itself—the Antichrist was to become incarnate and appear armed, as it were, with all but almighty power. With such foes the faithful felt wholly unfit to do battle. With the rage and hostility of man they could cope, but with their ghostly enemy and his myrmidons about to manifest themselves with soul- and body-compelling powers they dared not engage. And so just on the eve of this epiphany of Satan, God seals His servants on their foreheads to show that they are His own possession.

Satan has not been idle until this point; the seals have unmasked demonic activity all along. Now, in Charles's perception, the world must brace for the "epiphany of Satan." Will the epiphany show Satan as Satan, no longer masked and secretive? On which horse will he ride, the "red," the "black," or the "sickly green"—or, heaven forbid—on the "white horse"? Will he trust mayhem and "the haunting horrors" to work for him this time, or will he yet again, and now more than ever, try to make the "epiphany of Satan" seem as though it is a genuine epiphany, an "epiphany of Christ" or an "epiphany of God"?

Charles's perception of a movement toward a certain point in time, a climax of history, is not contrived, but the perception must be circumscribed. The movement toward an "epiphany of Satan" preserves a role for Satan in the events of history that he is often denied in the theological tradition. A

131

final thrust on his part—and a final exposé on the part of God—*this is how Revelation represents reality.* On the other hand, "sealing" cannot apply to a point in time only, as though it has not been necessary earlier or as though God at a given point provides protection and preferential treatment at a level not available in the past. The broad view, therefore, must be that the "sealing" of the believer is at all times God's foremost concern.

To receive **the seal of the living God** (7:2) is best understood as an inward matter.

> In its deepest sense this sealing means the outward manifestation of character. The hidden goodness of God's servants is at last blazoned outwardly, and the divine name that was written in secret by God's Spirit on their hearts is now engraved openly on their brows by the very signet ring of the living God. In the reign of the Antichrist goodness and evil, righteousness and sin, come into their fullest manifestation and antagonism. Character ultimately enters on the stage of finality. (Charles 1920, 1:205–6)

*Timing* and *meaning* will not at any point part company. With re-reader awareness, "the seal of the living God" (7:2) is the protective counterpoint to "the mark of the beast" (19:20; cf. 13:6; 14:9–11; 15:2; 20:4). For either side, being "sealed" or "marked" signifies a movement toward completion (Charles 1920, 1:360).

No stone is left unturned to make human beings invulnerable to ambush or attack from the other side. Two details invite special comment. First, "the seal of the living God" (7:2) has to be placed "on their foreheads" (7:3), speaking of the believers. "The mark of the beast" (19:20), by contrast, can be put "on the right hand *or* on the forehead" (13:16). If "the forehead" signifies intelligence, thought, and active participation, and "the right hand" alone means participation that owes less to reflection, this could be an important distinction. Second, "the four winds" are held in check until the sealing has been completed (7:1–3). A broad reading of this scenario, taking "the four winds" to represent external forces and circumstances, suggests that nothing in a person's circumstances will stand in the way of being "sealed."

Who, then, are these people, and how many are they?

> **And I heard the number of those who were sealed,**
> **one hundred forty-four thousand,**
> **sealed from every tribe of the people of Israel.** (7:4, 5–8)

We have earlier read of "those who say about themselves that they are Jews and are not" (2:9; 3:9). Here, we have people who do *not* say about themselves that they are Jews but *are* (C. Smith 1990, 116). We have disputed the notion of Jewish ethnicity for the "Jews" in the messages to the communities in Smyrna and Philadelphia (2:9; 3:9). Now we have the flip side. Ethnicity is not the main concern, but inclusion in a "tribe of Israel" is. Various observations have been made on how the list of names resembles or differs from the list of Jacob's sons and the tribes of Israel in the OT (e.g., Gen. 29:31–30:24; Exod. 1:1–4; Num. 1:5–15; Ezek. 48:1–29; C. Smith 1990; Bauckham 1991), but the most interesting features are neither the names nor their order. The "one hundred and forty-four thousand," twelve tribes times twelve thousand, is a symbolic number for completeness (7:5–8). The history of Israel, marked by disappointment and failure, turned out well after all! God's purpose in history, even when represented in the history of Israel, came out right. Against a background of apostasy and exile, Revelation presents a picture of faithfulness and liberation. All the tribes are represented (Bauckham 1991, 101), the good and the bad. The descendants of the concubines count as much as the children of Leah and Rachel. And all of them are there in an equal number even though the census at the time of the exodus shows vast differences in terms of numerical strength (Num. 1:20–46).

### Homecoming (7:9–17)

**7:9–17. After this I looked, and wow! an enormous multitude that no one could count, from every nation [*ethnous*], from all tribes and peoples and languages, standing before the throne and before the Lamb, dressed in white robes, with palm branches in their hands** (7:9–10). The pairing is striking, first a small, numbered group represented as though it is complete and now an infinitely large group that "no one could count" (7:9)! "The contrast is obvious in two respects," notes Richard J. Bauckham: "the 144,000 are counted, whereas the great multitude cannot be counted; the 144,000 are from the twelve tribes of Israel, whereas the great multitude are from all nations, tribes, peoples and languages" (1991, 103). What is the purpose of the strange pairing?

Even though "the people of Israel" and the "enormous multitude that no one could count" do not break along ethnic lines, the mention of "Israel" and the name of each tribe spelled out in loving detail show that the story of Israel in the OT is neither irrelevant nor in vain. The redemption of Israel alone was never the goal to begin with. The promise to Abraham that "in you all the families of the earth shall be blessed" has materialized (Gen. 12:3; Kelly 1986, 290). In this regard, Isaiah's influence on Revelation is incalculable. With reference to the scope and extent of the Servant's mission, we find Isaiah saying, "It is too light a thing that you should be my servant to raise up the tribes of Jacob and to restore the survivors of Israel; I will give you as a light to the nations, that my salvation may reach to the end of the earth" (Isa. 49:6). Revelation declares this vision fulfilled. Here, between the sixth and the seventh seals, we have a preview of what "mission accomplished" looks like: "an enormous multitude that no one could count" (7:9). Israel and the nations, all of them, becoming what they have always been, a great indivisible human family.

In the ensuing scene of gratitude, ascription counts more than description (7:10). Salvation is ascribed to God even though it would make good sense to say that the beneficiaries are the ones to whom **salvation belongs**. That is true, too, but the focus is on the One who made it happen. Moreover, "salvation" is a form of vindication. The multitude has "palm branches in their hands" (7:9), and this is only one of the allusions to the Feast of Tabernacles in the OT (Exod. 23:14–17; Lev. 23:34–44; 25:8–23; Zech. 14:16–21; Draper 1983). These allusions envision a time when all humanity will celebrate the Feast of Tabernacles, palm branches and all (Zech. 14:16–21). Theology, once the surest thing to divide the human family, is now the element that unites.

Scenes of unity and celebration encompass earth and heaven, yet another example of the cascade of jubilation that infuses the story (7:11–12). A literal reading puts the angels in the outer circle among the beings standing **around the throne** (7:11). It is not certain that John intended it to be read that way, but an ordered, cascading jubilation spreading from group to group is fitting. The various elements in the tribute may at first sight suggest that John lacks any selection criteria for the terms he employs. But each word counts, especially since God has been at the receiving end of a relentless campaign of slander on the part of "the Mudslinger" (12:9; 20:2). From the viewpoint of earthly reality, each word takes on special meaning. Is the existence of evil proof that God is *unwilling* to prevent it and therefore *malevolent*, as philosophers from Epicurus (341–270 BCE) to David Hume (1711–76) suggested (Larrimore 2001, xviii–xi; Hume 1992, 100; Tonstad 2016a, 10–12)? No, say **the angels, the twenty-four elders, and the four living creatures**, giving **the blessing and the glory** to God—above all—because of God's self-giving love (7:11–12). Does the reality of evil prove that God is *unable* to prevent it and therefore *impotent*? No, they say again, praising God for **the power and the might** (7:11–12). "Whence then is evil?" asks Hume (1992, 100), with God's very existence now in jeopardy. Does the heavenly council know the answer to this question?

They do. But they know it only descriptively, not causally. Revelation describes what happened, how it happened, and who did what. It does not say *why* it happened; it cannot say *why* it happened without giving evil a causal explanation. Blame is due "the Mudslinger" for embarking on a course that was causally unjustified (12:7–12). Epicurus and Hume laid out "the problem of evil" along the axes of love and power. There must either be a love deficit or a power deficit on the part of God for evil to exist. Their simplistic equation concentrates on these terms alone. *Freedom* does not occur to any of them, whether the relationship between *freedom* and *power*, on the one hand, or the connection between *freedom* and *love*, on the other. Has God, then, been blindsided for lack of intellectual acuity, caught like a deer in the headlights by a clever philosopher? No, **the angels, the twenty-four elders, and the four living creatures** proclaim once more (7:11). **The wisdom**, too, belongs to God

(7:12). God has not been outdone whether in the realm of the intellect or values. Questions raised in the domain of earthly philosophy are answered in the heavenly council even though these questions are only of peripheral concern to councillors. For them, the problem at the center is still "the rebellion of Satan which is paralleled by rebellion on earth" (A. Collins 1979, 39). Every single word of praise is an answer to the crisis. "Worship" of this kind is not obligatory adulation but the believer's gratitude to God.

While John absorbs what is going on, a participant in the scene turns to *him*, the visitor. **And one of the elders asked me, saying, "These who are dressed in white robes, who are they, and from where have they come?"** (7:13). Why would a being in heaven ask this question of John on earth? The reason cannot be that the elder does not know the answer. Instead, it must be that he is seeking an opening to draw attention to the wonderful subject once more.

> And I said to him,
>   "My master,
>   you are the one who knows."
> Then he said to me,
>   "These are the ones
>   who have come out
>     of the great tribulation;
>   they have washed their clothes
>     and made them white
>     in the blood of the Lamb.
> For this reason they are before
>   the throne of God,
>   and they worship him
>     day and night
>     within his temple,
>   and the one who is sitting on the throne
>   will shelter them." (7:14–15)

The question asked earlier, "Who is able to stand?" (6:17), is now answered. During the darkest hour, the prospects of the faithful looked dim, but the "sealing" worked. The language here is colorful and counterintuitive: How can a garment turn out white if washed in blood? This representation has two aspects, *cleansing* and *commitment*. In the OT, turning a piece of soiled clothing white is a frequent metaphor for spiritual cleansing. Theologians use words like *forgiveness* and *transformation*, but the OT prefers the metaphors of clothes and color when describing how sin is neutralized and removed (Isa. 1:18; Zech. 3:3–5; 13:1). Spiritual clothing will not be clean unless it is washed and made white "in the blood of the Lamb" (7:14). *Cleansing* is not the whole story, however. "The Lamb" is a victim of violence (5:6), and the believers have followed "the Lamb" on the path of *commitment* and victimhood (Perry

2009, 216). Revelation makes this aspect explicit, explaining that the redeemed prevailed by "the blood of the Lamb and by the word of their testimony, for they did not love their lives even at the cost of death" (12:11). *Cleansing* has not disappeared from the picture but *commitment* to a stance of nonviolence, even if it means death, adds fuller meaning to the statement (7:14).

Both aspects, *cleansing* and *commitment*, are included in what "the ones who are dressed in white robes" do (7:13). They stand "before the throne of God," but their focus is on qualities in God, not assets in themselves, and they are represented as people in a state of need. For the qualities in God, "they worship him day and night within his temple" (7:15). For the state of need, "the one who is sitting on the throne will shelter them" (7:15). "Day and night" of this seems tiring and tedious, but it will not be tedious for people who are aware of "the accuser of our brothers and sisters," the person "who accuses them before our God *day and night*" (12:10; cf. 4:8; Ps. 134:1). At a time when voices of proclamation and acclamation dominate, the voice of accusation is not forgotten.

In the closing tableau, before "the Lamb" opens the seventh seal, neither cleansing nor virtue, neither commitment nor devotion features in the description of the redeemed. They are represented solely from the point of view of *need*.

> They shall hunger no more,
>    and they shall thirst no more;
> the sun shall not hit them,
>    nor any heat;
> for the Lamb
>    in the middle of the throne
>    will be their shepherd,
> and he will guide them
>    to springs of the water of life,
> and God will wipe away
>    every tear from their eyes. (7:16–17)

It would not be necessary to mention hunger, thirst, or exposure if these were not features of existence with which the redeemed are acquainted. These features can be experienced materially, existentially, and spiritually. The same logic applies to the need for a shepherd, access to water, and the tears in their eyes (7:17). There would be no need for a shepherd except for vulnerability and danger; no need for access to water except for scarcity and thirst; and no need to have tears wiped away except for the fact that they have experienced loss and grief. God has been on their side in the trials of life—this much is certain.

Three additional features deserve comment. First, this text echoes the most soaring promises and prospects in the OT (Isa. 4:5–6; 25:4–9; 41:17;

49:9–10; Ezek. 34:23; Ps. 121:6). Second, the depiction in Revelation shares conspicuous thematic territory with the Gospel of John—the shepherd, the danger, the impostor, the vulnerability, and the promise of abundance (John 10:1–15; 21:15–17; cf. Draper 1983, 140). Third, already here, at the close of the "interlude" between the sixth and the seventh seal, John gives the reader an expansive view of the ending of the book: "springs of the water of life," a preview of the last chapter (7:17; 22:1–3); God wiping away "every tear from their eyes," a glimpse from the next-to-last chapter (7:17; 21:4).

A seventh seal remains. Do we need it? Has not the whole story been told? The cycles of the trumpets (8:1–11:19) and the bowls (15:1–22:5) are yet to come. Do we need them? Have we not already seen the ending?

Strictly speaking, we don't need it. *The whole story has been told*. If we "need it," the reason must be that there is need for repetition, recapitulation, and clarification. Revelation believes that we need *that*. On a time line, however, laying out the message along the axis of time, neither the trumpet nor the bowl sequence takes the story to a point beyond where the sequence of the seals has not already taken it (7:17).

### The Seventh Seal (8:1)

**8:1.** And then—one of the strangest verses in the Bible! **And when the Lamb opened the seventh seal, there was silence in heaven for about half an hour** (8:1). Without a doubt, "the seventh seal" springs an ambush on the most watchful reader. Most interpreters see it as a signifier of *continuation*, not as *completion* and *climax*, but there is no consensus regarding the meaning of the silence. The two categories most in favor are as far apart as "judgment" and "prayer." Robert Mounce (1977, 179) hears the silence as "a dramatic pause which makes even more impressive the judgments about to fall upon the earth." To G. K. Beale (1999, 447), likewise, the silence represents "the horror of divine judgment, which has such an awesome effect that no human is able to verbalize a response" (cf. Stefanovic 2009a, 253). A variant of the judgment theme anticipates the silence that, according to Jewish sources, will be recapitulated in connection with the new creation. "The mood is one of great solemnity and even dread" (Fabny 1992, 75).

In the category of prayer, R. H. Charles (1920, 1:224) suggests that "the praises of the highest orders of angels are hushed that the prayers of *all* the suffering saints on earth may be heard before the throne" (see also Bauckham 1993a, 70–83; Wick 1998). In this scenario, enforced silence is necessary in order that expressions of earthly need shall not be drowned out. These options, as noted, seek the meaning of the silence in the *continuation* of Revelation's story. They veer from best practice by failing to give the OT the requisite billing.

Silence is the most striking feature of the OT scene that has the greatest bearing on how best to understand the silence in heaven (8:1).

> Just as there were many
> who were *astonished at him*
> —**so marred was his appearance,**
> **beyond human semblance,**
> **and his form beyond that of mortals**
> —so he shall startle many nations;
> *kings shall shut their mouths because of him;*
> for that which had not been told them
> they shall see,
> and that which they had not heard
> they shall contemplate. (Isa. 52:14–15, emphasis added)

This text depicts silence—the silence of shock and awe in the face of an unexpected discovery. But what is the cause of the silence? To what or to whom are all eyes turned that has such an impact? They "were astonished *at him*," the text answers (Isa. 52:14). When this detail is applied to the mystery in Revelation, the cause for the silence will not be the events that are disclosed or events still to be disclosed—whether the terrors of judgment or the prayers of the saints (Kraft 1974, 132–33; U. Müller 1984, 184–85; Wilcox 1991). Perhaps our eyes have been on the horses and their riders, white, red, black, and "sickly green" (6:1–8); on the prayers of the victims of violence (6:9–10); or on the cosmos falling apart (6:12–14). None of this has been lost on the members of the heavenly council, but the eye-opener to them has been "the Lamb in the middle of the throne" (7:17; cf. 5:6–8). When human and cosmic reality is held up to what he is and what he reveals God to be, they are at a loss for words.

The setting within which this takes place in the OT background text is "a court of law, where a dispute about the view to be taken of a certain person is under consideration" (Baltzer 2001, 398). In this setting, the Revealer "shall be exalted and lifted up, and shall be very high" (Isa. 52:13). "*Lifted up*" is an ambiguous term, whether we see it in Isaiah or in the use of this text in the Gospel of John (John 12:32); it combines humiliation and exaltation. Mostly it envisions a path that runs contrary to all expectations and yet turns out well. "Look, my servant shall succeed," is an appropriate translation for the person described (Isa. 52:13). His success, too, is depicted in the currency of silence (52:14).

By this logic, "the seventh seal" does not lack content even though it is often seen that way. It signals completion, not continuation. Heaven's half an hour of silence is a measure of the impact of "the Lamb in the middle of the throne" (7:17; 5:6).

### Theological Issues

The *open heaven* and now the *open scroll* represent a challenge to a theological tradition that has emphasized God's *inscrutability* (Tonstad 2016a,

## Franz Kafka and the Quest for Access

Nothing is more demeaning to Joseph K. than *the lack of access, the complete lack of transparency* depicted in *The Trial*.

> *"As he looked round, he saw the top floor of the building next to the quarry. He saw how a light flickered on and the two halves of a window opened out, somebody, made weak and thin by the height and the distance, leant suddenly far out from it and stretched his arms out even further. Who was that? A friend? A good person? Somebody who was taking part? Somebody who wanted to help? Was he alone? Was it everyone? Would anyone help? Were there objections that had been forgotten? There must have been some. . . . Where was the judge he'd never seen? Where was the high court he had never reached? He raised both hands and spread out all his fingers."* (Kafka 1984, 228)

3–21). It is also a hopeful contrast to the existential despair and philosophical predicament that have found expression in the most influential writers of the twentieth century, among them Franz Kafka (1883–1924).

Amid ambiguity that added the word "Kafkaesque" to the English language, the predicament of the main character is not only legal, political, or existential. It is also *theological* (see sidebar). The veil of inscrutability persists all the way to the character's inexorable demise at the end—in body language suggestive of a crucifixion. Revelation speaks to this predicament, in distinction from a tradition that does not. God offers *access* and *transparency*, the essential building blocks of trust in civil society—and now in demand in theology, as well.

When heaven's door opens (4:1–2), contrary to all convention, the heavenly council is found to be in a crisis mode (5:1–4). The scroll that is "sealed with seven seals" distills the subject matter of the crisis (A. Collins 1979, 39). Except for the first seal, perhaps, the link between the symbol and the reality reflected by the symbol is straightforward: *deception, war, famine, death—* and *justice*, absent or deferred (6:1–11). The human condition has not been doctored or covered up. Revelation *does not portray reality prettier than it is or—indeed—other than it is.* Likewise, *God does not shut down questions* (6:9–11). The subject matter, now articulated as the discrepancy between expectations and reality (6:9–11), explains why there is a crisis. Questions of a similar kind appear in Ivan Karamazov's outrage at the suffering of children in *The Brothers Karamazov* (Dostoevsky 2002, 236–64; Tonstad 2016a, 22–35, 327–43; see sidebar), and they rise to a high decibel in the wake of the Holocaust and Hiroshima. By this criterion, heaven and earth share the same concerns. Faith is not a foregone conclusion even by heaven's point of view. A revelation is necessary to break the impasse, and this is exactly what happens (5:5–6).

## Ivan Karamazov and the Suffering of Children

*"Listen to me: I took children only so as to make it more obvious. About all the other human tears that have soaked the whole earth through, from crust to core, I don't say a word, I've purposely narrowed down my theme. . . . But then there are the children, and what am I going to do with them? That is the question I cannot resolve. . . . Besides, they have put too high a price on harmony; we can't afford to pay so much for admission. And therefore I hasten to return my ticket. And it is my duty, if only as an honest man, to return it as far ahead of time as possible. Which is what I am doing. It's not that I don't accept God, Alyosha, I just most respectfully return him the ticket."* (Dostoevsky 2002, 243–45)

When Jesus breaks the seven seals, he broadens the options with respect to *agency*. Visions of retribution dominate interpretations, but they lack depth. The calamities of the seal sequence occur at the point where divine *permission* intersects with demonic *commission*. The exposé of demonic agency continues in greater detail in two more cycles, the trumpets (8:2–11:19) and the bowls (15:1–16:21). Even when the exposé is complete, however, it does not put to rest questions over God's permissiveness. For this, the Lamb "in the middle" of the story is heaven's remedy (Ellul 1977, 154). There was no relief—high or low—until "the Lamb" appeared "in the middle" (5:3, 6).

This is easily the most critical issue in the book and the key to its theology. To focus on the Lamb that breaks the seals matters more than the content of the seals, especially when we concede that the content, in qualitative terms, brings very little that is new. The entrenched scenario of *retribution* yields the ground to scenes of *revelation*, and the Revealer is in his own person the one who transforms perceptions. At the end, the silence in heaven "for about half an hour" (8:1), represents the awed and subdued silence of insight, not the silence of fearful anticipation, or silence enabling prayers to be heard, or silence in the wake of seven waves of new information. Before the first prayer, if that were the point, God's Revealer was ready with a revelation in hand; before human need came to expression, there was a knock on the door even of houses unaware of need (3:20). Crucially, the *paideia* of Revelation does not bypass the needs of the world or humanity's most pressing questions.

# Revelation 8:2–11:19

## The Seven Trumpets

### Introductory Matters

It is over, isn't it? It is over—all the way to the day when God wipes "every tear from their eyes" (7:17; 21:4)? Why does the story continue when we already know the ending? For the story is certainly continuing.

The cycle of the seven trumpets begins with a spirited temple scene of mediation and prayer (8:2–5). Are we to expect a blast of *retribution*, as most scholars see it, or more scenes of *revelation*? The latter will emerge as the best interpretation by far—so much so that it will be in place for good (8:6–9:21). The OT allusions and bizarre, overwrought imagery have a diabolic entity in their sights (9:1–21): the calamities are not "acts of God" but the handiwork of God's opponent. The torrent of evidence makes for theological clarity. It is one of the most puzzling aspects of Revelation studies that this has not yet happened.

As in the cycle of the seven seals, the trumpet cycle also has a "digression"

> **Revelation 8:2–11:19**
> **in the Rhetorical Flow**
>
> Incentive to read (1:1–20)
> To the one who has an ear (2:1–3:22)
> The seven seals (4:1–8:1)
> ▶ The seven trumpets (8:2–11:19)
>   Mediation and prayer (8:2–5)
>   The first six trumpets (8:6–9:21)
>     The first four trumpets (8:6–13)
>     The fifth and sixth trumpets (9:1–21)
>   Digression (10:1–11:14)
>     Mission (10:1–11)
>     Method (11:1–14)
>   The seventh trumpet (11:15–19)

or "intercalation" between the sixth and the seventh elements in the cycle (10:1–11:14). The "digression" this time is twofold, the first centered on mission (10:1–11), the second concerned with the method to be used (11:3–10). The symbolism used to describe the method will tax the resources of the interpreter to the utmost. Once mastered, however, the reader will be left to ponder how the counterintuitive means can bring about such a profound change in sentiment and such world-transforming results (11:1–2, 11–13). The trumpet sequence ends on a note of jubilant completion and expectant preview (11:15–19).

## Tracing the Train of Thought

### Mediation and Prayer (8:2–5)

**8:2–5.** At the outset of the trumpet sequence, **the seven angels** are introduced as though they are a familiar entity or group (8:2). That they are *seven* is a matter of course. To the "seven communities" (1:11) and the "seven seals" (5:1, 5–6), we can now add "seven trumpets" (8:2) in the column of big-time "sevens," in addition to "seven lampstands of gold" (1:12, 20), "seven stars" (1:16, 20), "seven horns" (5:6), and "seven eyes" (5:6), as lesser themes. Yet to come are "seven bowls" (15:7) with the "seven last plagues" (15:1, 7) for the column of big-time "sevens," complemented by "seven thunders" (10:3), "seven heads" (17:7), "seven mountains" (17:9), and "seven kings" (17:9), as lesser ones.

The other item at the beginning of the trumpet sequence is deafening sound. A trumpet blast is hard to ignore. In the Torah, the Day of Atonement was heralded by the blowing of trumpets (Lev. 23:24; 25:9). In the prophets, the trumpet is the instrument of choice for the end-time summons (Isa. 27:13), for the decisive moment in time (Joel 2:1, 15), and for warning (Ezek. 33:3–6). Isaiah is particularly poignant. "All you inhabitants of the world, you who live on the earth, when a signal is raised on the mountains, look! When a trumpet is blown, listen!" (Isa. 18:3). "Thunder" and "a trumpet" are linked in the theophany at Mount Sinai (Exod. 19:16, 19). "As the blast of the trumpet grew louder and louder, Moses would speak and God would answer him in thunder" (19:19).

These examples contribute important background information to the trumpets in Revelation. The Sinai allusion suggests that a *revelation* is in the making. This allusion marks the opening scene in the heavenly council (4:5; Exod. 19:16–20), and it is now repeated before the first trumpet (Rev. 8:5). This imparts a melody to the noise—a theme: God is making an appearance.

Images of *mediation*, first, and *prayer*, second, precede the blowing of the trumpets (8:3). John notices hectic activity near **the altar**, a conspicuous piece of the sanctuary imagery that abounds in Revelation (8:3; cf. 6:9; 8:5;

9:13; 11:1; 14:18; 16:7). Whether this is the altar under which "the victims who had been killed with violence" cry out (6:9) and whether it is heavenly or earthly have been subject to debate (May 2009). Nothing is lost by seeing the heavenly altar in both places, and a both-and relationship has merit. In the latter scenario, the victims are killed on a Roman altar, but they are remembered at the altar in heaven. Such a notion is as old as the blood of Abel crying out to God from the ground (Gen. 4:10). Prayer is the main business of the altar in heaven (8:3, 5), and in that sense the cries of those "who had been killed" belong to that altar (6:9). "Incense" and "prayers" are linked so closely that incense *is* prayer, as noted in the seal cycle (8:3; cf. 5:8). Living beings *under*, *before*, and *around* the altar enliven the prayers of human beings, but the heavenly reality does not conform to expectation. In the bowl sequence, the altar itself *speaks* as a living, sentient entity (16:7)! If the throne and the altar have sentience and discernment built into their warp and woof, heaven is surely an unusual place.

Much is made of the cry from under the altar of those "who had been killed with violence" (6:9), but they will not be the only ones "praying." Indeed, their "prayer" is not called prayer as such. On the one hand, the cry of the victims of violence is "unsealed" by the Lamb who was himself "killed with violence" (5:6; 6:9–11). On the other hand, the scene that introduces the trumpet sequences suggests that prayer connects earth and heaven. These prayers must be the petitions, yearnings, and needs *of the living*. They reflect the everyday contact between earth and heaven, and the imagery is reassuring. While incense is prayer (5:8), "bowls full of incense" in the seal sequence and **a large quantity of incense** in the trumpet sequence magnify **the prayers** (8:3; cf. 5:8). Heaven pays attention to earthly need; the earthly signal is refined and amplified on its way; heaven is abuzz, aware, and ready to assist even though heaven's response does not come as immediate deliverance (6:9–11). **And the smoke of the incense—with the prayers of the saints—***rose before* **God** from **the hand of the angel** (8:4; cf. Ps. 141:2). God must be the architect and choreographer of this arrangement. Does God know or notice? Texts describing the plight of the Israelites in Egypt bear on the subject. "The Israelites groaned under their slavery, and cried out. Out of the slavery their cry for help *rose up to God*. God heard their groaning, and God remembered his covenant with Abraham, Isaac, and Jacob" (Exod. 2:23–24, emphasis added).

A response should be expected to these prayers and petitions. We know what form it took in Exodus (6:1–12:51). What form will it take now? This is a critical question, one of the most crucial in the entire book. Interpreters agree that there are allusions to Exodus in the trumpet sequence (Aune 1996–98, 545; Beale 1999, 467; Stefanovic 2009a, 293). It is assumed that if the language is similar, the meaning must be, too. By this logic, God will do to those who harass God's people what God did to the Egyptians in the past. This is the logic behind the drumbeat of retribution that reverberates across a wide array of interpretations. "The terrors about to intensify upon the earth are not caused by independent powers. All proceeds ultimately from the sovereign hand of the one God" (Boring 1989, 135). Of the poisoning of the waters at the third trumpet, we are told that "God poisons the water and thereby destroys the place where these people live" (Roloff 1993, 111). Retribution escalates until "the limited warning judgments of the trumpets give place to the seven last plagues of God's wrath on the finally unrepentant" (Bauckham 1993a, 204). David E. Aune (1996–98, 545) notes the motif of Israel's deliverance from Egypt, then adds that the purpose of the trumpet plagues "is not to elicit repentance but to exact punishment." With reference to the same motif, it is said that "the literary resemblance of the trumpets with Egypt's plagues tells us that the trumpets are in essence not natural disasters or general calamities, but God's covenant curses on His enemies" (LaRondelle 2007, 128). On the assumption that there is a straight line from the plagues in Exodus to Revelation, G. K. Beale (1999, 467) writes, "The trumpets must ultimately be understood as punishments that further harden the majority of people." These comments support the expectation that God "is preparing to bring his righteous judgments and vengeance upon those who viciously harassed and oppressed the faithful" (Stefanovic 2009a, 292). Critical and evangelical commentaries agree that the trumpet sequence depicts a punitive reality, foreclosing on other possibilities.

Commentators make much of the similarities between the trumpet sequence in Revelation and the plagues in the Exodus account, but they say too little about the differences (Koester 2014, 445–46). The differences do not make the similarities irrelevant, but they reduce their explanatory power. John does not cut and paste from the exodus story in a way that puts Exodus in control of his message with no need for further comment. In Exodus, the first plague turns the Nile into blood (Exod. 7:14–21). In Revelation, the first trumpet brings "hail and fire mixed with blood," and "a third of the earth was burned up, and a third of the trees were burned up, and all green grass was burned up" (8:7). At the second trumpet, "an object like a flaming mountain was thrown from heaven, and a third of the seawater turned to blood" (8:8–9). There is no "flaming mountain" in Exodus. At the third trumpet and again at the fifth, "a star" falls from heaven to earth, wreaking havoc to such an extent that its demonic character becomes the most important feature in the entire sequence (8:10–11; 9:1–11). There is no such "star" in the exodus story; no significant agent executing the calamities other than God. Pharaoh is an important figure in Exodus, but the cosmic ramifications of Revelation are absent. Applications of the Exodus plagues to the trumpet sequence of Revelation risk the perils of "parallelomania" (Sandmel 1962). "Two passages may sound the same in splendid isolation from their context, but when seen in context reflect difference rather than similarity" (Sandmel 1962, 3). The links between Exodus and Revelation are a case in point.

This weakens the underpinnings for the theology of retribution, and it makes it easy to see that God "is not the only one who is at work in this world—as the Apocalypse makes so abundantly clear" (Vögtle 1976, 383). Who else is at work—if not the "star that had fallen from heaven to earth" at the blast of the fifth trumpet (9:1)? What else is happening—not as punishment inflicted by God but as instigation of unimaginable evil by someone other than God (9:1–11)?

Third, the crisis in the heavenly council captures the discrepancy between expectations and reality, explored at length in the previous chapter (A. Collins 1979, 39). This concern looms large at the level of human experience in the cry of the victims of violence (Biguzzi 1998b, 212; Ellul 1977, 158; Heil 1993). How does God close the gap? Do we see God's action brought in line with expectations in the form of retribution? The surprise of the trumpets shows God bridging the gap, not by making the gap *smaller*—*not by ensuring that expectations are met*—but by making it *bigger*. All conjectures are shattered when God places everything within a new framework. Contrary to widely held views, the gap will be bridged by *revelation*, and *the content of the revelation is not retribution*. A reader in the twenty-first century may, for reasons of context, be wise to listen to Carl Jung (2002, 119) before proceeding: "We have experienced things so unheard of and so staggering that the question of whether such things [a theology of retribution] are in any way reconcilable with the idea of a good God has become burningly topical."

The angel's next move has the tenor of a revelation about to burst forth, and it is reminiscent of the most momentous moment of revelation in the OT (Exod. 19:16–20): **And the angel took the censer and filled it with the fire from the altar, and he threw it on the earth; and there was thunder, and booming voices, and flashes of lightning, and an earthquake** (8:5; cf. 4:5; 11:19; 16:17–18).

### The First Six Trumpets (8:6–9:21)

#### The First Four Trumpets (8:6–13)

**8:6–13. And the seven angels who had the seven trumpets made themselves ready to blow them** (8:6). Readers can reciprocate by getting ready to look and listen. By way of repetition, among questions that ought to be asked are the following: What is happening when the trumpets are blown: is it good or bad? Who executes the action? Are there oddities or idiosyncrasies in the sequence? Does the re-reader have advantages by being aware of matters that appear later in Revelation? What can the verbs tell us, whether at the level of simple description or by way of the larger theme of Revelation? Are there allusions to the OT that need to be mined in their original context to help unlock the message?

The events unfolding upon the blowing of the first trumpet are bad (8:7). For this scene, the link to the Exodus plagues is tenuous. Intensifying elements

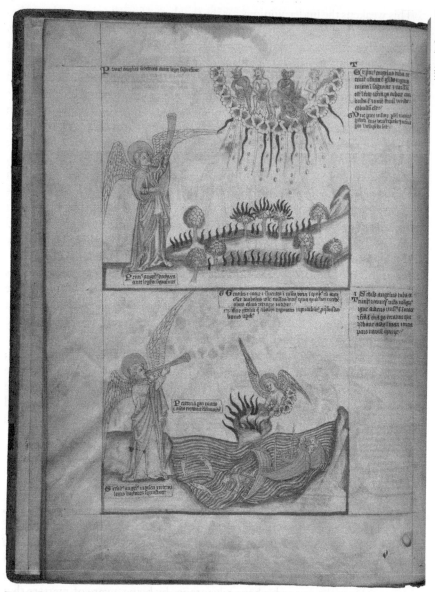

Figure 14. This ancient and anonymous depiction of the first trumpet sees (1) a bad action and (2) a demonic agent.

suggest a sinister power at work. **Hail and fire mixed with blood** (8:7) are no ordinary concoction, and divine agency is not the explanation that should first come to mind.

Who, then, executes the action, given that all the important verbs are in the passive voice? The brew of "hail and fire mixed with blood" suggests devastation, with "fire" as the dominant feature. It results in **a third of the earth, a third of the trees, and all the green grass** being reduced to ashes. The text has its share of oddities or idiosyncrasies, none more enigmatic than the curious **third** (8:7). This fraction of the whole will be mentioned a full thirteen times in the trumpet sequence, fourteen if an implied mention is included (8:7, 8, 9, 10, 12; 9:15, 18), to which must be added a single occurrence in chapter 12 (12:4). What does it mean? Does the "third" have a *quantitative* function, the most obvious meaning, or is it better understood in a symbolic, *qualitative* sense?

A re-reader perspective will prefer the second option. In chapter 12, Revelation describes "a great red dragon, with seven heads and ten horns" (12:3). This is an obvious reference to Satan, who is a dominant figure in the chapter. John says of the "great red dragon" that "his tail dragged along a *third* of the stars of heaven and threw [*ebalen*] them to the earth" (12:4). The curious "third" is here, too! It is tempting to regard it as a measure of quantity, but *quantity* is a moot point. Of all the "thirds" in Revelation, the most important "third" is here, when the dragon's tail drags heavenly beings with him (12:4). When this text is admitted as the key to understanding why the trumpet sequence never stops talking about "a third" (8:7, 8, 9, 10, 12; 9:15, 18), the issue will be *agency*, not *quantity*. By the time the trumpet sequence has gone through all its "thirds," the notion of quantity has all but vanished.

What else? Putting re-reader insight to further use, the verbs burst with explanatory power. John says that "there came hail and fire mixed with blood" at the first trumpet, and it ***was thrown*** [*eblēthē*] **to the earth** (8:7). "Heaven" is not mentioned, but a movement from heaven to earth is evident. In chapter 12, John describes the action of the dragon on the "stars of heaven": he "threw [*ebalen*] them to the earth" (12:4). Still on the same subject, John writes that "war broke out in heaven" (12:7). The war had a winner and a loser: "The great dragon *was thrown out* [*eblēthē*], that ancient serpent, who is called the Mudslinger and Satan, the deceiver of the whole world—he *was thrown* [*eblēthē*] to the earth, and his angels *were thrown out* [*eblēthēsan*] with him" (12:9). The verb of interest in these verses is *ballō*, occurring a full five times in the texts above. This verb has two nuances that are relevant to the subject. First, it means "to cause to move from one location to another through use of forceful motion, *throw*." Second, it means "to force out of or into a place, *throw (away), drive out, expel*" (BDAG 163–64, βάλλω). John's verb depicts something or someone having to relocate from heaven to earth by "forceful motion"; the "someone" in question is *driven out* and *expelled*. This is language symbolic for *conflict*. The dragon and the stars of heaven are "thrown out" (12:4, 9). The same type of action applies to "hail and fire mixed with blood" in the trumpet sequence (8:7). The latter are part of the "throwing out" of "the Mudslinger" (12:9) and the reason for the terrible distress that afflicts the earth (12:12). God has a hand in expelling and exposing "the Mudslinger," but the reality that follows in his wake is authentically the work of God's opponent. Wherever he moves, destruction and mayhem follow. "Hail and fire mixed with blood" are apt metaphors for demonic activity.

Revelation's interest in stars falling from heaven to earth (12:3–6), the notion of combat (12:7–9), and the terror befalling the earth (12:10–12) has OT antecedents that provide "background" and magnify the cosmic, nonhuman character at the center of the conflict. These texts are already explicit in Revelation's depiction of the third (8:10–11) and fifth (9:1–11) trumpets. No text of this kind is more important than Isaiah's poem about "the Shining One" (Isa. 14:12–20; K. Schmidt 1951; A. Collins 1979, 81–82; Graham 2001, 161–79). This poem has been praised for its exquisite literary qualities (Skinner 1915, 120; Kaiser 1974, 29), befitting the idea that when the prophets wanted to say something really important, their idiom was poetry.

> How you are fallen [*exepesen*] from heaven,
> O Most Brilliant Star, son of the Morning!
> How you are cut down [*synetribē*] to the ground,
> you who weakened the nations!
> You said in your heart,
> "I will ascend to heaven;
> I will raise my throne above the stars of God;
> I will sit on the mount of the heavenly council
> on the heights of the Far North;
> I will rise up to the tops of the clouds,
> I will make myself like the Most High."
> But you are brought down to Hades,
> to the utmost depths of the Death Hole. (Isa. 14:12–15, my trans.)

The character at the center of this text became Lucifer in Jerome's Latin translation and has remained Lucifer ever since, but the description in Isaiah highlights the character's exceptional brilliance: *He is the star that can be seen in broad daylight.* He aspires to traverse the divide between created reality and the Creator: *I will make myself like the Most High* (Isa. 14:14). All the aspirations have an upward trajectory—"*ascend . . . raise above . . . rise up*"—and the pinnacle at the top has many names: "*heaven . . . the stars of God . . . the mount of the heavenly council . . . the heights of the Far North . . . the tops of the clouds.*" The initial movement is *ascent* and self-exaltation toward a goal that is preposterous, unmerited, and out of reach. The final movement is *descent*, the character not going to the highest heaven but to earth and then descending further into the Death Hole (Isa. 14:15). If we look at the verbs used for the character's descent, including their metaphorical meaning, they picture someone who is collapsing and imploding. He has *fallen,* to be sure, but he has not fallen only in a spatial sense. His ambition has caved in and collapsed upon him, as a character who *shrinks* or *shrivels* (Isa. 14:12; *HALOT* 709–11, נפל). The "shattering" connotes someone who fractures and dissolves into pieces. The Greek translation resorts to the word "send" (*apostellō*), suggesting a subversive character going forth on a mission of malice to the nations of the earth (Isa. 14:12). Hans Wildberger (1978, 550) notes perceptively that "war" lies behind his expulsion from heaven. Isaiah's language is not irenic in English, but translation mutes the intensity of the struggle. The character that is "cut down" has not surrendered willingly (Isa. 14:12, 15). Lucifer "must have been involved in a severe struggle" (Wildberger 1978, 552–53).

The second trumpet is fully as bad as what preceded it (8:8–9), the circle of calamity expanding. Who is doing the terrible things remains the most important question. Are we witnessing divine retribution or another scene of *revelation,* an action that combines *expulsion* and *exposé?* Everything favors the second option. Craig R. Koester (2014, 499) says helpfully that the fiery mountain "can best be understood as a star." What seems like an object behaves like a subject—the "enormous mountain" needs to be personified to get it right. Again, the critical verb "throw" returns with the enigmatic "thirds." The bringer of calamity **was thrown** [*eblēthē*] **into the sea**—inflicting death and devastation on **a third of the sea, . . . a third of the creatures, . . . and a third of the ships** (8:8–9). Repetition and hyperbole nudge readers away from a preoccupation with quantity to a recognition of agency. Jeremiah's "destroying mountain" in the OT is less consequential than Revelation's "enormous mountain," but its tenor is useful. "I am against you, O destroying mountain, says the LORD, that destroys the whole earth; I will stretch out my hand against you, and roll you down from the crags, and make you a burned-out mountain" (Jer. 51:25).

**And the third angel blew his trumpet, and an enormous star fell** [*epesen*] **from heaven, burning like a torch** (Rev. 8:10). From here on, the "who" question gets easier. A "star" was thinly veiled as an "enormous mountain" in the second trumpet (8:8), but the veil is coming off. In the third trumpet, the star conforms to its representation in the OT, a glorious, "enormous star" (8:10; Isa. 14:12). **And it fell** [*epesen*] **on a third of the rivers and on the sources of water,** says John (Rev. 8:10). The "fall" has a spatial dimension, from heaven to earth, but the "fall" is also moral and existential. A star that was brilliant for its capacity to illuminate (Isa. 14:12) is now the agent of slash-and-burn on the earth, the verb in question doing double duty with respect to burning as a source of light and burning in the sense of "burning up" (BDAG 499, καίω). "Flaming out" is an appropriate term. Isaiah's brilliant star "fell," on the one hand, and was "cut down," on the other (Isa. 14:12–15). These are two sides of the same reality, "fell" describing the star's activity with respect to itself and "cut down" its fate in relation to others.

## Avalanche of "Thirds" in the Trumpet Sequence

**First trumpet**  "a *third* of the earth . . . a *third* of the trees" (8:7)

**Second trumpet**  "a *third* of the sea . . . a *third* of the living creatures . . . a *third* of the ships" (8:8)

**Third trumpet**  "a *third* of the waters" (8:10)

**Fourth trumpet**  "a *third* of the sun . . . a *third* of the moon . . . a *third* of the stars . . . a *third* of their light . . . a *third* of the day and likewise the night" (8:12)

**Sixth trumpet**  "a *third* of humanity . . . a *third* of humanity" (9:15, 18)

And the name of the star is Wormwood [*Apsinthos*]. And a third of the waters became wormwood, and many people died from the water, because it was made poisonous (8:11). More "thirds" drive home the demonic identity. The star poisons "a third of the rivers" and "a third of the waters" (8:10–11). This can be construed in material and ecological terms, as a blighting influence on the earth, and this option should not be dismissed. But the reference to "sources of water" has spiritual overtones (8:10). Water and light carry spiritual meanings in the OT, and in the NT they are characteristic of the Gospel of John (3:5; 4:10, 13; 7:38; 19:34). Water is now degraded and poisoned—curiously—by a falling star. "Wormwood" had a medicinal use in the treatment of intestinal worms but was not lethal to humans (BDAG 161, ἀψίνθιον). However, the taste was proverbially bitter. Revelation's depiction has two consequences. Water is degraded to become unfit for human consumption. *This* water is lethal even though wormwood normally is not. But "Wormwood" is now a surname; the falling star is Mr. Wormwood, and his errand in the world is to make water undrinkable and toxic. Recalling the information available to the re-reader, the "third of the rivers" and the "third of the waters" shall henceforth signify agency rather than quantity (8:10–11).

The world of the trumpets is increasingly in a bad shape, and things are about to get even worse. And the fourth angel blew his trumpet, and a third of the sun was struck [*eplēgē*], and a third of the moon, and a third of the stars, so that a third of their light was darkened [*skotisthē*]; a third of the day did not appear, and likewise the night (8:12). Water, physical and spiritual, is degraded in the wake of the third trumpet. Now comes the turn to damage the sources of light. The "thirds" come thicker and faster than ever, affecting entities that normally cannot be quantified in such terms: "a third of the sun," "a third of the moon," and "a third of the stars" are easier to comprehend than "a third of their light" or "a third of the day." Who is capable of such feats? Notions of divine agency are in retreat, and the Roman Empire is too small for this type of impact. *The world is getting darker,* and the dimming of the light affects "the night" as much as "the day." A legitimate variant will say, intriguingly, that "a third of the day did not appear." By this criterion, time itself is contracting, not only the light.

**And I looked, and I heard a vulture [*aetou*] crying with a loud voice as it flew in midheaven, "Woe, woe, woe to the inhabitants of the earth, at the blasts of the other trumpets that the three angels are about to blow!"** (8:13). The cry of the vulture adds to the apprehension and terror. While it is possible to perceive the vulture as "an eagle," the darkness and desolation that blight the world turn it into a landscape of death and the home of vultures. In this landscape, the cry of the vulture will be heard as fearsome, bone-chilling shrieks (cf. 19:17–18). The tiny word "woe" should not be overlooked (8:13; 9:12; 11:14; 12:12), although its full significance will not sink in until later. At the point when Satan realizes his defeat, we hear the "woe" that electrifies all the other woes (12:12). The re-reader is aware of this "woe" upstream in the text even though the trumpet sequence precedes it in the narrative. When we adjust the woes to the appropriate English idiom, the ill-omened shriek of the vulture echoes from midheaven, How awful! How awful! How awful! (Rossing 2005, 168). Readers are advised to brace for the worse that is to come.

### The Fifth and Sixth Trumpets (9:1–21)

**9:1–12.** *Fifth trumpet.* The trumpets have so far been bad, the "badness" intensifying qualitatively and expanding quantitatively (8:7–12). When "the sun" and "the moon" and "the stars" are struck under the fourth trumpet (8:12), the cosmic scope is evident.

But the text has made the greatest strides with respect to the "by whom" question. What little additional proof may be needed will be presented in less enigmatic terms in the fifth and sixth trumpets (9:1–19). Here, the announcements are much longer, far more detailed, the language more overwrought, and the echoes of the OT louder than ever.

**And the fifth angel blew his trumpet, and I saw a star that had fallen [*peptōkota*] from heaven to earth, and the key to the shaft of the bottomless pit was given [*edothē*] to him** (9:1). The fifth trumpet continues a teaching method suitable for kindergarten and slow learners. No stone will be left unturned with respect to the "by whom" question. It is as if the storehouse of images has been emptied, requiring reuse and recycling. Alternatively, the storehouse has a favorite that must be called upon more than once because it is the most representative image. At the third trumpet, "an enormous star fell [*epesen*] from heaven" (8:10). The fifth trumpet plays from the same music sheet, except that the temporal perspective is now a completed action with lasting consequences for the present: "had fallen."

**Fallen Star: Echoes of Isaiah**

| Isaiah 14:12–20 | Revelation 9:1–11 |
| --- | --- |
| great star | great star |
| heaven | heaven |
| fierce struggle | fierce struggle |
| fallen (ejection) | fallen (ejection) |
| earth | earth |
| pit | pit |
| destroyer | destroyer |

Even more important, the perfect tense conveys the *entirety* of the completed action. On this logic, we have the run-up to the "fall" of the star, the circumstances surrounding the actual "fall," and the lasting consequences now that the star "had fallen" (9:1). These are the key ingredients relative to an object that will behave like a subject in the verses to follow. The blast of the fifth trumpet repeats the OT background story (Isa. 14:12–20), compressing most of it into one single verse (9:1).

Earlier, we prioritized the "what" question because it comes first. From here on, the "by whom" question is the consuming preoccupation. *He*, the "star that had fallen" (9:1), goes to work with ruthless determination. **He opened** [*ēnoixen*] **the shaft of the bottomless pit, and from the shaft rose smoke like the smoke of a great furnace, and the sun and the air were darkened** [*eskotōthē*] **with the smoke from the shaft** (9:2). "Solar eclipse," figuratively speaking, has already been tried (8:12), and there is more of it here. The darkness has spiritual connotations. John's word for "darkened" is in the passive voice, using third-person singular where a plural would be appropriate. But the use of the singular may not be the result of incompetence or carelessness. The passive voice veils the one causing the darkness, but the singular form makes it a see-through veil, and the first part of the sentence is in the active voice (9:2). To Mr. Wormwood at the third trumpet, we can now add Mr. Darkness, and the darkness will be so dense that it can be touched.

**And from the smoke came locusts on the earth, and they were given** [*edothē*] **authority like the authority of scorpions of the earth** (9:3). If we conceive of this as polluted air, the particles consolidate from smoke into hard matter, and the hard matter turns into living organisms—"locusts." The connotation of locusts is insufficient for the phenomenon, however, giving way to yet another metamorphosis. Suddenly "the locusts" look like "scorpions," and the "scorpions" go to work, energized by the *permission* given to them. At this stage, we are reminded that the trumpet cycle is not independent of the seven seals that preceded it. **It was said to them**—the "locusts" or "scorpions"—**not to damage the grass of the earth or any green growth or any tree, but only those people who do not have the seal of God on their foreheads** (9:4; cf.

7:1–3). This instruction must have God as its source, given that "the seal of God" protects believers from harm. Mere material or physical harm cannot be the main issue. This is a spiritual conflict that centers on perceptions and loyalties, with the stakes so high that they are represented in material terms. Revelation describes a demonic reality. Nature has no creature like this, and the scorpions known in nature do not have capabilities to inflict harm like the "scorpions of the earth" in Revelation (9:3). Scorpions may maim and kill, but these scorpions inflict protracted torture. **They were given [*edothē*] permission to torture them** [the people who do not have the seal of God] **for five months, but not to kill them, and their torture was like the torture of a scorpion when it stings someone** (9:5). Neither by anatomical nor by physiological criteria can one find a creature that behaves like the one coming to view. An agent that takes pleasure in torturing without offering death as a way out takes a precise measure of the demonic, whether we think of the demonic in terms of worldview, doctrine, or character. **And in those days people will seek death, and they will not find it; they will long to die, and death will flee from them** (9:6).

This would seem quite enough, but Revelation piles on even more demanding metamorphoses. Did not "smoke" turn into "locusts"? Did not the "locusts" transform themselves into "scorpions"? How bizarre will this get? **In appearance the locusts were like horses made ready to go to war [*eis polemon*]** (9:7). Cosmic war has raged all along, and the parties are bracing for the final showdown. For evil to appear in all its horrors, the "smoke" turned "locusts" turned "scorpions" turned "horses" are further embellished. **And on their heads there were what looked like crowns of gold; and their faces were like human faces, and they had hair like women's hair, and their teeth were like lions' teeth; and they had scales like iron breastplates, and the noise of their wings was like the noise of many chariots with horses rushing to war [*eis polemon*]** (9:8–9). What are these creatures now, a composite of "smoke," "locusts," "scorpions," and "horses"? Even the most accomplished artist will have a hard time drawing it. "Human face," "women's hair," "lions' teeth," "iron breastplates," "wings"—we will not find this horse in the nearest zoo; its mix of human and animal attributes is meant to show its demonic character. "Crowns of gold" on the one hand, "rushing to war" on the other—both features indicating that the demonic side is dedicated to winning or, at the very least, able to pose as a winner. "Scorpions" have tails, but now "they," meaning the horses, **have tails like scorpions, with stingers, and in their tails is their power to harm [*adikēsai*] people for five months!** (9:10).

"Tails" will resurface as an anatomic detail of interest when the battle is joined under the sixth trumpet (9:19). For now, Revelation has assembled a stockpile of evidence as to the identity of the leader of this infernal army, and it is ready to name names. **They have as king over them the angel of the bottomless pit; his name in Hebrew is Abaddon, and in Greek he has the name**

**Apollyon** (9:11). "They"—meaning the "smoke" turned "locusts" turned "scorpions" turned "horses" with "human faces," "women's hair," "lions' teeth," and "tails like scorpions"—have a leader. Translators mean well by not giving the English for the Hebrew and Greek name given to "the angel," but we cannot leave it untranslated here. His name in both Hebrew and Greek is **Destroyer** (9:11). Revelation's kindergarten pedagogy might be useful even for sophisticated readers. With Isaiah as the background text for this "star" and this "angel," John has hit the nail on the head. In Isaiah's funeral dirge, the final stanza runs like this:

> You will not be joined with them
> in burial,
> because you have *destroyed* [*apōlesas*]
> your land,
> you have killed [*apekteinas*]
> your people. (Isa. 14:20; cf. Rev. 9:11)

This is what it does—it destroys and kills. And how does it end? We can hardly avoid the impression that the destruction that is at work also entails self-destruction.

The first "how awful" has come and gone. There are still two "how awfuls" to come (9:12).

**9:13–21.** *Sixth trumpet.* **And the sixth angel blew his trumpet, and I heard a voice from the four horns of the golden altar before God, saying to the sixth angel who had the trumpet, "Release the four angels who are bound at the great river Euphrates"** (9:13–14). The "four angels" must be related to, or identical with, the "four angels" who were mentioned in relation to the sealing (7:2). Instruction to restrain now becomes direction to let go of restraint. "Euphrates" is a new element. It will reappear in exactly the same language in the sixth bowl (16:12). A process coming to completion is suggested in both places (9:14; 16:12). Again, the altar seems to be speaking (9:13), as though heaven is a place of thoroughgoing sentience (Aune 1996–98, 536; Koester 2014, 465).

Revelation does not teach determinism (Mazzaferri 1989, 382–83), but it views reality through the lens of hidden aims and intentions. A *purpose* is at work in the world, and the purpose is so unwavering that it can be condensed into a point in time. **And the four angels were released, who had been made ready for the hour, the day, the month, and the year, in order to [*hina*] kill a third of humankind** (9:15). The word translated "in order to" can also be translated "so that" or "with the result that" (BDAG 475–77, ἵνα). *Readiness* is an indicator of intent, and the intent at this point has two sides: readiness on the part of God to see *God's* purpose brought to completion, and readiness on the part of the adversary. The restraint that is loosened applies to the battle readiness of "the Destroyer," who commands "many chariots with horses rushing to war" (9:9). The war will not suddenly collapse into single agency and unified command. David E. Aune's (1996–98, 537) view is needlessly confusing: "These are angels of punishment whose task it is to lead a demonic army to punish the people of the world." Again, the armies of good, presumably the "angels of punishment," are not likely to cooperate with "a demonic army" for the purpose of inflicting punishment on the world. As earlier in the trumpet sequence, *revelation* is the key word, not punishment.

The hyper-particularity of the time element is startling: "the hour, the day, the month, and the year" (9:15). It does not say which date from which to start the reckoning or which date at which to end it. We are left with certainty of intent, not a date on the calendar. Much has happened since John wrote Revelation, but he operates with quantities that suffice for us as much as for the first century. Armies are far larger now than when Roman and Parthian armies fought each other, but nothing like *this* army has ever been seen. **The number of the troops of cavalry was two hundred million; I heard their number** (9:16). "Two hundred million horses and two hundred million riders" are less an army than the swarm of "locusts" and "scorpions" that John described earlier (9:3). By responsible estimates, the population of the whole earth was about two hundred million at the time when Revelation was written. A demonic reality needs a number to match its subject. "I heard their number," John adds, as if to make sure that we do not think him guilty of exaggeration.

John's earlier description of the demonic horde seems enough to fill an Encyclopedia of Overwrought Imagery to overflowing (9:3–9), but there is more. **And this is how I saw the horses in my vision and those sitting on them: they had breastplates of fire and of sapphire and of sulfur; the heads of the horses were like lions' heads, and out of their mouths came fire and smoke and sulfur** (9:17). No one has seen horses like these. In an ordinary army, the rider is more important than the horse: *the rider is the warrior, not the horse.* In this army, the horse is fiercer than its rider. Rider and horse together deal in the same currency. "Fire" and "sulfur" characterize the rider, but the horses do it better: they have "lions' heads, and fire and smoke and sulfur came out of their mouths" (9:17). Detail work pays off. Does it need to be said that all hell is loose—and mean it—or that this is a demonic reality? **By these three plagues a third of humanity was killed, by the fire and smoke and sulfur coming out of their mouths** (9:18). The "three plagues" are "fire and smoke and sulfur," all of them elements in the toolbox of Satan. Overwrought particularity, including a pointed "hour" in the shapeless flow of time (9:15), suddenly shifts to subtler implements. The detail that attracts attention is "their mouths," repeated three times in the span of three verses (9:17–19). "Their mouths" control the conflagration, and the mouth is part of a larger story. **For the power of the horses is in their mouths and in their tails; their tails are like serpents** [*homoiai ophesin*]**, having heads, and with them they inflict harm** (9:19). What leaps of memory and imagination! These "horses" have "heads" at both ends, in the front, where there should be one, and "in their tails," normally not a body part where a head would be expected. "Their tails," in turn, "are like serpents," with "heads" and "mouths" and all. *Like serpents!* The verbal jolt is high voltage. The dots connect to the serpent in Genesis (Gen. 3:1), but it is best to reach Genesis by way of *"the Ancient Serpent"* in Revelation (12:9; 20:2). The antagonist in the cosmic conflict may breathe "fire and smoke and sulfur" in Revelation's exposé; he may acquire chameleon characteristics— "locusts" one day, "scorpions" another day, then "horses"—but he never lets go of his core identity. The sting of the serpent is related to its mouth, and the poison spewing forth is not snake venom but *words* (Gen. 3:1). David E. Aune's (1996–98, 540) link to the fire-breathing Leviathan in Job is well taken, a link that strengthens if we recognize that Leviathan is no ordinary animal any more than are the sulfur-breathing "horses" in Revelation (Tonstad 2016a, 256–61).

> From its mouth go flaming torches;
> sparks of fire leap out.
> Out of its nostrils comes smoke,
> as from a boiling pot and burning rushes.
> Its breath kindles coals,
> and a flame comes out of its mouth. (Job 41:19–21)

Six trumpets have passed, all of them an exposé of demonic activity. With respect to bringing about a change in perceptions and allegiances, the reader of the exposé is wiser, but the result is otherwise disappointing (9:20–21). We had probably expected more, a repudiation of Mr. Wormwood (8:12) and Mr. Darkness (9:1–11) and everything he represents, but this is what we have. Can anything be done to turn things around?

### Digression (10:1–11:14)

#### Mission (10:1–11)

**10:1–11.** It will be a while before "the seventh angel" blows the last of the seven trumpets (11:15). The "pause" is conspicuous, and it parallels the long delay between the sixth and the seventh seals (7:1–17). In neither case is there a lull in the action, but the structure is remarkable. Various terms and explanations have been proposed, with "digression" claiming strong support (Perry 2009, 39–52). While there is no time-out with respect to action, there is a time-out for thought. The narrative is momentarily diverted to clarify the needs and obligations of the believing community. In the sequence of the seals, the digression concerns the need for *protection* and *readiness* (7:1–8, 13–17). In the trumpet sequence, the digression between the sixth and the seventh trumpets emphasizes *mission* and *method* (10:1–11; 11:1–14). The believing community may be under siege, but it will not face the world in a state of passivity, resignation, or withdrawal. "These interludes are not so much pauses in the actual sequence of events as they are literary devices by which the church is instructed concerning its role and destiny during the final period of world history" (Mounce 1977, 205).

*Mission* is in the body language of the figure next to appear. **And I saw another mighty angel coming down from heaven, clothed in a cloud, with the rainbow around his head; and his face was like the sun, and his legs like pillars of fire** (10:1).

Appearance and importance must be two sides of the same coin. By this logic, this figure is a Very Important Person. The splendor approximates that of a divine being (Beale 1999, 522). Here, the description of the angel conflates elements used in the description of the human *and* angelic figure in Daniel (10:5–6; 12:6–9) and the risen Jesus in the first vision in Revelation (1:13–15; cf. J. Collins 1974; Rowland 1980; 1985; Gieschen 1998). The stature of the figure is matched by the importance of his errand. **And he had a little opened scroll** [*biblaridion ēneōgmenon*] **in his hand** (10:2). The scroll is the medium of a message; it is "opened" (10:2); it must be internalized (10:8–9); and it must be proclaimed (10:11). But what is the message?

| **The Seven Trumpets** |
| --- |
| **Mediation and prayer (8:2–5)** |
| **The first six trumpets (8:6–9:21)** |
| **Digression (10:1–11:14)** |
|   Mission (10:1–11) |
|   Method (11:1–14) |
| **The Seventh Trumpet (11:15–19)** |

We have three main options for the meaning of the scroll. First, it could be the "scroll written on the inside and on the back and sealed with seven seals" that we encountered in the heavenly council (10:2; 5:1), as Richard Bauckham argues (1993a, 243–57). In support of this view, we have a candidate scroll in the preceding chapters in Revelation; it has been opened; it resembles the scroll in Ezekiel (2:9–10), whose scroll, like the scroll in Revelation, is to be *eaten* (Ezek. 3:1–3; Rev. 10:9–10). On the other hand, the absence of the definite article is puzzling, precisely because Revelation has featured "a scroll" and made it the crux of the crisis in the heavenly council (5:1–8). If this is the same scroll, it should be "*the* scroll"; indeed, it should be "*the* opened scroll" and not simply "a scroll." Moreover, while the "mighty angel" is a figure of importance and the "scroll" important, too, neither the angel nor the scroll seem to be at the level of "the slaughtered Lamb" and "the scroll" in the heavenly council (5:5–7). *That* scroll seems henceforth inseparable from "the Lamb," and its errand is already brought to completion (P. Müller 2005, 303–4). This is especially true if the "mighty angel" must be distinguished from Jesus.

As a second alternative, therefore, the "scroll" (*biblaridion*) in the hands of the "mighty angel" is *not* the same as the "scroll" (*biblion*) before the heavenly council. To Leslie Baynes (2010b, 806–15), the latter corresponds best to the flying scroll in Zechariah (5:1–4), and the scroll in the hand of the "mighty angel" is the scroll in Ezekiel (2:8–3:3). The command to eat the scroll (Ezek.

3:1–3; Rev. 10:9–10) and significant patristic support in the writings of Origen and Oecumenius favor this view (Baynes 2010b, 806–15).

The third option draws upon the link between Daniel and Revelation.

1. Similar appearance of the angel in Revelation and the counterpart in Daniel (Rev. 10:1; Dan. 10:5–6; 12:6–9)
2. Strikingly similar stance, body language, and speech (Rev. 10:2–3; Dan. 12:6–7)
3. Focus on *time* and progression in time: in Daniel, a distant future; in Revelation, imminence (Rev. 10:6–7; Dan. 12:9, 13)
4. Progression from a message that will remain "secret [*katakekalym-mena*] and sealed [*esphragismena*] until the time of the end" in Daniel to "a little *opened* scroll" and a message no longer "secret and sealed" in Revelation (Rev. 10:2, 7, 11; Dan. 12:9)

In fact, Daniel ends with a scroll being rolled up and sealed (Dan. 12:4; cf. Rev. 22:10). Bauckham (1993a, 251) captures the movements from distant future to imminence and from "secret" to disclosure when he writes that "Daniel wrote for an eschatological future that was far distant from him, that same eschatological future now impinged directly on John and his readers." Likewise, "while Daniel's visions were to be kept secret until the time to which they applied, John's were to be made public at once" (Bauckham 1993a, 251). The arguments against this view, if any, relate to nuances more than to substantive objections. One implication of these links is not only that there is a forward movement in time but also a sense of time's compression: "*time [chronos] is no longer*" (10:6).

The "classified" information, nondisclosure of **the seven thunders**, is a striking exception to Revelation's policy of complete transparency (10:2–4). What could be the reason for nondisclosure? Revelation reveals all that is necessary to know but not necessarily all there is to know. In the same vein, knowing comes with benefits but also with risks; it can allay anxiety but also aggravate it, like an abnormal laboratory test of uncertain significance in the doctor's office. The nondisclosure of the message of "the seven thunders" may belong to a category of things best left unsaid.

On the other hand, the exception to policy might actually improve vigilance and enhance interest in what follows (10:5–7). The importance of **the angel** is not lessened by his posture, the solemn oath, and the credentials of the One in whose name the oath is taken. In a cosmic conflict perspective, the reminder that God **created the *heaven* and what is in it** (10:6) restores perspective to the aspiration of the heavenly being who made it his goal to cross the divide between the Creator and created reality (Isa. 14:12–15). God is the Creator of all things, including things and beings in heaven. Daniel's (12:7) depiction of the "man clothed in linen" is reflected in John's description of "the angel," and the connection is noteworthy for the shared interest in time and a process brought to completion: **then will be brought to completion the mystery of God, in line with the good news announced to God's servants the prophets** (10:7; Dan. 12:7–9). **No more time** may be read as "no more delay," as in the NRSV (Rev. 10:6), but the options are complementary and not mutually exclusive. From the perspective of prolonged waiting and unmet expectations (6:9–11), "no more delay" is reassuring, but if the concern is that God's purpose may be frustrated by contingencies in time, "no more *time*" is better. "The mystery of God" awaiting completion is a concept introduced by Daniel (Dan. 2:18, 19, 27, 30, 47). *God* is the subject of "the mystery of God," and "the mystery" cannot be accessed by any other means than God's self-disclosure. In this regard, the role of "God's servants the prophets" is not minor. Revelation affirms the importance of the OT voices, and the link goes beyond the relationship between promise and fulfillment. At the deepest level, these voices hold in common that God is committed to transparency and accountability: "the Lord GOD does nothing, without revealing [*apokalypsē*] his teaching to his servants the prophets" (Amos 3:7 LXX, my trans.; Paul 1991, 113).

At this point things get personal, and the name for it is *mission* (10:8–10). The imagery of taking the scroll and eating it goes back to Ezekiel (3:3), "'Mortal, eat this scroll that I give you and fill your stomach with it.' Then I ate it; and in my mouth it was as sweet as honey." If the scroll represents a message, as seems certain, eating it suggests appropriation of the message. Walther Zimmerli (1979, 1:136) sees it as an "act of ordination," in which case commission and readiness for mission become explicit. This thought is echoed by Craig R. Koester (2014, 482), who takes eating the scroll to mean "empowerment to communicate God's word." The call to mission is made enticing by the thought that "the sweet taste of honey refers to the emotions of joy and delight" (Aune 1996–98, 572). Thus far Ezekiel—and so far, so good.

In Revelation, however, sweetness is short-lived, and "joy and delight" will be, too. **When I had eaten it, my stomach was made bitter**, says John (Rev. 10:10). Bitterness stands in contrast to sweetness. By this criterion, "emotions of joy and delight" turn to feelings of grief and disappointment. The passage suggests an experience beginning with commission, then delight, then grief, and then renewed commission (10:8–11). Ezekiel hints at this possibility (Ezek. 3:14; cf. Charles 1920, 1:268), but it is explicit in Revelation. The disappointment could be so severe that it spells the end of the mission. The path from joy to dejection might be intrinsic to mission on the logic that "God's purposes will be accomplished in part through the suffering and witness of his people" (Koester 2014, 483). While this cannot be ruled out, it is prudent to ask whether the scroll that has been consumed has explanatory power for John's experience. Whether we see it as the "scroll . . . sealed with seven seals" (5:1) or as the "little opened scroll" (10:2) that might be the book of Daniel (Dan. 12:7–9), there are reasons to wonder whether elements specific to these books precipitate an experience where joy turns to disappointment. It is not necessary to answer this question conclusively to understand the recommission at the point when "the little opened scroll" turns bitter in the stomach. **And they [pl.] said to me, "You *must* [*dei*] proclaim again the inspired revelation, addressing it to many peoples and nations and languages and kings"** (10:11; BDAG 890, προφητεύω).

Details abound here, too, one in the form of proclaiming "*again.*" The commission suggests a vocation that is to be resumed or a message that needs to be repeated. The latter possibility, taken as a command to John to repeat the message one more time, turns the digression in Rev. 10:1–11:13 into a major suture line in the book (M. Hall 2002, 278–96). If John embarks on a retelling that compasses the rest of the book, rereading is built into the literary structure. Nevertheless, it seems more likely that the call to "proclaim again" happens in the context of disappointment. The recommission has the force of *necessity*, necessity welded to the fact that time is running out and proclamation is therefore more urgent than ever (10:6, 11). The call to mission is certain and explicit (10:11; cf. 14:6). Revelation now turns to the question of method (11:1–14).

### Method (11:1–14)

**11:1–14.** On the surface, a whole new topic is introduced that appears to have little relation to the preceding subject. **And a measuring rod like a staff was given to me with the instruction, "Get up and measure the temple of God and the altar and those who worship there. But the court outside the temple—leave that out and do not measure it because it has been given to the nations, and they will trample the holy city for forty-two months"** (11:1–2).

The material and architectural elements—what to "measure" and what to leave out—include "the temple of God," "the altar," "the court outside the temple," and "the holy city" (11:1–2). All the terms have the definite article, suggesting that they do not need to be explained. The commission to "measure," first (11:1), "and do not measure," second (11:2), require a figurative reading (contra Siew 2005, 89–107). Normally inanimate "things" may in Revelation be animated and sentient, as suggested when the altar is heard *speaking* later in the book (16:7). A similar logic is likely for all the items about to be measured. Among the material elements, "the holy city" is the easiest to locate. Unless the reference here is an exception, "the holy city" is the favorite term for "the New Jerusalem" (3:12; 11:2; 20:9; 21:2, 10, 15; 22:19). In a conversation about earthly real estate, the three most important things are "location, location, location." This priority works for spiritual real estate, too.

John will see "the holy city, the New Jerusalem, coming down out of heaven from God, groomed as a bride made beautiful for her husband" (21:2; cf. 21:10; 3:12). This city has its spatial point of origin in heaven, but its ultimate

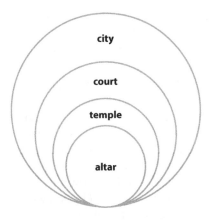

Figure 15. This diagram shows the demarcations of space in Revelation 11. Notice the expanding spheres, with the sphere at the center diffusing into all the other spheres.

destination is the earth (21:1–4). Talk about animation is not misplaced: a city "groomed as a bride" is made of people and not of brick and mortar (Gundry 1987). Yet again key elements belonging to the ending of the story appear earlier, without being fully explained. Moreover, "the holy city" is the largest spatial or architectural entity in the text, larger than "the temple of God," "the altar," or "the court outside the temple."

"Measure" is a key verb in the passage. But the two other verbs are equally important, and they contrast sharply. John speaks of those who "worship" and those who "trample" (11:1, 2). Their stances could not be more different, one group in a posture of reverence and the other in an attitude of deliberate disrespect. Those who "worship" belong to the inner circle: they worship *there*, by "the altar" (11:1). A line of demarcation may be imagined between "the temple" and "the court outside the temple," setting the inner circle apart from the rest. The forceful order regarding "the court outside" (*exōthen*), telling John to "throw it outside" (*ekbalē exōthen*), suggests a well-defined boundary line. However, if "the holy city" is the outermost perimeter, compassing all the others, we have the prospect that those who "trample" have no qualms about trampling all over the place—and do.

Physical space cannot be the chief concern despite the materiality of the language. The distinction between heaven and earth blurs, too. Those who "worship there," worship at an altar located in "the holy city" in heaven, and those who "trample" encroach on the same space. Only by animating the space is the incongruity resolved. People are divided between those who "worship" and those who "trample": they are the sole categories of interest. The plight of the worshiping group is elsewhere attributed to "slander," a form of "trampling" that covers misrepresentation of the God in whom people believe and of those who believe (13:6). Such "trampling" is first mentioned in Daniel, where "the sanctuary" (i.e., "temple") and "host" (i.e., "those who worship there") are "trampled" (Dan. 8:13), as they are in Revelation (11:2). "Trampling" is by this logic a form of disrespect and contempt.

This background makes it easier to understand the command to "*measure the temple of God*" while also specifying to "leave out" and "*not* measure . . . the court outside the temple" (11:1–2). A person who is *trampled* needs protection. This is the first and best option for what it means to "measure the temple of God" (Aune 1996–98, 604). However, protection does not stop the trampling. It follows that "those who worship" *are protected even though they are trampled*. In the melee of being trampled, it is difficult to tell who is who. *Measuring* takes care of that: God knows who is who, and "those who worship" are known to God. Koester (2014, 483–84) puts it well, if we assume that trampling is not taken out of the equation: "Measuring will define the place where true worship takes place and show that it is protected."

Two OT passages further illuminate this text. First, we have a long vision in Ezekiel that begins like this: "When he brought me there, a man was there, whose appearance shone like bronze, with a linen cord and a measuring reed in his hand; and he was standing in the gateway" (Ezek. 40:3). This text expands in the next eight chapters into a vision of restoration that includes sacred space, people, and God's presence (43:1–13), climaxing in a spectacular vision of healing (47:1–12).

Second, Zechariah belongs to the background material and may, in fact, be even more important.

> I looked up and saw a man with a measuring line in his hand. Then I asked, "Where are you going?" He answered me, "To measure Jerusalem, to see what is its width and what is its length." Then the angel who talked with me came forward, and another angel came forward to meet him, and said to him, "Run, say to that young man: Jerusalem shall be inhabited like villages without walls, because of the multitude of people and animals in it. For I will be a wall of fire all around it, says the LORD, and I will be the glory within it." (Zech. 2:1–5)

To understand what it means to "measure the temple" in Revelation, we must take this text into account, especially since John's next allusion (Rev. 11:3–5) comes from the same book. In Zechariah, the focus is on interiority. The man "with a measuring line in his hand" is about to measure what cannot be measured because size and numbers and the nature of what is to be measured will defeat him (Zech. 2:3–4). The makeup of "Jerusalem" will not be objectified. It is big, to be sure, but it is also elusive. Recalling that "the holy city" is the largest and most encompassing space in Revelation (11:2), Zechariah confronts readers not with the profane intruding on sacred space—*trampling* it—but by showing that the sacred diffuses into the domain of the profane.

There can be no doubt that the sacred aspires to reclaim and take possession of all space. "Run, say to that young man" (Zech. 2:4) reflects the fear that the young man will mark off a space that is too small to accommodate what God has in mind; it will create lines of demarcation that limit more than they protect. Protection, in turn, is conceived entirely in spiritual terms by placing God as "the glory within" and as "a wall of fire all around it" (Zech. 2:5). We thus begin with a hopeful and optimistic vision for mission that outlines the means and the results already at the outset (Goldsmith 2011, 17).

Confirmation that mission and method are linked, if such confirmation is needed, will soon become certain. **"And I will entrust [dōsō] to my two witnesses to proclaim an inspired revelation for one thousand two hundred sixty days, dressed in sackcloth." These are the two olive trees and the two lampstands that stand before the Lord of the earth** (11:3–4). God commissions "two witnesses" to carry out the mission, the commission including the call and the mandate. The time period for the commission is a favorite in Revelation, "one thousand two hundred and sixty days," mentioned a number of times in more than one variant (11:2, 3; 12:6, 14; 13:5; cf. Dan. 7:25; 12:11). The meaning of this time period is contested, but we can—in this book of symbols—rule out that the period refers to literal days. Other than "forever and ever," "one thousand two hundred sixty days" (11:3; 12:6) and its variants, "forty-two months" (11:2; 13:5) and "time, times, and half a time" (12:14), is the time period most frequently mentioned.

> **Time in Revelation: First Half**
>
> Half an hour (8:1)
> Three and a half days (11:9, 11)
> Ten days (2:10)
> Five months (9:5, 10)
> The hour, the day, the month, and the year (9:15)
> Forty-two months (11:2)

Prophets are "dressed in sackcloth," not in suit and tie or other festive clothing, and the "sackcloth" is a reminder that the prophet does not see it as his/her calling to tell the world to stay the course. But the "two witnesses" are also "the two olive trees and the two lampstands" (11:3–4). We have seen "lampstands" earlier as a representation of the believing communities (1:12, 13, 20). These are genteel images, and the lampstand connection shows that the believing communities are represented as witnessing bodies. Being *two*, not one, and not seven, points back to the two olive trees in Zechariah (Zech. 4:1–6) and the figures of Moses and Elijah that will be described in greater detail (11:5–6).

> The angel who talked with me came again, and wakened me, as one is wakened from sleep. He said to me, "What do you see?" And I said, "I see a lampstand all of gold, with a bowl on the top of it; there are seven lamps on it, with seven lips on each of the lamps that are on the top of it. And by it there are two olive

163

trees, one on the right of the bowl and the other on its left." I said to the angel who talked with me, "What are these, my lord?" Then the angel who talked with me answered me, "Do you not know what these are?" I said, "No, my lord." He said to me, "This is the word of the LORD to Zerubbabel: 'Not by might, nor by power, but by my spirit, says the LORD of hosts.'" (Zech. 4:1–6)

Prophetic pedagogy cannot take anything for granted; it breaks down the lessons in small pieces. "The two olive trees" provide the supply of oil. They signify that God works in the world through witness, "not by might, nor by power." This will be spelled out in greater—albeit paradoxical—detail.

**And if anyone wants to harm them, fire goes from their mouth and consumes their enemies; if anyone wants to harm them, in this manner he must be killed** (11:5). Where is the paradox? Did we not just learn by way of "the two olive trees" that God's way is "not by might, nor by power"? How, then, can the irenic "two olive trees" and "two lampstands" suddenly turn into a fire-spewing killing machine? The easy pedagogy of the previous verse now springs a surprise. Focus is still on *method*, and the method is specific and to the point: "*in this manner he must be killed*" (11:5). There is no literal killing of enemies and no actual fire. The weapon to be used is *witness*, but the witness has the force of a consuming fire. "Is not my word like fire, says the LORD, and like a hammer that breaks a rock in pieces?" asks Jeremiah, the main source for the imagery (Jer. 23:29). "Behold, I am making my words in your mouth a fire, and this people wood, and the fire shall devour them," he says again (Jer. 5:14; cf. 20:9). Thus, "the motif of fire emanating from a person's mouth was used as a metaphor for speaking forth the word of God" (Aune 1996–98, 613). While there should be no doubt regarding the divine method—*not by might nor by power*—there should also be no doubt about its efficacy.

**These have authority to shut the heaven, in order that no rain may fall during the days of their proclamation of the revelation, and they have authority over the waters to turn them into blood, and to strike the earth with every kind of plague, as often as they wish** (Rev. 11:6). "The two witnesses" are morphing into familiar OT characters. "No rain" recalls the prophet Elijah (1 Kings 17:1). Turning water into blood recalls Moses's confrontation with Pharaoh (Exod. 7:17–21). Two of the greatest personalities of the OT appear as a team in Revelation, a "dream team" if there ever was one! Apparently, they are free to withhold rain for years on end, turn water into blood, and strike the earth "with every kind of plague"—and this "as often as they wish." This seems strikingly at odds with the ideology of the Lamb that was killed with violence (5:6) and the cry of the victims under the altar (6:9–11). Is the contrast real or only apparent? "There is no tradition that associates either Elijah or Moses with fire that comes from the mouth and destroys enemies" (Aune 1996–98, 613). Once more, John resorts to metaphor: "the two witnesses" have the *mandate* and *authority* of Moses and Elijah, but their *method* is different. What they *can* do is not what they do any more than God does what God *can* do. A scrutiny of the Moses and Elijah narratives in the OT shows that already in the original setting the stories carry within themselves the revisionary vision that is explicit in Revelation (Tonstad 2016a, 163–82; 202–16).

Victimhood is as intrinsic to their witness as it is to "the testimony of Jesus" (1:2, 9; 12:17; 19:10); it has not been eliminated by the powers that have been granted to "Moses" and "Elijah" (Herms 2015). **And when they bring their testimony to completion, the beast that comes up from the bottomless pit will make war on them and win over them and kill them** (11:7). This is proof that victimhood is not a thing of the past! The digression running through Rev. 10:1–11:14 relates to the whole of the book even more than to the trumpet sequence. "The bottomless pit" is the headquarters of the "star that had fallen from heaven" (9:1; cf. 9:2, 11; 11:7; 17:8; 20:1–3). To "make war," "win over them," and "kill them"—these actions recapitulate the story of "the Lamb" in the lives of "the two witnesses." It is projected against the backdrop of the cosmic conflict (12:7–12). "The setting of the story is cosmic rather than local" (Koester 2014, 506). This is surely the case.

**And their dead body [sg.] will lie in the street of the great city, the one that is spiritually called Sodom and Egypt, where also their Lord was crucified** (11:8). John should be tired of crafting sentences with such a concentration of metaphors, but he does not let up. "The two witnesses," now dead, lie unburied and in a state of abject dishonor "in the streets of the great city" (11:8). Many interpreters wish to define "the great city" in historical and geographical terms, in which case a line is drawn between "Babylon" and imperial Rome (Koester 2014, 500). This logic runs into difficulty when John proceeds to emphasize that "the great city" is "the one that is spiritually called Sodom and Egypt" (11:8). We shall be hard pressed to imagine a set of more negatively charged appellations, and the meaning is clear. John is concerned about theology and ideology, not about geography (de Villiers 1988; Harker 2011). If spiritual realities had spatial parameters, "Sodom and Egypt" would be the point on the map farthest from the ideal. David E. Aune (1996–98, 618) says that "an original reference to Jerusalem appears most likely" for the street of the great city. This may well be true, but it threatens to take a metaphor hostage to geography. No one forgets that Jesus "was crucified" in Jerusalem. From a spiritual point of view, the beloved Jerusalem turns into "Sodom and Egypt."

Old Testament prophets used similar language about Israel in their time (Isa. 1:9–10; 3:9; Jer. 23:14; Ezek. 16:46–56). Revelation's ideological lines are even more distinct. If "Jerusalem" serves as a metaphor for the use of violence in defense of piety—with the one who "was crucified" as the foremost exhibit—the "pious" person is on the level of the most faithless. By the same token, Rome and Jerusalem are indistinguishable from each other, and "Sodom and Egypt" belong to the same family. The focus is not on location but on the deed and its underlying ideology. In which city, then, is the "dead body" of "the two witnesses" on display, given John's assertion that "the two witnesses" are now lying dead in the city "where also their Lord was crucified"? We are expected to answer this question in a way that brings ideological clarity. Nothing less than a global or cosmic stage will suffice: the residents and spectators include "the inhabitants of the whole world—all the peoples" (Koester 2014, 500). *His* story now finds embodiment in *their* witness.

To "make war on them and win over them and kill them"—the power inhabiting "the bottomless pit" is not playing games (Rev. 11:7). It did not work when the tactic was used on Jesus (12:1–6). Will it work this time? The question is meant to suggest that the account of "the two witnesses" is prescriptive and not only descriptive: it *prescribes* the method of the mission. And the prescription recapitulates the story of Jesus right down to the city and street "where also their Lord was crucified" (11:8). **And they—from the peoples and tribes and languages and nations—shall gaze at their body for three and a half days, and they refuse to let the dead bodies be placed in a tomb** (11:9). This looks like victory for the enemies of "the two witnesses," and they make the most of the moment. Indeed, **the inhabitants of the earth will rejoice over them and be delighted and exchange presents with each other, because these two prophets had exasperated the inhabitants of the earth** (11:10). On the surface, this looks like success for the opposing side. The joy suggests a sense of relief, as though "the inhabitants of the earth" have fallen into line with "the beast that comes up from the bottomless pit" to the point of celebrating the latter's improved fortune in the cosmic war.

But this is not the end of the story. **And after the three and a half days, the breath of life from God entered into them, and they stood on their feet, and fear [*phobos*] fell on those who saw them** (11:11). A story of death and resurrection, of victimhood and victory, is now playing out in the streets and in the city that is "spiritually called Sodom and Egypt" (11:8–11). Who had expected this? Who had imagined victimhood to be the path to victory? It looks like sentiments are shifting, too. A reappraisal is taking place, and the impact of the witness is directly linked to victimhood. "Fear" (*phobos*) is an ambiguous word, but ambiguity means that there is more than one way of looking at it. The NRSV says that "those who saw them were terrified" (11:11). This suggests people seeing the event in negative terms. But "fear" may also have a positive meaning, capturing the sentiments of people who are in the process of changing their minds. Fear of this kind is better perceived as reverence and respect, even admiration (BDAG 1062, φόβος). In another image of mission, "an angel flying in midheaven with eternal good news" will say "to those who live on the earth—to every nation and tribe and language and people, 'Fear [*phobēthēte*] God and give God glory'" (14:6, 7). The word goes forth to "fear God," and the connotation is utterly positive. *This is what* *the world should have done all along, and now it does* (11:11). The passage calling on people to "fear God" is related to the verse saying that "fear fell on them" even though the result comes before the cause is fully laid out (11:9–13; 14:4–6; cf. Bauckham 1993a, 278).

For "the two witnesses," victimhood turns to vindication. **And they heard a loud voice from the heaven saying to them, "Come up here!" And they went up into heaven in a cloud, and their enemies saw them** (11:12). Who hears the "loud voice"? "The two witnesses" hear it, but so must "their enemies" (11:12). Who else "went into heaven," given Revelation's love of types and models? Elijah, that is who, one of "the two witnesses" (2 Kings 2:1–12). Jesus did, too (12:5). His story counts the most because the witnesses are traversing the ground prepared and pioneered by him. **And at that hour there was a great earthquake, and a tenth of the city fell, and seven thousand people were killed by the earthquake, and the rest feared** [*emphoboi*] **and gave glory to the God of heaven** (11:13; cf. 14:6–7). The verse is packed, but the bottom line shows *mission accomplished precisely because of the method chosen.* "There should be no doubt that the end of 11:13 refers to genuine repentance and worship of God by the pagan world which is symbolized by the great city" (Bauckham, 1993a, 278). Richard Bauckham points to telling contrasts between Revelation's depiction and OT antecedents—in the book of Esther, the enemies of the people of God are slaughtered (Esther 9:11–15); in Revelation, the people of God are slaughtered; in the story of Elijah, the faithful seven thousand are spared (1 Kings 19:18); in Revelation, seven thousand are killed. He proposes a rationale that is as close to the truth as we are likely to get. "The reason why, in the final period of world history, God will not deliver his faithful people by the slaughter of their enemies, as he did in the days of Moses, Elijah, and Esther, but instead will allow them to be slaughtered by their enemies, is that this is the way the nations will be brought to repentance and faith, and the sovereignty over them transferred from the beast to the kingdom of God" (Bauckham 1993a, 282).

Another telling contrast is just as remarkable. At the end of the sixth trumpet, amid scenes of battle and mayhem, "the rest . . . *did not turn* from the works of their hands; . . . they *did not turn* from their murders or their sorceries or their fornication or their stealing" (9:20–21). Here they do "turn." We see a witness that is far-reaching in its impact despite means that seem ineffectual. Now, with the work of "the two witnesses" complete, "fear fell on those who saw them" (11:11), and "the rest feared and gave glory to the God of heaven" (11:13). Their mission has not been in vain. And the method, counterintuitive in the extreme, turned out well.

**The second woe has passed,** says John, and it has not been all bad (11:14; cf. 11:13). **Look, the third woe is coming soon,** he warns (11:14). This is ominous, but there is reason to believe that the events accompanying "the woes," bad though they may be (8:13; 9:12; 11:14; 12:12), will not be unopposed.

### The Seventh Trumpet (11:15–19)

**11:15–19.** No matter the terror in much of the trumpet cycle, it ends on a high note. **And the seventh angel blew his trumpet, and there were loud voices in the heaven, saying, "The kingdom of the world has become the kingdom of our Lord and of his Anointed One** [*tou Christou autou*]**, and he will reign forever and ever"** (11:15). Nothing is gloomy in this announcement. "Six angels have blown trumpets in a threatening manner, but the seventh sounds a festive tone" (Koester 2014, 512). A transfer of power from incompetent to competent hands is suggested. God's anointed is a figure in the line of David (Pss. 18:50; 20:6; 28:8), and his approach to governing is fully laid out (Isa. 11:1–10; 42:1–9; 49:1–9; 50:4–9; 52:13–15). The specifics of the transfer of power draw heavily on the visions in Daniel (Dan. 2:44; 7:14, 18, 27). The Reign of Terror is over, to be replaced by the Reign of Joy. This is cause for further celebration, carrying forward the jubilation that began in connection with the seven seals (5:8–14). To these joyous scenes the seventh trumpet now returns (11:16–18).

> And the twenty-four elders who sit on their thrones before God fell on
>     their faces and worshiped God, saying,
> "We thank you, Lord God Almighty,
>     who are and who were,
> for you have taken [perf.] your great power
>     and reigned [aor.].
> The nations were wrathful [*ōrgisthēsan*],
>     and your wrath [*hē orgē sou*] has come
> —and the time for judging the dead [has come],
> to give the reward to your servants,
>     the prophets and believers
>     and all who fear [*tois phoboumenois*] your name,
>     both small and great,
> and to destroy [*diaphtheirai*] those
>     who destroy the earth." (11:16–18)

Gratitude is due for what has come to light, but what is it? The verbs describing what God has done, "have taken" and "reigned," are not in the same tense (11:17). This can be remedied by saying "have taken" . . . "and *begun* to reign," and this is a legitimate translation (Aune 1996–98, 643). Two caveats nevertheless apply. First, the faithful rejoice not only over the *result* of what God has done but also for the *way* God has done it (5:8–14; 15:1–4). Second, there was never a point at which God did not reign even if Revelation here seems to suggest otherwise (Aune 1996–98, 643).

A bigger issue is at stake in John's description of the stance of "the nations" and the stance of God (11:18). The verb used to describe the sentiment of the nations is linguistically matched to a noun describing God. "The nations *raged [ōrgisthēsan],*" says the NRSV (11:18). To keep the words in the same key, we should say that "your *rage [hē orgē sou]* has come." Other options for the word pairings might be, respectively,

| Nations | God |
|---|---|
| raged | rage |
| were angry | anger |
| were irate | ire |
| were furious | fury |
| were wrathful | wrath |

Will this work? Does the rage of the nations have a counterpoint or corollary in "the rage of God," using this or one of the other terms on the list? The options that seem most obvious—equivalence in wrath—need other possibilities. "And the dragon was enraged [*ōrgisthē*] with the woman," says John (12:17), utilizing the same verb that was used to describe the sentiments of "the nations" (11:18), but now with Satan as the subject of the verb. For "the nations" and "the dragon," the rage must have the same valence, and the stronger the word the better. Both are *irate*, consumed by a fury that has resentment and revenge on its mind. In this constellation, it is necessary to see "the dragon" as the instigator and "the nations" in a secondary role.

"The dragon" has put a spell on "the nations" that God confronts and breaks (A. Hanson 1957, 170, 173). By this logic God's "wrath" and the rage of "the nations" stand in sharp contrast to each other. In fact, the announcement that "*your* wrath has come" will in this scenario be a message of liberation and hope, and the outworking of God's "wrath" is a matter to be watched with keen and suspenseful interest. The same need for nuance applies to the time that has come "to destroy those who destroy the earth" (11:18). Who are "those who destroy the earth"—other than the demonic horde that has been Revelation's unrelenting concern throughout most of the trumpet sequence? Who are they, if not first and foremost the "star that had fallen from heaven to earth" and his cohorts (9:1, 11; Isa. 14:12–20)? If God destroys "those who destroy" (11:18), by what means does God do it? The opposing side in the conflict has already made a good beginning of destroying itself and the earth and is poised to bring it to completion (9:1–20). In the song, the praise to God has greater depth and exuberance if we recognize—as in the earlier outbursts of praise and in songs yet to come (5:8–14; 12:10–12; 15:1–4)—that beings in the entire cosmos praise God for prevailing in the cosmic war (Grabiner 2015, 136–41).

Other items in the song—"the time for judging the dead," the time "to give the reward to your servants" (11:18)—belong to the future and provide a rough synopsis of the rest of the book (Stefanovic 2009a, 373). A big-picture conception might describe these items as *accountability* and *vindication*. By this logic, John caps the trumpet cycle by signaling the continuation of an unfinished story rather than its completion.

But *completion* insists on having the last word. By criteria explained earlier, the choreography of sound and light in the book is accompanied by *revelation* (4:5; 8:5). **And the temple of God in the heaven was opened, and the ark of God's covenant was seen in God's temple; and there were flashes of lightning, booming voices, peals of thunder, an earthquake, and heavy hail** (11:19). To *open* things is precisely what this book does—*open* door (3:8), *open* heaven (4:1), *open* scroll (5:5–7; 10:2, 8)—and now *open* temple! The holiest of holy is laid bare for all to see. Many things are signified by "the ark of God's covenant," and one of them is God's *commitment* (Exod. 25:8–22). The trumpet cycle, too, reveals the kind of person God is. On this stable thesis, the cycle ends on a note of completion.

> **The Seventh Trumpet (11:15–19)**
>
> Completion and continuation
>
> Completion: Looking back
>
> Continuation: Looking forward
>
> Festive tenor

### Theological Issues

All the time- and event-oriented schools of interpretation run into serious trouble in the trumpet sequence. Which events in the preterist scheme are prefigured if we assume that Revelation sees history headed for the day of Nero's return (Dochhorn 2010, 52–53, 115)? Does the historicist succeed in an attempt to match the symbol to a specific event in time, whether it be the barbarian king Odoacer in the fourth century (U. Smith 1884, 487–88) or the emergence of "rationalism, skepticism, humanism, and liberalism . . . and rise of secularism" in the seventeenth century (Stefanovic 2009a, 303), both ideas promoted for the symbols under the fourth trumpet? Should we, as in one futurist scheme, acknowledge that "a Cobra helicopter fits the composite description very well," referring to the monstrous phenomenon under the fifth and sixth trumpet (Lindsey 1984, 138–39)? This bizarre view originated in a conversation between a widely revered interpreter and an American soldier returning from duty in Vietnam. "I've seen hundreds of them in Viet Nam," said the soldier (Lindsey 1970, 139). For all, and especially for futurist suggestions, speculative and trivializing interpretations compromise the symbols. The yearning held in common by the "schools" sacrifices Revelation's representations of reality on the altar of historical specificity. These time-bound interpretations fail as "history," too, because the selections are speculative, arbitrary, and often trite. By contrast, the message of the trumpets will not become obsolete even if time extends beyond the present. As with the seven seals, readers may throw at them the worst that comes to mind—only to find it matched, in a material conception, by the trumpets' "scorpions," "horses," and "serpents."

"What" and "who" (or "by whom") are in the trumpet sequence more important questions than "when," even though "when" is the preoccupation of the main schools of interpretation. The "by whom" question has been neglected with the result that many readers send the bill for the calamities in the trumpet sequence—and in the world—to the wrong address. The horrors are *not* a series of God-orchestrated judgments, as many interpreters argue. God has *not* calibrated destruction in quantitative terms in the form of calamities affecting "only *one-third* of the specified parts of the world (8:7–12), while two-thirds of the cosmos and its inhabitants survive until a final round of tribulations" (Aune 1996–98, 546). Attention to the other side of the conflict, especially the falling and fallen star in the third and the fifth trumpets (8:10–11; 9:1–11), shows a power at work other than God. The author of Revelation spares no effort to bring out the demonic identity of this power.

This discovery determines the theological meaning. Strong and conclusive evidence is found in the overwrought, preternatural symbols that are especially forceful in the long descriptions in the fifth and sixth trumpets. Subtler—yet not particularly subtle—clues are marshalled in the repetitious "one-third" that dots the entire trumpet sequence (8:7, 9, 10, 12; 9:15, 18; 12:4). These are signifiers of agency and not primarily markers denoting "*one-third* of the specified parts of the world" (Aune 1996–98, 546). Interpretations that fail to see the demonic fingerprint have been too sloppy about the detail work that is essential to mapping out crime scenes. The pedagogy of the trumpet sequence feeds the answer to the reader teaspoon by careful teaspoon: it finds *Mr. Wormwood* at the scene in the third trumpet (8:10–11), *Mr. Darkness* in the fourth trumpet (8:12), and *Mr. Destroyer* in the fifth trumpet (9:2, 11)—the same agent appearing as the perpetrator of ever more grotesque actions. John's overriding interest in this figure reduces the importance of knowledge of history and the advantage of the resident expert that is a fixture in all the schools of interpretation.

The rhetoric of the trumpets is not descriptive of how evil looks to the naked eye but how it is assessed from the vantage point of *revelation*. One item of interest stands out: "the power of the horses is in their mouths and in their tails; their tails are like serpents, having heads; and with them they inflict harm" (9:19). The composite image is grotesque, but the message is subtle. Evil is construed as a theological project that works through words and representations, not as a military venture culminating in Cobra helicopters. "Serpents" and "mouths" that "inflict harm" echo the serpent's representation of God in Genesis (3:1). Interest in the "mouth" of the opposing side persists throughout the book (9:17, 18, 19; 12:15; 13:2, 5, 6; 16:13): it is the "mouth" of the loathsome threesome on the opposing side that commands attention all the way to the climactic showdown at Armageddon (16:12–16). Trumpet rhetoric may seem overwrought and bizarre, but it will not seem overwrought for the way it puts the demonic reality under the microscope. "Mouths" that "inflict harm," understood in theological terms, is a repudiation of the serpent's representation of God and the God thus represented. Such a conception of the trumpets creates a bridge to the concern for the integrity of the seven communities in Asia Minor and their witness. A "synagogue of Satan" in Smyrna (2:9), a "throne of Satan" in Pergamum (2:13), "deep things of Satan" in Thyatira (2:24), and a "synagogue of Satan" in Philadelphia (3:9)—all locate the threat within the communities and not only as an external menace that is easy to see. Again, when the smoke of locusts and the sting of scorpions in the trumpet sequence become theological conceptions, they trap human life in the vise of an unending, existential horror. Such suffering is not simply material and cannot be neatly circumscribed in historical time, even though Revelation attaches a time element. "And in those days people will seek death, and they will not find it; they will long to die, and death will flee from them" (9:6). This vision, as *theology*, provides tools with which to scrutinize theology, including the Christian theological tradition.

Despite the repulsive ugliness of the symbols, idols can be alluring objects of worship even when they are spectacularly undeserving. Germans did not flock to Adolf Hitler's side although they knew he was bad; they did so *because they thought he was good*. This is hard to accept after the carnage of World War II, but the mystery of all "bad" movements is how they manage to look good. Saul Friedländer (2008, 656–57) says that the main question after World War II "is not what personality traits allowed an 'unknown corporal' of the Great War to become the all-powerful leader Adolf Hitler, but rather why tens of millions of Germans blindly followed him to the end, why many still believed in him at the end, and not a few, after the end." This mystery is not resolved even when the trumpet exposé has run to completion: despite the ruin and mayhem, "the rest . . . *did not turn* from the works of their hands. . . . They *did not turn* from their murders or their sorceries or their fornication or their stealing" (9:20–21).

The surprising absence of impact suggests that *revelation as exposé* is necessary, but it is not sufficient. If this is correct, the section describing *mission* and *method* is more than an afterthought (10:1–11:14). Only here are the exploits of the bad side reversed and routed. Structurally, the sequence is the same as the "digression" in the seal sequence, a shift of focus from "the world" to the believing community. Striking similarities between Revelation and Daniel suggest that the commission to *mission* is influenced by Daniel (10:1–11). Zechariah emerges as the most significant OT voice with respect to *method* (11:1–14). These texts describe and *prescribe* the life and work of the witnessing community under the auspices of God. Everything is so counterintuitive that it becomes believable only by the force of revelation. To measure what cannot be measured (Rev. 11:1–2); to be assured of protection while being trampled (11:1–2); to have limitless power and yet fall as a powerless victim (11:3–10): the ways of God in the believing community track closely to the story of Jesus who is depicted as a victim of violence (5:5–6). And yet this is the story that makes the world "turn" (11:11–13). Revelation as *revelation*, working itself out in the life of Jesus and his witnessing community, succeeds where revelation as exposé fell short (11:11–13). The work of the two witnesses is patterned on the witness of Jesus. As in the case of the Lamb "killed with violence" (5:6), success happens in the path of apparent defeat (11:11–13).

# Revelation 12:1–14:20

## The Cosmic Conflict from A to Z

### Introductory Matters

Revelation does not tell its story in a linear mode from start to finish (Boxall 2002, 10). It fits the evidence better to imagine the story line fanning out from the middle of the book, with chapter 12 as the anchoring point. This view is well established (Gollinger 1971, 119; Feuillet 1978; Beale 1999, 131). And yet the notion of a circumscribed anchoring point is submerged in a composition that is fluid, symphonic, and assumptive. Boundaries exist, but the content within each boundary spills over into the adjacent textual territory. Symphonic features are evident by themes that wax and wane within the composition, without serving clear-cut notice of the theme's beginning and ending. Assumptive elements—things taken for granted—mean that the composer springs concepts on the listener that are not explained until later and never explained in a didactic manner.

Nevertheless, the centrality of chapter 12 justifies the view that content is matched to structure. Wilhelm Bousset (1906, 335) called Rev. 12–14 "the pinnacle of the apocalyptic prophecy." Here, at the structural midpoint, it becomes explicit "for the first time that the combat myth is the conceptual framework which underlies the book as a whole" (A. Collins 1976, 231). What is true for Revelation has been said for the Bible as a whole. "Now we hear for the first time in the Holy Scriptures the original history [*Urgeschichte*] of Satan and his fall" (Hammer 1958, 97).

Adela Yarbro Collins's claim on behalf of the combat theme rests on firm evidence within the text. Looking back to the beginning of the book, we have

## Chapter 12
## The Hub of the Wheel

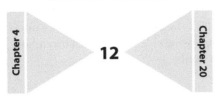

Figure 16. The pivotal influence of Revelation 12. The story in Revelation 12 influences the preceding chapters (4–11) just as much as the chapters following (13–20).

concern about Satan widely diffused in the messages to the seven believing communities (2:9, 13, 24; 3:9). The crisis in the heavenly council is illuminated by the combat theme: "The problem facing the heavenly council is the rebellion of Satan" (A. Collins 1979, 39). This undergirds the exposé accompanying the breaking of the seals (6:1–17), and it is reinforced by the intermission between the sixth and the seventh seal (7:1–17). Spheres interact in the text and in reality. Here, the theme of *marking* (13:15–18; 14:9–11; 16:2; 19:20) is assumed by the scenes describing the *sealing* in the sequence of the seven seals (7:1–3), and the *sealing* in that part spills over into the scenes describing the *marking* in the present section (13:15–18).

Looking forward and downstream from chapter 12, the narrative flow is more conventional and easier to follow, but there is no change in theme or "conceptual framework" (A. Collins 1976, 231). There is integration and spillover here, too, notably

> **Revelation 12:1–14:20 in the Rhetorical Flow**
>
> **Incentive to read (1:1–20)**
>
> **To the one who has an ear (2:1–3:22)**
>
> **The seven seals (4:1–8:1)**
>
> **The seven trumpets (8:2–11:19)**
>
> ▶**The cosmic conflict from A to Z (12:1–14:20)**
>
>   **Clash of the pregnant woman, the dragon, and the male child (12:1–6)**
>
>   **Origin and synopsis of the war in heaven (12:7–12)**
>
>   **Synopsis of the culmination of the conflict (12:13–18)**
>
>   **War by surrogacy and imitation (13:1–18)**
>
>     The beast from the sea (13:1–10)
>
>     The beast from the earth (13:11–18)
>
>   **Previewing victory: The redeemed and the Lamb on Mount Zion (14:1–5)**
>
>   **Final proclamation: God's reaction to the dragon's action (14:6–13)**
>
>     The first angel (14:6–7)
>
>     The second angel (14:8)
>
>     The third angel (14:9–11)
>
>     The faithfulness of Jesus (14:12–13)
>
>   **Hope and horror: Triumph and implosion (14:14–20)**

the striking similarities between the trumpet sequence (8:6–9:21) and the seven bowls (15:1–16:21). From the point of origin of the conflict in heaven (12:7–9), through the drama of conspiracy, identity theft, and double-dealing on earth (13:1–18; 17:1–18:24), the story marches on to the capture, release, and demise of the opposing side (20:1–10). Throughout, the cosmic scope of the story is never in doubt.

### Tracing the Train of Thought

*Clash of the Pregnant Woman, the Dragon, and the Male Child (12:1–6)*

**12:1–6.** Since the images of Revelation are not projected in chronological order, subdivisions of the text are tricky. While the three divisions in chapter 12 are clear (vv. 1–6, 7–12, 13–18), their sequence is not. Clear, however, is the importance of "the dragon," or "the ancient serpent," in all three phases. A sequence arranged according to what happens first advises the following order: (1) the war in heaven (12:7–12); (2) the birth of the male child (12:1–6); (3) and the war on "the rest of her children" (12:13–18).

**Center of the Center
"Epicenter"**

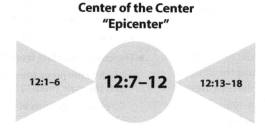

Figure 17. Revelation 12:7–12 is the "epicenter" in the context of chapter 12 as a whole.

The chapter begins on the Maternity Ward of the Ages (12:1–2). How the world has waited for this pregnancy! Genesis 3:15–20 "dominates this chapter" (Sweet 1979, 203; Minear 1991), and echoes of Genesis are particularly striking with respect to the birth scene. In the background passage, God tells Eve that "I will greatly increase your pangs in childbearing; in pain you shall bring forth children" (Gen. 3:16). *Pain* is a conspicuous element in the birth process in Revelation; *grief* may be, too (Gen. 3:16 LXX). For the magnitude of the moment to emerge, God's prior address to the serpent is indispensable. *That* the child is born is important; *why* he is born is not left out. "The LORD God said to the serpent, 'Because you have done this, cursed are you among all animals and among all wild creatures; upon your belly you shall go, and dust you shall eat all the days of your life. *I will put enmity between you and the woman, and between your offspring and hers;* he will strike your head, and you will strike his heel'" (Gen. 3:14–15, emphasis added). Among allusions to the OT in Revelation, this one is hard to surpass. Revelation seems to endorse Gen. 3:15 as the *protevangelium* (S. Driver 1904, 48). **A great sign** [*sēmeion mega*] . . . **seen in the heaven** (12:1) means that heaven is open, and the "sign" is an element of *revelation*. The **woman** is a composite figure, carrying within herself elements of Eve, the community of faith, Israel, and even the Virgin Mary (Braun 1955). As Eve, she is a woman transfigured. Everything about her projects importance, majesty, and promise (Hauret 1979). According to Genesis, *he*—the woman's *offspring*—will bring about the defeat of the serpent (Gen. 3:15). She is also the woman whose son will be "God with us" (Isa. 7:14; Feuillet 1978, 675). At the moment of birth, John switches to the historical present: she *cries out* (12:2), not "cried out," as though speaking from a point near and present. The cry has an apocalyptic tenor—a call to attention, a call to draw near. John tells the story in a *telescoped* fashion, many layers of narrative and long eons of time compressed into one decisive moment (Feuillet 1959, 56).

And now to the mortal danger on the Maternity Ward (12:3). This is the other side of the revelation. It, too, is called a **sign** (*sēmeion*). The murderous intruder is a monster by at least four criteria. First, he is **a dragon** (*drakōn*) and thus a frightening creature. This might seem enough, but the word by which he is identified as "a dragon" can also mean **a serpent** (Foerster 1932, 304). Second, he is **red**, and the color alone signals malice (Braun 1954, 64). Third, he has **seven heads**, the profusion of heads suggesting *confusion* with respect to his identity, *staying power*, and *completeness* (cf. 17:8–12). Which head is the core, if there is a core? Fourth, the **seven diadems** show a figure of importance.

Neat chronological order is not on offer, not even here (12:4). John keeps mixing up the tenses of the verbs. His storytelling looks back (*Rückblick*) and forward (*Vorblick*) in a demanding temporal perspective (Foerster 1932, 303–4). For the action of the serpent's **tail**, John again makes use of the historical present. The verbs in the sentence are in the active voice, meaning that agency is unambiguous. This is the work of "the dragon," soon to be known as "the Ancient Serpent" and "the Mudslinger" (12:9). "His tail" wreaks havoc among **the stars of heaven; his tail . . . threw them to the earth** (12:4). A dragon's tail might under normal circumstances seem like a crude instrument of war, but Revelation has already featured tails that "are like serpents, having heads" (9:19) and heads that have "mouths" (9:17, 18, 19). We have also seen monstrous tails that have "stingers" (9:10), by which weaponry they "inflict harm" (9:10, 19). The "tails" in the trumpet sequence bear more than a casual relation to the "tail" that here stirs up trouble. These anatomical subtleties move the story from the crude realm of mythology to the delicate realm of theology and ideology. In temporal terms, the upheaval in the cosmic order comes early, before the story of the woman about to give birth (12:1, 2). An echo of Isaiah is evident in the movement from heaven to earth (Isa. 14:12–15), and there is telescoping. But a time line is nevertheless discernible: he did *that* first, in *heaven* (Rev. 12:4), and now he will do *this*, on *earth* (12:13). Without this background and progression, it is impossible to make sense of what "the dragon" will do next.

What comes next is told in the perfect tense of a verb that means to "set" or "establish" or "stand," depending on the form that is used and whether the form carries an object (BDAG 482–83, ἵστημι). Here, the verb's objective is not to describe someone who *stands* but the relation between the one who stands and something else. We capture it best by seeing the enemy in a combat posture, ready to pounce. **And the dragon took up his position in front of the woman who was about to give birth in order—at the exact moment that she would give birth—to devour her child** (12:4). A "woman," a "child," a "birth"—and a "dragon": the glimpse into the Maternity Ward of the Ages brims with vulnerability.

Born, acknowledged, and gone (12:5)! John tells the story in bullet points. We have used the word "telescoping" earlier, and this is telescoping in the extreme. Rapid-fire images feature three stages in the child's career: his birth, his removal **to God's throne**, and his role as **shepherd to all the nations** (12:5; Ps. 2:8–9; Isa. 42:1–9; 49:1–9). As in the message to the believing community in Thyatira, there is **a rod of iron** (Rev. 12:5; 2:26–27). This symbol of protection and rulership echoes Ps. 2:8–9. In both instances, the shepherd stands as the protector of the sheep. Revelation omits describing the death of Jesus, but some elements are told more effectively by leaving them implicit. That the child **was seized away** or **snatched away** does not mean that he slipped through the back door in the nick of time. There was confrontation—to the point of being "killed with violence" (Rev. 5:6). Going **to God** captures the victorious outcome without betraying how the victory was achieved. John's compressed account is demanding, but all the elements of the Christian story are there.

What about the mother? The thought that she has been "left behind" is wrong, but hardship awaits her (12:6). Already in the first section (12:1–6) there is an overview of the whole conflict—the beginning (12:3–4), the decisive middle (12:1–2, 4–5), and the ending (12:6). What lies ahead for "the woman" is life in **the wilderness** (12:6). Flight is necessary because of ongoing danger (12:13–17). The measures taken on behalf of "the woman" imply that God works at the stage of "preparing" and at the point of "taking care of her": God is *they* (the acting subject of *trephōsin*, **that they may feed her**, 12:6) in the sentence (Koester 2014, 23). The escape into the wilderness recalls Elijah's flight under conditions of life-threatening adversity (1 Kings 17:2–3; 19:3–4). This creates a paradox because the flight into the wilderness suggests retreat while "Elijah," one of "the two witnesses" in the trumpet sequence, was staunchly in a "no flight" posture (Rev. 11:3–6). The two perspectives are complementary, and they are marked off within Revelation's signature time period, **one thousand two hundred and sixty days** (12:6; 11:3; cf. 11:2; 13:5; cf. also 12:14).

To "the assimilated arsenal of Christian proclamation" (Gollinger 1971, 126) belongs a narrative featuring a cosmic struggle between fallen and unfallen angels (12:4, 7–9), a God-like person incarnated in humanity (12:2, 5), and a fierce conflict, all this presented as the story of real beings. The characters on both sides emerge from the mist of mythology into the realm of history. Earth beware!

### Origin and Synopsis of the War in Heaven (12:7–12)

**12:7–12.** Heaven is not a residue of mythology in this story. When the cosmic conflict theme moves into high gear, the location of interest is precisely *heaven*, and the parties to the conflict do *not* belong to the human realm. **And war [*polemos*] burst forth in heaven: Michael and his angels had to wage war [*tou polemēsai*] with the dragon** (12:7a; cf. Charles 1920, 1:322). The announcement is abrupt, and the temporal relation to the preceding section is blurred. One interpreter says that the second tableau (12:7–12) is "distinctly raised from the rest by virtue of its content" (Lohmeyer 1926, 100), another that "the course of the narrative is interrupted here in a way that appears to be most ungrounded" (Roloff 1993, 148), a third that the second tableau is "an intrusive narrative fragment" (Aune 1996–98, 691). These are legitimate observations, and they are accounted for by "John's penchant for inserting a short scene that summarizes the action of major sections of the book" (D. Barr 1998, 124). A big-picture, telescoped projection compensates for the lack of a tidy time line (Beale 1999, 639; D. Barr 1998, 124). *Sequence* is nevertheless important enough to warrant a comment. A straightforward chronological reading of chapter 12 gives an implausible story line. If the chronological and narrative sequence walked in lockstep, "the Ancient Serpent" (12:9)—with no notification of background—first appears when he tries to destroy the male child on earth (12:4). Failing that (12:5), he goes to war "in heaven" (12:7), determined to achieve what he was unable to accomplish under more favorable circumstances on earth (Metzger 1993, 74; Mounce 1977, 240). Failing in this arena, too (12:8), he is confined to the earth for good (12:9). This sequence is contradicted by the clear implication that "the dragon" has a history prior to the attack on the woman (12:2, 4).

Second, the removal of the child "to God and to God's throne" (12:5) renders a battle in heaven meaningless: the removal of the child to heaven slams shut the prospect for success *in heaven*. The adversary can still do harm, but a heavenly battle is pointless. A *primordial* heavenly battle, on the other hand, is not only plausible but necessary for the elements in the story to add up. In the early part of the twentieth century, two of the foremost interpreters of this story document the widely held view in late Palestinian

Judaism that the primordial fall of Satan did not bar him completely from the heavenly council (Bousset 1906, 341; Charles 1920, 1:323). He was banished, but he still had access. This view is compatible with Revelation's perspective. John's wording about the war that "burst forth in heaven" catches the conflict at its point of origin (12:7). A showdown with "Michael" *after* the safe removal of the child "to God and to God's throne" is implausible and anticlimactic (12:5, 7).

"Michael and his angels had to wage war [*tou polemēsai*] with the dragon" (12:7) is odd grammar in Greek, but it is precise for the way it captures the causal relations in the conflict (Charles 1920, 1:322; Aune 1996–98, 692). The nominatives "Michael and his angels" stand before an infinitive in uncharacteristic and wooden Greek, quite possibly "a literal Greek reproduction of a pure Hebraism" (Charles 1920, 1:322; N. Turner 1963, 141). And yet it is to good purpose because the text distinguishes the instigator from the responder, and the "Semitic imperatival" *lamed* [ל] with the infinitive points to conditions of necessity (BDF §400.8, p. 207). "Michael and his angels" are doing what *must* be done.

Who, then, was the instigator? It was not "Michael and his angels." They were the *responders*, drawn into a war started by "the dragon." The formulation assigns blame to Satan. An emergency arose to which Michael's response became a matter of necessity. **The dragon waged war and his angels, but they were not strong enough, neither was a place found for them in heaven** (12:7b–8). Not being "strong enough" works as a metaphor that does not measure the two sides by muscle or physical might; the suggestion that the dragon "did not get the upper hand" is a helpful alternative (Dochhorn 2010, 232). A *battle of ideas* is the best proposition, in which case not being "strong enough" proves the dragon to have a weak case. Moreover, a physical battle, even if we assume the dragon to be a formidable foe, would be irrational in the extreme. The dragon's search for "a place" is told in the passive voice. In the active voice, the sentence would read, "They—the dragon and his cohorts—searched for a place in heaven but did not find any." The exclusion could mean that henceforth "the dragon and his angels" are unwanted or that they no longer see heaven as a good place to be. For both options, "not strong enough" and not finding "a place in heaven" would be two sides of the same coin, neither a matter of physical strength but of "irreconcilable differences."

John does not use language that can be taken literally, but his terms are not haphazard. **And the great dragon was thrown down [*eblēthē*], the ancient serpent, who is called the Mudslinger and Satan, the deceiver [*ho planōn*] of the whole world, he was thrown [*eblēthē*] to the earth, and his angels were thrown out [*eblēthēsan*] with him** (12:9). Here action is taken against the instigator of the conflict. The piling up of synonyms suggests that John is "consciously attempting to expose the real role of this antagonist of God throughout cosmic and human history" (Aune 1996–98, 697). Expulsion at the hand of a superior power is a legitimate inference, but the text offers other options. In the first tableau (12:1–6), the tail of the dragon dragged down "the third of the stars of the heaven." *It*— not God—"threw [*ebalen*] them to the earth" (12:4). The dominant verb, "throw" (*ballō*), is the same in both verses (12:4, 9). This verb occurs three times in the passive voice in connection with the expulsion of the dragon (12:9) and once in the active voice in connection with the action of the dragon upon "the stars of heaven" (12:4). This diminishes the role of divine agency at the point of origin in the conflict: the Mudslinger is acting and acted upon as though he plays an active role in his own expulsion.

> **Key Cosmic Conflict Texts**
>
> • Psalm 82
> • Isaiah 14:12–20
> • Ezekiel 28:11–20
> • Revelation 12:7–12
> (Morgenstern 1939)

Isaiah is the most important background voice but not the only one (Gunkel 1895, 30–114; Morgenstern 1939; Pope 1955; Clifford 1972; Page 1996; Jensen 1997, 343).

Like the poem about the fall of "the Shining One" in Isaiah, there is a parallel in the grief poem about "the covering cherub" in Ezekiel (28:12–19). This poem, too, is notable for its literary qualities (Fisch 1950, 188). The text mixes past and present, earth and heaven, the fall of the highest angel and the fall of human beings, but at the core stands a heavenly being (Greenberg 1997, 588–89).

Thus says the Lord GOD:

> "You were the seal of perfection,
> Full of wisdom and perfect in beauty.
> You were in Eden, the garden of God;
> Every precious stone was your covering:
> The sardius, topaz, and diamond,
> Beryl, onyx, and jasper,
> Sapphire, turquoise, and emerald with gold.
> The workmanship of your timbrels and pipes
> Was prepared for you on the day you were created.

> You were the anointed cherub who covers;
> I established you;
> You were on the holy mountain of God;
> You walked back and forth in the midst of fiery stones.
> You were perfect in your ways from the day you were created,
> Till iniquity was found in you.

> By the abundance of your trading
> You became filled with violence within,
> And you sinned;
> Therefore I cast you as a profane thing
> Out of the mountain of God;
> And I destroyed you, O covering cherub,
> From the midst of the fiery stones." (Ezek. 28:12–16 NKJV)

This being is of the same order as "the Shining One" in Isaiah (Isa. 14:12; K. Schmidt 1951). Like him, there is perfection and beauty (Ezek. 28:12), but there is also decline, dismissal, and descent—a precipitous downward movement from "the mountain of God . . . to the earth" (Ezek. 28:16, 17, my trans.; Isa. 14:12; Rev. 12:7–9). Ezekiel's covering cherub loses his way because of excessive self-regard (Ezek. 28:17). Translation of the poem is difficult. One version renders the key phrase as "You, O Serpent of perfection" (Ezek. 28:12; van Dijk 1968, 118). This option strengthens the link to the serpent in Genesis. Whether the subject is designated as "the far-covering cherub" (Fisch 1950, 192), "a wing-spread cherub" (van Dijk 1968, 119), or "a great shielding cherub" (Greenberg 1997, 579), the expression evokes the *cherubim* in the most holy place of the Israelite tabernacle (Exod. 25:20; 37:9; 1 Chron. 28:18; 1 Kings 8:7). The "great shielding cherub" occupies a position in God's immediate presence and has God's interests at heart.

The subtlety of Revelation's story becomes more striking when "the Ancient Serpent" is given its due (Jensen 1997, 343). In Isaiah, the topic of interest is what "the Shining One" says secretly about *himself* in his heart (Isa. 14:13–14). In Genesis, by contrast, we are told what the serpent says publicly about *God*. "Now the serpent was more subtle than any other wild animal that the LORD God had made," we read in Genesis (3:1). Despite views to the contrary, this "serpent" is more than a clever *animal* (Tonstad 2016a, 95–100). More than animal intelligence is at work when the serpent says to the woman, "Did God say, 'You shall not eat from any tree in the garden'?" (Gen. 3:1, my trans.). This is "the Ancient Serpent" speaking. Genesis supplies two of the characteristics that appear explicitly in Revelation. He is the *serpent*, and he is the *deceiver* (Gen. 3:1, 13; Rev. 12:9). *Deception* explains why Revelation calls him "the Mudslinger" (12:9): he brings slander to bear on *God*. God had not commanded humans not to eat of "*any tree* in the garden" (Gen. 2:16–17; 3:1). In the serpent's version, the divine command turns into an all-out prohibition, ruling out the possibility that the command might entail good things like *permission, provision, promotion*, or *protection* (Tonstad 2016a, 87–103). Variant translations bend to the task of conveying the force of the misrepresentation.

"Did God really say?" (Gunkel 1997, 16)

"Ay, and so God has said!" (Skinner 1910, 73)

"Is it true that God has said?" (R. W. L. Moberly 1988, 6)

"Though God said, you shall not eat from any tree of the garden—." (Alter 1996, 77–78)

The speaker cleverly distorts the original statement. In fact, the serpent "first distorts the prohibition, and then affects surprise at it when thus distorted" (S. Driver 1904, 44–45). This fits the claim that the serpent is a *subtle* character. The calibrated distortion of God's command will be resistant to correction.

> Instead of "You may certainly eat from every tree of the garden" we have "You shall not eat from any tree of the garden" attributed to God. Why should the serpent say something which, as the woman duly points out, is clearly not the case? Apart from the fact that the serpent thereby engages the woman in debate, the main point lies presumably in the *implication* of the serpent's words. What matters is not that the serpent's words are obviously false, but that they imply that a total prohibition is the sort of unreasonable prohibition that one might expect from God, who is to be seen as more interested in restriction than in freedom. (R. W. L. Moberly 1988, 6)

A God who dislikes freedom—is this the first taste of the *Mudslinger* at work? If God meant the tree of knowledge as a *provision* (freedom) or as *protection* (in the face of danger), the Mudslinger construes it as a hard-fisted *prohibition*. What God intended as a positive is turned into a negative (Tonstad 2016a, 87–103). For this problem there will be no quick fix because the innuendo "is not dismissed simply by pointing out the obvious inaccuracy of the serpent's words" (R. W. L. Moberly 1988, 6).

But here, in Revelation, "the great dragon was thrown down," says John (Rev. 12:9). The timing is more than a moot point, given that the instigation of the conflict and the serpent's defeat do not converge in a single instant. While John concentrates on the defeat of Satan as "an eschatological event" (Aune 1996–98, 695), the *primordial* fall of Satan is assumed. The adversary could be neither "serpent" nor "ancient" apart from the primordial background. Conceptions in circulation at the time of John make it easier to understand the connection between the primordial event (Lucifer's "fall from innocence") and his apocalyptic expulsion (Lucifer's "fall from influence"). In Jewish tradition, "Satan was cast down from heaven in the beginning of time, but according to a widely attested belief he had still access to heaven" (Charles 1920, 1:323; Beale 1999, 656; Tonstad 2006, 55–107). Loss of access is in this scenario the last, or the next-to-last, nail in the coffin.

A mixture of thematic conflation and temporal telescoping explains the next scene best (Beale 1999, 639). **And I heard a loud voice in heaven, saying, "Now has come the salvation and the power and the kingdom of our God and the authority of God's Anointed One because the Accuser of our brothers and sisters is thrown down [*eblēthē*], who accused them before God day and night"** (12:10). Here, again—and stronger than ever—comes a reminder that the battle in Revelation must be understood in terms of ideology and theology, not power and force. In what way or by what means is "the Accuser . . . *thrown down*," emphasizing not only expulsion but loss of influence? He is "thrown down" in an absolute sense by the event that took place on the Maternity Ward of the Ages (12:1–2, 5). In this scene, the stance of the dragon is power and violence and the child an easy conquest. And yet the child, despite his vulnerability, triumphs (12:4–5), securing the defeat of "the Ancient Serpent" and "the Deceiver of the whole world" (12:9). We learn from this, at the very least, that the hallmark of God in the conflict is neither power nor violence.

In Revelation's fast-paced telling of the story, the child was not snatched away unharmed (contra Gunkel 1895, 174–75). He became a grown-up man, and he left blood on the ground as proof that his earthly life was more than a cameo appearance. The war in heaven in this chapter cannot be separated from the crisis in the heavenly council in chapter 5 (A. Collins 1979, 39); the solution to the crisis is also the reason for the victory here (5:5–6; 12:7–12). Moreover, Revelation does not call the adversary "the Ancient Serpent and "the Deceiver of the whole world" for nothing. Genesis contributes his name(s) *and* the plot. Just as the self-giving of Jesus is his means by which "the prince of this world" is defeated in the Gospel of John (John 12:20–32; Tonstad 2008b), so here. Likewise, the scenes of jubilation in Rev. 5 have the same focus as the celebration in chapter 12 (5:7–14; 12:9–12). A child, yes (12:5), but also "the Lamb . . . killed with violence" (5:6). This is how "the Ancient Serpent" is defeated and why he is "thrown down" (12:9–10).

The Accuser's loss of innocence is not the cause for celebration, but his loss of influence is. From henceforth, his sphere of operation contracts (12:13). Earth is a beneficiary, too, even though Satan's domain will now be the earth. The "loud voice in heaven" says that believers on earth **have won the war against him through the blood of the Lamb and the word of their testimony, and they did not love their life even until death** (12:11). The subject of the believers' witness is "the blood of the Lamb," understood as Jesus's violent death in combat, and this will be the pattern for discipleship. Thematic, temporal, and spatial boundaries dissolve not only because heaven and earth are interrelated space but also by fast-forwarding to the triumph over "the Deceiver" on the part of hard-pressed believers on earth.

Heaven is henceforth liberated space, a place where the innuendo of the adversary no longer resonates. **For this reason rejoice, the heavens and those who dwell in them!** is a statement that confirms as much (12:12a). Prospects are worse for the earth, at least short term. **How awful** [*ouai* = woe] **for the earth and the sea because the Mudslinger has come down to you, consumed with great rage because he knows that he has little time!** (12:12b). This "woe" (12:12), like the "third" of the stars "thrown down" (12:4), drives home the *retroactive* influence of Rev. 12 on the chapters preceding it, in particular the many "thirds" in the trumpet sequence and its mind-numbing woes (8:13; 9:12; 11:14). In this depiction the *Mudslinger* is already defeated. "Rage" [*thymos*] describes his state of mind because he refuses to concede defeat, and he is running out of time (12:12).

*Synopsis of the Culmination of the Conflict (12:13–18)*

**12:13–18.** The third tableau in chapter 12 links logically to what has just preceded it. Resolve, pursuit, and persecution are in view on the part of **the dragon** (12:13): **he pursued** [*ediōxen*] **the woman,** described by a verb that shows him to be in a hurry (BDAG 254, διώκω). Although Revelation pictures him as a defeated foe, he is still capable of causing harm. The identity of "the woman" is getting clearer. She is no longer an individual on the order of Eve but is best understood as the believing and witnessing community. The purpose-driven stance of "the dragon" indicates that he is determined to silence "the woman" and—if possible—destroy her. We have already been informed that she will not be left to fend for herself (12:6).

What lies ahead takes the form of a compressed synopsis of the next eight chapters (12:13–18). Speed is of the essence to bring the woman to safety: God gives her **the two wings of the Great Eagle** (12:14a), an image that recalls Israel's deliverance from Egypt "on eagles' wings" (Exod. 19:4). Here the image is particularized as though "the Great Eagle" is a person ready to help her. That "person" can hardly be anyone other than God (cf. Deut. 32:10–12; Isa. 40:31; cf. Koester 2014, 553). The pursuer is represented as "the Serpent," confirming that this term and "the dragon" are interchangeable, with greater suggestiveness for the former term. Just as God led Israel through "the wilderness" and later made it a place of refuge for the prophet Elijah (Exod. 16:1; 1 Kings 17:1–7; 19:4–8), so here. "The wilderness" is God's ally in the conflict and a counterpoint to the society that threatens "the woman" (Rev. 17:5–6). The period of flight is once again laid out on a time line, **a time and times and half a time** (12:14b). This term originates in Daniel (7:25; 12:7), and it recurs in three variants in Revelation (11:2, 3; 12:6, 14; 13:5). It should be seen as a period for witness *and* as a time of persecution. As with several of Revelation's other time elements, it intimates a considerable period.

What will the Serpent do to the woman? Revelation says that he **threw out** [*ebalen*] **water like a river from his mouth after the woman to carry her away by the flood** (12:15). John again resorts to one of his favorite verbs, "threw out" (*ebalen*). The same verb is used for Satan's expulsion from heaven (12:9, 10) and his complicity in the expulsion of other beings (12:4). The pursuit proves that the Serpent will not leave the woman alone in her place of refuge. A word combining "river" with "carry" is as descriptive as it comes (BDAG 856, ποταμοφόρητος). This adjective occurs only here in the NT, and the meaning has at least two possibilities: the adversary will overwhelm her by *persecution*, or he will do her in by *subversion*. In several OT texts, flooding signifies warfare (Isa. 8:7–8; Dan. 11:10, 40; cf. Pss. 32:6–7; 124:1–5). Water in this sense is a metaphor for deadly persecution. *People*, especially *enemy people*, are the means deployed.

The second possibility is subtler, and it centers on the fact that "the Serpent threw out water like a river *from his mouth*" (12:15). The mouth—as speech—is from the beginning the most characteristic feature of the serpent (Gen. 3:1–2). What is the "mouth" up to this time? "From the serpent's mouth issued rivers of deceit," says Paul S. Minear (1991, 72; Koester 2014, 553). Dochhorn (2010, 249) suggests the same strategy: "As elsewhere in the Apocalypse so now the mouth functions as the seat for a weapon." The trumpet sequence depicts "heads" and "mouths" in the most usual places in the forces of the adversary (Rev. 9:17–19). The terms are used not because they are strange but because they are to the point: these are the favored means by which the demonic forces "inflict harm" under the sixth trumpet (9:19) and again here (12:15). The Serpent has not given up on deception. This sets up the scenario that "the woman" *will not only be subject to persecution but is also at risk of being deceived.* Either way, her existence is in grave danger.

"The woman" made it into "the wilderness" on "the two wings of the Great Eagle" (12:14). Who else will help her against the "river" that is bearing down on her? John says that **the earth [*hē gē*] came to the rescue of the woman; it opened its mouth and swallowed up the river that the dragon threw out [*ebalen*] from his mouth** (12:16).

For "the river" as hostile people, simple curtailment will be enough, akin to the earth swallowing up the pursuing Egyptians in the time of Moses (Exod. 15:12). Another analogy is found in the action taken against those who rebelled against the leadership of Moses in Numbers. "The earth opened its mouth and swallowed them up" (Num. 16:30–32; 26:10; Deut. 11:6; Aune 1996–98, 707). In this scenario "the earth" is not only a refuge but an active and effective protector (Dochhorn 1997).

In the story of Cain's murder of Abel, by contrast, the earth swallows the (good) victim, not the (bad) perpetrator (Gen. 4:11). But the earth still sides with the victim. It acts in the threefold capacity of *receiving, resisting,* and *recording.* By *receiving,* the earth offers terminal refuge to the battered victim, a resting place where no more harm can be done. The earth is also *resisting,* taking it upon itself to make Cain "cursed from the earth" (Gen. 4:12; Tonstad 2016a, 118–21; Minear 1991). There is also the earth *recording.* The blood of Abel may be spilled and hidden in the depth of the earth, but the earth will take care that no one tampers with the evidence. Job sees the earth acting in this capacity when he cries, "O earth, do not cover my blood; let my outcry find no resting place" (Job 16:18). In an echo of the murder of Abel in Genesis, Isaiah anticipates the day when "the earth will disclose the blood shed on it, and will no longer cover its slain" (Isa. 26:21). These scenarios have meaning for an "earth" that acts protectively toward "the woman."

For "water" gushing forth in the form of deception, a more complex dynamic is necessary. In the foregoing (Rev. 12:15), first "the wilderness" and then "the earth" are marked off as friendly territory. They represent a domain that is aware of the woman's plight and ready to help. Perhaps it is territory where the threats of "the Serpent" are off-limits or can be neutralized (12:14, 16). It would be good to find this confirmed as a reliable assumption, but evidence to the contrary lies ahead. One surprise will arise from "the earth" (13:11), the other in a "wilderness" (17:3). In the initial phase, "the earth" appears to defuse the danger (12:16). Long term, this may not be the case.

*Rage* describes the state of mind of "the Mudslinger" upon his expulsion from heaven (12:12). Thwarted in his first attack on "the woman" (12:13–16), his rage intensifies. **And the dragon was seething with rage toward the woman and went away [*apēlthen*] to make war on the rest of her children, those who keep the commandments of God and have the testimony of Jesus** (12:17). The wrath gets worse within the constant theme of waging "war," precisely the term used for the war that began in heaven (12:7, 17). What, now, does it mean that "the dragon . . . *went away*"? Did he leave point A to go to point B, his movements easily traceable from the point of departure to the destination? Or, more subtly, does it suggest that he *vanished* after leaving point A? The verb hints at the latter possibility. What follows confirms it. He "*went away*" in a "motion away from a reference point with emphasis upon the departure, but without implications as to any resulting state of separation or rupture" (L&N 15.37, p. 187, ἀπέρχομαι). The prospect of a vanishing act, the dragon going underground, is the best option. The target of his rage is not in doubt: he is determined to destroy "the testimony of Jesus" (12:17), the "testimony" that sealed his expulsion and loss of influence in the heavenly realm (12:10). We have the strong hypothesis that he mobilizes to prevent the same from happening on earth.

In the lead-up to the next move, there is a parallel to the commissioning "mighty angel" in the trumpet sequence (10:1–10). This suggests that two opposing forces contest the same ground. That angel set "his right foot on the sea and his left foot on the land" (10:2). Here, **the dragon took his stand [*estathē*] on the sand of the sea** (12:18), land and sea again in view. He is a posture of battle readiness and determination. A demonic commission will match the angelic commission and the work of "the two witnesses" seen earlier (11:3–4). And, indeed, the dragon will also field *two witnesses*!

### War by Surrogacy and Imitation (13:1–18)

#### The Beast from the Sea (13:1–10)

**13:1–10.** The first feat upon the vanishing act of "the dragon" makes it seem like he has not gone away at all (13:1)! **Coming up from the sea** is a look-alike, a power that is not the dragon even though it looks like him. The **seven heads** and **ten horns** are there; the main difference is only that the **diadems** are now on the "horns" and not on the "heads" (13:1; cf. 12:3). David E. Aune (1996–98, 732) says perceptively that the dragon "has come to a standstill on the shore of the sea to await, or perhaps even to summon, the emergence of the beast from the sea described in 13:1–10." Emergence from "the sea" also suggests a point of origin in "the abyss" and thus serves as further proof of the demonic affiliation of **the beast** (11:7; cf. 9:1–11). Much more will be said about "the beast," but its essential character is announced from the start. It has **slanderous names** [*onomata blasphēmias*] written **on its heads** (13:1). The most appropriate reading for the "blasphemy" is *slander, misrepresentation,* and *mudslinging.* By this criterion, there is no change in the basic characteristics of evil's enterprise, only in its manifestation. Given that the dragon was frustrated in his initial attack (12:15–16), he fine-tunes his operation to ensure greater success. A closer look confirms the suspicion of *novelty* as well as *continuity.*

We have seen continuity at the level of appearance (13:1). Now the continuity extends to historical phenomena. **The beast** (13:2a) is a composite of the four beasts coming out of the sea in Daniel (Dan. 7:1–8). Here, one beast will do, as though the sea beast in Revelation has absorbed into itself all the main characteristics of Daniel's four empires. In Revelation, the fearsome fourth empire is transformed into the sum of all the imperial powers in Daniel's representation (Koester 2014, 569–70). This could refer to Rome, of course, as most scholars believe, but it also fits a transhistorical final embodiment of what the prior powers represented, as suggested in a later note of its deeds (Rev. 18:24). The Danielic background text does not discount the continuity, but it focuses, laser-like, on *novelty.* Daniel says—four times—that the fourth beast will be as follows (emphasis added):

"*different* from all the beasts that had preceded it" (Dan. 7:7)

"*different* from all the rest" (Dan. 7:19)

"*different* from all the other kingdoms" (Dan. 7:23)

"*different* from the former ones" (Dan. 7:24)

In Daniel, the fourth empire "is sharply differentiated from the other three" (J. Collins and A. Collins 1993, 299). How is it different, especially from the perspective of Revelation? Daniel scholars consider the fourth empire of Daniel to be the Greek Empire of Alexander the Great, but this will not work for Revelation. If John's Daniel-like beast refers to Rome or some transhistorical composite of all world empires, we need to find room for the oft-repeated assertion that this power "was different from all the rest" (Dan. 7:19; cf. 7:7, 23, 24). Continuity *and* novelty together are legitimate and necessary conceptions for what has so far been described (Rev. 13:1–2).

The phenomenon coming up from the sea is under commission: **the dragon gave to it his power and his throne and great authority** (13:2b). This is not a Gospel Commission, and there is no Good News. But it is a commission writ large, a "Fake Gospel Commission." The sea beast resembles the dragon to make the two almost indistinguishable, and the dragon commissions it to perform important work. The entire story is henceforth fixated on what this beast is up to, the first of the "two witnesses" to appear on behalf of the dragon. "One of the most shocking things about this third story is that God is no longer the main actor," says David Barr (1998, 102). "The dragon *acts* and God *reacts*," he notes. "This is the dragon's story" (D. Barr 1998, 102).

These are perceptive comments even though they make too little of the demonic features in the tableaus of the seven churches, the seals, and the trumpets. Nevertheless, as we are now entering "the dragon's story" at a level not seen so far, with elements exceeding our wildest expectations, the observation is timely.

The first novelty is enough to prove the point (13:3). The beast deals in death and resurrection! **One of its heads seemed to have received a violent death blow, but the death stroke was healed** (13:3a). The "violent death blow" suggests that "the beast" is doomed, but it returns from the dead. Onlookers are won over. **And the whole earth was dumbfounded, wandering after the beast in amazement** (13:3b). This is no mean feat for a cause that seemed hopeless (12:13–16). Did not the dragon pursue the woman into the wilderness to no avail? Here, the tide turns. "Going away" now looks like a brilliant strategy.

Readings of this chapter now face a fork in the road. Many interpreters see the Roman Empire as the beast from the sea. With this conviction comes a candidate for the head that "received a violent death blow": the emperor Nero and the myth of Nero's return (Bousset 1906, 360–62; Aune 1996–98, 738–40; Barclay 1959). This verse (13:3) is considered one of the strongest pieces of evidence by those who see the myth of Nero in Revelation. A number of features call this interpretation into question.

First, the language used to describe the mortal wound of the beast is identical to the portrayal of Jesus. Just as Jesus appears as "a Lamb . . . killed with violence" (*arnion hōs esphagmenon*, 5:6), one of the heads of the beast is represented "as if violently killed" (*hōs esphagmenēn eis thanaton*, 13:3). This parallel is better appreciated "in the context of the 'imitation motifs' within the Antichrist theme" (Rissi 1966, 66). The Nero myth works as parody, but it does not work as imitation. The symbols suggest that *imitation rather than parody is at work.*

Second, "to kill with violence" (*sphazein*, 13:3) is not the term one would use to describe a self-inflicted wound or a suicide, as in the case of Nero. The word connotes violence inflicted from without (Johns 1998, 780). Nero, the murderer of his adoptive father, his brother, his mother, and at least two of his wives, approached death at his own hand with all the fear and panic that his ungallant self-absorption could muster (Champlin 2003, 1–6). The tenor of the verb "simply forbids thinking of Nero's suicide, but rather a blow from an enemy's hand" (Rissi 1966, 66). *Imitation* remains the main thing in this scenario, and it does not lead to Nero.

Third, that the beast is "violently killed" points to a crucial constituent of its identity (Beale 1999, 689). Just as "the Lamb" is inseparably linked to being "killed with violence" (5:6, 9, 12; 13:8), so with "the beast" (13:3, 12, 14). This, too, points to imitation.

Fourth, while the *wound* is part of the identity of the beast, *it is the healing of the wound* that is the source of the beast's projected resurgence (emphasis added):

"its death-stroke *had been healed* [*etherapeuthē*]" (13:3)

"whose death-stroke *had been healed* [*etherapeuthē*]" (13:12)

"that had been wounded by the sword and yet *came back to life* [*ezēsen*]" (13:14)

The emphasis on the healing of the wound makes the Nero hypothesis even more doubtful.

> Now there is little evidence that the rumored resuscitation of Nero actually had any such effects. It did not induce either Roman citizens or Christians "to follow the beast with wonder." It did not enhance the seductive worship of the dragon, nor did it aid the dragon in his deadly war against the saints. In fact, the legend of Nero's pending return from Parthia was considered a threat to the empire and the line of emperors. If we are to understand the wounded head, therefore, we should look not so much for an emperor who died a violent death, but for an event in which the authority of the beast (and the dragon) was both destroyed and deceptively restored. (Minear 1953, 97)

On the keenest reading of the evidence, the dragon produces a look-alike, and the look-alike is best understood within the imitation motif. The difference with "different" (Dan. 7:7, 19, 23, 24) is precisely that it is *different*. In the history of empires, not much is different about the Roman Empire except for size and staying power, and much less is different about Nero, one of the most odious rulers in the annals of tyranny. If Satan's masterstroke is to conjure up a *parody* of Jesus, this is indeed a parody! On the other hand, if Satan's masterstroke is to call up an *imitation* that tracks Jesus so closely that it is taken to be the real thing, the world and the believing community have a serious problem on their hands. The imitative aspiration of the "white horse" in the seal sequence (6:1–2) and the similarities between Revelation and the Synoptic apocalypse corroborate this perspective. Such parallels include Revelation within "the essential consistency of eschatological thought" in the NT (Cranfield 1982, 510). The beast "coming up from the abyss" (11:7; 13:1) aims for nothing less than the obliteration of "the testimony of Jesus"

(12:17). In this scenario, imitation is a more important element than the notion of authority lost and restored (Minear 1953, 97).

The impact in the world is immense and devastating, described as devotion and worship (13:4). Behind the edifice of influence stands the dragon, whose scheme has brought him coveted success.

And now, as expected, *speech* becomes the focus of attention (13:5). This should be understood as speech occurring at a point when the influence of "the beast" is firmly in place. Again we have **a mouth**; again we have *speech*: the mouth spews forth **exceedingly big words and slander** (13:5a; cf. 9:17–19). Scholars tend to read the passive construct **was given** as a "divine passive" in almost all instances, but this is one-sided and simplistic. A few sentences earlier John says that "the *dragon* gave to it" (the beast from the sea) "his power and his throne and great authority" (13:2). This sentence is in the active voice, and the "giver" is not concealed. Who, then, is the "giver" of the "mouth speaking exceedingly big words and slander"? The text points to *the dragon*. This verbal form is not a *divine* passive despite the arguments for this view (Pezzoli-Olgiati 2002, 231; Aune 1996–98, 743). Rather, it is a *diabolic* passive. The dragon commissions speech in the form of misrepresentation and slander (13:5), and the period allotted to this activity, **forty-two months** (13:5b), equals the time allocated to "the two witnesses" in the trumpet sequence (11:2–3).

There is a Semitic, solemn, and prophetic texture to the statement **It opened its mouth** (13:6a). This is how a voice projecting authority speaks, in "an official, formal manner" (Aune 1996–98, 744). But the content of the speech rises from a familiar script. The beast "opened its mouth" **to slander God, slandering God's name and God's dwelling, that is, those who dwell in heaven** (13:6b). By now it is no surprise that the mouth is "the beast's most important organ" (Roloff 1993, 157; Schlier 1936, 117). "Slander" is a form of "blasphemy" when God is the target, but the point is not simply hostile speech directed at a transcendent entity. This is "speech that denigrates or defames," with "slander" as one of the lexical options (BDAG 178, βλασφημία). The undertaking misrepresents God, "God's dwelling," and "those who dwell in heaven" (13:6). The commissioner has entrusted the task of attacking the divine economy to an entity that is his alter ego and an imitation of Jesus! Satan will be represented by a Jesus-like figure to silence "the testimony of Jesus" (12:17). For this to happen, Satan deploys a beast that bears his ideological imprint (13:1–2) but was killed with violence like Jesus (13:3). Confirmation of the thesis is needed, but this view respects the symbolic representation in Revelation.

Subversion works hand in hand with persecution. Revelation's concept of "war" is at its core ideological and subversive, meaning that words are more important than weapons. Subversion is not absent in the announcement that the beast **was permitted to make war on the saints and to win over them** [*nikēsai autous*] (13:7a). In the first of the seven seals, John used similar language for the rider that "set out conquering with the intent of winning the war" (*nikōn* *kai hina nikēsē*, 6:2). And success now seems within reach. The beast from the sea gets permission to exercise **authority over every tribe and people and language and nation** (13:7b), and **all the inhabitants of the earth will worship it** (13:8a). This looks like success.

John mentions knowledge or activity already in place **from the foundation of the world** (13:8b). Does this refer to the time when names are written in **the Book of Life** and thus make a statement about divine foreknowledge? This possibility cannot be ruled out on semantic grounds, and it is preferred in translations. Alternatively, does the phrase point to **the Lamb killed with violence**, with this possibility evident "from the foundation of the world"? On semantic grounds, this option is as valid as the other, and it has stronger theological warrant. Being killed with violence "from the foundation of the world" could, on God's side, refer less to foreknowledge than to willingness, and the willingness was there. "Willingness" will in this conception be synonymous with a self-giving disposition. There is also a "dragon-side" in the text, and this option has significant explanatory power. Was there a potential killer, a figure of violence—*from the foundation of the world*? This possibility is rarely considered, but it has support in the Gospel of John. Jesus says of Satan that "he was a murderer *from the beginning*" (*ap' archēs*, John 8:44). Revelation's "foundation of the world" corresponds to "the beginning" in John (Rev. 13:8; John 8:44). In both cases, the story that culminates in "the Lamb killed with violence" begins in primordial time. John's Gospel contributes greatly to this scenario by adding that the would-be killer did not initially make his intention known: "he was a liar" (John 8:44). In this scenario, nevertheless, *knowledge* differs from *foreknowledge*. "Foreknowledge" should be reserved for something belonging to the future. What God possessed, however, was *knowledge* of a reality already present at that time: God saw what was brewing in the mind of the adversary "from the foundation of the world" (13:8).

The call to attentive hearing reverberates like a mantra in the messages to the seven communities, and now it sounds again. **If anyone has an ear, let him/her hear** (13:9). What is to be heard requires the apparatus for hearing to be in a state of high alert, and extraordinary spiritual sensitization. If what has preceded the call has not shown why, what follows will. **If anyone (is to go) into captivity, into captivity he/she will go; if anyone is to be killed with the sword, with the sword he/she will be killed** (13:10a; cf. Koester 2014, 575). The sentence may be in "impossible Greek" (Aune 1996–98, 750), but the witnessing ethos also belongs to the realm of the impossible. Like "the Lamb . . . killed with violence from the foundation of the world" (13:8), believers look to share the same fate. Violence on one side and nonviolence on the other are markers of identity even if the two sides in the conflict are look-alikes.

**Here** [*hōde*] **is a wake-up call to perseverance and faithfulness on the part of the believers!** (13:10b). The sentence needs an exclamation mark to convey that "here" is "a scarcely hidden call to attention" (Lambrecht 2002, 345). In the communities reading it aloud, this is direct speech. We can imagine John establishing eye contact with the audience through the assigned reader. And there is plenty about which to be perplexed: the beast arising from the sea (13:1); its resemblance to the dragon (13:1); the dragon-given mandate (13:2); the mortal wound (13:3); the resurrection (13:3); and the spectacular success (13:4–7). This is the sketch of the first of "the two witnesses" called into action by the dragon (13:1–10). It will be followed later by a further in-depth description (17:1–18:24). A second witness is now to appear.

### The Beast from the Earth (13:11–18)

**13:11–18.** The violent death and resurrection of the first beast highlights its imitative character (13:3). More imitation is evident when the second "witness" takes the stage. **And I saw another beast that came up from the earth, and it had two horns like a lamb and it spoke like a serpent** (13:11). Three elements in the sentence are the kind to arouse deep anxiety. First, this beast "came up *from the earth!*" This is unsettling because "the earth" was earlier an ally of the endangered community: "the earth came to the rescue of the woman" (12:16). No such rescue this time around! Now "the earth," too, is beset with danger. "The vision is saying, in the region of apparent safety the dragon will work deceptively to continue its warfare against the woman" (Johnsson 1992, 27–28). Peril appears where it is least expected!

Second, the beast looks like "a lamb" (*arnion*). This is the word used to describe Jesus earlier in Revelation (5:6). With this, the imitative aspiration of the opposing side is firmly established.

Third, speech will give him away, but only to a point. The conjunction "and" (*kai*) in the sentence is often given an adversative force: "*but* he spoke like a serpent" (13:11). This suggests a discrepancy between appearance and reality—a disconnect between the way a creature looks and the way it behaves. This impression is understandable, but it misses the mark. *Appearance* and *speech* are both deceptive. To speak "like a serpent" is a skill of exceptional order, with the allusion to Genesis serving as a reminder of what serpent speech can accomplish (Gen. 3:1). Revelation treats "the dragon" and "the serpent" as synonyms (12:13, 15), and this is also reflected in the Greek word that is used (Barclay 1976, 2:98; Hendriksen 1998, 148).

Serpent speech is *theological* speech. A "witness" that looks like "a lamb" and speaks like "a serpent" projects an attempt to undermine the achievement of the real "lamb" featured in this book. The plot structure in Revelation is on this point crystal clear: the child born to the woman (12:1–5) came to defeat "the Ancient Serpent" (12:9)—and did (12:10; cf. Gen. 3:15). "The Ancient Serpent" cannot win the war, but he can harass "the woman," try to kill her (12:13–16; 13:7–9), and—above all—direct his ire against "the testimony of Jesus" (12:17). Through all this *speech* is crucial, echoing the debut of serpent speech in Genesis, "Did God really say, 'You shall not eat from any tree in the garden'?" (Gen. 3:1, my trans.).

Serpent speech is lying speech, but it is lying at a level of skill that makes the lie believable (Gen. 3:1–6). In Genesis, the *residue* of the lie rather than the lie itself gives proof of the serpent's subtlety. A mere residue of the original misrepresentation is sufficient to ensure success (Tonstad 2016a, 88–92, 100–102). According to the lie's residue, God is "more interested in restriction than in freedom" (R. W. L. Moberly 1988, 6). Within the lie's residue the serpent's innuendo remains intact: *God is not a giving Person* (Gen. 3:1).

The second "witness" works in close coordination with the first "witness," both commissioned to make the aim of the Serpent a success (13:12). Chronologically, it is at the point when the "death blow" of the first beast has "been healed" that the second beast enters the fray. This detail represents another weak spot in the Nero hypothesis (Minear 1953, 97). The imitative characteristics of the two witnesses indicate that humanity will face deception on steroids.

Intent to deceive is evident in the very first move of the second "witness."

> And it performs spectacular signs, so that it even makes fire come down from heaven to earth in the sight of people, and it deceives those who dwell on the earth through the signs that it has been commissioned [*edothē*] to perform before the beast, saying to those who live on the earth to make an image to the beast—the beast that was struck by the sword and yet came to life again. (13:13–14)

The second "witness" spares no effort to convince the world that it is in the service of God. In these packed verses, three features stand out. First, the second beast serves the interests of the beast "that was struck by the sword and yet came to life again" (13:14). The relationship between the beast from the sea and the second beast is so close that it is best to describe the activity of the latter in terms of *commission*—a diabolic passive—and not simply *permission*—a divine passive (contra Aune 1996–98, 760). Second, the spectacular sign replicates Elijah's calling down of fire from heaven in his fateful showdown with the prophets of Baal on Mount Carmel (1 Kings 18:20–39; Rev. 13:13). At the time of the face-off in the OT, both sides agree that "the god who answers by fire is indeed God" (1 Kings 18:24). Elijah's God triumphs decisively. In the process, Elijah creates the impression that powerful signs are a reliable indicator of what is true and what is false (Tonstad 2016a, 215). Revelation does not adopt the Carmel paradigm of power—it repudiates it. Fire comes down from heaven, but God has nothing to do with it.

Third, the persuasive impact of the sign is intact, only now it works to the advantage of falsehood (13:14). If the "spectacular signs" are proof of God's activity in the world, it would be logical to heed the commission "to make an image to the beast" (13:14). This conception is modeled on the OT story of King Nebuchadnezzar (Dan. 3:1–6). This king, in a crude pushback against the reality of finitude and transience, erects a gigantic image. He commands everyone to worship the image. Those who refuse to submit have a death sentence on their heads (Dan. 3:6, 15; Aune 1996–98, 761). In Revelation, those who do not succumb to deception will likewise be forced to submit (13:14–15).

Fire from heaven is spectacular, but the "witness" in Revelation has more up its sleeve—and more than King Nebuchadnezzar could muster. The lamb-like beast from the earth **was commissioned [*edothē*] to give breath to the image of the beast in order that the image to the beast might even speak (!) and to ensure that those who would not worship the image to the beast would be killed** (13:15). A *diabolic passive* in the sense of *commission* makes better contextual sense than permission. *Breath* given to inanimate matter hints at a replay of the creation of human beings from the dust of the earth, where God breathes "the breath of life" into the nostrils of the first human (Gen. 2:7). In Revelation, the lamb-like "witness" appears to impart life and speech to the "image of the beast" in an apparent imitation of God. A statue thus coming to life is shocking; hearing it speak is astounding (Tonstad 2016a, 94–99). But this, too, fits the story in Genesis (Gen. 3:1–5), where a serpent *even speaks*— and, of all things, speaks about God (3:1). Even for a rational human being, it will be hard to stay unmoved in the face of such staggering feats.

The foregoing assigns priority to the *biblical* antecedents for the phenomena attributed to the "witnesses" in Rev. 13. In comparison to these OT anchoring points, a Roman imperial referent seems far less consequential. Are the "spectacular signs" attributable to well-known "staged cultic wonders" in the form of moving statues and "lightning and amazing fire signs," as Steven J. Scherrer (1984, 600–601) suggests (cf. Kraybill 1996, 26; Aune 1996–98, 762)? Does the gadgetry of the cult ceremonial rise to the level of sophistry found in the biblical antecedents? Secular descriptions of the Roman contraptions do not doubt that the cult "wonders" represented trickery. Lucian (*Alexander the False Prophet* 26) describes "a talking god," the miracle made possible by connecting cranes' windpipes together and passing them through the head of the statue, with a voice supplied from the outside. The difference between Lucian and Revelation "is that Lucian rationalized his account, telling us it was all mere trickery, whereas John apparently believes that the wonders are real, but that Satan is behind them" (Scherrer 1984, 601–2). Was the disbelieving secular observer on this point more discerning than John? A spiritual book committed to distinguish the true from the false now proves to be inferior to the pagan sources describing the same phenomena. Unlike Lucian, who did not believe in Satan and who understood that the signs and wonders of the cult he lampooned were produced by means of mechanical manipulation, John naively holds to the notion that the signs are real and that a supernatural agent is at work (Scherrer 1984, 602).

If, on the other hand, John describes an inanimate object coming to life on the order of the story of creation (13:15; Gen. 2:7), sees a mute object that can "even speak" on the order of the serpent (13:15; Gen. 3:1), and watches fire coming down "from heaven to earth" on the order of Elijah on Mount Carmel (13:13; 1 Kings 18:38)—then it will be necessary to admit a level of sophistication surpassing the feats of the imperial cult. The choice between *parody* and *imitation* is still on the table, but the weight of evidence tilts heavily in favor of imitation.

This does not mean that a power that thrives on imitation will stop being itself. The "self" part has shown itself in measures taken "that those who would not worship the image to the beast would be killed" (13:15). Such measures in the sphere of religion would normally be out of character with Greek and Roman practice (Aune 1996–98, 765). As further proof that the "witness" is true to itself, **it causes all—the small and the great, the rich and the poor, the free and the slaves—to be marked with a mark [*charagma*] on the right hand or on the forehead, and this in order that no one will be able to buy or sell except the one who has the mark [*to charagma*], that is to say, the name of the beast or the number of its name** (13:16–17). This account of "marking" could well be exhibit A for how thoroughly integrated Revelation is with respect to texts that are far apart in the book. Here, the counterpoint is found in God's determination to put "the seal of God" on the foreheads of believers in the sequence of the seven seals (7:3, 4; 9:4). Once the intent of both sides is brought into the open, they stand as mutually exclusive options for the earth's inhabitants (Aune 1996–98, 768). A person is either "sealed" or "marked." To be a "marked man" or a "marked woman" will in this context signify what it means in everyday speech.

The competing "marks" have a representative function. For both symbols, whether the "seal" or the "mark," they represent the *name* of the reality to which they point. This warrants the view that the sealing (and the marking) "symbolizes the central dilemma of the Apocalypse" (Resseguie 1998, 179).

|  | Seal of God | Mark of the Beast |
|---|---|---|
| **Text** | "Do not hurt the earth or the sea or the trees, until we have sealed the servants of our God with a seal on their foreheads." (7:3) | "And it causes all . . . to be marked with a mark on the right hand or on the forehead." (13:16) |
| **Relation to *name*** | "And with him were one hundred forty-four thousand having his name and the name of his Father written on their foreheads." (14:1) | "No one will be able to buy or sell except the one who has the mark, that is to say, the name of the beast or the number of its name." (13:17) |
| **Meaning** | representative protective not coercive | representative not protective coercive |

An imperial referent is too parochial compared to the cosmic and climactic tenor of Revelation's imagery. "Roman" candidates have been found, but they fall short of being persuasive. For a Roman emblem to match the word *charagma*, translated "mark," one option is "the name of the imperial seal, giving the year and the name of the reigning emperor, and found on bills of sale and similar documents of the 1st and 2nd centuries" (Deissmann 1901, 246). Another says that "the word for 'mark' was used for brands on animals" and "was also a technical term for the imperial stamp on commercial documents and for the royal impression on Roman coins" (Ladd 1972, 185). A longer but still tentative list includes (1) "the tattooing of slaves, soldiers, or the devotees of a particular deity"; (2) "Roman coins used to buy and sell commodities"; and (3) "imperial seals" (Aune 1996–98, 767). None of these options meet the criteria of being *revelatory, representative, universal*, and *climactic*. There is as yet no record that any of these possibilities were ever put into practice. George Eldon Ladd (1972, 246) admits as much, saying that "we know of no ancient practice which provides adequate background to explain the mark of the beast in historical terms" or a "historical situation associated with emperor worship which explains this prophecy."

Old Testament antecedents for the imagery of "sealing" exist. The Israelites were told to bind the commandments "as a sign [*'ôt*] on your hand, fix them as an emblem [*tōṭāpōt*] on your forehead" (Deut. 6:8). This was hardly intended as an outward emblem. Although it has found such expression among ultraorthodox Jews, there, too, it is part of a pedagogical system meant to help a person internalize the commandments. In symbolic terms, notions of internalization, understanding, and practice apply. *Choice* and *consent* do, too. It could be more than a coincidence that "the seal of God" can only be placed "on the forehead" (Rev. 7:3; 14:1) while "the mark of the beast" can be placed "on the right hand *or* on the forehead" (13:16; 14:9; 20:4).

The description of the second "witness" is almost finished except for **the number of the beast** (13:18a). John, or the one speaking to him in the text, is told to figure out "the number," **for it is a human number, and its number is 666** (13:18b).

Few riddles have engaged interpreters more than this. Should we look for a number that matches someone's name, as many scholars do? Or, looking in a different direction, is it wiser to think in terms of a scheme, an ideology, a comparison, and *not* a person (Lenski 1963, 411–17; Minear 1968, 123)? Criteria that look for something that is *representative, universal*, and *climactic* favor the second option even though the first approach boasts impressive support. "The gematria [referring to the number 666] does not merely assert that Nero is the beast: it demonstrates that he is," says Richard Bauckham (1993a, 389). For this view to work, Nero's name must be retroverted into Hebrew letters with an *n* added to the end. The reference to 666, correctly spelled and deciphered in Hebrew lettering, is by this logic a numerical code for *Neron kaisar* (Bauckham 1993a, 389).

*Gematria* and *isopsephy* are technical words for numerical representations of someone's name. With respect to the number 666, one strand of textual evidence suggests that the number was 616, and the original referent was Caligula (Birdsall 2002). This option has not dislodged 666, but even slight uncertainty with respect to the number weakens the certainty of the application (Blumell and Wayment 2016, 125). Accepting 666 as the best number, Claudius has been promoted as a more plausible referent—and better than Nero (J. Schmidt 2002). The myth of Nero is absent from the earliest available interpretations. Irenaeus, one of the most ancient sources, left out Nero from his short list of possibilities even though he had the biographical prerequisites to be a valued source (*Haer.* 5.30.1). Irenaeus's birthplace was Smyrna, one of the seven cities of Revelation, and he was well connected (Grant 1997, 2). It is likely that he was born no later than 140 CE (Frend 1984, 244), close in time to the historical setting of Revelation. But the myth of Nero's return is not on Irenaeus's horizon. G. K. Beale (1999, 719) makes this omission one of his main arguments against the Nero hypothesis, given that "such a lack of consideration is striking since Nero's infamous reputation as a persecuting tyrant would still have been well known." While Nero appears early in patristic interpretations, he is not the earliest suggestion or the only one (Gumerlock 2006). By the best computation of the evidence, "there was not a single dominant tradition of interpretation regarding the identity of 666 in the first few centuries" (Blumell and Wayment 2016, 135). The lack of certainty is well advised in view of the fact that the majority view (Nero) "asks us to calculate a Hebrew transliteration of the Greek form of a Latin name, and that with a defective spelling" (Mounce 1977, 264–65).

The number 666 is so peculiar that the yearning to turn it into a person's name should be resisted. The call to "calculate" or "figure out" is best undertaken at a higher level of abstraction. First, "the number" is closely related to "the name" (13:17; 15:2; 20:4), the two converging as representative expressions of the underlying reality. A big, broad, and theologically significant conception should be sought. Second, "the number" has an imitative aspiration. A number consisting of three consecutive sixes conjures up the implied counterpoint. *Seven*, not *six*, is the number for completion in this book and in the OT. On this logic, too, the number 666 signifies an imitation that is a stunning *incompletion*. David Barr (1998, 128) suggests that the number is an imitative multiple of the perfect number seven and thus something that is "incomplete and imperfect." Third, given that "the Ancient Serpent" proposed to fix a defect in the divine economy (Gen. 3:1), "the name of the beast" and "the number of his name" reek with the opposite of *improvement*. *Six* is not an improvement on *seven*, and 666 is triple proof that "the Ancient Serpent" fails to deliver (13:16–18). This 666 shows the fake, ersatz character of the project. At the level of rhetoric, and left uninterpreted at the level of rhetoric, the world of "the Ancient Serpent" is a world that bears the imprint of 666.

Who can read this without feeling that the number itself signifies fallacy and deficiency writ large?

Suggestive confirmatory evidence for this view abounds in the Synoptic apocalypse. Jesus's warning in Mark to "beware that no one leads you astray" (Mark 13:5; cf. Matt. 24:4; Luke 21:8) is followed immediately by the thought that "many will come *in my name* and say, 'I am he!' and they will lead many astray" (Mark 13:6). "False messiahs and false prophets will appear and produce signs and omens, to lead astray, if possible, the elect," he cautions (Mark 13:22; cf. Matt. 24:24). These sayings make use of the same words and phrases as Revelation, envisioning influences that will deceive (*planaō*), signs (*sēmeia*) that will have a persuasive impact, and a role for a false prophet (*pseudoprophētēs*) either in the singular or in plural. In Mark, Jesus takes the signs and wonders of the deceptive influence to be of such a quality as "to lead astray, if possible, the elect" (Mark 13:22; cf. Cranfield 1953; Geddert 1989, 235).

This parallels the false "witness" in Revelation, who "performs spectacular signs, so that it even makes fire come down from heaven to earth in the sight of people" (13:13). It signifies power and subtlety, all with the tenor of imitation and executed at a level of sophistication far exceeding the feats of the imperial cult. Simply to identify the second beast "with a priestly cult of John's day, whether it be the heathen priesthood or the imperial priesthood of the provinces, is too restrictive" (Vos 1965, 133). Thus also the question, "But if this *beast* represents propaganda for the emperor cult, how could it be lamb-like enough to deceive Christians?" (Sweet 1979, 241; Hooker 1991, 317).

| Revelation | Mark 13 |
|---|---|
| it *deceives* (*planā*) the inhabitants of earth (13:14) | they will *deceive* (*planēsousin*) many (13:6) |
| it performs great signs (*sēmeia megala*, 13:13) | and produce *signs* and omens (*sēmeia kai terata*, 13:22) |
| from the mouth of the *false prophet* (*pseudoprophētou*, 16:13) | *false prophets* (*pseudoprophētai*) will appear (13:22) |

Revelation will describe the two "witnesses" in greater detail (17:1–19:21). This is one reason to put the quest for the connection between the dragon's two "witnesses" and history on hold until the fuller account has been processed. Some judgments are nevertheless possible at the level of representation. The "witnesses" accomplish subversion by imitation (13:3, 11); they practice "serpent speech" (13:5–6, 11); they build credibility by "spectacular signs" (13:13–14); and they practice coercion (13:7–8, 15–17).

### Previewing Victory: The Redeemed and the Lamb on Mount Zion (14:1–5)

**14:1–5.** Revelation's tableaus are not arranged according to chronological sequence. We saw this in chapter 12, and we see it again in chapter 14. Here a scene from the end (14:1–5) comes before the witness preceding the end (14:6–12). The third tableau is also a scene from the end (14:13–20), culminating in one of the most off-putting texts in the entire book (14:20). The two "end scenes" differ, the first positive and hopeful (14:1–5), the second negative and fearful (14:13–20). The tableau lying between the two (14:6–12) might be construed as the center of a chiasm and by this criterion the most important part.

The first tableau begins with a celebratory scene of the end. **And I looked, and wow! the Lamb was standing on Mount Zion! And with him were one hundred forty-four thousand having his name and the name of his Father written on their foreheads** (14:1). A body "pierced" (1:7) and "a Lamb . . . killed with violence" (5:6)—and now "the Lamb . . . standing on Mount Zion!" (14:1). The details are subtle, but "the Lamb" was "standing" in the initial representation, too (5:6). *Standing* is the body posture of the winner: in the context of the cosmic conflict, "the Lamb" *is the last one standing*. Mount Zion is mentioned frequently in the Psalms and in the prophetic books, especially Isaiah. Here the connotation is victory, revelation, and restoration. In one important entry, God stands toward believers as a liberator and protector, and Mount Zion is the place of origin for good news (Isa. 40:9–11). God is the ultimate Good Shepherd. In that capacity,

> He will tend his flock like a shepherd;
>   he will gather the lambs in his arms;
> he will carry them in his bosom,
>   and gently lead those that are with young. (Isa. 40:11, my trans.)

More proof that Revelation is a tightly knit text is evident by the mention of the 144,000. This group came to view during the "digression" between the sixth and seventh seals (7:1–8). Adela Yarbro Collins (1984, 127–28) suggests that the 144,000 "are not Christians in general" because (1) they are numbered, (2) they sing a song that no one else knows (14:3), (3) they are firstfruits (14:4), and (4) they seem to have suffered untimely deaths. David E. Aune (1996–98, 804) holds out the possibility that the number in Rev. 14:1–5 might refer to "the remnant of Christians who survive to the end." Craig R. Koester (2014, 607), by contrast, writes that they "can best be understood as the whole Christian community," and this seems more persuasive. A symbolic understanding is necessary for all the options. The end-time connotation is strengthened when the figure "144,000" is put alongside the "200 million" strong force marshaled by the other side in the conflict (9:16; 14:1). This makes for an extreme numerical mismatch, but it might also be a contrast between cohesion (7:4–8) and chaos (9:16).

The celebration of the 144,000 is represented in an auditory image vastly exceeding any known sound, symphonic or otherwise (14:2). **Are many waters**

(14:2a) meant to conjure up waterfalls or the waves of the ocean? **Loud thunder** suggests a transcendent and majestic reality. If "many waters" and "loud thunder" do not normally produce exquisite harmonies, **harpists playing on their harps** (14:2b) make up the difference (lit., "harpists harping on their harps"). Good theology set to music is meant to soar. The lyrics are not disclosed at this point, but we may have heard it already, in the "new song" sung in the heavenly council (5:9–14), and we will hear more in the song sung on the "sea of glass" (15:2–4).

Here, the focus is on the singers more than on the song except that it is **a new song** (14:3). The restricted opportunity to **learn the song** can be seen from several angles. If the pedagogy of "learning" includes experience, participation, and execution, the apparent exclusivity is understandable. In medical training, the skill progression operates by the rule: "See one, do one, teach one." "Seeing" is entry-level learning, "doing" takes learning to a higher level, and "teaching" brings learning to completion. "No one could learn the song" suggests that learning is restricted to those who participate in the experience that is the subject of the song. John implies that this is an experience worth having. The points noted above apply broadly to the divine pedagogy, refined by the end-time orientation of the scene.

Problems emerge when this group is described in greater detail, beginning with the (alleged) negative representation of women and possibly of sex (14:4–5). Can the text escape the stigma of "deep misogyny" for exhibiting a biased, male perspective (Pippin 1992, 50–53)? **Not defiled** and **virgins** are taken to refer to "actual sexual practice," highlighting sexual continence "as a quality of the ideal Christian life" (A. Collins 1984, 127–31). A symbolic interpretation is more in line with Revelation's overall character, although the possibility of male bias and sexual apprehension is not fully muted. A search for OT antecedents finds promise in one of the most enigmatic passages in Genesis (Olson 1997). In the preflood era, "the sons of God" became enamored with "the daughters of humans," "and they took wives for themselves of all that they chose" (Gen. 6:1–2, my trans.). This strange story is elaborated in The Book of Watchers in *1 Enoch* (chaps. 6–19), where there is illegitimate comingling between heavenly and earthly beings like the text in Revelation describes.

> The single line "these who have not defiled themselves with women, for they are virgins" serves effectively as a trigger to call up an entire narrative from outside the book. It has the marks of a literary allusion: the words are vivid, and they grab the reader's attention, but nothing can be found elsewhere in Revelation to which they point. Events of some kind are implied, and one naturally wants to ask, What defilement is meant? Which women? What opportunity for defilement have these male virgins passed over? The reader wonders whether these remarks refer to some episode known to John and his readers but lost to the modern audience. In short, Rev 14:4 sends one off looking for a story. In the [Book of

Watchers] that story is found. The references to the watchers' defilement of themselves with women are anything but obscure: the tale is told in careful detail, and language of "defilement" is used to describe the angels' actions no fewer than six times in eight short chapters. (Olson 1997, 500)

These background passages do not have misogyny or sexual asceticism as their concern. With the help of the story in Genesis and the Book of Watchers, Revelation has added one more piece to the theme of cosmic conflict. The 144,000 are characterized by what they are *not* twice and by what they *are* three times. With respect to the latter, they are "virgins"; they **follow the Lamb wherever he goes; . . . in their mouth no lie is found, and they are blameless** (14:4–5). With respect to what they are *not*, **they have not defiled themselves with women** (14:4). Each term matters, but all comes down to a single reality. Virginity "stands precisely for . . . purity of teaching" (Zimmermann 2003a, 160), and the last characteristic says the same thing to remove all doubt. Amid mudslinging and misrepresentation by the other side, "no lie is found" in the mouth of this group (14:5). The common OT contrast between virginity and harlotry, or faithfulness and infidelity, is also in view (Isa. 57:7–8; Jer. 3:6, 14–22; Ezek. 16:25–28; Zimmermann 2003b; Koester 2014, 611). Although it is not explicit, a nuptial connotation is implied. This is not only a shepherd taking care of the sheep but also a bridegroom ready to meet the bride.

### Final Proclamation: God's Reaction to the Dragon's Action (14:6–13)

**14:6–11.** The scene on "Mount Zion" may be extraterrestrial, but the target audience in the next tableau is earth (14:6–11). Notions of "earlier" and "later" are fluid in a story that switches back and forth in time, uses telescoping, and allows scenes yet to happen to pop up in the present. Allusions to the OT continue, as expected, and the network of intra-textual allusions keeps expanding. Above all, the reality of *conflict* does not go missing at the point when three messengers take the stage (14:6–11).

#### The First Angel (14:6–7)

Revelation has earlier reported loud and ominous activity "in midheaven" (8:13). Now it has more—but a very different tune. **And I saw another angel flying in midheaven, with an eternally valid good message to proclaim to those who live on the earth—to every nation and tribe and language and people** (14:6). Good news goes head-to-head with bad news. After the fourth trumpet, "an eagle" or "a vulture" flying *in midheaven* announced a threefold, "How awful! How awful! How awful!" with reference to events in the trumpet sequence (8:13) and the demonic reality being exposed (8:13; 9:1–21). The three messengers now "flying in midheaven" are not operating in a vacuum (14:6–11). Every word, sentence, or flap of the wing is a contrast to the damage perpetrated by the adversary. "Awful" on one side (8:13), "good" on the other (14:6)—these are necessary conceptions for the drama taking place.

Three contrasts are especially important. First, the three angels are God's response to the activities of the dragon in the immediate context (12:1–13:18). The framework fits the conception that "the dragon acts and God reacts" (D. Barr 1998, 102). This means that the "two witnesses" working on behalf of the dragon, the "witness" from the sea (13:1) and the "witness" from the earth (13:11), will not have the stage to themselves.

Second, the three angels belong to the same domain as God's "two witnesses" in Rev. 11 (11:3–13). This is one more instance where Revelation describes the result before laying out the cause (11:11–13). Throughout, the tenor of conflict is acute. John calls the message of the first angel "an eternally valid message" or "enduring good news" (Aune 1996–98, 825). The word *euangelion* does not have the article and should not be confused with the "gospel" in NT usage elsewhere (Charles 1920, 2:12). A traditional conception for the "good news" will thus miss the mark. An OT influence is again at work, this time from the Psalms (Bauckham 1993a, 286–87).

> O sing to the LORD a new song;
> > sing to the LORD, all the earth.
> Sing to the LORD, bless his name;
> > tell of his salvation *from day to day.*
> Declare his glory among the nations,
> > his marvelous works among all the peoples.
> For great is the LORD, and greatly to be praised;
> > he is to be revered above all gods.
> For all the gods of the peoples are idols,
> > but the LORD made the heavens, . . .
> Ascribe to the LORD the glory due his name;
> > bring an offering, and come into his courts.
> Worship the LORD in holy splendor;
> > tremble before him, all the earth. . . .
> Then shall all the trees of the forest
> > sing for joy before the LORD;
> for he is coming,
> > for he is coming to judge the earth.
> He will judge the world with righteousness,
> > and the peoples with his truth. (Ps. 96:1–13)

The Psalm is telling for emphasizing enduring good news that will go forth "from day to day." This phrase corresponds to Revelation's "eternally valid message" (Ps. 96:2 [95:2 LXX]; Rev. 14:6). God's worthiness is the theme throughout: there is a call to ascribe glory to God (Ps. 96:6–7); to worship God (96:8); and to reckon with God's right-making judgment (96:12–13). Above all, *the affirmation of God's worthiness happens against the backdrop of the unworthiness of other "gods"* (96:5). This backdrop is far more pronounced in Revelation, but it is not absent in the OT. God's worthiness is affirmed in a context where God has been slandered (13:5–6, 11). False "witnesses" make deep inroads by pretending to speak for God (13:1–18). The heaven-sent messenger has a rebuttal, **saying in a loud voice, "Fear God and give him glory, for his hour has come—the critical moment** [*hē hōra tēs kriseōs autou*]—**and worship him who made heaven and earth, the sea and the springs of water** (14:7). Much of this is mentioned in the Psalm (96:1–13). To "fear God and give him glory" means to speak well of God, rejecting the adversary's slander. The parallel to the Gospel of John is unmistakable (John 12:20–33). There, too, is an "hour of judgment," but the "hour" is not only the moment in time when God will sit in judgment of humanity (Tonstad 2008b). Judgment is a matter of *revelation*, the time when forces and phenomena will declare themselves and be exposed for what they are. At the "hour of judgment," conceived in revelatory terms, "those who live in the earth" face a mortal danger from an enemy who is plotting against them. The notion of a "critical moment" is pertinent to the impending crisis, arising from a scenario of events that differs from judgment conceived in judicial terms.

Third, only a musical conception of Revelation will be spacious and fluid enough to capture the symphonic relations in the messages of the three angels. The first angel initiates a communication relay that culminates in the message of the third angel (14:9–11). This angel warns against accepting "the mark of the beast" (14:9), the "mark" representing the dragon's name and ideology (13:16–18; 16:2; 19:20). The "mark" does not stand alone, as we have seen; it is the counterpoint to "the seal of God" introduced in the sequence of the seven seals (7:1–3). When "the hour of judgment" in the message of the first angel is understood in *revelatory* terms—as "*the critical moment*"—we perceive better what is at stake. "And so just on the eve of this epiphany of Satan, God seals His servants on their foreheads to show that they are His own possession" (Charles 1920, 1:205–6).

If the first messenger appears "on the eve of this epiphany of Satan," at "the critical moment" (14:7), as now seems certain, he is engaged in a work meant to *prepare* the world for the satanic epiphany and to provide *clarity* and *security* (14:6).

The call to "worship him who made heaven and earth, the sea and the springs of water" (14:7) resorts to the language of the fourth commandment (Exod. 20:11). This allusion indicts the dragon in at least three ways. On the most obvious level, "the Ancient Serpent" cannot match *that*: he did not create "heaven and earth, the sea and the springs of water" (Exod. 20:11). The "size gap" between God and "the Ancient Serpent" is insurmountable. The call to worship "the one who made" is, reversely, a call *not* to worship "the one who did *not* make" (14:7).

Equally incriminating is the contrast between "the one who *made*" (14:7) and the one who *destroys*. The name of the adversary is in English "Destroyer" (9:11; Isa. 14:20), the leader of "those who destroy the earth" (11:18). The respective contributions of the two sides is pinpointed. God "made . . . the springs of water" (14:7) while the other side destroys "the springs of water" (8:10), in the final exposé turning "the springs of water" into "blood" (16:4). To worship *him* (God) happens in the charged contrast between "the Maker" and "the Destroyer," which is also a contrast between an economy of life and an economy of desolation (Isa. 14:20).

In a third application, the angel's use of the language of the fourth commandment echoes the most important OT affirmation about God (Tonstad 2009, 35–36). God is not only the One who *is* or the One who has *created* everything. The commandment in Exodus (20:8–11) and the story of God's rest at creation (Gen. 2:1–3) affirm God's *commitment*. "God is he who is *with* someone" (E. Jacob 1971, 52). But this affirmation, too, sounds against the backdrop of slander and misrepresentation, whether in the version that God is absent or that *God*, rather than the Destroyer, could be the one who destroys.

A juridical reading of the angel's message obscures the interactive contrast within which "the dragon acts and God reacts" (D. Barr 1998, 102), and it collapses the action into single divine agency. Judgment as "juridical event" is not a foreign idea in Revelation (20:11–15), but here, on the threshold of the final showdown, the judgment has the tenor of a "critical moment" (14:7).

### The Second Angel (14:8)

The interactive tenor continues with the second angel, but now with a new word: **Babylon the Great** (14:8a). "Babylon" will appear five more times (16:19; 17:5; 18:2, 10, 21), with two full chapters devoted to its exposé (17:1–18; 18:1–24). The lack of an explanation at the first mention might seem ill-conceived. But this is a problem only for the first-time reader without the need to suspect an "intent to omit" on the part of the writer. In a re-reader perspective, "Babylon" encompasses the two "witnesses," the beast from the sea (13:1) and the beast from the earth (13:11). Their intent to deceive is the initial *action* to which the message of the first angel is the *reaction*—or better—the *pre-action*. When the second angel proceeds to indict "Babylon" head-on, he is not changing the subject.

To many interpreters, the message is not difficult: The double **Fallen! Fallen!** (14:8a) proclaims "the certainty of the fall of Babylon-Rome, which, from the standpoint of the speaker, is an event that has not yet occurred" (Aune 1996–98, 829). Echoes of the OT (Isa. 21:9; Jer. 50:2; 51:8) contribute to the conviction that this will be a replay of "the conquest of Jerusalem by Babylon in 587 BC and the conquest of Jerusalem by Rome in AD 70" (Aune 1996–98, 830). This view originates within the framework of *parody*, with ancient Babylon as a model for Rome.

As noted earlier, this view is imprecise and simplistic for a construct that envisions *imitation*. It is perilous to apply the Babylon versus Jerusalem contrast as though the two nations serve as the pattern for the relationship between imperial Rome and the believing community in Asia Minor. There is *novelty* in the paradigm, and no novelty is greater than the Lamb "killed with violence" (5:6). Neither for "Babylon" nor for "Jerusalem" can a straight line be drawn to the new situation. God "made us a kingdom, priests to his God and Father," John says to the seven churches, alluding to the commission to ancient Israel (Rev. 1:6; Exod. 19:6). The vocation is now fulfilled in the believing community; it does not have reference to a political entity, nation-state, or geographic location. If Rome can be located on the map, "Jerusalem" cannot. Jerusalem of old has been transformed into metaphor.

The same goes for "Babylon." When Jeremiah speaks of the fall of Babylon, he is referring to the military defeat of Jerusalem's historic enemy (Jer. 50:2; 51:8). John's "Babylon," by contrast, is not an entity that can be fought in military terms, and this insight will strengthen in the exposé yet to come (18:1–24). Revelation is not indifferent to the demise of "Babylon" in absolute terms, but its main interest lies in the spiritual aspiration of "Babylon." **Babylon the Great . . . made all nations drink of the wine of her passionate immorality,** says the second messenger (14:8b). This is not the language for *Babylon* in the OT. In the eyes of the OT prophets, *Israel* is the nation that is charged with unchastity. Israel has "fallen" because of illicit relations with other powers, gods, and values (Jer. 2:20; 3:2, 9; 13:27). Babylon is charged with self-aggrandizement and conceit (Isa. 47:8; Jer. 50:24, 31), and it is called to account because of unspeakable cruelty (Isa. 47:6; Jer. 50:17). "Passionate immorality," on the other hand, is *Israel's* sin. When Revelation ascribes the sin of "passionate immorality" to "Babylon," it conflates the characteristics of ancient Israel and Babylon.

In the OT, Babylon's fall signifies that the danger is over (Isa. 21:9; Jer. 50:2). In Revelation, a similar-sounding announcement means that the danger is approaching the critical point. Revelation's "Babylon" has ramifications akin to the "falling away" described in 2 Thessalonians (Tonstad 2007, 133–51).

**Terms for the Enemy**

- Balaam
- Jezebel
- Sodom
- Egypt
- Babylon

"Balaam" in Pergamum (Rev. 2:14) and "Jezebel" in Thyatira (2:20) are "insider" threats meant to put the church universal on notice. In his account of the "two witnesses" (11:3–6), John describes "the great city that is spiritually called Sodom and Egypt, where also their Lord was crucified" (11:8). Here John is not guilty of a memory lapse; he knows well where his Lord "was crucified." His hyperbole is value laden, conveying ideological and theological collapse from *within*. Within the scenario of imitation, the dragon's two "witnesses" (13:1, 11) are not raised up from outside, from virgin, imperial soil. They are the dragon's remedy for the lack of success on his first try

(12:13–17), recruited and groomed from within as proof that the dragon did better when he "went away" (12:18).

Revelation turns a host of historical references into metaphors. Such conceptions apply to "Babylon," too. When the obituary is read over "Babylon" in Revelation, the closing sentence brings out the deed that clinches the verdict. "And in her was found the blood of prophets and of holy ones, and of all who have been killed with violence on the earth" (18:24). Rome is consequential and has innocent lives on its conscience, but it is not big enough to fit this measure of "Babylon." Rome is guilty enough, but it is less guilty of persecution of believers in the first century than has commonly been assumed, and it is not guilty of the lives "of all who have been killed with violence on the earth" (18:24). For this, we need an entity that is transhistorical and climactic in ways Rome is not. And we need a phenomenon that was born and bred to be good but now is "fallen"—and "fallen" indeed.

### The Third Angel (14:9–11)

To understand the third angel, the context matters more than ever (14:9–10). John says that the three messengers *follow each other* (14:8–9). This suggests thematic, situational, and referential continuity. The threefold sequence builds toward a climax—beginning with the "critical moment" announced by the first angel (14:7). When the second angel announces that "Babylon the Great" is "fallen," it does not signal that "Babylon" has ceased to be a threat. On the contrary, the threat represented by "Babylon" consists precisely of the fact that it is "fallen."

John concludes his account of the two "witnesses" with the second "witness" causing "all—the small and the great, the rich and the poor, the free and the slaves—to be marked with a mark on the right hand or on the forehead" (13:16). God's *reaction* does not beat around the bush with respect to the danger. **If anyone worships the beast and his image and receives a mark on his/her forehead or on his/her hand, he/she will drink the wine of God's wrath (14:9).**

The third message emerges as the most pointed and explicit *reaction* to the dragon's *action*. Reading it as the final element in the sequence, it confirms that the messages belong in the *action-reaction* framework. We are also reminded that the two sides are represented by a *sign* and that there is a sharply focused *confrontation*.

But who is doing what in the confrontation? What is action, and what is reaction? How much of what is thought to be God's action is God's *reaction* to the action of the other side? In most interpretations, *everything collapses into divine action*. The warning that the person who **worships the beast . . . and receives a mark on his/her forehead . . . will drink the wine of God's wrath, poured unmixed into the cup of God's anger (14:9–10a)** is turned into a picture of human beings in the hands of an angry God for failing to respond to God's summons. Beale (1999, 759) says that while "the intoxicating effect of

Babylon's wine seemed strong, it is nothing in comparison with God's wine." God's alleged role is not a matter for discussion, and this view is seconded in the following sentiment. "The wine in God's cup is much more potent than anything Babylon/Rome may have concocted" (Blount 2009, 275). God's story and the dragon's story seem to converge at the deepest ideological level with respect to the use of torture, the only difference being that God strikes the heaviest blow.

When the pattern of *action* and *reaction* is respected, a different view appears. Readers must not forget where we have been and what has happened so far. First, the crisis in the heavenly council centers on God's conduct in the cosmic conflict (5:1–3). The Lamb "killed with violence" solves the crisis in the council (5:6), *but the Lamb does not close the gap between reality and expectations.* On the contrary, God's revelation in the Lamb *upholds and widens* the gap. This is stunning, but God's side will henceforth be identified with the Lamb "killed with violence" (Bauckham 1993b, 64). Second, victimhood is prescribed for the believer, too; *victimhood* is the pattern for faithful discipleship (13:10).

Third, in the seals and the trumpets, God acts toward the other side in the posture of *Revealer* (6:1–17; 8:6–9:21) and *Restrainer* (7:1–3; 9:13–14). All the calamities in the trumpet sequence must be ascribed to the demonic side—with God imposing *restraint.* Progression to the final stage is pictured as the loosening of restraint (9:13–14). The story shows how "God's wrath" operates. A process is coming to completion (A. Hanson 1957, 165). In this process, "wrath" that is "unmixed" suggests that God allows the other side to operate without restraint (14:10). Corroborating evidence will come in the harvest scene in this chapter (14:14–20), in the story of the seven bowls (16:1–21), in the detailed account of the collapse of "Babylon" (17:1–18:24), and—above all—in the account of the enigmatic capture, release, and undoing of Satan at the end (20:1–10). These scenes uphold Jacques Ellul's (1977, 65) claim that it is "the action of these Satanic powers that in every circumstance provokes death in the Apocalypse, and not at all, never directly, the action of God upon men." But the mountain of evidence stacking up *downstream* in the book, important as it is, counts for less than the revelation found *upstream.* No scene equals the anchoring revelation of the Lamb "killed with violence" (5:6).

When "God's wrath" is understood as removal of restraint, someone other than God will be the perpetrator of horror. To receive "the mark" (14:9) is to be at the mercy of the one whose name and character are expressed in "the mark" (13:15–17): **they will be tormented with fire and sulfur in the presence of the holy angels and in the presence of the Lamb (14:10b).** Revelation reverts to the passive voice, as is its custom, but we need not hesitate in calling this a *demonic* passive. Torture has so far been a signature statement of the demonic (9:4–5). "Fire and sulfur," likewise, are the telltale signs of demonic activity (9:17–18). What happens "in the presence of the holy angels and in the presence of the Lamb" shows the culmination of satanic activity. John captures self-destruction working itself out, and in every facet his account is consistent with its antecedent in Isaiah. "You have destroyed your land, you have killed your people" (Isa. 14:20).

And yet it is not unimportant that these things happen "in the presence of the holy angels and in the presence of the Lamb" (14:10). In the emerging scenario, the Lamb is not the agent of the torment, and it misses the mark to see the Lamb "and the holy angels" as indifferent spectators. As noted in the introduction, Frilingos's (2004, 81) assertion that "the gash in the Lamb's body, so apparent earlier, disappears from view" is misguided, frightening, and a striking example of what happens when the cosmic-and-conflict aspect of the story is compromised. In the contrastive reading, the torment "with fire and sulfur" shows the work of the dragon, but the deed has *witnesses* (Aune 1996–98, 835). Witnesses confirm and remember the horrific result of an aspiration that has run its course to completion. At the point of completion, the contrast between "the Mudslinger" (12:9; 20:2) and "Jesus Christ, the faithful witness" (1:5) has never been greater. Nothing has disappeared from the heart of God, the Lamb, or "the holy angels." On the contrary, "the gash in the Lamb's body" shines more luminously than ever.

Time will not live down the horrors that "the Ancient Serpent" inflicted on the world (14:11). The background imagery is the demise of ancient Edom, described as a fire that shall not be quenched; "its smoke shall go up forever" (Isa. 34:10; cf. Gen. 19:28). The text gives a figurative meaning to smoke that goes up **forever and ever** (Rev. 14:11a; Caird 1999, 186), but the framework of the dragon's action and divine reaction makes duration a moot point. Interpreters of various hues assign agency to God (Stefanovic 2009a, 462; Osborne 2002, 540–41), and many, without blinking, read the text as though God penalizes the dragon and his followers with eternal torment (Koester 2014, 614). "Furious indeed is the divine reaction to idolatrous worship. . . . It requires endless torments," says one (Boxall 2002, 209). This misses the careful line of demarcation between the two sides in Revelation. On display is the dragon's action—its calamitous character and results—the smoke of its terror never to be forgotten. To think otherwise is to concede the success of the dragon's determination to make "the testimony of Jesus" of no effect (12:17).

**And they do not have rest day or night, those who worship the beast and its image and anyone who receives the mark of its name** (14:11b). This is the final take-home message in the warning of the third angel. "Rest" is a deep concept that denotes completion, plenitude, and the presence of God (Gen. 2:1–3). Absence of rest goes to the heart of the experience of "those who worship the beast." The problem is not that God takes their rest away but that the dragon does not offer rest. Worse yet, the problem is not only what the dragon fails to offer but what he takes away. The sentence is a study in contrasts. We are, as we have been all along, in "the dragon's story," where fear and apprehension are rampant, where everyone is an enemy and a potential threat, and where "rest" is nowhere to be found.

**"Day and Night," in the Throes of Conflict**

| Four living creatures | *Day and night* without ceasing they sing (4:8) |
|---|---|
| Loud voice in heaven | The accuser ... has been thrown down, who accuses them *day and night* before our God (12:10) |
| Third angel | There is no rest *day or night* for those who worship the beast (14:11) |

By contrast, the initial call to worship God in this passage is couched in the language of the rest of creation, urging people "to worship him who made heaven, and earth, and the sea, and the fountains of waters" (14:7; Gen. 2:1–3; Exod. 20:8–11), the God whose distinctive is nowhere more evident than in the offer of *rest*. "*No rest*" is by this criterion a state of deprivation, just as the number 666, billed as "the number of its name" (13:17, 18; 15:2), is a number of mind-numbing incompletion.

### The Faithfulness of Jesus (14:12–13)

**14:12–13.** Conclusions are critical. Without a conclusion, the story ends in limbo. But conclusions also impose controls on the message of the story, sometimes sending the reader back for a remedial session because the conclusion does not fit the story line. The conclusion following the messages of the three angels is another call to attention, clarity, and perseverance (Lambrecht 2002, 345). Here [*hōde*] is a call for the perseverance of the saints, those who keep the commandments of God as revealed by the faithfulness of Jesus [*tēn pistin Iēsou*] (14:12; cf. Tonstad 2006, 159–94). The call is necessary because of commitments that are under siege. The believers have accepted the risk of victimhood, a possibility etched into the bedrock of their pledge, and this commitment is nourished by the story of Jesus. The dual phrase "the commandments of God" and "the faithfulness of Jesus" are not to be read as law and gospel in the usual sense (Tonstad 2006, 168–75). The phrases relate to each other in an explanatory fashion, the second phrase explaining the first (H. Strathmann, *TDNT* 4:500, μάρτυς; Mazzaferri 1988, 120). Whether "the word of God" (1:2, 9; 6:9; 20:4) or "the commandments of God" (12:17; 14:12), they are explained by "the testimony of Jesus" (1:2, 9; 12:17; 20:4) or "the faithfulness of Jesus." Using the attention-arousing word *hōde* as the lead word, translated "here" (NKJV, NASB, NRSV), "this calls for" (NIV), "this is why" (NJB), or "under these circumstances" (14:12), John signals unremitting awareness of the terror that comes from the other side. "What matters under these circumstances is the perseverance of the believers, those who keep the commandments of God as revealed by the faithfulness of Jesus" (14:12).

We cannot miss that the appeal links *story* and *practice*. With respect to the latter, Blount offers the translation, "Here is the nonviolent resistance of the saints, those who keep the commandments of God, that is, the faith of Jesus" (2009, 276). There is no stage II, plan B, or violent phase to make up for what many find lacking in God's conduct of the war—just as there is no stage II, plan B, or violent phase on the part of God at the level of story. God's work is revealed in "the faithfulness of Jesus" from the beginning to the end of the conflict.

No further mention of this seems necessary, but there is more. **And I heard a voice from heaven saying, "Write! Blessed are the dead who die in the Lord from now on"** (14:13a). This is heaven's imprimatur on the meaning of nonviolence and victimhood. **"Yes," says the Spirit, "they will rest from their labors, for their deeds follow them"** (14:13b). This snippet of the heavenly dialogue is fully in line with the story so far. Death is normally a negative, but dying "in the Lord" is a different matter. The line that is drawn across time—"from now on"—has an apocalyptic and eschatological ring to it. On the far side of the line, and on the far side for those "who die in the Lord," waits vindication (12:7–12).

### Hope and Horror: Triumph and Implosion (14:14–20)

**14:14–20.** Revelation 12:1–14:20 is itself a complete account of the cosmic conflict, the story from A to Z. The progression through these key chapters is discernible although some elements require side-glances to sections lying upstream and downstream. The account of the end offers unique challenges in this regard, as will now become apparent (14:14–20).

John describes a harvest scene of grain and grapes (14:14–17). Harvest means the culmination of a process. In agricultural terms, there cannot be harvest unless the crop is ripe. This is also the case in Revelation. The splendid figure **seated on the cloud** is readily recognizable from Daniel, where he appears as the Right-maker (14:14; Dan. 7:13). He has already been featured in Revelation with an exclamation mark (1:7; cf. 1:13). The **golden crown** is a symbol of majesty, the **sharp sickle** an instrument of harvest (14:14).

A person of lower rank, an **angel**, calls out to a person of higher rank, Jesus, to begin harvesting (14:15–16). For a chain-of-command structure, this is odd. The person of higher rank should tell the lower-ranked person what to do, but it is less odd if the angel has a mediating role. This angel has ascertained that **the harvest of the earth is ripe** (14:15; cf. Joel 3:13). It is possible to construe **the one who sat on the cloud** (Rev. 14:14, 16) as someone other than Jesus, but no rival candidate is in sight. Angelic features do not exclude that he is a divine being. Craig R. Koester (2014, 623) uses the term "redemptive ingathering" for this part of the harvest.

The harvest happens in two cycles, or phases, each with a separate angelic commissioner. This suggests that two kinds of harvests are in view (14:17–18).

The "redemptive ingathering" is followed by a harvest without hope of redemption. The first sickle is in the hands of "the one who sat on the cloud" (14:15–16), the second in the hands of an **angel** (14:17–18). The connection between this "angel," the "altar" (*thysiastērion*), and the "fire" (*pyros*) recalls the scene introducing the trumpet sequence (8:2–6). As with the first cycle, the grape harvest does not begin before it is certain that the "grapes are ripe."

At this point the harvest scene turns almost impenetrably dense. **And the angel sent forth his sickle over the earth and gathered in the vintage of the earth, and he threw it into the great winepress of God's anger. And the winepress was trodden outside the city, and blood went forth from the winepress, as high as the bridles of the horses, for about one thousand six hundred stadia** (14:19–20).

What a mixture of the general and the hyper-particular! "Harvest" is a well-established concept. A "sickle" and a "winepress" are familiar instruments for harvesting. But the rest is jarring. In this "winepress," the grape juice turns into "blood," and the amount of blood is copious and ominous. The blood reaches "as high as the bridles of the horses," and it gushes forth by a measurement that is a multiple of four, suggesting not only a worldwide scope but also a destructive force at work (Koester 2014, 626). The distance equals "about two hundred miles," but the number entails more than a certain quantity (14:20; Aune 1996–98, 847–48). In quantitative terms, the wave of blood is at least five feet deep (Koester 2014, 625), reaching from where I am sitting east of Los Angeles to beyond the Mexican border. Moreover, all this takes place "outside the city." How does this shed light on "God's anger"?

The second harvest is not a "redemptive ingathering." It is described in terms borrowed from Joel: "Go in, tread, for the wine press is full. The vats overflow, for their wickedness is great" (Joel 3:13; see also Isa. 63:3). "In this vision the earth's violence, or 'blood,' has reached a horrific level," says Koester (2014, 626). "The river reveals how much blood the earth contains, showing the need for God's judgment against it." This view lacks perspective for the implication that God compounds the carnage. What, instead, if the "judgment" adds nothing to what the forces inflict on themselves? Harvest and judgment are closely related in the sense that things will be known for what they are. Scenes of destruction earlier in the book now come to a head in a judgment that signifies the "culmination of the process" (A. Hanson 1957, 164).

Readers need to take a broad look to make sense of the bizarre, composite picture (Rev. 14:20). R. H. Charles (1920) demonstrates that the city outside of which the winepress is trodden is not "Babylon" or the earthly Jerusalem. Instead, the city is "the New Jerusalem." Revelation 14:17–20 is "a proleptic summary" not only of the battle scene to come in Rev. 19:11–21 but still more of the battle in Rev. 20:7–10 (Charles 1920, 2:25; Swete 1908, 192; Ford 1975, 251; Roloff 1993, 178–79; Beale 1999, 781). We have a conflation of endings, one superimposed upon the other, confusing to the reader who wonders which end is in view, but with clear priority, nevertheless, for the ultimate ending. The city is "the beloved city" (20:9), "the holy city" (21:2, 10), and the ending is the end of all things. Reading Revelation from back to front, a strategy recommended by David C. Steinmetz (2003), explains the identity of the city and the battle transpiring outside its walls. If we line up these verses in the opposite order of their occurrence, it resolves the puzzle so well that one may wonder why John did not do it in the first place.

"And I saw the holy city, the New Jerusalem, coming down out of heaven from God, made ready as a bride adorned for her husband." (21:2)

"They marched up over the breadth of the earth and surrounded the camp of the saints and the beloved city." (20:9)

"And he will tread the winepress of the anger of the wrath of God the Almighty." (19:15)

"And the winepress was trodden outside the city." (14:20)

These texts settle the location of the carnage, but the action remains an enigma. Knowing that Revelation has two kinds of horses, whose horses are these? On the one hand, we have "the rider on the white horse" and his entourage. He is "faithful and trustworthy," and "he judges and makes war in righteousness" (19:11). It falls to him to "tread the winepress of the anger of the wrath of God the Almighty" (19:15).

On the other hand, Revelation depicts swarms of locusts looking like "*horses prepared for battle*" (9:7). Under the sixth trumpet, "the number of the troops of cavalry was two hundred million; I heard their number" (9:16). The horses are on a demonic mission; "fire and smoke and sulfur" come out of their mouths. Bloodshed and mayhem follow: "a third of mankind was killed, by the fire and smoke and sulfur coming out of their mouths" (9:18). Horses are a staple of the demonic force, but the battle is not going well. A complementary passage offers a revolting depiction of birds eating "the flesh of horses and their riders" (19:18). The army is routed in a defeat so complete that it takes the repulsive description in Rev. 14:20 to portray it.

Although "the rider on the white horse" treads "the winepress of the anger of the wrath of God the Almighty" (19:15), the two sides are not engaged in hand-to-hand battle. The weapon of the rider is the sharp sword that comes forth from his mouth (19:15). "By upright means [*en dikaiosynē*] he makes decisions and wages war" (19:11), and "his name is called the Word of God" (19:13). The battle "outside the city" is a battle of futility: *the word proves superior to the sword*. Only in a figurative sense is "the rider on the white horse" the one who treads "the winepress" (19:11, 15).

The torrent of blood in Revelation parallels the description in *1 Enoch*, with a clear theological implication.

> In those days, the father will be beaten together with his sons, in one place; and brothers shall fall together with their friends, in death, until a stream shall flow with their blood. For a man shall not be able to withhold his hands from his sons nor from (his) sons' sons in order to kill them. Nor is it possible for the sinner to withhold his hands from his honoured brother. From dawn until the sun sets, they shall slay each other. The horse shall walk through the blood of sinners up to his chest; and the chariot shall sink down up to its top. (*1 En.* 100.1–3, *OTP* 1:81)

Putting the pieces together, the horses and riders of the losing side turn on each other. No shot is fired from the other side; no sword is lifted. While there is a battle raging "outside the city," the redeemed "will not go out to the outside any more" (3:12). Blood flows "from the winepress" (14:20), "blood in such quantity that the horses are almost drowned in it" (Prigent 2001, 453), a "shoreless sea of blood" (Kiddle 1940, 286). This transpires "in the presence of the holy angels and in the presence of the Lamb" (14:10), and they know what it means: "this is the dragon's story" (D. Barr 1998, 102).

## Theological Issues

The central section in Revelation—the hub of the wheel—is a remarkable composition (12:1–14:20)—allusive, shocking, and enigmatic. For the category of enigmatic, the number 666 (13:18) and blood flowing "for one thousand six hundred stadia" (14:20) are challenging conceptions. All the crucial elements of the story are found in this section—Lucifer's fall from innocence (12:3–4, 7–9), his fall from influence (12:1–2, 7–12), and his rage-filled lunge to snatch victory from the jaws of defeat (12:13–18). This is laid out in symbols that overwhelm the referential capacity of the Roman Empire and the myth of Nero's return. The beast that looks like it was "killed with violence" (13:3) and the beast that "looked like a lamb" (13:11) are best understood as imitations. Their aim is to revive false representations of God (13:5–6). The theological character of the story is compromised by a small-screen, Roman frame of reference.

The weakness of the Nero hypothesis throws the door open to other possibilities. Rising now from the symphonic composition is the story of "the Ancient Serpent" and his project of false speech. This figure retains prominence in the story line till the end of the book and is equally a premise of the first half of the book. The cosmic scope does not mean that human institutions and power structures are absent. Bauckham (1993b, 44) does not abandon the Nero hypothesis, but he sees it as "one of the deepest ironies of Christian history that, when the Roman Empire became nominally Christian under the power of the Christian emperors, Christianity came to function not so very differently from the state religion which Revelation portrays as Rome's idolatrous self-deification." A "Christian" empire is by the symbolic parameters of Revelation a stronger candidate than the secular version.

In the fourth century, Eusebius developed a new template for the Christian view of the state (*Hist. eccl.* 10.9.9). Henceforth, the interests of the state matched the goals of the church. Caveats are absent: the bishop's vision contains "no wistful regret at the blessings of persecution, no prophetic fear of imperial control of the Church" (Greenslade 1954, 10). The emperor Constantine is to Eusebius proof of the workings of divine providence. A deep change of forms and allegiances in matters of religion and politics walks hand in hand with an even deeper revolution in the self-understanding of the community of faith.

To Peter Brown, this change moves to the top of the Richter scale of significant changes in history.

> From being a sect ranged against or to the side of Roman civilization, Christianity had become a church prepared to absorb a whole society. This is probably the most important *aggiornamento* in the history of the Church: it was certainly the most decisive single event in the culture of the third century. For the conversion of a Roman emperor to Christianity, of Constantine in 312, might not have happened—or, if it had, it would have taken on a totally different meaning—if it had not been preceded, for two generations, by the conversion of Christianity to the culture and ideals of the Roman world. (P. Brown 1971, 82)

If the symbolic world of Revelation were to supply a criterion for the magnitude of the change, nothing takes its measure as much as the adoption of coercion by the Christian community. Augustine (354–430) became the first person to write a full justification "of the right of the state to suppress non-Catholics" (P. Brown 1967, 235; Bowlin 1997). On this point, the practice of the "Christian" empire exceeded what the pagan empire had done. W. H. C. Frend (1984, 505) says that the ancient world "exchanged the guardianship of one set of divine masters, capricious but generally tolerant, for another that would brook no opposition." Other accounts of ideological and institutional continuity are legion, few rivaling Peter Brown's (1971, 135) poetic verve: "like the last warm glow of evening, the late Roman Senator's love of *Roma aeterna* had come to rest on the solemn façade of papal Rome."

Revelation operates at the level of symbols and representations. Drawing lines from the symbols to historical realities is a fraught enterprise, as all the dominant schools of interpretation prove. But the symbols favor a paradigm of *imitation* over *parody*; they fit notions of a *future* threat better than danger actualized in the *present*; and they suggest the near-unthinkable for what happened when "the dragon went away" (12:17). In the nearly unimaginable scenario, the dragon's two "witnesses" are not mercenaries recruited and

215

trained in a distant land, plotters scheming against the community of faith from *without* (13:1, 11). Subversion precedes imitation. "At the end Satan's attack must be launched from a beachhead within the Church, where the earth-beast not only carries on priestly activities but displays the credentials of a prophet," says Paul Minear (1968, 119).

Few images put the Roman paradigm under pressure as much as the idea that the Lamb "was killed with violence from the foundation of the world" (13:8); few images deserve more to have the final say concerning the theology of the book. Leonard Thompson speaks of this with sensitivity that makes it a fitting end to these chapters in Revelation:

> There is a permanence to the crucified Lamb that cannot be captured by locating the crucifixion in time, for example under "Pontius Pilate" or "in the first century of the Common Era." To put it differently, the crucifixion is much more than a momentary event in history. That permanence is captured in the book of Revelation through spatial, not temporal imagery. The "slain Lamb" appears not only on earth but also in heaven, close to the throne (5:6). The Lamb was not slain at a particular moment in time; rather the Lamb was slain before time. The seer describes that time in spatial language: the Lamb was slain "from the foundation of the world" (13:8; cf. 17:8). The crucifixion is enfolded in the "deep," permanent structures of the seer's vision, and it unfolds in the life of Jesus and those who are his faithful followers. (L. Thompson 1990, 85)

It cannot be said better than this—a reality "enfolded in the 'deep,' permanent structures of the seer's vision," his eyes now transfixed on the mind and disposition of God.

# Revelation 15:1–16:21

## The Seven Bowls

### Introductory Matters

Endings in Revelation come almost like beads on a string—in the knock on the door in the messages to the seven churches (Rev. 3:20), in the silence in heaven at the end of the seven seals cycle (8:1), in the announcement that "the kingdom of this world has become the kingdom of our Lord and his anointed" in the trumpet cycle (11:15), and in the scene of ending "outside the city" (14:20) in the previous chapter. And yet the story continues. The seven plagues (15:1) recapitulate the now-distant trumpet sequence point by point except for being more severe (16:1–21; 8:6–9:21). There must be a point, a message, and not repetition that is to no purpose. If Revelation's *paideia* at times seems demanding, we should assume that it maps out a learning curve tailored to our ability, first, and also to our need.

To one interpreter, there is a compelling reason for the seven bowls. "The wicked have to experience the final wrath of God in its full strength, without mercy and grace. . . . They have to drink from the cup of God's wrath" (Stefanovic 2009a, 485). Another voice is less blunt but no less modest with respect to understanding the bowls. "The eschatological wrath of God expressed against the inhabitants of the earth in Revelation presupposes a universal divine law or standard, repeated violations of which are now thought to have caused a final eschatological manifestation of the wrath of God" (Aune 1996–98, 870). The logic "is the anticipation that those who violate the laws of God will be punished" (Aune 1996–98, 870).

These sentiments are of a piece with a similar view of the seven trumpets, and they perpetuate the same misreading. If the acting subject in the trumpet sequence is demonic, who is the acting subject when the seven bowls recapitulate a scenario even worse? If the theology of the trumpets is revelatory, what is the theology of the seven bowls? Readers cannot afford to come empty-handed to a sequence announcing itself as the completion of a process already at work (15:1). Everything is related to the crisis in the heavenly council (5:1–5).

**Trumpets and Bowls: Common Ground**

| | |
|---|---|
| 1 | Damage to the *earth* |
| 2 | Damage to the *sea* |
| 3 | Damage to *rivers and fountains of water* |
| 4 | Damage to the *sun* |
| 5 | *Darkness* and severe *pain* |
| 6 | Activity at *the great river Euphrates* |
| 7 | *Loud voices in heaven* announcing the end |

The bowls should not be disconnected from the trumpet sequence whether with respect to agency, meaning, or theology. A punitive logic falls on hard times in the trumpets. Must it be reinstated for the bowls? My answer is a firm no, and we shall find additional reasons to temper the tendency to assign the bowl horrors to God. We have within this cycle proof of demonic agency in ever more spectacular rounds of revelation quite apart from the connection to the trumpets. Should doubts arise about the viability of this thesis, the Battle of *Har-magedōn* (Armageddon) will set the record straight (16:12–16).

### Tracing the Train of Thought

#### Revelation and Response: The Song of Moses and the Lamb (15:1–4)

**15:1–4.** The sense of process, forward movement, and march to completion is felt right from the beginning of the bowl sequence (15:1). "Signs" (*sēmeia*) have a revelatory significance when performed by the other side, too (12:1, 3; 13:13, 14; 15:1; 16:14; 19:20). Here, another revelation is about to begin, **great and astonishing**, the adjectives suggesting that the revelation will surpass expectations (15:1). The **seven plagues . . . are the last**, suggesting that there have been other and earlier plagues. The best candidate for plagues that might be called "first" in contrast to "last" is the trumpet sequence. This possibility is strengthened by the striking parallels to the trumpets, including the likelihood that the angels might be the same. **The wrath of God . . . brought to completion,** now added to the statement that they "are the last," confirms that we have come to the end of a process. Where the demonic activity earlier was operating under restraint (9:13–15), it is now untethered. This understanding of "the wrath of God" means *permission* and *the loosening of restraint*, on the one hand, and *revelation*, on the other.

Location matters, and the location is the sea of glass (15:2), the transparent expanse in front of the heavenly throne (4:6). Bits and snippets from previous tableaus reappear—"the sea of glass" from the initial entry into the heavenly council (4:6; cf. 21:8), the harps of God from the scene on "Mount Zion" (14:1–2), and the beast, its image, and the number of its name from "the dragon's story" (13:11–18). A victory celebration is afoot, staged by and for those who had won the war (15:2). The term signifies victory, whether for the believing communities in Asia Minor (2:7, 11, 17, 26; 3:5, 12, 21) or for the church universal (5:5; 12:11; 17:14; 21:7).

**Revelation 15:1–16:21 in the Rhetorical Flow**

Incentive to read (1:1–20)

To the one who has an ear (2:1–3:22)

The seven seals (4:1–8:1)

The seven trumpets (8:2–11:19)

The cosmic conflict from A to Z (12:1–14:20)

▶ The seven bowls (15:1–16:21)

Revelation and response: The song of Moses and the Lamb (15:1–4)

Open heaven: Preparing for the seven bowls (15:5–8)

The seven bowls: Aka the "seven blows" (16:1–21)

The first five bowls (16:1–11)

The sixth bowl (16:12–16)

The seventh bowl (16:17–21)

When "those who had won the war" break out in song (15:2–3), they confirm that song is the best reflection of their state of mind and the most delicate expression of Revelation's message. Hymns burst to the surface at critical points in the story (5:9–13; 14:1–5)—and here, yet again (15:2–4). The hymns are a key element in Revelation's *soteriology* (Jörns 1971) and a critical constituent of the book's high *Christology* (Ford 1998), but they speak primarily to *theology*: the kind of person God is. The crisis in heaven is captured, refined, and resolved in the hymns (Carnegie 1982). Massive choirs in an ever-widening circle of participants offer a gripping response to what has been revealed (Jörns 1971, 167). In this sense, surely, "the hymns of the Apocalypse are essential to its very plot" (Ford 1998, 211).

The thought aspect of Revelation's songs reaches a new high in the song now about to be sung (15:3–4). Here, the OT background texts are many and wide-ranging (cf. Pss. 22:3; 86:9; 111:2; 139:14; Amos 4:13; Jer. 10:7; Deut. 32:4; Lohmeyer 1926, 131), but the composition is sharply focused.

And they sing the song that Moses sang, the servant of God, which is also the song sung by the Lamb:

Great and counterintuitive are your actions,
Lord God the Almighty!

219

> Right-making and trustworthy are your ways,
>> King of the nations!
> Lord, who will not fear you
>> and speak well of your name?
> For you alone are faultless.
> All nations will come and worship before you,
>> for your notion of "right act"
>> has been revealed. (15:3–4)

The translation above leads to a specific context and point of origin for "the song that Moses sang" in Deuteronomy (Deut. 32:1–43; Fenske 1999). "Now therefore write this song, and teach it to the Israelites," God tells Moses as his ministry is ending, "Put it in their mouths, in order that this song may be a witness for me against the Israelites" (Deut. 31:19). And Moses did, posthaste. "That very day Moses wrote this song and taught it to the Israelites" (31:22). "Then Moses recited the words of this song, to the very end, in the hearing of the whole assembly of Israel," says Deuteronomy (31:30).

The song of Moses in Deuteronomy must be understood as a reflection of Moses's personal experience (Tonstad 2016a, 174–82). It is *his* song, originating in the twilight years of his ministry. The immediate background is his demotion after striking the rock when God had told him to speak to it (Num. 20:7–11). Despite Moses's plea to stay on and complete the journey into the promised land, his dismissal was upheld (Num. 27:12–14; Deut. 3:26–27). "You did not show my holiness before their eyes at the waters," God tells him (Num. 27:14). The details of the story bear on the meaning of the song and its import in Revelation. Diana Lipton notes Moses's evident rage at the rock incident, particularly his use of the word "rebels" (Num. 20:10), most likely shouted at full decibel. "By this hurled insult, his suggestion that he and Aaron will provide water for the people, and his impatient striking of the rock, Moses implies that he no longer numbers himself among them" (Lipton 1996, 87). Moses fails as a representative of the God whose chief attribute is to be with someone (E. Jacob 1971, 52), and he fails to embody the God who does not shout in anger. By his irate outburst, Moses becomes what the people are: a rebel. God tells him as much, "You rebelled against my command" (Num. 20:24; 27:14). God's verdict fits the gravity of Moses's failure. Moses is disconnected from the people and out of tune with the God he was commissioned to represent.

Against this background, the original "song of Moses" makes the song an admission of failure to represent God correctly. What Moses got wrong in life, however, he gets right in the song. One of the stanzas in Deuteronomy is the most important contribution to the hymn in Revelation.

> For I will sing the LORD's renown.
> Oh, proclaim the greatness of our God!

> The Rock—how faultless are his deeds,
>   how right all his ways!
> A faithful God, without deceit,
>   how just and upright he is! (Deut. 32:3–4 NAB;
>     see Skehan 1951, 157)

The hymn in Revelation is so indebted to Moses that it bears his name, billed as the joint composition of Moses and Jesus (Aune 1996–98, 872–73; Beale 1999, 793)! The two sing the same tune, theologically speaking. Revelation's version is more cheerful than the song in Deuteronomy, but the Mosaic contribution is liberally acknowledged. The translation favored above brings out three key elements. First, this is "the song that Moses sang," and it is also "the song sung by the Lamb" (Rev. 15:3). For this to work, we have the words supplied from a literal song in the OT with a figurative meaning: Moses composed a song for the ages, and it was certified and amplified by "the Lamb." The composition arises from the same ideological point of view, and the phrases have the sense of "legacy."

Second, the song in Revelation answers a bigger question than in Deuteronomy, but the setting in Deuteronomy has more in common with Revelation than is generally understood. "There is much in this song that gives the idea that it took place in Yahweh's heavenly court," says John M. Wiebe (1989, 140) of the song in Deuteronomy. In Revelation, the hymn is sung in answer to the crisis in the heavenly council—in the wake of the revelation. Perplexity and lack of confidence in God's ways change to understanding, admiration, and acclaim (5:1–4; 15:1–4).

Third, the affirmations in the song are deep and underappreciated. What the adversary in the cosmic conflict said about God was not true, but what is true is not what was expected. Transcendence sprang a surprise on the world (5:5–6). Nothing conformed to expectations, whether the self-giving of the Lamb "killed with violence" (5:6) or the permission given to the other side to stage its own demise (14:17–20). Just as "the lion of the tribe of Judah" conjures up an image altogether different from the sight of the Lamb "killed with violence" (5:5–6), "the wrath of God" must be reimagined by the displays of demonic activity under the billing "wrath" (6:16, 17; 11:18; 14:10, 19; 15:1, 7; 16:1, 19; 19:15). These are warnings not to draw conclusions simply based on what something is called.

The vocabulary of the song of Moses is a case in point. *Surprise* is the tenor from the very beginning, most translations preferring "amazing" or "astonishing" for the word *thaumastos*. The preference here, "*counterintuitive*," is a poor choice from the point of view of poetry, but it is well suited for a disclosure that is contrary to logic or expectations.

The song calls the ways of God *dikaiai* (sg. *dikaios*), usually translated "just" or "righteous." This is lexically legitimate, but it falls short of the dynamic of

221

this term in the OT. God's "righteousness" is God's main attribute. When it is applied to the human situation, we need to expand its meaning to cover the resultant action. God's *dikaiai* are *"right-making"* and *"right-setting"* and not only a form of legal redress (Tonstad 2016b, 275–77, 372–76; Skinner 1898, 90–91; P. Hanson 1995, 42). A similar and even more demanding logic applies to *alēthinai* (sg. *alēthinos*), generally translated *"true."* Here, *"trustworthy"* is the word of choice.

**Vocabulary of the Song of Moses**

| Greek word | Usual translation | My translation |
|---|---|---|
| *thaumastos* | amazing, astonishing | counterintuitive |
| *dikaios* | just, righteous | right-making |
| *alēthinos* | true | trustworthy |
| *doxazō* | glorify | speak well of |
| *hosios* | holy | faultless |
| *erga* | deeds, works | actions |
| *hodoi* | ways | ways |
| *dikaiōmata* | judgments | sense of "right act" |

This is easily defended on lexical grounds (BDAG 43, ἀληθινός), but the word must not be shorn of its range of meanings whether we view it from a background of Hebrew or classical Greek. Etymologically, *alēthinos* is the counterpoint to forgetfulness, "the removal of the curtains of forgetfulness in the mind" (Frye 1982, 135; cf. B. Williams 2002, 273).

This works for the message in Revelation, but forgetfulness was not the main problem. Truth was lost because of a smear campaign. As *true*, *alēthinos* will be the remedy for *false* (B. Williams 2002, 272–73). No conception of *true* in Revelation can afford to miss this contrast. Still, the preference for *trustworthy* stands. When *false* has surrendered to *true* with respect to a person, that person is *trustworthy*, and more so when the person in question has done the hard work to separate the true from the false. Lesser but still important notions are *care*, *precision*, *order*, and *coherence* (B. Williams 2002, 276). These are profound concepts, and the word is not made lesser by adding *sincerity* and *authenticity*. *Trustworthiness* in the context of the song of Moses has not been attained on the cheap.

The last word for which an explanation is needed is the word *dikaiōmata*, usually translated "judgments" (NRSV), "righteous acts" (NIV, NASB), or "saving justice" (NJB), all of which are legitimate lexical options. Nevertheless, it is necessary to specify that it is *God's notion* of what constitutes *"right act"* that has come to light, not simply a "righteous act" with reference to previous ideas of "right" (G. Schrenk, *TDNT* 2:221–22, δικαίωμα). On this logic, the song of Moses comes full circle: the *counterintuitive* surprise at the beginning is confirmed by a singular, hitherto unknown category of *right act* at the end. If another reason for these preferences is needed, let it be that "the song sung by Moses" is also "the song sung by the Lamb" (15:3).

### Open Heaven: Preparing for the Seven Bowls (15:5–8)

**15:5–8.** The song anticipates the action that is to come, comprising the seven bowls within the body of facts to which the song speaks (15:5–6). Sanctuary imagery is extensive in Revelation, and **the tent of witness** fits the revelatory thrust, especially with the additional mention that "the tent of witness" *was opened* (15:6). We may have seen **the seven angels** before, in the trumpet sequence. Even more to the point is the throwback to **the four living creatures** (15:7). We have a meandering but unbroken line from the time of entry into the open heaven (4:1) until this scene (15:7–8), first with a door in heaven thrown *open* (4:1; 11:19; 15:6), then the setting on "the sea of glass" (4:6; 15:2), and now with "the four living creatures" again acting in a key capacity (4:6–9; 5:6–14; 6:1–7; 15:7). This establishes continuity reaching from the seven seals to the seven bowls and not only between the trumpets and the bowls, where continuity is less likely to be missed. Adding this up, three cycles address the same problem; they are variants of the same theme; they have the same theological valence; and they have a revelatory purpose.

John says that **the temple was filled with smoke from the glory of God and from God's power** (15:8), suggesting the fullness of God's presence. There is nothing ominous about the fact that **no one could enter the temple** when the reason is the undimmed glory of God's presence. Old Testament antecedents describing God filling the temple to the point of curtailing all other activity are positive (Exod. 34:34–38; 1 Kings 8:10–12; 2 Chron. 7:1–2; Aune 1996–98, 881). It is unnecessary to give the scene in Revelation a different slant (contra Aune 1996–98, 882). The process coming to completion reverberates with finality. To this end, God throws the final revelation into the fray.

### The Seven Bowls: Aka the "Seven Blows" (16:1–21)

#### The First Five Bowls (16:1–11)

**16:1–11. And I heard a loud voice from the temple saying to the seven angels, "Go and pour out the seven bowls of the wrath of God on the earth"** (16:1). Readers shall be forgiven if, when reading this, we conclude that God is about to do something terrible. Something terrible is indeed about to happen, but the identity of the agent is not the foregone conclusion that it is taken to be. The box illustration repeats points that have been argued earlier: the setting in the heavenly council (4:1–6; 15:1–2); the participants (4:6; 15:7); the crisis

(5:1–6); the Lamb killed with violence as the *Revealer* (5:6; 6:1–17); acts of *revelation* in the seals and the trumpets now carrying over into the seven bowls; and the solution to the crisis at the end, the most articulate proof of which is the song of Moses (15:2–4).

### Seven Bowls as Revelation

| | Seven seals | Seven trumpets | Seven bowls |
|---|---|---|---|
| Setting | heavenly council | heavenly council | heavenly council |
| Participants | four living creatures | | four living creatures |
| Issue | crisis of confidence | crisis of confidence | crisis of confidence |
| Answer | revelation | revelation | revelation |
| Focal image | Lamb killed with violence | | Lamb, in the song of the Lamb |
| Conclusion | resolution of crisis | resolution of crisis | resolution of crisis |

Just as the first trumpet targets the *earth*, so does **the first angel** in the bowl cycle (16:2). The *kind* of action is straightforward. The bowl brings suffering to **those having the mark of the beast.** Many scholars have noted the similarity between the bowl plagues and the plagues afflicting the Egyptians in Exodus (Richard 1995, 77; H. Maier 2002, 152; Aune 1996–98, 884). The sequence is not the same, and the cosmic ramifications in Revelation are of a different order, but we do well to take something away from the language. In the context of Exodus, Terence Fretheim (1991, 386) notes "an extravagance of language, perhaps even a failure of language, in an effort to speak of the increasing intensity in the final plagues: every tree, all the fruit, no one can see, not a single locust, the whole land. Everything is affected or nothing. A hyperbolic way of speaking has taken control of the narrative." This characterization is perceptive, and it should be extended to how we read the bowl plagues in Revelation. Here, too, "a hyperbolic way of speaking has taken control of the narrative."

On this logic, the language itself is the best clue to identifying the cause. The line of demarcation between the two warring parties is similar to the Gospel of John. "The thief comes only to steal and kill and destroy," Jesus says of his opponent in John (10:10). By contrast, he says of himself, "I came that they may have life, and have it abundantly" (10:10). The action accompanying the first bowl, **an evil and vicious sore** (Rev. 16:2), is by this criterion easily assigned to the demonic side.

Each calamity reflects the quality of the object of veneration of "those having the mark of the beast" (16:2). Richard Woods (2008, 67) conceives the bowls as "physical and spiritual hurt to the natural systems of the world but especially the human inhabitants." "Plague" (*plēgē*) language is widely diffused (9:18, 20; 11:6; 13:3, 12, 14; 15:1, 6, 8; 16:9, 21; 18:4, 8; 21:9; 22:18), and it brings a sense of calamity: a blow, a life-threatening wound, or a beating.

Thus, "the Seven Plagues of Revelation could more accurately be called 'the Seven Wounds of Creation'" (Woods 2008, 67).

Mindful of the hyperbole, there is a trend and a theme: the demonic brand is losing its luster. In the first bowl, the "vicious sore" is reminiscent of the "loathsome sores" that Satan inflicted on Job (Job 2:7). The second bowl will not be better. Like the second trumpet, the second bowl strikes **the sea** (16:3; cf. 8:9): **it became blood like that of a corpse, and every living creature in the sea died** (16:3). Death and ruin are at work in the world on a large scale. The demonic economy is stripped of all pretense: death is everywhere. The death economy is contrasted with God's economy of life and abundance. Some readers are rightly impressed by the ecological character of the plagues—damage to "the sea" (16:3; 8:9), damage to **the rivers and the springs of water** (16:4; 8:10–11), and scorching by "fierce heat" as the sun's rays beat down on the world with increasing intensity (16:8–9; cf. 8:12; Hawkin 2003; C. Johnson 2014; Moo 2015). The vocabulary of global warming is recent, but we will be hard pressed to match Revelation's descriptive powers even if we are ecologically attuned. Such concerns lose nothing by the fact that John ascribes the ecological horrors to demonic incitement.

The third bowl also has ecological ramifications (16:4). Sources of life that were once pristine now reek with death. In the Gospel of John, Jesus begins his ministry by turning water into wine in a miracle celebrating God's gift economy (John 2:1–11; cf. Tonstad 2016a, 282–85). Here, the water turns into **blood**. The contrast is striking, and it clarifies further who is doing what. While the third bowl appears to add little to what happens in the second bowl, one detail needs further comment. Damage to "the rivers and the springs of water" means harm to elements of life lovingly created by God, the creator of "the sea and the springs of water" (14:7). Now, in the second and third bowls, these vital constituents turn into "blood," a telling metaphor for death. Whereas John in the trumpet sequence takes great care to describe the connection between the great star that "fell from heaven" and the damage done to "the rivers and . . . the springs of water" (8:10–11), less needs to be said here. The devastations speak for themselves.

But the comment that follows the third bowl does *not* speak for itself, at least not the way it is commonly read.

> And I heard the angel of the waters say,
> "*You* are in the right,
>> you who are with us and always were,
>> the Irreproachable One,
> for the way you adjudicate these things.
> Because they poured out the blood
>> of saints and prophets,
>> you have given them blood to drink.
> They are in balance!"

> And I heard the altar respond,

> "Yes, O Lord God, the Almighty,
> trustworthy and right-making
> are your decisions!" (16:5–7)

My translation is close enough to the most common versions to highlight what the exclamation by "the angel of the waters" does *not* mean. The idea that the plagues are "covenant curses" like the curses in Lev. 26 or Deuteronomy does not do justice to the story line in Revelation (contra Gallusz 2008, 35; Koester 2014, 647–48). The notion that "one is punished by the very things by which one sins" has merit (Koester 2014, 648). Nevertheless, it falls short of the mark, given that the frame of reference for "the angel of the waters" is something other than punishment.

Ecologically oriented readings disavow the notion of punishment while affirming the correspondence between deeds and consequences: "They are in balance!" (W. Foerster, *TDNT* 1:379–80, ἄξιος). In broad terms, this reflects the moral order God has instituted, and by this criterion the consequences are God's work. In the context of Exodus, Fretheim (1991, 394) says that "the theological grounding for the plagues is an understanding of the moral order, created by God for the sake of justice and well-being in the world." Nahum Sarna (1989, 28) describes it as "moral ecology" that proves the interrelatedness of human and nonhuman reality (cf. Lev. 18:24–28; 20:22; Deut. 28:41). Barbara Rossing (2008, 372) puts these insights to use with respect to the plagues in Revelation:

> When waters and springs turn to blood in the third bowl plague, the angel ("messenger") of the waters interprets this through the logic of natural consequences, as a boomerang-like effect: "You are just, O Holy One, . . . for you have judged these things. Because they shed the blood of saints and prophets, you have given them blood to drink. It is axiomatic" (*axios estin*, Rev 16:6). Today, what is axiomatic is that if we continue on our perilous path we will inflict our own demise.

These comments affirm the moral framework of human existence. They are timely for pointing out ecological effects, but they are not fully attuned to Revelation's theological concern. Three features of the angel's exclamation restore perspective. First, "the angel of the waters" repeats and deepens the affirmations of the song of Moses (15:3–4). Both songs echo the *theological* thrust that pervades the story. The setting and the participants at the beginning of the bowl sequence are reminders that the bowls cannot be dissociated from the crisis in the heavenly council (15:2, 7). Crucially, the songs are not affirming a view of God widely known to be true; they are proclaiming a point of view that seemed unsupported by evidence.

Second, the similarity between the trumpets and the bowls is stronger than the assumed link to Exodus, and it is more important with respect to determining the theology of the bowls. In the trumpet sequence, the demonic power carries out infernal deeds. A tsunami of misery floods the world, its demonic character made manifest in deliberately overwrought imagery. Revelation controls the story line, not Exodus, and the movements of the acting subject are closely monitored.

Third, when "the angel of the waters" speaks, he—like those who sing the song of Moses—uses words and sentiments from the OT (Staples 1972). Already in the OT the text upends a theological convention and not only when "the angel of the waters" repeats it (Jer. 12:1). Rather than speaking *for* God, Jeremiah speaks *to* God in a manner reminiscent of a lawsuit (Holladay 1963). He raises his voice in protest because he is perplexed by the discrepancy between expectations and reality. The text is subtle, and translations tend to under-project the unusual message.

Righteous art thou, O Lᴏʀᴅ, when I plead with thee. (Jer. 12:1 KJV)

You will be in the right, O Lᴏʀᴅ, when I lay charges against you. (Jer. 12:1 NRSV)

You are no doubt innocent, if I ever enter suit against you. (Holladay 1963, 281)

At face value, Jeremiah and "the angel of the waters" both say, "You are righteous" (Jer. 12:1; Rev. 16:5). But a face-value reading is trite and deceptive. As William Holladay (1963, 281) notes, "Jeremiah is not pleading his case before Yahweh. Rather, he is *passing judgment* upon him." This is unusual, to put it mildly: "It is blasphemous to suggest that a prophet can enter suit against God" (Holladay 1963, 282). Considering the complete text and context in Jeremiah, the prophet does not address God as though God is the judge before whom he pleads his case. Instead, God is "a defendant against whom Jeremiah has a quarrel" (Holladay 1986, 375–76). The tenor of the text is reproach and censure as though Jeremiah confronts "the all-righteous Judge with a legal challenge and with judgments the prophet himself has made" (Lundbom 2008a, 643).

When we add this up, "You are righteous" does not repeat a timeless theological axiom. On the contrary, it is "the formula for the declaration of acquittal pronounced in a law court" even though "to pronounce an acquittal on Yahweh is to be bitterly ironic" (Holladay 1986, 375).

Who expected this, whether in Jeremiah or in Revelation? Who expected the rightness of God to be in doubt? Who, indeed, was ready to hear "the angel of the waters" pronounce a verdict of acquittal on *God*?

*Revelation, that is who!* In the relevant OT passages, "an obvious question mark has been placed against the (alleged!) righteousness of God" (Staples 1972, 284).

"Let me put my case to you," Jeremiah says in his lawsuit, "Why does the way of the guilty prosper? Why do all who are treacherous thrive?" (Jer. 12:1). Questions like these are also heard in Revelation, at a higher decibel (6:9–11). The legitimacy of this question and its variants are at the center of the crisis in the heavenly council. When we bring these insights to bear on the exclamation of "the angel of the waters," the translation of the first sentence depends mostly on the boldness of the translator. Should it be "You are innocent" or "You are acquitted" or "*You* are in the right," spoken in awareness that there has been a process and that God at the beginning of the process seemed *not* to be in the right?

A logic of consequences is a valid ecological inference. A punitive interpretation misses the mark. The blood given to the perpetrators of violence "to drink" is the axiomatic outworking of violence. In this sense Isaiah is on the same page. "I will make your oppressors eat their own flesh, and they shall be drunk with their own blood as with wine" (Isa. 49:26). But the gist of the song is the vindication of God by the revelation of God's ways. "*You* are in the right" implies and invites the admission "*We* were in the wrong; *we* were mistaken; *we* did not know."

Damage done to "the rivers and the springs of water" in the third bowl jeopardizes the prospect for life on earth (16:4). This trend gets more ominous when **the sun** is struck in the fourth bowl (16:8). The sun is also the target in the fourth trumpet along with the moon and the stars, but in the trumpet sequence the problem is darkness (8:12). Here, the sun *scorches* **the people with fire** (16:8). It is not necessary to invoke modern notions of global warming for this depiction, but global warming it is. Causal relations are misperceived or deliberately falsified by those affected by the heat. They **slandered the name of God** as though this is God's doing, and they **did not turn to speak well of God** (16:9). The first angel's message in chapter 14 calls on people to "fear God and give God glory" (14:7). Here, the people do not **give God glory**, or, as in my translation, do not "speak well of God" (16:9). Interpreters who see divine agency in this plague create the expectation that scorching by **intense heat** will induce people to change their minds (16:9). This is not persuasive, and the reason is intuitive. Who would want "to speak well of God"—sincerely—while being scorched "with fire"? Those who experience the plague could just as easily be viewed as recalcitrant *climate-change deniers*, metaphorically speaking, not because they deny the fire but because they are unwilling to admit the cause. Mark Bredin (2008, 84) says that "the plagues represent the consequences of living by deception and accusation, the way of Satan's rule. The inhabitants cannot see that they have caused their own torment, and they cannot live with that knowledge. They blame those who expose them to the truth."

Reality is closing in on the opposing side in the fifth bowl (16:10–11). In the trumpet sequence, the hyperbole is most overwrought in connection with the fifth and sixth trumpets (9:1–21). It is less convoluted here, but the imagery leaps and twists so restlessly that the demonic referent is not any less in view (16:10–11). Is darkness a cause of *pain*? Or of *sores*? Neither one is logically connected to literal darkness, but they connect perfectly as descriptions of demonic activity. The bowls seem to be cumulative and not sequential, as they are in the Exodus plagues (Sweet 1979, 204). Darkness is common to the fifth trumpet and the fifth bowl (9:2; 16:10), and the connection is worth pursuing. Where is **the throne of the beast** located except in "the bottomless pit," the place where the fallen star set up headquarters (9:1; 16:10)? And what is the most characteristic product of "the bottomless pit" if not darkness? The mixture of metaphors works for a physical reality, but the spiritual overtones predominate. The causal explanation offered by those who are affected by this plague is as dubious as the reason given for the fourth plague. John says that people **slandered** [*eblasphēmēsan*] **the God of heaven because of their pains and sores, and they did not turn from their deeds** (16:11). *Slander* is a constant in the strategy of the adversary, and the essence of slander is to misrepresent a person.

### The Sixth Bowl (16:12–16)

**16:12–16.** The sixth bowl stands apart by its length, the eye-catching convergences, and the opportunity it provides for assessment and clarity. Crucial threads from earlier points in the narrative converge in the form of "the great river Euphrates" (9:14; 16:12); the mobilization for war by the dragon, the beast from the sea, and the beast from the earth (13:1–18; 16:13); the performance of signs (13:13; 16:14); the coming of "the great day of God"—all coming to a head "at the place that in Hebrew is called *Har-magedōn*" (16:16). The text must be read unabridged.

> And the sixth angel poured his bowl out on the great river Euphrates, and its water was dried up in order that the way be prepared for the kings coming from the rising of the sun. And I saw coming from the mouth of the dragon, and from the mouth of the beast, and from the mouth of the false prophet three unclean spirits like frogs. For these are demonic spirits, performing signs [*sēmeia*], who go forth to the kings of the whole world, to gather them for war [*eis ton polemon*] on the great day of God the Almighty. "Look, I am coming like a thief! Blessed is the one who stays awake and keeps his/her clothes so as not to go around naked that they might see his/her shame!" And they gathered them at the place that in Hebrew is called *Har-magedōn*. (16:12–16)

This is the longest, most detailed, and most enigmatic description in the bowl sequence. By itself, the term "Armageddon" or "*Har-magedōn*" has spawned an industry in disciplines as diverse as theology (Walvoord 2007; Weber 2004; Sizer 2004; Jewett 2009; Kierulff 1991), history (Falls 1964; Hastings 2005; Painter 2008), dark humor (Horne 2010), national politics (Morris and McGann 2016), and searing existential concerns (Vonnegut 1991; 2008).

In January 2017 a Google search on the word yielded 24,900,000 entries, and a simple entry on Amazon.com returned 25,134 results. "Armageddon" might well be Revelation's most successful contribution to popular perceptions of its message. But the word is not self-explanatory: it could be a prime example of a misperception, the one thing everyone knows that isn't what it is thought to be.

The sixth bowl is de facto the last because the seventh bowl is mostly a concluding declaration (16:17–21). It represents a striking parallel to the sixth trumpet. Both feature "the great river Euphrates" as the sixth element in the respective sequence (9:14; 16:12). Intention, finality, and ultimacy resound in both sequences, counting down to "the hour, the day, the month, and the year" in the trumpets (9:15) and to "the great day of God the Almighty" in the bowls (16:14). All stops are pulled—in the trumpets by cavalry of "two hundred million horses" on the demonic side (9:16) and in the sixth bowl by the demonic triumvirate summoning "the kings of the whole world, to gather them for war" (16:14). Both sequences conjure up world-historical scenes befitting the end of all things rather than a showdown that can be accommodated within Roman imperial realities.

No feature is more striking than the resilience, vigor, and ambition of the demonic side. If we yield momentarily to the idea that the first five bowls describe divine retribution, there should not be much vitality left on the demonic side. Instead of God unleashing a last strike, however, there is a climactic offensive orchestrated by the demonic side. The conspiring triumvirate is alive and *acting*; it is not simply *acted upon* by God. "*They*"—meaning "the dragon, the beast, and the false prophet"—"gathered *them* at the place that in Hebrew is called *Har-magedōn*" (16:16). In this translation, *they* represent the summoning and mobilizing element in this confrontation, and the pronoun *them* represents the people who are summoned and mobilized (de Villiers 2005, 209). Neither the one summoning nor the ones summoned show God directly at work.

Everyone is there, seemingly in the open: the dragon who "went away to wage war" (12:17), the beast from the sea with the mortal wound (13:1), and the lamb-like beast from the earth (13:11), here described as "the false prophet" (16:13; Aune 1996–98, 894; Koester 2014, 658). Once more, the mouth is the most conspicuous anatomic feature of the deceitful triumvirate (16:13). The unflattering allusion to Exodus is another telling tentacle: "three unclean spirits *like frogs*" (16:13; Exod. 8:2–7). In plain language we are told that "these are *demonic* spirits," capable of "performing signs" with the intent of persuading "the kings of the whole world" to join the false side (16:13–14).

"*Har-magedōn*," the location for the final gathering, is a strange "place" (16:16). For a good beginning summary, the word "occurs only here, where it represents the mythical apocalyptic-world mountain where the forces hostile to God, assembled by demonic spirits, will gather for final battle against God and his people" (Aune 1996–98, 898). The search for a "place," whether in biblical or geographical terms, has been inconclusive (and misguided). Etymology (word derivation) has favored the strategically located city of Megiddo in ancient Israel as the OT background, but this is unsatisfactory. There is no significant mountain at Megiddo (Day 1994), and the words are dissimilar. A composite word leading to the story of Cain is even less persuasive (Oberweis 1995). *Har-magedōn* may be elusive for a reason: the word was not conceived with an eye to earthly geography.

Words are important, but they are in the service of the story that is told. Stories have beginnings and endings, and the story in Revelation is no different. It is to be expected that the ending of the story will have some connection to the beginning, ensuring that the problem laid out at the beginning is resolved. Allusions to the war in heaven in Isaiah have been noted earlier (Isa. 14:12–20; Rev. 8:10, 11; 9:1–11; 12:7–9). This remains the best option for the meaning of Armageddon without the need to base everything on word derivation. Revelation takes the reader to the climax of a process and not to an earthly battlefield. C. C. Torrey (1938, 237–38) proposed that *Har-magedōn* is best understood as the Mount of Assembly (*har mô'ēd*) in Isaiah (14:12–13), the mountain upon which the cosmic rebel wanted to sit. This is a coherent suggestion even though it is not a perfect match. Marko Jauhiainen (2005) argues in favor of the same passage in Isaiah (14:12–20) but for a different reason. In his view, the story peeking out behind John's expression is the story of the one who was "cut down" (Isa. 14:12, 15).

"Armageddon," or "*Har-magedōn*," will in this scenario be the name for an ending that has not forgotten the beginning. "The sixth bowl unmasks evil as it is expressed in the arrogant war of the kings. . . . The evil triad organizes a great war" (de Villiers 2005, 209). In plain language, *the bowls describe demonic horror and not divine terror, and the demonic horror in the sixth bowl is the crowning deception.* This view of agency applies to the seals, the trumpets, and the bowls, all carrying a revelatory message. In the bowls, the climactic unmasking has been held in suspense until the next-to-last item in the last cycle. The unexpected interjection in the middle of the sixth bowl serves as a reminder to be vigilant and not fall victim to the scheme set in motion by the false triumvirate (16:15).

The frantic activity of the demonic side at *Har-magedōn* does not mean that God is idle. For a time line, the mobilization leading to *Har-magedōn* is best located *before* the drying up of the Euphrates, an event accompanying the arrival of "the kings coming from the rising of the sun," that is, "from the east" (16:12). These "kings" are the good kind: this is God at work. On intratextual terms, the angel carrying "the seal of God" also came "from the rising of the sun" with a seal of protection in preparation for the final crisis (7:2). Here, in the run-up to *Har-magedōn*, the great things from the east must be understood in the light of OT antecedents. "Who has raised up a righteous one from the east and calls him to follow?" Isaiah asks about a deliverer who is to appear (Isa. 41:2; McKenzie 2008, 26). A judgment is approaching, a final contest between the false and the genuine (Baltzer 2001, 87, 89). "I have aroused one from the north, and he has come; from the rising of the sun he will call on My name," says Isaiah of the same figure (Isa. 41:25 NASB). This, too, happens in the context of a legal contest: "the challenge here is addressed not to the nations but to their gods" (McKenzie 2008, 34–35). "It is I who says to the depth of the sea, 'Be dried up!' And I will make your rivers dry," Isaiah says again (44:27 NASB), another token that the other side will go down to defeat.

### Har-magedōn, Exposé of Intent

| Intent at the Beginning | Reality at the End |
| --- | --- |
| I will sit on the mount of assembly [har-mô'ēd] . . . I will make myself like the Most High. (Isa. 14:13–14) | And they gathered them at the place that in Hebrew is called Har-magedōn. (Rev. 16:16) |

The dense and demanding poetry of these chapters in Isaiah echoes in Revelation. As in Isaiah, the confrontation at *Har-magedōn* heralds a theophany: God will make an appearance (Baltzer 2001, 212). The forces of chaos dry up (Baltzer 2001, 263). Cyrus, the promised deliverer in Isaiah, is in Revelation a type of the Messiah. The Euphrates of history was a reliable water source, never known to have dried up (Aune 1996–98, 890–91), but now it does. Other possible antecedents are the parting of the Red Sea in Exodus (Exod. 14:21; Isa. 11:15; Jer. 51:36) and the alleged diversion of the river Euphrates by Cyrus at the time of his conquest of Babylon, as told by Herodotus (*Hist.* 1.192). This "memory" lacks historical support, and Revelation exercises tight control over its own imagery. In the chapter to come, John sees a woman "seated on many waters" (17:1), and his guide explains that "the waters that you saw . . . are peoples, and multitudes and nations and languages" (17:15). For such a conception of a river that dries up, the prospect is that the summons to "the kings of the whole world" (16:13) culminates in failure and loss of support (16:12). Most important is the idea that "the drying up of rivers is one of the responses of nature to the coming of God" (Isa. 50:2; Hosea 13:15; Nah. 1:4; Aune 1996–98, 891). This means hope; it means that *hope* is writ large in the text describing the calamity known as Armageddon.

### The Seventh Bowl (16:17–21)

**16:17–21.** "Armageddon" is such a dominant image in the bowl sequence that it is tempting to go no further. But there is a seventh bowl (16:17). In ecological terms, the bowls have laid waste the three mainstays of life, "the earth" (16:1), "the sea and the springs of water" (16:3, 4), and "the air" (16:17), and "the sun" has turned hostile toward earthly life (16:8–9). There is no new calamity after the sixth bowl, but there is an announcement: **"It is done!"** (16:17). What, now, is *done*? *Revelation* has run its course to completion. The scene is analogous to the announcement at the cross in the Gospel of John, "It is finished!" (John

19:30). Both places capture the moment of completion by a single word in the perfect tense. The choreography of revelation that accompanies the cycles of seals, trumpets, and bowls is now unleashed one last time (16:18).

### Scenes of Completion

|              | Greek       | English          |
| ------------ | ----------- | ---------------- |
| **John's Gospel** | *tetelestai* | "It is finished!" |
| **Revelation**    | *gegonen*    | "It is done!"     |

What follows may be included in the bowl sequence, but it is also a summary of what is left to tell and a point of transition. **And the great city became three parts, and the cities of the nations collapsed. And Babylon the Great was remembered before God to give to her the cup of the wine of the fury of God's wrath** (16:19). Elements in this description can be traced to things we have read earlier, but most of it awaits further elaboration. Collapse is a key feature. To be "remembered" means to be called to account. Here, the most elaborate and charged expression of "God's wrath—the wine of the fury of God's wrath"—is likely to revive concerns that divine agency is shortchanged. More is to come on this subject, too. Things are falling apart on the earth and in the cosmos, but the descriptions owe more to theology than to cosmology or ecology. **And every island fled away, and no mountains were found. And large hailstones, each weighing about a hundred pounds, came down from heaven on people** (16:20–21a). Chaos and dissolution have the upper hand. Disorder and distress are the order of the day even when we factor in hyperbole and the need to think in theological terms. Hailstones "weighing about a hundred pounds" are another clue that this is a demonic reality and not a natural disaster. John should be excused for putting out a round figure that to him was huge beyond belief. It is modest, however, if we imagine that the objects falling from heaven in the twenty-first century are not "large hailstones" but bunker-busting bombs, each weighing up to 30,000 pounds. The need for the imagination to reconsider long-held views is especially urgent for a story that time and again finds the opposing side guilty of misrepresenting the actual causal connections. This is the bottom line here, too. **And they slandered** (*eblasphēmēsan*) **God for the plague of the hail, for the plague was very severe** (16:21b).

## Theological Issues

### Two Songs

The most consequential elements in the bowl sequence are the two songs (15:2–4; 16:5–7) and the movements culminating "at the place that in Hebrew

233

is called *Har-magedōn*" (16:16). The songs are similar, the first song sung by "those who had won the war over the beast" (15:2), the second by "the angel of the waters" (16:5). Earth and heaven are on the same page, preoccupied by the same vexing concerns. "What happens does not take place in heavenly remoteness," Klaus Baltzer (2001, 212) says of Isaiah's contribution to important passages in the bowl sequence. "Heavenly and earthly spheres are related to each other to a degree hardly found elsewhere." If there is an "elsewhere" that shows even closer interaction, it is here, in Revelation.

The song of Moses extols what is the *"right act"* in *God's* eyes (15:4); it does not praise God's "righteous act" according to an everyday notion of "right." God has taken "right" and "right-making" into territory that shatters prior conceptions. When "the angel of the waters" announces a verdict of acquittal on *God* (16:5, 7), there is hyperbole, but the séance would be odd if not for the crisis in the heavenly council (5:1–3). The *singularity* of God's ways in Revelation is also a major topic in Isaiah's background texts: no one counseled God to do what God has done (Isa. 40:13). Indeed, the course chosen originated with God *alone* (Baltzer 2001, 68).

The songs confirm that the crisis has been resolved. God is theologically at home plate. God's approach to right-making has won the day.

### Armageddon Timeout: A Brief Excursus

Crude versions of "Armageddon" have made it into popular culture to such a degree that they define the message of Revelation. In the crudest versions, Armageddon means unprecedented violence (LaHaye and Jenkins 2003, 285–342). In the United States, "Armageddon theology" has established a foothold in large circles of conservative Christians and in the political establishment drawing support from these groups. Key features of American "Armageddon theology" are fear of communism, uncritical support for Israel, and the belief that Armageddon is a military confrontation fought on Israeli soil in the vicinity of ancient Megiddo (Weber 2004; Sizer 2004). "Armageddon" sentiments are "resistant to federal authority, hostile to the traditional American politics of compromise, rejecting government controls over the banking and business systems, and profoundly suspicious of international law and peacekeeping" (Jewett 2009, 67). "Armageddon" is the Christian version of holy war, and turmoil is condoned for its theological significance (Kierulff 1991).

In the aftermath of World War II, the German pastor and scholar Helmut Gollwitzer (1973) wrote a reflection based on the central cosmic conflict text in Revelation (12:7–12). Gollwitzer, appalled by massive Christian support for Hitler, had been part of the resistance. In his reflection, belief in the use of force that is at the center of "Armageddon theology" and similar belief systems is proof that evil is winning over good. It is proof, too, of the seduction against which Revelation is the most forceful antidote in the NT.

For we resort to force even though we ought to confess that the power of good which is at our disposal does not arise against the power of evil. Everyone has become a captive of a fateful illusion that believes itself able to drive out evil by force. In this world where we everywhere marshal force against force, we must learn that force at best may succeed in containing a few manifestations of evil, but it can never conquer or eliminate evil. On the contrary, the force with which we fight evil, has mainly the consequence that we ourselves become the victims of evil. As we resort to force against others, evil attacks us from behind and makes us evil ourselves. (Gollwitzer 1973, 128)

Subtler perceptions of Armageddon do not leave out war, catastrophe, or the notion of a decisive event, but they focus on ecological, economic, and psychological currents. In these reflections, the bowls of Revelation do not impose on human reality what isn't there. Damage to the oceans to the point that *"every living creature* in the sea died" (16:3), as in the second bowl, has yet to be seen, but marine life is seriously threatened.

### "Armageddon": Which One, What Kind?

| Scenario | Construct | Proponent |
| --- | --- | --- |
| retribution | "Armageddon" not specified | common scholarly view |
| retribution | "Armageddon" linked to the myth of Nero's return | common scholarly view |
| military battle in Valley of Megiddo, with retribution | literal reading of texts, "Armageddon" linked to Megiddo | evangelical and dispensationalist communities |
| revelation | climax in the biblical narrative of cosmic conflict | view of this commentary |
| radical change or cataclysmic event | "Armageddon" used as metaphor | historians, writers, polemicists |

No one knows for sure what the tipping point might be. Damage to "the rivers and the springs of water" (16:4), conceiving the third bowl in ecological terms, is in the twenty-first century such a pressing concern that access to drinking water will soon be a major determinant for world peace (Hynes 1972; Salzmann 2013). For the fourth bowl, describing permission given to the sun "to scorch the people with fire" (16:8–9), the imagination will not draw a blank. There is more than symbolic convergence between the fourth bowl and Auschwitz, in one part of the world, and between the fourth bowl and Hiroshima, in another. The crematoria in the extermination camps in Europe, the firebombing of Dresden, and the fiery mushroom clouds over Hiroshima and Nagasaki are not fictions: they are real-life displays of the power to "scorch the people with fire" (16:8). These events conform poorly to divine retribution, but they revive the conviction that a humanistic and naturalistic view of evil

235

is inadequate (Graham 2001, xv, 161). Human reality in the twentieth and twenty-first centuries keeps pace by acts of cruelty as heinous as in Revelation.

Dresden in February 1945 and Hiroshima in August of the same year call for a pause in our reading of Revelation. These events lay claim to our attention on their own merits, by offering examples of the power to "scorch people with fire" (16:8), and because witnesses to these events could not help themselves: *they thought they saw Armageddon.*

Kurt Vonnegut (2008, 36–37), the American novelist, was in Dresden as a captive US soldier when the firebombing was unleashed:

> In February, 1945, American bombers reduced this treasure to crushed stone and embers; disemboweled her with high-explosives and cremated her with incendiaries. The atom bomb may represent a fabulous advance, but it is interesting to note that primitive TNT and thermite managed to exterminate in one bloody night more people than died in the whole London blitz.

Fire was the weapon of choice, the intensity of the bombing so extreme that it created superheating akin to a nuclear blast. The experience led Vonnegut to write another essay titled "Armageddon in Retrospect" (in Vonnegut 2008, 208–32). Like his most famous book, *Slaughterhouse Five* (1991), the essay is noteworthy for the author's awareness that language is inadequate for the reality it seeks to convey. Calling it a *retrospect* is telling: it means that Armageddon is not an event relegated to the future. It is here, in *present* experience, with the author casting himself as an eyewitness (Vonnegut 2008, 209).

"Armageddon in Retrospect" differs from Revelation's showdown. Vonnegut appears to say that the world would be happy to recognize the devil and thus have the option of blaming the ills of the world on him. His concern is the devil within that human beings find hard to acknowledge. Still, his meditation is not wasted. There is depth to his irony, and he takes evil seriously. In a century that saw proof of ferocity on a demonic scale, neither Auschwitz nor Dresden nor Hiroshima did much to raise the status of the devil—*within* or *without.*

To James H. Foard, the nuclear bomb that annihilated many of the students of the Ichijo School in Hiroshima is another twentieth-century Armageddon.

> On the morning of August 6, 1945, the 669 students and ten teachers from Ichijo were between one and two hundred yards from the hypocenter, where most were exposed to temperatures of perhaps 2,000 degrees centigrade. Nearly all died instantly, although some who were sheltered probably died in the subsequent fireball, and their bodies largely disintegrated into the shattered white bones that remain after cremation. Immediately after the bombing staff from the school went to the site to search for remains and check for the girls at relief stations. All they could find were the bodies of a teacher and a few students in a cistern, where they may have jumped or been thrown. These bodies had exploded from

the heat and were "without eyes," so that while they were recovered they could not be individually identified. (Foard 1997, 5)

Dresden and Hiroshima have in common incineration by a blast of fire that consumed everyone and everything in its path. These events give proof that the power to "scorch people with fire" (16:8) is real, in Dresden at one thousand degrees Celsius, in Hiroshima at one million degrees Celsius inside the fireball, at ground level briefly four thousand degrees (Ham 2014, 317). But the historical realities do not fit the category "divine retribution" and might, by themselves, temper interpretations that see the bowls as God-ordained carnage. Civilian nuclear disasters at Chernobyl and Fukushima have shown real-life horrors worthy of the seven last plagues even though they happened in peacetime. As one firsthand account of Chernobyl put it, "Chernobyl is like the war of all wars. There's nowhere to hide. Not underground, not underwater, not in the air" (Alexievich 2005, 45).

Despite the fascinations of the Armageddon industry, the text must be pulled back to its theological moorings. The seven bowls have as their main goal to expose and curtail the Reign of Slander—till the day a loud voice goes forth "from the temple, from the throne," saying, "It is done!" (16:17).

# Revelation 17:1–18:24

## The Woman and the Beast

### Introductory Matters

Revelation prepares the reader for the beast that "was and is not and is to come" (17:8), but the profusion of new details in chapter 17 is still overwhelming. Once again it is legitimate to ask why the story continues after the emphatic "It is done!" of the bowl cycle (16:17). If things are *done*, the telling of it is not, and not by far.

Continuity at the level of mediation is conspicuous. "The four living creatures" played a key role in the opening scenes in the heavenly council (4:6). They are in the communication chain for "the seven bowls," too (15:7). And the "bowl angels" do not disappear just because they finished pouring out the bowls. They stay on, doing "commentary and clarification" until the end of the book (17:1; 21:9).

Continuity of content also runs deep. The "woman," or at least *a woman*, is important in the continuing story. So is "wilderness" (17:1–3). When the characters and issues in the present story began in earnest (12:13–17), John saw a "woman" fleeing into "the wilderness" (12:14). The dragon pursued her, and "the woman" made a narrow escape. Is there more than a narrow *escape* to the story? The dragon, "seething with wrath toward the woman," concocted a new plan. He "*went away* to make war on the rest of her children" (12:17). How did the new plan turn out? To say that chapter 17 is an elaboration of chapter 13 is so much to

**Enigmas Old and New**

- 666 (13:18)
- Armageddon (16:16)
- "beast that was and is not and is to come" (17:8)
- "it is an eighth and it is of the seven" (17:11)

the point that the two chapters should be read back to back (King 2004, 305; Mucha and Witetschek 2013). There is *war* here too (17:14), a sign of continuity with the war that began in heaven (12:7–9). Insights gained at the Battle of Armageddon in the previous chapter (16:12–16) will be indispensable to understanding the battle in this chapter (17:14, 16).

The new items add two new enigmas that have sent interpreters scurrying in all directions (17:8, 11; see sidebar).

But the main novelty in the next two chapters is the *woman* (17:1–18:24). John depicts her as (1) *distinct* from "the beast" (17:3); (2) *colluding* with "the beast" (17:3, 12); (3) and *destroyed* by "the beast" (17:16; cf. 18:1–24). The pictures on the next leg of the journey will be strange and demanding.

## Tracing the Train of Thought

*Stunned in the Wilderness: A Woman Colluding with the Beast (17:1–6)*

**17:1–6.** A *woman* is now the focus of attention. And one of the seven angels who had the seven bowls came and said to me, "Come, I will show you the verdict on the great prostitute who is seated on many waters, with whom the kings of the earth have engaged in sexual immorality, and the inhabitants of the earth have become drunk with the wine of her immorality" (17:1–2). Here the angel is cast in the role of a tour guide or *interpreting angel* (*angelus interpres*), the function of whom is to make sure that the revelation is understood (Reichelt 1994, 5–68; 211–13). The lesson for the day is a woman who is declared to be "the great prostitute" and has "engaged in [consensual] sexual immorality with the kings of the earth" (17:1–2). She is "seated on many waters." For audiences less attuned to symbols, the angel explains that "the waters that you saw . . . are peoples, and multitudes and nations and

> ### Revelation 17:1–18:24 in the Rhetorical Flow
>
> Incentive to read (1:1–20)
>
> To the one who has an ear (2:1–3:22)
>
> The seven seals (4:1–8:1)
>
> The seven trumpets (8:2–11:19)
>
> The cosmic conflict from A to Z (12:1–14:20)
>
> The seven bowls (15:1–16:21)
>
> ▶The woman and the beast (17:1–18:24)
>
> > Stunned in the wilderness: A woman colluding with the beast (17:1–6)
> >
> > Explanation and exposé (17:7–18)
> >
> > > Items of interest: Seven heads, seven kings, seven mountains
> > >
> > > Blurred identities: The one, the other, and the eighth
> > >
> > > The woman destroyed by the beast
> >
> > Exposé continued: Babylon (18:1–24)
> >
> > > Predatory trade
> > >
> > > And trade in slander
> > >
> > > The blood of all who were killed with violence

languages" (17:15). This means that the woman is in a position of influence in relation to "the kings of the earth" and individual human beings (Aune 1996–98, 959–60).

Who is the woman? She is "Babylon the Great," of course, as the tour guide will soon point out (17:5). This is the same "Babylon the Great" that was targeted in the message of the second angel (14:8) and again in the transition between the bowl sequence and the present chapter (16:19). But these antecedents are only marginally helpful. "Babylon" belongs to concepts that require re-reader competency. While the concept has been featured earlier, it has not been fully explained.

Or has it? David E. Aune (1996–98, 829) says, without apparent need for caveats, that Babylon is "a symbolic name for Rome," given that "both were centers for world empires and both captured Jerusalem and destroyed the temple." Koester (2014, 675) affirms the parallel but is less emphatic. "The parallel suggested that Rome was a kind of Babylon." These statements might be enough to curtail further inquiry, but it is wise to regard them as suggestions and not as conclusions.

Why, first, does the angel launch an intricate show-and-tell on the *distinction* between the woman and the beast if they are the same entity, both symbols of imperial Rome? What does "she" add to what has already been said—other than more inflammatory rhetoric with which to disparage Rome? The idea that the woman is the city of Rome and the beast the Roman Empire is not a fully satisfactory solution. As one discerning reader puts it, "Rome cannot be seated upon Rome" (Ford 1975, 285; see also King 2004, 306).

**Characters and Concepts**

- Woman
- Beast
- Kings
- Waters
- Wilderness
- Immorality
- Slanderous names
- Babylon

Second, why does the most scathing put-down fall on the woman and *not* on the beast, at least not yet (17:6, 9, 18)? All along, the *distinction* between the two is a key feature in the angel's show-and-tell.

Third, what is the big deal about the "sexual immorality" in Revelation's indictment? If the woman signifies Rome, "sexual immorality" reflects Rome's character with little need for commentary and less need to be shocked (17:1–3; 18:3, 9). To make this scenario work, it is necessary to redefine "sexual immorality" away from idolatry and apostasy to illicit forms of "political intercourse" (Fiorenza 2006). It goes without saying that this would not be an imperial novelty and not very shocking.

Fourth, therefore, why is John so shocked (17:6–7)? Had he expected better if *Rome* were the subject of the exposé? Is the economic predation of Rome a subject in need of *revelation*? These reservations are enough to posit other options than the fast answer given by most interpreters. Jacques Ellul (1977, 188–89) sees a subtler referent than the "easy" one:

The problem at bottom is that of symbol. We interpret in a completely superficial fashion that if Babylon is the symbol for Rome; then the seven heads that are seven kings are the symbols for Roman emperors. But here we simply confound the symbol and the coding. . . . When we have "deciphered" that Babylon is Rome we have not explained the symbol in the least; we have simply situated the text historically, given its historical references, which is a wholly different thing.

Ellul (1977, 189) accepts that Rome might be "an actualized symbol, the historical presence of a permanent, complex, and multiple phenomenon," but he rejects the notion of a simple code. In the decoding scenario that many interpreters take for granted, the language is obscure for strategic reasons. The writer has a "hidden transcript" that will elude the hostile reader but will serve the friendly audience well (Scott 1990). Coded language is used to "hide the revolutionary character of the text from the eyes of the 'police'" (Ellul 1977, 188). The language in Revelation's alleged code, however, turns out not to be all that obscure. Just think of the "seven mountains" (17:9), assumed to be a code for the seven hills of Rome! By this expression, John supposedly drops a hint "so heavy that it would surely be sufficient to earn him a further spell on Patmos if it were to come to official notice!" (O'Donovan 1986, 83). This view assumes the existence of "thought police" in the empire, but it also suggests a dull "thought police." Ellul's alternative view, where the symbol is more than a code, is attuned to the tenor of the representation.

> **The Woman (and the Beast)**
>
> - Woman *separate*
> - Woman *indicted*
> - Woman *unfaithful*
> - Woman *startling*
> - Woman *seduced*

Fifth, and now to the detail work, is there a connection between the woman fleeing the serpent into "the wilderness" (12:13–14) and the woman sitting on the "scarlet beast" in this chapter? The vulnerability and predicament of the fleeing woman begins with a preview of the rest of the book (12:13–18). The summary is expanded into the detailed story that we have in chapters 13–20. This view is easily defended (Koester 2014, 554). In the synopsis, "the serpent" fails to destroy "the woman" on his first try (12:13–16). But he does not give up (12:17–18). Furious, he *goes away* "to make war on the rest of her children" (12:17). Plan A made use of persecution and failed (12:13–16). Plan B stakes everything on seduction (12:17–18; 13:1–18). Does seduction succeed where persecution fell short? This possibility is already present in chapter 13, and it will not be weakened in this chapter. John says of "the woman" that "the inhabitants of the earth have become drunk with the wine of her immorality" (17:2; 14:8; 18:3). This suggests a woman as seductress. Was she, the fleeing woman, herself seduced? Could this be why the angel is eager to tell the story and why John is horror-struck (17:1–7)? We shall soon get the answer.

**And he carried me away in the spirit into a wilderness, and I saw a woman sitting on a scarlet beast that was full of slanderous names, having seven heads**

**and ten horns** (17:3). Amid scenes that have an urban flavor, it is surprising that the angel heads for "a wilderness" (17:3). This "wilderness" lacks the definite article, and it is tempting to distinguish it from "the wilderness" where the fleeing woman earlier sought refuge (12:6, 14; Ford 1975, 287). But the difference is not decisive. The wilderness connection, and with it a woman and a beast, cannot marginalize the earlier story (12:13–17). The reason for leaving out the article need not be that this "wilderness" is new but that it is the scene of an unexpected discovery. This—the element of surprise—is better preserved by omitting the article until John has caught on. As for "the beast," recognition is facilitated by the equivalent of a mug shot: "seven heads and ten horns" (17:3). These features call to mind the dragon with "seven heads and ten horns" (12:3) and the beast from the sea, also having "ten horns and seven heads" (13:1). "Our" beast is further distinguished by the "purple" [*kokkinon*] color and by "slanderous names" (17:3). The color puts it close to the dragon (12:3), the "slanderous names" close to the beast from the sea (13:1). These two beings, already *almost* indistinguishable, are now even harder to tell apart. Conflation at the level of description foreshadows conflation at the level of identity.

The theological aspiration of the beast resides in the name, and the name is stable as bedrock. "Slanderous names" remain a fixture with respect to the activity of the adversary in Revelation (2:9; 13:1, 5, 6; 16:9, 11, 21; 17:3). "We must not forget that the first meaning of blasphemy is to defame," says Ellul (1977, 191). Exactly! While the "slanderous names" amount to one thing and one word would do, the plural is necessary. This creature does slander on an industrial scale (13:1; 17:3).

John now turns to describing the woman, the new character in the drama (17:4–5). Once again, the wilderness setting is puzzling for a disclosure that reeks with urbanity. Earlier in this story, "the earth" seemed like a safe place (12:16). But the beast "that came up *from the earth*" shattered the illusion of safety by location of origin, its lamb-like appearance, and by speaking "like a serpent" (13:11). So much for "the earth" as a region of safety!

By appearance and place the woman is in a position of power. While she may be vulnerable to the whims of the beast, the initial impression puts her in collusion with the beast. She might serve the beast, or the beast could be subservient to the woman. **Purple and scarlet** with **gold and jewels and pearls** make her a royal figure and a woman of the world (17:4; Ford 1975, 287). "Gold and jewels and pearls" can be adornments meant to enhance attractiveness and signal availability. Moreover, jewelry can be part of the preparation for marriage (Isa. 61:10). If this is the connotation, the jewelry magnifies the *unfaithfulness*. Given that the color scheme of the woman matches the color of the beast (17:3) and the dragon (12:3), we have ideological unity. These details are not indicators of good taste but signifiers of a common character and purpose.

The "golden cup" is sinister, already described as the instrument by which to make human beings "drunk" (17:2). The intoxicating element is not alcohol: the cup is "full of abominations and the indecencies of her sexual immorality" (17:4). This makes seduction the modus operandi of the woman, but this is the lesser concern. The most important question is whether the seductress has herself fallen victim to seduction (12:17). Her persona parades seductiveness. She, not the beast, is the one dishing it out to society. Her given name is **Babylon**, but the term needs an explanation: she is **the mother of prostitutes and the abominations of the earth** (17:5). Does this conception apply to ancient Babylon, preceding Rome by six centuries? Does it fit imperial Rome, making Rome *the mother*? "Babylon" in Revelation is best understood as an entity that transcends the specific historical situation, whether it be ancient Babylon or imperial Rome (Ellul 1977, 188–89); it is revelatory for a phenomenon that deserves to be called "the mother of prostitutes." This makes her the ultimate expression of the reality thus represented. Prostitution goes hand in hand with "abominations" (*bdelygmatōn*). So far in this chapter, the woman has not said anything, but she knows how to talk. The "golden cup" filled with "abominations" corresponds to the "slanderous names" that define the beast. Both are mediators of speech. If purple clothing and the golden cup are images from the sanctuary service in the OT, they imply a priestly function, and the import of this priestly ministry is shattering (Ezek. 16:43–45; Ford 1975, 287–88).

The word "abominations" (*bdelygmatōn*) conjures up the crowning revulsion in Daniel (8:13; 9:27; 11:31; 12:11). This connection is enhanced and made relevant to NT eschatology when Jesus in the Gospels speaks of "the abomination [*to bdelygma*] of desolation which was spoken of through Daniel the prophet" (Matt. 24:15; Mark 13:14 NASB). In the Synoptic warning, "the abomination" is "set up where it ought not to be" (Mark 13:14 NRSV) and that place—of all places—is "the holy place" (Matt. 24:15 NRSV). In all these instances—Daniel, the Synoptic apocalypse, and Revelation—the exhortation to "understand" recurs in similar urgent terms (Dan. 8:16–17; 9:21–22; Mark 13:14; Matt. 24:15; Rev. 17:9). The ministry of *abominations*, like the woman, must be understood as symbol and metaphor, not as intrusions in a literal temple, but it is surely activity taking place "where it ought not to be" (Mark 13:14). The call to understand is well taken (Rev. 17:9).

How does this add up? The woman is not a "prostitute" only, and she is not "the mother of prostitutes" in a sexual sense. In the sweep of events that runs from Rev. 12 through chapter 20, the impression gathering steam is that the prostitute bears some relation to the woman fleeing the serpent (12:13–16). The woman has a history! A *mother of prostitutes* represents the epitome of unfaithfulness. If this scenario now confronts the reader, what happened? Has *that* woman, the one fleeing for her life from the serpent, changed masters to become the seductress of the world? On first thought, this seems inconceivable, but it is a stronger theory than that the woman represents "Rome seated upon Rome" (Ford 1975,

243

285). Shocking as it seems, it is not without precedent. Pagan cities depicted as prostitutes can be found in the OT (Nah. 3:4–5), but it is far more common to take *Israel* to task for "sexual immorality" (contra Biguzzi 2006). Texts to this effect are too numerous to count (Exod. 34:15–16; Num. 25:1–2; Deut. 31:16; 2 Chron. 21:13; Pss. 78:37, 56–64; 106:39; Isa. 57:3; Jer. 3:1–9; Ezek. 16:1–63; 23:1–49; Hosea 1:2; 2:4; 3:1). Isaiah offers a case in point about Judah.

> How the faithful city has become a whore!
> She that was full of justice,
>    righteousness lodged in her
>    —but now murderers! (Isa. 1:21)

For an entity guilty of "sexual immorality," the best candidate is the woman of high expectations (Rev. 12:13–16). The problem with "Babylon" is not that she takes promiscuity to a new level but that *she—she* of all conceivable candidates—is the one to do it (Ford 1975, 285).

It is not strange, therefore, for John to say that "on her forehead was written a name, a *mystery*" (17:5). Revelation has used this term before, and the prior use has explanatory power (1:20; 10:7; 17:5, 7). A mystery is a riddle that does not have an obvious explanation; it brings to light a phenomenon "in need of interpretation" (Aune 1996–98, 936). Revelation has already used terms that reflect on the quality of a deed without concern for the geographical connotation of the word (11:8). "Babylon" falls into the same category. The mystery "concerns the meaning of the name" (Koester 2014, 674).

### Woman and Rome: Some Problems

- Problem of *concept*
- Problem of *evidence* (history)
- Problem of *logic*
- Problem of *story*

The meaning, if not yet obvious, now rises in inconceivable horror. **And I saw that the woman was drunk with the blood of the believers and the blood of the witnesses of Jesus** (17:6a). While interpreters see this as an indictment of Rome, the lead-up to this text has unearthed other options.

As noted, there is a *conceptual* problem in the separate identities of the woman and the beast. Murderous conduct is now ascribed to *the woman* even though *the beast* showed itself perfectly capable of persecution and murder (13:5–7). A Rome "seated upon Rome" is to this scenario a serious objection because the text makes an enormous investment in the *distinction* between the woman and the beast.

Next, the absence of evidence for large-scale imperial persecution raises a *historical* problem (L. Thompson 1990, 171–201). This, the main thing in the indictment, threatens to be unmoored from reality. A woman "drunk with the blood" suggests not only killing on a large scale but as a fundamental characteristic even if we assume a measure of hyperbole.

Third, in the traditional interpretation John's astonishment must be directed at the magnitude of the killing and not the identity of the perpetrator (17:6). This option runs afoul of *logic* and *narratival* elements, a problem that persists even if we invoke Nero's persecution of Christians in Rome some thirty years before Revelation was written (Koester 2014, 676).

The alternative scenario does not run into these difficulties. There is no *conceptual* problem because we have a compelling reason to make the woman distinct from the beast. Second, there is no *historical* problem. If Revelation's horizon exceeds Roman imperial reality in the first century, murder of "the believers and . . . the witnesses of Jesus" will not be in want of historical evidence. And there is no affront to *logic*, beginning with the novelty of the woman and ending with John's disbelief (17:6). In this scenario, the identity of the perpetrator matters more than the number of victims.

It is hard to do justice to the depiction of John's surprise. **And I was extremely horrified** [*ethaumasa*] **with a great horror** [*thauma mega*] **when I saw her** (17:6b). This, advisedly, is stronger than saying, "I was very perplexed" (Aune 1996–98, 938), or even, "I was greatly amazed" (17:6 NRSV). The terms used are related to the word "see," and they describe the response to *seeing*, a *vision*, even a *revelation*. The surprise can go in two directions, expressing "an attitude of criticism, doubt, and even rejection, though it may also express inquisitiveness and curiosity" (G. Bertram, *TDNT* 3:28, θαῦμα). *Criticism*, *doubt*, and *rejection* are in John's case better matches than *inquisitiveness* or *curiosity*, and the terms also include incomprehension. In Job, *thauma* captures "the horror which grips those who, without being directly involved, must watch the judgment of God fall" (G. Bertram, *TDNT* 3:31, θαῦμα). In Daniel, the word conveys the idea of "being startled" into a state of disquiet and alarm (Dan. 8:27). The magnitude of the surprise is proportional to expectations. On this logic, a negative valence is unavoidable. John is "extremely horrified with a great horror" (17:6). "Oh, no! This can't be true!"

### Explanation and Exposé (17:7–18)

**17:7–18.** The reason for the surprise must be inferred, and yes, *the unthinkable is true*! **And the angel said to me, "Why are you so horrified? I will tell you the mystery of the woman and of the beast carrying her, the one having seven heads and ten horns"** (17:7). From the point of view of the angel, seeds have been planted to the effect that John should be prepared for what is coming (17:8). But the rebuke is mild, and it is followed by the promise of a remedial lesson. For readers who are still bewildered (as many are), this is good news. The angel pledges to tutor John about "the mystery of the woman" as well as "(the mystery of) the beast" (17:7).

Wilhelm Bousset (1906), the chief architect of the role of the Nero myth in Revelation, gave the answer that still dominates the scholarly view of the beast that **was, and is not, and is about to ascend from the bottomless pit and go** to destruction (17:8a). "The beast that returns from the abyss is the expected Nero redivivus, concerning whom people in later times were convinced would come back from the netherworld" (Bousset 1906, 405; Aune 1996–98, 960; Koester 2014, 677). Objections to this view are substantial, however, many of them reviewed in connection with Rev. 13. Here, the need for better alternatives arises with renewed urgency.

First, does the Nero myth meet the *ontological* measure of the text? This should be the primary concern, and it is an in-your-face feature. "The beast . . . was and *is not* and is to come" (17:8) contrasts with God "*who is and who was and who is to come*" (1:4, 8). *Is not* might be a contrast in the realm of chronology or history or even strategy, but it is best seen as a contrast at the level of being. On this logic, Nero is a mismatch. It must be asked seriously: Does Revelation cast *Nero*, of all conceivable characters, human and nonhuman alike, as the ultimate counterpoint to the One "*who is and who was and who is to come*" (1:4, 8)?

### Matching God and the Opponent

| God | Opponent |
|---|---|
| who is and who was and who is to come (1:4) | was, **and is not**, and is about to ascend (17:8) |
| who is and who was and who is to come (1:8) | it was **and is not** and is to come (17:8) |
| the Alpha and the Omega, the first and the last, the beginning and the end (22:13) | the beast that was **and is not**, it is an eighth but it belongs to the seven (17:11) |

If the beast in question is not Nero, who is it? The cosmic outlook of Revelation has a candidate whose foot is better matched to the story's titanic shoe. On all counts, the Ancient Serpent is that candidate (12:9; 20:2). How did competent readers lose sight of *him*, substituting Nero in his place?

A move from the realm of *being* (ontology) to the domain of *time* (chronology) does not weaken the demonic element. The beast that "*was* and *is not*" corresponds to the point when the dragon "*went away*" to wage war by other means (12:17–18). As noted earlier, *went away* suggests a vanishing act, going undercover. The dragon's success during the vanishing act lays the groundwork for making an implausible return (13:3–4, 8, 13–15). He is "about to ascend from the bottomless pit," John is told, repeating the same thought in slightly different wording: "it was and is not and is to come [*parestai*]" (17:8). In chronological terms, the expression suggests three phases, each phase translating into *presence*, then *absence*, then *presence*. The latter is confirmed by the verb used, leading to the following enhanced reading: *it was (present) and is not (present) and is to be present* (BDAG 773–74, πάρειμι; cf. Aune 1996–98, 939). The underlying thought is not death but absence and concealment. Nero's prospects, already weakened by ontological feet of clay, can work only if conceived as death and resurrection. Indeed, it works only

246

as a *purported* event, not as disclosure of careful *intent*, and then as *actualized event*. Scholars' investment in the Nero myth confronts the additional problem of nonfulfillment. "John's probable expectations with regard to historical events were not fulfilled" (A. Collins 1979, 122; cf. Minear 1953, 97). Nonfulfillment will not be a problem for an interpretation that sets its sights on a higher order of being: "*it is to be present again*" (17:8).

The tutoring angel outlines four phases, not only three, and the fourth stage writes large the cosmic perspective. We are twice told that the beast "*goes to destruction*" (17:8, 11). This is the ending of the story. The description comes charged with OT background that has already put its stamp on the account. In the trumpet sequence, the star that "had fallen from heaven" is named. "His name in Hebrew is Abaddon, and in Greek he has the name Apollyon" (9:1, 11): he is the "Destroyer" (9:11). This fits exactly the trajectory set for the fallen star in Isaiah's poem: "You have *destroyed [apōlesas]* your land, you have *killed* your people" (Isa. 14:20). In the present setting, going "*to destruction*" suggests the same unstoppable, self-destructive momentum (17:8, 11), here with the tenor of finality. The character that "goes" is not minor. Revelation is focused on a larger story than Roman history, its vocabulary primed for an epic account that will not settle for Nero. *Time* in the broadest conception is also evident when the angel draws a line between the culmination of history and **the foundation of the world** (17:8b; 13:8). The perspective in widescreen vastly exceeds what may be imagined for a scenario centered on the nonevent of Nero's return.

### The Beast in Four Stages

| | Stage 1 | Stage 2 | Stage 3 | Stage 4 |
|---|---|---|---|---|
| 17:8 | was | is not | is about to ascend | goes to destruction |
| 17:11 | was | is not | is an eighth | goes to destruction |

Important *spatial* parameters close the loop. John is told that "the beast . . . is about to ascend *from the bottomless pit*" (17:8). This location has been mentioned four times, three times in connection with "the star that had fallen from heaven" (9:1, 2, 11) and once during the "digression" between the sixth and the seventh trumpets (11:3–13). In the latter instance, John says that "the two witnesses" fall prey to "the beast that comes up *from the bottomless pit*" (11:7; 17:8, 11; cf. Isa. 14:15, 19). The spatial parameters make "the star that had fallen from heaven" the main person of interest.

One item needs further clarification. Revelation appears to blend the identities of the dragon and the beast. This is suggested by the beast in Rev. 17 appearing in a *purple* or *red* color, a feature that puts it even closer to the dragon than it appeared to be earlier (17:3; 12:3). "The bottomless pit" is the domain of the fallen star and thus the home base of the dragon (9:1). It is from "the bottomless pit" that *the beast* will ascend (17:8). In its first official appearance, as the lead surrogate of the dragon, the beast comes up "from the sea" (13:1). Here, it comes from "the bottomless pit" (17:8), a location that differs from the former manifestation, at least verbally. Merging identities—or identities becoming indistinct—for the dragon and the beast are also suggested by the statement that "the beast was and is not and is to come" (17:8; Lohmeyer 1926, 139). If "is not" refers to the vanishing act of the dragon, how can one keep the dragon and the beast apart?

The angel must say more to resolve the puzzle—and will. But the difficulty must be acknowledged. As in Rev. 13 (13:10), the person who reads the message out loud in the communities makes direct contact with the audience to instill respect for the difficulty. **Here [*hōde*] is need for a mind that has wisdom!** (17:9a). This is another call to attention—a "wake-up call" (13:10, 18). The need for discernment will not be less by noticing that the very same expression occurs in connection with the number 666 (13:18). For now, the best counsel is not to fall for the first idea that comes to mind.

This warning applies to the statement that **the seven heads are seven mountains [*orē*] on which the woman is seated** (17:9b). While this seems to place imperial Rome at the center (Koester 2014, 677), the number "seven" is not a matter of convenience. It is unlikely that in this instance John takes this "seven" from popular speech when he otherwise employs the number for theological reasons. *Seven* is the number for totality and completion. Two authorities who see the number as a reference to Rome regard it as a possible addition to the text, perhaps to cement the Roman connection (Charles 1920, 2:68–69; Aune 1996–98, 944). By the alternative logic, however, the beast does not have "seven heads" because John had in mind seven Roman emperors, and the woman is not seated on "seven mountains" because there are seven hills in Rome. The symbolism conjures up a transhistorical entity that is larger than Rome. A "mountain" can symbolize a nation or a power, often a power standing in opposition to God (Ps. 68:15–16; Isa. 57:7; Jer. 51:25). If there is "need for a mind that has wisdom," the "Seven Hills of Rome" set a low bar for the wisdom required—and much lower than the call in connection with the number 666 (13:18). Earlier we concluded that Nero is not adequate for the number 666, and the conclusion will be similar here: the "seven mountains" are not a coded reference to imperial Rome.

"Seven" stays in focus as a term for completeness when the same "seven heads" are found to be "seven kings" (17:10). If the "seven mountains" were a no-brainer, as most interpreters believe (O'Donovan 1986, 83), the "seven kings" bring interpretations into disarray. History fails to supply a list of seven kings or seven empires about which interpreters can agree. Invariably, the list is replete with conjectures and arbitrary omissions that are necessary to whittle the list down to seven. When the tutoring angel begins to break it down (17:10), the predicament gets worse. Increasing specificity in the text calls for commensurate specificity in the interpretation, but the latter proves elusive. Craig R. Koester's (2014, 678) approach illustrates the problem. "Identifying the seven heads with seven kings summarizes imperial rule," he says, opting first for a nonspecific approach to the "seven kings." Then, as the demand for specificity in the text is raised a notch higher, he acknowledges that the sixth king must be the ruler at the time of John's vision. And then things stall. "Many interpreters have tried to determine who this king might be without reaching a satisfactory solution" (Koester 2014, 678). David E. Aune (1996–98, 947) computes the various attempts at making a list of Roman emperors that stops at seven. He despairs at the result and the lack of cogency for any of the options. "For several reasons, the *symbolic* rather than the *historical* approach to interpreting the seven kings is convincing," he concludes (1996–98, 948). We might agree—to a point—but it follows that a *symbolic* rather than a *geographical* approach is the wiser option for the "seven mountains" too.

The alternative approach looks for the key in Revelation and its use of the OT, first, and at the historical clues, second. The angel tells John that the **seven heads also are seven kings** (17:9c). Then begins a remarkably detailed breakdown concerning the "seven kings," here played in slow motion.

> **The five [*hoi pente*] have fallen.**
> **The one [*ho heis*] is.**
> **The other [*ho allos*] has not yet come,**
> **and when he comes,**
> **he must [*dei*] remain a little while. (17:10)**

All the important words in this verse have the definite article. We have "*the* five" that have "fallen"; "*the* one"; and "*the* other." "The one" and "the other" are promising specifics, a twosome that stands out not only as numbers six and seven among the "seven kings" but also as *two of a kind* that seem to be linked. This possibility gets stronger when we review earlier clues.

First, we recall the Ancient Serpent seeking reinforcement in the form of "a beast rising out of the sea" and a second beast rising "out of the earth" (13:1, 11). The cooperation and reciprocity between the beasts is striking from the beginning (13:12, 14–15), as is the relationship between the dragon and "the first beast" (13:2, 4, 12).

Second, there is precision in the enumeration of the beasts at the point when they first come onstage. John says of the second beast that he saw "another beast" (*allo thērion*, 13:11). In the passage we are studying, he talks about "the other" (*ho allos*) with the implication that this might be the "other" mentioned earlier (17:10).

Third, the connection *and* the distinction between the two persist throughout. After introducing "another beast," John is careful to keep track of the first, specifying it as "the *first* beast" or "the beast, the *first* one" (13:11–12).

Fourth, in further installments on the topic, the three beast-like beings are closely linked: it is all about them (16:13; 19:20; 20:2).

Fifth, as the story ends, two of the three are singled out as "the beast" and "the false prophet," in the same verse described as "these two" (*hoi duo*, 19:20).

Sixth, in this chapter we have paid heed to the contrast between the One "who was and is and is to come" (1:4, 8; 4:8; 11:17) and the beast that "was and *is not* and is to come" (17:8; Lohmeyer 1926, 142). Concern that the dragon suddenly is absent is unwarranted: *this is the dragon.*

Seventh, while the three entities on the opposing side work in closely co-ordinated fashion, in the end they are made to go their separate ways. The "duo" in the story stay together, but the Ancient Serpent covers the last leg all by himself (20:1–10). Whatever significance "these two" have had (19:20), they were no more than instruments and never the main concern.

When we put these observations to use for the identity of "the one" and "the other," clarity is within reach. The beast from the sea must be "the one," and the beast from the earth is "the other" (17:10; cf. 13:1, 11). This brings narratival and conceptual clarity that has been lacking in interpretations that rush from the text to history, or from history to the text. Revelation is not interested in "the five" that "have fallen" (17:10). One consequence of this interpretation is the implied time line for "the one" and "the other." Revelation says of "the other" that "it has not yet come" (17:10). In the Nero scenario, the beast from the sea, as the Roman Empire, and the beast from the earth, as the imperial cult, are contemporaries.

New details are added to the picture. **And the beast that was and is not, it is an eighth, but it is of the seven, and it goes to destruction** (17:11). Again, the crucial ontological distinction is implied between God and the adversary (1:4, 8; 4:8). Beyond the ontological contrast, the beast is "to ascend from the bottomless pit" (17:8; 11:6), the home base of the "star that had fallen from heaven" (9:1). This being "is to be present (again)" (17:8).

The notion that there is a time when "the beast . . . *is not*" must be taken with a grain of salt because "the one *is*" even if "the beast . . . *is not*" (17:8–11). By this criterion, the dragon will at no point lack representation in the world even though at some point it "*is not*." The language describes absence, but absence does not mean nonexistence. With the dizzying idea that "the beast . . . is an *eighth* but it is of the seven," the angel breaks the rules of arithmetic (17:11). "Seven" is the axiomatic number, and it is equally manifest that the beast has "seven heads" (17:3, 7). Suddenly, there is "an eighth" that "is of the seven" (17:11). This anomalous "eighth" is now in full conceptual height as "the beast that was and is not and is to come" (17:8, 11)—coming up "from the bottomless pit" (17:8; cf. 9:1; 11:7). At the level of representation, "an eighth" is pure *novelty*, so unexpected that it cannot be integrated into the entity "that was and is not" and so detached from symbolic and historical

Figure 18. The strange beast in Revelation 17. This diagram represents the seven heads of the beast, with John's descriptions of the sixth and seventh heads.

antecedents that it appears never to have existed before. And yet the beast that "is to come" is not a novelty: it is "the beast" that "was and is not" (17:8, 11).

"And it goes to destruction" (17:11; cf. 17:8; 9:11; Isa. 14:19–20), the angel tells John. Ernst Lohmeyer (1926, 142), in a rare move among interpreters, shows sensitivity to the grand sweep of the vision.

> It has not been demonstrated that the beast "that was and is not and is to come" is historically determined and should be understood in a historical sense. It "ascends from the bottomless pit" and "goes to destruction." These are mythical expressions regarding a God-hating demonic power, and the words "it was and is not and is to come" read like a demonic mimicking of the divine title: "who was and who is and who is to come." It follows that the "surprise" of those who "are not written in the Book of Life" makes it necessary to conclude in favor of a satanic and not a political power. For this reason, it lies close at hand to attempt to compass all the visionary sketches within a framework of the demonic myth and explain them on that basis.

George Keough (1944, 47–48) also concludes that "the only person who is said to ascend out of the abyss is Satan himself. . . . The seven heads are his heads. . . . But the eighth king is the beast himself, and not one of the seven heads." Despite wide support for the view that this head "does indeed represent Nero and reflects the Nero redivivus legend" (Aune 1996–98, 950; cf. Koester 2014, 678), we have deal-breaking evidence to the contrary—with more to come.

Detail and density do not let up in the angel's show-and-tell (17:12). Now that "the seven heads" have been explained, attention shifts to **the ten horns**. Pictorially, it might be expected that the horns are distributed evenly across "the seven heads." Perhaps they are, but in this representation, "the ten horns," said to be "ten kings," all belong to the future: they **are ten kings who have not** yet received a **kingdom** (17:12). This contrasts with the heads, five of which "have fallen," but it echoes the seventh head ("the other"), which "has not yet come" (17:10). At face value, the future orientation of these disclosures contests the view that almost everything in Revelation refers to realities that are contemporary to John.

A formidable *gathering* is in the making, reminiscent of the gathering in the verses referring to Armageddon (16:12–16; Aune 1996–98, 953). **These are of one mind and purpose in giving their power and authority to the beast** (17:13). With the beast now a demonic conception, this is a stunning change of fortune because the "ten kings" seem committed in thought and action to the task at hand (Aune 1996–98, 952). What that task is should not come as a surprise: **they will make war** [*polemēsousin*] **on the Lamb** (17:14; cf. 16:12–16). This is shorthand for "the Lamb" as it is represented in the believing community, and the close connection between "the Lamb" and the community is spelled out. The outcome is also a matter of knowledge: **the Lamb will win over them, for he is Lord of lords and King of kings, and those with him are called and chosen and faithful** (17:14; cf. Dan. 2:37, 47). The Armageddon connection is not contrived. There, too, the spectacle describes a mobilization for war (16:13–14, 16). In the former text, nothing is said about the outcome of the war. Here, there is no doubt. Despite the determination of the dragon and his two cohorts, John is told that the Lamb "will win over them" (17:14).

Other things to be explained follow in rapid succession. **And he said to me, "The waters that you saw, where the prostitute is seated** [*kathētai*]**, are peoples and multitudes and nations and languages"** (17:15). This is a broad, comprehensive, universal conception, a similar phrase indicating that the two sides in the cosmic conflict are in intense competition for the same target group (13:7; 14:6). Being "seated" suggests enthronement and authority over "kings," as representatives of nations, or simply over people in general (17:1, 3, 9, 15). This idyllic picture will not last very long.

The genial conditions are shattered already in the next verse—and shattered thoroughly (17:16). Until now the relationship between the woman and her partners has been one of unity and single-minded purpose. Suddenly the relationship turns sour, and "the prostitute," in particular, bears the brunt of the hatred bursting forth. The text does not go into motives, and the cause must be inferred. We get the impression that **the prostitute** has played a con game that unravels. Sentences in the passive voice dominate in Revelation, but this sentence is in the active voice. All the verbs bristle with rage: **these will** *hate*; . . . **they will** *lay her waste* [*erēmōmenēn*] **and naked**; . . . **they will** *consume* **her flesh**; . . . **(they) will** *burn* **her up with fire** (17:16). Why the unbridled

> ### "I Will Tell You the Mystery"
>
> - "The one": The beast from the sea
> - "The other": The beast from the earth
> - "An eighth": The dragon

rage? "The prostitute" has been engaged in a ministry of deception on behalf of "the deceiver of the whole world" (12:9). The merging of identities of the dragon and the beast, first, and the unity of purpose between "the prostitute" and the beast, second (13:1; 17:3)—these incriminate every element in the constellation that deceives the world. When *these* and *they*, meaning *people*, suddenly rise to "hate," "lay waste," "consume," and "burn" the woman turned "prostitute," it has the feel of vengeance for wrong done to them (17:16). When the deception is exposed, the victims turn on the woman, determined to annihilate her (17:16). As the attempt at coalition building and deception unravels, it falls apart *from within*, and the result is best understood as an *implosion*. This fits a logic of retribution as far as the relationship between the deceiver and the deceived is concerned, but it does not represent the logic of God's action. The "theology" of the scene is compatible with *revelation* but not with divine *retribution*.

And yet God is not left without a role. **For God has given it into their hearts to carry out God's purpose [***gnōmēn***] and bring about one single purpose [***gnōmēn***]: to give their kingdom to the beast, until the words of God will be brought to completion** (17:17). There is an outworking in history that has a theological rationale after all. It is important not to miss the explanatory intent, looking back to the Indian summer when there was unity of purpose and action before the great scheme fell apart (17:12, 13). Again, it is inadequate to make this drama culminate in the myth of Nero's return. Craig R. Koester (2014, 683–84) hedges, not ready to abandon the Roman application, but he advises that "the vision depicts forces that extend beyond Rome. . . . The whore is Rome, yet more than Rome." The divine "purpose" or "mind" (*gnōmēn*) is on display, to be understood as "mind-set," "way of thinking," and "resolution" (BDAG 202–3, γνώμη). But this is God's "way of thinking" in the broadest sense, with the crisis in the heavenly council as background. The imagery is fluid, more concerned about ideology and principles than in preserving clear boundaries between the dragon and the beast. Fluidity will not count as imprecision for a scenario that pictures the dragon *going away* (12:17) in order to *return* and *be present* in a spectacular fashion (17:8, 11). It is *his* return, not the return of his surrogate, that counts. Revelation presents the strange idea that God's "way of thinking" consists in making the schemes of the power players in the world equal God's purpose. This does not mean that God and the power players share the same values. On the contrary, it confirms God's determination to allow the opposing forces to stage their own defeat. Throughout, this is the logic of revelation.

The next verse marks a transition, looking back to what has been explained up to this point but also looking ahead to what is yet to be explained. **The woman you saw is the great city that rules over the kings of the earth** (17:18). Given that more is coming, further speculation is unwarranted. We shall soon enough be told.

*Exposé Continued: Babylon (18:1–24)*

**18:1–24.** "One of the clearest facts regarding these chapters is that they concern one and the same entity," says one reader of the connection between chapters 17 and 18 (Edgar 1982, 333). That entity is "Babylon." Beginning in Rev. 16:19, this entity is described as "the great city" (16:19; 17:18; 18:16, 18, 19, 21); "Babylon the Great" (16:19; 17:5; 18:2); "the great prostitute" (17:1; 19:2); "the prostitute" (17:16); and "the great city, Babylon" (18:10; Edgar 1982). Reviewing findings so far, our reading has sought to understand (1) how Babylon and the beast are intimately related and how they are distinct; (2) Babylon as genuine "mystery" (17:5, 7); and (3) the reason why Babylon is called "the prostitute" (17:16), even "the great prostitute" (17:1; 19:2).

On the third point, Babylon is no longer a simple code word for the historical city of Rome. A wider, more fluid, and more shocking conception is necessary, not of *Rome* committing heinous acts but of *Babylon* as "the great *prostitute.*" The key element in this conception is not the seduction of the world by ancient Rome but the serpent's pursuit of "the woman" and his determination to undo *her* (12:13–16). Revelation's plot fractures if the reader loses sight of the serpent's design on "the woman" and his success in making *that* woman the seductress of the world. Seeing *her* explains John's body language. "And I was extremely horrified with a great horror when I saw her" (17:6).

These caveats do not render Rome irrelevant. Revelation's interest in Babylon as an agent of economic predation accommodates more than one conception of Babylon (18:3, 7, 11–19). With the charge that "the merchants of the earth have grown rich from the allure of her luxury" (18:3), Revelation offers a societal and economic critique whether the referent is Rome or the modern capitalist economy (Bauckham 1993a, 338–83; Callahan 1999; 2009; Moore 2006, 97–121; Koester 2008; Zerbe 2003). The economic message is broadly relevant at the level of *analogy*: "the injustice, poverty, and mass death of the Roman regime correspond to the injustice, poverty, and mass death of our global economy" (Callahan 1999, 51). John's description of an economic system that is exploitative, unsustainable, and doomed by its own inner structure shall not be irrelevant to systems that exhibit similar characteristics.

We are about to enter territory with distinctive literary characteristics (18:2–24), a different diction, and the absence of peculiar Greek constructs otherwise found (Charles 1920, 2:94; Aune 1996–98, 983). This need not mean a separate source (Charles 1920, 2:94) or a different time of composition (Aune 1996–98, 983–84), but the distinctive diction is worth noting. Most of it can be ascribed to copious use of OT texts that exceeds what is normal even for John. Two voices, Jeremiah and Ezekiel, get greater exposure here than anywhere else in Revelation. These texts pack colossal rhetorical punch in the original setting, and the impact is not diminished in the story within which they are now used. All the voices contribute to accelerating the momentum and the sense of finality.

And yet it is precisely these features—and these texts—that fashion Babylon into a more ominous spectacle. At the human level, "the woman" was seduced and is now the seducer, akin to Israel in the days of Jeremiah (Jer. 7:32–34; 16:9; 25:1–10). She—*that woman*—"is the great city that rules over the kings of the earth" (17:18). A Babylon known for self-aggrandizement, commerce, and cruelty is not unknown in the OT (Isa. 21:9; 41:1–11; Jer. 50:29–32; 51:8–9; cf. also Ezek. 27:2–36), but a *prostitute* conjures up a failed spiritual community. A "Babylon" of this kind is exposed and indicted *for the sin of not being what she was;* for this reason, *she is called "the great prostitute" and "the mother* [= *epitome*] *of prostitutes"* (17:5). "Babylon must not be reduced to a simple code or steno-symbol for Rome since John uses the name Babylon in order to evoke a whole range of scriptural-theological-political meanings" (Fiorenza 1998, 220). Although in favor of a political and economic reading, Elisabeth Schüssler Fiorenza (1998, 220) adds that the "prostitute" metaphor is in the OT language "that indicts Jerusalem and the people of Israel for idolatry" (see also Hylen 2003, 212).

This prospect demands that OT conceptions of *prostitution* be preserved, and it changes the story line. By this criterion, it is not strange why "the woman" is depicted as separate from "the beast" in John's depiction. The *mystery* aspect becomes intelligible by the same logic (17:5). Most important by far is the discovery that the dragon, that is, the Ancient Serpent, makes "the woman" a tool for his aims (12:13–18).

The recapitulation and expansion of the story in Rev. 13 means that this is still "the dragon's story" (D. Barr 1998, 102). "Babylon" is native to the earlier "dragon's story" in Revelation (14:8), and it is a key word in "the dragon's story" in the OT. Isaiah's depiction of the cosmic rebellion, as noted numerous times in this commentary, begins as a funeral poem about "the king of *Babylon*" (Isa. 14:4). The poem echoes in the proclamation that Babylon is "fallen" (Rev. 18:2; Isa. 14:12); that it "will be thrown down" (Rev. 18:21; Isa. 14:12); and that the nations were "deceived" (Rev. 18:23; Isa. 14:12). In this conception "Babylon" is neither the city of Rome nor the woman that was seduced into prostitution. At the deepest level, "Babylon" embodies the story of "the Shining One" in enthralling poetic language (Isa. 14:12–20).

Ezekiel explores the same notions in his poem about "the covering cherub" (Fisch 1950, 188). Here, the guise is "the king of Tyre" (Ezek. 28:12–19). The text conflates past and present, earth and heaven, the fall of the highest angel and the fall of human beings, but the core of the story concerns a heavenly being (Jensen 1997, 343; Morgenstern 1939, 111–12; Zimmerli 1979, 2:94; Eichrodt 1970, 392; Rolin 2012). In Ezekiel's poem, the cherub was "the seal of perfection, full of wisdom and perfect in beauty" (Ezek. 28:12 NASB); "the anointed cherub who covers" (Ezek. 28:14), or simply the "covering cherub" (Ezek. 28:16 NASB). A "seal *on* perfection" (Carley 1974, 190) suggests a being who was the standard by which perfection is measured. Flawlessness was matched by intimacy with God. Like "the Shining One" in Isaiah, the cherub is expelled from his original abode, cast "as a profane thing out of the mountain of God" (Ezek. 28:16). Throughout, the spatial parameters found in Isaiah and in Revelation are preserved. "I cast you to the earth" (Ezek. 28:17, my trans.).

The poet's subject adds up to more than the city-state of Tyre. *That* Tyre was at no point "the measure of perfection." Origen of Alexandria (185–254 CE) reflects the early Christian view of these passages (Tonstad 2004). As Origen explains, Ezekiel's poem has a nonhuman creature in its sights.

> Who is there that, hearing such sayings as this, "You were a signet of likeness and a crown of honor in the delights of the paradise of God," or this, "from the time you were created with the cherubim, I placed thee in the holy mount of God," could possibly weaken their meaning to such an extent as *to suppose them spoken of a human being, even a saint, not to mention the prince of Tyre?* (Origen, *Princ.* 1.5.4, trans. Butterworth 1936; see also Origen, *Cels.* 6.44, trans. Chadwick 1965; Origen, *Hom.*, trans. Borret 1989, 411–13)

Beyond "Tyre," Origen sees an angelic being, and this figure counts the most. Isaiah does the same for "Babylon" (Isa. 14:12–20). Ancient Rome engaged in rapacious commerce, as did Tyre and Babylon centuries earlier, but the items traded in these poems are not only material goods.

> You *were* without fault in your ways
>> from the day you were created,
>> till malice was found in you.
> By *the abundance of your trading in slander,*
>> you became filled with violence within,
>> and you lost the way. (Ezek. 28:15–16, my trans.)

"Trading," yes, but this is "trading" done by a peddler or huckster (*HALOT* 1237, I. רכל). The economic connotation should not be ignored, but more than economy is on the line. The merchandise of this trader consists of thoughts and ideas and not only conventional cargo. On etymological grounds, too, the stock-in-trade of this merchant is *slander*. Armed with this background, the exploits of Babylon with respect to trade and commerce demand a cosmic perspective.

The subject in Ezekiel's poem is afflicted by inexplicable and unwarranted self-regard (Ezek. 28:17). His course of action is fundamentally self-destructive and cannot succeed.

> By the multitude of your iniquities,
>> by the dishonesty of your traffic in slander,
>> you spoiled your sanctuaries.
> So I brought out fire *from within you,*
>> *it* consumed you.

And I allowed you to turn to ashes
on the earth
in the sight of all who saw you. (Ezek. 28:18, my trans.)

Ezekiel uses poetry, the idiom for "theological thinking at its keenest and deepest" (Terrien 1978, 278), to tell the story of the downfall of the most exalted of all created beings. The inexplicable turning inward, the traffic in slander, the prostitution of gifts and talents for an unworthy cause—all are packed into the poem. Translations fail to convey the force of these metaphors, especially the traffic in slander. Likewise, the description of the cherub's demise has not been given its due. Three of the best translations make the point (Ezek. 28:18).

I brought forth a fire from the midst of thee; it hath devoured thee. (Fisch 1950, 193)

So I brought forth fire from the midst of you; it consumed you. (van Dijk 1968, 219)

So I caused fire to break out from your midst; it consumed you. (Greenberg 1997, 580)

Here is one detail we cannot afford to miss: *the covering cherub is felled by his own action.* "The evil in the midst of Tyre will be the flame which reduces her to a heap of burnt ruins" (Fisch 1950, 193). Likewise, "fire from your midst" signifies "evil causing its own destruction" (Greenberg 1997, 587). Walther Zimmerli (1979, 94) makes the point with even greater emphasis, saying that there is in Ezekiel "the additional idea that the fire of judgment bursts forth from the very place of the sin itself and destroys it."

The foregoing corrects, redirects, and enriches traditional readings of Rev. 18 on at least three counts. First, we are reminded of the need to think in cosmic terms and not to limit the focus to the cities of Babylon or Tyre in the distant past—or Rome during the time of John. Second, the "commerce" language in Revelation makes it necessary to carve out room for illicit theological trade in texts otherwise thought to be concerned with economics only (18:11–18). Third, clearer than in virtually any other text on the topic, the poem in Ezekiel perceives the self-destructive dynamic working itself out in the covering cherub (Ezek. 28:18).

**After this I saw another angel coming down from heaven, having great authority; and the earth was illuminated [*ephōtisthē*] with his splendor** (18:1). As usual, the stature of the messenger is matched to the importance of the message. Another message, at this late hour, indicates that heaven is still open for business. But it also means that the story continues to turn back on itself or return to an earlier stage. "After this" does not signify a tidy chronological sequence for the events reported but has John's sequence of "seeing" in view.

257

Love of light is a characteristic of God: no reader of the Bible will fail to notice that light is God's first work or that light debuts by driving back the domain of darkness (Gen. 1:1–3). Here, "the earth was illuminated" again (18:1), not so much by physical light as by *revelation*.

When the angel begins speaking, the message is a blast of truth-telling about the other side in the cosmic conflict (18:2). Why the **loud** exclamation—here for the second time in Revelation (14:8; 18:2)? What is the real cause of heaven's sense of alarm? The angel "coming down from heaven" is an agent of revelation, sent to inform the world of something not ascertainable by other means. Reminiscences of the demise and ruin of ancient Babylon, turning it into a **roaming ground** for wild animals, are serviceable for a material conception of Babylon (Isa. 13:19–22; 21:9; Jer. 50:39; 51:37). In a deeper stratum, "Babylon" is a spiritual community that has lost its way. This is the import of the double declaration: **"Fallen, fallen is Babylon the Great!"** (18:2a).

The announcement draws on the OT poem about the lead character in the cosmic conflict (Isa. 14:12–20; Ezek. 28:12–19). "How you are *fallen* [*exepesen*] from heaven!" says the poet (Isa. 14:12). "Fallen! [*epesen*] Fallen! [*epesen*]," proclaims the angel in Revelation (18:2). "How you are *cut down* to the earth!" exclaims the poet (Isa. 14:12). "With such a violent rush Babylon the Great shall be *thrown down* [*blēthēsetai*]," says John (Rev. 18:21; cf. 12:7–9). "You . . . laid the nations low," says Isaiah (14:12), with Ezekiel adding that there was "trading in slander," even *dishonest* "traffic in slander" (Ezek. 28:16, 18, my trans.). "By your sorcery all nations were deceived [*eplanēthēsan*]," says Revelation (18:23). These statements belong to the core curriculum of the cosmic conflict. When this is taken into consideration, the demonic reality embedded in "Babylon" moves from the background into the foreground. *That* reality gives the most cause for alarm and—when the day comes—the greatest reason for rejoicing. "Babylon" is the "roaming ground" of everything that is repulsive, debasing, and demeaning. It is now **a dwelling place for demons** and the home base for the promotion of evil (18:2b).

A bifocal lens is necessary to sort these things out. **Sexual immorality** is mentioned twice (18:3). As noted, "sexual immorality" is a favored term for unfaithfulness among the people of God. Betrayal of trust, disloyalty, and conduct equivalent to "prostitution" are also ascribed to the cherub in Ezekiel's poem (Ezek. 28:15–18). The elements holding court in Babylon—"unclean, foul," and "detestable" (18:2)—show the distance between pretension and reality.

The exposé happens for a purpose. **And I heard another voice from the heaven saying, "Come out of her, my people, so that you do not have fellowship with her in her sins, and so that you do not experience her plagues; for her sins have reached the point of touching heaven, and God has taken note of her iniquities"** (18:4–5). "Babylon" compasses space inhabited by everyone. A physical flight from the city of Rome does not do justice to the intent of the text (Aune 1996–98, 991). But the summons to flee drives home the need to distance oneself from "Babylon" in its fallen and falling state. And who are "my people"? Do they know who they are? Do those who are *not* "my people" know who is out and who is in? A similarly worded call addressed earlier "those who dwell on the earth," that is, "every nation, tribe, tongue, and people" (14:6–8). This version has the feel of "To whom it may concern"; God speaks to the world as though all human beings are "*my* people." Along this line of thought, "my people" are not a group defined in advance but a community that is constituted by the call. They will not physically move from point A to point B, but they will need separation from "Babylon" in thought and deed. This is what it means to "come out" (Jer. 51:45; Isa. 52:11). As the house of the opposing side comes tumbling down, there is a realignment of loyalties and commitments away from the false side.

Hyperbole works in overdrive in this text, and nowhere more than in the running commentary on Babylon's demise. **"Give back to her as she herself has given, and double to her double for her deeds; in the cup she mixed mix double"** (18:6). As a measure of fairness, giving back "double" is a dubious proposition. The basic premise of lex talionis in the OT is proportionality: the punishment must fit the crime (Exod. 21:23–25; Lev. 24:19–20; Deut. 19:21). Moreover, the concern of the OT injunctions is precisely *not* to punish to excess, in a retaliatory spirit. Revelation's apparent exhortation to "double to her double" must therefore be appreciated for its *rhetorical errand* rather than *judicial precision*. Adela Yarbro Collins (1984, 152–61) accounts for the language not as descriptions of actual events but as *catharsis*. "Catharsis" is what the victim wishes upon the oppressor, and it will give a sense of closure even if everything happens in the imagination.

Such sentiments have emotional legitimacy, but the implied morality and theology are disconcerting. A legal case for giving back double is repudiated in the OT, and yet the pattern of "giving double" is affirmed. Isaiah is told to "speak tenderly to Jerusalem" and to "cry to her . . . that she has received from the LORD's hand *double* for all her sins" (Isa. 40:2; cf. Jer. 16:18; 17:18; Ezek. 21:14). Sins resulting in a doubling of the negative consequences have a counterpoint in doubling the reversal. Thus, at the point of Israel's restoration, "their shame was *double*; . . . therefore they shall possess a *double* portion" (Isa. 61:7; Zech. 9:12). This has been called a "dramatic inversion modality" (Strand 1986), speech driving home the magnitude of the reversal. In Revelation, the cry to "double to her double" conveys seriousness as well as certainty, but it is not a quantitative and strictly legal measure. We can leave the "doubling" intact, and the *dis*proportionality will make a nonlegal point that reflects the way things work in the real world. What "Babylon" dished out will come back to her, and it will come back "double" because the cycle of injury and terror escalates, spinning out of control.

When the exposé gets down to specifics, economic realities loom large. History, reality, and the human community have kept score. What comes back to haunt "Babylon" reflects what she has meted out (18:7–8). In this representation, the repercussions seem proportional, and the adherents are blindsided by consequences that they have failed to foresee. Reality's ambush on the illusion of stability echoes the OT (Isa. 47:7–9; Ezek. 28:2–10), but it also anticipates the language of rulers in recent human history as though Revelation eavesdropped on them centuries before they opened their mouth. **For in her heart she says, "I rule as a queen; I am no widow, and I will never see grief"** (18:7). This is Babylon's self-image of durability and invincibility and—conversely—her lack of humility. So deluded, so wrongheaded—and yet so representative! The surprise stands in proportion to the self-delusion; indeed, the self-delusion manufactures the blow. It **will hit** *in a single day* (18:8a), not only by springing an ambush on the unprepared but also by the concentrated boom. What comes around, however, is what goes around: **death, and grief, and famine** (18:8b) now come knocking on doors that formerly inflicted these things on others.

**And she will be burned with fire** (18:8c). It is said almost as an afterthought, in parenthesis, and here in the passive voice. Whence the fire this time? Entities that once embraced the woman and colluded with her are now the ones who *"will lay her waste"* and *"consume her flesh"* and *"burn her up with fire"* (17:16). God is *not* the agent that makes Babylon burn, but God has not disappeared from the moral equation and the revelatory reality at work. *This is God's way, the way of revelation* (17:17). "**For rock solid** [*ischyros*] **is the Lord God who exposes her and ensures that justice is done**" (18:8c). The "justice" being done relies on revelation to make its case.

The stance of those who witness these scenes borders on eerie. **And the kings of the earth, who committed sexual immorality and lived it up with her, they will weep and mourn inconsolably over her when they see the smoke of her burning** (18:9). This is freakish, a scene reeking with insincerity. Are not these the same kings who earlier *colluded* in creating the monstrosity (17:13)? Are not the mourners the ones who bring about Babylon's demise? Did we not read of "ten horns" that "are ten kings," and did not the angel explain that "the ten horns . . . will lay her waste and . . . burn her up with fire" (17:12, 16)? For the mourners to do that, they must have been as close to "the woman" as Cassius and Brutus were when they murdered Julius Caesar.

But look now! **Far off they will stand, petrified at her torment, saying, "How awful! How awful! the great city, Babylon, the strong city! For in one hour your moment of truth has come"** (18:10). Now, they stand "far off," the body language suggesting that they expect distance and expressions of grief to place them beyond suspicion of complicity.

A calamity of this order needs witnesses. For this, many OT antecedents model the appropriate emotional reaction (Jer. 19:8; 49:17; 50:13; Ezek. 5:14–15; 36:34; Aune 1996–98, 997). The witnesses are not incidental passersby. They cooperated willingly with "Babylon" before they killed her (17:12–16).

Measured by the criterion of repentance, their tears are crocodile tears, like the son who has murdered his parents and now complains that he is an orphan (Blount 2009, 333). If fear of being implicated in sins that "have reached the point of touching heaven" plays a part (17:5), distance helps the feigned posture of innocence. On the other hand, the mourning approaches incoherence if they are the ones who brought "Babylon" down (17:16). Rhetorical priorities appear to trample on logic, but it is better to say that the rhetoric prioritizes *revelation*: "Babylon" has been exposed, as have those who enabled her, turned on her, and now mourn her (18:9–10).

Modern terms like "economic crisis" and "market collapse" fit Revelation's description (18:11–13). "Bankruptcy" also works. G. K. Beale (1999, 904) weighs in that **the merchants** (18:11a) voice "despair over economic loss," and this captures the situation at face value. One interpreter says that the problem of "Babylon" is neither sexual debauchery nor the idolatrous cult but hard-nosed commerce (Rolin 2012, 58). Thomas R. Edgar (1982, 340) makes a "what-it-is" and "what-it-isn't" argument, insisting that "Babylon" should *not* be understood in political or ecclesial terms, but in relation to economics. Attempts at defining "what-it-isn't" are difficult to sustain based on the text, and they are unwise and unnecessary apart from the text, given that religion, politics, and economics represent a continuum of interrelated power spheres. Callahan (1999, 46) calls it a "critique in apocalyptic idiom of the political economy of imperial Rome." Focusing specifically on Roman slave trade, Craig R. Koester (2008, 766) calls Rev. 18 "a climactic moment" in the book's repudiation of "economic life under imperial Roman rule."

The tendency to see a Roman referent is predictable, but the predatory and acquisitive trade practices attributed to Rome have wide application. Callahan (2003, 271) again notes that "Revelation goes on to itemize the goods traded for the gratification of the powerful: luxuries—those commodities that all want, few have, and none need" (cf. Woods 2008). Such a system exists for the benefit of the few at the expense of the many, and it is neither fair nor sustainable. John's long list of luxury goods that are beyond the reach of most people is at once impressive, monotonous, and sleep inducing until one gets to the last item on the list: *bodies—and human beings* (18:13). Both terms refer to human beings that are subject to the slave trade; both imply loss of dignity; and both are the high point of an economy that spots a commodity in beings that move as much as in the things that don't, including "human beings" (18:13). "What dominates the reign of Satan is consumption" (Bredin 2008, 82). "Bodies—and human beings" have in this economy become a commodity and items for consumption.

All the items listed are the subject matter of revelation, but all things are not equal. "Bodies—and human beings" stand out on the list. Politics, religion, and economy cannot be separated from each other in an exposé that joins them together just as they are joined in human affairs otherwise. And just as economy and ecology, too, are tightly knit, they express the underlying *theology*. It goes without saying that the theological underpinnings of a system that trades in "human beings" have by Revelation's standard *fallen*. This can be said with even greater force when the religious character of "Babylon" is recognized. More evidence to this effect is about to come.

**And the fruit which you desired** [*epithymias*] **has slipped from you, and all your brightness and your splendor are lost to you, never to be found again!** (18:14). How far back in the biblical narrative should we go to grasp this sorrowful statement? To the garden of Eden and the woman who "saw that the tree was good for food, and that it was a delight to the eyes, and that the tree was to be desired to make one wise" and then "took of its fruit and ate" (Gen. 3:6)? Should we go further back still—to the Shining One, the covering cherub, whose assets were incomparable brightness and splendor put to wrongful use (Isa. 14:12–15; Ezek. 28:12–17)? More than Rome is in view in texts that wrap up the larger story and march on to expose a misguided aspiration brought to grief.

Three rounds of action and reaction are distinguishable, each rising from the same script of failure (18:9–14, 15–17a, 17b–19). "The kings of the earth" lead the mourners (18:9–14), and those who follow go through the same motion with little variance. **The merchants of these goods** are next (18:15), also standing **far off**, also **petrified**, also **mourning**, also reading from the same script, **"How awful! How awful!"** (18:15–16). The third group, the **shipmasters and those in the way of the sea**, take it a notch higher, throwing **dust on their heads** in a posture of grief that rivals the reaction of Job's friends (18:17b–19; Job 2:12). They, too, **stood far off**, like the others **weeping and mourning**, and like the others singing the same tune, **"How awful! How awful!"** (18:17b–19).

"How awful"? The mourners have said it a full six times (18:10, 16, 19), "the merchants" and "all shipmasters" possibly sincerer than "the kings." But here, too, the beholder must beware. Some spectators do not share the mourners' grief. For them, this is the moment for which they have waited. If the mourners have tears streaming down their cheeks, all faces are smiling on the other side. **Rejoice over her, heaven, and the believers, and the apostles, and the prophets! For God has decided for you from her** (18:20a).

It is humane to participate in another person's grief, but this obligation does not apply here. Expressions of grief at the demise of "Babylon" lack merit and dignity. Liberation and vindication for the oppressed—this is what counts. The rejoicing has a cosmic tenor befitting the end of the conflict and not only the demise of imperial Rome. There is a subtlety in the text, the perception of which is necessary for its theological treasure to come to light. We see and hear *vindication*, first as the vindication of "the believers, and the apostles, and the prophets," but the text is mainly a tribute to *God*. God—translating it literally—*has judged your judgment out of her* (18:20b; Strand 1986, 44).

In plainer English, God has *not* brought judgment *against* "Babylon" with a direct hit from on high but has accomplished something far more difficult at the level of imagination, cost, and execution. The "judgment" came *"out of her (Babylon),"* making *her* be the case against *herself.* Conversely, the judgment in favor of the believers is also a judgment rising *out of her.* Kenneth A. Strand's (1986, 44) reading is perceptive, and the link to Ezekiel's poem about the covering cherub is telling. "So I brought forth fire from within you; it consumed you" (Ezek. 28:18). According to this logic, judgment was not idle or slothful, but it aimed for more than a legal verdict "for you against her." It bided its time; it did not stray from its ideology; it kept the surprise waiting. And there it was—an outcome making the cosmic rebellion the lead witness against the rebellion.

Body language matched to words makes for powerful communication, and the playacting that accompanies the undoing of "Babylon" soars. **And a mighty angel took a stone like a great millstone and threw [*ebalen*] it into the sea, saying, "With such violent force Babylon, the great city, will be thrown down [*blēthēsetai*], and will be found no more"** (18:21). To be "thrown down" is a recurring scenario in the cosmic conflict: of the Shining One in Isaiah's poem (Isa. 14:12–15); of the star under the fifth trumpet (Rev. 9:1); of the dragon when "war burst forth in heaven" (12:7–9). Now, one last time, "Babylon . . . will be *thrown down*" for good (18:21). She is brought down by forces at work within herself, and knowledge of her demise is a matter of *revelation.* "Babylon . . . will be found no more" (18:21), just as the covering cherub comes "to a dreadful end and shall be no more forever" (Ezek. 28:19).

"No more" is now a theme word, embedded in poetry of finality and relief. For, John says,

> the sound of harpists and musicians and flutists and trumpeters
> will be heard in you *no more*;
> and traders of any trade
> will be found in you *no more*;
> and the sound of the millstone
> will be heard in you *no more*;
> and the light of a lamp
> will shine in you *no more*;
> and the voice of bridegroom and bride
> will be heard in you *no more*. (18:22–23)

At last "the great city" falls silent. Industry, commerce, and culture come to an end. Domestic and public life cease. But "the great city" that descends into silence is described by evocative OT passages taking stock of the decline of *Jerusalem* (Jer. 7:34; 16:9; 25:10; cf. Ezek. 26:13; Isa. 24:8). This is not incidental, as though John helped himself to texts irrespective of the original context. Rather, the story of apostasy in the OT finds a parallel in Revelation.

The OT provides an antecedent and "proof of concept" for "the woman" who becomes "Babylon" in Revelation's story (Isa. 14:12–20; Ezek. 28:12–19). In the OT, God says of Jerusalem "that there will be a cessation of the continuity of the community: no temple, no one left to bury, no one left to marry" (Holladay 1986, 270). Again—still referring to the Jerusalem community in the days of Jeremiah—the eeriness is intense. "Dead silence during the day, uninterrupted by any human sound; unearthly darkness during the night, unillumined by any gleam of a lamp—in its concise characterization this is a quite wonderful depiction of complete barrenness and desolation, which could be achieved only by a poet of God's grace" (Holladay 1986, 668). In Jeremiah's time, the Jerusalem community became "Babylon" to the point that the descendants of the patriarchs sacrificed their children to Baal and Moloch (Lev. 20:1–5; Jer. 7:31; 19:5–6; 32:35; Acts 7:43; cf. Lundbom 2008a, 501–2). As in Jeremiah's depiction, "the millstone" in the morning and the "lamp" in the evening are complementary symbols of domestic life: "one is *heard* in the *morning*, the other *seen* in the *evening*" (Jer. 25:10; Rev. 18:22, 23; cf. Lundbom 2008b, 249). A community where "the voice of bridegroom and bride" is no longer heard is not only a community deprived of cherished seasons of celebration. The expression is a metaphor for death—a community threatened with extinction (Lundbom 2008a, 760).

The need to see "Babylon" as a theological enterprise remains. It is driven home further when Revelation says that **your merchants were the great men of the earth, and all nations were deceived** [*eplanēthēsan*] **by your magic spells** [*tē pharmakeia sou*] (18:23b; L&N 53.100, p. 545, φαρμακεία). Material goods and unsustainable economic practices need not be taken out of the equation, but theology will be left out at the cost of missing the main point. This is an entity that trades in falsehood, and it is good at it: "all nations were deceived" (18:23; Gen. 3:13). Deception has been hard at work by the concept from which the words *pharmacy* and *pharmacology* are derived (*pharmakeia*): a form of misleading that is subtle, clever, and intentional.

At this point John shifts from the second person, *addressing* "Babylon," to the third-person singular, *describing* "Babylon" for the benefit of someone else. We can imagine this as the report of a forensic pathologist writing the final report about the most incriminating evidence that has been uncovered. The investigator looks up from the subject under investigation to share with the public what he/she found. **And in her was found** [*heurethē*] **the blood of prophets and of believers, and of all who have been killed with violence on earth** (18:24).

The bottom-line indictment is immense and shocking. First, taking the verse to be the conclusion concerning the most incriminating evidence, mention of "the blood of prophets and of believers" seems odd considering the historical evidence. It is not illegitimate to call Rome to account for persecution and murder of "prophets." However, the surprise in recent scholarship is the dearth of evidence for large-scale persecution of Christians—the fact that there is so little to report (L. Thompson 1990, 95–115). Second, the investigator ascribes responsibility to "Babylon" for "*all* who have been killed with violence on earth" (18:24). Really? This is either immoderate hyperbole (Koester 2014, 711), a wild exaggeration, or yet another incentive to rethink the terms of the subject. If "Babylon" is Rome at the time of John, is it fair to blame it for "*all* who have been killed with violence on earth"?

A possible allusion to Jeremiah's indictment of Babylon has been recognized (Jer. 51:49), but this does not put to rest the disquiet interpreters ought to feel. Ancient Babylon was called to account for well-known incriminating conduct, no investigation necessary, and the Roman track record was similar. Besides, the statement in Revelation aims to capture *earthly* affairs in its totality; it is not limited to imperial *Roman* conditions. *This* "Babylon" needs an investigation because there is a discrepancy between pretensions and reality, on the one hand, and a gap between expectations and reality, on the other. For these concerns in the text, the verbs must be scoured for meaning in the most wide-ranging clues available in the OT. Like "Babylon" in Revelation, Ezekiel says of the covering cherub that "you were blameless in your ways from the day you were created, until iniquity *was found* [*heurethē*, LXX] in you" (Ezek. 28:15). A eureka moment as big as that is the subject in Revelation: "in her *was found* [*heurethē*] the blood of prophets and of believers" (18:24). This is the element lying between pretension and reality because "the Shining One" and "the covering cherub" did not present himself as a murderer even though that is what he is found to be. What *was found*, therefore, is the most revealing discovery about the instigator of the cosmic conflict. The murderous character of the pretender has come to light (13:8; 18:24; cf. John 8:44).

At the lesser, human level, "Babylon" takes stock of the story of the fleeing woman (12:13–16). Rome as city and the Roman Empire as power constellations fail to capture the drama and shock of Revelation's exposé. Here, too, the OT is in the know. But its subject is Jerusalem, not Babylon: *it tells the story of "Jerusalem" losing its way until it behaves like the villain* (cf. Isa. 1:21; 5:7; 57:3; Jer. 2:20–28; Ezek. 22:1–13). This leads to the following enhanced translation of the closing word on "Babylon" in Revelation. "And in *her*—*in her of all places*—was found the blood of prophets and of believers, and of all who have been killed with violence on earth" (18:24).

## Theological Issues

"And Babylon the Great was remembered before God" (16:19). Thus begins the story told in demanding detail in Rev. 17 and 18. An assessment that takes the symbols seriously must acknowledge that the identity of "Babylon" is less the foregone conclusion than interpretations make it appear. At the level of

265

*representation*, these chapters blur the line of distinction between "the dragon" and "the beast," but they take great care to distinguish "the woman" from "the beast" (17:1, 3, 7). The close connection between these chapters and the story of the two beasts in Rev. 13 is widely acknowledged (King 2004, 305; Mucha and Witetschek 2013). Revelation 13 projects a story of *imitation*, the imitation grounded in images of Jesus and the defining event in *his* story (13:3, 11). This unfolds in the context of the dragon "going away" (12:17), following his last-ditch effort to destroy "the woman" (12:13–17). The account of "the woman" and "the beast" in Rev. 17 is thus another chapter in the same story, with the "woman" now the center of attention. She is represented as a *fallen* woman, a "prostitute" (17:1–4) and "the mother of prostitutes," the latter best understood as "the epitome of prostitutes" (17:5). She and "the beast" traffic in *slander* (17:3), a commodity that also looms large in the exposé of Babylon's trading practices. And she is a "mystery" (17:5, 7). As "mystery," John's surprise seems perfectly reasonable (17:6). More surprising, therefore, is the angel's admonition that he should not be amazed (17:7). Why not? Should he, as most interpreters believe, have grasped that this is an exposé of imperial Rome and that there is not much about which to get surprised? Or should he, in an alternative conception, have understood the profoundly subversive character of the dragon's war against the woman's offspring (12:13–17)? In the latter conception, it is easy to understand John's astonishment—although the angel's corrective stands (17:7).

In this representation of the dragon's war on the woman and "the rest of her offspring" (12:17), *seduction* is in Rev. 17 the ideological and strategic linchpin, much like *imitation* is the main thing in chapter 13. This summons the mind to accept that the dragon achieves a measure of success in his war. He has a seductress to show for his effort (17:1–3). She becomes the seducer-in-chief, for some time operating in lockstep with the beast until the coalition unravels (17:16). Seduction may be her strategy, but she breeds violence and feeds on it (17:6; 18:24): resort to violence is a core element in her character.

All this unfolds along a future-oriented time line. We read of "the beast . . . *that is to come*" (17:8, 11) as the critical, climactic reality not yet present. We read that "the other has *not yet* come" (17:10) and of "ten kings . . . who have *not yet* received a kingdom" (17:12). The *not yet* caveats, like so much in these disclosures, have a horizon that is future and a tenor of finality. These are weighty reasons not to accept that Revelation returns the same answer, mantra-like, to the questions raised by its symbols: "Rome. Rome. Rome." The challenge, instead, is to accommodate "the woman" in an interpretation that does justice to the symbol, the cosmic perspective, the plot structure, and the suggestive biblical antecedents—and thus overcome the mismatch between the metaphorical shoe and the Roman foot that is supposed to fill it.

This does not mean that the Bible disparages history. On the contrary, historical analogies are extremely helpful for these chapters in Revelation. According to the OT, the descendants of the patriarchs might become—and did become—devotees of Baal and Moloch (Lev. 20:1–5; Jer. 7:31; 19:5–6; 32:35). Jesus voices the same concern in his parting word to his followers: "Beware that no one deceives [*planēsē*] you. For many will come in my name, saying, 'I am the Christ,' and they will deceive [*planēsousin*] many" (Matt. 24:4–5, my trans.). By this analogy the history of "the woman" and "the beast" in Revelation may be understood as the actualization of the unthinkable. John's body language and choice of words are to the point (17:6). In the implausible partnership between "the woman" and "the beast," there is intimacy before there is enmity; collusion precedes collapse; and at the end the common cause fragments and implodes (17:13–16).

For a historical reality describing a faith community (the woman) tightly but unwisely entwined with the state (the beast), Eusebius in the fourth century offered his stamp of approval. A banquet hosted by the Emperor Constantine is a tone-setting scene. "Not one of the bishops was wanting at the imperial banquet. . . . The men of God proceeded without fear into the innermost of the imperial apartments. . . . One might have thought that a picture of Christ's kingdom was thus shadowed forth, a dream rather than a reality" (*Vit. Const.* 3.15). In this uncritical perception, the state will be the protector of the faith, and the faith sees the state favorably disposed to its mission. Providence is at work, and the reality is better than anyone dared to dream (Greenslade 1954, 10).

Even if we read Revelation as analogy rather than prophecy, the options explored here do not conform to Eusebius's congenial view. Revelation's values and commitments are meant to place the believing community in a posture of vigilance toward attempts to seduce it. To Stephen D. Moore (2006, 115), "Revelation epitomizes, and encapsulates for analytical scrutiny, the larger and later process whereby Christianity, . . . [after the] Constantinian period, paradoxically *became* Rome." This view envisions a "Babylon" that "sits upon the political power," and it includes the prospect that "it is the political power that will destroy her" (Ellul 1977, 118). Even if we think Fyodor Dostoevsky guilty of exaggerating the extent to which the church adopted violence against dissent, it should be seen as a matter of principle. There is more than a drop-let of truth to Ivan Karamazov's scornful "poem" about the Christian world to which Jesus returns in the fifteenth century: "My action is set in Spain, in Seville," says Ivan, "in the most horrible time of the Inquisition, when fires blazed every day to the glory of God" (Dostoevsky 2002, 248).

Lord (Sir John) Acton, writing as a Roman Catholic historian, applies a value judgment to Christianity that by this criterion comes close to Revelation (18:24). In correspondence between him and Mandell Creighton, a British Protestant historian later to become a bishop in the Church of England, Lord Acton (1972, 333) puts his eggs in the basket deemed most important:

> We all agree that Calvin was one of the greatest writers, many think him the best religious teacher, in the world. But that one affair of Servetus outweighs the

nine folios, and settles, by itself, the reputation he deserves. So with the medieval Inquisition and the Popes that founded it and worked it. That is the breaking point, the article of their system by which they stand or fall.

Lord Acton's perception of "the breaking point" is telling. He had in mind Calvin's role in the burning of Michael Servetus at the stake for holding to a heretical Christology, and as the defining principle of the deed, the approval of persecution, coercion, and executions in defense of the faith (Schaff 1910, 462–65; Bainton 1953). The Inquisition had a different rationale but the same policy (Acton 1972, 58–87). The policy became so entrenched, the connection between faith and state so seamless, that it came as a shock on the Christian community when Roger Williams (1603–83), like Lord Acton, made this "the breaking point." Upon his arrival in the New World, Roger Williams (1848, 2) declared that "an enforced uniformity of religion throughout a nation or civil state, confounds the civil and religious, denies the principle of Christianity and civility, and that Jesus Christ is come in the flesh."

Revelation projects a similar standard by which to judge whether an entity stands or falls. In the final paragraph of its forensic report, we read that "in her was found the blood of prophets and of believers, and of all who have been killed with violence on earth" (18:24). This "Babylon" is judged to be "fallen" (14:8; 18:4). If we find ourselves stymied by the many challenges in these chapters, the criterion by which to ascertain "fallenness" is clearly laid out (18:24).

What did victims of oppression experience at the zenith of Christian power in Europe, computed in economic terms? Six million people died of starvation in the course of one generation during the reign of Louis XIV (1643–1715), one of the most callous tyrants in European history and also the most "Christian" (Acton 1972, 100). What did they experience—if not poverty, suffering, and death at the hand of pious entities "made rich" at others' expense (18:14–16)? This sordid and "Christian" chapter in history plays out as the story of a religious-political structure puffed up and living it up with abandon, the arms of the church all over the state, and vice versa. Likewise, in the same period, as colonial powers fanned out in the world, they brought with them the pursuit of profit and fortune at the expense of the millions whose misfortune was the flip side of their prosperity. The economic implications of Revelation's indictment seem descriptively adequate for the exploitation committed by the colonial merchants in the eighteenth century.

A mentality foreign to the conventional economy inspired these traders. Their attitude, characterized by a hazardous quest for profit, transformed the warring spirit into a ruthless determination to vanquish competitors and made speculation the mainspring of their activity. With them appeared certain characteristics of what we call capitalism—concentration of capital and business concerns so that exploitation could be rationalized, a development that gave this economic technique cardinal importance in the rise of European civilization. (Lefebre 1962, 1:24)

This involved trade in "*bodies—and human beings,*" too (18:13), now as the actual slave trade of "Christian" nations that march forth under the banner of Christianity. Africa was "'the ebony reservoir' for the New World" (Lefebre 1962, 1:8) and slavery a key element in its prosperity. Half of the story is still untold, says Edward E. Baptist (2014) in a book that has the subtitle *Slavery and the Making of American Capitalism*. These dehumanizing realities are at least serviceable *examples* of the kind of predation Revelation has in mind.

In Revelation, everything plays out in the seeing presence of the heavenly council. It is easy to forget that John processes reality from the perspective of "up there" (Rev. 4:1). Reminders of continuity are evident all along, especially by "the four living creatures" who are present (4:6–8; 5:6; 14:3), who participate (6:1, 3, 5, 7; 15:7), and who pass judgment on what they see (5:8–14; 7:11–12; 19:1–4). In the heavenly perspective the "Babylon" that "is fallen" in human terms matters less than the enemy at work behind the scenes. When the nonhuman agent is called to account, the violent shedding of "the blood of prophets and of believers" (18:24) shows a policy of coercion and cruelty that is in sharp contrast to the ways of God. To implicate *this* murderous agent in the deaths of "all who have been killed with violence on earth" (18:24) is not an exaggeration, an inflation of the numbers, a mismatch between ideology and deeds, or a failure to do precise chronology. Throw in two thousand years of human history; throw in the Crusades; throw in the Holocaust and Hiroshima, too: the underpinnings of the text will not cave in under the weight. The murderer that has been on the loose in the world cannot be represented in human terms alone, but he has now been exposed. In the heavenly perspective, the Shining One is the one who has "fallen" (Isa. 14:12–20), and the covering cherub is the one in whom the most horrendous iniquity "was found" (Ezek. 28:15; Rev. 18:24).

# Revelation 19:1–21

## The Wedding, the Rider, and the Supper

### Introductory Matters

The first nine verses of Rev. 19 are a response to, and a celebration of, the scenes that have been depicted in the preceding two chapters (Rev. 17 and 18). Ideally, the exposition of these verses should proceed without the artificial suture line that a new chapter entails.

On the other hand, the reaction needs breathing room to make its point clear, respectful of the limitations of expositors and readers alike. A fresh start is well advised for reasons of digestion even if it runs against the grain of the text. When we acknowledge that the text flashes back and forth, revisiting earlier scenes as well as giving glimpses of things yet to come, no suture line should lay claim to cutting the text in the right place. Two of the three tableaus in this chapter are scenes of endings, at one end an alluring wedding (19:1–9), at the opposite end a sickening "supper" (19:17–21). Wedged between these two tableaus is another compelling description of how God "makes decisions and wages war" (19:11–16).

### Tracing the Train of Thought

#### Celebration and Wedding: The Marriage Supper of the Lamb (19:1–9)

**19:1–9.** Before describing the wedding, there is another burst of singing (19:1–2). Like songs heard earlier (5:8–14; 15:2–4; 16:5–7), this song has also

---

### Revelation 19:1–21 in the Rhetorical Flow

Incentive to read (1:1–20)

To the one who has an ear (2:1–3:22)

The seven seals (4:1–8:1)

The seven trumpets (8:2–11:19)

The cosmic conflict from A to Z (12:1–14:20)

The seven bowls (15:1–16:21)

The woman and the beast (17:1–18:24)

►The wedding, the rider, and the supper (19:1–21)

    Celebration and wedding: The marriage supper of the Lamb (19:1–9)

    Who is who: The angel and the testimony of Jesus (19:10)

    The end and the means: The rider on the white horse (19:11–16)

    Desolation and horror: The great supper of God (19:17–21)

---

the tenor of an appraisal. The "appraisal" has God as its subject, and it is a retrospective: the singers find confirmed about God what seemed in doubt. *Song* and *story* are inseparable. The songs celebrate not only the solution to the crisis but a solution that differs sharply from what anyone expected.

> After this I heard what seemed like a loud sound of a great multitude
>    in the heaven, saying,
> "Hallelujah!
> The victory [*hē sōtēria*] and the renown and the power
>    are due our God,
> for trustworthy [*alēthinai*] and right-making [*dikaiai*]
> are God's decisions [*hai kriseis autou*];
> God has exposed [*ekrinen*] the great prostitute
>    who corrupted the earth
>    with her sexual immorality,

---

### Important Nuances

To preserve the dynamic character of the action deemed to be *dikaios*, I have chosen "right-making" rather than "just" or "righteous" to render the Greek word *dikaios* (BDAG 246–47, δίκαιος). While *krisis* entails judgment in a legal sense, Revelation brings to light God's governance, thus "God's decisions" for *hai kriseis autou* (BDAG 569, κρίσις). On the same broad logic, God "has judged [*ekrinen*] the great prostitute," but the judgment is revelatory, and thus God "has *exposed* the great prostitute" (BDAG 567–69, κρίνω).

---

> and God has vindicated [*exedikēsen*]
> the blood of God's servants
> shed by her hand." (19:1–2)

As noted, this is not the first occasion of earnest celebration (4:9–11; 5:9–13; 7:10–12; 11:15; 12:10; 15:2–4). The celebratory scenes follow in succession, each reinforcing the others, all cognizant of fierce conflict, all in awe of the path taken by God. Although the celebrations are inspired by the relief brought to human beings and the world, the focus is on God and on heaven's point of view. God's conduct in the cosmic conflict seemed to have nothing to commend it (5:1–2), but a new way of seeing is taking hold: *God's* decisions are trustworthy; *God* has exposed the great prostitute; *God* has made it up to the victims of violence (19:1–2). The song echoes the question to which the song is the answer.

> *Cry of the victims of violence*: "How long . . . will it be before you act justly [*krineis*] and vindicate [*ekdikeis*] our blood (shed) by those who dwell on the earth?" (6:10)
>
> *Sound of great multitude*: "God has vindicated [*exedikēsen*] the blood of God's servants shed by her hand." (19:2)

God has indeed "acted *justly*" insofar as *God's* notion of just action is preserved. When this is appreciated, it matters less which emphasis is preferred for the rest of the text. Concern that God neglects to punish the perpetrators is less distressing than the possibility that God forgets the victims. Acting "justly" by way of *retribution* competes for ownership of the text with God acting justly by way of *vindication*. What becomes of the victim in the earth's cycle of violence, beginning with Abel in Genesis (Gen. 4:10; Tonstad 2016a, 104–24)? Is victimhood remedied by retribution, or is it better alleviated by God making it up to those who felt abandoned? The text in Revelation moves the second of these options to the top of the list. *By this criterion acting justly is a matter of right-making* (19:1–2). Allusions to the OT lend support to this reading (Aune 1996–98, 1025; Koester 2014, 727). In Revelation, the focus is on the hand by which the blood of the victims was shed, just as an OT text expresses concern for "the deaths of my servants the prophets and the deaths of all the servants of the Lord *at the hand of Jezebel*" (2 Kings 9:7 LXX, my trans.). This means "that blood was shed 'by [the hand of] Jezebel,' not that vengeance would be taken upon her" (Aune 1996–98, 1025). When the same reasoning is applied to the text in Revelation, the accent falls on the plight of the victim without losing sight of the perpetrator.

"Babylon" and its side in the cosmic conflict have come to naught. **And they said it again, for the second time, "Hallelujah! The smoke of her ascends forever and ever"** (19:3). This is poignant language for a memory that will not be erased. Just as there was celebration in the earlier scenes in the heavenly council

(5:8–14), so here (19:4). Discretion with respect to **the One who is seated on the throne** (12:4; see also 4:2, 3, 9; 5:1, 7, 13), if usually indeterminate, is now made explicit. *God* is the one "who is seated on the throne" (19:4). Doubts about the trustworthiness of God have vanished. The misrepresentations of the adversary in the cosmic conflict have gone up in smoke.

And a **voice called out from the throne, saying, "Praise our God, all you God's servants, and those who speak well of God, small and great"** (19:5). The heavenly antiphony is impressive, on cue, and on topic, a vivid contrast to the prior depiction of a heavenly council in a state of distress and disarray (5:1–4). That the voice calls out "from the throne" does not mean that God is the one talking, given the presence of created beings "in the middle of the throne" (4:6; 5:6). The verbs are best seen as synonyms befitting Hebrew poetic conventions. This makes the call to "*praise* [*aineite*] our God" and the exhortation to "those who fear [*hoi phoboumenoi*] God" synonymous. What do people who *praise* do, other than "speak well of" the person they praise (19:5)? The terms describe a community that has been constituted by the call of the three angels earlier in Revelation (14:6–12) and by the loud call coinciding with the fall of Babylon (18:4). Most important, the scenes reverberate with a sense of reversal. All the slander of the Ancient Serpent has come to grief. Insights internalized by the beings closest to the throne are picked up and processed in the idiom of praise by countless others (19:6).

Good news? This is what the wave of praise and well speaking fanning out among intelligent beings conveys. We do not have good news in the sense that God is something that God has not been until now. *God is seen to be what God is against a background of conflict.* The crisis gives depth and verve to the exclamations. The exclamations, in turn, are captured in language aware of its inadequacy: **the sound of a great multitude; the sound of many waters; the sound of mighty peals of thunder** (19:6a). The tenor of all the sounds is admiration and gratitude, and the whole of the well-speaking is greater than the sum of its parts.

And the voice calling out from the throne is not done. **Let us be grateful, and let us be overjoyed, and let us give God the glory, for [*hoti*] the marriage of the Lamb has come, and his bride has made herself ready** (19:7). There is joy over what has been described until now, and still more joy in anticipation of "the marriage of the Lamb" (BDAG 731–32, ὅτι). The voice speaks of "the marriage of the Lamb" as though it is a known and widely anticipated event within the text. Readers, however, have not had advance notice. "The mention of a wedding at this point is entirely unexpected," David E. Aune (1996–98, 1021) admits. Those in the know have been aware how this will end, and the three verbs conveying the excitement prove as much. By Johannine criteria, the thought of Jesus as *bridegroom* is not new. Other Gospels use nuptial imagery (Matt. 22:1–12; 25:1–13; Luke 12:36), but the Gospel of John is unique for seeing Jesus as the bridegroom; unique, too, in perceiving a wedding at the end of the story (John 3:29). The theological tradition is skeptical of analogies between human experience and knowledge of God, but the prospect of *marriage* in our text cannot be freed from all we associate with the term. Marriage at its best (1) implies *appreciation* and *longing* of one for the other; (2) speaks of *commitment*; (3) belongs to the domain of *joy*; (4) is a *communal* experience, imparting a surplus to all participants; (5) and anticipates *consummation*. Marriage that includes these elements will be the end point and the zenith of experience.

These elements can safely be imagined for the nuptial imagery in Revelation. In *this* marriage *appreciation* and *longing* of one for the other are enhanced by the long alienation (Gen. 3:1–6). In Genesis, there is a marriage between Adam and Eve, a union with primacy for the human realm (Gen. 2:21–25). In Revelation, "the marriage of the Lamb" suggests primacy for the relationship between human beings and God (Rev. 19:7). Revelation's marriage is also a *communal* experience, but with the difference that the entire community is constituted as *bride*. We are in the realm of metaphor, but the exclusionary zones of marriage in human experience—*only* her, or *only* him, or *only* the other one—to the exclusion of everyone else, some single, some disappointed, and some widowed or divorced, are now erased by a marriage embracing all.

*Consummation* entails *intimacy* and *ecstasy*. Is this connotation of marriage off-limits when the subject is "the marriage of the Lamb"? We may leave out a sexual connotation but not *intimacy* or *ecstasy*. Jesus is on record in the Gospels to the effect that marriage and procreation in human terms are not a feature of the life to come (Matt. 22:23–32; Mark 12:18–27; Luke 20:27–39), but the prospect is not diminished joy or ecstasy. If anything in this regard can be inferred from the phrase used in Revelation—"His bride has made herself ready"—we are enticed not only to contemplate a marriage ceremony but also a *consummation. This couple will go all the way.* Johannine language of *perichoresis*—the indwelling of one in the other—complements the marital imagery in Revelation. "As you, Father, are in me and I am in you, may they also be in us, so that the world may believe that you have sent me" (John 17:21). The OT also describes the relationship between God and human beings in marital terms (Hosea 2:19–20; Isa. 62:5; Ezek. 16:8), and it envisions a celebration like no other (Isa. 25:6). A "marriage of the Lamb," nevertheless, is a conception never before imagined.

The clothing described must be interpreted with care (19:8). Earlier, the victims of violence "were each given [*edothē*] a white robe" (6:11; cf. 3:5; 7:13–14). The robe of **fine linen, bright and pure**, has also **been given** (19:8a). Ernst Lohmeyer (1926, 152) intimates that the explanatory note has been added ill-advisedly because it suggests that the believers' earthly works are meritorious. This interpretation is unwarranted. Even if the notion of being *ready* includes a person's mind-set, the focus is on compatibility, not merit. The moral tenor of the explanatory note—**the fine linen is the righteous deeds** of the believers (19:8b)—is a comment on fact and not a hint of an earned reward (Aune 1996–98, 1030–31). While the redeemed have suffered adversity, perseverance is not construed as merit (7:13–14; 12:10–12).

No prospect is brighter than participation at "the marriage of the Lamb." This is on the mind of the angel who now speaks again, **"Write! How fortunate are those who are invited to the marriage supper of the Lamb!"** (19:9; Aune 1996–98, 1031). The command to write is concerned to get the word out, and it highlights the certainty of God's commitment. A word that is *written* has an official, irrevocable tenor that the spoken word cannot match. The call to write occurs at some of the most critical points in the story (1:11; 14:13; 19:9; 21:5). Even though declaring a person to be "fortunate" is not a comment on subjective happiness, no privilege is more to be desired. Participation is by invitation, "to request the presence of someone at a social gathering" (BDAG 502–4, καλέω). And who are invited? How big is the tent, how wide-ranging the inclusion? The emphasis must be that "those who are invited" are fortunate, not that some are invited and some left out, even though this idea runs deep in the theological tradition. "Many more are condemned by vengeance than are released by mercy," Augustine wrote unwisely (*Civ.* 21.12, trans. Fredriksen 2010, 351).

Invitation to this event is attractive on its own merits without needing to be contrasted to anything else, but there is "something else." At the "great supper of God" (19:17–18), cannibalistic scenes define horror the way "the marriage supper of the Lamb" defines joy. Revelation has been in this territory earlier, particularly in the promise to the community in Laodicea. "If anyone hears my voice and opens the door, I will come in to eat supper with him/her, and he/she with me" (3:20). These are images of closeness, communion, and community.

### Who Is Who: The Angel and the Testimony of Jesus (19:10)

**19:10.** What follows next is unexpected, but it is unwarranted to dismiss it as an interpolation (Longenecker 2000, 230–37). **And I fell down at his feet to worship him. But he says to me, "Watch out! I am a fellow servant with you and your brothers and sisters who hold the testimony of Jesus. Worship God! For the testimony of Jesus is the spirit of prophecy"** (19:10). "Watch out!" is more literal and to be preferred than the implied meaning "Don't do that!" (BDAG 719–20, ὁράω). Either way, should not John know better? Is the sight of an angel enough for him to lose sight of the distance between the Creator and a created being? We are tempted to read this with an air of superiority, but humility is advised. Neither John nor his first readers had the benefit of two thousand years of acrimonious controversy over the status of Jesus in Christian thought. One facet of the problem is found in Revelation. Revelation is not afraid to represent Jesus as an angel even though he belongs to the God-side of beings that exist (J. Collins 1974; Gieschen 1998; Rowland 1980; 1985). Angelic representation of Jesus poses a risk to his standing, superficially speaking, but it does no harm to his self-giving character. Why would a person who shares in the divine identity appear as though he is less than that—and less than God—unless it is God's disposition to behave that way? John mistakes *this* angel as someone worthy of worship, and it is a big mistake, but it would not be a mistake to worship someone who has the appearance of an angel if that person is Jesus. And—in short—that person *could* be Jesus. New Testament representations of Jesus do not stop at angelic appearance but go on to promote worship of someone who appears as a human being (Rev. 1:13–15; 12:7–10; Dan. 7:13–14; 10:5; 12:1; Tonstad 2016a, 67–83).

A view more respectful of John's ability to tell who is who could interpret the scene as though John playacts the problem facing the human community with respect to objects of worship. He, too, gets enticed, as it were; he, too, rushes to the wrong conclusion; even he misses the point and needs a strongly worded corrective while standing in the full blaze of revelation. David E. Aune (1996–98, 1035) notes that "mistaking a human being for a deity appearing in human form is a motif found frequently in Greek and Hellenistic literature," but the problem in Revelation is the reverse. In Revelation, the being in question is not only the deity in human *form* but also a genuine human being.

"The testimony of Jesus" [*martyria Iēsou*] has earlier appeared as a synonym and explanation of "the word of God" (1:2) and "the commandments of God" (12:17). This function persists and expands whether the term is seen as the "personal testimony of Jesus" (Mazzaferri 1988, 119), the sum and consummation of God's communication to human beings, or a term that puts the self-giving of Jesus at the center: Jesus is a *martyr* even in the modern sense of the word (Vassiliades 1985). By all these criteria "the testimony of Jesus" is "the spirit of prophecy," and "the spirit of prophecy" is best understood as a comprehensive term for revelation that leads to, and culminates in, Jesus (19:10).

### The End and the Means: The Rider on the White Horse (19:11–16)

**19:11–16.** An "open heaven" greets John—and the reader—over and over in the book (4:1; 11:19; 15:5). Here it happens again. **And I saw the heaven opened, and look! A white horse! And the one sitting on *it* is called Faithful and Trustworthy, and by upright means [*en dikaiosynē*] he makes decisions and wages war** (19:11). A "white horse" has been seen before, at the breaking of the first seal—and with the same wording (6:2). The article is lacking in both instances (6:2; 19:11). This is not a problem for the first occurrence, but it is a clue for the second. While the nonuse of the article at the second occurrence may not be conclusive evidence, it makes it more likely that it is not the same thing. White horses in Revelation are not self-explanatory. Their identity and what they are up to are defined by the rider and his activity rather than the color of the horse. On this occasion, the rider is a witness wielding a sword (19:15);

he is not a conqueror armed with a bow (6:1–2). To make the contrast show in the translation, points of emphasis will be necessary. This "white horse" is identified by the character of its rider: "the one sitting on *it*," that is, "the one sitting on *this* white horse," is different from the rider on the white horse in the seal sequence (6:2). *That* white horse belongs to a group, spearheading their activity. By that criterion, it is a symbol of *deception*, and is followed by horses "red," "black," and "sickly green" (6:4, 5, 8). The rider of this "white horse," by contrast, is not a deceiver: he "is called Faithful and Trustworthy." Deceit rides the first white horse; faithfulness and trustworthiness the second. The text continues as a study in contrasts. Any means will work for the false side, beginning with deception and violence (6:2, 4), but *this* rider is distinguished by his principles: "by upright means [*en dikaiosynē*] he makes decisions and wages war" (19:11). Nothing sets the causes of the two sides apart as much as the means they use. "In righteousness he judges and wages wars," as most translators put it, is fine if we perceive the distinctive means of the warrior. John's use of the historical present conveys immediacy and timelessness. The rider's way of conducting business has no boundaries in time because it is a matter of character; it applies to how he *deliberates, governs, reveals, exposes, makes decisions*, and *passes judgment*. And—indeed—all plays out in the context of conflict. This is how the rider wins the war.

The rider is the subject of interest, and his identity is not in doubt (19:12; 1:14, 17). The **diadems** suggest majesty, authority, and possibly victory, but the latter is less certain, given that the dragon and the beast from the sea also boast "diadems" (12:3; 13:1). The external features, while important to the rider's identity, are leading up to the point that matters more. **And he has** [lit., *having*] **a name that no one knows but him** (19:12).

This is stunning. The name stands for the person's character: how he thinks, what he is like, and what he is up to. And the rider's *name*—and by inference *God's name*—is unknown. The rider takes the stage in a world that does not know what God is like. Just as Athens had an altar dedicated "to an unknown god" (Acts 17:23; cf. Exod. 6:3), the God of Revelation is unknown: "no one knows" the name "*but him*" (19:12). Intuitive, religious, and philosophical assumptions are inadequate with respect to the subject at hand. To know the rider's name, and *God's name*, too, requires *revelation*.

This is not a new thought, but it is given heightened emphasis. Once again, the revelation brings out a startling image. **And he is dressed in clothing dipped** [*bebammenon*] **in blood, and his name is called The Word of God** (19:13). Even for a book abounding in images, this one stands out. Clothes "*dipped in blood*"? Whose blood is it, that of the rider's enemies (Aune 1996–98, 1057) or his own blood (Koester 2014, 755–56)? The two alternatives are miles apart, one casting Jesus as a perpetrator of violence, the other as a victim. To many, Isaiah's liberator is the presumed background image. The liberator comes from Edom "in garments stained crimson," and the question is raised, "Why are your robes red, and your garments like theirs who tread the wine press?" (Isa. 63:1–3). This link has led to the conclusion that in Revelation "the blood is not the actual blood of Jesus which he poured out for sinners, but rather the blood of God's enemies" (Roloff 1993, 218).

But the blood-stained garment in Isaiah can have other meanings. The liberator has "trodden the wine press *alone*, and from the peoples *no one* was with me" (Isa. 63:3; cf. 59:15b–21). Why is he *alone*? Why is no one stepping up to help him? Singularity and abandonment dominate the depiction, suggesting that he is alone and on his own in the conception of the mission and its execution. In addition to the conspicuous aloneness of the Warrior, the wider context in this part of Isaiah is the *inner* enemy, the chronic rebelliousness of Israel (Isa. 59:12–21; 63:17; 64:5–7). Can that enemy be defeated (Oswalt 1998, 591–99)? The metaphors in Isaiah, too, invite options other than that the liberator prevails by killing his enemies.

A text more explicit for clothing "dipped" in the blood of the rider is found in the story of Joseph. Genesis says that his brother "took Joseph's robe, slaughtered a goat, and dipped the robe in the blood" (Gen. 37:31). Joseph is not killed by his brothers, but Jacob takes the robe "dipped in blood" as evidence that Joseph has been violently killed. "It is my son's robe!" he exclaims. "A wild animal has devoured him; Joseph is without doubt torn to pieces" (Gen. 37:33). This association reinforces the presentation of Jesus "in the middle" of the heavenly council (Rev. 5:6). He solves the crisis because he was "killed with violence" and has clothing "dipped in blood" (5:6; 19:13). Revelation defines discipleship in the same terms: believers "have won the war . . . through the blood of the Lamb and the word of their testimony, and they did not love their life even until death" (12:11).

Clothing "dipped in blood" and knowledge of the *name* are closely related: "*his name is called The Word of God*" (19:13). The clothing is synonymous with the *name*, and the name reveals what the person is like. There is little left to do when these dots have been connected. The rider on the white horse is a self-giving person who puts his life on the line. As "the Word of God," he is the embodiment of what God is like. The text roams in the same territory as the Gospel of John (John 1:1–18). "Only here in Revelation does 'word' (*logos*) function as a title for Christ" (Koester 2014, 756), but it is enough to be a Johannine giveaway. "It describes the highest thing that can now be said about Jesus insofar as it expresses his relationship to God: in him God reveals himself in word and act; he is the executor of God's word and will" (Roloff 1993, 218–19).

Conventional ideas about warfare have nothing to contribute in relation to this war, its ideology, and its method (19:14). "Following" is a key concept; in an earlier glimpse of the same group, the redeemed "follow the Lamb wherever he goes" (14:4). Heaven's ideal is in view more than the mere conviction that God will win the war (19:15). In what body part is the rider's weapon located?

The critical body part is the **mouth,** and the weapon is a **sharp sword** (19:15a). Both belong to the realm of speech, and speech has a synonym in this book: *revelation.* The rider will prevail among the nations by witness, not by violence.

This idea is also found in the Gospel of John (John 12:46–50). A "shepherd" who wields **a rod of iron** (Rev. 19:15b) is equipped to handle dangers to the sheep (cf. Rev. 2:27; 12:5; Ps. 2:9). If we exchange "rule" for "shepherd," as many translations do, the image is not harsh. In the psalm from which the image is drawn, the subject is not God's harshness but the *futility* of plotting against God (Ps. 2:1–12).

This idea helps the transition to the winepress metaphor: **and he (alone) will tread the winepress of the fury of the wrath of God the Almighty** (Rev. 19:15c; 14:19–20). The text does not say "he *alone,*" strictly speaking; it says *he* or that *"he is the one."* When Isaiah's depiction of the winepress is heard, the message is surely that he had to do it *alone* (Isa. 63:1–3). Why the need to say that he had to do it *alone*—if violence were his method? Use of violence has many supporters—and many perpetrators—including the adversary in the cosmic conflict. Why his perplexity that "from the peoples no one was with me"; that he looked, "but there was no helper"; that he stared, too, "but there was no one to sustain me" if not to drive home the singularity of God's ways (Isa. 63:3, 5)?

**On his clothing and on this thigh a name is inscribed: "King of kings and Lord of lords"** (Rev. 19:16). For the third time in the span of just a few verses, "the *name* of the rider is mentioned, and the mode of expression makes it clear that this is an explanation of the secret name mentioned in v 12" (Aune 1996–98, 1062). The text has taken the reader from the *unknown* to the *known:* the rider is the Revealer.

### *Desolation and Horror: The Great Supper of God (19:17–21)*

**19:17–21.** Images of the rider on the white horse are wedged between two "supper" scenes, "the marriage supper of the Lamb" (19:9) and "the great supper of God" (19:17). The first is a celebration, the second a scene of abject wretchedness (19:17–18). This is the third time Revelation draws attention to beings flying "in midheaven" (8:13; 14:6; 19:17). The posture of the angel and the call going out to **all the birds that fly in midheaven** signify an important and public event (19:17). But the rest is dismal—a "supper" that has human flesh on the menu (19:17–18). Like vultures, the birds called to the scene are indiscriminate in their food preferences, and the tenor is desolation and death. This "supper" offers the **flesh of all,** and the birds do not distinguish between **the flesh of horses** and the flesh of **those who sit on them** (19:18). Hyperbole is at work in the overwrought details, intent on showing the death-making character of the opposing side.

The cannibalistic imagery owes a debt to Ezekiel (39:17–20; cf. 1 Kings 14:11; 16:4; 21:24). Like Revelation, the background text loves hyperbole. The subject is the demise of "Gog, of the land of Magog" (Ezek. 38:1–2), but the hyperbole does not hide what is most important from a theological point of view: *the armies of Gog will self-destruct* (Irwin 1995, 106). "I will summon the sword against Gog in all my mountains, says the Lord GOD; the swords of all will be against their comrades" (Ezek. 38:21). In Revelation, the same dynamic unfolds in battle scenes in a way that preserves the tenor in Ezekiel (Rev. 19:19). Glimpses of a decisive, final battle have appeared in the trumpet sequence (9:14–16); in the Battle of Armageddon (16:12–16); in the exposé of Babylon (17:12–16; 18:21); and now here (19:19). The pedagogy is demanding, but the master pedagogue does not stray from his subject. At every stage, the opposing side is the aggressor, a restless warmonger always imagining a loophole that can be turned to his advantage. This ambition has failed, and it fails again (19:20).

*Fire* has been a staple in the armamentarium of the opposing side (9:17–18; 13:13; 16:8; 17:16; 18:8). This makes evident its self-consuming character, in line with Origen's assertion "that every sinner kindles for himself the flame of his own fire and is not plunged into a fire which has been previously kindled by someone else or which existed before him" (*Princ.* 2.20.4, trans. Butterworth 1936). In Revelation, the underpinning of destruction is situated in the very being of the opposing side.

John captures the action in these climactic scenes in a barrage of powerful verbs that are all in the passive voice. The result is a careful and masterful balancing act between scenes of defeat and demise and the means God uses to bring it about.

The beast *was caught* and with it the false prophet. (19:20a)

These two *were thrown* [*eblēthēsan*]. (19:20c)

"The rest *were killed*." (19:21)

*Caught . . . thrown . . . killed*—the verbs suggest muscular and definitive actions (19:20–21). But the widely held perception that these are "divine passives" (Aune 1996–98, 1069; Koester 2014, 760) is too simplistic. As noted earlier, the passive voice has functions other than the wish to use God's name sparingly. Within a scenario of *self-destruction*, forces other than God will be at work. Fortunately, we are not left guessing as to God's role. *Revelation* is the centerpiece, and the last verse spells it out. **And the rest were killed by the sword of the one sitting on the horse, the sword that came from his mouth; and all the birds were gorged with their flesh** (19:21). Images of dead bodies left exposed and unburied inspired horror in the ancient world, here coupled with birds feeding on the bodies (Aune 1996–98, 1067). This is how desolation and wretchedness look in Revelation, and the scenes are revolting to our imagination, too. When we try to pin down God's role in the carnage, notions of divine violence run into fierce headwinds. We read again that "the rest were killed *by the sword* of the one sitting on the horse, *the sword that came from his mouth*" (19:21). The winning side has *witness* as its weapon; it wins by the word and not by violence; it counts on revelation to make its case. "To be slain by the sword that projected from the mouth of the warrior on the white steed certainly invites metaphorical interpretation; i.e., the 'sword' must be the words spoken by the warrior" (Aune 1996–98, 1067). It cannot be stated more clearly, and the parallel to the Gospel of John is striking (John 12:47). "His word—the word that is scorned, ignored, rejected—will judge such a person, and then not on some mythical last day, but right now, as we know only too well in our solitude before God" (Haenchen 1984, 101).

## Theological Issues

The concern that God has failed to "act justly" is heard in the heavenly council when the Lamb "opened the fifth seal" (6:9). This, broadly speaking, is also the reason for the crisis in the heavenly council (5:1–4). Throughout, God has charge of the subject matter. God allows the question to be heard; God brings it up; *God does not feel threatened by the subject*. The alarm of those who have been "killed with violence" is processed and resolved in the heavenly council by the Lamb that was "killed with violence" (5:6). By Revelation's order and priorities, the revelation that takes place by the hand of the *victim* (the Lamb) absorbs and integrates the question of the *victims* (the martyrs) into the experience of Jesus. History will have a say in answering their question, too, but history already *had* a say. No line is thicker or more important than the line that runs between the *victim* and the *victims*, the connection between *his* horror and *theirs*. While there is more than one thread in this tapestry, it is shortsighted to soften the connection between Jesus as a victim of violence and the experience of his followers. What happened to *him* transforms the meaning of what happens to *them*. "Divine identification makes the victim's experience of horrors so meaningful that one would not retrospectively wish it away," Marilyn McCord Adams (1999, 167) says boldly. "Let me add the Biblical footnote that such dual solidarity explains why it is 'the Lamb that was slain' who is worthy to open the meaning of history (5:6–10)," she writes (1999, 174). This is well said, a legitimate inference of the most important scene in Revelation. By this logic, the Lamb is the principal subject of the revelation, not only the instrument.

The celebration in the text in this chapter (19:1–2) builds on the celebrations that began early in the book (4:9–11; 5:9–14) and are interspersed throughout (7:10–12; 11:15; 12:10; 15:2–4). The short version of the songs is the conviction that God has "acted justly." The exuberant affirmation takes place against a

281

horizon that made it appear that God had failed to "act justly," on the one hand, and on the other hand, that "acting justly" must be understood on the terms of the revelation and not by some other, prior criterion. God's "just act" did not put an end to victimhood, but it promised vindication for the victim (6:9–11). The nuptial imagery in Rev. 19 suggests that God succeeds in making it up to the victims.

At chapter's end, the beast and "the false prophet" are captured and put away (19:20–21). This is a pivotal moment in the story. We can put it in perspective by reviewing the preceding events.

First, there is striking thematic continuity. John has crisscrossed the subject for seven full chapters. The beast that came up from the sea (13:1) and "the false prophet" that "looked like a lamb" (13:11) have now reached the end of the line (19:20).

Second, the story projects on a widescreen canvas. The two beasts were recruited to advance the interests of "the Ancient Serpent" (12:13–17), one of the names for the angel who began the war in heaven (12:7–12). The two beasts owe their success to passing themselves off as imitations of the Lamb (13:1–18).

Third, the story does not forget the issues that are at the heart of the cosmic conflict. What comes to a head in the Battle of Armageddon (16:12–16) or here, in another glimpse of the same battle (19:19–20), cannot be disconnected from the beginning. In formal terms, eschatology reflects protology: the ending remembers the beginning.

Fourth, untangling the passive voice remains critical (19:20–21). If *God* is the one who catches "the beast and the false prophet," God does it by means of the rider on the white horse and "the sword that came *from his mouth*" (19:15). This is *revelation* at work.

And yet the offenders may also be "caught" in a literal sense. When the deception unravels, there is a price to be paid by the deceiver. If the deceived turn on the deceivers, we have a clean line between the crime and the consequences. The rage of the former is veiled in the passive voice (cf. 17:16).

Readers of Revelation have never had a stronger reason for believing that the conflict now is over. It stands as one of the book's biggest surprises that it is not.

# Revelation 20:1–15

## The Thousand Years and Then

### Introductory Matters

In Rev. 20, Satan occupies the center—alone. He is *captured* and then *released* (20:1–10). This is a strange prospect even by Revelation's standard, and it invites three observations.

First, it matters that Satan now has the stage to himself. *At the end, it is only about him.* Revelation treats him as an important character, not as a mere appendix to the human drama (Tonstad 2006, 41–54).

Second, the *binding* and *release* of Satan is a reason to rethink the plot (20:1–3, 7–10). *Binding?* By all means! *Release?* Not in a million years! Even if the *binding* could be made a ho-hum matter, the thought of his *release* will elicit disbelief and consternation. Why, therefore, does Revelation describe Satan's release not only as a *certainty* but as a *necessity*?

Third, *Satan is again represented as a deceiver* (20:1–3). Revelation remembers him as the original purveyor of *fake news* (12:9; 20:2; cf. Gen. 3:1–6; John 8:44). There is no letting up in this regard (Rev. 20:7–10). He now takes his last stand. To what extent will the ending echo the beginning? Deception, curtailment, and exposé are packed into the verses we are about to read (20:1–10). Is there a pattern, a key, or a logic to the puzzling turn of events?

In ways too numerous to count, commentators are at a loss in this chapter because (1) they treat Satan dismissively, sometimes as no more than a rhetorical construct; (2) they concentrate on human and historical aspects at the expense of the cosmic perspective; and (3) they pay little or no attention to Satan's theological brand, ignoring what he says. On all these counts, this commentary comes better prepared to grapple with the enigma of Satan's capture and release.

## Tracing the Train of Thought

### Satan Captured and Released, with a Thousand Years in Between (20:1–10)

**20:1–10.** In the sequence of the seven seals, victims of violence clamor for God to intervene on their behalf (6:10). Their plea assumes a systemic defect in God's economy, a bigger problem than incidental inaction. Here, suddenly, there is action.

> And I saw an angel coming down from heaven, having the key to the abyss and a huge chain in his hand. And he seized the dragon, the Ancient Serpent, who is the Mudslinger and the Antagonist (that is, the Devil and Satan), and he tied him up for a thousand years, and he threw him into the abyss and locked and sealed it over him, in order that he would not deceive the nations any more until the thousand years are ended. After that he must be set free for a short time. (20:1–3)

The verbs in this passage are muscular and impressive, and they are all in the active voice. Notions of inaction are put to rest when a heavenly messenger *seizes, binds, throws, locks,* and *seals,* resolutely curtailing the activity of the adversary in the story (20:1–3). But the second part of the "action" obliterates the impact of the first part. *Satan is bound and—heaven forbid—released!* Even when we allow for symbolic language and hyperbole, this is enough to make a reader choke. Many interpreters have additional discomfort for failing to take an interest in the Ancient Serpent in the first place. Even though the questions now arising fail to make up for the lack of interest in Satan earlier in the story, they are nevertheless pertinent.

> "But why is Satan merely bound and why is he ever to be loosed again?" (Farrer 1964, 202)

> "Why, *must* he *be let loose* to wreak further havoc?" (Caird 1999, 249)

> "Why could he not have been liquidated from the beginning?" (Sweet 1979, 290)

> "Just why this is done, and by whom, is an undisclosed mystery." (Metzger 1993, 93)

> "What is the point?" (Talbert 1994, 95)

It is the *release* of Satan that throws the reader off. Satan ought *not* to be released (Farrer); he will surely "wreak further havoc" (Caird); God should have liquidated him earlier (Sweet). The notion of Satan's *release* is so strange that an answer is probably out of reach (Metzger). To escape the predicament, some scholars suggest that there must be a mistake in the text or a lapse in the concentration of the author. In the former category, R. H. Charles (1920, 2:144–47) postulated that the original composer must have died an untimely death! His unfinished composition was taken over by an "unintelligent disciple." This accounts for the strange bend in the story, and the reader can justifiably relax his/her effort with respect to finding a reasonable explanation. In the second category, some interpreters suggest that the author at this point is tired and not able to perform at his best (Lohmeyer 1926, 161). A variant of this view holds that the author lost interest in his material (Kraft 1974, 258). These views offer a partial alibi for not offering substantive exegesis of the passage. Prior lack of interest in Satan is also reflected in answers that do not raise objections to the text as we have it.

> **Revelation 20:1–15 in the Rhetorical Flow**
>
> Incentive to read (1:1–20)
>
> To the one who has an ear (2:1–3:22)
>
> The seven seals (4:1–8:1)
>
> The seven trumpets (8:2–11:19)
>
> The cosmic conflict from A to Z (12:1–14:20)
>
> The seven bowls (15:1–16:21)
>
> The woman and the beast (17:1–18:24)
>
> The wedding, the rider, and the supper (19:1–21)
>
> ▶ **The thousand years and then (20:1–15)**
>
> Satan captured and released, with a thousand years in between (20:1–10)
>
> Judgment by the book (20:11–15)

One answer appeals to *inscrutability*. "There is a necessity for it, founded on some mystery of the Divine Will" (Swete 1908, 261; cf. Roloff 1993, 228; MacLeod 1999, 483). This sounds like the counsel of despair. When everything seems put to order, Revelation throws the bombshell that Satan "*must be released* for a short time" (20:3)! We read this in a book that bears the name *revelation* (*apokalypsis*, 1:1). Are we expected to accept that the revelation in progress leaves us stranded on the island of *inscrutability*?

A second option sequesters the problem by treating it as a *contaminant* in the text. "The origin of this doctrine is not specifically Christian but is to be found in certain Jewish beliefs about the Messianic age which were common in the time after 100 B.C." (Barclay 1976, 2:186). This view is in the same class as the idea that John died or that he lost interest in the story and is equally untenable. All the books of the NT contain apocalyptic sentiments that are "contaminated" by the same implied and invalid "norm" (Käsemann 1969, 102). Revelation develops apocalyptic themes more fully than other books, but its worldview is essentially the same as the rest of the NT. The binding and release of Satan cannot be dismissed as a foreign body that fails the

"Christian" test (Rudnig-Zelt 2016; Korpel and de Moor 2015). To this must be added that John's version is not borrowed. "The representation of Satan first bound and then released for a brief period which is to end in his final doom is not found in earlier literature, Jewish or Christian" (Beckwith 1919, 736).

A third view claims to see *free will* at work. Satan "represents man's free will, the capacity God has given for sin, and the terrible reality of the consequences" (Sweet 1979, 290). By this criterion, Satan owes his longevity to the need for symbolizing "free will" in the human realm. His status as a distinct nonhuman being is doubtful. "*This* heaven and earth cannot exist without him" (Sweet 1979, 290). The alleged link between Satan and "free will" suggests that "free will" is a negative quality and that human beings will one day be delivered from its burden.

A fourth view argues that the passage seeks to assign *responsibility* to the right agent. Sin is curtailed when Satan is bound, but it returns in force upon his release. This is said to prove "that humans cannot blame their sinfulness on their environment or circumstances" (Talbert 1994, 95). For this to work, "Satan" must again be reduced to a component *within* the human structure. If he is more than that—if he is a real being and the sine qua non for sin to happen—his release does not expose "the radical evil of the human heart" or show that we "are without excuse" (Talbert 1994, 95). We are left with the opposite conclusion: *circumstances matter, and we have an excuse.* Human beings would do fine if Satan were not part of the environment.

A fifth option imagines the need for *stage effects* to suit the occasion. John is "preparing to present before our imagination a picture of the ultimate destruction of evil and needs for this scene antagonists to God who are larger than life" (Boring 1989, 209–10). According to this view, "Satan" appears because it makes for good theater. Will this explanation work? Indifference toward Satan earlier in the story is a barrier to making him look significant in the ending. Even as a literary ploy, this option fizzles.

A sixth option casts Satan's binding and release as a demonstration of God's *sovereignty*. "The main intent of this description of the arrest, binding, and incarceration of Satan is to assert God's sovereignty even over Satan, chief instigator of evil" (S. Thompson 1999, 265; cf. MacLeod 2000, 205). This view can count on support in the action-packed verbs in the text, and it is well matched to the doctrines of divine sovereignty and human depravity that are part of the Christian tradition. But the weaknesses of this view, too, are crushing. "Sovereignty" is too easy and too unsubtle to fit the hyperbole in the text, and it suggests arbitrariness on God's part with respect to timing as well as means. Why did God not intervene by force earlier if force is now the solution? "Sovereignty" fits the *language*, superficially speaking. Does it fit the *plot*? "Sovereignty" might also account for the *binding* of Satan. Does it fit the idea that Satan "must be *released*" (20:3)? In sum, "sovereignty" works no better than the options that cast doubt on Satan's ontological status—whether as theological contaminant, a cipher for free will, a figure of speech for responsibility, or a rhetorical device by which to create stage effects.

A seventh option is hiding in plain sight: *revelation*. The story marches with ever-increasing suspense toward the ending of the disclosure, faithful to the theme of revelation, certain of Satan's ontological status, cognizant of the plot to be resolved, consistent in its use of terms, with no confusion or stumbling in the face of the enigma of Satan's release. Two specific value judgments concerning Satan are evident from the outset. "Seizing and binding was used for criminals" (Koester 2014, 769). This counts as an unmasking because Satan has posed as something other than a criminal throughout the story. The criminal element is highlighted further by having him locked up in a "prison" (20:7). *Sealing* is the second tantalizing element. This "did not physically strengthen the closure but deterred unauthorized people from attempting to open the door unobserved, as a broken seal would show tampering" (Koester 2014, 770). The process in motion is tamper-proof. Deceit will not get the defendant off the hook this time.

A larger revelation is embedded in the plot. It is "the Ancient Serpent" that is caught (20:2), "the master and the instigator" of evil in Genesis (Cuvillier 1984, 346). The concentration of names is not redundant or haphazard—the one caught is "the dragon, the Ancient Serpent, who is the Mudslinger [the Devil] and the Antagonist [the Satan]" (20:2). Name, identity, character, story, and track record are compacted into the forensic detonation now taking place. Attention to *that* part of the story—the *beginning*—holds the key to understanding *this* part of the story—the *ending*. The serpent in Genesis will be known as a *deceiver* (Gen. 3:13). In Revelation, curtailment of *deceit* coincides with the binding of Satan and is therefore a momentous occasion: the Ancient Serpent is put out of commission "in order that [*hina*] he *would not deceive* [*planēsē*] the nations any more" (20:3). But this pointed explanation merely intensifies the enigma of Satan's release: "And when the thousand years have come to an end, Satan *will be released* from his prison, and he will set forth to *deceive* [*planēsai*] the nations at the four corners of the earth" (20:7–8a). No one can read this without recognizing the role of deceit in the plot now coming to an end.

David E. Aune's (1996–98, 1083) comment is too little and too late, but it is an excellent description of the nature and function of deception: "This is extremely important from a theological perspective, for the notion of deception presupposes that a person or group previously held the correct views or behaved in the appropriate manner *until they were tricked or deceived and in consequence led astray*. This purpose clause is an example of the author's insertion of an explanatory comment into a vision narration." When we apply this understanding to the deception in Genesis, things will be less mysterious. Human beings held "correct views or behaved in the appropriate manner *until they were tricked*" (Aune 1996–98, 1083). Then came the deception, promoting a daring and maliciously *incorrect* view. *God prohibits! God exacts! God prefers restriction to freedom!* This is the gist of the deception in Genesis (3:1). Coherence is in sight if we keep this in mind. For now, it suffices to acknowledge that Revelation remembers the deception and that deception is at the center in connection with Satan's binding and release.

The next verse revisits many of the key themes in Revelation (20:4). John saw **thrones and those sitting on them** (20:4a). This is not surprising because John has earlier seen intelligent beings "in the middle of the throne" (4:6; 5:6), and Jesus promised the believers in Laodicea "a place with me on my throne" (3:21). The throne arrangement implies participation and empowerment. Human beings do not knock in vain on the door of divine sovereignty (3:8; 4:1; 11:19; 19:11).

"Those sitting on them" are the former victims of violence. **They came to life**, John says, **and they reigned with Christ for a thousand years** (20:4d). The God-ordained structure of power sharing and coregency is predicated on God taking human beings seriously. Revelation defaults to the passive voice when it says that **the mandate to pass judgment was given to them** (20:4b), but there is no doubt who gives the mandate. God endows human beings with the ability to understand, and "the mandate to pass judgment" need not be limited to matters in the human realm. Indeed, it cannot be limited to that sphere because the question deals with matters in God's realm (6:9–11). The broad mandate begins with *participation*, then *vindication*, then *vindication of their question*, and lastly *access to answers*. Wrenching existential questions, including the possibility that God may be at fault in relation to the world (5:1–4; 6:9–10), suggest that "the mandate to pass judgment" is *retrospective* rather than *prospective*. The task is not to run the heavenly bureaucracy for a thousand years *prospectively* but to have a say about God's conduct in the cosmic conflict. The typical features of judgment in a judicial sense are lacking in this passage (Aune 1996–98, 1079). When the victims "came to life," *vindication* takes the form of *resurrection* of the victim, not *retribution* upon the perpetrators. This fits heaven's initial response to the predicament of the faithful victim (6:11).

The believers **had been beheaded for the sake of the testimony of Jesus** [*tēn martyrian Iēsou*] **and the word of God** (20:4c). It is not wrong to say that the believers suffered because they bore testimony to Jesus, but this is the secondary sense. The paired phrase, appearing with slight variations in other places (1:2, 9; 6:9; 12:17; 14:12; 19:10), puts "the testimony of Jesus" in an explanatory relationship to "the word of God." These matters belong to the future from the vantage point of John.

John says that the believers "reigned with Christ *for a thousand years*" (20:4). This time period is mentioned only here in the NT but is referred to a full six times in the span of six consecutive verses (20:2, 3, 4, 5, 6, 7). Revelation is rich in temporal elements, and the thousand years are the longest specific period in the book (see table). In the present context, it should be seen not only as a long time but also—for its purpose—a *long-enough* time.

### Time in Revelation Updated

| | |
|---|---|
| **Qualitative** | "the time is near" (1:3; 22:10)<br>"his time is short" (12:12)<br>"a short while" (17:10)<br>"soon" (22:12) |
| **Point in time** | the hour, the day, the month, and the year (9:15) |
| **Quantitative** | half an hour (8:1)<br>one hour (17:12; 18:10, 17, 19)<br>a single day (18:8)<br>three and a half days (11:9, 11)<br>ten days (2:10)<br>five months (9:5, 10)<br>forty-two months (11:2; 13:5)<br>one thousand two hundred and sixty days (11:3; 12:6)<br>time, times, and half a time (12:14)<br>a thousand years (20:2, 3, 4, 5, 6, 7)<br>forever and ever (1:6, 18; 4:9; 5:13; 7:12; 10:6; 11:15; 14:11; 15:7; 19:3; 20:10; 22:5) |

All this fits the notion of revelation. "The thousand years" have a *before*, a *during*, and an *after* perspective (20:2, 3, 4, 5, 6, 7). The *after* perspective has been the subject of a book-length study (Mealy 1992), and the author's interest is well taken. It is only "when the thousand years are completed" that the final showdown in the cosmic conflict will take place (20:7).

**And the rest of the dead did not come to life until the thousand years were ended. This is the first resurrection** (20:5). Here, the second sentence ought to come before the first. "The first resurrection" is *not* the one that happens at the point when "the thousand years were ended." Resurrection is a core belief in the NT. The concept of *two* resurrections receives a hint in the Gospel of John (5:29), but it is explicit only in Revelation (Aune 1996–98, 1090). The two resurrections are not only separated in time but are meant for two distinct groups (Koester 2014, 773). By Revelation's sentiment, "the first resurrection" is the better part by far, highlighted by another beatitude (20:6). Revelation has covered much of this ground already: resurrection, vindication, and reigning with Christ (20:4). A "*first* resurrection" implies that there will be a *second*. And there is, but the reader is expected to keep track without further cues. Selection to become **priests of God and of Christ** (20:6) is closely related to the notion of coregency. By this criterion, the priestly function blends with a political role—never a happy combination in human society—but Revelation has figured out how to do it the right way. In either capacity, priest or coregent, the person holding the office has a representative function. He/she is entrusted the task of representing God. This is not a trivial mandate in a story that makes misrepresentation of God the main problem.

We are now back to the most puzzling item, the release of Satan (20:7–9). The task of understanding will be helped—again—by trying to "draw the picture which the seer saw" (Flowers 1930, 526). We will need to draw the picture slowly to get things right with regard to place, time, and meaning. David E. Aune (1996–98, 1084–85) says that the appearance of disorder "results both from the author's tendency to use the literary device *hysteron-proteron*, that is, reversing the logical order of narrative events . . . and from his tendency to describe *where* an individual or group of people sits before describing them." An author should not be putting the *latter* before the *former*; he should keep his chronology and sequence of events straight. John's excuse might be that *meaning* does not run on parallel tracks with *sequence*. To the questions asked earlier, two more should be added. How, precisely, does evil come to an end in this book? And what does the ending tell us about God?

First, Revelation says that there will be a final battle, and this is the main point in these verses (20:7–10). The battle is to happen **when the thousand years have come to an end**, at which time **Satan will be released from his prison** (20:7). Even though the language abounds in symbols and metaphors, the parameters of the story must also make sense on the material, nonsymbolic level.

Second, we have been told that "the rest of the dead did not come to life until the thousand years were ended" (20:5). The release of Satan and the resurrection of "the rest of the dead" coincide in time, as two sides of the same coin. This group, "the rest of the dead," are not invulnerable to death and deception, like those who have a part in "the first resurrection" (20:4–5). When Satan goes forth to **the four corners of the earth . . . to gather them for war** [*eis polemon*] (20:8), his target group consists of those who have been raised from the dead. He now has the liberty and the people needed to launch the final battle.

Third, the battle is going to take place outside **the beloved city** (20:8–9). We need re-reader mastery in order to draw this feature. John does not describe the descent of "the New Jerusalem, the beloved city," until the very end (20:7–10; 21:1–2). This is a striking example of his tendency to reverse the logical order.

Fourth, the city that comes down "out of heaven" (21:2) is a city full of people (Gundry 1987). It is not necessary to deny that "the beloved city" is *space*, too, and not only *people*, as Gundry does, but the essence of a city is *people*. This view is corroborated by the fact that the New Jerusalem is "made ready as a bride beautified [*kekosmēmenēn*] for her husband" (21:2; 19:7). The bride that is "beautified" is described by the verb from which our word "cosmetics" is derived. It means, then and still now, "to cause something to have an attractive appearance through decoration" (BDAG 560, κοσμέω). The timing of the battle—and the descent of the city—is now fixed to the point "when the thousand years have come to an end" (20:7). With respect to *space*, the descent "out of heaven from God" is a critical feature because the city and its inhabitants have until now been in heaven.

How does this fit the eschatology of the NT and, more widely, perceptions of its eschatology? On the one hand, Revelation does *not* say explicitly that the redeemed "go to heaven," although "the two witnesses" earlier in the story do that in a sense that may be more than a metaphor (11:12). Revelation's distinctive story line is demanding and underappreciated. In the end, the redeemed *come down from heaven* to earth as "the holy city" (21:2)! This prospect is possible only if the redeemed did "go to heaven" at some point. We now have a scenario that *assumes* (implicitly) the redeemed "going to heaven" and *states* (explicitly) that the redeemed *come down from heaven*. At the end, therefore, the address of the redeemed at journey's end is the earth (21:2).

On the other hand, key texts in the NT suggest (explicitly) that the redeemed "go to heaven" (1 Thess. 4:16–17; 1 Cor. 15:51–52; John 14:2–3; 17:24), an all-but-certain scenario if we take into consideration the perception of these texts in the Christian tradition. They do not teach a bodiless, intermediate state when a person dies (Sumney 2009), but they envision being "taken up" at the second coming (Plevnik 1984). In one comment on Paul's view in 1 Thessalonians, the message "indicates the termination of the present earthly existence" (Plevnik 1984, 280). The "heaven" part remains even if we focus more on the end of separation than on "location." It is difficult to argue otherwise when Jesus says in John that "I will come back and take you to be with me that you also may be where I am" (John 14:3 NIV). Paul writes that those living and those raised from the dead "will be caught up in the clouds together . . . to meet the Lord in the air; and so we will be with the Lord forever" (1 Thess. 4:17). End of separation—and "going to heaven"—seem to be in view in both scenarios (McCaffey 1982; Haenchen 1984, 124). What is not in view in these texts, in contrast to Revelation, is the prospect of *returning* to earth.

Fifth, the resurrection of believers in Revelation happens at the beginning of "the thousand years" (20:4–6). What then? Where do the resurrected go after the resurrection? In the Gospel of John and the Letters of Paul, there is neither a bodiless state nor an earthly interregnum (John 14:1–3; 1 Thess. 4:16–17), leaving only the option that the believers "go to heaven." The same movement is assumed in Revelation (11:12; 21:2). What is new in Revelation, alone among the books in the NT, is that *heaven is only a temporary residence*. After the thousand years, the New Jerusalem, as a city of people, comes down to earth to make *the earth* the permanent dwelling place of the redeemed (21:1–2; 22:1–3). Christianity's heaven-centered view is corrected by Revelation's earth-bound orientation (L. Thompson 1990, 85; Russell 1996, 208; Rossing 2005).

Sixth, wedding imagery runs on parallel tracks with images of war (19:7–8; 21:2; 20:7–10). Satan begins the march on the city just when a marriage is taking place. Wedding and war happen simultaneously, each reflective of the quest driving the parties. The wedding is not arranged; it is not coerced; it is sheer joy for the bridegroom and the bride. The union that is in the making exceeds the relationship between God and human beings at the beginning of the story. Instead of a permanent separation, there is an intimate, unending union (19:7). Outside the city, a vast army is marching in the posture of war, but no one in the wedding party leaves the wedding to confront the advancing army in a physical sense (20:8–9; 3:12; 21:2, 10).

Seventh, it is now evident that the muscular account of Satan's capture must be read as a passage bursting with hyperbole (20:1–3). If (1) "the first resurrection" is a resurrection of the redeemed only (20:4–6); and (2) the redeemed go to heaven (11:12; 14:14–16; 1 Thess. 4:16–17; John 14:2–3); and (3) the unredeemed are resurrected only "after the thousand years" (Rev. 20:5); and (4) the redeemed return to earth with the New Jerusalem "after the thousand years" (21:1–2); then (5) the action-filled "binding" of Satan is not a display of power (20:1–3). Satan will be "bound"—of that there is no doubt—but he is bound by force of circumstances and not by coercive means. The "binding" of Satan, as curtailment of his activity, is better understood as people being removed from his reach than as him being removed from a society that is otherwise flourishing.

Eighth, Satan commits to one last round of warfare as soon as he is "released from his prison" (20:7–10). His target is "the beloved city" (20:9). If the hand that draws the picture gets this part right, it promises to put an end to one of the most enduring misperceptions in the Christian tradition. In John's vision, Satan goes forth **to deceive the nations at the four corners of the earth, Gog and Magog, to gather them for war** (20:8–9). The text is sparse with respect to detail, but it shows Satan amassing a force of great numbers: **the number of them is like the sands of the sea** (20:8). This unexpected turn of events rarely gets the reflection it deserves, chiefly because Satan is treated as a cardboard character and partly because the text is held hostage to the speculative futurist interpretations.

My reflection begins by recognizing that a cardboard character cannot at this stage of the conflict bring about the awe-inspiring mobilization seen in this text. The notion that "he shall go forth" (20:8) suggests intent and determination. *Why does he do it?* Should not Satan be ready to concede? The text does not explain his state of mind, and we are left to look for an analogy in human affairs. Perhaps there is one in the story of Adolf Hitler's inability to rein in his inclinations during World War II despite being offered the opportunity to do so. Joachim Fest (2005) pictures Hitler as a man trapped within his own character, hell-bent on continuing a disastrous war even when it is obvious that he is destroying his country. When Joachim von Ribbentrop, his foreign minister, tried to persuade Hitler to enter into a truce with the Soviet Union in 1943, at a point when the war already was unwinnable, Hitler replied, "You know, Ribbentrop, if I were to come to an agreement with Russia today, I would attack them again tomorrow—I can't help myself" (Fest 2005, 134). The lead character on the losing side of Revelation's cosmic conflict is similarly trapped and similarly unable to help himself.

Next, Satan "will go forth *to deceive the nations*" (20:8). This is hard to believe. Deceive the nations? Again? Have not "the nations" been thoroughly *un-deceived*? *How does he do it?* Even though Revelation conditions readers to be aware that Satan is a wizard of deceit (2:20; 12:9; 13:14; 18:23; 19:20; 20:3, 8, 10; cf. John 8:44)—indeed, that *Deceiver* can be construed as one of his names (12:9; 20:10)—it is hard to fathom his actions. The how-question matters, and the answer available to readers must be sought in the occasions when the Antagonist *talks* (Gen. 3:1–6; Job 1:6–12; 2:1–6; Matt. 4:1–11; Tonstad 2016a, 100–103, 238–63, 264–81). How he *will do it* in Revelation is illuminated by how he *did it* on other occasions. This question has an answer: he did it by going negative. His brand of deceit is slander and misrepresentation of the other side. Resentment and enmity are at the heart of Satan's theological merchandise. *The other side is the enemy even if the other side is God. It is us against them; it is us or them. It is now or never.* For this, too, there are plausible human analogies and ample proof that "going negative" works.

Revelation says that "the number of them is like the sands of the sea" (20:8). *How could it succeed?* Again, we fall back on imperfect human analogies. How could Napoleon succeed in winning over the French, jubilantly, after his return from forced exile on the island of Elba? The most perplexing warning was quoted earlier, Saul Friedländer's (2008, 656–57) saying that the main question after World War II is not about Hitler as a person but "why tens of millions of Germans blindly followed him to the end, why many still believed in him at the end, and not a few, after the end." In the aftermath of the calamity, the question is not only what he was but what we are. A reflection of this kind is a form of introspection, proving that Revelation's ending deals in figures that aren't cardboard.

In this tableau, a terrifying march of death unfolds in tight progression. It should be imagined or produced in cinematic version, set to military music that stirs the patriotic heart, more fervent than the religious devotion of the Nazis on Zeppelin Field outside Nuremberg during the "happy" part of the Hitler years. Just look and listen, with attention to who is who and what is what in the drama.

- Up they march, headed for "the beloved city" behind the newly energized leader (20:8).
- Up they march, striding majestically **over the breadth of the earth** until they surround **the camp of the saints and the beloved city** (20:9a).

- Up they march, "as numerous as the sands of the sea" (20:8).
- Up they march, with body language exuding confidence (20:8, 9).
- Up they march, heading brazenly in the direction of the unnamable *ḥašmal* of Ezekiel's vision, the fiery center of God's presence (Ezek. 1:4); "the holy mountain of God" and "the stones of fire" (28:14–16)—an emanation so intense that God appointed an "anointed cherub who covers" to lessen the dazzling impact of God's unveiled glory (28:14 NASB).
- Up they march, advancing under the spell of the fallen cherub toward the One whose unveiled face no mortal can see and live (Exod. 33:20).
- **And fire came down from heaven and consumed them** (Rev. 20:9b).

The last sentence is the most quoted and the one best remembered. If fire from heaven is all we take away, however, we miss the carefully stitched picture of self-destruction that pervades Revelation's depiction; we miss the suicidal character of the marchers; and we miss the *revelation* that here, too, is the main theme.

Before we get to that point in the story, we have convulsive movements in time and space: the *binding* of Satan before "the thousand years" (20:1–3), his enigmatic *release* when "the thousand years are ended" (20:7), the *descent* of "the beloved city" (20:9; 21:2), the *mobilization for war*, and the *march* against "the beloved city" (20:9). And then the war itself, culminating in the combatants' *turning on each other*, described in imagery of mayhem and bloodshed so extreme that nothing escapes the destroying hand (Ezek. 38:21; Rev. 14:19–20). This part is left out in the final description, but it has been told in numerous earlier flashes (9:13–21; 14:19–20; 17:16; 19:17–18), and it cannot be left out from the reader's reconstruction of what is taking place. A *revelation* is in the making, with God and the Lamb and the redeemed secure in "the camp of the saints and the beloved city" (20:9), on the one hand, and Satan's last deceptive push melting in the blaze of revelation, on the other. Unmasking, futility, and implosion are legitimate words for the collapse of the advancing army. In *1 Enoch*, self-destruction is described in revolting detail in a scene reminiscent of the carnage "outside the city" in Revelation (14:20): "In those days, the father will be beaten together with his sons, in one place; and brothers shall fall together with their friends, in death, until a stream shall flow with their blood. . . . From dawn until the sun sets, they shall slay each other. The horse shall walk through the blood of sinners up to his chest; and the chariot shall sink down up to its top" (*1 En.* 100.1–3, *OTP* 1:81). After this, what is left for the fire to do?

What is left is mostly to reclaim "fire" as a metaphor. This view looms large in Revelation (8:7–8; 9:17–18; 18:8), and there is almost no end to texts describing damage by "fire" in the OT (Prov. 6:27; Isa. 33:11; 47:14; 50:11; Ezek. 19:14). Fire is also an image for God's presence, with intriguing twists in its usage (Exod. 19:18; Deut. 5:25; Ezek. 1:4). Light and fire seem to be the reason why Moses will not see God's face: "You cannot see my face; for no one shall see my face and live" (Exod. 33:20, my trans.). In Ezekiel's opening vision, the best he can do to describe God is a rare word that combines light and heat (Ezek. 1:4).

Ninth, God does not need to play another card than *revelation* to counter the forces advancing on "the beloved city" (20:9). Much is written between the lines describing the final movement and the "fire." In a scenario of revelation, **the Mudslinger** is not **thrown into the lake of fire** by a God who is angry for what he did but by beings who are enraged at what he did to *them* (20:10). There is torment and the unbridled intent to torment, but everything happens within the framework of revelation. The Christian tradition was too willing to cast God as the tormentor and make **forever** mean conscious torment that has no end (20:10). "Christian theology invincibly confirms this, in that it tells us that the torments of the damned will be eternal and continuous, and as strong at the end of one hundred thousand years as they were the first day," Pierre Bayle wrote in the seventeenth century in a classic work on suffering in the Christian tradition (1965, 171). The statement accurately reflects the tradition, but it does not do justice to Revelation. As in the OT, "forever" is often a figure of speech for finality and closure, not for duration (Jer. 15:14; 17:4; Gen. 19:28; Isa. 34:10). A reading that imagines God keeping the devil and his followers on life support to torment them fails to capture the implosion in this chapter as well as the restoration and healing in the chapters to come. In Ezekiel, "the covering cherub" is destroyed by fire, but the fire does not come from without. "I made fire come out *from within you*; *it* consumed you; I reduced you to ashes on the earth in the eyes of all who see you" (Ezek. 28:14, 18, my trans.). This is revelation at work.

Tenth, returning to the most puzzling element and the question raised at the beginning of this chapter, "Why is Satan merely bound and why is he ever to be loosed again?" (Farrer 1964, 202). Revelation knows the answer. There is more than a casual connection between "the serpent" at the beginning and "the Ancient Serpent" at the end (12:9; 20:2); more than a stippled line between the problem in Genesis and the resolution in Revelation; more, too, than a flimsy link between the malice of the serpent and God's last response to the malice at the end of "the thousand years."

> *Problem*: "Now the serpent was shrewder than any other wild animal that the LORD God had made. He said to the woman, 'Did God really say, "You shall not eat from any tree in the garden"?'" (Gen. 3:1, my trans.)

In this pivotal scene from the beginning, the serpent threw the entire divine economy into the basket of prohibition (Tonstad 2016a, 87–103). Was it true, even slightly? It was not true, not even slightly. Revelation's story line is puzzling, but it is not incoherent or pointless when we remember the misrepresentation in Genesis.

> *Resolution*: "And after these things, he must be *released* for a short time."
> (20:3)

By itself, the release of Satan is strange. We need only to think of criminals given the death penalty, or convicts serving a life sentence—or alleged terrorists indefinitely incarcerated—to put Satan's release into perspective. How naive of God, how reckless! This would be a fair assessment until we ponder again the original innuendo in the serpent's charge that God is more interested in restriction than in freedom (Gen. 3:1; R. W. L. Moberly 1988, 6).

If we think less in terms of conventional law enforcement and more in terms of blistering theological propositions, we get a different picture. The plot that culminates in Satan's release is anchored at the beginning of the biblical narrative. No statement will be adequate, but let the following serve as a start: *When the voice of the Ancient Serpent was heard in Genesis, it made lack of freedom a characteristic of God's government (Gen. 3:1). This, we now see, was false. In Revelation, it is the logic of freedom that leads to Satan's release. Let it be said again: it is the logic of freedom that leads to Satan's release. Within the logic of freedom—precisely the quality said to be lacking in God—Satan goes forth to work his own undoing* (20:7–9; Tonstad 2006, 155).

### Judgment by the Book (20:11–15)

**20:11–15.** The judgment before the **great white throne** that now follows might seem unnecessary considering what has just transpired (20:11). It comes with the risk that it will eclipse the revelation taking place outside "the beloved city" (20:9). The pedagogy is at this point more conventional. "The throne and the One who sat on it" were John's first sighting upon his entry into the open heaven (4:1–2). In that respect we have come full circle. Here, the throne is "great" and "white," images that reinforce the importance of the throne and the dignity of the occupant. In our time, it can serve as the counterpoint to William Butler Yeats's (1996, 458) feeling that "things cannot hold; the center falls apart," and "mere anarchy is loosed upon the world."

"Mere anarchy" does indeed seem to be on the loose in the world, but Revelation claims that there is a center. And the center holds. When push comes to shove, the center is the only thing that holds and the one thing *that is.*

For the judgment now unfolding (20:11–15), it is wise to think of narrative priorities: the inanimate world vanishes so as not to distract from the encounter between God and lived lives (20:11). The scene drives home transcendent realities *and* the stupendous significance of human beings. "Is what John describes here something new and unprepared for, something which is to be understood as happening after the end of the (apparently completed) story of 4.1–20.10?"

asks J. Webb Mealy (1992, 57). "Or does it function as an amplification of, or a new viewpoint upon, something in the story that has already been related?" (Mealy 1992, 57). The second alternative is better, the same reality appearing in ever clearer representations. A similar cosmic dissolution is attested in the OT. "All the host of heaven shall rot away, and the skies roll up like a scroll," said Isaiah (34:4; cf. 51:6)—with like-sounding descriptions in Jeremiah (4:23, 28), Ezekiel (32:7–8), and Joel (2:10, 30, 31; 3:15–16).

Revelation has already described the resurrection—or the *resurrections* (20:1–6). This is the subject again, now told from a different angle (20:12). The judgment "before the throne" does not stand alone as the sole means with which to represent accountability (20:1–10). And what is the tenor of the judgment? "The judgment being never juridical but revelatory, it is not the expression of the servile terror of men, but of their comprehension of the divine reality," says Jacques Ellul (1977, 172). The entire book has been a painstaking advance toward "comprehension of the divine reality." Although the throne scene is distinctive, all the disclosures take place in the immediate vicinity of the throne. Revelation at one end, comprehension at the other: this is how the book works. Majesty and sovereignty are surely in view when **the earth and the heaven fled from his presence, and a place was not found for them** (20:11), but the throne now filling the screen does not come with a clean slate. "In the middle of the throne," now and forever, "the divine reality" that is to be comprehended centers on God revealed in "the Lamb . . . killed with violence" (5:6).

The summons includes **the great and the small**, the people of significance and "the little people" in equal measure. There is equality before the law, and no one is too small in God's eyes. **Books** are *opened* (20:12), yet another instance of "open" and "openings" that carry the story line and show forth God's ideology (3:7–8; 4:1; 5:5, 9; 11:19; 15:5; 19:11). "Books" are the material ingredients of transparency, due process, and objectivity. The judgment happens *by the book*, suggesting that everyone may know where he/she stands. "At the last judgment people are accountable for their actions as inscribed in the scrolls of deeds, but they are saved by grace by having their names in the scroll of life" (Koester 2014, 780). No book in the Bible speaks more clearly about salvation "as a gift" (22:17), but the gift does not cancel out accountability. Understood as judgment in a conventional sense, *books* signify "that God's judgment is not arbitrary but is based on written evidence" (Koester 2014, 791).

Material conceptions of judgment in the form of a throne and books and witnesses have a counterpoint in psychological, existential, and personal realities. *Eyes* are opened, too, making the judgment a moment of self-knowledge. "The judgment at this moment is then: to be what one has actually wished to be but seeing in the light of God what it was" (Ellul 1977, 176). Is that it? Will the judgment show nothing other than what a person wanted to be while making what the person wanted to be seem like a surprise to that person? John R. Sachs (1993, 626) envisions a similar scenario in the teachings of Origen in the third century. "On the day of judgment," he says, "when face to face with God, in the purity and perfection of divine love, sin will manifest its own true nature with a burning clarity. Sinners themselves will be their own accusers and the evil they have done will ignite within them, as a fever takes hold of a person who has indulged in bad food or intemperate, unhealthy behavior." These suggestions are helpful for the care with which they avoid notions of arbitrary judgments and outcomes that cannot be explained.

With the judgment come *return*, *resurrection*, and *restoration* (20:13). Think of all who went missing and seemed to be lost for good! Think of watery graves and the feeling of being abandoned! Think of points of no return! Think of cruelty covered up or generosity unacknowledged! Then read that **the sea gave back the dead that were in it. Death and Hades gave back the dead that were in them** (20:13). Human beings given up to "the sea" or to "Death and Hades" are now *returned*, *resurrected*, and *restored* when "the sea" and "Death and Hades" see the prey wrested from them. For victims, hope resides in restoration rather than in seeing the perpetrator of violence punished (6:9–11; 13:10).

In the end, "Death and Hades" also face obliteration (20:14–15). To put this into perspective, it is necessary to review the role of this fearsome twosome in Revelation, paying attention to *text*, *agent*, and *meaning*.

### Death and Hades

| Revelation text | Agent | Meaning |
|---|---|---|
| I have the keys of Death and of Hades (1:18) | Jesus | promise to bring Death and Hades to naught |
| the one who sat on it had the name Death, and Hades followed him (6:8) | Satan | reign of Death and Hades described and exposed |
| Death and Hades gave back the dead (20:14) | Jesus | defeat of Death and Hades |
| Death and Hades were thrown into the lake of fire (20:15) | Jesus | end of Death and Hades |

The term "Death and Hades" needs three more points of clarification. First, both members of the paired phrase have the article. A better translation might be **the Domain of Death** and **the Domain of Hades** (20:14–15; cf. 1:18; 6:8), both belonging to the portfolio of Satan and both representative of his ideology and activity. His "Economy of Death" contrasts with God's "Economy of Life" in the book—as in "tree of life" (2:7; 22:2, 14), "crown of life" (2:10), "Book of Life" (3:5; 13:8; 17:8; 20:12, 15; 21:27), "water of life" (7:17; 21:6; 22:1, 17), and "breath of life" (11:11).

Second, the paired phrase is a metaphor for evil, material as well as theological. In this conception, "Death" is not only physical death, and "Hades" is not only the place where the dead are buried. "Hades" is not empty space (6:8; 9:1). As occupied space, it is the abyss that disseminates darkness and misperceptions into the world (9:1–11). Terms suitable for this reality are "Death and Hellishness." To this demonic enormity, Jesus brings "the keys of Death and of Hades" by mediating *revelation* and *reversal* (1:18). Third, attention to *sequence* and *agency* is crucial in the last verses of the judgment scene (20:14–15). We have been put on the alert that John resorts to the literary device *hysteron-proteron*, "reversing the logical order of narrative events" (Aune 1996–98, 1084–85). When we make use of this insight without losing sight of the two sides in the conflict, order and meaning will walk in step.

**And Death and Hades were thrown [*eblēthēsan*] into the Lake of Fire. (20:14)**

**And if anyone was not found written in the Book of Life, he/she was thrown [*eblēthē*] into the Lake of Fire. (20:15)**

Two things can be inferred from this sequence. First, as we have seen on numerous occasions, verbs in the passive voice anonymize the acting subject. This caveat comes in addition to the need to desist from a strictly literal reading of a symbolic text. For the passage at hand, the battle raging outside "the beloved city" (20:7–10) complements the judgment scene before "the great white throne" (20:11–15). In the former scenario, Satan's assault on "the beloved city" faces meltdown in the presence of revelation. The attackers turn on each other (Ezek. 38:21; *1 En.* 100.1–3). The evil enterprise implodes. Rage on the part of the deceived against the deceiver is more than a hypothetical possibility in Revelation (17:16). Similar sentiments should be expected in this scene. This possibility erodes the anonymity of the acting subject, especially because *deception* and reaction to deception loom large in the text. "And the devil who deceived them was thrown into the lake of fire and sulfur," says John (Rev. 20:10). When this is included in "the picture which the seer saw" (Flowers 1930, 526), it implores the reader to have more than one candidate on his/her short list for who is doing the throwing.

Second, in the sequence adopted, "Death and Hades" conclude the judgment scene. The vicious twosome and its demonic sponsor are the subject of the last "throw." When they are "thrown," they are gone. This emphatic move is conveyed by means of the most telling verb in the cosmic conflict, *to throw* (12:9; cf. 8:7, 8; 12:4, 10, 13; 18:21; 19:20; 20:3, 10, 14, 15). It comes here, for the last time, with the connotation of finality and closure. An exclamation mark, not a period, is necessary to drive the point home. "Death and Hades" will not be around with no end in sight to their blight; there is no "forever" in this conception of the last "throw." It must be said advisedly that no reading of Revelation has done more harm to the Christian theological tradition than its failure to take the requisite measure of the final "throw" (e.g., Lambrecht 2000).

## Theological Issues

While the ontological status of Satan and his role in the message of Revelation are theological issues throughout the book, they are never as acute as in this chapter. Failure to invest in his character earlier explains the scrambling taking place among scholars: corrupted text, tired author, or foreign element in one category; "free will" and "responsibility" in another (but only as *human* qualities); inscrutability in a third category; stage effects in a fourth. The proposals seem speculative, and even the best bears scant relation to the plot.

To many readers, *sovereignty* has seemed like a viable option among attempts at explaining the enigma of Satan's binding and release. On closer examination, however, it may easily end up as the least persuasive. Will a story line featuring the Ancient Serpent, at one end anchored in the serpent's misrepresentation of God and its aftermath (Gen. 3:1–15), bend to the notion of "sovereignty"? If assertion of "sovereignty" solves the cosmic conflict, why didn't it happen earlier? Overall, "sovereignty" tends to delegitimize questions; it is less an explanation than the reef on which questions run aground. Revelation's report of Satan's release, described as a necessity (20:3), suggests subtler qualities and answers.

One objection to "sovereignty" is historical and intuitive. Adolf Eichmann was entrusted with the logistics of "the Final Solution" during World War II. Bettina Stangneth describes a meeting between Eichmann and Jewish leaders in Vienna in 1938, Eichmann then a strapping young officer in a black SS uniform. "His behaviour, too, was godlike: he was master of *arresting* and then *releasing* people, of banning institutions and then allowing them to resume," writes Stangneth (2014, 9, emphasis added). The key words in the analogy are "arresting" and "releasing" and the notion that a person who can "arrest" and "release" at will is "godlike." Is God, Eichmann-like, engaged in a game of binding and releasing that offers positive proof of God's sovereignty? In this context "godlike" is not a compliment to Eichmann—or to God—and the appeal to "sovereignty" for the binding and release of Satan becomes unattractive.

A plot construct anchored in Genesis sees a theological reason behind Satan's release (20:3). Misrepresentation is corrected by revelation, and the *Misrepresenter* (Mudslinger) finds himself cornered by his misrepresentation. Few things should be less expected than Satan's release and few things less anticipated than how he is defeated. What dooms the Antagonist is not that God restrains him but that God doesn't. OT texts bring much with which to answer these enigmas. Satan's defeat "is similar to Ezekiel's oracles concerning Gog, who devised battle plans against Israel (Ezek. 38:11–12) only to find that God used Gog's own schemes to defeat him (Ezek. 38:4, 17; 39:2)," Craig R. Koester notes perceptively (2014, 771; cf. Bøe 2001, 302).

For communities committed to futurist schemes in the United States, "Gog and Magog" are shorthand for theological and political convictions similar to

"Armageddon theology" discussed earlier. These include causes that oppose relaxation of international tensions, a dislike of liberal democracy, militarism, and belief in a literal battle in the Middle East (Railton 2003, 42). Like "Armageddon," the term "Gog and Magog" represents "a presence in literary reception history that far out-weighs their slender beginnings" (Swindell 2016, 27). Daniel I. Block (1992, 156) spots a heavy dose of hyperbole in the "Gog and Magog" passages in Ezekiel, and this is a good start for sober-minded exegesis. The OT background thus understood imagines "a cosmic event" (Zimmerli 1979, 314), and the enemy "cloaked in ambiguity" represents "the most fierce and powerful enemy that one could ever imagine" (Irwin 1995, 106). How it ends, or one element of how it ends, is foreshadowed already in Ezekiel: the assailants turn on each other (Zimmerli 1979, 313).

"Death and Hades gave back the dead that were in them," says John (Rev. 20:13). His words resonate in the exquisite poem of another John (Donne 1996, 202), with Revelation as more than a distant contributor to the conviction expressed.

> Death, be not proud, though some have called thee
> Mighty and dreadful, for thou art not so;
> . . . . . . . . . . . . . . . . . . . . . . . . . . . . . . . . . . .
> One short sleep past, we wake eternally
> And death shall be no more; Death, thou shalt die.

# Revelation 21:1–27

## Journey's End

### Introductory Matters

What now is told has been told already, but it has not been told fully until now: only now is it told without distractions (21:1–27). In the context of the seven seals, it was said that "God will wipe away every tear from their eyes" (7:17). But when Revelation now says that "God will wipe every tear from their eyes" (21:4), adding that "death will be no more nor grief nor wailing nor pain will be any more" (21:4), it is as though we hear it for the first time. Only now do we have a fuller account of "the Holy City, the New Jerusalem, coming down out of heaven from God" (21:2) even though we have already seen a hostile army marching up "over the plain of the earth" with the intent of surrounding "the camp of the believers and the beloved city" (20:9). *That* battle takes place *after* the descent of "the beloved city" (20:9). Only now do we have an uncluttered view of its descent and a much fuller account of the Holy City as "the bride, the wife of the Lamb" (21:9).

All this confirms *recapitulation* in the telling of the story. The account is convoluted, moving back and forth, with flashbacks to primordial time and fast-forwards to the life to come, but it is steadily headed for journey's end. What John sacrifices with respect to an easy-to-follow chronology, he makes up to the reader in the form of striking images that will be processed separately to get the message across. The last two chapters of Revelation are a case in point.

Continuity at the level of mediation is evident and important (21:9), and yet this is only a surface feature of a composition that abounds in deep and enduring continuities. "The new earth" does not mean that "the old earth" has been discarded, and "the New Jerusalem" does not make "the old Jerusalem" irrelevant. Images of earth and community project tight, unbreakable interdependence. Theology blends so intimately with ecology that it is impossible to have one without the other. Creation, as depicted in Genesis, is vindicated in the new creation, and Israel, as its story is told in the rest of the OT, is finally at home in a promised land and a Holy City that exceed anything imagined in the past. These images and other pairs like them emerge in scenes from "the new earth" (21:1–8) and "the New Jerusalem" (21:9–27).

## Tracing the Train of Thought

### New Earth and God as Earthling: Proof That God Is the One Who Is with Someone (21:1–8)

**21:1–8.** A vast scope is apparent right from the start (21:1), cosmic and all-encompassing (Russell 1996, 199). **New** contrasts logically with "old," and **first** contrasts with "second" or "last," but the emphasis falls on *the state of things* rather than *the things as such* (21:1). We do not have "new" versus "old" in a temporal sense only but a contrast between "whole" and "broken." The old *order* is sent into oblivion, not the earth (L. Thompson 1990, 85; du Preez 1992, 7; Rossing 2005, 170).

This is underscored by the word *kainos*. The *new* earth is not a replacement earth but an earth that is "new in nature," "different from the usual, impressive, better than the old, superior in value or attraction" (J. Behm, *TDNT* 3:447, καινός). This understanding of "new" suggests "fresh life rising from the decay and wreck of the old world" (Swete 1908, 275), and it favors the translation **I saw a *renewed* heaven and a *renewed* earth** (21:1a; L. Thompson 1990, 85). John's announcement means that the *broken* heaven and the *broken* earth had passed away (21:1b).

A "broken *earth*" is not hard to visualize, but a "broken *heaven*"? Does John throw "heaven" into the mix for good measure or for a genuine theological reason? Only the second option

---

**Revelation 21:1–27 in the Rhetorical Flow**

Incentive to read (1:1–20)

To the one who has an ear (2:1–3:22)

The seven seals (4:1–8:1)

The seven trumpets (8:2–11:19)

The cosmic conflict from A to Z (12:1–14:20)

The seven bowls (15:1–16:21)

The woman and the beast (17:1–18:24)

The wedding, the rider, and the supper (19:1–21)

The thousand years and then (20:1–15)

▶Journey's end (21:1–27)

New earth and God as earthling: Proof that God is the one who is with someone (21:1–8)

New Jerusalem as theology, completion, and a familiar place (21:9–27)

works. "Heaven" was broken, too; it was "heaven" that broke first; "war broke out *in heaven*" (12:7–9; Isa. 14:12–15). Material and physical healing is writ large in these chapters, but the cosmic crisis carries the story line. John volunteers that **the sea was no more** (21:1c), but his interest is not primarily geography, topography, or oceanography. This detail, too, has theological meaning.

> "Sea" often exists in relationship to evil powers such as the beast or dragon within the Book of Revelation (cf. 13:1, 6–7). In Dan. 7:3ff., four beasts came up out of the sea, and Isaiah associates the wicked powers with "the tossing sea which cannot rest, whose waters toss up mire and dirt" (Isa. 57:20). . . . Consequently, "no more sea" does not mean the vanishing of this earth but rather of the evil power. This is the natural result of the total defeat of the satanic trinity in 16:6–16, 17:13–14, 19:11–21 and 20:7–10. (Lee 2001, 269)

By this criterion the sea that is "no more" is a way of saying that the cosmic conflict is over and the cosmos liberated from the forces causing turmoil. God *redeems* and *renews*; God does not *discard* or *replace*.

Other background texts corroborate this perspective (Isa. 65:17; 66:22–23). These texts take an expansive view of the future, and the future they envision is *earthly*. No OT voice had it in him/her to imagine the abolition and abandonment on earth in favor of an immaterial existence in *heaven*. And yet "the new heavens and the new earth" belong together; *heaven* is not left out any more than that *earth* will cease to matter. The *earth* and the *heavens* together are the matrix within which a redeemed and restored existence will emerge, and the material parameters have a *theological* errand. David Russell (1996, 208) and Barbara Rossing (2005, 170) have shown that the new world is primarily characterized by pointed negations of the most demeaning features of the old *order*.

1. The *sea* was no more (Rev. 21:1).
2. *Death* will be no more (21:4).
3. *Grief* . . . will be no more (21:4).
4. *Wailing* . . . will be no more (21:4).
5. *Pain* will be no more (21:4).
6. *All things accursed* will be no more (22:3).
7. *Night* will be no more (22:5; cf. 21:25).

Woven into all these texts is the conviction that the blighting influence, with "the sea" as the first example, will be defeated and vanish. God, who is about to "create new heavens and a new earth" where "the former things shall not be remembered or come to mind" (Isa. 65:17), consigns the old *order* to oblivion. "The sea" tops the list, and "night" concludes it, both elements expressing a blight that is theological more than physical (Koester 2014, 795–96; T. Schmidt 1994; Mathewson 2003a; Moo 2009).

If we enlarge the frame for the texts echoing in Revelation, the *cosmic* and *theological* concerns become even more striking. Isaiah's "new heavens" and "new earth" are a case in point.

> For behold, I create new heavens
>     and a new earth;
> And the former things
>     shall not be remembered
>     or come to mind. (Isa. 65:17 NKJV)

The influence of this text on Revelation is well established (21:1), but there is more to Isaiah's vision of the new order. Within the enlarged frame, in the same chapter and context, Isaiah draws a line of exclusion. Why mention *the serpent*—emphatically?

> The wolf and the lamb
>     shall feed together,
> the lion shall eat straw
>     like the ox;
> *but the serpent*
> —*its food shall be dust!*" (Isa. 65:25)

Isaiah is a layered text, but the book has profound thematic continuity. This text from the end of the book echoes a scene from the book's earlier vision of what the world will look like when the Right-maker has completed his mission (Isa. 11:6). Crucially, the intervention arising from "the stump of Jesse" brings about cosmic, ecological, and zoological harmony (Isa. 11:1–10). This is the background text for the pivotal moment when "the root of David" appears "*in the middle*" as the solution to the crisis in the heavenly council (Rev. 5:5–6). The agent, the *who* behind this turn of events, is the insignificant figure made significant in Isaiah (11:1, 10).

Isaiah describes the means as well as the results (11:1–10). In the second iteration, one creature is pointedly left out (Isa. 65:25; Blenkinsopp 2003, 286; Oswalt 1998, 662). Why, in Isaiah's final depiction of the restoration, is *the serpent* mentioned only to exclude it? The answer, of course, lies in the story about the serpent in Genesis. True to the character of allusions, only a snippet of the original story echoes in Isaiah and Revelation, but the link is clear (Gen. 3:14; Isa. 65:25; Rev. 21:1).

In ecological terms, the earth is damaged, but it is not doomed. Revelation does not envision a replacement earth. *Renewed* is the meaning of *new*; *healed* is the remedy for *broken*. Even more important, *heaven* is not the address at journey's end. The final address, resoundingly, is *earth* (21:1–5). The vision blends the earth and the urban, meaning that a city will occupy the center in the transformed reality (21:2; Rossing 1998, 496). For this verse, too, Isaiah remains the most significant background voice (Isa. 65:18–19).

**Echoes of Healing**

| | Who | What | Theology |
|---|---|---|---|
| **Isaiah** | root of Jesse | new heavens and a new earth | but the serpent—its food shall be dust |
| **Revelation** | root of David | a new heaven and a new earth | the sea was no more; night will be no more |

Two aspects of **the Holy City** (21:2a) need special emphasis, initially by way of review. First, "the Holy City" is a city of *people* (Gundry 1987). John thus sees *people* **coming down out of heaven from God** (Rev. 21:2b). How odd and counterintuitive is this, given that the traditional Christian account envisions a permanent departure of the redeemed *from* earth *to* heaven, never again to set foot on earth and the earth no longer of interest! Here, the mind is directed in the opposite direction on both counts: *the earth is retained and enhanced, and the earth—not heaven—will be the address at journey's end.* Second, "the Holy City" comes down "out of heaven from God" *before* the cosmic conflict is over. This was the subject of the previous chapter, and this, too, is a feature left out or glossed over in traditional accounts.

And now to the meaning of the city "coming down." "What does the fact that it is a city essentially mean?" Jacques Ellul (1977, 221) asks. The first meaning, he answers, "is that we observe a total contrast between the first creation and the second. In the first, God had created a garden for man. . . . In the second, he is installed in a city." Revelation does not leave out images of *return*, specifically images of "Paradise Regained" (22:1–4), but "the Holy City" was not a feature of the garden of Eden (Gen. 2:1–25).

> Thus we do not observe a return to the origin. It is not the preservation of God's primitive plan. The biblical God is not the abstract God who, having had an idea at the beginning, maintains it over against everything and again makes a garden because it was his plan at the beginning. Here we are in contradiction to all the other religions: for all those, without exception, which have a view of the future, of paradise, of an "afterlife," there is uniquely a return to a lost primitive age of gold. Here the situation is radically reversed. (Ellul 1977, 221–22)

As phenomenon, the city's history begins with Cain and is from the first "but a constant succession of revolts against God" (Ellul 1970, 50). In the book of Daniel, for instance, empires rise and fall, but they do not rise and fall in ever-improving expressions of strength and ingenuity. On the contrary, the successor is inferior to the empire preceding it; the trajectory declines from gold to silver, from silver to bronze, from bronze to iron, and from iron to clay (Dan. 2:29–45). In Daniel's representation, the entire edifice rests on feet that have clay as their most conspicuous component (2:31, 41–43). The result is given: "The kingdom shall be partly strong and partly brittle" (2:42); "they will not hold together" (2:43); they "were all broken in pieces and became like the chaff of the summer threshing floors; and the wind carried them away, so that not a trace of them could be found" (2:35). Images of failure play out against a horizon of ever-increasing determination to succeed. Nebuchadnezzar (in Babylon) responds to Daniel's message of impermanence with an imperious, gravity-defying counter-representation (3:1–7), and he counts on coercion to hold reality at bay (3:8–23). In Isaiah, "Babylon" says, "I shall be mistress forever" (47:7–8). Revelation's "Babylon" is similarly convinced of its own indestructibility. "I rule as a queen; I am no widow, and I will never see grief" (Rev. 18:7). The entity saying this is oblivious to the futility breathing down her neck. And failure it is: "for this reason her blows will hit in a single day—death, and grief, and famine—and she will be burned with fire" (18:8).

Despite the aspirations of the city builders in the Bible, they never succeeded. The city is not only an expression of rebellion but also of *failure*. This includes Israel's failure, too, and the failure of its city, the "old" Jerusalem (Isa. 1:21; 5:7). In our time, it extends to the precarious state of cities that are too big to fail and almost certain to do so. "Man had never succeeded; he had always experienced failure, and the actual urban monstrosity is striking testimony to this" (Ellul 1977, 224).

God turns the city, the Bible's embodiment of rebellion and futility, into a symbol of reconciliation, community, and permanence. Nothing captures this better than the announcement that the New Jerusalem is "the bride, the wife of the Lamb" (21:9). "Communion" vies with "community" as the best way to describe the new existence. Aspiration exceeds reality for all the cities in history except one: the city not built on and by force (Ellul 1970, 13; cf. Dan. 2:34, 45). And yet failure too must be redeemed.

> The symbol of Jerusalem is the strongest sign we can have that the biblical God is a God who accompanies man in his history. He does not pursue his independent design, he pursues his design in and with the history of men. And that which men have freely, voluntarily, created they are going to find again in Jerusalem. (Ellul 1977, 222)

This is a staggering thought. God will redeem and renew the old world; God will reverse past failure in the New Jerusalem. This suggests that God redeems human *history* too: *history* will not be discarded and annulled any more than the *earth*. That is the *people*—the *human* part.

What about God? Exclamation must be the mode of expression for "the *God* part" now proclaimed from on high.

> And I heard a loud voice from the throne saying,
> "Look!
> The dwelling place of God
>     is among human beings.
> He will dwell with them,
>     and they will be his people,
> and God himself
>     will be with them.
> And God will wipe
>     every tear from their eyes,
> and death will be no more
>     nor grief nor wailing nor pain
>     will be any more,
> for the former state of things
>     has passed away. (21:3–4)

"The Holy City" comes down "out of heaven from God," but this does not mean that human beings will resume life on earth as before or that God will resume business as usual in heaven. God, too, comes down! *The dwelling place of God is among human beings!* This is without precedent in Greco-Roman thought (Gilchrest 2013, 267–68).

A close reading of Genesis leads to the realization that the "new" arrangement is prefigured in the old, specifically in the blessing of the seventh day in the creation story (Gen. 2:1–3). "By resting on the seventh day, God is thereby shown to have entered into the time of the created order," says Terence Fretheim (2005, 63; Rossing 1999, 149). To Jürgen Moltmann (1985, 279), the seventh day in Genesis means that God "adopts the community of creation as his own milieu." Shimon Bakon (1997, 84) perceives divine commitment and not human obligation as the meaning of the seventh day. John Dominic Crossan (2009, 211) finds in this arrangement a decentering of human beings and a re-centering of God that highlights God's commitment. These unfamiliar perspectives lessen the surprise that God relocates from heaven to earth in Revelation. Instead, they suggest that God makes good on a commitment that existed from the beginning (Gen. 2:1–2).

No one makes more of this than Moltmann (1996, 266), who sees the seventh day of the first creation as "*the presence of God* in the *time* of those he has created or, to put it more precisely, the dynamic presence of eternity in time, which links beginning and end, thus awakening remembrance and hope." On this logic hope is anchored in memory. Indeed, he adds, "Sabbath and Shekinah [God's actual presence] are related to each other as promise and fulfillment, beginning and completion. In the Sabbath, creation holds within itself from the beginning the true promise of its consummation" (1996, 266).

These are not musings about trivial matters. Revelation is classified as "apocalyptic literature," and the link between Genesis and Revelation supports the idea that *vindication* is a key element in apocalyptic thought (Beker 1982, 14, 15, 32). Theologically, the new heaven and the new earth represent God's faithfulness to creation, not its abandonment (Koester 2014, 803). The relevance of this in the twenty-first century—seared by the sense of God's absence at Auschwitz, Hiroshima, and other sites of horror—is immeasurable.

Revelation makes God a welcome presence in the human community and—by extension—portrays the New Jerusalem as "a welcoming city" (Rossing 1998, 498; Koester 2014, 797). There is no need to keep distance. God's presence guarantees healing and plenitude and the complete reversal of the accumulated burden of loss and grief and pain in human experience (21:3–4). Again, it is the former *state* that will vanish, not the world as such. In the Sabbath perspective explored above, humans will flock to the God who has come to them. Craig R. Koester (2014, 802) notes that "nearly every verse in this section recalls passages from the prophets, weaving older themes into a new vision of promise" with Isa. 65:17–19 as the dominant passage. Isaiah bequeaths the prospect that "from sabbath to sabbath, all flesh shall come to worship before me" (66:23). John, who helps himself to large chunks of Isaiah's vision for his view of the world made new, did not miss this part, given that he alludes to it in the song sung on "the sea of glass" (Rev. 15:1).

> All nations will come and worship before you,
> for your sense of "right act" has been revealed. (15:4)

God is not making "all new things," working from a blank slate (21:5). It will be **all things new** in the sense of renewal, applying heaven's powers of healing to broken conditions (21:5). That **these words are trustworthy and true** reassures those who doubt that God can pull it off, and they stand in contrast to words that are neither trustworthy nor true. The interactive tenor between God and the reader (21:5) and God and John (21:5–6) marks a transition to greater urgency and emotional intensity.

### Look! (21:5) Write! (21:5) Done! (21:6)

*"Done!"* has been said before, at the close of the seventh bowl (16:17), a revelation as final and definitive as this one (21:6; cf. John 19:30). Why the need to say it again? "Done!" we hear twice, loud and clear, once in the singular (Rev. 16:17) and once in the plural (21:6). The exclamations occur at points of completion, but they refer to different realities. "Done!" in the context of the seven bowls signals the undoing of the opposing side (16:17). "Done!" in the context of the new heaven and the new earth marks the full extent of God's commitment and self-giving (21:6). For both realities, "Done!" is a good word.

What God does cannot be separated from what God is. God is **the Alpha and the Omega** (21:6). David E. Aune says that the divine title "has a cosmological rather than a temporal significance" (1996–98, 1126), suggesting that space is more important than time. By either measure, we can think of it as ontological preeminence. But there is more to it. God, as "the Alpha and the Omega," is a giving Person. The haste to get from what God is to what God does implies a title that is less about time and space than about giving. **I will give to the thirsty from the spring of the water of life as a gift** (21:6; Isa. 55:1–3). This is reassuring in a general sense. In the context of conflict, recalling the serpent's portrayal of God as someone who withholds and prohibits (Gen. 3:1), the emphasis on *giving* has much deeper resonance. The recipient of the gift is "the thirsty." Thirst is a metaphor for *need*. This must be how God sees the human condition, with *need* as the only requirement. A person who has nothing but need to show for himself/herself, has what it takes. "Thirst was a metaphor for the need for God" (Koester 2014, 799), but "thirst" is best left broad and unspecified. A host of texts inside and outside Revelation highlight this (Rev. 7:17; 21:6; 22:17; Isa. 55:1–3; John 4:10, 14; 7:37–38).

Allegiances to one or the other side in the conflict loom larger than scenes from the courtroom (20:7–9, 11–12). Choices made can be described as "shares" (21:8), and "share" may be the equivalent of "thing" in everyday language. (What is your "thing"?) God gives "to the thirsty from the spring of the water of life as a gift" (21:6). By contrast, the other side offers a share **in the lake that burns with fire and sulfur** (21:8). We recoil from this prospect, but John's main point is the emergence of utterly different realities, God's gift-and-life economy in contrast to the adversary's economy of deception and death.

### New Jerusalem as Theology, Completion, and a Familiar Place (21:9–27)

**21:9–27.** The guide is in a hurry to show John more. **"Come! I will show you the bride, the wife of the Lamb"** (21:9). Why it falls to one of the bowl angels to do this is not explained (Aune 1996–98, 1150), but it shows continuity. Perhaps, too, the angel is more eager to show some things than others. **And he carried me away in the spirit to an enormous, high mountain, and he showed me the Holy City, Jerusalem, coming down out of heaven from God** (21:10). The descent of the New Jerusalem has been the subject briefly and *explicitly* in this chapter (21:2). It has been told *implicitly* in earlier chapters, as "the city" (14:20) and "the Holy City" (20:9), but the most extensive exposition is coming now (21:9–27). Being "carried away" is not new. John was "carried away" by a bowl angel to "a wilderness" to get the truth about the "woman sitting on a scarlet beast" (17:3). He is now "carried away . . . to an enormous, high mountain" (21:10; cf. Ezek. 40:2). The subject of the previous excursion was "Babylon," the unfaithful city (Rev. 17:5). The subject now is "the New Jerusalem," the faithful city (21:10). This is additional proof that there are two sides to the revelation. The combination of *wilderness* and *mountain* has external links to the tour of reality given to Jesus by Satan in the Synoptic Gospels (Matt. 4:1–11; Luke 4:1–13). A contrast may not be intended, but one can easily be inferred. In the Synoptic account, Satan tries to entice Jesus with a false view of reality, including a visit to "the holy city" and a panoramic view of the world from the top of a high mountain (Matt. 4:5–11; Luke 4:5–13). The "enormous, high mountain" in Revelation is the last mountain featured in the Bible, providing an unmatched vision for the way it blends materiality and theology.

We have, first, a city "coming down out of heaven from God" (21:10). This is a *city of people*, and *people* are therefore "coming down out of heaven" instead of the familiar idea of "going to heaven." The redemptive symbolism of the city extends to more than people. Jacques Ellul (1977, 222) again expands the vision to include people *and their work*:

> Consequently, the history of humanity is not in vain, annulled by a stroke of the pen, as if nothing of our efforts, our suffering, our hopes, had ever existed: on the contrary, *all* is gathered up. Then man is saved *with his works*. Paradise is not a formless cloud, a rose and blue fog and "nonplace"; it is a good city, a solid place, where the whole creation of man is re-created. Thus in the judgment, God destroys history but without anything being lost; and he synthesizes that same history. He judges the works, purified, borne to the absolute of grandeur and perfection. Perfect, and nevertheless the same.

Can this be true? In the world to come, must not Bach be supplanted by more melodious music, Michelangelo by paintings more exquisite, Milton by poetry more sublime, or Einstein by superior insights into the workings of the physical world? Will there not be buildings more splendid than the Mezquita, the great mosque in Cordoba that sought to blur the line of demarcation between secular and sacred space? Perhaps—or probably, or even certainly—but Ellul's perception that "*all* is gathered up" should not be dismissed.

For "Babylon," there is cessation of commerce and culture, like this:

> the sound of harpists and musicians and flutists and trumpeters
>     will be heard in you no more;
> and traders of any trade
>     will be found in you no more;
> and the sound of the millstone
>     will be heard in you no more;
> and the light of a lamp
>     will shine in you no more;
> and the voice of bridegroom and bride
>     will be heard in you no more. (Rev. 18:22–23)

But this is not the whole story. The *broken* city falls silent and disappears, but another city will appear, "coming down out of heaven from God" (21:10). In this city, culture, commerce, and celebration do not cease, whether "harpists playing on their harps" (14:2)—the harps even described as "the harps of God" (15:2)—or light (21:22–23) or trade (21:24). In the negation called Babylon, "the voice of bridegroom and bride will be heard . . . no more" (18:23). But it is precisely "the voice of bridegroom and bride" that *will be heard* at journey's end, in the city "made ready as a bride beautified for her husband" (21:2; cf. 19:7–8; 21:9–10).

When John proceeds to describe various features of the city in terms that are strange even for symbolic language, these impressions are confirmed and deepened. Architecture is now a vehicle for theology, aesthetics blends with ethics, and the transparent politics of heaven is exported to earth.

*Glory* (21:11). In material terms, "glory" implies splendor and beauty (21:11). These will not be lacking in the Holy City, but its main interest lies elsewhere. Is this "glory" bestowed or "glory" reflected? It must be both—and therefore a city within which God's ideal is actualized. The Gospel of John is similarly preoccupied with "glory" that has been lost and is reclaimed (John 1:14; 2:11; 12:23, 28; 17:1, 4, 5). In Romans (3:23), Paul captures the human predicament as a case of "lacking the glory of God." In all three cases—John, Romans, and Revelation—the "glory deficit" begins with misperception and misrepresentation of God. In the Holy City, there is no such misperception: the city **has the glory of God** (21:11). And the city is **clear as crystal**, suggesting light and brightness as elements of theology. By this criterion, the "shining city on the hill" that inspired the early pilgrims coming to America and their dream about a New Israel and a New Jerusalem on the American continent is in for serious competition (Barry 2012, 120–35). A city that is "clear as crystal" is a city known for its transparency. *This* city has nothing to hide.

*Wall* (21:12–13). What is the point of the **enormous high wall** (21:12–13)? If we assume that walls are for protection, this city will be a tall order for anyone wishing to harm it. The hostile army marching on the city should think twice before proceeding (20:8–9). "Protection," however, is not likely to be the meaning, and the subject is best left for later (Rossing 1998, 498). The profusion of gates is out of character with ancient cities: if the "high wall" were for protection, the **twelve gates** squander the advantage (Aune 1996–98, 1154). For this item, it is necessary to think of OT antecedents (Ezek. 48:31–34) and ponder the symbolism. **Twelve gates, twelve angels,** and then **the twelve tribes of Israel,** each one with its name **inscribed on the gates** (Rev. 21:12–13), mean that nothing has been lost. A central concern in Jewish thought, *"the restoration of the twelve tribes of Israel"* (Aune 1996–98, 1155), has been solved even though many tribes in ancient times never made it back from captivity. Old Testament ideals are vindicated at the level of ideology (as in the song of Moses), and hopes are brought to fulfillment at the level of *story*. To find "inscribed on the gates . . . the names of the twelve tribes of the Israelites" ensures continuity and completion. In the seal sequence, the twelve tribes are *sealed* to make sure that no tribe will be lost in the final crisis (7:4–8). Here, "the names of the twelve tribes" are *inscribed* to let it be known that no tribe was lost (21:12–13). Physical grandeur has a role, but it is mostly about *people*.

*Foundations* (21:14). More "twelves" are pouring forth, this time **twelve foundations** and **the twelve names of the twelve apostles** (21:14). The number is *complete*, and this is not scribbled graffiti. At the level of ideology, "twelve tribes" (21:12) and "twelve apostles" (21:14) link the message of the OT with the message of the NT (cf. Eph. 2:20; Aune 1996–98, 1157). But "the twelve names of the twelve apostles" go beyond ideology. They are the names of *people*—and more than inscriptions on a plaque that is to be admired until time erodes the names. Not the ideology only but the *person* constitutes the foundation of the city; not the memory but the man and the woman themselves are in view. "Here the emphasis is apparently on their *persons*," David E. Aune (1996–98, 1157) says perceptively. The tenor is not the word or the deed but the person.

*Size and shape* (21:15–18). **Twelve thousand** is another instance of **twelve**, and **one hundred and forty-four** is twelve multiplied by twelve (21:15–18). Who will contest that theology trumps architecture and geometry in these representations? A city shaped like a cube is unlikely to appeal to anyone's aesthetic sensibilities, especially if the vertical side of the cube is fifteen hundred miles long. This is a *very big* city even though symbols are not literal representations. At the level of metaphor, the city will be even bigger. In theological terms, the cubic shape suggests that the Holy City is patterned on the Most Holy in the sanctuary (Koester 2014, 816; Aune 1996–98, 1160; Mathewson 2003b, 106). If this is the case, this holy place is gigantic; it is not a tiny place within a gigantic city but the city itself. Sacred space has diffused into secular space to erase the boundary or, in the reverse conception, the distinction between sacred and secular is no longer meaningful. Second, therefore, the angel's task of measuring cannot end merely with a city that is very big. It is necessary to think of the measured space not as a portion of the whole but as the whole. "Where God's glory once filled the holy of holies, it now fills New Jerusalem," says Craig R. Koester (2014, 816; Exod. 40:34; 1 Kings 8:11; Rev. 21:23–24). "The massive size of the cubic city exhibits holiness on a cosmic scale" (Koester 2014, 816). By this logic, all space is sacred space; indeed, all space is now the Most Holy (Rissi 1972, 62; Beale and Kim 2014, 139). This fits the conception in Zechariah, a measured space that turns out to be immeasurable and a city that "shall be inhabited like villages without walls, because of the multitude of people and animals in it" (Zech. 2:4–5; R. Smith 1984, 197). In this conception, the "high wall" (21:12) is a concession to a theological message and not a feature of protection. There is no need for protection where all space is sacred.

*Foundations, gates, and street* (21:19–21). On yet another walk-through of the city, John describes things mentioned earlier in greater detail: **the**

**foundations of the wall of the city,** with nothing spared with respect to making it beautiful and lasting; **the twelve gates,** with nothing left to chance with respect to material and workmanship; **the street of the city,** as though there is only one street and this is the new Main Street (21:19–21). And still nothing shady is going on because this street is **transparent as glass** (21:21). The background texts combine primordial and priestly conceptions (Ezek. 28:13; Exod. 28:17–21).

*Temple* (21:22). In medicine, one of the most important tools is the concept "pertinent negatives." These are items looked for but not found. Sometimes the item is expected to be there, and its absence is even more remarkable. What is not found narrows the options, easing the path to a precise diagnosis. Here we have what could well be theology's most "pertinent negative" (21:22). All ancient cities had temples, often more than one, and Jerusalem was no exception. John expects to see a temple (Aune 1996–98, 1166, 1168). In fact, he expects the temple to be the most conspicuous feature of the city. Instead, the conspicuous feature is what he does not see. Our surprise may be muted by the groundwork John has done up until this point. Where would the temple be when all space is sacred? Why the need for sequestered space dedicated to the contemplation of God when **the Lord God . . . is her temple—and the Lamb** (21:22)? Temples are not only sequestered spaces devoted to religion; they are also expressions of the need for mediation between God and human beings. The absence of a temple signifies God's *unmediated* presence (Gilchrest 2013, 268–69). As Celia Deutsch (1987, 115) notes, "There will be no need for a separate place to symbolize, or even mediate, encounter between God and the community. . . . The Temple, as symbol of access to the divine presence, is replaced by the Presence itself."

*Illumination* (21:23). John does not say that he did not see the **sun** or the **moon,** but he marginalizes these heavenly bodies as sources of illumination (21:23). This, too, is a pertinent negative if not quite as dramatic as the absence of a temple. From the point of view of physics or astrophysics, this negation could be the unpardonable sin, but the reduction of the sun and the moon to matters of relative unimportance is not proof of ignorance. God, not the sun, is for John the premise for life, and **the Lamb,** as the Revealer, is the prerequisite for finding the way.

As a place, the New Jerusalem is at once paradise, holy city and temple. As paradise it is the natural world in its ideal state, rescued from the destroyers of the earth, reconciled with humanity, filled with the presence of God, and mediating the blessings of the eschatological life to humanity. As holy city, it fulfils the ideal of the ancient city, as the place where heaven and earth meet at the centre of the earth, from which God rules his land and his people, to whose attraction the nations are drawn for enlightenment, and in which people live in ideal theocentric community. As temple, it is the place of God's immediate presence, where his worshippers see his face. (Bauckham 1993b, 132)

*Trade* (21:24). The secular and the sacred now occupy the same sphere, with hints of international relations ("nations") and trade ("kings"). The city is not only *illuminated*; it also *illuminates*: **the nations will walk by its light, and the kings of the earth will bring the best they have** [*tēn doxan autōn*] **into it** (21:24). The reclamation of all space is a reminder that God has prevailed in the cosmic conflict, and the orientation of "the nations" and "the kings of the earth" prove that God's intervention has not been in vain (Aune 1996–98, 1173). Here, too, a spiritual application must be uppermost. The covering cherub in Ezekiel was engaged in trade practices with a theological overtone, trading in falsehood and indicted for "the dishonesty of your trading" (Ezek. 28:18 NJB), "the iniquity of your trading" (NKJV), or "the unrighteousness of your trade" (NRSV). By this criterion, notions of "fair trade" will mean the reclamation of truthful speech about God.

*Safety measures* (Rev. 21:25). Isaiah (60:11) envisioned a city where the gates would always be open, Zechariah (14:7) a time of "continuous day" (Aune 1996–98, 1172). Gates that never shut are risky under conditions of hostility and danger. Here, hostility and danger are at an end. Open gates and continuous light are features of restoration (21:25), and **no night** (21:25) means more than a change in the diurnal cycle. All these conditions transmit a theological message.

*Community and commerce, and theology* (21:26–27). A city like this must be community at its best, as John's images suggest—community, culture, and commerce all contributing to the common weal (21:26–27). The notion of bringing good things into the city (21:26) suggests gratitude, reciprocity, and dependence. We have been told that "the nations will walk by its light" (21:24). This, surely, is not only physical light, or some source of renewable energy that is much in demand in the world today. Above all, it is the light of revelation: "for the glory of God illuminates it, and its lamp is the Lamb" (21:23).

**The New Jerusalem**

| Symbol | Meaning 1 | Meaning 2 |
|---|---|---|
| city | people | culture, history, redemption |
| bride | people | trust, intimacy, consummation, joy |
| glory of God | revelation of God complete | no more misrepresentation |
| wall and gates | people | story of Israel and its witness |
| foundation | people | story of apostles and their witness |
| size | people | all as the Most Holy; all space sacred |
| temple absent and superfluous | God's unmediated presence | revelation completed |
| sun and moon superfluous | God and the Lamb the source of light | revelation completed |
| gates open day and night | end of danger | end of lies |

This enables a community of truthful speech, peace, and plenitude. The prophetic vision has been actualized. "Nations shall come to your light, and kings to the brightness of your dawn" (Isa. 60:3; Bauckham 1993a, 313). John brings in a third pertinent negative for emphasis, and who can blame him? What will *not* enter this community are the things that brought turmoil in the first place. The corroding influence has many names and more than one mode of operation, but one thing is clear as crystal (21:18, 21): **And into her will not enter . . . anyone who . . . promotes a lie** (21:27).

## Theological Issues

Among the books in the NT, Revelation by itself represents one of the most far-reaching correctives to the Christian theological tradition. Earth, not heaven, is journey's end, and the usual one-way passage *from* earth *to* heaven is in this book turned upside down. The traffic at the very end goes *from* heaven *to* earth, first when the Holy City comes down, and then God, too, comes to earth (21:1–4). The vision of the new earth is more than a feast of materiality and earthiness. It also makes for a moment of theological reflection. Which is greater, human beings going up to heaven or God coming down to earth? By this criterion Revelation's embrace of materiality is less impressive—and a lesser corrective—than its vision of God.

### Matter and the New Creation

*"In this universe, space, time and matter are all mutually interlinked in the single package of general relativity. It seems reasonable to suppose that this linkage is a general feature of the Creator's will. If so, the new creation will also have its 'space' and 'time' and 'matter.' The most significant theological consequence of this belief is that there will be 'time' in the world to come."* (Polkinghorne 2002, 117)

If Revelation's embrace of materiality differs from the theological tradition, where do the chips fall with respect to suffering? In John's vision, "death will be no more nor grief nor wailing nor pain will be any more" (21:4). Is that the whole story or only one half? Is death *no more*—except in hell? Do grief and wailing and pain persist for all eternity *on the outside*? The theological tradition has been dis-affirming of materiality, but it has not held back with respect to suffering in the world to come. Could this be Revelation's second and weightiest corrective to the tradition, now with the promise that all suffering will come to an end? Cosmology, theology, and psychology will want to have a say, cosmology with the claim that there is no permanent *outside* in a cosmos where *all* space is to be sacred; theology with the claim that God brings an end to *all* grief; and psychology by safeguarding the connection between happiness and compassion. The idea that awareness of the suffering of others increases the bliss of the saved can hardly be correct, can it, despite the attestation of Thomas Aquinas (*Summa Theologiae* III, q. 94, art. 1)? "Blissful, in the kingdom of heaven, they will see the sufferings of the damned so that their bliss should be more delightful to them" (Nietzsche 1918, 33; Tonstad 2016a, 351). This view made Albert Camus (1991, 57) say that there "is no possible salvation for the man who feels real compassion." How Revelation is read on this question is no small matter.

A concern remains even if we conclude that Revelation envisions an end to suffering. Leonard Thompson (1990, 200) alleges two defects in the book. One assumed defect concerns the book's "cognitive exclusiveness," the claim that its vision and nothing else is the truth (22:18–19). The other alleged defect is that the cosmic dualism in Revelation is overcome by the defeat and demise of the hostile forces, not by reconciliation and reunion. Even if it is settled that Revelation does not predict an *everlasting* "outside," should a healthy and mature vision ensure that the outside be brought inside?

> We are dealing here in part with the place of revenge and retribution in the Book of Revelation—with the confidence that those outside the circle of true knowledge cannot succeed, that they must be outside the city gate and beyond the temple wall. . . . Is there hope for those outside? Is the city gate of the New Jerusalem closed forever on such people? Can God be all in all if the gate is closed for eternity? (L. Thompson 1990, 200)

This view constrains the options, offering "revenge and retribution" on one side, not revelation and implosion of the opposing side, as in a more nuanced reading. Still, is there a defect in John's vision of God's love? Did his redemptive imagination fail by letting the forces of evil come to grief in an orgy of self-destruction *outside* the city (14:20; 20:7–9)? This concern invites a broad discussion about love, freedom, and responsibility in God's economy. Revelation's representation tracks closely with the conflict in the Gospel of John. There, Jesus describes his opponent as "a liar and the father of the lie" (John 8:44), a term that makes "the lie" seem an inseparable and permanent resident in the person, an element integral to his identity. Indeed, says Jesus, "there is no truth in him" (John 8:44). These are strong words concerning the reality against which Jesus is fighting. *They come with the implication that the liar is unable to stop promoting the lie.* The person thus described is also "a murderer from the beginning" (John 8:44). "The lie" and its promotion are inseparable from a disposition to kill whatever stands in its way. And what is God's remedy? "Now is the critical moment of this world, now the prince of this world will be cast out," Jesus says in John (12:31; cf. Rev. 12:7–12). "Cast out" he will be, but the means by which "the prince of this world" will be "cast out" is contrary to expectations. "And I—when I am lifted up—I will draw all people to myself" (John 12:32). "Lifted up" is in Johannine diction what happens when Jesus dies on the cross as a victim of violence. God overcomes "the father of the lie" not by killing the liar but by allowing the liar to kill.

To call this surprising and *counterintuitive* would be an understatement. John is not the only one to place the violent death of Jesus in a cosmic perspective. Paul does it, too, and he does it in a context that compares "wisdom" in familiar Greco-Roman terms, as philosophy and eloquence, to the "wisdom" of his message (1 Cor. 1:18–2:13).

> Yet among the mature [*teleios*] we do speak wisdom. But this is not a wisdom of this age or of the rulers of this age, who are rendered powerless. No, we speak God's wisdom, in a mystery hidden to ordinary sight, which God determined before the ages for our glory. None of the rulers of this age comprehended this. For if they had comprehended, they would not have crucified the Lord of glory. (1 Cor. 2:6–8, my trans.)

"The ruler of this world" in John (12:31) and "the rulers of this age" in Paul's letter describe the same category of being. "The rulers" were caught off guard and defeated by the very means by which they intended to overcome "the Lord of glory" (Conzelmann 1975, 63). Revelation portrays incomprehension not only in the camp opposed to God but also on God's side in the conflict (Rev. 5:3). Similarly, when the rider on the white horse appears late in the story, "he has a name written that no one knows but himself" (19:12). States of incomprehension in the realm of created beings do not relate to insignificant matters. Reason finds itself stymied by God's disposition. The promoter of "the lie" is stymied, too, because his pursuit of self-interest cannot fathom the depth of God's self-giving.

And yet, as we see in Revelation's account of the final battle (20:7–10), there is no change of heart on the part of Satan, no backing down, no evidence of remorse, only one more attempt to conquer "the camp of the believers and the beloved city" (20:9). His disposition sets up the last "outside" before the story ends (21:27; 22:15). It is as though we hear him say, like Adolf Hitler, "If I were to come to an agreement with Russia [God] today, I would attack them [God] again tomorrow—I can't help myself" (Fest 2005, 134). "The lie" will cease when the liar does. It is not Revelation's smallest surprise that the Deceiver is brought down by his own action, as this commentary contends.

A story is not the same as an explanation. And yet we are left to derive "explanations" from the story that is told. When Leonard Thompson (1990, 200) spots a defect in Revelation's final vision, an alleged failure to bring the outside to the inside, he faults the story. I have pondered his objection attentively and concluded, respectfully, that the defect is not in the story. It must be on our side. John and his NT allies tell a story that is a challenge to reason but not because it shows a failure of love. The wisdom accessible to "the mature" (1 Cor. 2:6) surpasses normal thought. It is trite to say again that Revelation's ending shows how love works in *freedom*. Let less be said by specifying what it does *not* show. It does *not* demonstrate the failure of wisdom, it does *not* represent an immature vision, and it does *not* prove a deficit of love.

In Revelation's vision of the end, God extends an invitation to the thirsty: "I will give to the thirsty from the spring of the water of life as a gift" (21:6). *Thirst* is a metaphor for *need*. But can *need* be all? Is there not also the need for virtue, faithfulness, courage, and perseverance? *Need*—and acknowledgment of need—plays out in a context. Society is under siege from influences that are hostile to God. The adversary is especially unfriendly to "the need for God" as God is revealed in the Lamb that was "killed with violence" (5:6). *Need* alone suffices before God, but the conflict demands of each person to choose sides and take a stand even to the point of paying for the commitment with one's life (12:11; 13:10; 14:3–4). This does not mean that *need* was insufficient or that "the one who wins the war" is someone other than the person said to be thirsty (21:6–7). Still, need is discovered, admitted, and held on to against forces determined to keep human beings in the dark, oblivious to need and unmindful of opportunity. There is an implied contrast between "the one who wins the war" and the one who doesn't win. The trait that counts is unusual and unique with respect to lists of vices and virtues in the NT. David E. Aune (1996–98, 1131) says that the list in Rev. 21:8 "has parallels with the Ten Commandments and traditional applications of the Ten Commandments, including other early Christian vice lists." This is true, but the differences matter more: "the two words *deiloi* [δειλοί] and *apistoi* [ἄπιστοι], 'cowards' and 'unbelievers,' occur only here in Revelation and are found in no other vice lists in the *NT*" (Aune 1996–98, 1131). Why are these traits included, and why do they rise to the top of the list? The best answer must be that courage in some form is essential. "Rather than beginning with classic vices, John leads with cowardice and faithlessness, which were issues for Christians facing both overt and subtle pressures to compromise their commitments" (Koester 2014, 809).

We need not look far for clues to how this works in real life. In the aftermath of World War II, the Protestant pastor Martin Niemöller (1892–1984) wrote these well-known words.

> First they came for the Communists, and I did not speak out—Because
> I was not a Communist.
> Then they came for the Trade Unionists, and I did not speak out—
> Because I was not a Trade Unionist.
> Then they came for the Jews, and I did not speak out—Because I was
> not a Jew.
> Then they came for me—and there was no one left to speak for me.

In the early Nazi years, Niemöller was a supporter of Hitler and a shareholder in the anti-Semitic sentiments that carried Hitler's movement forward. But his repentance was heartfelt, and it came early enough to land him in Hitler's prison camps for seven years. Someone to take a stand, someone to speak out, someone to withhold allegiance—history has time and again asked for such a person. Revelation does too (18:1–4; 21:7–8). Saul Friedländer's (2008, xxi) verdict on European sentiments before and during the Holocaust years serves as another example that the problem is less a failure of virtue before *God* than failure of commitment in the presence of *reality*.

> Not one social group, not one religious community, not one scholarly institution or professional association in Germany and throughout Europe declared its solidarity with the Jews (some of the Christian churches declared that converted Jews were part of the flock, up to a point). . . . Thus Nazi and related anti-Jewish policies could unfold to their most extreme levels without the interference of any major countervailing interests.

Figure 19. Undeserved adulation. Women celebrate Adolf Hitler with uncritical acclaim (1937).

Figure 20. A lone dissenter appears among the men saluting Adolf Hitler (1936). Do you see him?

Here, the enabler of evil ends up in the same category as the initiator, and the bystander becomes a participant precisely for imagining that it is enough to stand on the sidelines. Certain situations do not offer the option of neutrality, with Revelation as another case in point.

In the first picture reproduced here, we see a crowd of people enthusiastically offering their allegiance to one of the most notorious leaders ever to appear in human history. All seem to do it, with no exceptions.

In the second picture, all do it too, with one exception. He stands in the middle of the crowd with his arms crossed. Is he merely indifferent? Is he amused? Or is he aghast at the spectacle, with its mind-numbing discrepancy between the intensity of devotion and the unworthiness of its object?

Could he be our role model for the need to take a stand that links a person's sense of need with a certain kind of courage? The verdict of history clouds our judgment of these scenes because at that time the object's unworthiness was to many not a foregone conclusion. What is lacking is the stance of dissent. By these criteria the words "coward" and the "faithless" refer to a person who stays on the sidelines and who, fearing the cost of commitment, risks being swept up by the opposing side. Revelation's "vices" are to some extent variants of the theme struck by the first two. In light of the cosmic conflict, certainty of healing at the end does not cancel the need for commitment.

# Revelation 22:1–21

## *The Healing of the Nations*

**Introductory Matters**

The last chapter in Revelation repeats things mentioned in the next-to-last chapter, but the repetitions are significant expansions, and much is new.

The first five verses represent a new vision (Rissi 1972, 80). Three things stand out in these verses. First, there is a center, a *middle* (Rev. 22:1–2). This is reminiscent of the garden of Eden in Genesis, the original book of "sacred geography" in the Bible (Gen. 2:8–14; 3:1; Fishbane 1979, 112; Wyatt 1981, 10). Eden had a *garden* with two unique trees and a *stream* flowing "as from a navel" into the surrounding world (Fishbane 1979, 112). In one compressed representation, "Eden" was like a mountain, "the mountain of God," and "the covering cherub" was walking back and forth *"in the middle"* (Ezek. 28:12–14; cf. NKJV). The cherub's presence "in the middle" came to an end; he was barred "from the mountain of God" and banished *"from the middle"* (Ezek. 28:16, my trans.; Greenberg 1997, 579). By this criterion "the middle" is the sacred center and ground zero in the cosmic conflict.

Second, it is not the *location* of the garden "in the east" that matters (Gen. 2:8). The term taken as a signifier of location is better seen as a *temporal* reference: "in the beginning" (Stordalen 2008, 41). The temporal emphasis puts the garden and its life-giving *middle* at the beginning and the end of the story. Genesis and Revelation are the bookends of the Bible by their place in the canon and similarities that lie on the surface, but they are thematic next-door neighbors in a deep sense. Genesis transmits to Revelation the *problem* that must be solved, and Revelation broadcasts to the world how God did it. Revelation's ending cannot be understood apart from the dispute that blights the beginning (Tõniste 2016, 132–98).

Third, the story in Revelation unfolds against the horizon of *promise* and *expectation* in Genesis. This contrasts with the blunt assertion that Gen. 3 is "one of the most non-eschatological texts of the Bible" (Schmid 2008, 74). In the noneschatological scenario, "the angels with their sword stand for the conviction that the paradise is lost forever," as Konrad Schmid puts it. "There is no way back, never ever" (Schmid 2008, 74). Reve-

> **Genesis and Revelation: Distant Bookends *and* Next-Door Neighbors**
>
> Space: all eyes on *the middle*
> Time: *beginning* reflected in the *ending*
> Plot: *conflict, crisis,* and *closure*
> Story: *pledge* and *attainment*

lation, however, builds on the markers of hope already evident in Genesis (3:15). *There is a way back precisely in the text from which John draws his most important images.* John is a keen reader of the ancient texts, not missing that God's speech to the serpent in Genesis promises reversal of the loss and defeat for the serpent (Gen. 3:15; Rev. 12:1–5). John is not the first person in the Bible to see it that way (Isa. 65:25) although he will be the one to track it to completion in greater detail than any other writer in the Bible.

The epilogue comes with a smattering of repetitions (22:6–21), not from the previous chapter this time but from the beginning of the book (1:1, 3, 4, 9, 18). The chapter has a final blast of allusions to the OT. At the very end, the boundary between the speaking voices blurs, but it is possible to distinguish between the voice of the accompanying angel (22:10–11) and Jesus (22:12, 13, 16). When "the Spirit" speaks, God must be speaking, and when "the bride" joins in, God and the believing community are joined in the final mission outreach in the canon (22:17). Revelation's ending has the feel of direct, unmediated speech from God. If the message of the Bible could be condensed into one word, we have it here, when "the Spirit and the bride say 'Come'" (22:17).

## Tracing the Train of Thought

### The Means of Healing (22:1–5)

**22:1–5.** John's tour of the world to come continues, still with one of the bowl angels as his guide (21:9). **And the angel showed me the river of the water of life, bright as crystal, flowing from the throne of God and of the Lamb** (22:1). First on the final tour, the angel stops at the *river*, "the river of the water of life" (22:1). This scene makes *life* the heartbeat of God's economy. A river "bright as crystal" adds *light* to life. Such a river must be beautiful, too, a *see-through* river that cannot be depicted in words except to say that we have entered a world without defects. John "cannot have the river flowing from the temple since there is no temple in the New Jerusalem (21:22), so he substitutes the throne of God for the temple" (Aune 1996–98, 1177). The effect of this is to *personalize* life and light and beauty. The stream "flowing from the throne of God and of the Lamb" specifies that God is the source of the life and the light—God as God is revealed in "the Lamb." While life and light are evident in the economy of creation, the link to God is less explicit in Genesis: "A stream would rise from the earth, and water the whole face of the ground" (Gen. 2:6, 10).

Familiar material elements convey a theological message. **In the middle of her street and the river** [that is, in the middle], **on either side is the tree of life making twelve kinds of fruits, producing its fruit every month, and the leaves of the tree are for the healing of the nations** (22:2). The items on the guided tour are like—but also unlike—the story at the beginning (Gen. 2:1–14). What is the most striking difference? There are differences aplenty at the level of detail, but the main contrast is the *representation*. In Genesis, the serpent professed to see a defective world (Gen. 3:1). Revelation returns to the garden of Eden, or better, it *returns* the Garden. But it finds nothing to support the serpent's fault-finding view. Sights bursting with life and plenitude rebut the serpent's assertions: *what he said must have been false!* God's world projects gift, not prohibition; plenitude, not restriction; abundance, not deprivation (22:1–2). When we keep this in mind, we understand better why Jesus calls his opponent "the father of *the* lie" in the Gospel of John (John 8:44, my trans.; Tonstad 2008b) and why Revelation names him "the Mudslinger and . . . the deceiver of the whole world" (12:9; 20:2). Revelation's description is a damning verdict on the serpent's negative representation.

John's final vision is also influenced by the life-giving river and the life-mediating trees in Ezekiel's vision of healing (Ezek. 47:1–12; Rev. 22:2). This river begins as a modest trickle. One thousand cubits from the site of origin—equal to five hundred yards—it is only ankle-deep (Ezek. 47:3). A thousand cubits more, it is knee-deep; another thousand cubits, and the water is up to the waist (Ezek. 47:4); a thousand cubits more, "and it was a river that I could not cross, for the water had risen; it was deep enough to swim in, a river that could not be crossed" (Ezek. 47:5). This is strange because there are no tributaries, and the river courses through arid land (Block 1998, 692). A river with no tributaries should not get deeper and wider downstream than it is at the source. When we add this image to the life and light that come from God, the life is not static and inert. It is an expanding, *life-generating*, burgeoning reality (Ezek. 47:8–10).

It is wise to move slowly through these scenes. The journey will soon be over, and there is no need to rush for that reason alone. More important, the story that is ending requires close attention to how the account began. Thus, when John mentions the tree "in the middle," the bells of memory start ringing. Earlier in the book, the throne of God is located "in the middle" (Rev. 4:2–6; 6:6), and "the Lamb" is "in the middle of the throne" (5:6; 7:17). Here, "the throne" can be nowhere else than "in the middle" (22:1–2), but now "the tree of life" is also "in the middle" (22:2). "The middle" is getting crowded because "her street and the river" are "in the middle" (22:2), and "the tree of life" that is "in the middle" occupies both banks "of the river of life."

These phrases put the focus on the trees in the garden of Eden in Genesis.

> Out of the ground the LORD God made to grow every tree that is pleasant to the sight and good for food, the tree of life also *in the middle* of the garden, and the tree of knowledge of good and evil. (Gen. 2:9, my trans.; cf. Rev. 22:2)

> The woman said to the serpent, "We may eat of the fruit of the trees in the garden, but God said, 'You shall not eat of the fruit of the tree that is *in the middle of the garden*, nor shall you touch it, or you shall die.'" (Gen. 3:2–3)

In Genesis, "the tree of life" is located "in the middle of the garden" (Gen. 2:9). Also in the middle is "the tree of knowledge of good and evil" (Gen. 2:9; 3:3). Revelation has not lost interest in "the middle" (Rev. 22:2). Where, however, is "the tree of knowledge"?

Norman Habel (2011, 54) explains that "'good and evil' does not refer specifically to an ability to discern morally between good and evil but is an idiom that means more broadly 'knowing everything' about a subject: knowing the 'good and bad' or both sides of the issue." By this criterion, more than "forbidden knowledge" is in view: the warning was meant to protect against a bad experience. In a more abstract application, the prospect of "comprehensive knowledge" entails the temptation of rising above the limitations of finitude and erasing the difference between the creature and the Creator.

Nahum Sarna (1966, 27), reflecting a Jewish tradition, argues that the Bible relegates *the tree of life* to an insignificant role. In his view, Scripture "dissociates itself completely" from the implied preoccupation with immortality associated with this tree (Sarna 1966, 27). Instead, the concern of the story in Genesis "is with the issues of living rather than with the question of death, with morality rather than mortality." By this criterion, it is the tree of knowledge that matters, *and this tree is not mentioned in Revelation*. But the either-or proposition is not shared by everyone. "I have argued, then, that the central theme of the story of the garden of Eden, along with the theme of knowledge of good and evil, is the theme of immortality," says James Barr (1992, 14). By this criterion, pride of place goes to the tree of life. The two trees in Genesis are in this line of thought assigned distinctive meanings. In the realm of experience, *morality* (the tree of knowledge) will by Sarna's criterion be more important than *immortality* (the tree of life). If he is correct, why does Revelation put "the tree of life" at the center while saying nothing about "the tree of knowledge"? Does this book value *immortality* more than *morality*?

Such questions do not become less critical when we consider how these trees have been understood in the Christian tradition. To the first Christians, the tree of knowledge represented freedom (Pagels 1985, 67–99). Origen (185–254 CE), the greatest Christian apologist before Augustine, held strongly to this view. He wrote that God "will subject all rational creatures to himself through *persuasion*, not through constraint, and thus bring their freedom to fulfillment in obedience to the divine will" (Sachs 1993, 628). Freedom, as Origen saw it, is "the most general of all the laws of the universe" (Daniélou 1955, 205–6).

Gregory of Nyssa (ca. 334–ca. 394 CE) was a great admirer of Origen, but he did not share Origen's regard for "the tree of knowledge" or the tenor of freedom that belongs to it. Gregory wrote at a time when Christianity was poised to become the religion of the state. The change of fortune for the Christians had an impact on exegesis. Gregory catches the transition at a critical point. To Gregory (*Hom. Cant.*, preface, GNO 6:10.17–11.5), "the tree of knowledge" faces geometric obstacles. It is impossible to have *two* trees "in the middle."

> But if another center is set alongside the center, the circle must necessarily be shifted along with its center, with the result that the former center is no longer the midst. Since, then, the Garden in that place is one, why does the text say that each of the trees is to be treated as something separate, and that both of them are at the center, when the account which tells us that the works of God are "very good" teaches that the killer-tree is no part of God's planting? (Norris 2002, 220; cf. Ska 2008, 10)

Thus begins a subtle denigration of "the tree of knowledge" in Christian theology. Not only will Gregory push "the tree of knowledge" off-center. He also stigmatizes it as "the killer-tree." He follows through by claiming that this tree "is no part of God's planting." By his terms alone, Gregory intimates that "the tree of knowledge" is a defect in God's creation. This trend accelerates with Augustine (354–430 CE). Like Gregory, he made the trees in the garden of Eden his subject matter, and he offers options that revise the script. "The tree of life is the holy of holies, Christ; the tree of the knowledge of good and evil, the will's free choice" (*Civ.* 13.21). The shift in emphasis means a 180-degree turn for theology. The serpent tempts Adam with the lure of liberty, and the forbidden fruit symbolizes "personal control over one's own will," says Augustine (*Civ.* 13.21). The change in wording may seem small, but the change in meaning is dramatic. "What earlier apologists celebrate as *God's* gift to humankind—free will, liberty, autonomy, self-government—Augustine characterizes in surprisingly negative terms" (Pagels 1985, 78; cf. Clark 1992, 250). The new perspective coincides in time with political changes. The church, long a threatened minority, was by now in the driver's seat. Augustine revised the map of interpretation to fit the new political landscape. The change happened without apparent awareness of its magnitude, as though, from the point of view of the church, it was a win-win situation. To one historian, it meant "the capitulation of all who held to the classical proclamation concerning human freedom, once regarded as the heart of the Christian gospel" (Pagels 1985, 99). Theology would soon be reflected in policy (Tonstad 2016a, 9, 335–47) and was when the great theologian and apologist wrote "the only full justification, in the Early Church, of the right of the state to suppress non-Catholics" (P. Brown 1967, 235).

"The tree of knowledge," not "the tree of life," is at the heart of these defining and course-setting reflections. There is also a missing element. Neither Gregory nor Augustine pay attention to how the tree is represented by the serpent (Gen. 3:1). In hindsight, their account of the tree resembles the serpent's view. The serpent uses the tree as his *instrument*, but he must *misrepresent* God to make it work (Tonstad 2016a, 87–103). Gregory cannot make "the tree of knowledge" a "killer-tree" without distorting the original meaning. We can only guess at the motives for Gregory's omission, but the hole in his account cannot be covered up. His depiction of the fateful moment in the Garden falls short because "its plausibility depends on the one thing Gregory cannot allow; namely, the existence *apart from human choice* of some factor or reality that by its intrinsic magnetism or attractiveness deceives the mind, overwhelms the will, and so orients human loving away from the authentic Good" (Norris 2002, 239–40). Gregory has inexplicably left out the nonhuman voice and the deception that recasts the tree as a negative. Revelation's glimpses of the future world come full circle—to the God who put "the tree of knowledge" in the Garden (Gen. 2:9), to the serpent who made the tree a pretext for a reproachful view of God (Gen. 3:1), and to the contest over the meaning of "the tree of knowledge" in the theological tradition.

Was the tree a "killer-tree" and therefore a mistake (Gregory of Nyssa)? Has *immortality* suspended *morality*, at least in the sense that *morality* in Revelation is off-center and unseen (cf. Sarna 1966, above)? Has God, in Paradise Regained, acknowledged that a mistake was made at the beginning and taken measures to correct it? On the final leg of John's tour, "the river of the water of life" is there, "in the middle," and there, still "in the middle," is "the tree of life" (Rev. 22:2). Where is "the tree of knowledge"? If the tree is absent in the world to come, does it follow that God demotes freedom?

Allusions are pliable elements in a text, but it is in the nature of allusions to economize, leaving to the reader to remember and supply more than the textual echo says. Nonmention of "the tree of knowledge" does not mean that it has been discarded or that the world to come prioritizes *immortality* at the expense of *morality*. Christians did not make a mistake when they saw "the tree of knowledge" as a "freedom tree," and nonmention does not mean that freedom has been downgraded. Perceptions of the *single* tree straddling "the river of life"—a tree that is "in the middle" and "on either side of the river" (22:2)—are completed in the imagination by uniting the two trunks at the top. Gregory of Nyssa's geometric quandary of *two* trees in the middle can be solved, and with it the suspicion that the second tree is a "killer-tree" (Habel 2011, 54). But the second tree has run its course as "the tree of knowledge of good and evil." *Oneness* of representation broadcasts *oneness* of experience under another depiction. With an eye to the story in Genesis, it may be possible to see "the tree of knowledge" as a *morality tree* and "the tree of life" as a separate *immortality tree* or to see the former as a *freedom tree* and the latter as a *life tree*. But the single tree resists sharp distinctions: it is not possible to separate *morality* from *immortality*, and it is even harder to drive a wedge between *life* and *freedom*. By these criteria, love and life and freedom are seamless qualities in God's economy.

James Barr (1992, 14) did not think much of the story in Genesis, but he describes its take-home message well: "The person who comes out of this story (Gen. 3) with a slightly shaken moral record is, of course, God." John has not overread or overinterpreted Genesis on this point. Like the discussion of the meaning of "the tree of knowledge" in Genesis (3:1), *Revelation makes representation of God its main concern.* The terms of human existence laid down earlier are not repudiated or changed, but the serpent's negative representation of God is silenced. All that is necessary for a life of dignity and plenitude, including notions like morality and mortality, or freedom and responsibility, or love and life, are assumed in the pictures on John's canvas. His life-and-light-infused imagery silences even the possibility of a negative representation.

"Healing" is Ezekiel's gift to Revelation (47:1–12), but John incorporates it as a homegrown topic. Where *healing* is needed, the underlying problem must be medical, to be distinguished from a problem that is primarily moral or legal. *Healing* and the need for healing assume *disease.* Where there is illness, a person faces contingencies beyond his/her control, and the diseased person is better seen as a victim than a villain. Conversely, a problem defined in moral terms lays out a person's life along an axis of culpability and guilt. In a legal framework, culpability looms even larger. Revelation is not indifferent to moral or legal categories, but "the tree of life" does not only address the problem of *mortality*, and "the tree of knowledge" is not simply a "morality tree." In the homestretch of Revelation, the horizon is *brokenness* and *healing*, not sin and punishment. Among items broken and in need of repair are not only human beings and the world. There is a sense in which *God* also was "broken" (Gen. 3:1–6), and this part of the brokenness is not lost on Revelation. God is at the center of its message, in awareness that nothing is more in need of healing than humanity's view of God (Rev. 22:4).

Much of this is evident in the echoes of Ezekiel's river in Revelation, a stream that also has ecological meaning. Despite running into salt-infested land, "I saw on the bank of the river a great many trees on the one side and on the other," says Ezekiel (47:7). When the river enters the sea of the Arabah, described as "the sea of stagnant waters" (47:8), "its waters are healed" (47:8 NKJV), and "everything will live where the river goes" (Ezek. 47:9). The result bears reading unabridged:

> On the banks,
> on both sides of the river,
> there will grow
> all kinds of trees for food.
> Their leaves will not wither
> nor their fruit fail,
> but they will bear fresh fruit
> every month,
> because the water for them
> flows from the sanctuary.
> Their fruit will be for food,
> and their leaves for healing. (Ezek. 47:12)

In these scenes theology brings hope to ecology, and ecology mediates healing. This is hopeful for broken human beings, and it is hopeful for the earth. Above all, it corrects entrenched misperceptions of God (Gen. 3:1). In a world in need of healing, the God of Revelation is a Healer.

Why, however, does John say that "the leaves of the tree are for the healing *of the nations*"? Interpreters struggle with this detail (Rev. 22:2). "The allusion is simply mechanical, however, since there is no real place in the eschatological scheme of Revelation for 'the healing of the nations' construed as their conversion," says David E. Aune (1996–98, 1178). This is not a good explanation for a writer who is as careful as John. If this were strictly a vision of the future, there should be no need for healing, and "the nations" would be an anachronistic concept (Mounce 1977, 387). Somewhat better is the suggestion that "the glory of the age to come is necessarily portrayed by means of imagery belonging to the present age" (Mounce 1977, 387). Ranko Stefanovic (2009a, 604) suggests that the imagery "refers figuratively to the removal of all national and linguistic barriers and separation." From the vantage point of present reality, the leaves of the tree "will heal all wounds—racial, ethnic, tribal, or linguistic—that have torn and divided humanity for ages" (Stefanovic 2009a, 604).

These are sensible suggestions, but they do not take advantage of the *nonmechanical* option that lies close at hand. Ezekiel is not singing solo in Revelation's last vision. Here, at the point of climax, Isaiah joins him in a duet that is poignant, rousing, and *revelatory*.

"The nations" echoes Isaiah, and it is close to a theme word. The importance of this word is not lessened by finding it in an Isaianic echo that underlies Revelation's most important scene (Rev. 5:5–6; Isa. 11:1–10). An array of texts show that "the nations" matter in Isaiah.

> **"The Nations"**
>
> • Echo of Isaiah
> • Same revealer
> • Same emphasis on revelation
> • Same focus on healing

A shoot shall come out from the stump of Jesse, and a branch shall grow out of his roots. (Isa. 11:1)

On that day, the root of Jesse shall stand as a signal to the peoples; *the nations* [Hb. *gôyim*; Gk. *ethnōn*] shall inquire of him, and his dwelling shall be glorious. (Isa. 11:10)

I have given you as a covenant to the people, a light to *the nations* [Hb. *gôyim*; Gk. *ethnōn*]. (Isa. 42:6)

I will give you as a light to *the nations* [Hb. *gôyim*; Gk. *ethnōn*], that my salvation may reach to the end of the earth. (Isa. 49:6)

See, my servant . . . shall startle many *nations* [Hb. *gôyim*; Gk. *ethnē*]; kings shall shut their mouths because of him; for that which had not been told them they shall see, and that which they had not heard they shall contemplate. (Isa. 52:15)

*Nations* [Hb. *gôyim*; Gk. *ethnē*] shall come to your light, and kings to the brightness of your dawn. (Isa. 60:3; cf. 60:5, 11; 66:12, 19)

All of Isaiah envisions a mission of revelation *to the nations*, echoes of which exercise a commanding influence on Revelation (Bauckham 1993a, 307–18; Koester 2014, 824). As we have seen over and over, this Healer is the figure who appears "in the middle" of the heavenly council (Rev. 5:6–7). He is the one who "has won the war to open the scroll and its seven seals" (5:5). He is the mediator of revelation (5:6), the promised Revealer (Isa. 11:1), and the hope of *the nations* (Isa. 11:10).

Isaiah describes not only *what* "the root of Jesse" will do or *how* he will do it but also *that he will succeed* (Isa. 11:10; 49:6; 52:15; 60:3). Like the river in

Ezekiel's vision, the Revealer in Isaiah is commissioned to accomplish things that seem to exceed his resources. When his mission is completed, no one will "hurt or destroy on all my holy mountain; for the earth will be full of the knowledge of the LORD as the waters cover the sea" (Isa. 11:9).

"*The nations*" are an integral part of the vision. "On that day, the root of Jesse shall stand as a signal to the peoples; *the nations* [Hb. *gôyim*; Gk. *ethnē*] shall turn to him *inquisitively*, and his dwelling shall be glorious" (Isa. 11:10, my trans.; Wildberger 1991, 461). In the Hebrew text, the nations [*gôyim*] flock to the root of Jesse with their questions; in the Septuagint, the nations [*ethnē*] will pin their hopes [*elpiousin*] on him. In both scenarios, *the nations are bewildered, at a loss, and in a state of need.* Against this background, "the healing of the nations" *is a vision of mission and of mission accomplished.* Jesus, "the root and the descendant of David" (Rev. 22:16; Isa. 11:1, 10), did not go back on his commitment to bring healing to the earth. The nations [Gk. *ethnē*] and the coastlands that were waiting for God's revelation have not been waiting in vain (Isa. 42:4; cf. Tonstad 2016b, 350–83).

And yet the mission is not only a matter of human *need*. God's intent at creation does not unfold according to a scenario of *need* only (Gen. 2:1–3). In Revelation, God's intent is brought to completion in the announcement that "the dwelling place of God is among human beings. . . . God will dwell with them, . . . and God himself will be with them" (Rev. 21:3; cf. Moltmann 1996, 261–67). It is stupendously kind of God to make this move, and it must be in character for God to be kind. But the last part of the text in Isaiah is not only concerned about *human* need. The concluding sentence describes the "resting place" of the one who rests and the "rest" God gives to the restless (Isa. 11:10; Hb. *mənūḥâ*; Gk. *anapausis*). For both sides of the coin of "rest," the prophet says that they "are glorious" (Isa. 11:10). According to the first option, God has needs too. When the revelation is completed and the earth full of the knowledge of the Lord, there shall be a homecoming for God: in Jewish thought God's wandering is over. *Rest* [*mənūḥâ*] is the presence and participation of God with creation. This conception of rest is integral to the theology and meaning of the Sabbath (Wirzba 2006, 32–34) and the climax of Revelation (Rev. 21:3; 22:3). God's need has been met, and it is "glorious."

*All* (that is) accursed [*pan katathema*] will not be any more can also be rendered *nothing* accursed will be any more (22:3a). Echoes of Genesis are again unmistakable. "Cursed are you," God says to the serpent (Gen. 3:14). "Cursed is the ground because of you," God explains to Adam and Eve (3:17). These are not penal reactions but descriptions of the state that came about because of views promoted and choices made (Combs 1988; Tonstad 2016b, 192, 249). All this is reversed down to the item most *accursed: the serpent's misrepresentation of the divine command* (Gen. 3:1). Where the scope is *all*, where *nothing* is excepted, the implied spatial limitation in the NRSV is unwarranted: "Nothing accursed will be found *there* any more" (Rev. 22:3). The curse will not be found *there* or anywhere else. The curse that is so intimately related to the serpent and the accursed falsehood means that the serpent is included in what "will not be any more" (22:3; Isa. 65:25). How this happens has been told already (20:1–10). When we gather the threads, there is symmetry between the beginning (Genesis) and the ending (Revelation), the problem and the solution, the distortion and the right-making.

**But the throne of God and of the Lamb will be in it, and his servants will cherish** [*latreusousin*] **him** (22:3b). God's presence in the middle of the human community is now the chief attraction. The disposition of God's servants can be described as "serve" or "worship." Given all that has come to light, we should also include words like "revere," "admire," and "cherish." The words are devoid of obligation. God's servants are happy that God is in their midst.

The latter thought is confirmed in what best shows the magnitude of the reversal. **And they shall see God's face, and God's name shall be on their foreheads** (22:4). God's encounter with Moses is a striking contrast to the text in Revelation, "You cannot see my face; for no one shall see me and live" (Exod. 33:20, 23). But images from Genesis show the contrast most clearly:

And the man and his wife hid themselves from the presence of the LORD God among the trees of the garden. (3:8)

I heard the sound of you in the garden, and I was afraid, because I was naked; and I hid myself. (3:10)

In Genesis, human beings become hostages to distrust, alienation, fear, and the need to keep distance. In Revelation, the reversal is complete. To look into someone's face is a demanding form of intimacy. The *face* and the *name* are linked, suggesting that *seeing* and *knowing* are indistinguishable. What pertains to the outside (face) also applies to the inner reality (name). Crucially, God's name is not on *God's* forehead; "God's name shall be on *their* foreheads" (22:4). Knowing the other and likeness to the other go hand in hand. Ignorance and incapacity are overcome. "The phrase 'seeing the face of God' is a metaphor in Judaism and early Christianity for a full awareness of the presence and power of God" (Aune 1996–98, 1179). Revelation seen and appropriated has accomplished this in a way that resembles the Gospel of John (John 1:18; 5:37; 6:46; 14:9–10; Exod. 24:9–11; Num. 12:8). The text has rightly impressed readers. "Christ alone has seen God, and those who have seen Christ have the possibility of seeing God" (Aune 1996–98, 1180). Bauckham (1993b, 142) says it even better: "Nothing expresses this immediacy more evocatively than the words 'they shall see his face.'"

**And night shall be no more,** John continues, **and they do not have need of light of lamp or light of sun because the Lord God shall shine upon them** (22:5). Much of this has been said earlier (21:23, 25). The scene does not promise "energy independence" as such; there is no independence in relation to God. Nevertheless, light in a material sense is less important than the illumination that God brings. The knowledge imparted must be the basis for the promise that they will reign forever and ever (22:5). Here, too, Genesis can be seen in the distance. The dominion that was lost is reinstated (Gen. 1:28; Rev. 22:5).

### Epilogue and Invitation (22:6–19)

**22:6–19.** Normally an epilogue is expected to take readers into calmer waters. This is not the case in Revelation. Hardly any book in the Bible matches the emotional tenor of the closing verses of this book. There is first a "farewell scene" (22:6–9) involving John and the angel who has accompanied him through the last two chapters. But the departure point for the beginning of the epilogue must be set at Rev. 22:6. From here onward, the ending recapitulates the beginning of the book (Aune 1996–98, 1188).

**And he said to me, "These words are trustworthy and true, and the Lord, the God of the spirits of the prophets, sent his angel to show his servants what must soon take place"** (22:6). This is like the opening verse (1:1) except that it is *retrospective* and comes with an assertion regarding veracity. A question has been raised concerning the identity of the angel—whether this is the one who is implied at the beginning (1:1) or the one who has accompanied him in the New Earth vision (21:9–22:5). More important is the other voice that breaks in, showing that mediated, secondhand communication is coming to an end. **"Look! I am coming soon! Blessed is the one who keeps the words of the prophecy of this book!"** (22:7; cf. 1:7). A similar line was spoken in the third person at the beginning of the book (1:7). The person whose credibility is on the line is Jesus (22:7). To "keep" the book can be seen in ethical terms, as a form of practice, but it also means to "cherish" or "preserve." "Keeping" in the latter sense means to cherish and safeguard the revelation of God in Jesus (12:17; 14:12).

The voice breaking in from nowhere falls silent, leaving room for John to identify himself to his readers as he did at the beginning (22:8; cf. 1:9). His subsequent action is puzzling given that an almost identical exchange took place earlier (22:8–9; 19:10). Is the repetition proof of authorial carelessness, a feature of redaction, or simply evidence that John repeats the same mistake twice (19:10; 22:8–9)? Should not a person of his caliber and theological acumen know what counts as a legitimate object of worship? The two incidents are troubling, but there may be a point to them. Everyone is in this together, meaning that all are susceptible to undeserving objects of devotion. John may have been sincere in his inclination to "worship" the angel. If so, he deserved the rebuke—with the qualification that far less worthy objects of devotion have won acceptance. Or was he playacting, going through a certain motion for pedagogical reasons? I would like to think that this option explains the anomaly best.

From here on, the speaking subject can be either the angel or Jesus, but the next statement probably comes from the angel. **And he said to me, "Do not seal up the words of the prophecy of this book, for the time is near"** (22:10). Daniel's influence on Revelation runs deep, and here we see it again. The diplomat-in-exile had a message addressing a distant future, preserved in a book that was to be "sealed" and closed to comprehension (Dan. 8:26; 12:4, 9). By contrast, John assumes imminence (22:10; 1:3), and comprehension will not be deferred (22:10). This is followed by another instance of "temporal telescoping": events that are separate in time seem to occur simultaneously. **Let the wrongdoer still do wrong, and the unclean still be unclean, and the upright still behave redemptively, and the wholehearted still pursue wholeheartedness** (22:11). This could be the angel speaking (Aune 1996–98, 1217), but why does he speak like that? Is not his purpose to effect change? Should he not tell "the wrongdoer" to *stop* doing wrong and "the unclean" to *change* his/her ways? The pronouncement makes sense only if we place it *after the message has been proclaimed and completed its work*. The Revealer has spoken. Now he can rest his case. A deadline is not an arbitrary dramatization. It is meant to precipitate decisions. When the revelation has done its work, further delay is pointless. An idea of "closing time" has played in my memory ever since I went on my first trip abroad at the age of twenty. I was on my way to study in Beirut, Lebanon, traveling from Oslo, Norway, by way of several stopovers. The first leg on my trip was to Copenhagen, Denmark, and then Zurich, Switzerland. A voice on the speaker system called out that Scandinavian Airlines flight 601 bound for Copenhagen and Zurich was ready for boarding. The voice repeated the same message a couple of times. At last the message changed to something like this: "Final call, SK 601 for Copenhagen and Zurich, at gate 12." This was not a contrived whim by an unfriendly airline. The plane was leaving. If I wished to go, I would have to take the time window seriously. Revelation thus hints of a time after which things will stay the way they are; that hint is neither cynical nor hysterical. The voice we hear is caring, urgent, and persistent, but it is not codependent.

**"Look! I am coming soon, and my reward is with me, to give to each according to his/her work"** (22:12). This must be Jesus speaking, not the angel. "Reward" and "work" are fraught terms in theology even when Jesus is using them. A mercenary connotation is excluded: Jesus does not promise a bountiful payday for deeds that have accumulated merit. A reward can be a form of vindication. Perhaps a certain life commitment seemed ill advised and pointless? Perhaps the expectation that goodwill to come hangs by a thread? Perhaps a person's hope was dashed to pieces? Jesus speaks reassuringly of a hope that will not disappoint. A Johannine mode of thought is likely. To critics concerned about the "work" required of them, Jesus answers in John, "This is the work of God, that you believe in him whom he has sent" (John 6:29). This conception of "work" entails more than a certain form of piety or moral quality even though Jesus does not disparage either. Revelation's "work"—and there is one—centers on acceptance of "the testimony of Jesus" (6:9; 12:17; 14:12; 19:10).

**"I am the Alpha and the Omega, the first and the last, the beginning and the end"** (22:13). This is Jesus talking; it cannot be anyone else. Similar statements have occurred earlier (1:8; 21:6). The self-identification "the Alpha and the Omega" applies interchangeably to God and Jesus (Bauckham 1998a, 53–54; Aune 1996–98, 1219). The person who offers hope and healing to human beings is not a nobody. Ontology matters—no one else is in the same category—but character and disposition matter, too. Jesus wins in that category, as well. The one who is "the Alpha and the Omega, the first and the last, the beginning and the end" is also "the Lamb . . . looking as though it had been killed with violence" (5:6). He now rolls out the welcoming mat for the last time in the book, urging hearers to take advantage of the offer. **Blessed are those who wash their robes, so that they will have the right to the tree of life and may enter by the gates into the city** (22:14). A lot is compressed into this verse: it is the seventh and last beatitude in the book (Aune 1996–98, 1219), it makes access to the tree of life tremendously attractive, and it echoes the Good Shepherd passages in the Gospel of John (John 10:1, 2, 9). Entry "by the door"—or "by the gates"—is proof of legitimacy and good intentions (John 10:1; Rev. 22:14). The one who "climbs in by another way is a thief and a robber" (John 10:1; cf. NKJV). There is "a thief and a robber" in Revelation who cares nothing for entry "by the gates," but this city has no other avenue of entry. The beatitude deems those "who wash their robes" to be in an enviable state (22:14).

A robe is clothing worn on the outside, but in biblical thought it describes more than exterior matters (Zech. 3:1–4; Matt. 22:11–12; Rev. 19:8). A robe in need of washing must be dirty, and this admission requires introspection. In the "intermission" between the sixth and the seventh seals, Revelation calls attention to people "dressed in white" (7:13). John was told that these people "have washed their robes and made them white in the blood of the Lamb" (7:14). The answer provides "washing instruction" with respect to how to get a white robe, but the language is evocative, not analytical. The imagination has to do the rest. If the robe reveals the truth about the person, his/her inside as much as the outside, no single term will suffice for the process of washing. Words like "forgiveness" and "transformation" should come to mind; in theological speech, this would be "justification" and "sanctification." Psychologically, the imagery may be used to describe a new self-awareness. *I have not been the kind of person I should have been. I am not the kind of person I ought to be—or would like to be.* "The blood of the Lamb" is the prescribed remedy: it brings the possibility for *deep cleaning* and *deep healing*, but it is not a formulaic conception. To internalize and take possession of the meaning are a mysterious and personal matter.

The King James Version bypasses these challenges with the translation "Blessed are they that do his commandments" (22:14). This suggests a requirement for entry that condenses everything into an ethical standard. There is textual basis in Greek for this alternative, but it does not have the support of the best sources (Metzger 1994, 690). To "wash their robes" or "do his commandments" are verbally dissimilar options in English, but the translations derive from like-sounding words in Greek.

A simple moral equation does not do justice to the differences between those who "enter by the gates" and those who remain "outside" even if the description of the "outside" group seems heavy with moral liability. **Outside are the dogs and the sorcerers and the sexually immoral and the murderers and the idolaters, and everyone who loves and promotes a lie** (22:15). Nothing is flattering about the group "outside." Let the view stand that there is an "outside" for reasons that do not represent a defect in John's theology (contra L. Thompson 1990, 200). His rhetoric makes use of images that stir the viscera as much as the mind. A similar list has appeared earlier (21:8). "New to this list are dogs" (Koester 2014, 842). Roaming bands of dogs "outside the city" were a common sight in the ancient world—and in modern cities, too. These "dogs" are people, and the epitaph conveys contempt toward something seen as unclean. Stray dogs inside and outside the cities are unattached, ownerless animals, unloved and unloving, scrounging for something to eat, frightened and frightening. I saw my share of such dogs in Baghdad in better, prewar days when doing my morning run along the river Tigris during a six-week stay. On an unclaimed portion of land along the river was a band of large, roaming dogs. Their body language deepened my considerable fear of dogs. I was as scared of them on the first morning as on the last. Such a beast is also unattached theologically, a homeless creature in the most far-reaching sense of the word. A "theological" (as contrasted to a "moral") reading is also appropriate for the remaining characterizations. It is too simplistic to dismiss the description as a scene from the red-light district, from the crime-infested section of a large city, or from a legal no-man's-land like Guantanamo Bay. The "outside" group is better seen as ordinary people who, on the value scale of Revelation, are guilty of an extraordinarily serious sin: a person "who loves and promotes a lie" (22:15; cf. 21:8). When we complement this description with other images of what takes place "outside the city" (14:20; 19:15; 20:9; 21:8), the "outsiders" are not milling about in half-bored chaos. The most important complementary scene depicts a large army assembled from "the four corners of the earth," striding across "the broad plain of the earth" until they surround "the camp of the saints and the Beloved City" (20:8–9). The hostile forces "left out" are hell-bent on annihilating the city.

Little is left to say, but the best is saved for last. For the best, the address must be direct and personal, the words well chosen, and the emotional tenor unambiguous. It begins with the personal. "**I, Jesus, sent my angel to you with** this testimony for the churches. I am the root and the descendant of David" (22:16a–b; cf. 1:1–3). How does he do it? I mean, how does he manage to be personal and at the same time flash glimpses on the screen that summarize the entire book—all in one verse? Picking up themes announced at the beginning of the book, there is *Jesus*, as the source; the *angel*, as the messenger; the *testimony*, as the message; and *the churches*, as the recipients (1:1–3). But there is more. As "the root and the descendant of David," Jesus ensures fulfillment of the OT promise of perennial kingship for a "descendant of David" (2 Sam. 7:12–16; Ps. 89:3–4, 35–36; Isa. 9:7; 53:10; Jer. 23:5–6; 33:14–16), and he will, in the end, be king (Rev. 15:3; 19:16). It is not an error to put kingship in the picture, but Revelation makes "king" the lesser portfolio. In the original context in Isaiah, the shoot that "shall come out from the stump of Jesse" and the branch that "shall grow out of his roots" is most of all a *revealer* (Isa. 11:1–10). As Revealer, he breaks the seals (Rev. 5:5; 6:1–8:1). But he is also the content of the revelation, appearing "in the middle" as "a Lamb looking as though it had been killed with violence" (5:6). In this capacity, as *revealer*, Jesus is introduced as "the root of David" (5:5; Isa. 11:1, 10). His closing claim to being "the root and the descendant of David" recapitulates the most important part of the story.

There is another surprise. "I am . . . the bright morning star" (22:16c). For this to resonate, the field of vision cannot be limited to earthly politics and a Davidic line of succession. The scope must be cosmic, and there must be awareness of conflict. "The bright morning star" used to be the favored title for God's most illustrious creature (Isa. 14:12). The exquisite poem we have explored several times exclaims,

> How you are fallen from heaven,
> O Most Brilliant Star, son of the Morning! (Isa. 14:12, my trans.)

Revelation knows this figure well: his origin, background, fall from innocence, misrepresentation of God, and demise. No book appreciates as well that Lucifer, as "Most Brilliant Star," was a *revealer*, a person who knew how to represent God. *That* "Most Brilliant Star" is brilliant no longer; *that* "bright morning star" has flamed out like a meteor in the night (Rev. 9:1). Revelation applies the title that was *his* to Jesus, or rather, *Jesus* claims the title for himself. We can read his claim as a generic statement and still retain the sense that Jesus is the Revealer, "I am . . . the bright morning star" (22:16). But we can also—and we should—read it as a retrospective on the conflict fought over how God should be represented. If we take this route, we hear Jesus say with emphasis, "*I* am . . . the bright morning star" (22:16). *I*, not *he*.

Other voices have waited their turn. Now they speak up in an antiphony of proclamation, acclamation, and invitation that marks the high point in Revelation's astounding choreography. John retains control of the narration, but he cannot do this part by himself. There is direct speech—just one single verb in the imperative—but the voices exclaiming it are many. For this part only a performance in the community will do.

> And the Spirit and the bride say,
> "Come!"
> And let the one who hears say,
> "Come!"
> And the thirsty
> —let him/her come.
> And the one who would like to have it
> —let him/her take
> the water of life
> as a gift. (22:17)

The auditory aspiration of this verse exceeds the capacity of the imagination. "The Spirit" is a single, heavenly voice, the first one to speak. "The bride" is a collective, earthly voice, made up of people who know the score as well as the theological foundation underlying it. Together the single voice of "the Spirit" and the collective voice of "the bride" speak in the present tense. The present tense means an action that continues to be actualized *in the present*: it is a word heard *now*. The heavenly voice and the earthly voices come off the same page, but it is necessary to make a distinction and to lay out a temporal sequence to perceive that the word spoken by the single heavenly voice is received and amplified by the collective earthly voices: *"Come!"*

The vocabulary of the Bible encompasses many important words. Theology has many, too, some of them big words that are not used in everyday speech. Revelation knows the biblical vocabulary well. The nouns have had their turn—information, revelation, exposé, explanation, and clarification. The verbs, as a livelier order of speech, have had their turn, too. We have heard many of the important words, *Hear! Look!* and *Write!* along with lesser ones, such as *Wake up! Remember! Turn!* and *Keep!*

But here, at the book's closing, the word is *"Come!"* Quite likely the mind that authorized this to be the final word assumed that there would be hearing, looking, and writing, and—after that—discovery, understanding, and insight. Revelation attempts no quick fix or shortcut, but it has a conclusion and a final word. *"Come!"* is not the speech of a tongue-tied messenger who does not know what to say. *This* suitor knows exactly what to say, and he has "the bride" say it with him, compressing it into a simple, comprehensible proposition.

"The one who hears it" must be someone other than "the Spirit" or "the bride," but it is expected that he/she will say it, too, expanding the circle, turning up the volume, giving increased momentum to the cascade of influences that is in the making. Revelation is the most interactive and performative book of the canon (Vanni 1991; Kavanagh 1984). Its performative mode of communication, the explicit and dynamic dialogue, is meant to facilitate appropriation. At the far end of the vision is *participation* and even *vocation*. There is a charge to "the one who hears: let him *say*" (22:17). A vision of vocation is explicit, complete with a commission to go forth to the nations on a mission of healing in the world.

The Spirit: *"Come!"*
The bride (many): *"Come!"*
Those who hear (many): *"Come!"*

*"Come!"* is a word addressed specifically to the thirsty: "And the thirsty—let him/her come." Thirst, as we have seen, is existential, intuitive, and universal. It also reflects a need that does not easily break into intellectual propositions. This says a lot for one of the most intellectually demanding books in literature. While *thirst* expresses *need* at an elemental level, here it may be thirst brought about by revelation. The Bible is aware of fake healers and snake-oil salesmen who heal the wounds of humanity superficially (cf. Jer. 6:14; 8:11). In this sense, Revelation aims to relieve a need that *revelation* has created, and only the remedy found in Revelation can relieve the need.

This book ends at the level of *need* and in the currency of *need*. The exhortation to people to "wash their robes" comes with the risk of having to meet a standard to "make it" (22:14), but the closing invitation concentrates on *need* alone (22:17). For the person who has nothing but need to show for himself, the solution must come as a gift. And it does!

And the one who would like to have it
—let him/her take
the water of life
as a gift. (22:17)

Revelation's final call is not diminished by the sound of Isaiah's unwearied voice in the background, "Ho, everyone who thirsts, come to the waters; and you that have no money, come, buy and eat! Come, buy wine and milk without money and without price" (Isa. 55:1; cf. 44:3).

"The water of life" is a constituent of the world to come and an item beckoning from a point in the future (22:1–2), but Revelation broadens this conception. It makes "the water of life"—"the water of the river of life"— available in the present (Lord 2012, 70). A reality that belongs to the lush land of the future breaks into the arid land of the present: the most important transaction happens now.

While going over this material one last time before submitting it to the publisher, I received a note from Dana Stelian, one of my former students. We had studied the Gospel of John in a graduate-level class and then Revelation. Dana's grasp of the Johannine idiom is exceptional. Now a chaplain ministering to patients in California, she sent me these words.

> Today, one of my patients died while I was reading to her Revelation 21. Her son laid down in bed next to her, holding her hand. I was kneeling down on the other side, with my hand on her shoulder. It was a sad and sacred moment. (personal communication, October 21, 2017, used with permission)

Dana's note is testimony to Revelation's power, its capacity to illuminate the present with comfort and hope in circumstances where vulnerability, transience, and grief are most acutely felt.

A sternly worded warning follows right after the invitation to "come" (22:18–19). The transition is jarring, and the reading up to this point should be momentarily paused so as not to let the warning mute the force of the prior invitation. "The Apocalypse is rewritten scripture, and yet it ends with a strict warning against rewriting," says Robert Royalty (2004, 292), implying that John claims a privilege for *his* book that he has not observed in his own treatment of the books of others. But this is hardly the point. The warning and its wording confirm that there is real danger, and the danger threatens from *within*. Neither the content nor the timing of the warning is accidental. Revelation's message has shown God to be a giving person, and it concludes with the offer of a gift (22:17). The gift and the terms for receiving it are not the kind of which there are many in the world's religions or in world affairs otherwise. It is not logic, common sense, or tradition that put their heads together to make the offer of a *gift* the breaking point in human experience. If we preserve the connection between the warning and the offer preceding it, the warning is predicated on (1) a threat from *within*; (2) a threat to the *gift*; and (3) yet another *reminder* that John's horizon is not limited to the first century of the Christian era.

I write these lines as the world marks the five-hundredth anniversary of the Protestant Reformation. It was triggered by a posting on the door of the Castle Church in Wittenberg on October 31, 1517. The material concern in the Ninety-Five Theses, stated in ninety-five different ways, was the loss of the *gift*. Martin Luther's protest focused on a gift that was turned into a commodity that (in its crudest version) could be bought with money or (in its subtler version) had to be earned. Heiko A. Oberman (1989), explaining the reason for Luther's courage and refusal to compromise, settles on the battle for the *gift*.

> The whole indulgences issue, this selling of insurance as protection against the wrath of God, is the appalling consequence of Rome's assiduous efforts at securing inward and outward dominion over the people of God. The Papal States must be expanded and holy wars must be fought for the honor of God and the growth of the Church—thus runs the shameless propaganda. (Oberman 1989, 72)

To Luther, the Reformation was *preceded* by a counterreformation. The devil successfully ambushed the church, wreaking havoc with the gift and with

God as a Giver. Revelation's closing warning could be distilled to the same concern: *Woe to anyone who tampers with the gift* (22:18–19).

### RSVP Sent and Answered (22:20–21)

**22:20–21.** Revelation's mode of communication is interactive throughout, and especially toward the end. When the time comes to say farewell, the line of communication between heaven and earth is direct and unmediated—no go-between in the person of John or an angel. **The one who testifies these things says, "Surely, I am coming soon!"** (22:20a). This is less a "goodbye" than a "see you later": *Auf Wiedersehen* in German. Here it is actually "See you soon." To those who read this almost two thousand years later, the meaning of "soon" will be a subject of discussion, but the word is "soon." Revelation never lets go of the notion of imminence even if it risks the charge of misleading readers over the meaning of "soon." In the currency of time and chronology, "soon" means as soon as the things described in the book are completed (cf. Dan. 12:6–7). As disposition, it means that the speaker is eager to come and cannot find a better word than "soon" to express it. As hope, given the instability of the world and the fragility of human existence, heaven is ready to bring relief, and it will happen "soon."

The breaks in the sentences and paragraphs are uncertain at this point—whose word should be assigned to whom—but there is no doubt about the interaction. "Surely, I am coming soon!" is heaven's last word in the Bible (22:20). The earth responds in John's revelation and the community to which the revelation is addressed, **"Amen! Come, Lord Jesus!"** (22:20b). *Hope* has a name in this book—and a name among "the nations" (22:2). "On his name the nations shall pin their hope" (Isa. 11:10 LXX). A string of words that have "certainty" as their theme stumble over each other in the last two verses: *Nai. Amēn. Amēn.* These words entail a "strong affirmation of what is stated" (BDAG 53–54, ἀμήν). "*Surely. Surely. Surely*" (Rev. 22:20–21).

"The grace of the Lord Jesus be with all the saints," as the NRSV translates it, gives the last line to John, the implied letter writer (22:21). Perhaps "the saints" are implied in the greeting, but this word is not in the Greek. For a book that has as its theme that God is a giving person despite slanderous rumors to the contrary, a more literal translation should be preferred, and "the saints" should be left out. There is *gift*, there is a *Giver*, and there is *need*. **The gift of the Lord Jesus with all** (22:21).

## Theological Issues

### "All's Well That Ends Well"

It ends well in the last book of the Bible, but the saying does not merit Revelation's endorsement—not if "ending well" reduces all that went before to irrelevance. While it "ends well," the path to the happy ending is slow, tortuous, and painstaking. John's account sometimes makes it seem, like history itself, that the end is indefinitely deferred. Through sequences of letters, seals, trumpets, and bowls the reader is nudged to think about the problem that needs to be resolved, and the path to the end is not less important than the end. Above all, images of a happy ending in the last chapters of Revelation are anchored in the beginning of the story, particularly the first chapters of Genesis. Two of Külli Tõniste's (2016, 133–34) observations are hugely important for how to understand the ending of the last book in the canon. First, *"endings depend on the rest of the story,"* and second, *"endings reveal the full meaning of what went on before."* For this to work, the ending must not be an anesthetic, a compensation, or payment of reparation but a resolution to the problem defined at the beginning: *"endings resolve the crisis and show what the characters have learned"* (Tõniste 2016, 136). In such a conception, the beginning and the middle of the story are not phased out by the blaze of the ending. As Gordon Graham (2001, 167) puts it, "What we want to know is not what God is going to do about these things now that they have happened, but why they were ever permitted in the first place." The narrative parallels between the beginning of Genesis and the ending of Revelation are in this sense less a vision of a happy ending than proof that the problem in Genesis has been addressed and resolved (Tõniste 2016, 135). A notion of "compensatory bliss" fails to capture John's agonizing story and the meaning of the ending (Graham 2001, 167).

This point is often passed over lightly, and it may come as a surprise that serious thinkers consider a "happy ending" scenario unconvincing and even offensive. One such thinker is Ivan Karamazov in *The Brothers Karamazov*, whose "poem" was briefly mentioned in chapter 8. In his analytical approach to the problem of suffering, Ivan dismisses the notion of "compensatory bliss" as a moral travesty (Dostoevsky 2002, 244–45).

> I absolutely renounce all higher harmony. It is not worth one little tear of even that one tormented child who beat her chest with her little fist and prayed to "dear God" in a stinking outhouse with her unredeemed tears! (Dostoevsky 2002, 245)

Ivan's outrage is caused by the suffering of children. Fyodor Dostoevsky, the author, certifies Ivan's example as a true story (Tonstad 2016a, 23), one of four or five other true stories that Ivan brings up in a conversation that rattles his believing brother, Alyosha. The "tormented child who beat her chest" was a five-year-old girl who sometimes wet her bed at night. For this, she was flogged and beaten by her parents "until her whole body was nothing but bruises" and then locked up in a freezing outhouse all night after having her face smeared with excrement. "And it was her mother, her mother who made her!" Ivan shouts (Dostoevsky 2002, 242).

How can a happy ending make up for such suffering? What is the moral meaning of "harmony" in relation to suffering that should never have happened? This is the subject of Ivan's outrage in one of the most searing protests in literature. In Dostoevsky's rendition, Ivan even makes use of passages from Revelation to put his outrage in perspective, and he is not unaware of the problems and contradictions in the Christian narrative. "Harmony" is not sufficient for suffering that should not have happened, and "harmony" is much less than it is claimed to be. "And where is the harmony, if there is hell?" Ivan scoffs, knowing full well the Christian answer (Dostoevsky 2002, 245).

Revelation's subject matter has more in common with Ivan's concerns than many realize. Reading the books together would be time well spent, if only to discover that the older book is well matched to questions thought to be recent, uniquely modern—and pressing. Revelation ends with a vision of final harmony, but it does not buy harmony on the cheap. John does not leave out what led to loss of harmony in the first place; he covers ground that closely parallels key ideas in *The Brothers Karamazov*; and, as the present interpretation has sought to show, he is not caught flat-footed by Ivan's sharpest barb, "Where is the harmony if there is hell?"

### *"God Is in Control"*

This is another prized saying in the Christian tradition, and it is often heard in relation to Revelation. At face value, what could be more reassuring than to say that God is in control? But the statement fits Revelation no better than the saying "All is well that ends well." Too much in this book is not compatible with a facile *God-is-in-control* scenario. As the crisis in the heavenly council shows (5:1–4), God seems *not* to be "in control." At the very least, God appears *not* to be "in control" in the way that is expected. Revelation's ending returns explicitly to the garden of Eden, its life-giving river, and its tree(s). If, as this chapter suggests, we have a "freedom tree" rather than a "control tree," "control" is not the best term for God's economy. Gregory of Nyssa's disdain for the "killer-tree," directly, and for freedom, indirectly, raised a Christian objection to the status of freedom in Christian belief. But Gregory's critique is mild compared to the scorn Ivan Karamazov heaps on freedom. Ivan cannot bear the suffering of children. After a heated monologue and many examples of atrocious suffering, he tells Alyosha that he has written a "poem." This is no ordinary poem but a scathing evaluation, first of God and freedom, and second of Jesus and freedom. Ivan's poem is called "The Grand Inquisitor" and is the best-known chapter in *The Brothers Karamazov*. Ivan imagines Jesus appearing unexpectedly in the city of Seville fifteen hundred years after his ascension. The Grand Inquisitor recognizes him, orders him arrested, then goes to the prison in the evening to interrogate the prisoner. "Was it not you who so often said then: 'I want to make you free'?" the Grand Inquisitor begins. This is said as an accusation, not as a tribute. "For fifteen hundred years we have been at pains over this freedom," he laments, expressing a point of view that shows the church and Jesus to be in serious disagreement (Dostoevsky 2002, 251).

To Gregory of Nyssa, somewhat, and to the Grand Inquisitor in a bigger way, God betrayed the world by putting a "killer-tree" in the middle of the garden. Jesus's freedom-loving ways made the problem even worse. "Instead of taking over men's freedom, you increased it and forever burdened the kingdom of the human soul with its torments," says the Grand Inquisitor (Dostoevsky 2002, 255). The church tried to remedy the mistake. The Grand Inquisitor wonders whether Jesus will approve of the work the church has done to fix the damage.

"We corrected your deed and based it on *miracle, mystery*, and *authority*," the Grand Inquisitor continues, claiming the moral high ground for taking the church on a path of less freedom. Allusions to Revelation are part of his argument. "You objected that man does not live by bread alone, but do you know that in the name of this very earthly bread, the spirit of the earth will rise against you and fight with you and defeat you, and everyone will follow him exclaiming, 'Who can compare to this beast, for he has given us fire from heaven!'" (Dostoevsky 2002, 252–53). This two-sided allusion mixes "bread" in the temptation story in the Synoptic Gospels with "fire from heaven" in Revelation (13:13). As the Grand Inquisitor sees it, the world owes no debt to the freedom-loving maniac God turned out to be. Humanity will be grateful to the church for correcting the terrible deed of freedom. Once corrected, "mankind rejoiced that they were once more led like sheep, and that at last such a terrible gift, which had brought them so much suffering, had been taken from their hearts," he says (Dostoevsky 2002, 257).

Ivan's poem does not operate in a theological no-man's-land. Interpretations of the trees in Genesis played a central role in the theology and self-understanding of the church, and the tree(s) make a final appearance in Revelation (22:1–2). We may wonder whether an ancient book like Revelation is capable of such consequential meanings. When we review the book, however, for one last time we might feel that the subject stirring the heavenly council concerns consequential meanings (5:1–4). Indeed, we may not be far off the target if we perceive the crisis to break along an axis of "control" versus "lack of control." In flawed human speech, it is almost as if the heavenly council is calling on God to take control.

In the realm of thought, philosophers from Epicurus to David Hume wondered whether evil and apparent chaos in the world expose a power deficit or a love deficit in God (Hume 1992, 100; Tonstad 2016a, 10–12). Their predicament plays out within a *God-is-in-control* scenario, or rather, a scenario within which God is not in control. To these thinkers, a God of love would have prevented evil, and a God of infinite power would surely have done it. In light of Revelation, the sight of the Lamb who was killed with violence (5:6) makes it difficult to argue that there is a love deficit in God. At the end, when

God raises the dead, even if the person had vanished to the lowermost crevice of the ocean floor (20:13), the concern about a power deficit will also be less. This concern might dissipate completely considering the promise that God is capable of renewing the heavens and the earth (21:1). Neither one of the two elements in the philosophers' account, lack of love or lack of power, has much traction when Revelation describes a city of people "beautified as a bride for her bridegroom" (21:2) and the joy of those who "see God's face" (22:4). And yet it is not the notion of "control" that carries the day; "control" is not the cornerstone of assurance. Throughout, despite so much that is strange and unexpected, nothing seems more certain than that God set things right by a measure that exceeds all expectations. To say that God complied with the practical imperative expressed by Immanuel Kant is to say too little, but it should be said, because God may be the only one who did no less than that: "So act as to treat humanity, whether in thine own person or in that of any other, in every case as an end withal, never as means only" (Kant 2004, locs. 736–37 of 1410, Kindle).

To be certain of this requires transparency on the part of the governing authority and access on the part of the governed. The ending of Revelation is the ending of a revelation. This puts John in dialogue with a book that to many describes human experience in the twentieth and twenty-first centuries. If Dostoevsky's *Brothers Karamazov* is one of the keenest texts ever written on the problem of God and suffering, *The Trial* by Franz Kafka will be the key text for the problem of concealment, confusion, and lack of access.

We read in this book that Joseph K. was arrested one fine morning by warders who will not say who sent them; he is charged with a crime and never gets to know what it is; he is tried before a court he never gets to see; he is sentenced without a definite hearing and even without knowing for certain whether there has been one; and he is executed in the dark of night in a monstrous ceremony devoid of empathy. In his last hour, nothing is more demeaning than *the lack of access—the complete lack of transparency.* Joseph K. will die, but his questions linger as one of the most pressing dilemmas of human existence.

Was he alone? . . . Would anyone help? . . . Where was the judge he'd never seen? Where was the high court he had never reached? He raised both hands and spread out all his fingers. (Kafka 1984, 228)

Revelation's ending is also the ending of a *revelation*, as noted, and the *revelation* expresses a commitment to transparency. Unlike the predicament in Kafka's book, a soul-crushing plight that also has a theological tenor, John describes an open door (4:1), an open heaven (4:1; 19:11), an opened book (5:1–8:1), and an open temple (11:19; 15:5). "Open" is the opposite of "closed" and the counterpoint to concealment. With the open door comes an invitation to *come up* at the beginning (4:1) and a second invitation to *come home* at the end (22:17). These are unparalleled metaphors for transparency, on the one hand, and access, on the other. Revelation promises to remedy the problem of bewilderment, lack of transparency, and denial of access. To the dying Joseph K.'s questions, Revelation answers them one by one. *You are seen. Someone is taking part. There is one who wants to help. You are not alone. Nothing has been forgotten. There is no hidden judge and no inaccessible high court that is out to get you.* With this comes the invitation to enter through the open door for a seat at the table where scrutiny and understanding meet.

These are big issues, suitable for university-level study, but they deal equally with existential questions that arise within the experiences of everyday life. Revelation is at home in both realms, and it blends the two into one. If there is a preference for one over the other, the lowly takes priority over the lofty, and the near and personal come across in terms that have little need for explanation. We have it here, at the end, when "the Spirit and the bride" raise their voices, saying, "Come!" (22:17), and we hear it even better in the last of the messages to the seven believing communities in Asia Minor, another of Revelation's many endings. The one who is the subject matter of the mail delivered to the seven communities is also the mailman. God makes house calls in this book; there is more than virtual presence. "Look! I have taken up my position at the door, and I stand there knocking. If anyone hears my voice and opens the door, I will come in to eat with him/her, and he/she with me" (3:20).

This is how Revelation represents the relationship between a misperceived God and a needy world.

# Bibliography

Achtemeier, Paul J. 1986. "Revelation 5:1–14." *Interpretation* 40:283–88.

Acton, Lord (Sir John). 1972. *Essays in Freedom and Power.* Edited by Gertrude Himmelfarb. Gloucester, MA: Peter Smith. Originally published, 1887.

Adams, Marilyn McCord. 1999. *Horrendous Evils and the Goodness of God.* Ithaca, NY: Cornell University Press.

Albertini, Francesca. 1999. "Èhyèh Ashèr Èhyèh: Ex 3,14 according to the Interpretations of Moses Mendelssohn, Franz Rosenzweig, and Martin Buber." Pages 19–26 in *Jewish Studies at the Turn of the 20th Century: Proceedings of the 6th EAJS Congress, Toledo, July 1998.* Vol. 2 of *Judaism from the Renaissance to Modern Times.* Edited by Judit Targarona Borrás and Angel Sáenz-Badillos. Leiden: Brill.

Albertz, Rainer. 2002. "The Social Setting of the Aramaic and Hebrew Book of Daniel." Pages 171–204 in vol. 1 of *The Book of Daniel: Composition and Reception.* Edited by John J. Collins and Peter W. Flint. Boston: Brill.

Alexievich, Svetlana. 2005. *Voices from Chernobyl: The Oral History of a Nuclear Disaster.* Translated by Keith Gessen. London: Dalkey Archive Press.

Alter, Robert. 1996. *Genesis.* New York: Norton.

Aulén, Gustav. 1931. *Christus Victor: An Historical Study of the Three Main Types of the Idea of Atonement.* Translated by A. G. Hebert. London: SPCK. Repr., Eugene, OR: Wipf & Stock, 2003.

Aune, David E. 1983. "The Influence of Roman Imperial Court Ceremonial on the Apocalypse of John." *Biblical Research* 28:5–26.

———. 1986. "The Apocalypse of John and the Problem of Genre." Pages 65–96 in *Early Christian Apocalypticism: Genre and Social Setting.* Edited by Adela Yarbro Collins. Semeia Studies 36. Decatur, GA: Scholars Press.

———. 1996–98. *Revelation.* 3 vols. Word Bible Commentary. Nashville: Nelson.

Bainton, Roland H. 1953. *Hunted Heretic: The Life and Death of Michael Servetus, 1511–1553.* Boston: Beacon.

Bakon, Shimon. 1997. "Creation, Tabernacle and Sabbath." *Jewish Bible Quarterly* 25:79–85.

Baldwin, J. G. 1978. *Daniel: An Introduction and Commentary.* Tyndale Old Testament Commentaries. Downers Grove, IL: InterVarsity.

Baltzer, Klaus. 2001. *Deutero-Isaiah: A Commentary on Isaiah 40–55.* Hermeneia. Minneapolis: Fortress.

Band, Alan S. 2011. "Patterns of Prophetic Lawsuits in the Oracles to the Seven Churches." *Neotestamentica* 45:178–205.

Baptist, Edward E. 2014. *The Half Has Never Been Told: Slavery and the Making of American Capitalism.* New York: Basic Books.

Barclay, William. 1959. "Great Themes of the New Testament: Revelation xiii." *Expository Times* 70:260–64.

———. 1976. *The Revelation of John.* 2 vols. Philadelphia: Westminster.

Barr, David. 1998. *Tales of the End: A Narrative Commentary on the Book of Revelation.* Santa Rosa, CA: Polebridge.

Barr, James. 1956. "The Word Became Flesh: The Incarnation in the New Testament." *Interpretation* 10:16–23.

———. 1992. *The Garden of Eden and the Hope of Immortality.* London: SCM.

Barry, John. 2012. *Roger Williams and the Creation of the American Soul: Church, State and the Birth of Liberty.* New York: Viking.

Bauckham, Richard J. 1982. "The Lord's Day." Pages 221–50 in *From Sabbath to Lord's Day: A Biblical, Historical, and Theological Investigation.* Edited by D. A. Carson. Grand Rapids: Zondervan.

———. 1991. "The List of the Tribes in Revelation 7 Again." *Journal for the Study of the New Testament* 42:99–115.

———. 1993a. *The Climax of Prophecy: Studies in the Book of Revelation.* Edinburgh: T&T Clark.

———. 1993b. *The Theology of the Book of Revelation.* New Testament Theology. Cambridge: Cambridge University Press.

———. 1998a. *God Crucified: Monotheism and Christology in the New Testament.* Carlisle, UK: Paternoster.

———. 1998b. "John for Readers of Mark." Pages 147–71 in *The Gospels for All Christians: Rethinking the Gospel Audiences.* Edited by Richard J. Bauckham. Edinburgh: T&T Clark.

———. 2006. *Jesus and the Eyewitnesses: The Gospels as Eyewitness Testimony.* Grand Rapids: Eerdmans.

———. 2007. *The Testimony of the Beloved Disciple: Narrative, History, and Theology in the Gospel of John.* Grand Rapids: Baker Academic.

Bayle, Pierre. 1965. *Historical and Critical Dictionary: Selections.* Translated by Richard H. Popkin. New York: Bobbs-Merrill.

Baynes, Leslie. 2010a. "Horses of Heaven: Equine Imagery in John's Apocalypse." Paper presented at the annual meeting of the Society of Biblical Literature, John's Apocalypse section, Atlanta, November 2010.

————. 2010b. "Revelation 5:1 and 10:2a, 8–10 in the Earliest Greek Tradition: A Response to Richard Bauckham." *Journal of Biblical Literature* 129:801–16.

————. 2012. *The Heavenly Book Motif in Judeo-Christian Apocalypses, 200 BCE–200 CE.* Leiden: Brill.

Beacham, Richard C. 1999. *Spectacle Entertainments of Early Imperial Rome.* New Haven: Yale University Press.

Beale, G. K. 1999. *The Book of Revelation.* New International Greek Testament Commentary. Grand Rapids: Eerdmans.

Beale, G. K., and Mitchell Kim. 2014. *God Dwells among Us: Expanding Eden to the Ends of the Earth.* Downers Grove, IL: IVP Books.

Becker, Eve-Marie. 2007. "'Patmos': En nøgle til fortolkningen af Johannes' Åbenbaring." *Dansk Teologisk Tidsskrift* 70:260–75.

Beckwith, I. T. 1919. *The Apocalypse of John.* New York: Macmillan.

Beker, J. Christiaan. 1982. *Paul's Apocalyptic Gospel.* Philadelphia: Fortress.

Bellinger, W. H., and W. R. Farmer, eds. 1998. *Jesus and the Suffering Servant: Isaiah 53 and Christian Origins.* Harrisburg, PA: Trinity Press International.

Berger, P.-R. 1985. "Kollyrium für die blinden Augen, Apk 3:18." *Novum Testamentum* 27:174–95.

Biguzzi, Giancarlo. 1998a. "Ephesus, Its Artemision, Its Temple to the Flavian Emperors, and Idolatry in Revelation." *Novum Testamentum* 40:276–90.

————. 1998b. "John on Patmos and the 'Persecution' in the Apocalypse." *Estudios Biblicos* 56:201–20.

————. 2006. "Is the Babylon of Revelation Rome or Jerusalem?" *Biblica* 87:371–86.

Birdsall, J. Neville. 2002. "Irenaeus and the Number of the Beast: Revelation 13,18." Pages 349–59 in *New Testament Textual Criticism and Exegesis: Festschrift J. Delobel.* Edited by A. Denaux. Louvain: Leuven University Press.

Blenkinsopp, Joseph. 2003. *Isaiah 56–66: A New Translation with Introduction and Commentary.* Anchor Bible 19B. New Haven: Yale University Press.

Blevins, James L. 1990. "Revelation 1–3." *Review and Expositor* 87:615–21.

Block, Daniel I. 1988. *The Book of Ezekiel: Chapters 25–48.* New International Commentary on the Old Testament. Grand Rapids: Eerdmans.

————. 1992. "Gog in Prophetic Tradition: A New Look at Ezekiel XXXVIII." *Vetus Testamentum* 42.2:154–72.

Bloom, Harold. 1988. "Introduction." Pages 1–5 in *The Revelation of Saint John the Divine.* Edited by Harold Bloom. Modern Critical Interpretations. New York: Chelsea House.

Blount, Brian K. 2000. "Reading Revelation Today: Witness as Active Resistance." *Interpretation* 54:398–412.

————. 2009. *Revelation: A Commentary.* New Testament Library. Louisville: Westminster John Knox.

Blumell, Lincoln H., and Thomas A. Wayment. 2016. "The 'Number of the Beast': Revelation 13:18 and Early Christian Isopsephies." Pages 119–35 in *Book of Seven Seals: The Peculiarity of Revelation, Its Manuscripts, Attestation, and Transmission.*

Edited by Thomas J. Kraus and Michael Sommer. Wissenschaftliche Untersuchungen zum Neuen Testament 363. Tübingen: Mohr Siebeck.

Bøe, Sverre. 2001. *Gog and Magog: Ezekiel 38–39 as Pre-text for Revelation 19,17–21 and 20,7–10.* Wissenschaftliche Untersuchungen zum Neuen Testament 2/135. Tübingen: Mohr Siebeck.

Bonhoeffer, Dietrich. 1959. *Creation and Fall: A Theological Interpretation of Genesis 1–3.* Translated by John C. Fletcher. London: SCM.

Boring, M. Eugene. 1986. "The Theology of Revelation." *Interpretation* 40:257–69.

———. 1989. *Revelation.* Interpretation. Louisville: John Knox.

———. 1992. "Narrative Christology in the Apocalypse." *Catholic Biblical Quarterly* 54:702–23.

Bornkamm, Günther. 1937. "Die Komposition der apokalyptischen Visionen in der Offenbarung Johannis." *Zeitschrift für die neutestamentliche Wissenschaft* 36:132–49.

Borret, Marcel, trans. 1989. *Origen: Homélies sur Ézéchiel.* Sources chrétiennes 352. Paris: Cerf.

Bost, Hubert. 1984. "Le chant sur la chute d'un tyran en Esaïe 14." *Études théologiques et religieuses* 59:5–14.

Bousset, Wilhelm. 1906. *Die Offenbarung Johannis.* Göttingen: Vandenhoeck & Ruprecht.

Bovon, François. 2000. "John's Self-Presentation in Revelation 1:9–10." *Catholic Biblical Quarterly* 62:693–700.

Bowersock, G. W. 1972. "Greek Intellectuals and the Imperial Cult in the Second Century AD." Pages 179–212 in *Le Culte des Souverains dans l'Empire Romain.* Edited by Willem den Boer. Geneva: Vandœuvres-Genève.

Bowlin, John R. 1997. "Augustine on Justifying Coercion." *Annual of the Society of Christian Ethics* 17:49–70.

Boxall, Ian. 2002. *Revelation: Vision and Insight.* London: SPCK.

Bradley, K. R. 1987. *Slaves and Masters in the Roman Empire: A Study in Social Control.* New York: Oxford University Press.

Brant, Jo-Ann. 2011. *John.* Paideia. Grand Rapids: Baker Academic.

Braun, F.-M. 1954. "La femme et le dragon." *Bible et vie chretienne* 7:63–72.

———. 1955. "La femme vêtue de soleil (Apoc. XII)." *Revue Thomiste* 55:639–67.

Bredin, Mark. 2008. "God the Carer: Revelation and the Environment." *Biblical Theology Bulletin* 38:76–86.

Bright, John. 1976. *A History of Israel.* 2nd ed. Philadelphia: Westminster.

Brighton, Louis A. 1999. *Revelation.* Concordia Commentaries. St. Louis: Concordia.

Brod, Max. 1995. *Franz Kafka: A Biography.* Translated by G. Humphreys Roberts. New York: Da Capo.

Brown, Peter. 1967. *Augustine of Hippo: A Biography.* London: Faber & Faber.

———. 1971. *The World of Late Antiquity.* London: Thames & Hudson.

Brown, Raymond E. 1966. *The Gospel according to John (I–XII).* Anchor Bible 29. Garden City, NY: Doubleday.

Brown, Schuyler. 1966. "'The Hour of Trial' (Rev. 3:10)." *Journal of Biblical Literature* 85:308–14.

Browning, Robert. 1989. "A Death in the Desert." In *Selected Poems*. New York: Penguin.

Brox, Norbert. 1965. "Nikolaus und Nikolaiten." *Vigiliae Christianae* 19:23–30.

Bultmann, Rudolf. 1964. *Existence and Faith: Shorter Writings of Rudolf Bultmann*. Edited by Schubert M. Ogden. London: Collins.

Butterworth, G. W., trans. 1936. *Origen on First Principles*. London: SPCK.

Byrskog, Samuel. 2002. *Story as History–History as Story: The Gospel Tradition in the Context of Ancient Oral History*. Leiden: Brill.

Caird, G. B. 1999. *The Revelation of Saint John*. Peabody, MA: Hendrickson.

Callahan, Allen Dwight. 1999. "Apocalypse as Critique of Political Economy: Some Notes on Revelation 18." *Horizons in Biblical Theology* 21:46–65.

———. 2003. "Revelation 18: Notes on Effective History and the State of Colombia." Pages 269–85 in *Walk in the Ways of Wisdom: Essays in Honor of Elisabeth Schüssler Fiorenza*. Edited by Shelly Matthews, Cynthia Briggs Kittredge, and Melanie Johnson-Debaufre. Harrisburg, PA: Trinity Press International.

———. 2009. "Babylon Boycott: The Book of Revelation." *Interpretation* 63:48–54.

Camus, Albert. 1991. *The Rebel: An Essay on Man in Revolt*. Translated by Anthony Bower. New York: Vintage.

Carley, Keith W. 1974. *The Book of the Prophet Ezekiel*. London: Cambridge University Press.

Carnegie, David R. 1982. "Worthy Is the Lamb: The Hymns in Revelation." Pages 243–56 in *Christ the Lord: Studies in Christology Presented to Donald Guthrie*. Edited by Harold H. Rowdon. Leicester, UK: Inter-Varsity.

Carter, Warren. 2009. "Accommodating 'Jezebel' and Withdrawing John: Negotiating Empire in Revelation Then and Now." *Interpretation* 63:32–47.

Cary, Earnest, trans. and ed. 1925. *Dio Cassius: Roman History*. Loeb Classical Library. London: Heinemann.

Cashmore, David. 2004. "Laodicea and the Seven Churches." *Stimulus* 12:16–20.

Chadwick, Henry, trans. 1965. *Origen: Contra Celsum*. With an introduction and notes. Cambridge: Cambridge University Press.

Champlin, Edward. 2003. *Nero*. Cambridge, MA: Belknap.

Charles, R. H. 1920. *The Revelation of St. John*. 2 vols. International Critical Commentary. Edinburgh: T&T Clark.

Clark, Elizabeth. 1992. *The Origenist Controversy*. Princeton: Princeton University Press.

Clifford, Richard. 1972. *The Cosmic Mountain in Canaan and the Old Testament*. Cambridge, MA: Harvard University Press.

Collins, Adela Yarbro. 1976. *The Combat Myth in the Book of Revelation*. Missoula, MT: Scholars Press. Repr., Eugene, OR: Wipf & Stock, 2001.

———. 1979. *The Apocalypse*. New Testament Message 22. Dublin: Veritas.

———. 1981. "Dating the Apocalypse of John." *Biblical Research* 26:33–45.

————. 1984. *Crisis and Catharsis: The Power of the Apocalypse.* Philadelphia: Westminster.

————. 1996. *Cosmology and Eschatology in Jewish and Christian Apocalypticism.* Journal for the Study of Judaism in the Persian, Hellenistic, and Roman Periods: Supplement Series 50. Leiden: Brill.

Collins, John J. 1974. "The Son of Man and the Saints of the Most High in the Book of Daniel." *Journal of Biblical Literature* 93:50–66.

————, ed. 1979. *Apocalypse: The Morphology of a Genre.* Semeia Studies 14. Missoula: Scholars Press.

————. 1998. *The Apocalyptic Imagination.* 2nd ed. Grand Rapids: Eerdmans.

Collins, John. J., and Adela Yarbro Collins. 1993. *Daniel: A Commentary on the Book of Daniel.* Hermeneia. Minneapolis: Fortress.

Combs, Eugene. 1988. "Has God Cursed the Ground? Perplexity of Interpretation in Genesis 1–5." Pages 265–87 in *Ascribe to the Lord: Biblical and Other Studies in Memory of Peter C. Craigie.* Edited by Lyle Eslinger and Glen Taylor. Journal for the Study of the Old Testament Supplement Series 67. Sheffield: Sheffield Academic.

Conzelmann, Hans. 1975. *1 Corinthians: A Commentary on the First Epistle to the Corinthians.* Translated by James W. Leitch. Hermeneia. Philadelphia: Fortress.

Cook, Stephen L. 1995. *Prophecy and Apocalypticism: The Postexilic Social Setting.* Minneapolis: Fortress.

Court, John M. 1979. *Myth and History in the Book of Revelation.* London: SPCK.

Cranfield, C. E. B. 1953. "St. Mark 13." *Scottish Journal of Theology* 6:300–301.

————. 1982. "Thoughts on New Testament Eschatology." *Scottish Journal of Theology* 35:497–512.

Crossan, John Dominic. 2009. "Divine Violence in the Christian Bible." Pages 208–36 in *The Bible and the American Future.* Edited by Robert L. Jewett with Wayne L. Alloway Jr. and John G Lacey. Eugene, OR: Cascade Books.

Cuvillier, Elian. 1984. "Apocalypse 20: Prédiction ou Prédication?" *Études théologiques et religieuses* 59:345–54.

Damon, Cynthia, trans. 2012. *Tacitus: Annals.* London: Penguin Classics.

Daniélou, Jean. 1955. *Origen.* Translated by Walter Mitchell. London: Sheed & Ward.

Davis, Dale Ralph. 1973. "Relationship between the Seals, Trumpets, and Bowls in the Book of Revelation." *Journal of the Evangelical Theological Society* 16:149–58.

Day, John. 1994. "The Origin of Armageddon: Revelation 16:16 as an Interpretation of Zechariah 12:11." Pages 315–26 in *Crossing the Boundaries: Essays in Biblical Interpretation in Honour of Michael D. Goulder.* Edited by S. Porter and P. Joyce. Biblical Interpretation Series 8. Leiden: Brill.

Dehandschutter, Boudewijn. 1980. "The Meaning of Witness in the Apocalypse." Pages 283–88 in *L'Apocalypse johannique et l'apocalyptique dans le Nouveau Testament.* Edited by J. Lambrecht. Gembloux: Duculot.

Deissmann, Adolf. 1901. *Bible Studies.* Translated by Alexander Grieve. Edinburgh: T&T Clark.

den Hertog, Cornelis. 2002. "The Prophetic Dimension of the Divine Name: On Exodus 3:14a and Its Context." *Catholic Biblical Quarterly* 64:213–28.

Deutsch, Celia. 1987. "Transformation of Symbols: The New Jerusalem in Rv 21:1–22:5." *Zeitschrift für die neutestamentliche Wissenschaft* 78:106–26.

de Villiers, P. G. R. 1988. "The Lord Was Crucified in Sodom and Egypt: Symbols in the Apocalypse of John." *Neotestamentica* 22:133–35.

———. 2004. "The Role of Composition in the Interpretation of the Rider on the White Horse and the Seven Seals in Revelation." *Hervormde teologiese studies* 80:125–53.

———. 2005. "The Septet of Bowls in Revelation 15:1–16:21 in the Light of Its Composition." *Acta Patristica et Byzantina* 16:196–222.

de Waal, Kayle B. 2015. *An Aural-Performance Analysis of Revelation 1 and 11.* Society of Biblical Literature 163. New York: Peter Lang.

Dochhorn, Jan. 1997. "Und die Erde tat ihren Mund auf: Ein Exodusmotif in Apc 12,16." *Zeitschrift für die neutestamentliche Wissenschaft* 88:140–42.

———. 2010. *Schriftgelehrte Prophetie: Der eschatologische Teufelsfall in Apc 12 und seine Bedeutung für das Verstandnis der Johannesoffenbarung.* Wissenschaftliche Untersuchungen zum Neuen Testament 268. Tübingen: Mohr Siebeck.

Dodd, C. H. 1952. *According to the Scriptures.* London: Nisbet.

———. 1963. *The Apostolic Preaching and Its Development.* London: Hodder & Stoughton.

Donne, John. 1996. "Death, Be Not Proud." Sonnet 10 in *Selected Poetry.* New York: Oxford University Press. Originally written, 1633.

Dostoevsky, Fyodor. 2002. *The Brothers Karamazov.* Translated by Richard Pevear and Larissa Volokhonsky. New York: Farrar, Straus & Giroux.

Draper, J. A. 1983. "The Heavenly Feast of Tabernacles: Revelation 7:1–17." *Journal for the Study of the New Testament* 19:133–47.

Driver, G. R. 1956. *Canaanite Myths and Legends.* Edinburgh: T&T Clark.

Driver, S. R. 1904. *The Book of Genesis.* London: Methuen.

Duff, Paul B. 2001. *Who Rides the Beast? Prophetic Rivalry and the Rhetoric of Crisis in the Churches of the Apocalypse.* New York: Oxford University Press.

Dulk, Matthijs. 2006. "The Promises of the Conquerors in the Book of Revelation." *Biblica* 87:516–22.

Du Preez, J. 1992. *Eschatology and Ecology: Perspectives from the Book of Revelation; Third Lecture of the Institute of Missiological Research (ISWEN).* Pretoria: University of Pretoria.

Edgar, Thomas R. 1982. "Babylon: Ecclesiastical, Political, or What?" *Journal of the Evangelical Theological Society* 25:333–41.

Ehrman, Bart D., trans. and ed. 2003. *1 Clement, 2 Clement, Ignatius, Polycarp, Didache.* Vol. 1 of *The Apostolic Fathers.* Loeb Classical Library. Cambridge, MA: Harvard University Press.

Eichrodt, Walther. 1970. *Ezekiel.* Translated by Cosslett Quinn. Old Testament Library. London: SCM.

Ellul, Jacques. 1970. *The Meaning of the City.* Translated by Dennis Pardee. Grand Rapids: Eerdmans.

———. 1977. *Apocalypse: The Book of Revelation.* Translated by George W. Schreiner. New York: Seabury.

Evans, Craig. 2002. "Daniel in the New Testament: Visions of God's Kingdom." Pages 490–527 in vol. 2 of *The Book of Daniel: Composition and Reception.* Edited by John J. Collins and Peter W. Flint. Boston: Brill.

Fabny, Tibor. 1992. *The Lion and the Lamb: Figuralism and Fulfilment in the Bible.* Art and Literature. London: Macmillan.

Falls, Cyril. 1964. *Armageddon 1918.* London: Weidenfeld & Nicholson.

Farrer, Austin. 1964. *The Revelation of St. John the Divine.* Oxford: Oxford University Press.

Fenske, Wolfgang. 1999. "'Das Lied des Mose, des Knechtes Gottes, und das Lied des Lammes' (Apokalypse des Johannes 15,3f.): Der Text und seine Bedeutung für die Johannes-Apokalypse." *Zeitschrift für die neutestamentliche Wissenschaft* 90:250–64.

Ferguson, Everett. 2011. "Angels of the Churches in Revelation 1–3: Status Quaestionis and Another Proposal." *Bulletin of Biblical Research* 21:371–86.

Fest, Joachim. 1975. *Hitler.* Translated by Richard and Clara Winston. New York: Vintage.

———. 2005. *Inside Hitler's Bunker: The Last Days of the Third Reich.* Translated by Margot Bettauer Dembo. London: Pan.

———. 2012. *Not I: Memoirs of a German Childhood.* Translated by Martin Chalmers. New York: Other.

Feuillet, André. 1959. "Le Messie et sa Mère d'apres le chapitre XII de l'Apocalypse." *Revue biblique* 66:55–86.

———. 1978. "Le chapitre XII de l'Apocalypse: Son caractère synthétique et sa richesse Doctrinale." *Esprit et Vie* 49: 674–83.

Fiorenza, Elisabeth Schüssler. 1974. "Redemption as Liberation: Apoc 1:5f. and 5:9f." *Catholic Biblical Quarterly* 36:220–32.

———. 1991. *Revelation: Vision of a Just World.* Proclamation Commentaries. Minneapolis: Fortress.

———. 1998. *The Book of Revelation: Justice and Judgment.* 2nd ed. Minneapolis: Fortress.

———. 2006. "Babylon the Great: A Rhetorical-Political Reading of Revelation 17–18." Pages 243–69 in *The Reality of Apocalypse: Rhetoric and Politics in the Book of Revelation.* Edited by David L. Barr. Atlanta: Society of Biblical Literature.

Fisch, S. 1950. *Ezekiel: Hebrew Text and English Translation with an Introduction and Commentary.* Stuttgarter biblische Beiträge. London: Soncino.

Fishbane, Michael. 1975. "The Sacred Center: The Symbolic Structure of the Bible." Pages 6–27 in *Texts and Responses: Studies Presented to Nahum N. Glatzer.* Edited by Michael A. Fishbane and Paul R. Flohr. Leiden: Brill.

———. 1979. *Close Readings of Selected Biblical Texts.* New York: Schocken.

Flowers, H. J. 1930. "The Vision of Revelation IV–V." *Anglican Theological Review* 12:525–30.

Foard, James H. 1997. "Imagining Nuclear Weapons: Hiroshima, Armageddon, and the Annihilation of the Students of Ichijo School." *Journal of the American Academy of Religion* 65:1–18.

Foerster, W. 1932. "Die Bilder in Offenbarung 12f. und 17f." *Theologische Studien und Kritiken* 104:279–310.

Ford, Josephine M. 1968. "'The Son of Man'—a Euphemism?" *Journal of Biblical Literature* 87:257–66.

———. 1975. *Revelation: A New Translation with Introduction and Commentary.* Anchor Bible 38. Garden City, NY: Doubleday.

———. 1998. "The Christological Function of the Hymns in the Apocalypse of John." *Andrews University Seminary Studies* 36:207–29.

Fredriksen, Paula. 2010. *Augustine and the Jews: A Christian Defense of Jews and Judaism.* New Haven: Yale University Press.

Frend, W. H. C. 1984. *The Rise of Christianity.* Philadelphia: Fortress.

Fretheim, Terence. 1991. "The Plagues as Ecological Signs of Historical Disaster." *Journal of Biblical Literature* 110:385–96.

———. 2005. *God and the World in the Old Testament: A Relational Theology of Creation.* Nashville: Abingdon.

Freud, Sigmund. 2010. *The Interpretation of Dreams: The Complete and Definitive Text.* Edited and translated by James Strachey. New York: Basic Books. Original German edition, 1899.

Frieden, Ken. 1990. "Dream Interpreters in Exile: Joseph, Daniel, and Sigmund (Solomon)." Pages 193–203 in *Mappings of the Biblical Terrain: The Bible as Text.* Edited by Vincent L. Tollers and John Maier. London: Associated University Presses.

Friedländer, Saul. 2008. *The Years of Extermination: Nazi Germany and the Jews, 1939–1945.* London: Phoenix.

Friedrich, Nestor Paulo. 2002. "Adapt or Resist? A Socio-Political Reading of Revelation 2.18–29." *Journal for the Study of the New Testament* 25:185–211.

Friesen, Steven J. 1993. "Ephesus: Key to a Vision in Revelation." *Biblical Archaeology Review* 19:24–37.

———. 1995a. "The Cult of the Roman Emperors in Ephesos: Temple Wardens, City Titles, and the Interpretation of the Revelation of John." Pages 229–50 in *Ephesos, Metropolis of Asia: An Interdisciplinary Approach to Its Archaeology, Religion, and Culture.* Edited by Helmut Koester. Valley Forge, PA: Trinity Press International.

———. 1995b. "Revelation, Realia, and Religion: Archaeology in the Interpretation of the Apocalypse." *Harvard Theological Review* 88:291–314.

———. 2001. *Imperial Cults and the Apocalypse of John: Reading Revelation in the Ruins.* Oxford: Oxford University Press.

Frilingos, Christopher A. 2004. *Spectacles of Empire: Monsters, Martyrs, and the Book of Revelation.* Philadelphia: University of Pennsylvania Press.

Frye, Northrop. 1982. *The Great Code.* New York: Harcourt Brace.

Fuller, J. William. 1983. "'I Will Not Erase His Name from the Book of Life' (Revelation 3:5)." *Journal of the Evangelical Theological Society* 26:297–306.

Fyfe, W. Hamilton, trans. 1908. *Tacitus: Agricola*. Oxford: Clarendon.

Galinsky, Karl. 1996. *Augustan Culture: An Interpretive Introduction*. Princeton, NJ: Princeton University Press.

Gallusz, Laszlo. 2008. "The Exodus Motif in Revelation 15–16: Its Background and Nature." *Andrews University Seminar Studies* 46:21–43.

———. 2014. *The Throne Motif in the Book of Revelation*. Library of New Testament Studies 487. London: Bloomsbury.

Gardner, Jane F., trans. and ed. 1967. *Julius Caesar: The Civil War*. New York: Penguin.

Garrett, Susan R. 2008. *No Ordinary Angel: Celestial Spirits and Christian Claims about Jesus*. New Haven: Yale University Press.

Garrow, A. J. P. 1997. *Revelation*. London: Routledge.

Geddert, Timothy J. 1989. *Watchwords: Mark 13 in Markan Eschatology*. Journal for the Study of the New Testament Supplement 26. Sheffield: JSOT Press.

Gelzer, Matthias. 1968. *Caesar: Politician and Statesman*. Translated by Peter Needham. Cambridge, MA: Harvard University Press.

Giblin, C. H. 1974. "Structural and Thematic Correlations in the Theology of Revelation 16–22." *Biblica* 55:487–504.

Gieschen, Charles A. 1998. *Angelomorphic Christology*. Arbeiten zur Geschichte des Antiken Judentums und des Urchristentums 42. Leiden: Brill.

Gilchrest, Eric J. 2013. *Revelation 21–22 in Light of Jewish and Greco-Roman Utopianism*. Biblical Interpretation Series. Leiden: Brill.

Gingrich, F. Wilbur, and Frederick William Danker, eds. *Shorter Lexicon of the Greek New Testament*. 1965. 2nd ed. Chicago: University of Chicago Press.

Glasson, T. F. 1965. *The Revelation of John*. Cambridge: Cambridge University Press.

Gloer, W. Hulitt. 2001. "Worship God! Liturgical Elements in the Apocalypse." *Review and Expositor* 98:35–57.

Goldingay, John. 1998. *Daniel*. Word Biblical Commentary. Dallas: Word.

Goldsmith, Galen L. 2011. "The Cutting Edge of Prophetic Imagery." *Journal of Biblical and Pneumatological Research* 3:3–18.

Gollinger, Hildegard. 1967. "Das 'grosse Zeichen': Offb. 12—das Zentrale Kapitel der Offenbarung des Johannes." *Bibel und Kirche* 39:401–16.

———. 1971. *Das "grosse Zeichen" von Apocalypse 12*. Stuttgart: Echter Verlag.

Gollwitzer, Helmut. 1973. "Predigt über Offenbarung Johannes 12:7–12." Pages 125–32 in *Festschrift für Ernst Fuchs*. Edited by G. Ebeling, E. Jüngel and Gerd Schunack. Tübingen: Mohr.

Grabiner, Steven. 2015. *Revelation's Hymns: Commentary on the Cosmic Conflict*. Library of New Testament Studies 511. London: Bloomsbury.

Graham, Gordon. 2001. *Evil and Christian Ethics*. Cambridge: Cambridge University Press.

Grainger, John D. 2003. *Nerva and the Roman Succession Crisis of AD 96–99*. London: Routledge.

Grant, Robert M. 1997. *Irenaeus of Lyons*. London: Routledge.

Graves, Robert, trans. 1979. *Suetonius: The Twelve Caesars*. Harmondsworth: Penguin Classics.

Greenberg, Moshe. 1983. *Ezekiel 1–20: A New Translation with Introduction and Commentary*. Anchor Bible 22. Garden City, NY: Doubleday.

————. 1997. *Ezekiel 21–37*. Anchor Bible 22B. Garden City, NY: Doubleday.

Greenslade, S. L. 1954. *Church and State from Constantine to Theodosius*. London: SCM.

Grelot, P. 1956. "Isaïe XIV 12–15 et son arrière-plan mythologique." *Revue de l'histoire des religions* 149:18–48.

Gumerlock, Francis X. 2006. "Nero Antichrist: Patristic Evidence for the Use of Nero's Naming in Calculating the Number of the Beast (Rev 13:18)." *Westminster Theological Journal* 68:347–60.

Gundry, Robert H. 1987. "The New Jerusalem: People as Place, Not Place for People." *Novum Testamentum* 29:254–64.

Gunkel, Hermann. 1895. *Schöpfung und Chaos in Urzeit und Endzeit: Eine religionsgeschichtliche Untersuchung über Gen 1 und Ap Joh 12*. Göttingen: Vandenhoek & Ruprecht.

————. 1997. *Genesis*. Translated by Mark E. Biddle. Macon, GA: Mercer University Press.

Guttenberger, Gudrun. 2005. "Johannes von Thyateira." Pages 160–88 in *Studien zur Johannesoffenbarung und ihrer Auslegung: Festschrift für Otto Böcher zum 70. Geburtstag*. Edited by Friedrich Horn and Michael Wolter. Neukirchen-Vluyn: Neukirchener Verlag.

Habel, Norman. 2011. *The Birth, the Curse and the Greening of Earth: An Ecological Reading of Genesis 1–11*. Earth Bible Commentary. Sheffield: Sheffield Phoenix.

Haenchen, Ernst. 1984. *A Commentary on the Gospel of John*. Translated by R. W. Funk. Philadelphia: Fortress.

Hall, Mark Seaborn. 2002. "The Hook Interlocking Structure of Revelation: The Most Important Verses in the Book and How They May Unify Its Structure." *Novum Testamentum* 44:278–96.

Hall, Robert G. 1990. "Living Creatures in the Midst of the Throne: Another Look at Revelation 4.6." *New Testament Studies* 36:609–13.

Ham, Paul. 2014. *Hiroshima and Nagasaki: The Real Story of the Atomic Bombings and Their Aftermath*. New York: Picador.

Hammer, Josef. 1958. *Die geheime Offenbarung: Ein Schicksalsbuch der Engel und Menschen*. Stuttgart: Verlag Katholisches Bibelwerk.

Hamstra, Sam. 1998. "An Idealist View of Revelation." Pages 95–131 in *Four Views on the Book of Revelation*. Edited by C. Marvin Pate. Grand Rapids: Eerdmans.

Hanson, Anthony Tyrrell. 1957. *The Wrath of the Lamb*. London: SPCK.

Hanson, Paul D. 1979. *The Dawn of Apocalyptic*. Philadelphia: Fortress.

————. 1995. *Isaiah 40–66*. Interpretation. Louisville, KY: John Knox.

Harker, Andrew. 2011. "Spiritually Called Sodom and Egypt: Getting to the Heart of Early Christian Prophecy through the Apocalypse of John." *Tyndale Bulletin* 62:317–19.

Harkins, Paul W., trans. 1979. *Saint John Chrysostom: Discourses against Judaizing Christians*. Fathers of the Church. Washington, DC: Catholic University of America Press.

Hartman, Louis F., and Alexander A. Di Lella. 2005. *The Book of Daniel: A New Translation with Introduction and Commentary*. Anchor Bible 23. New Haven: Yale University Press. Original edition, 1977/78.

Hastings, Max. 2005. *Armageddon: The Battle for Germany, 1944–1945*. New York: Vintage.

Haupt, Paul. 1918. "The Curse on the Serpent." *Journal of Biblical Literature* 35:155–62.

Hauret, Charles. 1979. "Ève transfigure: De la Genèse à l'Apocalypse." *Revue d'histoire et de philosophie religieuses* 59:327–39.

Haussleiter, Johannes. 1886. "Die Kommentare des Victorinus, Tichonius und Hieronymus zur Apokalypse." *Zeitschrift für kirchliche Wissenschaft und kirchliches Leben* 7:239–57.

Hawkin, David J. 2003. "The Critique of Ideology in the Book of Revelation and Its Implications for Ecology." *Ecotheology* 8:161–72.

Hegel, Georg W. F. 1991. *The Philosophy of History*. Translated by J. Sibree. New York: Prometheus Books.

Heil, John Paul. 1993. "The Fifth Seal (Rev 6,9–11) as a Key to the Book of Revelation." *Biblica* 74:220–43.

Heiligenthal, Roman. 1991. "Wer waren die 'Nikolaiten'? Ein Beitrag zur Theologiegeschichte des frühen Christentums." *Zeitschrift für die neutestamentliche Wissenschaft* 82:133–37.

Hemer, Colin. 1986. *The Letter to the Seven Churches of Asia in Their Local Setting*. Journal for the Study of the New Testament Supplement 11. Sheffield: Sheffield Academic.

Hendriksen, William. 1998. *More than Conquerors*. Grand Rapids: Baker.

Hengel, Martin. 1989. *The Johannine Question*. Translated by John Bowden. London: SCM.

Herms, Ronald. 2015. "Πνευματικῶς and Antagonists in Revelation 11 Reconsidered." Pages 135–46 in *The Book of Revelation: Currents in British Research on the Apocalypse*. Edited by Garrick V. Allen, Ian Paul, and Simon P. Woodman. Wissenschaftliche Untersuchungen zum Neuen Testament 2/411. Tübingen: Mohr Siebeck.

Hofmann, Hans-Ulrich. 1982. *Luther und die Johannes-Apokalypse: Dargestellt im Rahmen der Auslegungsgeschichte des letzten Buches der Bibel und im zusammenhang der theologischen Entwicklung des Reformators*. Beiträge zur Geschichte der biblischen Exegese 24. Tübingen: Mohr.

Holladay, William L. 1963. "Jeremiah's Lawsuit with God: A Study in Suffering and Meaning." *Interpretation* 17:280–87.

———. 1986. *Chapters 1–25*. Vol. 1 of *Jeremiah: A Commentary on the Book of the Prophet Jeremiah*. Hermeneia. Philadelphia: Fortress.

Holtz, Traugott. 1962. *Die Christologie der Apokalypse des Johannes*. Texte und Untersuchungen 85. Berlin: Akademie-Verlag.

Hooker, Morna. 1991. *The Gospel according to St Mark*. Black New Testament Commentaries. London: Black.

Horne, Richard. 2010. *A Is for Armageddon: A Catalogue of Disasters That May Culminate in the End of the World as We Know It; Have a Nice Day*. New York: Harper.

Hort, F. J. A. 1908. *The Apocalypse of St. John I–III*. London: Macmillan.

Huesman, John E. 1961. "They Shall Mourn for Him." *Worship* 35:224–27.

Hume, David. 1992. *Dialogues concerning Natural Religion*. Oxford: Oxford University Press.

Humphrey, Edith M. 2007. *And I Turned to See the Voice: The Rhetoric of Vision in the New Testament*. Studies in Theological Interpretation. Grand Rapids: Baker Academic.

Hylen, Susan E. 2003. "The Power and Problem of Revelation 18: The Rhetorical Function of Gender." Pages 205–19 in *Pregnant Passion: Gender, Sex, and Violence in the Bible*. Edited by Cheryl A. Kirk-Duggan. Atlanta: Society of Biblical Literature.

Hynes, H. B. N. 1972. *The Ecology of Running Waters*. Toronto: University of Toronto Press.

Irwin, Brian P. 1995. "Molek Imagery and the Slaughter of Gog in Ezekiel 38 and 39." *Journal for the Study of the Old Testament* 62:93–112.

Iwamura, Jane Naomi. 2002. "The 'Hidden Manna' That Sustains: Reading Revelation 2:17 in Joy Kogawa's *Obasan*." *Semeia* 90–91:161–79.

Jacob, Benno. 1992. *The Second Book of the Bible: Exodus*. Translated by Walter Jacob. Hoboken, NJ: Ktav.

Jacob, Edmond. 1971. *Theology of the Old Testament*. Translated by Arthur W. Heathcote and Philip J. Allcock. London: Hodder & Stoughton.

Jauhiainen, Marko. 2002. "The Measuring of the Sanctuary Reconsidered (Rev. 11:1–2)." *Biblica* 83:507–26.

———. 2005. "The OT Background to Armageddon (Rev 16:16) Revisited." *Novum Testamentum* 47:380–93.

Jensen, Joseph. 1997. "Helel ben Shaḥar (Isaiah 14:12–15) in Bible and Tradition." Pages 339–56 in vol. 1 of *Writing and Reading the Scroll of Isaiah: Studies of an Interpretive Tradition*. Edited by Craig C. Broyles and Craig A. Evans. Supplements to Vetus Testamentum 70. Leiden: Brill.

Jewett, Robert. 2009. "Between Armageddon and the World Court: Reflections on the American Prospect." Pages 48–71 in *The Bible and the American Future*. Edited by Robert L. Jewett with Wayne L. Alloway Jr. and John G. Lacey. Eugene, OR: Cascade Books.

Johns, Loren L. 1998. "The Lamb in the Rhetorical Program of the Apocalypse of John." *Society of Biblical Literature Seminar Papers* 37.2:762–84.

———. 2005. "Conceiving Violence: The Apocalypse of John and the *Left Behind* Series." *Direction* 34:194–214.

Johnson, Curtis. 2014. "The Earth's Ethos, Logos, and Pathos: An Ecological Reading of Revelation." *Currents in Theology and Mission* 41:119–27.

Johnson, Luke Timothy. 1999. *The Writings of the New Testament: An Interpretation* Rev. ed. Minneapolis: Fortress.

Johnsson, William G. 1992. "The Saints' End-Time Victory over the Forces of Evil." Pages 3–40 in *Symposium on Revelation: Exegetical and General Studies, Book 2.* Edited by F. B. Holbrook. Silver Spring, MD: Biblical Research Institute.

Jones, Brian W. 1992. *The Emperor Domitian.* London: Routledge.

Jörns, Klaus-Peter. 1971. *Das hymnische Evangelium: Untersuchungen zu Aufbau, Funktion und Herkunft der hymnischen Stücke in der Johannesoffenbarung.* Gütersloh: Gütersloher Verlagshaus Gerd Mohn.

————. 1983. "Proklamation und Akklamation: Die antiphonische Grundordnung des frühchristlichen Gottesdienstes nach der Johannesoffenbarung." Pages 187–208 in *Liturgie und Dichtung.* Edited by H. Becker and R. Kaczynski. Sankt Ottilien: EOS Verlag.

Jung, Carl G. 2002. *Answer to Job.* Translated by R. F. C. Hull. New York: Routledge Classics.

Kafka, Franz. 1984. *The Trial: Definitive Edition.* Translated by Willa and Edwin Muir. New York: Schocken. Original German edition, 1925.

Kaiser, Otto. 1974. *Isaiah 13–39.* Translated by R. A. Wilson. Old Testament Library. London: SCM.

Kant, Immanuel. 2004. *The Fundamental Principles of the Metaphysics of Morals.* Translated by Thomas Kingsmill Abbott. London: Longmans, Green & Company, 1873. http://www.gutenberg.org/ebooks/5682. Original German edition, 1785.

Käsemann, Ernst. 1969. *New Testament Questions for Today.* Translated by W. J. Montague. Philadelphia: Fortress.

Kavanagh, M. A. 1984. *Apocalypse 22:6–21 as Concluding Liturgical Dialogue.* Rome: Pontificia Università Gregoriana.

Keener, Craig S. 2003. *The Gospel of John: A Commentary.* 2 vols. Peabody: Hendrickson.

Keller, Catherine. 1996. *Apocalypse Now and Then: A Feminist Guide to the End of the World.* Boston: Beacon.

Kelly, Balmer H. 1986. "Revelation 7:9–17." *Interpretation* 40:288–95.

Keough, George. 1944. *Studies in Revelation.* Washington, DC: n.p. Retrieved from Special Collections Library, Loma Linda University.

Kerkeslager, Allen. 1993. "Apollo, Greco-Roman Prophecy and the Rider on the White Horse in Rev 6:2." *Journal of Biblical Literature* 112:116–21.

Kermode, Frank. 1979. *The Genesis of Secrecy: On the Interpretation of Narrative.* Cambridge, MA: Harvard University Press.

Kiddle, Martin. 1940. *The Revelation of Saint John.* Moffatt New Testament Commentary. London: Hodder & Stoughton.

Kierulff, Stephen. 1991. "Belief in 'Armageddon Theology' and Willingness to Risk Nuclear War." *Journal for the Scientific Study of Religion* 30:81–93.

King, Fergus. 2004. "Travesty or Taboo? 'Drinking Blood' and Revelation 17:2–6." *Neotestamentica* 38:303–25.

Klauck, Hans-Josef. 1992. "Das Sendschreiben nach Pergamon und der Kaiserkult in der Johannesoffenbarung." *Biblica* 73:153–82.

———. 2001. "Do They Never Come Back? Nero Redivivus and the Apocalypse of John." *Catholic Biblical Quarterly* 63:683–98.

Koch, Klaus. 1972. *The Rediscovery of Apocalyptic*. Translated by Margaret Kohl. London: SCM.

Koester, Craig R. 2001. *Revelation and the End of All Things*. Grand Rapids: Eerdmans.

———. 2003. "The Message to Laodicea and the Problem of Its Local Context: A Study of the Imagery in Rev 3.14–22." *New Testament Studies* 49:407–24.

———. 2008. "Roman Slave Trade and the Critique of Babylon in Revelation 18." *Catholic Biblical Quarterly* 70:766–88.

———. 2014. *Revelation: A New Translation with Introduction and Commentary*. Anchor Yale Bible 38. New Haven: Yale University Press.

Korpel, Marjo C. A. and Johannes C. de Moor. 2015. *Adam, Eve, and the Devil: A New Beginning*. 2nd ed. Hebrew Bible Monographs. Sheffield: Sheffield Phoenix.

Köstenberger, Andreas J. 2014. "The Cosmic Trail Motif in John's Letters." Pages 157–78 in *Communities in Dispute: Current Scholarship in Johannine Epistles*. Edited by R. Alan Culpepper and Paul N. Anderson. Atlanta: SBL Press.

Kovacs, Judith, and Christopher Rowland. 2004. *Revelation: The Apocalypse of Jesus Christ*. Blackwell Bible Commentaries. Oxford: Blackwell.

Kraft, Heinrich. 1974. *Die Offenbarung des Johannes*. Handbuch zum Neuen Testament 16A. Tübingen: Mohr.

Kraybill, J. Nelson. 1996. *Imperial Cult and Commerce in John's Apocalypse*. Journal for the Study of the New Testament Supplement Series 132. Sheffield: Sheffield Academic.

———. 2010. *Apocalypse and Allegiance: Worship, Politics, and Devotion in the Book of Revelation*. Grand Rapids: Brazos.

Kreitzer, Larry. 1988. "Hadrian and the Nero *Redivivus* Myth." *Zeitschrift für die neutestamentliche Wissenschaft* 79:92–115.

Krüger, Thomas. 2008. "Sündenfall? Überlegungen zur theologischen Bedeutung der Paradiesgeschichte." Pages 95–109 in *Beyond Eden*. Edited by Konrad Schmid and Christoph Riedweg. Forschungen zum Alten Testament 2/34. Tübingen: Mohr Siebeck.

Kulka, Otto Dov. 2014. *Landscapes of the Metropolis of Death: Reflections on Memory and Imagination*. Translated by Ralph Mandel. New York: Penguin.

Ladd, George Eldon. 1972. *A Commentary on the Revelation of John*. Grand Rapids: Eerdmans.

LaHaye, Tim, and Jerry B. Jenkins. 1995–2007. Left Behind series. 16 vols. Wheaton / Carol Stream, IL: Tyndale House.

———. 1995. *Left Behind: A Novel of the Earth's Last Days*. Left Behind 1. Wheaton, IL: Tyndale House.

———. 2003. *Armageddon: The Cosmic Battle of the Ages.* Left Behind 11. Wheaton, IL: Tyndale House.

———. 2004. *Glorious Appearing: The End of Days.* Left Behind 12. Wheaton, IL: Tyndale House.

Lambrecht, Jan. 1979. "A Structuration of Revelation 4,1–22,5." Pages 77–104 in *L'Apocalypse johannique et l'Apocalyptique dans le Nouveau Testament.* Edited by J. Lambrecht. Gembloux: Duculot.

———. 1998. "The Opening of the Seals (Rev 6,1–8,6)." *Biblica* 79:198–220.

———. 1999. "Jewish Slander: A Note on Revelation 2,9–10." *Ephemerides theologicae Lovanienses* 75:421–29.

———. 2000. "Final Judgments and Ultimate Blessings: The Climactic Visions of Revelation 20,11–21,8." *Biblica* 81:362–85.

———. 2002. "Rev 13,9–10 and exhortation in the Apocalypse." Pages 331–47 in *New Testament Textual Criticism and Exegesis: Festschrift J. Delobel.* Edited by A. Denaux. Bibliotheca Ephemeridum Theologicarum Lovaniensium 161. Louvain: Leuven University Press.

Lane, William. 1974. *The Gospel of Mark.* New International Commentary on the New Testament. Grand Rapids: Eerdmans.

LaRondelle, Hans K. 2007. *How to Understand the End-Time Prophecies of the Bible: A Biblical-Contextual Approach.* Bradenton, FL: First Impressions.

Larrimore, Mark, ed. 2001. *The Problem of Evil: A Reader.* Malden, MA: Blackwell.

Lawrence, D. H. 1967. *Apocalypse.* New York: Viking.

Lee, Pilchan. 2001. *The New Jerusalem in the Book of Revelation: A Study of Revelation 21–22 in the Light of Its Background in Jewish Tradition.* Wissenschaftliche Untersuchungen zum Neuen Testament 2/129. Tübingen: Mohr Siebeck.

Lefebre, Georges. 1962. *The French Revolution: From Its Origins to 1793.* 2 vols. Translated by Elizabeth Moss Evanson. New York: Columbia University Press.

Lenski, R. C. H. 1963. *The Interpretation of St. John's Revelation.* Minneapolis: Augsburg.

Lenzi, Alan. 2009. "Secrecy, Textual Legitimation, and Intercultural Polemics in the Book of Daniel." *Catholic Biblical Quarterly* 71:330–48.

Lindsey, Hal. 1970. *The Late Great Planet Earth.* Grand Rapids: Zondervan.

———. 1984. *There Is a New World Coming.* Eugene, OR: Harvest House.

Linton, Gregory L. 2006. "Reading the Apocalypse as Apocalypse: The Limits of Genre." Pages 9–42 in *The Reality of Apocalypse: Rhetoric and Politics in the Book of Revelation.* Edited by David L. Barr. Atlanta: Society of Biblical Literature.

Lipton, Diana. 1996. "Inevitability and Community in the Demise of Moses." *Journal of Progressive Judaism* 7:79–93.

Lohmeyer, Ernst. 1926. *Die Offenbarung des Johannes.* Handbuch zum Neuen Testament 16. Tübingen: Mohr (Siebeck).

Lohse, Eduard. 1993. "Synagogue of Satan or Church of God: Jews and Christians in the Book of Revelation." *Svensk exegetisk årsbok* 58:105–23.

Longenecker, Bruce W. 2000. "Revelation 19,10: One Verse in Search of an Author." *Zeitschrift für die neutestamentliche Wissenschaft* 91:230–37.

Lord, Jennifer L. 2012. "The River Flows." *Word and World* 32:63–70.

Lundbom, Jack R. 2008a. *Jeremiah 1–20: A New Translation with Introduction and Commentary.* Anchor Yale Bible 21A. New Haven: Yale University Press.

———. 2008b. *Jeremiah 21–36: A New Translation with Introduction and Commentary.* Anchor Yale Bible 21B. New Haven: Yale University Press.

Lytton, Timothy D. 2002. "'Shall Not the Judge of the Earth Deal Justly?': Accountability, Compassion, and Judicial Authority in the Biblical Story of Sodom and Gomorrah." *Journal of Law and Religion* 18:31–55.

MacLeod, David J. 1999. "The Third 'Last Thing': The Binding of Satan (Rev. 20:1–3)." *Bibliotheca Sacra* 156:469–86.

———. 2000. "The Fifth 'Last Thing': The Release of Satan and Man's Final Rebellion (Rev. 20:7–10)." *Bibliotheca Sacra* 157:200–214.

Maier, Gerhard. 1981. *Die Johannesoffenbarung und die Kirche.* Wissenschaftliche Untersuchungen zum Neuen Testament 25. Tübingen: Mohr.

Maier, Harry O. 2002. *Apocalypse Recalled: The Book of Revelation after Christendom.* Minneapolis: Fortress.

Mandelbaum, Allen, trans. 2004. *Virgil: The Aeneid.* New York: Bantam Classics.

Marcus, Joel. 2000. *Mark 1–8: A New Translation with Introduction and Commentary.* Anchor Bible 27. Garden City, NY: Doubleday.

Martyn, J. Louis. 1968. *History and Theology in the Fourth Gospel.* New York: Harper & Row.

Mathewson, David. 2003a. "New Exodus as a Background for 'The Sea Was No More' in Rev 21:1C." *Trinity Journal* 24:243–58.

———. 2003b. *A New Heaven and a New Earth: The Meaning and Function of the Old Testament in Revelation 21.1–22.5.* London: Sheffield Academic.

May, David M. 2009. "Interpreting Revelation with Roman Coins: A Test Case, Rev 6:9–11." *Review and Expositor* 106:445–65.

Mayer, Jane. 2008. *The Dark Side: The Inside Story of How the War on Terror Turned into a War on American Ideals.* New York: Doubleday.

Mayo, Philip L. 2006. *"Those Who Call Themselves Jews": The Church and Judaism in the Apocalypse of John.* Princeton Theological Monograph Series 60. Eugene, OR: Pickwick.

Mazzaferri, David Frederick. 1988. "*Martyria Iēsou* Revisited." *Bible Translator* 39:114–22.

———. 1989. *The Genre of the Book of Revelation from a Source-Critical Perspective.* Beihefte zur Zeitschrift für die neutestamentliche Wissenschaft 54. Berlin: de Gruyter.

McCaffey, James. 1982. "John 14:2–3: A First Level of Meaning." *Proceedings of the Irish Biblical Association* 6:58–80.

McKenzie, J. L. 2008. *Second Isaiah: Introduction, Translation, and Notes.* Anchor Yale Bible 20. New Haven: Yale University Press.

Mealy, J. Webb. 1992. *After the Thousand Years: Resurrection and Judgment in Revelation 20.* Journal for the Study of the New Testament Supplement 70. Sheffield: JSOT Press.

Meeks, Wayne A. 1972. "The Man from Heaven in Johannine Sectarianism." *Journal of Biblical Literature* 91:44–72.

Melville, A. D., trans. 1986. *Ovid: Metamorphoses* II. Oxford: Oxford University Press.

Menken, Maarten J. J. 1993. "The Textual Form and the Meaning of the Quotation from Zechariah 12:10 in John 19:37." *Catholic Biblical Quarterly* 55:494–511.

———. 2007. "John's Use of Scripture in Revelation 1:7." *In die Skriflig* 41:281–93.

Metzger, Bruce M. 1993. *Breaking the Code: Understanding the Book of Revelation.* Nashville: Abingdon.

———. 1994. *A Textual Commentary on The Greek New Testament.* 2nd ed. Stuttgart: Deutsche Bibelgesellschaft.

Meyers, Carol L., and Eric M. Meyers. 1993. *Zechariah 9–14: A New Translation with Introduction and Commentary.* Anchor Bible 25C. Garden City, NY: Doubleday.

Michaels, J. Ramsay. 1991. "Revelation 1.19 and the Narrative Voices of the Apocalypse." *New Testament Studies* 37:604–20.

Miles, Rufus E. 1978. "The Origin and Meaning of Miles' Law." *Public Administration Review* 38:399–403.

Minear, Paul S. 1953. "The Wounded Beast." *Journal of Biblical Literature* 72:93–101.

———. 1968. *I Saw a New Earth.* Washington, DC: Corpus Books.

———. 1991. "Far as the Curse Is Found: The Point of Revelation 12:15–16." *Novum Testamentum* 33:71–77.

Moberly, Robert B. 1992. "When Was Revelation Conceived?" *Biblica* 73:376–93.

Moberly, R. W. L. 1988. "Did the Serpent Get It Right?" *Journal of Theological Studies* 39:1–27.

Moltmann, Jürgen. 1985. *God in Creation: An Ecological Doctrine of Creation.* Translated by Margaret Kohl. London: SCM.

———. 1996. *The Coming of God: Christian Eschatology.* Translated by Margaret Kohl. London: SCM.

Moo, Jonathan. 2009. "The Sea That Is No More: Rev 21:1 and the Function of Sea Imagery in the Apocalypse of John." *Novum Testamentum* 51:148–67.

———. 2015. "Climate Change and the Apocalyptic Imagination: Science, Faith, and Ecological Responsibility." *Zygon* 50:937–48.

Moore, Stephen D. 2006. *Empire and Apocalypse: Postcolonialism and the New Testament.* Bible in the Modern World. Sheffield: Sheffield Phoenix.

———. 2014. "Retching on Rome: Vomitous Loathing and Visceral Disgust in Affect Theory and the Apocalypse of John." *Biblical Interpretation* 22:503–28.

Morgenstern, Julian. 1939. "The Mythological Background of Psalm 82." *Hebrew Union College Annual* 14:29–126.

Morris, Dick, and Eileen McGann. 2016. *Armageddon: How Trump Can Beat Hillary.* Palm Beach, FL: Humanix.

Moulton, James H. 1908. *Prolegomena*. Vol. 1 of *A Grammar of New Testament Greek*. By J. H. Moulton, W. F. Howard, and N. Turner. 3rd ed. Edinburgh: T&T Clark.

Mounce, Robert. 1977. *The Book of Revelation*. New International Commentary on the New Testament. Grand Rapids: Eerdmans.

Moynihan, Daniel Patrick. 1998. *Secrecy: The American Experience*. New Haven: Yale University Press.

Mucha, Robert. 2014. "Ein flavischer Nero: Zur Domitian-Darstellung und Datierung der Johannesoffenbarung." *New Testament Studies* 60:83–105.

Mucha, Robert, and Stephan Witetschek. 2013. "Das Buch ohne Siegel: Zur zeitgeschichtlichen Referentialität der Johannesapokalypse." *Early Christianity* 4:96–125.

Müller, Peter. 2005. "Das Buch und die Bücher in der Johannesoffenbarung." Pages 293–309 in *Studien zur Johannesoffenbarung und ihrer Auslegung: Festschrift für Otto Böcher zum 70. Geburtstag*. Edited by Friedrich Wilhelm Horn and Michael Wolter. Neukirchen-Vluyn: Neukirchener Verlag.

Müller, Ulrich B. 1984. *Die Offenbarung des Johannes*. Ökumenischer Taschenbuch-Kommentar 19. Gütersloh: Echter Verlag.

Mussies, G. 1971. *The Morphology of Koine Greek as Used in the Apocalypse of St. John*. Supplements to Novum Testamentum 27. Leiden: Brill.

———. 1980. "The Greek of the Book of Revelation." Pages 167–77 in *L'Apocalypse johannique et l'Apocalyptique dans le Nouveau Testament*. Edited by J. Lambrecht. Paris-Gembloux: Duculot.

Nabokov, Vladimir. 1980. *Lectures on Literature*. Edited by Fredson Bowers. New York: Harcourt Brace.

Nauta, Ruurd R. 2002. *Poetry for Patrons: Literary Communication in the Age of Domitian*. Mnemosyne Supplements 206. Leiden: Brill.

Nietzsche, Friedrich. 1918. *The Genealogy of Morals*. Translated by Horace B. Samuel. New York: Boni & Liveright. Original German edition, 1887.

Norris, Richard A., Jr. 2002. "Two Trees in the Midst of the Garden (Genesis 2:9b): Gregory of Nyssa and the Puzzle of Human Evil." Pages 218–41 in *In Dominico Eloquio: Essays in Patristic Exegesis in Honor of Robert Louis Wilken*. Edited by Paul Blowers. Grand Rapids: Eerdmans.

Oberman, Heiko A. 1989. *Luther: Man between God and the Devil*. Translated by Eileen Walliser-Schwartzbart. New Haven: Yale University Press.

Oberweis, Michael. 1995. "Erwägungen zur apokalyptischen Ortsbezeichnung 'Harmagedon.'" *Biblica* 76:305–24.

O'Donovan, Oliver. 1986. "The Political Thought of the Book of Revelation." *Tyndale Bulletin* 37:61–94.

Olson, Daniel C. 1997. "'Those Who Have Not Defiled Themselves with Women': Revelation 14:4 and the Book of Enoch." *Catholic Biblical Quarterly* 59:492–510.

Osborn, Eric. 1999. "The Apologist Origen and the Fourth Century: From Theodicy to Christology." Pages 51–59 in *Origeniana Septima*. Edited by W. A. Bienert and U. Kühneweg. Louvain: Leuven University Press.

Osborne, Grant R. 2002. *Revelation*. Baker Exegetical Commentary on the New Testament. Grand Rapids: Baker Academic.

Oswalt, John. 1998. *The Book of Isaiah: Chapters 40–66*. New International Commentary on the Old Testament. Grand Rapids: Eerdmans.

Ozanne, C. G. 1965. "The Language of the Apocalypse." *Tyndale Bulletin* 16:3–9.

Page, Hugh Rowland, Jr. 1996. *The Myth of Cosmic Rebellion: A Study of Its Reflexes in Ugaritic and Biblical Literature*. Vetus Testamentum Supplements 65. Leiden: Brill.

Pagels, Elaine. 1985. "The Politics of Paradise: Augustine's Exegesis of Genesis 1–3 versus That of John Chrysostom." *Harvard Theological Review* 78:67–99.

———. 1995. *The Origin of Satan*. New York: Random House.

Painter, Nell Irvin. 2008. *Standing at Armageddon: The United States 1877–1919*. New York: Norton.

Parenti, Michael. 2003. *The Assassination of Julius Caesar: A People's History of Ancient Rome*. New York: New Press.

Parker, Floyd O., Jr. 2001. "'Our Lord and God' in Rev 4,11: Evidence for the Late Date of Revelation?" *Biblica* 82:207–31.

Parker, T. H. L. 1971. *Calvin's New Testament Commentaries*. London: SCM.

Pate, C. Marvin, ed. 1998. *Four Views of the Book of Revelation*. Grand Rapids: Eerdmans.

Paul, Shalom M. 1991. *Amos: A Commentary on the Book of Amos*. Hermeneia. Minneapolis: Fortress.

Paulien, Jon. 1988. *Decoding Revelation's Trumpets: Literary Allusions and the Interpretation of Revelation 8:7–12*. Berrien Springs, MI: Andrews University Press.

———. 1992. "The Seven Seals." Pages 227–34 in *Symposium on Revelation—Book 1*. Edited by Frank Holbrook. Silver Spring, MD: Biblical Research Institute.

Peake, Arthur S. 1919. *The Revelation of John*. London: Joseph Johnson.

Perry, Peter S. 2009. *The Rhetoric of Digressions: Revelation 7:17 and 10:1–11:13 and Ancient Communication*. Wissenschaftliche Untersuchungen zum Neuen Testament 2/268. Tübingen: Mohr Siebeck.

Pezzoli-Olgiati, Daria. 2002. "Between Fascination and Destruction: Considerations of the Power of the Beast in Rev 13:1–10." Pages 229–37 in *Zwischen den Reichen: Neues Testament und Römische Herrschaft*. Edited by Michael Labahn and Jürgen Zangenberg. Texte und Arbeiten zum neutestamentlichen Zeitalter 36. Tübingen: Francke Verlag.

Pippin, Tina. 1992. *Death and Desire: The Rhetoric of Gender in the Apocalypse of John*. Literary Currents in Biblical Interpretation. Louisville: Westminster John Knox.

———. 1995. "'And I Will Strike Her Children Dead': Death and Deconstruction of Social Location." Pages 191–98 in *Social Location and Biblical Interpretation in the United States*. Vol. 1 of *Reading from This Place*. Edited by Fernando F. Segovia and Mary Ann Tolbert. Minneapolis: Fortress.

Plantak, Zdravko. 1998. *The Silent Church*. London: Macmillan.

Plevnik, Joseph. 1984. "The Taking Up of the Faithful and the Resurrection of the Dead in 1 Thessalonians 4:13–18." *Catholic Biblical Quarterly* 46:274–83.

Polkinghorne, John. 2002. *The God of Hope and the End of the World.* New Haven: Yale University Press.

Pope, Marvin. 1955. *El in the Ugaritic Texts.* Supplements to Vetus Testamentum 2. Leiden: Brill.

Popkes, Wiard. 1983. "Die Funktion der Sendschreiben in der Apokalypse: Zugleich ein Beitrag zur Spätgeschichte der neutestamentlichen Gleichnisse (Rev 2–3)." *Zeitschrift für die neutestamentliche Wissenschaft* 74:90–107.

Popper, Karl R. 1989–90. *The Open Society and Its Enemies.* Vol. 1, *The Spell of Plato.* Vol. 2, *The High Tide of Prophecy: Hegel, Marx, and the Aftermath.* London: Routledge. Original edition, 1945.

Porter, Stanley E. 1987. "Why the Laodiceans Received Lukewarm Water (Revelation 3:15–18)." *Tyndale Bulletin* 38:143–49.

Porter-Young, Anathea E. 2011. *Apocalypse against Empire: Theologies of Resistance in Early Judaism.* Grand Rapids: Eerdmans.

Postman, Neil. 2006. *Amusing Ourselves to Death: Public Discourse in the Age of Show Business.* New York: Penguin.

Price, S. R. F. 1984. *Rituals and Power: The Roman Imperial Cult in Asia Minor.* Cambridge: Cambridge University Press.

Prigent, Pierre. 1959. *Apocalypse 12: Histoire de l'exégèse.* Tübingen: Mohr Siebeck.

———. 2001. *Commentary on the Apocalypse of St. John.* Translated by Wendy Pradels. Tübingen: Mohr Siebeck.

Radice, Betty, trans. 1969. *Pliny: Panegyricus.* Cambridge, MA: Harvard University Press.

Railton, Nicholas M. 2003. "Gog and Magog: The History of a Symbol." *Evangelical Quarterly* 75:23–43.

Ramsay, William. 1905. *Letters to the Seven Churches and Their Place in the Plan of the Apocalypse.* New York: A. C. Armstrong.

Reddish, Mitchell G. 2001. *Revelation.* Smyth & Helwys Bible Commentary. Macon, GA: Smyth & Helwys.

———. 2004. "Hearing the Apocalypse in Pergamum." *Perspectives in Religious Studies* 41:3–12.

Reichelt, Hansgünter. 1994. *Angelus Interpres—Texte in der Johannes-Apokalypse: Strukturen, Aussagen und Hintergründe.* Frankfurt: Peter Lang.

Reider, Joseph. 1966. *An Index to Aquila.* Revised by Nigel Turner. Supplements to Vetus Testamentum 12. Leiden: Brill.

Resseguie, James L. 1998. *Revelation Unsealed: A Narrative Critical Approach to John's Apocalypse.* Leiden: Brill.

Richard, Pablo. 1995. *Apocalypse: A People's Commentary on the Book of Revelation.* New York: Orbis Books.

Rissi, Mathias. 1964. "The Rider on the White Horse." *Interpretation* 18:407–18.

———. 1965. "Die Erscheinung Christi nach Off. 19,11–16." *Theologische Zeitschrift* 21:81–95.

———. 1966. *Time and History.* Translated by Gordon C. Winsor. Richmond: John Knox.

———. 1972. *The Future of the World: An Exegetical Study of Revelation 19.11–22.15.* Studies in Biblical Theology 2/23. London: SCM.

Rist, Martin. 1957. *Revelation.* Pages 345–613 in vol. 12 of *The Interpreter's Bible.* New York: Abingdon.

———. 1961. *The Modern Reader's Guide to the Book of Revelation.* New York: Association.

Robinson, John A. T. 1987. *The Priority of John.* Oak Park: Meyer-Stone.

Rolin, Patrice. 2012. "Gens qui pleurent, gens qui rient: Apocalypse 18." *Foi et vie* 111:53–65.

Roloff, Jürgen. 1993. *The Revelation of John.* Translated by John E. Alsup. Continental Commentaries. Minneapolis: Fortress.

Romm, James. 2014. *Dying Every Day: Seneca at the Court of Nero.* New York: Vintage.

Rossing, Barbara. 1998. "River of Life in God's New Jerusalem: An Ecological Vision for Earth's Future." *Currents in Theology and Mission* 25:487–99.

———. 1999. *The Choice between Two Cities: Whore, Bride, and Empire in the Apocalypse.* Harvard Theological Studies. Harrisburg, PA: Trinity Press International.

———. 2005. "For the Healing of the World: Reading Revelation Ecologically." Pages 165–82 in *From Every People and Nation: The Book of Revelation in Intercultural Perspective.* Edited by David Rhoads. Minneapolis: Fortress.

———. 2008. "'Hastening the Day' When the Earth Will Burn? Global Warming, Revelation and 2 Peter 3 (Advent 2, Year B)." *Currents in Theology and Mission* 35:363–73.

Rowland, Christopher. 1979. "The Visions of God in Apocalyptic Literature." *Journal for the Study of Judaism in the Persian, Hellenistic and Roman Period* 10:137–54.

———. 1980. "The Vision of the Risen Christ in Rev i.13ff.: The Debt of an Early Christology to an Aspect of Jewish Angelology." *Journal of Theological Studies* 31:1–11.

———. 1982. *The Open Heaven: A Study of Apocalyptic in Judaism and Early Christianity.* London: SPCK.

———. 1985. "A Man Clothed in Linen: Daniel 10.6ff. and Jewish Angelology." *Journal for the Study of the New Testament* 24:99–110.

———. 1993. *Revelation.* Epworth Commentaries. London: Epworth.

Royalty, Robert M., Jr. 2004. "Don't Touch *This* Book! Revelation 22:18–19 and the Rhetoric of Reading (in) the Apocalypse of John." *Biblical Interpretation* 12:282–99.

———. 2005. "Etched or Sketched? Inscriptions and Erasures in the Messages to Sardis and Philadelphia (Rev. 3.1–13)." *Journal for the Study of the New Testament* 21:447–63.

Rudnig-Zelt, Susanne. 2016. "Der Teufel und der alttestamentliche Monotheismus." Pages 1–20 in *Das Böse, der Teufel und Dämonen—Evil, the Devil, and Demons.* Edited by Jan Dochhorn, Susanne Rudnig-Zelt, and Benjamin Wold. Wissenschaftliche Untersuchungen zum Neuen Testament 2/412. Tübingen: Mohr Siebeck.

Rudwick, M. J. S. 1957. "The Lukewarmness of Laodicea (Rev. iii.16)." *Tyndale Bulletin* 3:2–3.

Ruiz, Jean-Pierre. 1995. "Revelation 4:8–11; 5:9–14: Hymns of the Heavenly Liturgy." Pages 216–20 in *1995 Seminar Papers: One Hundred Thirty-First Annual Meeting, November 18–21, 1995, Philadelphia Marriott and Pennsylvania Convention Center, Philadelphia, Pennsylvania*. Society of Biblical Literature Seminar Papers 34. Atlanta: Scholars Press.

Russell, David M. 1996. *The "New Heavens and New Earth": Hope for the Creation in Jewish Apocalyptic and the New Testament*. Studies in Biblical Apocalyptic Literature 1. Philadelphia: Visionary.

Sachs, John R. 1993. "*Apocatastasis* in Patristic Theology." *Theological Studies* 54:617–40.

Salzmann, James. 2013. *Drinking Water*. New York: Overlook Duckworth.

Sandmel, Samuel. 1962. "Parallelomania." *Journal of Biblical Literature* 81:1–13.

Sarna, Nahum. 1966. *Understanding Genesis: The Heritage of Biblical Israel*. New York: Schocken.

———. 1989. *The JPS Torah Commentary on Genesis*. Philadelphia: Jewish Publication Society.

Schaff, Philip. 1910. *Modern Christianity: The Swiss Reformation*. Vol. 8 of *History of the Christian Church*. New York: Charles Scribner's Sons.

Scheck, Thomas P., trans. 2001. *Origen: Commentary on the Epistle to the Romans; Books 1–5*. Fathers of the Church 103. Washington, DC: Catholic University of America Press.

Scherrer, Steven J. 1984. "Signs and Wonders in the Imperial Cult: A New Look at a Roman Religious Institution in the Light of Rev 13:13–15." *Journal of Biblical Literature* 103:599–610.

Schlier, Heinrich. 1936. "Vom Antichrist: Zum 13. Kapitel der Offenbarung Johannis." Pages 110–23 in *Theologische Aufsätze: Karl Barth zum 50. Geburtstag*. Munich: Chr. Kaiser Verlag.

Schmid, Konrad. 2008. "Loss of Immortality? Hermeneutical Aspects of Genesis 2–3 and Its Early Receptions." Pages 58–78 in *Beyond Eden*. Edited by Konrad Schmid and Christoph Riedweg. Forschungen zum Alten Testament 2/34. Tübingen: Mohr Siebeck.

Schmidt, Josef. 2002. "Die Rätselzahl 666 in Offb 13:18: Ein Lösungsversuch auf der Basis lateinischer Gematrie." *Novum Testamentum* 46:35–54.

Schmidt, K. L. 1951. "Lucifer als gefallene Engelmacht." *Theologische Zeitschrift* 7:161–79.

Schmidt, Thomas E. 1994. "'And the Sea Was No More': Water as People, Not Place." Pages 233–49 in *To Tell the Mystery: Essays on New Testament Eschatology in Honor of Robert H. Gundry*. Edited by Thomas E. Schmidt and Moisés Silva. Library of New Testament Studies 100. Sheffield: JSOT Press.

Scott, James C. 1990. *Domination and the Arts of Resistance: Hidden Transcripts*. New Haven: Yale University Press.

Shepherd, Michael B. 2006. "Daniel 7:13 and the New Testament Son of Man." *Westminster Theological Journal* 68:99–111.

Siew, Antoninus King Wai. 2005. *The War between the Two Beasts and the Two Witnesses: A Chiastic Reading of Revelation 11.1–14.5.* Library of New Testament Studies 283. London: T&T Clark.

Sizer, Stephen. 2004. *Christian Zionism: Road-Map to Armageddon?* Leicester, UK: Inter-Varsity.

Ska, Jean-Louis. 2008. "Genesis 2–3: Some Fundamental Questions." Pages 1–27 in *Beyond Eden.* Edited by Konrad Schmid and Christoph Riedweg. Forschungen zum Alten Testament 2/34. Tübingen: Mohr Siebeck.

Skehan, Patrick W. 1951. "Structure of the Song of Moses in Deuteronomy (Deut 32:143)." *Catholic Biblical Quarterly* 13:153–63.

Skinner, John. 1898. *The Book of the Prophet Isaiah 40–66: With Introduction and Notes.* Cambridge: Cambridge University Press.

———. 1910. *A Critical and Exegetical Commentary on Genesis.* International Critical Commentary. Edinburgh: T&T Clark.

———. 1915. *Isaiah 1–39.* Cambridge: Cambridge University Press.

Slater, Thomas B. 1998. "On the Social Setting of the Revelation to John." *New Testament Studies* 44:232–56.

Smith, Christopher R. 1990. "The Portrayal of the Church as the New Israel in the Names and Order of the Tribes in Revelation 7.5–8." *Journal for the Study of the New Testament* 39:111–18.

Smith, Morton. 1983. "On the History of ΑΠΟΚΑΛΥΠΤΩ and ΑΠΟΚΑΛΥΨΙΣ." Pages 9–20 in *Apocalypticism in the Mediterranean World and the Near East: Proceedings of the International Colloquium on Apocalypticism, Uppsala, August 12–17, 1979.* Edited by David Hellholm. Tübingen: Mohr.

Smith, R. L. 1984. *Micah–Malachi.* Word Biblical Commentary. Waco: Word.

Smith, Uriah. 1884. *Thoughts, Critical and Practical, on the Books of Daniel and Revelation.* Battle Creek, MI: Review and Herald.

Solove, Daniel J. 2007. *The Future of Reputation: Gossip, Rumor, and Privacy on the Internet.* New Haven: Yale University Press.

Solzhenitsyn, Aleksandr I. 1973. *The Gulag Archipelago, 1918–1956.* Translated by Thomas P. Whitney. New York: Harper & Row.

Speiser, E. A. 2008. *Genesis: Introduction, Translation, and Notes.* Anchor Bible 1. New Haven: Yale University Press.

Stangneth, Bettina. 2014. *Eichmann before Jerusalem: The Unexamined Life of a Mass Murderer.* London: The Bodley Head.

Staples, Peter. 1972. "Revelation 16:4–6 and Its Vindication Formula." *Novum Testamentum* 14:280–93.

Stefanovic, Ranko. 2009a. *Revelation of Jesus Christ: Commentary on the Book of Revelation.* 2nd ed. Berrien Springs, MI: Andrews University Press.

———. 2009b. "The Sealing of the Scroll in Revelation." Pages 367–76 in *Christ, Salvation and the Eschaton: Essays in Honor of Hans K. LaRondelle.* Edited by

Daniel Heinz, Jiri Moskala, and Peter van Bemmelen. Berrien Springs, MI: Andrews University Press.

———. 2011. "'The Lord's Day' of Revelation 1:10 in the Current Debate." *Andrews University Seminary Studies* 49:261–84.

Steinmetz, David C. 2003. "Uncovering a Second Narrative: Detective Fiction and the Construction of Historical Method." Pages 54–65 in *The Art of Reading Scripture.* Edited by Ellen F. Davis and Richard B. Hays. Grand Rapids: Eerdmans.

Stendahl, Krister. 1963. "The Apostle Paul and the Introspective Conscience of the West." *Harvard Theological Review* 56:199–215.

Stone, I. F. 1989. *The Trial of Socrates.* New York: Anchor.

Stordalen, Terje. 2008. "Heaven on Earth—or Not? Jerusalem as Eden in Biblical Literature." Pages 28–57 in *Beyond Eden.* Edited by Konrad Schmid and Christoph Riedweg. Forschungen zum Alten Testament 2/34. Tübingen: Mohr Siebeck.

Strand, Kenneth A. 1986. "Some Modalities of Symbolic Usage in Revelation 18." *Andrews University Seminary Studies* 24:37–46.

Sumney, Jerry. 2009. "Post-Mortem Existence and Resurrection of the Body in Paul." *Horizons in Biblical Theology* 31:12–26.

Sweet, J. P. M. 1979. *Revelation.* Philadelphia: Westminster.

Swenson, Kristin M. 2006. "Care and Keeping East of Eden: Gen 4:1–16 in Light of Gen 2–3." *Interpretation* 60:373–84.

Swete, Henry Barclay. 1908. *The Apocalypse of St. John.* 3rd ed. London: Macmillan.

Swindell, Anthony C. 2016. "Gog and Magog in Literary Reception History: The Persistence of the Fantastic." *Journal of the Bible and Its Reception* 3:27–53.

Syme, Ronald. 1960. *The Roman Revolution.* Oxford: Oxford University Press.

Talbert, Charles H. 1994. *The Apocalypse.* Louisville: Westminster John Knox.

Taylor, John B. 1969. *Ezekiel.* London: Tyndale.

Terrien, Samuel. 1978. *The Elusive Presence: Toward A New Biblical Theology.* New York: Harper & Row. Repr., Eugene OR: Wipf & Stock, 2000.

Thimmes, Pamela. 2003. "Women Reading Women in the Apocalypse: Reading Scenario 1, the Letter to Thyatira (Rev. 2.18–29)." *Currents in Biblical Research* 2.1:128–44.

Thomas, Michael L. 2004. "(Re)locating Domitian's Horse of Glory: The 'Equus Domitiani' and Flavian Urban Design." *Memoirs of the American Academy in Rome* 49:21–46.

Thompson, Leonard. 1990. *The Book of Revelation: Apocalypse and Empire.* Oxford: Oxford University Press.

———. 2000. "Lamentation for Christ as a Hero: Revelation 1:7." *Journal of Biblical Literature* 119:683–703.

Thompson, Marianne Meye. 2015. *John: A Commentary.* New Testament Library. Louisville: Westminster John Knox.

Thompson, Steven. 1985. *The Apocalypse and Semitic Syntax.* Society for New Testament Studies Monograph Series 52. Cambridge: Cambridge University Press.

———. 1999. "The End of Satan." *Andrews University Seminary Studies* 37:257–68.

Töniste, Külli. 2016. *The Ending of the Canon: A Canonical and Intertextual Reading of Revelation 21–22*. Library of New Testament Studies 526. London: Bloomsbury.

Tonstad, Sigve K. 2004. "Theodicy and the Theme of Cosmic Conflict in the Early Church." *Andrews University Seminary Studies* 42:169–202.

———. 2006. *Saving God's Reputation: The Theological Function of Pistis Christou in the Cosmic Narratives of Revelation*. Library of New Testament Studies 337. Edinburgh: T&T Clark.

———. 2007. "The Restrainer Removed: A Truly Alarming Thought (2 Thess. 2:1–12)." *Horizons of Biblical Theology* 29:133–51.

———. 2008a. "Appraising the Myth of *Nero Redivivus* in the Interpretation of Revelation." *Andrews University Seminary Studies* 46:175–99.

———. 2008b. "'The Father of Lies,' the Mother of Lies, and the Death of Jesus." Pages 193–210 in *The Gospel of John and Christian Theology*. Edited by Richard J. Bauckham and Carl Mosser. Grand Rapids: Eerdmans.

———. 2009. *The Lost Meaning of the Seventh Day*. Berrien Springs, MI: Andrews University Press.

———. 2016a. *God of Sense and Traditions of Non-Sense*. Eugene, OR: Wipf & Stock.

———. 2016b. *The Letter to the Romans: Paul among the Ecologists*. Earth Bible Commentary Series. Sheffield: Sheffield Academic.

Torrey, C. C. 1938. "Armageddon." *Harvard Theological Review* 31:237–48.

Trites, A. A. 1977. *The New Testament Concept of Witness*. Cambridge: Cambridge University Press.

Trocmé, Étienne. 1999. "La Jezabel de Thyatire (Apoc. 2/20–24)." *Revue d'histoire et de philosophie religieuses* 79:53–54.

Turner, Nigel. 1963. *Syntax*. Vol. 3 of *A Grammar of New Testament Greek*. By J. H. Moulton, W. F. Howard, and N. Turner. Edinburgh: T&T Clark.

———. 1976. *Style*. Vol. 4 of *A Grammar of New Testament Greek*. By J. H. Moulton, W. F. Howard, and N. Turner. Edinburgh: T&T Clark.

Turner, William Bennett. 2011. *Figures of Speech: First Amendment Heroes and Villains*. Sausalito, CA: PoliPoint.

Ulrich, Jörg. 1996. "Euseb, HistEccl III, 14–20 und die Frage nach der Christenverfolgung unter Domitian." *Zeitschrift für die neutestamentliche Wissenschaft* 87:269–89.

Ureneck, Lou. 2015. *The Great Fire: One American's Mission to Rescue Victims of the 20th Century's First Genocide*. New York: HarperCollins.

Valentine, Kendra Haloviak. 2015. *Worlds at War, Nations in Song: Dialogic Imagination and Moral Vision in the Hymns of the Book of Revelation*. Eugene, OR: Wipf & Stock.

van de Water, Rick. 2000. "Reconsidering the Beast from the Sea." *New Testament Studies* 46:245–61.

van Dijk, H. J. 1968. *Ezekiel's Prophecy on Tyre: A New Approach*. Rome: Pontifical Biblical Institute.

van Kooten, Geurt Hendrik. 2007. "The Year of the Four Emperors and the Revelation of John: The 'Pro-Neronian' Emperors Otho and Vitellius, and the Images and Colossus of Nero in Rome." *Journal for the Study of the New Testament* 30:205–48.

Vanni, Ugo. 1991. "Liturgical Dialogue as a Literary Form in the Book of Revelation." *New Testament Studies* 37:348–72.

van Unnik, W. C. 1962–63. "A Formula Describing Prophecy." *New Testament Studies* 9:86–94.

———. 1970. "'Worthy Is the Lamb': The Background of Apoc 5." Pages 445–61 in *Mélanges bibliques en hommage au R. P. Béda Rigaux*. Edited by Albert Descamps and André de Halleux. Gembloux: Duculot.

Varner, Eric R. 2004. *Mutilation and Transformation:* Damnatio Memoriae *and Roman Imperial Portraiture*. Monumenta Graeca et Romana 10. Leiden: Brill.

Vassiliades, Petros. 1985. "The Translation of *Martyria Iēsou* in Revelation." *The Bible Translator* 36.1:129–34.

Victorin de Poetovio. 1997. *Sur l'Apocalypse et Autres Écrits*. Translated and edited by M. Dulaey. Paris: Les Éditions du Serf.

Vögtle, Anton. 1976. "Der Gott der Apocalypse." Pages 377–98 in *La Notion biblique de Dieu*. Edited by J. Coppens. Gembloux: Duculot.

Volf, Miroslav. 2000. "Enter into Joy! Sin, Death, and the Life of the World to Come." Pages 256–78 in *The End of the World and the Ends of God: Science and Theology on Eschatology*. Edited by John Polkinghorne and Michael Welker. Harrisburg, PA: Trinity Press International.

Vonnegut, Kurt. 1991. *Slaughterhouse Five*. New York: Dell.

———. 2008. *Armageddon in Retrospect*. New York: Penguin.

Vos, Louis A. 1965. *The Synoptic Traditions in the Apocalypse*. Kampen: Kok.

Vriezen, T. C. 1970. *An Outline of Old Testament Theology*. Oxford: Basil Blackwell.

Wallace, Daniel B. 1996. *Greek Grammar beyond the Basics*. Grand Rapids: Zondervan.

Wallace-Hadrill, Andrew. 1982. "The Golden Age and Sin in Augustan Ideology." *Past and Present* 95:19–36.

———. 1989. "Patronage in Roman Society: From Republic to Empire." Pages 63–87 in *Patronage in Ancient Society*. London: Routledge.

———. 1995. *Suetonius*. London: Bristol Classical.

Walter, Nikolaus. 2002. "Nikolaos, Proselyt aus Antiochien, und die Nikolaiten in Ephesus und Pergamon: Ein Betrag auch zum Thema; Paulus und Ephesus." *Zeitschrift für die neutestamentliche Wissenschaft* 93:200–226.

Walther, James Arthur. 1995. "The Address in Revelation 1:4, 5a." *Horizons in Biblical Theology* 17:165–80.

Walvoord, John F. 2007. *Armageddon, Oil, and Terror: What the Bible Says about the Future of America, the Middle East, and the End of Western Civilization*. Carol Stream, IL: Tyndale.

Watson, John Selby, trans. 2015. *Quintilian: Institutes of Oratory*. Revised and edited by Lee Honeycutt and Curtis Dozier. Creative Commons License.

Wayne, Philip I. 1949. Introduction to Johann Wolfgang von Goethe, *Faust*. Part One. Translated by Philip Wayne. London: Penguin.

Weber, Timothy P. 2004. *On the Road to Armageddon: How Evangelicals Became Israel's Best Friend*. Grand Rapids: Baker Academic.

Welborn, L. L. 2009. "'Extraction from the Mortal Site': Badiou on the Resurrection in Paul." *New Testament Studies* 55:95–314.

Welch, Charles H. 1950. *This Prophecy: An Exposition of the Book of Revelation*. 2nd ed. Banstead, UK: Berean.

Wenham, David. 1981. "Paul and the Synoptic Apocalypse." Pages 345–75 in *Gospel Perspectives: Studies of History and Tradition in the Four Gospels II*. Edited by R. T. France and David Wenham. Sheffield: JSOT Press.

Westcott, B. F. 1978. *The Gospel according to St. John*. Grand Rapids: Eerdmans. Repr. of 1882 edition.

Wevers, John W. 1969. *Ezekiel*. New Century Bible Commentary. London: Nelson.

Whiteley, D. E. H. 1970. "The Threat to Faith: An Exegetical and Theological Reexamination of 2 Thessalonians 2." *Journal of Theological Studies* 21:168 (review).

Wick, Peter. 1998. "There Was Silence in Heaven (Revelation 8:1): An Annotation to Israel Knohl's 'Between Voice and Silence.'" *Journal of Biblical Literature* 117:512–14.

Wiebe, John M. 1989. "The Form, Setting and Meaning of the Song of Moses." *Studia Biblica et Theologica* 17:119–63.

Wilcox, Max. 1991. "'Silence in Heaven' (Rev 8:1) and Early Jewish Thought." Pages 241–44 in *Mogilany 1989: Papers on the Dead Sea Scrolls Offered in Memory of Jean Carmignac*. Edited by Zdzislaw J. Kapera. Krakow: Enigma.

Wildberger, Hans. 1978. *Jesaja 13–27*. Biblischer Kommentar Altes Testament 10:2. Neukirchen-Vluyn: Neukirchener Verlag.

———. 1991. *Isaiah 1–12*. Translated by Thomas H. Trapp. Continental Commentaries. Minneapolis: Fortress.

Wilkinson, Richard H. 1988. "The Stylos of Revelation 3:12 and Ancient Coronation Rites." *Journal of Biblical Literature* 107:498–501.

Williams, Bernard. 2002. *Truth and Truthfulness: An Essay in Genealogy*. Princeton: Princeton University Press.

Williams, Roger. 1848. *The Bloudy Tenent of Persecution for Cause of Conscience Discussed and Mr.Cotton's Letter Examined and Answered*. Edited by Edward Bean Underhill. London: J. Haddon. Original edition, 1644. Repr., Whitefish, MT: Kessinger Publishing's Rare Reprints, [2000s].

Williamson, G. A., trans. and ed. 1989. *Eusebius: The History of the Church*. London: Penguin.

Wilson, Mark W. 2005. "The Early Christians in Ephesus and the Date of Revelation, Again." *Neotestamentica* 39:169–200.

Wirzba, Norman. 2006. *Living the Sabbath: Discovering the Rhythms of Rest and Delight*. Grand Rapids: Brazos.

Witetschek, Stephan. 2012. "Ein weit geöffnetes Zeitfenster? Überlegungen zur Datierung der Johannesapokalypse." Pages 117–48 in *Die Johannesapokalypse:*

*Kontexte—Konzepte—Rezeption.* Edited by Jörg Frey, James A. Kelhoffer, and Franz Tóth. Wissenschaftliche Untersuchungen zum Neuen Testament 287. Tübingen: Mohr Siebeck.

Witulski, Thomas. 2013. "Das Zeugnis Papias und die Datierung der Johannesapokalypse." *Biblische Zeitschrift* 57:184–215.

Wolff, Uwe. 2007. "The Angels' Comeback: A Retrospect at the Turn of the Millennium." Pages 695–714 in *Angels: The Concept of Celestial Beings—Origins, Development and Reception.* Edited by Friedrich Reiterer, Tobias Nicklas, and Karin Schöpflin. Berlin: de Gruyter.

Woods, Richard. 2008. "Seven Bowls of Wrath: The Ecological Relevance of Revelation." *Biblical Theology Bulletin* 38.2:64–75.

Wyatt, Nicolas. 1981. "Interpreting the Creation and Fall Story in Genesis 2–3." *Zeitschrift für die alttestamentliche Wissenschaft* 93:10–21.

Yeats, William Butler. 1996. "The Second Coming." Page 458 in *Poem a Day.* Edited by Karen McCosker and Nicholas Alberry. Hanover, NH: Steerforth.

Yoder, Douglas. 2009. "Why Daniel 2 Is a Central Theological Text of the Hebrew Scriptures." Paper presented at the Society of Biblical Literature Annual Meeting in New Orleans, November 24, 2009.

Zanker, Paul. 1990. *The Power of Images in the Age of Augustus.* Translated by Alan Shapiro. Ann Arbor: University of Michigan Press.

Zerbe, Gordon. 2003. "Revelation's Exposé of Two Cities: Babylon and New Jerusalem." *Direction* 32:47–60.

Zimmerli, Walther. 1979. *Ezekiel: A Commentary on the Book of the Prophet Ezekiel.* 2 vols. Hermeneia. Philadelphia: Fortress.

Zimmermann, Ruben. 2003a. "Nuptial Imagery in the Revelation of John." *Biblica* 84:153–83.

———. 2003b. "Die Virginitäts-Metapher in Apk 14:4–5 im Horizont von Befleckung, Loskauf und Erstlingsfrucht." *Novum Testamentum* 45:45–70.

Zuntz, Günther. 1991. "Papiana." *Zeitschrift für die neutestamentliche Wissenschaft* 82:242–63.

Zwingli, Huldrych. 1939. *Huldreich Zwinglis sämtliche Werke.* Corpus Reformatorum 93. Leipzig: Verlag von M. Heinsius Nachfolger.

# Index of Subjects

# Index of Modern Authors

# Index of Scripture and Ancient Sources